THERAPEUTIC RIDING PROGRAMS

INSTRUCTION AND REHABILITATION

THERAPEUTIC RIDING PROGRAMS

INSTRUCTION AND REHABILITATION
A Handbook for Instructors and Therapists

Edited by
Barbara Teichmann Engel, M.Ed., O.T.R.

Major Contributor and Assistant
Margaret L. Galloway, M.A., B.H.S.A.I.

Foreword by
John Anthony Davies B.A., B.H.S.I.

Major Illustrator (SCW)
Stephanie C. Woods, B.F.A

Published by
Barbara Engel Therapy Services

It is expected that the procedures described in this book will be carried out by trained and qualified practitioners according to recognized standards in the field of Therapeutic Riding. No warranty, expressed or implied, is made regarding the content of this book by the editor, consultants, reviewers, or by its contributors. This book has been developed independently without the assistance of grants, sponsors or support of any organization. No endorsement has been requested or received from any foundation or organization.

❖ ❖ ❖ ❖ ❖ ❖ ❖ ❖

The opinions and/or experiences expressed in the articles of text are those of each author/contributor and do not necessarily represent the views of the editor, reviewer, or that of any organization. It is the intent of this text to present the reader with many viewpoints from people who have extensive experience in the field, with the purpose of expanding and challenging each reader's base of knowledge. The dynamic field of therapeutic riding will prove its value **only** when those in the field *share their experiences, question, search, develop and continue to expand knowledge. The end result will be validation of the values of this unique discipline.*

**Without question, there is no change;
Without change, there is no growth.**

Library of Congress Catalog Card Number: 92-71597

ISBN 0-9633065-0-2

Manufactured in the United States of America

Published by Barbara Engel Therapy Services
10 Town Plaza, Suite 238
Durango, CO 81301

Printed by Omnipress
2600 Anderson Street
Madison, WI 53704
USA

Cover photograph of young rider Dana Sussman
Courtesy of Pegasus Therapeutic Riding Inc. of Darien CT.

Acknowledgements

DETAILED CONTENTS

Foreword

Preface

This book is dedicated in the memory of my father
Walter O. Teichmann, M.D.
who instilled in me a drive to excel and to strive toward accomplishment

Contributors and Reviewers:

The contributing authors of this book are acknowledged for the many hours of hard work they gave to complete this book. Without their expert knowledge, endeavor, and patience, a book of this scope could not be produced. A thank you to all the reviewers who gave freely of their time and advice, especially to Joann Benjamin who not only collaborated on several articles but reviewed the complete text.

A special kind of acknowledgement must go to Jean Tebay who was the major advisor to the editor and spent a great deal of time reviewing and advising. Her enthusiasm and drive to better the field of therapeutic riding is unmatched.

To Stephanie Woods who worked diligently to illustrate the manuscript with specific details and to Octavia Brown who performed a very thorough final reading and gave final advice, many thanks.

Most of all, to Florence Cromwell who provided both expert technical guidance, encouragement, and a great deal of support through out the two and a half years it took to complete the manuscript. Without her assistance this book could not have been completed.

Finally to my husband, Jay who provided the technical computer assistance, editing, and encouraged and supported me throughout the many hours spent on this project itself, particular appreciation. I could not have done it without his help and support.

Barbara T. Engel, BS, MEd, OTR - Editor
Educational psychology; pediatric occupational therapist, private practice and consultant; 18 years administration, 24 years clinical and University instruction; extensive experience in the fields of pediatrics, psychiatry, and adult rehabilitation; equine-assisted practioner since 1980 and therapeutic riding--1963; consultant, lecturer in therapeutic riding since 1981; advanced hippotherapy course in Germany; member, Hippotherapy Curriculum Development Committee, member of Delta Society, NARHA, AVA, USDF, AHSA, CanTRA, FRDI; co-author *The Horse, The Handicapped, The Riding Team*; authored *A Bibliography for Therapeutic Riding in Sport - Education - Medicine*, and articles for professional journals; life long equestrian; active in dressage; vaulter-4 years; Special Olympic certified coach.

Ellen Adolphson, PT
Bryn Mawr Rehabilitation Hospital, equine-assisted therapy practioner since 1985; advanced hippotherapy course in Germany; member, Hippotherapy Curriculum Development Committee.

Elizabeth A. Baker, RPT
Physical Therapy Supervisor, Children's Hospital, Wrentham State School, MA.; physical therapist, Greenlock Therapeutic Riding Center, MA.; advanced hippotherapy course in Germany; member; Hippotherapy Curriculum Development Committee; member NARHA; equine-assisted therapy practioner since 1985; life-long equestrian; 1st VP, American Hippotherapy Association.

Terri Barnes, PT
Director, Rocky Top Therapy Center (PT & Hippotherapy,) Keller TX; advanced hippotherapy course in Germany; member, Hippotherapy Curriculum Development Committee; NARHA member; equine-assisted therapy practioner since 1984; national & international lecturer; equestrian since adolescence. Board member, American Hippotherapy Association.

Joann Benjamin, PT
NDT certified; NARHA & Delta Society member; involved in the field of therapeutic riding/hippotherapy as a physical therapy consultant since 1986 to several programs; equestrian.

Loretta Binder-Wheeler
Life-long equestrian - dressage/hunter-jumper; instructor certified, All Seasons Riding Academy; instructor, All Seasons Riding Academy; head instructor Cornerstone Equestrian Center; coach, International Cerebral Palsy Equestrian Games, Sweden; instruction therapeutic riding involvement since 1983.

Mary-Lu Bonte, BA, BHSAI
Human Movement and Equestrian Activities; Director of Equestrian program, Special Olympics; involved with therapeutic riding since 1982; life long rider; instructor of able-bodied and special riders since 1975.

Barbara J. Brock, MA, ReD
Associate Professor, Recreational Management, Eastern Washington University; researcher & programmer for physically disabled adult population; doctoral dissertation, *Effect of Therapeutic Horseback Riding on Physically Disabled Adults*-Indiana University, 1987; Produced a therapeutic riding video.

John H. Brough, OTR
Principal, Windward Preparatory School; founder with Nancy Winters of Wayne Dupage Ride & Hunt Club Program; past NARHA VP & Chair of Medical & Research Committee; Therapeutic riding involvement since 1975; national lecturer in learning disabilities; member of many professional advisory committees.

Octavia J. Brown, EdM
Executive Director, Somerset Hills Handicapped Riders Club; NARHA Certified Master Instructor; Cheff Center certified instructor; Special Olympics Equestrian coach & event director, 25 years teaching therapeutic riding; 16 years NARHA Board member, 1st VP of NARHA. NARHA member, committees.

Robin Hulsey Chickering, BS, MS
Teacher of hearing impaired, special school district of Saint Louis Country, MO; certified Cheff Center instructor; President & Head Instructor of Riding High Inc. since 1981; *Author: Horseback Riding for the Hearing Impaired.*

Jane C. Copeland, MA, RPT
Psychology; NDT certified; Executive Director, Pegasus Therapeutic Riding Inc, physical therapist; private practice; Hippotherapy Curriculum Development Committee, NARHA Medical Committee, Treasurer & Board Member Delta Society. NARHA member; Executive Committee, American Hippotherapy Association.

Florence S. Cromwell, MA, OTR, FAOTA
Past editor, Journal of Occupational Therapy in Health Care; past Chair, Depart. of Occupational Therapy, Univ. of Southern California; past President, American Occupational Therapy Association; consultant, educator, researcher, editor.

Gisela T. Dalrymple, MD
Pediatrician. Medical Director, United Cerebral Palsy Association Center of Nassau County, Roosevelt, NY.

John A. Davies, BA, BHSI
Equine Sciences; Director/trainer, St. James Farm Equestrian Facility; Instructor/Trainer/Examiner; 33 years international experience; Dressage-combined training-steeplechasing through advanced level; 40 years experience in the field of therapeutic horseback riding in England and the USA; 4th president of NARHA; NARHA member; Author: *The Reins of Life, Riding in Rhyme*, and *I Saw A Child* in addition to many articles.

Karen P. DePauw, PhD
Associate Dean, Graduate School, Professor Physical Education Sport Leisure Studies, Washington State University. Author & lecturer on therapeutic riding research and disabled sports & adaptive physical education.

Ruth Dismuke-Blakeley, MS/CCC-SLP.
Director, THNM/Skyline Therapy Services, speech/language-hippotherapy program; researcher, lecturer, & leader in equine-assisted therapy; NARHA and Delta Society member; life-long equestrian & trainer.

Sandy Dota
American Judging Association Certified Judge; therapeutic riding instructor; Somerset Hills Handicapped Riders Club; NARHA Board of Directors; since 1985, faculty for NARHA Workshops; national lecturer; NARHA member; International riding competitor.

Angela Dusenbury, PT
Therapist with Old Dominion School of Therapeutic Horsemanship, Great Falls, VA; NDT certified. Therapeutic riding/hippotherapy since 1986; advanced hippotherapy course in Germany; member, Hippotherapy Curriculum Development Committee; Translator, Reide: *Physical Therapy on the Horse* into English.

J. Warren Evans, PhD
Professor of Animal Sciences, Texas A & M Univ., Supervisor-therapeutic riding program, 3 years; Author: *The Horse*, and *Horses*. NARHA Board member.

Joy E. Ferguson, BA, Magr
NARHA Certified Instructor; Certified Instructor, Camp Horsemanship Association; Executive Director, Therapeutic Horsemanship of El Paso; Board Member, 2 term Past-President Lone Star Therapeutic Equestrian Network; National Recreation Park Association.

Gertrude Freeman, BS., MA., PT
Professor, Department of Physical Therapy, School of Allied Sciences, Univ of Texas Medical Branch; Consultant and member of Hippotherapy Curriculum Development Committee; Consultant, Hope Arena Therapeutic Riding Program, Galveston TX; Board member, American Hippotherapy Association.

Maureen Fredrickson, MSW
Deputy Director, Delta Society.

Fuller, Caroline, BA
Instructor, Coach & Administrator Great Falls Pony Club Vaulting Team since 1984, & Aft Us Up; Equestrian; Board member, American Vaulting Association since 1985; Vaulting Chair, USPC; member AHSA, published articles in Chronicle of the Horse, AVA Vaulting World, & USPC Newsletter. Vaulting Instructor for therapeutic & sports vaulting, 8 years. AVA and NARHA member.

Galloway, Margaret (Meg), MA, BHSAI
Special Education; Certified Therapeutic Riding Instructor, Fran Joswick Center; Maryland Horse Center; California Dressage Society Qualified rider; NARHA member; Instructor-BOK Ranch, CA; therapeutic riding since 1986; NARHA member; life long equestrian; co-author, *The Horse, The Handicapped, The Riding Team.*

Glasow, Barbara, BS
Pediatric physical therapist, private practice; hippotherapy practiner; promoted remedial vaulting nationally & internationally since 1975; leader in development of hippotherapy in the USA; author of many articles, video-*Challenged Equestrians*; advanced hippotherapy course, Germany. Member Hippotherapy Curriculum Development Committee; NARHA James Brady Professional Achievement; NARHA member. 1st secretary, American Hippotherapy Association.

Gonzales, Anthony Z
Master farrier for 21 years; developer of the PBM (proper balance movement) Protector Pads; lecturer; consultant; columnist & author, *PBM, a Diary of Lameness.*

Green, Celine, BS
Journalism; Ex-Director, Happy Horsemen Riding for the Handicapped; NAHRA Certified Master Instructor; NAHRA Instructor's committee, workshops faculty & program consultant; involved with therapeutic riding since 1979. 4H horse leader; Special Olympic certified instructor; member of NARHA, AHSA; therapeutic riding 1978.

Susan Greenall, BS
Animal Science; teaching certificate, science (retired), free lance writer. Somerset Hills Handicapped Riding Club; competitor, judge & TD, American Driving Society; NARHA Driving Committee & member.

Hilda Gurney
Dressage Trainer & authority, Moorpark CA; six time USET grand prix champion & Olympic Team medalist in dressage; an "I" Judge; 1992 US Olympic Dressage Team; regular writer for Chronicle of the Horse; author: *Selecting Your Dressage Horse; The ABC's of Basic Dressage* videos.

Victoria Haehl, PT, BS
NDT Certified (adult). Consultant Physical Therapist, All Seasons Riding Academy & other Bay Area therapeutic riding centers; member Bay Area Equines for Sports & Therapy & NARHA.

Robin R. Hall, BS, MS
Riding instructor, Equestrian Studies Program, Univ of Findley, Findley, OH; certified instructor, Fran Joswick Center; instructor of Equestrian Challenge Therapeutic Riding Program, Findley OH; NARHA member.

Gloria Hamblin, BS, RTR
Therapeutic Recreation; program director, Equestrian Therapy for Handicapped Riders, since 1975; Cheff Center certified head instructor, RTR at Woodview Calabassas Psychiatric Hospital, adolescent unit, 5 years; International Equestrian Therapeutic Riding Coach. NARHA member; equestrian competitor.

Kyle Hamilton, PT, MS
Sports Science; physical therapists; experience with therapeutic riding since 1985. Contributor to: *The Horse, The Handicapped, The Riding Team.*

Arthur S. Hansen, DDS
Rider; Volunteer; NARHA member; Woodside Board member; active member of dental associations; active equestrian.

Gundula Hauser, Physiotherapist
Headmaster of school for mentally handicapped and body injured children; President of the Austrian Kuratorium fur Hippotherapie Heilpadagogisches Voltigieren/Reiten u. Behindertenreiten; responsible for the education of professionals teaching remedial educational vaulting and riding; hippotherapy and vaulting practioner.

Nancy Hendrickson
Volunteer.

Judy Hilburn, OTR/L
Private practice; Sensory Integration International SIPT certified; equine-assisted therapy since 1985 in private practice; advanced hippotherapy course, Germany; member, Hippotherapy Curriculum Committee; Dressage rider.

Philippa (Pippa) Hodge, BS, PT, BHSAI
Physiotherapist; head riding instructor, Valley Therapeutic Equestrian Association; examiner, Canadian Therapeutic Riding Association; Board member, CanTRA; member Hippotherapy Curriculum Development Committee; advanced hippotherapy course, Germany; developed video, *Analysis of the Horse and Human Movement.* Board member, American Hippotherapy Assoc.

Jean Hoffman, BS
Animal Science; graduate student-Cal Poly Univ., CA; instructor, therapeutic riding, since 1988; American Trakehner Assoc; equestrian since high school.

Lita R. Hughes, BS
Pre-Veterinarian Science; teacher certificate; 5 years training with Sally Swift in Centered Riding; Caroll County Extension Service, therapeutic riding program; therapeutic riding with Baltimore Parks and Recreation; therapeutic riding since 1980; instructor in dressage; competitor in dressage and eventing; dog trainer; NARHA member.

Carolyn Jagielski, PT, MS
NDT certified; physical therapist, High Hopes Therapeutic Riding; member NAHRA Medical & Accreditation Committees; instructor, NAHRA instructor workshops; advanced hippotherapy course, Germany; member, Hippotherapy Curriculum Development Committee & NARHA.

Robert R. Johnson, BS, VMD
Animal Science; Veterinarian; North County Large Animal Practice; Veterinary care & applied physical therapy for R.E.I.N.S. handicapped riding program, San Marcos, CA & Helen Woodward Animal Care & Education Center Therapeutic Riding Program, Rancho Santa Fe, CA,.

Frances C. Joswick, MSW
NAHRA Certified Master Instructor; founder and Executive Director Emeritus, Joswick Therapeutic Riding Center, San Juan Capistrano, CA; senior faculty for instructor training course; Social Worker; co-author *Aspects and Answers.* NARHA member.

Lorraine "Frosty" Kaiser, BA, MA
Teaching Credential, learning disabilities; therapeutic riding program since 1976; Executive Director, American Riding Club; California Special Olympics Equestrian Director; established 1st all disabled equestrian drill team, NAHRA member, Special Olympics; Council for Exceptional Children; CA Jr. State parade champions, 8 times from 1983 to 1992. NARHA member.

Eleanor Kellon, VMD
Researcher & contributor to *Chronicle of the Horse*, authors many articles & scientific papers, *The Older Horse*, and *First Aid For Horses;* equestrian, trainer, instructor, and judge.

Kerrill Knaus
Co-Founder, President, Executive Director, H.O.R.S.E.S for the physically challenged; 14 yrs animal behavior; 12 yrs, adaptive riding for disabled persons; disabled equestrian.

Antonius Kroger, Physiologist
Headmaster of special education school; member German Kuratorium fur Hippotherapie Heilpadagogisches Voltigieren/Reiten u. Behindertenreiten; responsible for the education of and professional teaching remedial educational vaulting; international lecturer and researcher; author of many papers and videos on remedial vaulting; vaulting practitioner.

Prof. Dr. med Carl Kluwer
Psychoanalyst, President, The Federation of Riding for the Disabled International; member and consultant, German Kuratorium fur Hippotherapie; International lecturer, researcher, and writer on the subject of Hippotherapy.

Lawrence, Elizabeth Atwood, VMD, PhD
Professor of Environmental Studies; Veterinary Anthropologist, Tufts University School of Veterinary Medicine; specializing in research, writing and teaching human/horse relationships; author: *Rodeo: An Anthropologist Looks at the Wild and the Tame*; *Hoofbeats and Society: Studies of Human-Horse Interactions*; *His Very Silence Speaks: Comanche - The Horse Who Survived Custer's Last Stand*; *Horses in Society*; contributed to many books; Delta Society member.

Lawson, Marci
Disabled riding instructor and consultant; disabled rider; Board member, Therapeutic Riding Program; presenter 1990 at NAHRA; NARHA member.

Leff, Marty, BA, MA
NCTR instructor certification; instructor for National Center for Therapeutic Riding; instructor since 1985 remedial/psychoeducational riding, inner city public special education project (Washington D.C.); free-lance writer/editor in English and Spanish; NARHA member; co-author *Guide To Therapeutic Groundwork*.

Lingue, Molly, PT
Equestrian since grade school; advanced hippotherapy course in Germany; member, Hippotherapy Curriculum Development Committee; life-long equestrian. 1st Treasurer, American Hippotherapy Association.

Marshall, Nancy B
CCHHeeR instructor certification; program coordinator/head instructor, Acts 19:11 Therapeutic Horseback Riding; Colorado Council for Handicapped Horseback Riding (CCHHeeR); NAHRA member; 13 years experience in counseling with developmentally disabled.

Martin, Virginia H, BS
President and chief riding instructor: Borderland Farm Inc,; founder & executive director: Equus Outreach Inc; founder & consultant: Winslow Therapeutic Riding Inc; former NAHRA Board member; 4 years director: Metropolitan Therapeutic Equestrian Games, trainer of the 1984 U.S. Cerebral Palsy Team; trainer of New Jersey Special Olympics competitor at Indiana International Special Olympics. NAHRA certified master instructor.

Mayo, Liisa, BS, PT
NAHRA Driving Committee member; founding member of National Association of Driving for the Disabled; active therapist associated with Saratoga Therapeutic Equestrian Program; teaches carriage driving for the disabled.

Mazza, Virginia G, BA, MS
Special education teacher, 21 years; NAHRA member; member of Delta Society, O.C.D.A., U.S.E.T.; presenter, Winslow Therapeutic Riding seminars; president and a Board of Directors, Special Olympics: head equestrian coach and judge for 18 years.

McGibbon, Nancy H, PT
Physical therapist; Director of Therapy Services for Therapeutic Riding of Tucson; associated with TROT; 17 years experience in therapeutic riding and equine-assisted practioner; Hippotherapy Curriculum Development Committee, NAHRA workshop faculty; advanced hippotherapy course in Germany; lecturer; first president, American Hippotherapy Association.

McParland, Chris, BS
Adaptive Physical Education Specialist, credential general secondary; Cheff Center certified instructor; NAHRA Certified Master Instructor; director/instructor Project R.I.D.E. & Elk Grove unified school district; 13 years therapeutic riding instructor; co-author, *Aspects and Answers*; NAHRA's President's Award; NARHA Board member; long time equestrian.

Mitchell, Linda, BS, MS, PT
Special Education; Therapy Service Coordinator United Cerebral Palsy, Morriston, FL; NDT certified; instructor, TAMO (Tscharnuter Akademie for Movement Organization); owner of Working Walk, an equine-assisted therapy program; program committee member, Hole-in-the-Wall Gang-South; advanced hippotherapy course in Germany; member, Hippotherapy Curriculum Development Committee; Delta Society and NARHA member. Board member, American Hippotherapy Association.

Morin, Claudia, MS, OTR
Health Education; Director of Occupational Therapy, Medical College of Georgia Hospital and Clinics; Coordinator/Therapist for Special Equestrians of CSRA; advanced hippotherapy course in Germany; member, Hippotherapy Curriculum Development Committee; NARHA workshop faculty; presenter at NARHA, Delta Society and RDA Australia Conferences; NARHA James Brady Professional Achievement award; 2nd VP, American Hippotherapy Association.

Moore, J. Aston, Judge AVA (I), FEI (O)
Founded with Elizabeth Searle, the American Vaulting Association (AVA); technical advisor to the AVA, instructor and lecturer.

Nanaa, Andrew. Judge
Pleasure driving (A.D.S.); National Association of Driving for the Disabled; technical delegate, pleasure and combined driving/A.D.S.; secretary and certification instructor N.A.D.D.

Newman, June
Certified riding instructor; owner and director of Oakridge Riding Club; 5 years training and teaching dressage & combined; instructor with a private equine-assisted occupational therapy practice since 1987.

Olsen, Paulette J, BS, RPT
Health One Mercy Hospital; Workwell Program; Author *Applause: Body Mechanics for Children*.

Parker, Debi Ruth, MA
Special Education (visually impaired) NAHRA Certified Master Instructor; founded several programs; involved in therapeutic riding as instructor since 1980.

Pfifferling, Sunny, BS
Therapeutic Recreation; NAHRA Master Instructor; Cheff Center Head Instructor certified; Head equine trainer, International Special Olympics; Director/Head Instructor of Loveway Inc; therapeutic horseback riding since 1982.

Potter, John T, MS, PhD
Assistant professor/extension Horse Specialist, Department of Animal Science, University of CT; NAHRA Board member; NAHRA Public Relations Committee; NAHRA Co-Chair Research Committee; currently developing extension & research programs at the University of Conn.; assisted with therapeutic riding program at Texas A & M Univ.

Rafferty, Sandra, OTR, MA
Special Education; certified instructor, John Davies Course; occupational therapist and riding instructor with Therapeutic Horsemanship, St. Louis, MO; instructor/ head coach of the USA international disabled equestrian team; teacher of therapeutic riding since 1975.

Rector, Judy, BHSI
Professional horse trainer and instructor in English and Western horsemanship; co-owner of Sunrise Stables, CO; faculty in therapeutic riding courses.

Rector-Morken, Barbara, MA
Program coordinator, STIRRUP; certified therapeutic riding instructor; equine-assisted psychotherapist; Breathwork certification student with GROF's program; therapeutic riding since 1970; co-founder of TROT; advisory board, TROT, FETE, & NCEFT therapeutic riding programs; NARHA medical/educational research committee; dressage rider.

Renker, Lorraine, BS
Cheff Center instructor certified; NAHRA Certified Master Instructor; Director & Instructor of Special Friends- A Program for the Developmental Disabilities Inc; NAHRA Accreditation Committee Member, NAHRA networking co-chair, 25 years experience with horses.

Rogowski, Susan, OTR
Occupational therapist and riding instructor for Equine Outreach, Winslow, NY.; promoter for Polocrosse for riders with disabilities; presenter at the 7th International Riding Congress. Therapeutic riding involvement since 1982.

Rosenzweig, Marcee, BSc, PT
Consultant to CanTRA & OnTRA, Hippotherapy Development Committee Member, Hippotherapy course instructor, Hippotherapy practioner since 1981. Author: *Horseback Riding--The Therapeutic Sport*. Board member, American Hippotherapy Association.

Ross, Samuel B., Jr, PhD, BA, MA, EED (Hon)
Delta Society Board member; Executive Director: Green Chimneys Children's Services; 40 Years as Executive Director of a residential school with farm and horseback riding program; member of NARHA.

Ryan, Pegi
Director and Instructor of the Helen Woodward Animal Care and Education Center Therapeutic Riding Program, Rancho Santa Fe, CA.

Sayler, Patricia J, MA
VP Easter Seal Society of Lehigh, Monroe, and Northampton Counties, PA; Pocono Therapeutic Riding Instruction for Special Equestrians (R.I.S.E.), Hippotherapy Curriculum Committee Member; NAHRA Medical Committee; faculty, hippotherapy workshop; NAHRA general & instructor's courses; riding instructor since 1982.

Shugol, Wendy R, BS, MA
Special Educator; USA International Equestrian Team for Disabled Riders, more than 8 years; volunteer; Board of Directors, Old Dominion School of Therapeutic Horsemanship.

Spink, Jan, MA
Major in psycho-motor therapy/rehabilitation; certified head instructor in riding for the disabled; Founder/Director of New Harmony Foundation; 30 years riding experience, hunters, jumpers, dressage, combined training; 18 years, field work-lecturing/ researcher, education, national - international on therapeutic riding; created "Developmental Vaulting" which later evolved into the treatment method known as "Developmental Riding Therapy" or D.R.T.; helped input hippotherapy knowledge from Germany & co-presented first U.S. workshops. Member Delta Society.

Standquist, Jill A, OTR/L
Pediatric private practice, certified NDT, certified ski instructor for disabled; advanced hippotherapy course, Germany; member Hippotherapy Curriculum Development Committee; 8 years occupational therapist, Pegasus Therapeutic Riding Program; NARHA member.

Stanley, Sheila, BS
Interior designer; self employed, Certified Riding Instructor, Fran Joswick Center, president and 6 years instructor for Pegasus Riding Academy for the Handicapped, Board of Directors CalNET.

Sweet, Gigi, BA, MEd
Arizona teaching & supervisory certificate; director of instruction, Therapeutic Riding of Tucson Inc; 16 Years in Therapeutic Riding; NAHRA Accreditation Committee, NAHRA workshop faculty; raises and shows Appaloosas.

Szychowski, Eileen
Founder/Director Camelot Therapeutic Horsemanship Inc; former rehabilitation counselor & National Park Service Ranger; an equestrian with a disability; trained under Josef Rivers at the Dragon Slayers, CA.

Tebay, Jean M, BA, MS
Director Therapeutic Riding Services, Baltimore, MD; certified NAHRA Master Therapeutic Riding Instructor; certified Therapeutic Recreation Technician; 26 years, special riding populations; NAHRA Board of Directors; Delta Society Board of Directors; first NAHRA James Brady Professional Achievement award; Delta Society Distinguished Service Award; coordinator of NAHRA college curriculum project; Director of Hippotherapy Curriculum Development Project to train occupational/physical therapists as hippotherapy practitioners; member, special member task force for Riding for the Disabled International to develop an International Charter; initiated therapeutic riding programs in OH, Wash. DC, MD, and OR. Leader/teacher/lecturer for the advancement of therapeutic riding. Board member, American Hippotherapy Association.

Tedescdi, Philip, MSSW
Assistant Clinical Director, director-instructor of Therapeutic Riding; director of Sex Offender Programs Griffith Center, CO; certified NAHRA Master Instructor; WEMT; Cheff Center certified instructor; member of NAHRA Instructor Certification Curriculum Committee, Medical Committee, faculty of NAHRA workshops; Co-chaired NAHRA Research Committee; experience in therapeutic riding since 1981, exploring equine-assisted psychotherapy.

Tellington-Jones, Linda
Life-long equestrian and accomplished rider, having competing in combined training, hunters, jumpers, dressage, Western and English pleasure, steeplechasing and endurance ride competitions. Held a World Record for 7 years in 100-mile endurance racing; co-founder of Pacific Coast Equestrian Research Farm; Feldenkrais practioner; judge, teacher, trainer, researcher, and lecturer; developed the internationally known training technique of T.T.E.A.M. lecturing and training all over the world; co-auther of *Physical Therapy for the Athletic Horse, Endurance and Competitive Trail Riding, T.T.E.A.M Approach to Problem Free Training*, and *The Tellington-Jones Equine Awareness Method, Riding with Awareness, The Tellington TTouch*, and many manuals and articles; produced more than 12 videos and holds regular clinics in North America and many other countries; involved in riding with the disabled since 1958.

Tucker, Susan F
Certified Instructor Cheff Center; certified NAHRA Master Instructor; NAHRA program consultant; faculty NAHRA work-shop; NAHRA National accreditor; NAHRA Accreditation & instructor certification committees; presenter, International Congress on Therapeutic Riding, Denmark 1991; instructor for CCHHR.

Walsh, Mary-Beth, BS, PT
BS, PT/biology; BHSAI; Georgetown Univ. Hospital, Lift Me Up Riding Program; 3 years equine-assisted therapy practioner and therapeutic riding; instructs/treats able-bodied riders with low-back pain.

Walsh, Lisa
Member U.S.A Equestrian Team for Disabled Riders in Sweden and Holland; presenter, International Congress for Therapeutic Riding; Rider.

Wham, Jill, Dip OT/NZ, OTR
Occupational therapist in New Zealand; therapist with therapeutic riding program; presenter at the International Congress of Therapeutic Riding in Denmark, 1991.

Wiegand, Christine, RN, MA
Clinical child development; family & child counselor, C.A.M.F.T.; therapist with Hillsides Families Together Program; early intervention instructor - Exceptional Children's Foundation, CA.

Wiger, Nina, MA
Microbiology; independent instructor Dressage-vaulting; horse trainer; remedial vaulting; Horsepower, California Carousel 4-H Vaulters; National AVA Training Clinics; member, NCEFT in remedial & therapeutic vaulting; gives clinic throughout USA in training vaulting horses; writer, lungeing for *Chronicle of the Horse*; AVA member.

Woods, Stephanie C, BFA
California special secondary/art teaching credential; consultant public relations; product/graphics designer; co-editor & illustrator- *Aspects and Answers; A Manual for Therapeutic Horseback Riding*; developed brochure for National Center for Equine Facilitated Therapy; riding instructor/trainer/exhibitor in trail/Western pleasure; owner, SpeCial Worlds Unlimited.

Zanin, Colleen Clark, OTR
Pediatric occupational therapist; therapeutic riding instructor and equine-assisted therapy practioner; NDT certified; BHSAI; founder Old Dominion School of Therapeutic Horsemanship Inc.; advanced hippotherapy course, Germany; member Hippotherapy Curriculum Committee.

Zimmerman, Kate, BS, MBA, PT
Director of Rehabilitation, San Francisco General Hospital, taught 4 years at All Seasons Riding Academy; founder, director of Rehab Ranch Camp, residential therapy camp.

CONTENTS

FOREWORD

Over thirty years ago in Europe, horse and pony riding was first introduced as a viable alternative form of rehabilitation therapy for persons with physical disabilities. At that time, one of the most difficult tasks facing the early equestrian pioneers was to try to convince a then skeptical medical profession of the numerous therapeutic benefits that could be derived for persons with a multitude of disabilities while they attempted to control or "ride" a horse.

Provided the term "therapeutic" was not over-emphasized, medical advisors went along with what was then considered the brainchild of a few eccentric "horsey people". In spite of doubting the full extent of the benefits that were claimed early on, therapists grudgingly admitted that in fact "no harm could be done" given certain safety requirements and medical guidelines were followed. It took quite a few years of participation in operating programs before doctors, surgeons and therapists finally became convinced of its value, and began to recommend this new form of "treatment" for patients with a variety of physical disabilities.

A group of German medical and equestrian experts, following a visit to the Chigwell Center in England, finally recognized the multiple therapeutic benefits of the horse's movement and subsequently coined the phrase "Hippotherapy." This term now applies to treatment of patients whose degree of disability or involvement may contraindicate an actual progressive riding program, but who may benefit from specific mounted exercises. These exercises are determined by the therapist and the riding instructor, and utilize the rhythm of the horse's movement, the warmth of the horse, the rolling action of the horse's gait, and results in the adjustment necessary to maintain balance. These "patients" are now mainly recommended by a medical professional and do not necessarily ride by their own choice.

For persons whose ability enabled them, the emphasis was directed more toward the recreational and rehabilitative effects of influencing or controlling the horse, albeit minimally. The enjoyment and social integration aspects of treatment outside of the "clinical atmosphere" was also a prime consideration. At the initial joint assessment or evaluation the individual desires of the student were taken into consideration, provided they were mentally aware and capable of making their own decision to ride. Hence, the adoption of the Chigwell motto,"It is Ability not Disability that Counts!"

During the last twenty years a great deal has been written by different authors, separately on both aspects. To my knowledge, however, the two approaches have never been described or compiled so logically together, to explain the natural progression from Hippotherapy to Rehabilitative Riding, through all the natural transitions. This manual covers both in great detail. It is the result of close cooperation between experts from various fields, who have been involved in programs for many years and who have obviously learnt a great deal from their personal experiences. It also includes very comprehensively the opinions of riders with a variety of disabilities, who describe their own personal experiences. These I find particularly enlightening and informative.

Anyone who has the opportunity to read this manual can learn and apply these unique principles to teaching their own students, and thereby enable many more, who may choose, to take up and hold *"The Reins of Life"* !

John A. Davies

May 1991

Former Chief Instructor, Riding For The Disabled Trust, England, 1964-1973;
President, North American Riding for the Handicapped Association, 1976-1982.

Preface

Therapeutic Riding Programs: Instruction and Rehabilitation is a collection of essays assembled in chapters relating to specific topics. Each topic deals with a distinct base of knowledge which can influence instruction and rehabilitation with the person with disabilities. Bringing together the experiences of people in the fields of horsemanship and therapeutic horseback riding provides a dynamic paradigm and a base of knowledge to effectively improve any instructor's and therapist's performance.

This book was developed to expand the field of knowledge in therapeutic horseback riding, to promote thought, and to raise questions regarding present techniques used in sport, education, and medicine with the horse. Horseback riding for persons with disabilities has gained popularity throughout the world. It is time for **Therapeutic Horseback Riding** to move from amateurism to professionalism. By presenting many points of views, personal opinions, and a variety of techniques, the editor has intended to raise within the reader questions which should provoke thought and help to inspire research. For a field to become "professional," it must have a base of proven knowledge. Only then will therapeutic riding be accepted as a viable product for the consumer--the person with disabilities.

The reader looking at each of the disciplines of therapeutic riding becomes aware of the magnitude of the field. In order to serve those who come to us to the fullest extent of our ability, we must assimilate a great deal of knowledge. I hope this book is a step toward in depth exploration.

Barbara Teichmann Engel

Thou shall:

Practice " Safety First"

Do no harm to any rider

Present a professional appearance

Have a daily lesson plan appropriate to riders' disabilities

Be a task master; of yourself and those around you

Simplify words and actions

Be creative, be resourceful

Bring each rider to his full potential, challenge each rider

Recognize your own areas of strength, and limitations

Inspire confidence

Enjoy yourself while teaching, enjoy your riders

Jean Tebay

PART I HUMAN-HORSE BONDING

1 THE HUMAN-HORSE BOND

Elizabeth Atwood Lawrence, VMD, PhD.

> *"He who has seen the tree-tops bend before the wind or a*
> *horse move knows all there is to be known about dancing."*
> (Porter, 1989)

The vital role that the horse can play in human healing--both physical and mental--is a contemporary dimension of the equine animal's capacity to serve as an indispensable partner throughout the history of civilization. During the centuries following its domestication, no animal has been more closely intertwined with human life and culture. Wherever the horse's strength was utilized to confer power and mobility, it transformed people's way of life and contributed in countless ways to the improvement of human welfare.

Associated with the equine capacity for providing traction and transport have always been the horse's extreme sensitivity and an unusual potentiality for fine-tuned communication with people. In its role as a living vehicle, carrying human beings forward into space, the horse has provided new dimensions of experience and sensation. Also, by means of shared kinetic processes--the physical and mental merging of rider and mount--this has awakened the human spirit to fresh aspects of perception through its special qualities of pace and rhythm. The horse affords satisfaction for our species' profound fascination with motion, and has near-universal appeal to the human senses of sight, sound, and touch.

The fact that there are said to be more horses in America now, when their use is almost entirely restricted to pleasure, than there were during the age when the animals were the essential means of transportation demonstrates the appreciation that the present society has for horses. Part of their appeal is that horses confer a feeling of heightened self-worth that is reflected in the behavior and perceptions of people who interact with them. Throughout much of human social history it has been the general rule that horses, both in a literal and symbolic sense, elevate the status of those who ride and use them. As Walter Prescott Webb wrote,

> *"The horse has always exerted a peculiar emotional effect on both the rider and the*
> *observer: he has raised the rider above himself, has increased his power and sense of*
> *power, and has aroused a sense of inferiority and envy in the humble pedestrian...*
> *Through long ages the horse has been the symbol of superiority, of victory and triumph."*

The historian goes on to point out that *"A good rider on a good horse is as much above himself and others as the world can make him."* (Webb,1936)

A survey of horse-owning cultures of the world reveals a pervasive theme of high regard for the horse, which is almost universally recognized as the aristocrat among domestic animals, often identified with luxury, leisure, and power (Barclay, 1980). Evidence indicates that from earliest times, human relationships with horses have been especially meaningful. From the dawn of human consciousness, the horse has been a source of inspiration. Its beauty and strength were first immortalized in Paleolithic cave paintings. The admiration that all equestrian societies throughout history have felt for horses persists into modern times, for the aura of equine grandeur remains to grace the machine age. The term most frequently applied to horses is "noble." Again and again people reiterate the concept of the horse as the noblest of animals. Somehow the horse's traits--dignity and refinement, grace, beauty, and power--are felt to be transmitted to its human associates, for the equine animal seems to confer self-esteem and even ennoblement.

As a huge and powerful animal, the horse represents a paradox, for its strength can be guided and controlled according to human bidding. That mounts respond to people with such gentleness and dependability seems miraculous. Even more remarkable is the plasticity demonstrated by horses that allows them to adapt their behavior to the particular

1

rider and situation at hand. Differences in interaction with one rider as compared to another show the horse's capability for discrimination and individual experience. The sensation of riding, as described by one keen horseman who spent the early part of his life in the saddle each day from dawn to dusk, means that a horse is "not a mere cunningly fashioned machine" which *sustains us; but a something with life and thought, like ourselves, that feels what we feel, understands us, and keenly participates in our pleasures. Take, for example, the horse on which some quiet old country gentleman is accustomed to travel; how soberly and evenly he jogs along, picking his way over the ground. But let him fall into the hands of a lively youngster, and how soon he picks up a frisky spirit!* (Hudson, 1903).

Although the extraordinary intercommunication that takes place between people and horses has not been adequately explained, it continues to amaze those who observe it and experience it for pleasure and for healing.

Today, though mechanization has made the historic utility of horses for transportation and work virtually obsolete, and societies no longer revolve around them, contemporary people still turn to their traditional equine partner for important functions. Horses are companions of a different order than most other domestic species, for they provide an experience of motion that defies machinery. Equestrians can merge their own being with the rhythm and power of their mounts, bonding with a living creature in a participatory rather than a passive way. Communication between horse and rider is both physical and mental. The grace of movement of the horse somehow becomes possessed by the rider.

In our highly industrialized, mechanized age, horses have the unique role of leading us back to nature, back to our roots, back to the elemental rhythms and cycles of life. To ride a horse is to leave the cares of the mundane world behind and to become fused with the movements of a splendid creature that still belongs to the realm of nature, though it lends itself so willingly to humankind. The image of the centaur is deeply embedded in the human psyche, for it expresses the universal dream of unity with the animal world. And no other creature elicits or fulfills a deeper desire for that merging, that oneness with the elemental forces of nature, than the horse.

So wondrous is the bond between people and horses that it can never be definitively defined or wholly explained. Its richness and complexity give many facets to this age-old affective relationship. Mounted on a horse, the rider feels exhilarated in body and spirit. The animal not only provides an elevated position, but confers a heightened awareness that is an essential component of any type of healing process. The unbridled horse is a symbol of freedom, yet the equestrian, for a time, can direct the animal's path and share its swift flight, partaking of a marvelous adventure. But the benefits that horses bring to human life do not depend only on being ridden. Even the sound of equine hoofbeats may afford comfort and tranquility (Lawrence 1985). The feel of a horse's velvet-soft muzzle, the warm curves of its neck and flanks, the sight of its flowing mane and tail that blow in the wind, the sweet smell of its hay-scented breath--all these give solace to the horse lover that is like no other. In modern society, the horse has a role as healer--both for those who are weary of life's stresses and for those who have mental or physical handicaps to overcome. In some remarkable way, whatever quality an individual may lack, whether it is confidence, serenity, courage, or coordination, or whether it is health of mind or body, the horse willingly helps to evoke that quality so that it becomes the person's own possession. It is this complementarily that so endears the horse to human beings and cements the bond between them. An old adage states that "there is something about the outside of a horse that is good for the inside of a person." Folklore, which even many modern physicians believe, though they cannot explain it, holds that association with horses brings good health that leads to longevity. The extremely beneficial results that are being obtained through therapeutic horseback riding programs are evidence of the great effectiveness of healing through horses. Such programs demonstrate the adaptability of the horse in lending its many unique and wonderful attributes to the improvement of the quality of human life. The dramatically favorable results obtained from therapy using horses to promote human well-being depend upon and give testament to the enduring strength and power of the special bond between people and horses.

References
Barclay, H.B. (1980). *The Role of the Horse in Man's Culture*. London: J.A. Allen Co. 396-70.
Hudson, W.H. (1903). *The Naturalist in La Plata*. New York: E.P. Dutton & Co. 352.
Lawrence, E.A. (1985). *Hoofbeats and Society: Studies of Human-Horse Interactions*. Bloomington:Indiana Univ. Press. 145-46, 180-81.
Porter, V. (1989). *Horse Tails*. London: Guiness Publishing Ltd. 109.
Webb, W.P. (1936). *The Great Plains*. Boston: Houghton and Mifflin. 493.

photograph by Susan Earhart Feldman

THE HORSE-HUMAN BOND--Jan Spink and her horse

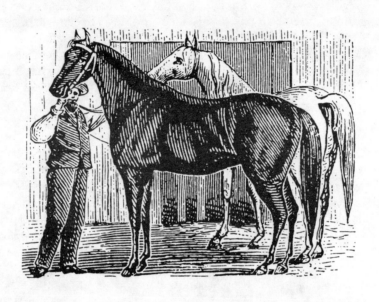

2   FROM THE RIDER'S POINT OF VIEW

2.01 RIDING AS ABLE, THEN DISABLED

Marci Lawson

I have been riding horses ever since I can remember. First they were farm horses that my cousins and I jumped onto bareback, and rode with a halter and lead rope. Next it was working at a stable and leading trail rides, always riding a rent string horse. Then came mucking stalls for the privilege of a "real" lesson from a trainer. And finally on down the line, came my own business which kept me on the show circuits with pleasure horses, hunters, jumpers, and a handful of junior riders to promote as well. Then came life in a wheelchair.

Like most people that go through a devastating change in their life, I wasn't quite sure what to do with myself. I spent the first year quite depressed. It seemed I had to give up everything I liked to do most: sports, riding, camping and worst of all my business. I could find absolutely nothing to do from a wheelchair. That is until I found a small article in the newspaper about a local program that offered horseback riding to--what--yes--disabled individuals. It took a few weeks to muster the courage to call the program as I wasn't sure what I could possibly do. Finally I did call to get more information and to see how I could be of any help. Little did I know then the possibilities that lay ahead of me.

After visiting the program and observing the first lesson, I knew that I was hooked. The program's founder and director and I became friends as she put me to work in various capacities based on my previous background in horsemanship. I immediately became a board member, primarily as a spokes-person for the disabled students, and represented them, as well as their families and friends. I still had many contacts in the horse world and had new ones throughout the general disabled community which helped to attract more riders into the program. My favorite capacity, though, was as a "disabled rider consultant." Many times I was asked to consult with a riding instructor and help problem solve a rider's particular problem. I often explained to the teacher what a handicapped rider's body was feeling, as I could relate the experience to how my own body would react in a particular circumstance. Often I could formulate ideas to make some process easier, or possibly more independent for the student in either grooming, mounting, riding, or dismounting procedures because of methods I had myself experimented with. It became quite a challenge to identify my limitations, as well as abilities, and to try to match them with other students to help improve their own skills.

It is truly amazing to me as a wheelchair user to realize exactly what a good ride, meaning the combination of the right exercises and activities, plus the right horse, can do to a disabled body. I have seen drastic changes in other riders, which, of course is always impressive, but when I can feel it happening to my own body it's unforgettable! I have a neuromuscular disease called familial spastic quadraparesis which can be similar in symptoms to many other types of neurological diseases including multiple sclerosis and Lou Gehrig's disease. As the name of my disease implies, there is a strong spastic component to my disorder which tends to keep my limbs rather stiff and makes moving in a coordinated fashion difficult. Some muscles are constantly tight and contracted. After a while the muscles begin to tire and although they tend to stay tight, they begin to ache as though I had a bad case of the flu. I take medicine for the spasticity and do some range of motion exercises to keep the muscles as loose as possible, but spasticity does not just disappear. You learn to live with it.

As the time finally neared for me to actually mount and ride a horse for the first time as a disabled person, I had a lot of mixed feelings and thoughts racing through my mind. As a person who craved independence, I realized that this would not be an independent feat in the least. I was still picturing myself on a 17 hand thoroughbred, galloping around the arena heading toward a 5 foot solid wall, ready to feel the adrenaline rush as my horse lifted his front feet and coiled like a tight spring in the rear, to leap over the obstacle looming in front of us. But as I was wheeled over to the wheelchair mounting ramp, I was suddenly snapped back to reality. I saw a large, broad horse standing patiently at the ramp with a leader at his head, a side walker at his off-side, and my second side walker and the instructor on the ramp ready to assist me onto the horse. As I have minimal trunk control I also required a fifth person to stabilize me on the horse. Imagine, five people just so that I could ride for ten minutes at the walk! I was feeling pretty humiliated by then.

My first conscious thought after I mounted was how wonderful it was to look down at my sidewalkers. Since I have been using a wheelchair, all I have done was look up at people, which can easily make you feel childlike again. To actually look down on all those around me was a most pleasant surprise! That first ride went very smoothly and was indeed quite pleasant, mainly riding on the rail at an even, long, and swinging stride. The horse was great. I remember how peaceful I felt and how comfortable and relaxing the long rocking rhythmic walk felt to my stiff body. It was at this point that I started to learn about, or maybe just be aware of, new aspects of riding.

As I worked mentally to get my body relaxed, I suddenly became aware of the cadence of the horse's foot falls. Not just the cadence, but also the actual sequence. We all know that the horse's walk is a four beat gait, but I had never been aware how much stronger the first and third beats are. I guess it makes sense, as those beats are from the rear legs which automatically imply some thrust and drive. But I had never noticed the difference until I rode as a disabled rider and my body reacted more to those first and third beats.

Another thing that I discovered was *that if a horse was at all lame, even just slightly off, it could ruin my whole ride in that my body would stiffen even more each time the horse would step down onto the affected leg.* It therefore became of utmost importance to pick the horse that I would ride on the soundness and purity of his gait. A nice long even swinging stride proved to be the best for me, and for that the horse needs to be fairly tall. What seems to work for me is to match the size of the horse relative and proportionate to the size of the rider. If I ride a horse under 15 to 15 ½ hands, the stride tends to be too short and the positive effect is not nearly as pronounced as if I ride a larger horse with a longer, flowing stride.

I think that the greatest thing for me about riding a horse now, is what it can do for my body. I can mount the horse being stiff and rigid, but when I dismount after a good ride I come off the horse similar to a wet, soggy noodle. To date I have found no other exercise or activity that can even approximate the extreme relaxation I get from riding. My body gets so relaxed that for a few minutes after my ride it is difficult to coordinate any voluntary movement and I must in fact be strapped into my wheelchair just to keep me from slipping right out onto the floor. It may sound terrible, but in reality it feels absolutely wonderful.

I have one suggestion to make to instructors of the disabled. My favorite lesson plan as a physically disabled rider is to have a three part lesson. The first part contains some mild stretching and exercising routines to limber and loosen up enough to perform the second part of the lesson, which can be anything from serious equitation to just fun and games. Whatever the second part consists of, make it challenging mentally as well as physically. Frequently physically disabled riders have few chances to be stimulated mentally, especially if they are unable to attend school or work. So challenge their brains and make them think and plan and concentrate within their lesson. The third and best segment of the lesson is the relaxation part.

I like to end the lesson and get off the horse feeling better both mentally and physically than when I got on. I believe to achieve complete physical relaxation, one must give up the reins and control of the horse to a leader, so that the arms can be free to relax as well. Depending on the rider and the disability, the technique used can vary from simple exercises to full hippotherapy. Find what works best with your student, then make it part of your lesson plan.

In summary, I guess that I would have to affirm that horseback riding is a great sport whether you do it from a wheelchair or as an able-bodied person. The parameters are different, but the challenges are always there. The challenge comes from what a person can feasibly do, not from what is realistically unattainable.

"My own challenge now comes not from facing a tough round of five foot jumps, but rather possibly doing an independent transfer from wheelchair to the horse. I will always continue to keep meeting the challenge!"

2.02 EDGING TOWARD FULFILLMENT

Eileen Szychowski

"Come to the edge," he said,
They said "We are afraid".
"Come to the edge" he said.
They came... he pushed them
And they flew!

Author Unknown

Standing on the narrow, swaying bridge, I savored the wind in my hair and watched it lift my horse's mane. This wonderful horse and the sublime world of the Inner Canyon made me forget I had just ridden seven hours on slim, winding trails that edged thousand foot cliffs. Instead, I felt that I had been carried into an unearthly world on the mist of the river--the great Colorado--which churned and roared sixty feet below.

It was hard to believe that a year previously I was denied, on the basis of handicap, the opportunity and the right to ride the Grand Canyon. I owed this historical ride and the confidence to do it to a wonderful teacher named Josef Rivers who operates a therapeutic riding program in California called the DRAGON SLAYERS. Josef was my first disabled role model and continues to inspire me today. Among the many special gifts he has given me was the knowledge that, despite crutches, leg braces and paralyzed hands, I could be or do anything! He also gave me several years of training and several magnificent horses to begin my own program, CAMELOT, here in ARIZONA.

What makes CAMELOT and DRAGON SLAYERS unique among handicapped riding programs is that they are among a handful of programs which are run by persons with disabilities. I have always felt that my handicap is my greatest asset in teaching. My disability experience increases my sensitivity to my students and also increases my expectations of them. Living with my own disability helps me in creatively overcoming obstacles while the heightened expectations enable students to discover their potential. Research shows that students will perform according to expectation. Disabled persons can and want to work hard. Indeed, there is therapeutic value in hard work and, if the truth be known, hard work is part of daily living with a disability. Don't be afraid to send us home tired. It will be a "tired" we can feel good about.

Growing up with a physical disability, I grew frustrated at programs which failed to challenge me, which treated me "special" when what I wanted and needed was to be treated equal. Those of us in the helping professions--including disabled riding programs--continue to make this mistake today, which results in limiting the potential of the people we serve.

Those of us who go into the field of disabled riding are, by nature, caring people who want to make life better for others. But let us begin by honestly examining our perceptions. Do we see the people we serve as our equals, having a unique combination of strengths and needs with the potential to become independent persons integrated into our community? Or do we see them as "kids" regardless of their age, who will always need us, who will never leave the lead line or show in anything but "special" shows. Do we see them in terms of possibility or disability? It is true that some disabled persons will go farther than others, but all of us with disabilities will go farther in a teaching environment which supports our right to explore risk and does not, however well intended, attempt to keep us separate or protect us from disappointment. We are failing a vast contingent of physically disabled persons who are not being appropriately served by our therapeutic recreation programs simply because of our own attitudes about risk and failure. And so, places like the Grand Canyon, the forests, shorelines, mountains and deserts which belong to all of us are accessible to only a few. When I began my lessons under Josef Rivers, I wanted more than a pony ride. I wanted to someday own a horse so that I could have complete access to nature, perhaps even to show, breed and

7

train horses. I wanted things to be made accessible to me--not made easy for me. And that is what I got: a tough but empowering teacher who did not give me ribbons just for being disabled but gave me the incentive to win or lose like anyone else. In this way, horses became the greatest equalizers in my life.

This experience of empowerment is what I seek to pass on to my own students at CAMELOT. Like the DRAGON SLAYERS, CAMELOT operates on a few basic truths. The first basic truth is that dreams are essential to quality of life. Dreams involve risk, risk is a basic human right. We must honor the need to dream and the right to risk by building challenge into our programs. Out of my frustration with programs and activities which failed to meet my needs for challenge and integration grew the commitment to design a curriculum with more emphasis on personal development than physical therapy. Frankly speaking, most of us have had therapy up the kazoo! Our parents, teachers and therapists have lovingly done their best to enhance our lives, but, all too often the development of muscle has been stressed while overlooking our human need for fun and the kinds of social interactions which lead to a healthy adult life.

CAMELOT is offered as a salute to disabled persons who want to pilot their own ship rather than be a passenger. Our students come with the desire to feel the wind in their faces, to ride the trail and experience the outdoors. We encourage them to set their own goals, reminding them not to think small. Most of our work is done outside the arena, moving always toward independence and goal fulfillment. All of this means, of course, increased risk which requires horses and staff that are absolutely exemplary, jewels which can only be found through rigorous screening and training. Accordingly, CAMELOT requires of staff a minimum age of 21 and some basic knowledge of horses. This means not everybody will be suitable as a rider assistant. We utilize them in other ways. Safety and challenge can happily co-exist but only when the strictest standards are adhered to.

Yes, this is especially difficult when we are all in need of more volunteers. At CAMELOT we make our commitment to do a small job well through a well-structured, individualized program rather than trying to serve everybody. (After all, the world is changed one life at a time). We have found that serious trail riding and horse trekking for the disabled can only be approached in this way, an approach which has led to several CAMELOT students acquiring their own horses or landing jobs in the horse industry. All of this comes back to our personal attitudes about dreams, risk and possibility. Another basic truth we believe at CAMELOT is that disabled persons should be in control of their own lives. CAMELOT, therefore, is a program where disabled persons provide their own leadership. Our teaching model is based on mentorship. This is not to say that able bodied instructors should not be operating programs or teaching disabled students. What I am saying is that the role model is a most powerful way of teaching. Cultivate this precious resource! Use your advanced riders as assistant instructors, advisors and board members to insure that you are hitting your mark. Solicit the input of the people you serve in all aspects of your program!

I am excited to see that programs are improving as the field of adaptive riding matures. We are all seeing more riders and they are asking more of us as their teachers. Let's continue to allow our disabled students to define their own horizons and when they have arrived, encourage them to go a step further. We will all grow in the process; after all, we are all both teacher and student. At CAMELOT we call this the Round Table philosophy.

HOW DOES IT WORK? They come..I push them...and WE FLY!

© 1990 E.S.

2.03 HOW THERAPEUTIC HORSEBACK RIDING WAS INSTRUMENTAL IN MY REHABILITATION

Sandy Dota

In 1980 while out trail riding, my horse was spooked by a dog, causing me to fall. The result of that fall was a spinal cord injury from a broken back. This injury left me a paraplegic. I have no use of my legs or control of my bodily functions from the waist down. When I came out of surgery, the doctor told me I would probably never walk again. I appreciated his honesty. Over the next few months, I would realize how my accident would create a major change in my life and that of my family. Not walking again would be only <u>one</u> of the many difficulties I'd have to learn to endure.

My main inconvenience has been loss of bowel and bladder control. Fear of incontinence or an embarrassing accident dictates where I can go and for how long. Usually, I didn't care to go anywhere at anytime. Being seen in public as a disabled person and in a wheelchair also made me extremely uncomfortable. During the first two years, I hardly left my house (except my excursions to the stable). Going to shopping malls was a horror because I felt everyone was staring at me. I no longer felt like a customer or typical shopper. I saw myself as this big clumsy obstacle in everyone's way. I got to the point where I just refused to go to stores which put an additional burden on my husband. I had lost all self-confidence and much self-esteem. This was not a good feeling.

I had a real need. I was not much good for myself or my family. Rehab and medical professionals were not much help. Their job was to constantly remind me of "reality" and the "real world" according to everyone else's point of view. I heard things like, "you've got to learn to adjust," or "you've got to learn to live with it." No encouragement was ever positive or upbeat. And you can just forget horseback riding, 'cause that doesn't fit into their reality at all; paraplegics CANNOT RIDE HORSES!

I was convinced of this until I came across an article in a newspaper about the Cheff Center for the Handicapped in Augusta, Michigan. The article focused on therapeutic horseback riding. From the information sent to me, I found out therapeutic riding is rehabilitative emotionally as well as physically, and at the same time it can be recreational. For me, just the thought of riding again was exciting and overwhelming. I was informed by the Cheff Center to contact Mrs. Octavia Brown at the Somerset Hills Handicapped Riding Club in Bedminster, N.J. After a "go ahead" from my surgeon, and a lot of "I hope you know what you are doing" from my family and friends, I was back in the saddle only ten months after my accident, this time on the back of a beautiful mare called Brandy. My own horse put me in the chair; Brandy took me out.

Animals have that innate ability to break through emotional barriers that drugs and the medical profession have difficulty accomplishing. Animals meet a human being's needs of honesty and affection, creating a valuable friendship. Most people would be astonished to think this is possible with a horse, but they have not met the horses and ponies in therapeutic riding programs.

My riding lessons had begun with a leader at Brandy's head and a side-walker on each side of me for balance and support. It took two years of lessons before I could be weaned of one side-walker, then the other, and finally the leader. I was now an independent rider again, just me and my horse, walking around the ring with an occasional bit of trotting. Although this was enough to make me happy, it was not enough for Brandy; she expected more of me. She taught me to trust her, and she would help me learn, by not always being consistent, to balance myself to increase my riding ability. Brandy was always totally tuned into my body and its needs. She ignored my distracting legs as they flopped and banged at her sides, all the while encouraging me to use my upper body for control and balance. She could transform the most timid personality into an assertive, self-confident individual. Although this horse may seem special or remarkable, almost every therapeutic riding program has a "Brandy." She is a representation of the personality and attitude required before a horse is accepted into a therapeutic riding program.

9

For me, Brandy represented a transition in my life, a kind of stepping stone. My weekly riding lessons with Brandy were all I looked forward to. She didn't care about my wheelchair or my disability; she responded only to my feelings for her. She made me feel worthwhile. Because she was so nurturing to me, I grew to trust her completely. In doing so, my riding improved dramatically. I was becoming more confident in myself and my capabilities, dwelling less and less on what I could not do. With Brandy, I began doing riding exhibitions and even started competing in horse shows. I couldn't imagine something like this was possible for any paraplegic, much less me. Through Brandy, I was allowed to find another reality, one I could learn to adjust to or live with; hers was not the reality of resignation and adjustment, but of "can do." Trust in her gave me the self-esteem I needed to progress and the self-confidence to follow through.

In 1985 I earned a position on the New Jersey Cerebral Palsy/Les Autres Equestrian Team and competed very successfully on the national level. We received the Governor's Trophy and New Jersey State Horse person of the Year award for 1985. This award had been given the previous year to the U.S. Olympic Equestrian Team. So as you can see, we were in pretty good company! Another rider from Somerset Hills and I were among fourteen top disabled riders in the U.S. who were invited to participate in Inspire '85, an event chaired by Nancy Reagan. We did three performances of a musical Pas de Deux on the Capitol Mall in Washington, D.C. My riding pursuits have since taken me and my family all over the U.S. and Canada. I have also taken an active interest in carriage driving and was reserve champion in 1988 at an ADS (American Driving Society) sanctioned show in New Jersey. When not competing in horse shows, I am working at them. I've been show secretary, scribe for dressage judges, and am also a judge myself (certified with the American Judging Association). I have also completed an instructors' training course to instruct horseback riding to people with disabilities and have been teaching since 1985. I have been on the faculty (in the instructor's position) of NARHA's[1] General Workshop and Instructor Workshop.

I currently have a horse that is being trained "in lightness" by Jean-Claude Racinet (a master of riding in lightness). This principle involves the absolute lightness of the horse to the hands, seat and legs of the rider. As the training progresses, the horse performs more and more in a self-maintained impulsion, carriage and collection, the rider practicing an almost permanent release of the aids. My personal goal is to perform higher level dressage exercises using the *lightness* approach, but the ultimate result will show how a horse trained in lightness can increase the abilities of disabled riders as well as able-bodied riders.

You are reading about the same person who several years ago could not handle being seen in public in a wheelchair, and at that time whose closest friend was a horse. True, even today when I go to shopping malls, people still stare. That's human nature. But, it's not my problem anymore. My chair is just a tool, something to make my life easier, just as eyeglasses are a tool to help someone see better. The point is, I go and I do. I now have the courage to at least try. My husband and my son are happy to have our household back to "normal" again. I've become very busy and totally committed to supporting and promoting therapeutic horseback riding and driving and their benefits.

"Who would have thought the same thing that put me in a wheelchair, namely horseback riding, would be the same thing to get me "back on my feet again" so to speak?

Sandy

---

[1] NARHA: North American Riding for the Handicapped Association, P.O. Box 33150, Denver, CO USA

2.04 THE VALUE OF HORSEBACK RIDING

Lisa Walsh

Horseback riding has played a large role in my life. I have been riding for the past 16 years and I couldn't imagine not having it be such a large part of my life. It is now not just an activity but it is part of my work week. I do not take it for granted; it is missed greatly if I cannot ride.

The value of horseback riding is priceless. When I began riding, I thought it would be great therapy for me. Little did I know how much else in my life riding could affect. I do depend on my horse's body warmth to stretch my muscles and allow them to lengthen. The horse's movement during his walk, trot, halt and other transitions have taught me how to "think ahead" and prepare my body for different actions. My balance has become keen both on horseback and on the ground, whether I am in my wheelchair, on a bench, or on the ground.

My eye-hand coordination has strengthened as I am now an independent rider and have gained positive thought process through the use of horseback riding. My spasticity can be overwhelming at times along with my athetoid movements. Through the use of horseback riding I have been taught a great philosophy--"MIND OVER BODY." My instructor and her many leaders have allowed me to accept my cerebral palsy and its many difficulties and utilize my strengths. It is not easy but this theory does work. If we put our minds before our actions, great things do happen! That's exciting and possible.

Horseback riding has increased my self-concept 110%. In the beginning, it gave me pride. Pride that I could do an activity that nobody else in my family would even think of doing. Sixteen years later, I would never have thought I'd be where I have been today:

1. I have traveled to the West Coast to demonstrate that horseback riding is a positive thing in a very therapeutic way.

2. I have competed locally, regionally and nationally against persons with my disability, with a different disabilities, and with no disability at all.

3. I have traveled abroad - once as an alternate member to the U.S. Equestrian Team to compete in the First World Championship held in Orust, Sweden. And once as a member on the U.S. Equestrian team to the Games for the Cerebral Palsied in Assen, Holland.

4. I was chosen to present a paper on horseback riding and its many positive attributes, with responses from other disabled riders, to the International Conference on Animal-Human Relationships held in Monaco in November 1989.

The above four activities focused greatly on how I felt about myself. Through horseback riding I am able to leave my disability behind and stress my abilities. It may have started with confidence that my horse will remain still as I mount, allowing my body to respond with awkward movements. I think as my body moves, everything will be fine, and I complete my movement while I am thinking about it. "MIND OVER BODY" can be powerful, and simply, it can work. As I try to keep in mind that very powerful theory and practice, I need to remember that nothing is perfect. Spasms do happen. Differences can be present. Above all, nothing is perfect.

Horseback riding has also taught me a great deal about relationships both between human and human and/or animal and human. With any relationship one must continue to give and take. I trust my family and I trust my horse. I acknowledge the presence of goodness in my friends and family. I see the gold upon my mount. As my horse moves, I need to allow him to feel as free as I do, yet acknowledge that I do have control with trust. With my friends and family, it takes more than just one person to get something good finished. Even better, to be independent, I have to acknowledge my needs and how they should be met.

As an adult rider, I believe that I have received top-notch instruction. Dressage is understood but I always can better my ride. My instructor has taught me how to use my abilities and deal with my disabilities. Upon a horse I have no limitations. I expect my instructor to accept me as I am, but teach me to ride as she teaches many others, disability or no disability.

In summary, horseback riding is priceless. It has given me dignity. I know that it is okay to be me, no matter what. I am proud of my past, my family, my friends and myself. It has allowed me to say "yes I use a wheelchair but yes I have many abilities." I am a teacher. I am disabled. I have a great number of friends and family who believe in me and my abilities as I do. I am a human being with dignity like everyone else.

I wouldn't give up horseback riding for the world!

2.05 A RIDER'S PERSPECTIVE

Arthur S. Hansen, DDS

Readers of this section should know that I am writing as a rider who is hemiplegic as a result of a right cerebral hemorrhage (CVA) in 1982 and subsequent brain surgery in 1983. Prior to the foregoing, I was an active dentist in a private practice and showed no signs of problems of the nature described. I also had no previous riding experience or contact with horses other than occasional "hack" rides as a teenager.

Since my surgery in 1983, I have attended rehabilitation sessions in which physical and occupational therapists used Bobath techniques. My riding began in 1984 during a particularly depressive period, more or less as a last resort. This last resort saved my life. The information I will share with you has been developed through a mentor/rider program, hippotherapy program and individual evaluation and experiment program. I ride for therapy; riding is secondary to therapy. **My riding has been "*my therapy*" whether it was hippotherapy, therapeutic riding or just riding on the Alaskan trails.**

The Horse
The horse is the most important element in therapy or therapeutic riding and the instructor must know and understand the horse. The ability of the horse will dictate the therapy that the rider will receive. In a controlled situation, the instructor must know how to engage the horse to gain the movement pattern that the therapist has requested for the rider. The instructor must know and understand the communications of the horse (i.e., tail swishing, head shaking) so as to develop the horse's potential for a rider. Not only must the instructor understand this aspect of the horse, but the horse's behavioral characteristics must be taught to the rider (if the rider is able to understand). This is an important aspect of rider improvement especially if sensory systems are impaired. The horse can replace these impairments to some degree if the rider and instructor are sensitive to the horse's actions. The higher the training level of the horse, the more this is true, due to the higher level of sensitivity of the horse to the rider's actions (i.e., leg pressure from high leg tone may cause the horse to do side passes or move sideways). The challenge in such a situation is for the rider to adjust the pressure or change position so as to stop or prevent unwanted movement of the horse. In this way the trained horse becomes the therapist by eliciting desirable activity from the rider. It cannot be over-emphasized how important the horse is to the rider.

The Horse Trainer
The trainer probably holds the key to the success of any therapeutic riding program or individual's therapy on horseback because it is the trainer who must be relied on to train the horse so it can be used to its fullest potential. The better the horse is trained, the greater it can be utilized in therapeutic riding. In order to do this, the trainer must understand how the horse is to be used by the rider and what must be done to draw the desired results out of the horse. In order to do this, the trainer must confer with the therapist, instructor and therapy team members.

The Therapist
The therapist must have determined a goal or several goals and a plan to attain them. The goals should be presented to the rider, instructor and the therapeutic riding team. Once this is done, the team can synergistically develop the best way to proceed. The therapist is the monitoring person for the rider to assure that the program progresses, is challenging, and that it is producing the desired results with the fewest side effects.

The Instructor
The instructor must instill confidence and enthusiasm for what the rider is doing. The primary goal of any therapeutic riding instructor should be to assist in integrating a medically, physically, or mentally compromised person into a society that considers itself "normal." It is to this end that all activities involving a client should be directed. In the process, the activities involved should in no way be demeaning or patronizing. Remember, riders are people too,

and should be treated as such. They are not "problems" housed in a body, but people with a problem. In many cases they are extraordinary people who show courage, perseverance and drive beyond the norm. It also must be remembered that were it not for these people and their needs, there would be no need for the therapeutic riding programs. These riders need the instructors, but it must never be forgotten that the program is for the riders and the benefits they derive from it and not vice versa.

Challenge plays an important part in eliciting therapeutic progress. It is important for the instructors to challenge the riders, but at the same time they must monitor and minimize risks involved. Risk removal should not be carried to extremes, however, so as not to stifle the inner need for challenge. The risk-taking is very important in eliciting progress from the client. A rider's program also should be dynamic. Push the limits of the rider at each session. Vary activities for or during each session to keep the rider's interest. If the rider is able to talk, involve him in the activities and get feed-back on the results.

Find out what the rider likes or does not like, whether he has pain or not. Don't forget, however, that the rider's reactions will change as he progresses. Don't assume that things are static. If the program established for the rider is dynamic and progressive, noticeable changes can take place in a week or two, or even during a session, depending on the duration and frequency of the sessions. This will depend on the rider and the trainer's ability to accommodate him or her in the program. Once goals have been achieved, new goals should be developed, but the old goals should be incorporated in the process of attaining the new goals so progress is not lost, but reinforced.

The Volunteer It is the volunteer's job to assist the instructors and/or therapist to see that the sought-after goals are achieved by the rider. At the same time goals are being pursued, it must be remembered that progress is not always forward. Many things such as illness, depression or other outside distractions may impede progress. The volunteer must realize this and adjust to it. The rider may or may not realize ground has been lost and it is often only the urging and persistence of the volunteer that carries the rider through the rough times. A friendly smile means more than one could ever realize when the rider is in need.

Possibly the greatest improvement in riders will be in the areas of psychological well-being and self-esteem. The volunteer can play an important role in this area by praising the rider when it is earned and by keeping the rider interested and focused on the riding session.

Accomplishment is an important part of improving one's sense of well-being and renewing self-esteem. It is an important aspect of the volunteer's job to reinforce this sense of accomplishment as goals are attained. This can be done by direct observation and comment or indirectly by starting at higher levels of difficulty as goals are attained. BE DYNAMIC, but above all, BE PATIENT, because progress is often painstakingly slow. The words of my instructor to "hurry slowly" seem appropriate. He was speaking of training horses, but I believe it applies equally well to the therapeutic rider.

The Rider
The rider, next to the horse, has the most important job of all. If therapeutic riding is going to be successful, the rider must communicate in his or her own way with the therapeutic riding team and the horse. The rider must be consistent and persistent in his or her riding activities if established goals are going to be attained. My experience, with input from others, shows that progress is slow in a once-a-week program and all efforts should be made to ride at least three days a week, or seven days a week if possible. Progress is patterned and sequential and the more the patterns can be repeated on a regular basis, the greater the progress.

Children and adult riders should not be mixed--this can be embarrassing and demeaning for the adults and hinder progress; even grouping persons with different disabilities can cause problems, i.e., hypertonic and hypotonic in the same class (each of these requires different activities). Be careful not to tell the rider he or she can not do something if he or she really can. It may be your or someone else's perception that he or she can not in order to remove a risk. It could also inhibit challenge-taking and stop progress. Neither safety nor a rider's need for challenge need be compromised, as long as thought is given to both for a progressive and dynamic therapeutic riding plan. This certainly requires a delicate balance at times, and all factors must be considered on a "value-to-the-rider" basis. For the rider, frequent and consistent therapeutic riding is an effective adjunct to clinic therapy. The therapy or therapeutic riding team (horse, trainer, instructor, therapist, and volunteers) must think in terms of progress and change in order to assist the rider to attain his full potential.

My riding has been "my therapy" whether it was hippotherapy, therapeutic riding or just hacking on the Alaskan trails. My horse is "my therapist" and facilitates my therapy with or without my own assistance or anyone elses."

2.06 FROM THE RIDER'S PERSPECTIVE

Wendy R. Shugol, MA

How do I begin to unfold the myriad of feelings and opinions which I have come to formulate over the years when it comes to the topic of therapeutic riding? So much has occurred, and horses have come to play such a very significant role in my life since I first became involved with a therapeutic riding program in 1976. As a result of this partnership with horses, I have become an owner, and a contender in both disabled and able-bodied competition on many different levels.

When I began riding, l had no idea what an impact it would have on me. I had always loved horses from the time I was a small child, and suffered from a terminal case of "Black Beauty Syndrome," (something many young people experience). I never outgrew it, and, as an adult, finally received my chance to be involved with a program where I could begin to see just whether or not I really wanted to ride. I became thoroughly engrossed in horses and the therapeutic riding program right from the beginning. I was able to ride independently almost by the end of the first lesson. This experience motivated me to the point where I wanted to get as much as I could possibly get as soon as I could get it. It was the biggest "pick-me-up" I had in a long time. Here was something that I could do that was unique to my able-bodied peers! Finally, something physical that put me on equal footing with them!

From the beginning, the sky became the limit. I spent every weekend with the program, learning all I could about horse management, grooming and tacking, equipment management, and how I needed to manipulate my environment to accomplish the tasks around the farm. I figured out how to muck out stalls from my wheelchair, bring horses in from the field, clean feet and fully groom horses of all sizes.

Then, my family donated a horse to the program I was involved in. Now I had a mount whom I could ride any time the program was in session. I continued to spend just about all my free time working with, and for, the program. However, as time wore on, my enthusiasm was waning. I continued to care for the horse donated by my family but something just was not the same. l could not put my finger on it right away, but it finally occurred to me what the problem could possibly be. The problem was that I was reaching the end of what the therapeutic riding program could offer me. I was ready to move on to a higher level of riding which the program could not provide. It was becoming time for me to move on.

By this time, I was now the proud owner of the horse which my family had donated. Not knowing how I would support him, I managed to get him involved with another therapeutic riding program so I could keep my expenses to a minimum and also, to give the program the benefit of a very suitable mount for all the aspects of their curriculum (hippotherapy, vaulting, and recreational riding). I had also sought out this group because of the dressage background which the instructor possessed. I had become involved with dressage and competition, and wanted to further my knowledge and ability level. Another situation arose at about this time in my riding career: the aspect of competition. This was truly the shot-in-the-arm that I was looking for. In 1979, the National Cerebral Palsy Games was hosting the first competition ever to be held in the United States for riders with disabilities. I suddenly had a goal to work for again as I began to set my sights on this new opportunity. This was to be my first show experience.

Being a rather competitive person by nature, riding competition appealed to me immediately. The instructor I was now working with helped me in every way possible. She provided me with extra riding opportunities in preparation for this, as well as letting me know when there was a horse show competition in the area that I might benefit from watching. All these experiences were beneficial in fostering my new interest. I "repaid" the program with additional volunteering and fund-raising hours. It was a very amicable (and successful) working agreement. I was, and continue to be, very motivated in this endeavor of competitive riding. It is an avenue which continually gives me a new goal to work for. With dressage, I will never run out of new things to learn. It is always a feeling of great accomplishment when I finally achieve a new skill. Each competition is a new challenge which I look forward to very much.

In the past several years, I have graduated from the therapeutic riding programs. I have received all the benefits I can derive from their expertise. It was unfair for me to continue to take up a space on their roster when I now had two horses (I had received a second horse as a gift), both of whom were being used extensively in the program, and I was fully "mainstreamed" most of the time. I was fortunate because the program borrowed space and horses from a private facility which provided lessons on a large scale to the non-disabled public. It was quite easy for me to make the transition into mainstream riding.

My current instructor (whom I have been with for the past several years) accepted me as a student as soon as I presented my case to her. Her philosophy was much the same as mine, so we decided to give it a trial. Needless to say, it has worked out. She has extracted performance levels from me that I never thought possible. Although she pushes me to my limit and beyond, I let her know when my abnormal neurological reflexes are going to impede my performance. Then I adapt my positioning to accommodate my disability in order to achieve the desired end result. We have established an extremely successful team.

However, despite my now more advanced level of riding, competition among those in my disability group (individuals with cerebral palsy) is limited. I am currently the top-seeded rider with my level of disability in this country. This is an honor I have held since the inception of the competitive movement in 1979. It is very difficult for me to attend the regional and national qualifiers when I am fairly sure that there really will not be much, if any, competition for me in my disability classification. My experience has been, in the many programs throughout the country which I have visited, that instructors are afraid to push their students with disabilities for fear that they might be hurt if something should happen. Riding is a controlled, high risk sport, and riders who undertake this endeavor know that they are taking a chance. More than anything else, we want the right to choose the route of competition just like any other rider. We know we are taking a risk to do this, but we deserve the same opportunity as anyone else. Too often I have visited programs where there were students, still dependent upon leaders and sidewalkers, who were more than able to be riding independently. When questioned, the instructor admitted that they were afraid to let the student go for fear they may have problems. But yet, they talk about wanting their students to have the experience of competition. Riders need the tools at the program level in order to be successful in the competition arena.

Then there is the subject of space availability within a program. What happens to the riders with disabilities once they have reached as high a level of achievement as they can in their therapeutic riding programs? I was one of the lucky ones who had developed a network of people who could help me find an instructor who was willing to accept a rider who needed different techniques of teaching in order to accomplish her goals. I was also extremely fortunate in that I was given a horse so I always had access to a mount. But this is rare. I have met so many people with disabilities who have said to me, "*Oh, I used to ride but once I graduated from the program, there was nowhere else for me go. Now I am no longer riding.*" It is a shame that there are so many riders out there who are singing the same song. *It should be a cooperative effort on the parts of both rider and instructors to help the rider to continue riding* (if this is what the rider desires).

"Competition and mainstreaming are there for those who wish to pursue it. There are many would-be talented riders with disabilities who just need to be provided with the tools and opportunities to make it happen."

PART II THE PROGRAMS IN THERAPEUTIC RIDING

This section will address how the field of therapeutic riding on a national and international basis has developed. It will show its relationship to the field of human-animal interaction and discusses the development of the use of the horse in sport, in education, and in medicine (health care).

3   WHAT IS THERAPEUTIC RIDING ?

3.01   THREE THERAPEUTIC ASPECTS OF RIDING FOR THE DISABLED

Jane Copeland, MA, PT

Therapeutic riding in the United States evolved from two directions -- the adapted sports model practiced in the British Riding for the Disabled programs, and the more clinical model of the Germans and Swiss which emphasizes treatment. The philosophical backgrounds of these two models differ in that the British model promotes mental and physical well-being through riding as a recreational sport, while the German and Swiss clinical model relies on a medical orientation which stresses postural alignment and symmetry as goals of equestrian activity.

In the United States these two approaches have been joined by a third approach which emphasizes educational goals. Each area--recreation, medicine, and education--encompass specific goals and techniques and yet all three overlap, complement and support each other (Figure 1). While riding for sport and recreation, a student also receives valuable physical benefits. For example, while he participates in an educational riding program, he also participates in an exciting sport.

The over five hundred therapeutic riding programs in the United States vary widely in the disabled populations they serve, the goals they set for their riders, and in how they deliver their services. Most programs place a high degree of emphasis on the combination of learning a rewarding activity while attaining the best physical and functional levels possible. Most programs in the United States choose to belong to the North American Riding for the Handicapped Association (NARHA) which sets accreditation standards for therapeutic riding programs and certification standards for instructors. NARHA makes liability and accident insurance available for riders, volunteers, and staff; holds seminars and conferences; and promotes education in therapeutic riding throughout North America.

It is easy to comprehend the social, recreational, and sport aspects of riding. This is one of the world's oldest and most popular leisure activities. Horseback riding is practiced in nearly every culture by men and women enjoying the close association with an animal. In therapeutic riding disabled clients come together with a professional instructor, horse leader, sidewalkers and their special mount to experience a pleasurable activity. They learn the rules of a sport, the techniques of horsemanship, and methods of controlling their bodies to make the human-to-horse interaction meaningful. Students can enjoy practicing skills in indoor and outdoor rings, trail riding, or progressing on to drill team participation, dressage, and equestrian competition.

Less obvious to the observer but of equal importance to the therapeutic riding team are psycho/educational goals such as right-left discrimination, sequencing, and following directions--goals which can be met by steering the horse through an obstacle course. A relay race challenges these same skills and asks the student to cooperate with the other students. Hurrying, becoming verbally or physically abusive, or quitting has immediate negative results with the horse withholding the desired behavior or with the student's removal from the highly motivating opportunity to ride. Students develop a rapport with their teammate, the horse, and concentrate to achieve the goals of their individual lesson.

19

The therapeutic use of the horse to treat specific movement dysfunctions is called hippotherapy -- literally "treatment with the help of the horse," from the Greek word hippos, meaning horse. Hippotherapy is carried out by a physical or occupational therapist, working with a riding instructor and a specially trained horse. The client role is not to influence or control the horse, but to respond by posturally accommodating to the horse's movement. The rider's center of gravity is continually displaced with each step the horse takes, causing the rider to accommodate to these changes with muscular activity and control to remain centered on his mount. Movement exploration including reaching and touching the moving horse, varying sitting postures, and performing vaulting exercises all accomplish goals of postural control and sensory integration in equine-assisted therapy.

Forming meaningful lesson plans by combining goals from the three areas of therapeutic riding is the usual versus the unusual circumstance. Every rider presents a unique set of abilities. The aim of therapeutic riding is to develop a lesson plan that addresses the capabilities of each rider. For example in one riding session, a Down Syndrome child could ride in a saddle with stirrups and work on the posting trot in preparation for competition in Special Olympics. In another session, he might ride on a sheepskin fleece, sitting erect without holding onto reins, and work on staying centered while the horse trotted on the longe line. It is this combination of interesting and challenging experiences that makes therapeutic riding so motivating for the rider and interesting for the professionals and volunteers. As is true in any activity, the participant's perception of accomplishment and joy in achievement are paramount. Therapeutic riding presents unique opportunities to achieve meaningful self-realization.

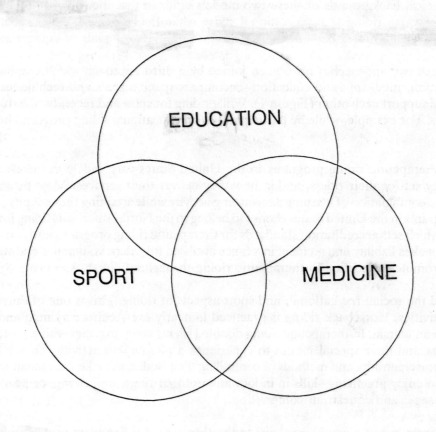

FIGURE 1. THREE CIRCLE DIAGRAM OF THERAPEUTIC RIDING

3.02 ESTABLISHING THERAPEUTIC RIDING AS A PROFESSION: DEVELOPING STANDARDS

Jean M. Tebay, MS

Why are Professional Standards Important?

This is a time in the history of the United States when the concern for excellence is at a high level of public consciousness. It appears that excellence in many areas of endeavor is in the minds not only of state and federal officials, but also educators and the public. One stimulus for such a phenomenon comes, perhaps, from product advertising--the biggest, the best, the most that money can buy.

The primary distinguishing characteristic of any profession is its willingness to commit itself to quality as well as to excellence, and to govern itself and its practitioners in the promotion of both, in order to protect the clients it serves. The development of standards of educational preparation and performance by a national organization is the enactment in reality of such a philosophical commitment. Without such policies, many disciplines--in our case therapeutic riding as conducted at the more than 450 operating centers registered by North American Riding for the Handicapped Association (NARHA)--may be viewed as a non-vocation, or an avocation. In addition, without such policies, the activities these operating centers offer are more likely to be regarded as para-professional in the eyes of professional practitioners, of the disabled communities served, and of the public in general.

Those active in therapeutic riding in the U.S., though a comparatively small entity, have answered a national call to join in this pursuit of excellence. Many individuals who engage in therapeutic riding have been influenced by the growing momentum and rising popularity of the activity and seek to serve as leaders in the field. They have acted together to professionalize both the field's activities and its personnel in their quest for excellence and quality.

Let us contrast with therapeutic riding for a moment, the venerable profession of nursing which, through nationally accepted policies, seeks to assure consistently trained personnel, who work in uniformly recognizable settings, governed by constantly updated sets of practice standards. Therapeutic riding, on the other hand, has within its ranks a variety of individuals who differ greatly in the strength and focus of their educational preparation and vocational qualifications. There is no unique type of setting in which they work, no nationally recognized goals for their work, and until recently no established standards to govern their service activities.

Therapeutic riding has reached a time in its growth and popularity when it has become more than a pleasant recreation for disabled individuals. It has established itself as a feasible rehabilitation tool used to make significant changes, both physically and psychologically, in the lives of disabled individuals. In the United States, many therapeutic riding practitioners have worked to make the field a viable profession. A vital step in this development process has been the establishment of standards, and an accreditation process for operating centers and programs which comprise the NARHA membership.

What Exactly are Standards?

Standards are a written set of mutually agreed-upon criteria providing a guideline or measure by which to evaluate an activity. For therapeutic riding programs, NARHA's comprehensive list of standards is helpful for assuring quality services to clients and in helping to define the scope and purpose of service. In addition, such standards assure personnel a safe, suitable work environment; and satisfy prospective clients, as well as outside agencies, of consistent operational quality.

The NARHA standards were developed by a committee within the organization, and subsequently submitted to a larger sample from the organization's total membership for review, verification of content, and comment. Following revision, the final standards were published as a manual and circulated to NARHA operating centers. Subsequently the standards will be reviewed and updated every three years. It is important to understand that compliance with such standards is now purely voluntary. Such standards are not enforceable until and unless adopted into state or federal law, or incorporated into health care regulations.

The *Manual of Standards* for therapeutic riding, recently updated by NARHA (1992), was prepared in order to meet several objectives:
- To provide guidelines for the planning and organization of therapeutic riding programs
- To provide an educational resource for orientation and training of staff and other personnel
- To provide organization and definition of activities on a level consistent with current knowledge and practice
-

To provide an authoritative source of information for use in program promotion
- To provide a set of requirements which would be met in order to be eligible for and subsequently retain accreditation
- To provide a means for on-going assessment and improvement
- To provide a resource for risk management and safety administration
- To provide for the health and welfare of animals involved in therapeutic riding programs

What are the areas in which standards were developed?
The current standards in therapeutic riding focus on both facilities and programs. Areas for future development include those for specific groups of professional personnel (for example, therapists) as well as for adjunct activities such as vaulting, driving, and hippotherapy.

Summary
With its first set of standards firmly in place, along with a well-established process for accrediting operating centers, the field of therapeutic riding, operating under the umbrella of NARHA, has joined the ranks of a full fledged professional discipline in the realms of therapeutic recreation and rehabilitation. The field has reached a first level of ongoing professional development in its determination to provide consistent quality service to its clients.

Sources
American Society of Association Executives. (1988). *Self Regulation: Accreditation, Certification and Standardization.* American Society of Association Executives: Washington, D.C.
Commission on Accreditation of Rehabilitation Facilities. (1988). *Standards Manual for Organizations Serving People with Disabilities.* Tucson, Az.
Joint Commission on Accreditation of Hospitals. (1985). Consolidated Standards Manual. Chicago, IL.
North American Riding for the Handicapped Association. (1992). The Manual of Standards for Therapeutic Riding. NARHA: P.O. Box 33150, Denver, CO 80233
Professional Standards in Special Education. (1987). ERIC Clearinghouse on Handicapped and Gifted Children. Reston, Virginia.
Riles, B. ed., (1989). *Evaluation of Therapeutic Recreation Through Quality Assurance.*
Voelkl, J.E. (1988). *Risk Management in Therapeutic Recreation.* American Therapeutic Recreation Association. State College: Venture Publishing, Inc.

3.03 STANDARDS AND ACCREDITATION FOR THERAPEUTIC RIDING PROGRAMS--A MODEL

Octavia Brown, EdM, NARHA Master Instructor
Jean M. Tebay, MS, NARHA Master Instructor

Introduction: The Need for Standardization

In most fields of human endeavor, there is a process of development that begins with a *good idea*. The pioneering work on that idea is usually done by energetic, visionary people who may or may not accurately document their progress and results. These are the revolutionaries, the makers of changes, the inspirers of others. This generation is followed usually by a less visionary, more practical-minded set of people who take the pioneering work and further the process of starting a new discipline. The *good idea* is no longer free to follow any path that appeals to its creators; it must be studied, its effects documented, the practitioners trained, a body of literature established, scientific research undertaken, and results published and applied in increasingly specialized ways.

Soon, there are so many people in the field that rules and regulations about how to use the *good idea* begin to be developed. Different schools of thought arise, each proposed by well-meaning, well-educated individuals. These people may or may not communicate with each other productively because their egos get involved with their *good idea*. The issue of "turf" becomes important: in the language of equines: "get away from that pile of hay: it's **MINE!**" Those wishing to enter the field, as well as the consumers of its products begin to wish there were a set of criteria by which the quality of the *good idea* could be judged.

Our *good idea,* of course, is <u>Therapeutic Activities with the Horse</u>. For the sake of clarity we will use the term "Therapeutic Riding" in this presentation to cover any and all equine activities that can be done by or for a person with a disability.

The United States Experience

In the United States, it became very clear in the mid 1980's that our national organization, the North American Riding for the Handicapped Association (NARHA), needed an organized system of controls and information that would result in consistent quality of service in therapeutic riding centers; a system that would ensure that the medical aspects of instruction or treatment are correct for each client; a system that would ensure adequate safety standards nation-wide.

In 1987, NARHA board adapted an organizational Long Range Plan which provided for the accreditation of all therapeutic riding centers by the end of 1991. An Accreditation Committee was created and made up of experienced therapeutic riding practitioners from varied educational and experiential backgrounds. They were charged with developing a set of **standards** for therapeutic riding centers with a process of <u>accreditation</u> based on those standards. This paper deals with how those in the United States developed both the standards and the accreditation process. The standards aspect will be discussed first.

Standards for Therapeutic Riding Centers

A set of standards is a series of specific rules of performance and quality against which a product can be measured. In our case, the product is **therapeutic riding**. Compliance with a set of professional standards currently is voluntary. The only exceptions concern rules that have been adopted into law by local, state or national entities. Developing a set of written standards for therapeutic riding was the first step in the creation of an accreditation system. Standards were needed to cover every aspect of the profession's activities so that those electing to abide by the standards could be aware of their responsibilities and be more certain of offering safe services to the disabled.

The process of creating actual Standards for Therapeutic Riding in the United States was as follows:

First, a committee was formed to undertake the job of writing them. Eight areas of activity were identified as needing definition:

- Administration/organization
- Equipment
- Facilities
- Horses
- Instructor/instruction
- Mounting/dismounting
- Therapist/Therapy
- Volunteers

Each committee member was assigned one area of activities on which to write a basic set of rules or standards. Sub-groups were then assigned to critique, add to, and improve on them. After a draft of the standards was produced it circulated to all committee members and to the Governing Board of NARHA for review and suggestions for change and improvement. An editor was then chosen who incorporated all of the comments from the Accreditation Committee and the Governing Broad to produce a cohesive document. The editor made final decisions on each standard to be included as follows:

a) Was it worded clearly and correctly?
b) Was it a necessary standard?
c) Had it been covered elsewhere in the document?

A revised draft of the standards was then sent to 30 randomly selected therapeutic riding centers for review and reaction. Staff of these centers were asked to evaluate each standard, using a critique form provided. Their comments were incorporated into the revision of the document which followed. Finally, in 1990, the first edition of the Standards for Therapeutic Riding Programs was sent to all therapeutic riding centers holding membership in NARHA, for information and in preparation for actual accreditation surveys.

One example of a standards, within the area of facility: "All therapeutic riding center buildings shall be maintained in a neat, safe, and sanitary condition."

The critique done by the therapeutic riding centers was conducted to ensure that the initial document was accurate and that standards set forth were seen as attainable. The now distributed, studied and accepted standards will be reviewed periodically by different therapeutic riding experts to be certain they remain current and valid.

How are the Standards now Used?

The NARHA standards are applied in three major ways:

- As a self-study guide for established centers. If the center can say "yes" to every one of the 160 entries, they know they are doing a great job. Where there is a "no," the center organizers can consider how to correct the problem. Where there is a "not applicable," consideration can be given to the necessity or practicality of changing their operation to include the item.
- As a guide for the creation of a therapeutic riding center. A facility hoping to qualify as a therapeutic riding center can be checked against that section: instructor and therapist can find a partial job description and list of responsibilities, physical facilities, and equipment can be examined and so on. Also, through the NARHA office, an aspiring group can find local help and advice on how best to meet the NARHA requirements before they make major commitment in plans and cost.
- As a guide to prepare for official accreditation

The NARHA Accreditation System.
How do the NARHA standards interfold with the accreditation system?

In the United States, development of the NARHA standards was done along with the development of an accreditation system. Each complemented the other, and the two responsible committees perforce had to work closely with one another. The group to be charged with accreditation consists of ten people knowledgeable in different areas of therapeutic riding: physical and occupational therapists, therapeutic riding instructors, driving-for-the-disabled experts and administrators are sought to create a well-rounded group. No individual serves longer than two years, and given the intensity of the work, that is enough! The group operates independently of NARHA's governing board, reporting four times a year to recommending which centers should be accredited. Accreditation is based on the quality of a center's performance in all areas. A center may be awarded a one, two or three year approval. At the end of that time, centers must be again reviewed, surveyed, and reaccredited.

What Must a Center do to Become Accredited?
Each center must submit an application which includes:
1. A completed comprehensive written questionnaire related to the standards content that covers all aspect of the program: the center's administration, horses used, facilities, categories of disabilities represented in the clients served, equipment used.
2. Detailed photographs of the facilities used--all locations, building, equipment used.
3. Video-tapes of each instructor or therapist conducting a session. If many different disabilities are represented among clients,tapes of each separate compatible group are also required. For example, a class of neurologically impaired people, a class of physically involved riders, and one for developmentally delayed clients would each require a separate video-taped session. Hippotherapy, developmental vaulting or driving would also require separate video-taped segments. When the therapeutic riding center has completed the questionnaire, photographs and video-tapes, this information is mailed to the NARHA office where it is sent out randomly to one of the committee members for evaluation.

The Evaluation and Decision Process
The primary surveyor then reviews all parts of the application. If specialized knowledge is needed he will send the material to someone else for a second opinion. At each accreditation committee meeting all reviewed applications are presented to the total group. Problem areas are analyzed. The Committee compiles the list of centers approved, with recommendations on the number of years of approval to be given. The Governing Board receives the accreditation committee's recommendations for final approval and ratifies or denies them at their discretion. A detailed report on the finding is then sent to each center indicating deficiencies if present. Video tapes are returned to encourage self-study. An appeal process is in place should a center contest the final decision on their status.

Centers whose performance indicates that they are not ready for accreditation are granted six months in which to correct deficiencies. In addition, these centers are visited by a trained therapeutic riding consultant. If problems are serious, one of the Accreditation Committee members may be sent for further consultation. The assumption is that, unless proven otherwise, people want their centers to improve and are not out to deceive the public nor the national organization. However, if a center repeatedly refuses to comply with the surveyor's recommendations, the center may lose the right to coverage under NARHA's insurance plan and to be listed in the national membership directory as an accredited program. It should be noted that in the United States, membership in NARHA cannot be denied to any who apply, but failure to be listed as an approved center can have negative P.R. consequences.

Results
The new system of accreditation by NARHA began in late 1988. In the summer of 1991, 269 therapeutic riding centers have been evaluated. Of these, 98 received three year approval; 89 received two year approval; 32 received one year approval. Designated as "not ready for accreditation" were 18 centers. Incomplete applications were received from 32 centers.

Does the Accreditation System Work?
In the past NARHA tried a system of visiting each therapeutic riding center. This worked well in the beginning, but as the numbers grew it became very expensive to train and maintain a large enough team of surveyors to cover our large country. Experience has shown that it is possible to use audio-visual materials to accurately determine the quality of a center's performance.

Advantages and Disadvantages:

Disadvantages have been found to include:

- Hazards, in the facility, can be hidden from the camera.
- It is possible to edit a video-tape to omit a dangerous situation.
- The exact condition of equipment (especially saddle and bridles) may be difficult/impossible to determine.

Advantages noted are:

- Large number of centers can be reviewed in a short space of time.
- The process is not expensive to conduct either for the center or for NARHA.
- Video-tapes are extremely revealing. Lack of knowledge and training are difficult to hide.
- Centers receive a through written evaluation of their performance including a detailed critique of the video-taped segments. This provides a basis for continued development and improvement.
- The group review process provides:
  - a more objective set of recommendations
  - a relatively uniform approach to judging of quality of performance.
  - apparent consistency in the use of the standards in evaluating each application.
- There is opportunity (and real need) for qualified members of the national organization to be trained and to serve as surveyors.

Response to the Standards and to the Accreditation Process

Many centers have written letters to NARHA describing the benefits they derived from using the standards and from bring a part of the accreditation process. One center wrote:

As we filled out the forms, worked on our video-tapes and took the required pictures, we were surprised and pleased at how much we learned about ourselves. Suddenly we saw things that we thought were o.k. but to our 'enlightened' vision were not acceptable. Things were not neat enough... we found equipment we forgot existed...NARHA helped us to move one step closer to our goal of safe, medically effective, and high quality therapeutic horseback riding program."

Conclusion

In June of 1985 an international organization, Riding for the Disabled International, was formed. A statement of purpose was written. In it each participating country agreed to set standards for improving the quality of its therapeutic equine programs. The secretary General of R.D.I., Jane Wykeham-Musgrave (of Great Britain?), wrote in March 1986:

"We are all striving for perfection, but it will take time. But 'second best' is insufficient for the many disabled individuals entrusted to our care. Only the very best will do."

In the United States quality of services in therapeutic riding is our primary goal. A set of standards and a process of accreditation of centers are two means by which to reach that goal. If each country involved in therapeutic riding sets its own standards and develops a process for enforcing them in its centers, the aims of Riding for Disabled International will have been supported. As a result, our equestrians with disabilities will gain even greater benefits.

3.04 THE FEDERATION OF RIDING FOR THE DISABLED INTERNATIONAL

Carl Kluwer, Prof. Dr. med.

In many nations in the last twenty years, and in some even before that, horseback riding as a therapeutic activity was developed. The sources of development varied from country to country. In some countries, the development evolved from Dressage, which is beneficial to the formation of personality. In most English-speaking countries, the interest to bring riding within the reach of the disabled resulted mainly from an increased sense of life through leisure riding and cross-country riding.In the Scandinavian countries, sports riding and competition were at the center of the development of therapeutic riding, In fact, Liz Hartel, a Scandinavian post-polio victim who won a silver medal in Dressage at the 1952 Helsinki Olympics, is credited with giving the concept of riding as therapy its modern day impetus.

In the German-speaking countries, the development was based more on medical experiences. For that reason the therapeutic aspect in its more scientific sense directed the early activities of therapeutic riding; including use of the Swiss term "Hippotherapy," which came into common use to describe therapeutic riding as a specialized medical treatment. Remedial-educational riding and vaulting, and riding as sport for the handicapped, described the non-medical specialties.

The International Congresses on Therapeutic Riding were differently oriented depending on the interests of the host country. The first congress in Paris in 1974, and the second in Basel in 1976, had for their titles "Riding as Therapy." Since then, the title has been changed in favor of the term Hippotherapy, in which scientific results were shown within the general scope of Riding for the Disabled, or therapeutic riding, which eventually became the generic, or umbrella, term.

The third international congress, held in Warwick, Great Britain, in 1979, highlighted the sportive and joyful enthusiasm of even the most severely disabled riders. At the fourth "International Congress on Therapeutic Riding" in Hamburg, 1982, an attempt was made to present an overview of a wide range of possibilities of the therapeutic use of the horse. Therefore the program was subdivided under three headings: 1) Hippotherapy, 2) Remedial- educational riding and vaulting, and 3) Riding as sport for the disabled. The results showed not only the very clear differences between these three specialties, but also the common orientation regarding the possibilities of the horse in therapeutic settings.

The contacts made during these congresses led the participants to want a continuing exchange of information between congresses. As a result, it was planned for the fifth international congress in Milan, in 1985, to create an administrative body to carry out such an exchange. During this congress the delegates of the different national associations met and discussed this issue. Some pleaded for the immediate foundation of an international association, while others felt that they did not know each other well enough to form a legally binding commitment. All agreed, however, that two tasks should be worked on immediately:

1)　　To set up a list of all national organizations who were concerned with therapeutic riding, and
2)　　To conduct a survey regarding national education and training programs for personnel in the field of therapeutic riding.

A loose cooperation was formed under the title RIDING FOR THE DISABLED INTERNATIONAL (RDI) and an Interim Executive Board was elected as follows:

President:	Dorothy Ames, Canada
	Task: Congress in Toronto, 1988
Secretary General:	Jane Wykeham-Musgrave, Great Britain
	Task: Editorial work for a newsletter, and distribution of information about national groups.
In addition:	Jean Tebay, United States of America
	Task: A manual about national education and training programs

These tasks were all promptly carried out. But it proved to be difficult to guarantee the financing of the newsletter because prospective sponsors asked for proof of a non-profit organization in the form of a constitution with appropriate statutes. In response, Jane Wykeham-Musgrave asked each participating nation for proposals regarding the statutes. What she received, however, was an enormous list of proposed wishes, but no workable draft of statutes. Finally, however, as a result of urgent international demand, in Germany a draft constitution was drawn up under the cooperative efforts of several German therapeutic riding specialists including H. Riesser, H. Wolf, myself, and particularly Gerlinde Hoffmann. This draft included all of the proposed wishes. Jane Wykeham-Musgrave then forwarded this document to all national organizations for review and comment.

At the next meeting of the national delegates of the RDI during the sixth international congress in Toronto, in 1988, this draft was discussed sentence by sentence and revised. As a Preliminary Constitution endorsed by an overwhelming majority of the 19 national representatives present at that meeting, it could then be legally examined and revised according to the requirements of international law.

In Toronto, the President and the Secretary General were re-elected to the Executive Board and in accordance with the new preliminary constitution, they were joined by:
Treasurer: Ad Van Vliet, Netherlands
Further members; Charlotte von Arbin, Sweden
                           Valerie Poplawski, Australia

The congress in Canada was a big success; however, the energies of the Executive Board were largely directed to solving the problems concerning drafting an international constitution, because British law set such complicated conditions for the acknowledgment of a charity, that there was finally no success in bringing all of the member organizations to a sufficient majority for agreement. In September of 1990, an extraordinary General Assembly was called in London, where a special committee was appointed to resolve the constitutional problems. This committee included:

J. Bromann, Denmark
A. Corrado, Italy
C. Kluwer, Germany
N. Pearce, Australia
J. Wykeham-Musgrave, Great Britain
J. Tebay, USA

This special committee met in Cologne, Germany, in December of 1990. The goals of this committee were to finalize a working draft of the constitution, to be presented at the seventh international congress in Aarhus, Denmark, in August 1991; and to locate a suitable country for the official organizational "seat" of the RDI.

Finally, at the General Assembly (International council, RDI) in Denmark, the result of the task force's work was passed nearly unanimously by the 21 national delegates entitled to vote for their representative national organizations.

Some characteristics of the newly accepted constitution deserve specific review:
- The official name of the organization became *The Federation of Riding for the Disabled International (FRDI)*,
- The Federation would be registered as an international not-for-profit organization according to Belgian law, with the official "seat" in Belgium,
- The Executive Board would be enlarged by a further member, to be of Belgian nationality,
- In addition to the status of Full Membership for national representation, there would be the status of Associate Membership. Associate membership does not carry the right to vote, but entitles the member to receive all information and to obtain a hearing on any issue.
- An annual membership fee was approved by the International Council:

Full Membership: 70,-   UK Sterling
Associate Membership   20,-   UK Sterling

A new Executive Board was elected:

President:	Dr. med. c. Kluwer, Germany
Vice-President:	Dr. D. Nicolas Citterio, Italy
Treasurer:	Dr. med. A. Van Vliet, Netherlands
Secretary General:	J, Baillie, Great Britain
Members:	J. De Buck, Belgium
	J. Tebay, USA
	N. Pearce, Australia

It became necessary to strengthen FRDI, as was shown at the latest congress in Denmark. At that congress, as a result of major efforts by a largely Scandinavian committee, a new group was founded on the initiative of the Disabled Sports Organization, This new group, International Paraolympic Equestrian Committee, (IPEC) was instrumental in organizing the splendid and world Dressage Championships for Disabled Riders at Wilhelmsborg, Denmark, just prior to the start of the International Congress. At this event, 11 coaches of national teams met to confirm the IPEC constitution, and elect its Board of Directors.

After intensive discussion between representatives of the IPEC and FRDI, the 26 delegates of the International Council of the FRDI came to the conclusion that the basic concerns of the specialty areas within therapeutic riding and the variety of approaches within the many countries practicing therapeutic riding, could not be adequately met by the IPEC, with its strong sport and competition orientation. It was decided by the International Council of the FRDI to develop good cooperation and communication with the IPEC, as with, for example, the Special Olympics Committee, and to support the mission of IPEC - riding as a sport for the disabled, especially regarding international competition. A. Van Vliet was appointed as the official liaison between FRDI and IPEC. Similarly, it was also decided that each national organization should promote contact with their national equestrian association and other national sport organizations for the disabled.

The FRDI as the international organization representing all aspects of the use of the horse to improve the quality of life for disabled individuals is beginning a new phase in its development, The FRDI strives to become the leading international service organization in the field of the therapeutic use of the horse. Individuals and organizations from all over the world may contact the FRDI for information and assistance regarding the therapeutic use of the horse. The FRDI provides consultation and assistance to all who seek its services.

The Eighth International Congress in Therapeutic Riding will take place in the third week of January, 1994, in Hamilton, New Zealand.

3.05 TERMS AND DEFINITIONS IN THE FIELD OF HUMAN-ANIMAL INTERACTIONS

Maureen Fredrickson, MSW, Deputy Director, Delta Society*

Under a grant from the SmithKline Beacham Foundation, the Definitions Task Force of the Delta Society Standards Committee (Renton, Washington) first developed a list of common terms generally associated with animal-assisted interventions. Members discussed the use of terms such as "pet therapy," "animal-facilitated therapy," "animal visitation" and "pet-fostering." Members then placed more than 30 terms into three separate categories based on whether they implied therapy, a therapeutic effect, or other interventions. Members agreed the term "therapy" implies diagnosis utilizing specialized criteria such as the DSM-4 or ICDM-9, involves prescribed treatment, requires professionals to be liable for actions and is billable to third-party payers such as insurance carriers. It was agreed the term "Animal-Assisted Therapy" should refer to programs offering therapy and must meet narrowly defined requirements. Other interventions - although therapeutic - would be identified by alternate terms.

The task force members discussed the use of terms for programs that were therapeutic in nature and determined that these focused on three aspects: recreational, educational, and motivational. Programs may serve one or all of these goals. "Animal-Assisted Activities" was the term assigned to this category of programs. Members agreed that the term "assisted" was preferred to "facilitated" because greater participation on the part of the animal was implied. Programs that reflected a recognition of the importance of the human-animal bond and focused on supporting and promoting the development of that bond were assigned the term "Human-Animal Support Services."

TERMS AND DEFINITIONS

ANIMAL-ASSISTED ACTIVITIES (AAA)--provide opportunities for motivational, educational ,recreational, and/or therapeutic benefits in a variety of environments by a specially trained professional, para-professional, and/or volunteer in association with animals that meet specific criteria.

ANIMAL-ASSISTED THERAPY (AAT)--is a goal-directed intervention in which an animal that meets specific criteria is an integral part of the treatment process. AAT is directed and/or delivered by health/human service professionals with specialized expertise, and is within the scope of practice of their profession. AAT is designed to promote improvement in human physical, social, emotional, and/or cognitive functioning. AAT is provided in a variety of settings, and may be group or individual in nature. This process is documented and evaluated. An alternate term to identify such action is "pet-facilitated therapy." A less acceptable term is "pet therapy."

HUMAN-ANIMAL SUPPORT SERVICES (HASS)--enhance and encourage the responsibility and humane interrelationship of people, animals and nature.

PERSONNEL

ANIMAL-ASSISTED ACTIVITIES (AAA)--A person who provides AAA possesses specialized knowledge of animals and the populations with which they interact in delivering motivational, educational, recreational and/or therapeutic animal-oriented activities. Volunteers are often involved in AAA. Individuals may work independently when they have specialized training. This group may include but is not limited to such individuals as:

activities directors	educators
nursing assistants/aides	riding instructors
animal health technicians	humane educators
occupational therapy assistants	student nurses
animal shelter workers	licensed practical nurses
pet visitation specialists	trained volunteers
camp counselors	licensed vocational nurses
physical therapy assistants	4-H leaders
recreational therapy aids	nature counselors
dog trainers	

ANIMAL-ASSISTED THERAPY (AAT)--Professionals who direct and/or deliver AAT comply with the legal and ethical requirements of their profession in the state or country in which they practice. Incorporating animals as a treatment modality that requires the professional have specialized expertise about animals. This may include but is not limited to such individuals as:

certified alcoholism counselors	physical therapists
school counselors	social workers
special education counselors	physicians
marriage, family & child counselors	speech pathologists
recreational therapists	psychologists
rehabilitation therapists	speech therapists
occupational therapists	psychotherapists
registered nurses	vocational rehabilitation counselors
pastoral counselors	

HUMAN-ANIMAL SUPPORT SERVICES (HASS)--Those who provide HASS may be professional, paraprofessional or trained volunteers working within the legal and ethical scope of their job description or practice. These services target support to the pet/animal owner. This might include but is not limited to such individuals as:

animal behaviorists	veterinarians
trainers	K-9 Units
self-help coordinators	● Police
grief counselors	● Army
pet fostering	● Rescue
trained volunteers	applied animal behaviorists
pet loss counselors	applied animal ethologists

Printed by permission. * Delta Society, P.O. Box 1080, Renton, WA 98057-1080

3.06 GLOSSARY OF TERMS USED IN THERAPEUTIC RIDING

ADAPTIVE EQUIPMENT

1) Riding equipment which has been changed in structure or form to allow a person with a disability to ride.
2) Equipment which has been specially developed to allow a physically disabled person to ride a horse.
3) Equipment which is used to elicit specific responses.

ADAPTIVE PHYSICAL EDUCATION

Physical education which has been modified for special populations who cannot take part in regular physical education activities.

ADAPTIVE RIDING

Horseback riding adapted for a special population.

ANIMAL-ASSISTED THERAPY

AAT professionals, who are specially trained in the use of animals, incorporate animals as a treatment modality, complying with the legal and ethical requirements of their profession.

BACKRIDING

When two people ride on a horse together. In therapeutic horseback riding, backriding is used in therapy to develop posture in the front rider--the client by the backrider--a therapist. To a limited basis, an instructor may backride a child until that child feels secure.

BONDING

The establishment of an attachment/union between two persons or a person and an animal.

CERTIFIED OCCUPATIONAL THERAPIST ASSISTANT

A person with credentials as an occupational therapy assistant who works under the supervision of a registered occupational therapist and treats disease and injury by the use of activities with emphasis on adaptation.

DELTA SOCIETY

An organization, headquartered in Renton, WA, that supports research studies and educates people on how companion animals benefit human physical and emotional well-being; establishes community programs to build a partnership between animals and people; operates the national information center and library for field of human-animal interactions.

DEVELOPMENTAL EQUINE-ASSISTED THERAPY

A specific treatment method, using NDT treatment techniques, which is carried out by a specially trained physical or occupational therapist during a treatment session with a client with neuromuscular dysfunction.

DEVELOPMENTAL VAULTING

Vaulting (gymnastic activities on the back of a horse) for persons with special needs, supervised by a vaulting instructor.

DISABILITY

Restriction or lack (resulting from impairment) of ability to perform an activity in the manner or within the range considered normal for a human being (World Health Organization, 1980).

EQUINE-ASSISTIVE THERAPY

Treatment with the use of the horse and the equine setting by a qualified health care professional.

HANDICAP

Disadvantage for a given individual, resulting from an impairment or a disability, that limits or prevents the fulfillment of a role that is normal (depending on age, sex, and social and cultural factors) for that individual (World Health Organization, 1980)

HIPPOTHERAPIST

A physical or occupational therapist who has been trained in the theory of classic hippotherapy, and in the use of equine movements in the treatment of neurological disorders; is able to apply this knowledge to augment his professional skills in physical therapy /or occupational therapy to treat clients with mild to severe movement disorders (Hippotherapy Curriculum Development Project 1988/Hippotherapy Section of NARHA 1991).

HIPPOTHERAPY

("Hippos" means horse in Greek. "Treatment with the help of the horse.") A treatment for clients with movement dysfunctions and/or neurological disorders used by physical or occupational therapists trained as hippotherapists. In classic hippotherapy, the horse influences the client rather than the client controlling the horse (Hippotherapy Curriculum Development Project, 1991). The therapist may use exercises or activities to achieve specific treatment goals.

HORSE HANDLER

A person who has had training in horsemanship skills and knows the psychological and physical needs of a horse.

HORSE LEADER

A person who has had training in horsemanship skills and knows the psychological and physical needs of a horse. In addition, he or she knows how to handle a horse with specific needs for the disabled rider.

HUMAN-ANIMAL BONDING

The attachment that develops between humans and animals involving strong feelings and psychological ties. Studies have supported that the love and attentiveness given by people to animals is reciprocal and both animals and people benefit (Anderson, 1983).

IMPAIRMENT

Loss or abnormality of psychological, physiological, or anatomical structure or function.

LEADER

Same as horse leader. One who leads the horse.

LONG REINING

A technique used in hippotherapy and training. The horse is "driven" from the ground by the use of reins that reach from the bit to one stride or more behind the horse. The client sits on the horse while the handler controls and reins the horse from behind.

METER

A unit of measurement in the metric system. A riding ring, such as a dressage arena, is measured by the metric system. 1 meter = 39.37 inches.

MOUNTING BLOCK

A device used for mounting a rider to the horse.

MOUNTING RAMP

A ramp designed for mounting a person onto the horse from a wheelchair. It is also used by ambulatory riders since it is kinder to the horse's back than ground mounting.

NORTH AMERICAN RIDING FOR THE HANDICAPPED ASSOCIATION (NARHA)

NARHA is a service organization created to promote the well-being of individuals with disabilities through equine activities.

OCCUPATIONAL THERAPIST REGISTERED /or licensed OTR-OTR/L

A person with a credential in occupational therapy who treats disease and injury by the use of activities with emphasis on adaptation (Clark & Allen, 1985).

PHYSICAL THERAPIST--PT

A person with a degree in physical therapy who treats disease and injury by physical means, such as light, heat, cold, water, ultrasound, massage and exercise, and with emphasis on mobility (Clark & Allen 1985).

PROBLEM SOLVING

The mental process by which one sequentially identifies a problem, interprets aspects of the situation, and selects a method to alleviate the problem (Fleming, 1991).

RECREATIONAL THERAPIST--RTR

A person with a degree in recreational therapy who treats disease and injury using usual or adaptive leisure activities.

REMEDIAL RIDING

Riding activities which are adapted to help the client gain educational and psychological goals under the direction of a specially trained educator or therapist.

REMEDIAL VAULTING

Vaulting which is adapted to help the client to gain educational and psychological goals under the direction of a specially trained educator or therapist.

RIDING THERAPY

The integration by therapists of neurophysical or psychosocial treatment procedures with exercises and horsemanship, to gain specific medical goals. Riding therapy is a part of equine-assisted therapy.

SCHOOLING FIGURES.

Circles, figure eights, straight lines, curves, and other patterns used in riding training to develop precise control of a horse through one's aids or actions.

SENSORY INTEGRATION (SI)

The ability of the brain to organize and coordinate sensation and behavior, which leads to adaptive responses that permit a higher level of function. Sensory integration procedures are initiated by the client with the therapist manipulating the environment to gain the therapeutic results. The sensory integration procedure is a part of occupational therapy practice and can also be carried out by specially trained physical therapists. Sensory Integration is a specific technique developed by A. Jean Ayres and her associates.

SENSORIMOTOR INTEGRATION

This term refers to a group of techniques used by therapists to treat neurological disorders. It may incorporate sensory integration methods along with other techniques to increase a person's function.

SHEEPSKIN

A pad made out of sheepskin secured with a surcingle. The pad is used with clients during exercises with a therapist or with riders who are more comfortable with the softness of sheepskin. It can be used with a standard surcingle or with a vaulting surcingle.

SIDEAID or AID, SIDEWALKER.

A person who has been trained to assist a rider. This person walks next to the horse, at the rider's side (so he or she can place his or her arm across the rider's thigh when necessary), may assist the rider with balance, provides necessary security, and/or help the rider carry through with a lesson. Sideaid is more often use by therapists since the term is more descriptive to the task.

SPECIAL EDUCATION

Educational programs which are adapted to meet learning needs for a population with special needs (and problems).

SPECIAL NEEDS POPULATION

Persons with special needs--these can be physical, psychological, psych-social, or a combination of these.

SPEECH AND LANGUAGE PATHOLOGIST

A person with a degree in speech and language pathology who treats persons with deficits in speech and language, both visual and audible.

SPORTS VAULTING

Same as vaulting. Gymnastics on horseback. Vaulting is carried out according to the primary six vaulting exercises and additional creative exercises called kur. Vaulting is an equine sport.

SUPPLING THE HORSE

Riding exercises to increase the flexibility and balance of the horse.

THERAPEUTIC VAULTING

Standard vaulting exercises performed at the level of the special vaulter. Sports vaulting for special needs vaulters.

THERAPY

The meaning employed in effecting the cure or management of disease. Implies diagnosis using special criteria (or diagnostic and procedural coding systems used in medicine for billing purposes); involves prescribed treatment by a health care professional who is liable for his or her actions according to the standards of his or her specialty, and is billable to third-party payor (i.e., insurance carriers). Hippotherapy and equine assisted therapy are recognized treatment procedures when used by especially trained physical and occupational therapist in a treatment situation by the American Physical Therapy Association and by the American Occupational Therapy Association.

T.T.E.A.M.

The Tellington-Jones Equine Awareness Method, a unique training protocol developed by Linda Tellington-Jones for the horse to make him safer, more attentive to the handler, less distracted by the environment, more pleasurable, less stressful to ride and a better performer. The training method involves a detailed step by step procedure (taught during a series of courses) which produces a friendly horse who is eager to learn (Tellington-Jones, Bruns 1988).

VAULTING

Gymnastics on horseback. Vaulting is carried out according to the primary six vaulting exercises and additional creative exercises called kur. Vaulting is an equine sport.

VAULTING SURCINGLE

A surcingle with handles. A vaulting surcingle used with a bareback pad or sheepskin, mainly for holding on, can be constructed of leather or webbing with two handles (internally secured to a metal plate) and can flex at the center. A vaulting girth used in gymnastic vaulting, must be constructed with a solid plate (internally) from well below the handle on one side, across the top to well below the handle on the other side. The construction of this vaulting girth is much stronger than the one required for "therapeutic riding".

VAULTING THERAPY

The integration by therapists of neurophysical or psychosocial treatment procedures with exercises and vaulting to gain specific medical goals. Vaulting therapy is a part of equine-assisted therapy.

Anderson, R.K. (1984). *The Pet Connection*. Center to Study Human-Animal Relationship and Environments, Univ of Minn. Minn., MN

Clark & Allen. (1985). *Occupational Therapy for Children*. St. Louis: C. V. Mosby Co.

Fleming, H.M. (1991). *American Journal of Occupational Therapy*. Nov. 45, 11, 989.

Gould Medical Dictionary. (1979).New York: McGraw-Hill Book Co.

Hippotherapy Section, *NARHA Conference*. Los Angeles. 1991

Hippotherapy Curriculum Development Project (1987-1991). Therapeutic Riding Services, Inc. Riderwood, MD. 21139

World Health Organization. (1980). *International Classification of Impairments, Disabilities, and Handicaps: A Manual of Classification Relating to the Consequence of Disease*. Geneva: World Health Organization.

3.07 THERAPEUTIC RIDING: ITS BENEFITS, PROFESSIONS, AND DIVISIONS

Barbara T. Engel, MEd, OTR

> **KEY WORDS**
> BONDING
> PHYSICAL
> RISK
> HEALTH
> AWARENESS
> TEAM

Therapeutic horseback riding parallels all horseback riding. It is a *strenuous sport* with *risk factors*. It gives the rider the opportunity to *bond* with a large responsive animal. It provides a *team sport*, the horse and the rider, that focuses on self improvement and not necessarily competition with other humans. All riding provides the rider a *physical activity* which increases *general health* in the same manner as tennis, golf, biking or swimming might do. Riding stimulates the cardio-vascular system, strengthens muscles, provides weight bearing, and increases balance, coordination and body awareness. Because it is a leisure sport with the companionship of an animal, horseback riding has a soothing mental and social effect which may provide the rider a feeling of well being.

It is important to remember that putting persons with disabilities on horses and teaching them to ride is therapeutic in the <u>same manner</u> as teaching able bodied persons to ride. This is sports riding. **THIS IS AN IMPORTANT FACTOR TO REMEMBER .** Many adult and child riders with disabilities will express their desire to ride, ride in a safe setting with safe horses and with instructors who understand their difficulties. They may tell you that they are not there for "therapy" but for the pleasure and exercise of riding. *A horse + a rider with a disability does not = "therapy" but rather sports riding. However, because of riders' unique needs, they may continue to require a modified or therapeutic riding setting for safety and understanding.*

SPECIFIC PROGRAMS CAN BE DETERMINED BY THE GOALS OF THE CLIENT AND THE TRAINING OF THOSE DIRECTING THE CLIENT.

Sports and recreational therapeutic riding has as its goal to <u>develop riding skills</u>. *Sports vaulting* and *developmental vaulting* have as their goals the <u>development of vaulting skills</u> according to the American Vaulting Association guidelines. These activities are carried out by trained riding and vaulting instructors. *Sports driving* has as its goals to develop driving skills.

Some clients need or want more than <u>sports riding</u>. They may come for *equine-assisted therapy* and work with a variety of professionals with specialized training including: a clinical psychologist or counselor; a physical, occupational, or recreational therapist; speech and language pathologist or therapist. *Equine-assisted therapy* (e.g., *hippotherapy, riding therapy, vaulting therapy, developmental equine-assisted therapy*) has as its goal <u>the rehabilitation of persons with **specific** health care problems</u>. The development of riding or vaulting skills is not a major goal or of primary concern. This therapy is carried out by health care professionals with specific training in the use of the horse in treatment who may use any aspect of the equestrian environment to accomplish their goals. The professional uses the horse or equine setting to assist him in achieving specific client treatment goals. Remember that equine-assisted therapy is a <u>treatment process</u> carried out by a <u>medical or health care professional</u> who is using the horse as a treatment tool and intervention for <u>specific</u> health care problems.

Remedial riding and *remedial vaulting* can be used by special educators who use equestrian activities for <u>specific education gains</u>. Again, horsemanship skills are not a primary goal.

Clients have different goals and may work with riding instructors, equine science specialists, special educators, vocational specialists, activity directors, recreation or camp leaders, or others with special skills that can be applied to the equine setting. The primary benefit may be educational, social, vocational, or for special project-oriented activities, such as 4-H clubs. These activities are *animal-assisted activities* and should not be misrepresented as riding therapy or equine-assisted therapy. Those latter sessions require trained specialists in particular fields to carry out and direct each unique approach. The results of these sessions can be impressive and provide the clients with many gains.

When working with a specific population, especially with people who have disabilities, one takes on specific responsibilities. An instructor who takes on the responsibility of a "therapeutic riding instructor" is saying - I AM QUALIFIED TO DO THIS JOB. Would your qualifications hold up in the legal system during a law suit? If the program states that it is doing therapy, (could this be implied by the program title?) can the documentation be provided affirm the qualifications of the staff and the propriety of therapy procedures which are normally used in the health care "therapy session?" The more one **is** involved with this dynamic method of treatment intervention, the more one **becomes** aware of its complexity and consequences.

The field of *therapeutic riding* is no longer in its infancy. It has a track record and has developed standards to ensure safety of the population it serves. Everyone involved in the field must abide by these standards and take the responsibility to up grade them as this becomes necessary. This is a professional responsibility which affects everyone in the field. One bad example can hurt other programs and possibly the national image of therapeutic riding. One can no longer put a child on a horse and call this therapeutic riding without putting oneself at risk. It is important to contact the agency that sets the standards for practice in your country for information and training. These include RDA, NARHA, CanTRA, Kuratorium fur Therapeutisches Reiten, Associazion Nazionale Italiana Di Riabilitazione Equestre, Austrian Kuratorium fur Hippotherapie and those in other countries around the world.

The term **THERAPEUTIC HORSEBACK RIDING** is an umbrella term referring to riding in a setting which is specially equipped to handle people with special needs. The instructors and assistants are trained not only in horsemanship but also:
- To understand problems presented by each disability and are comfortable with them
- To develop teaching techniques that accommodate special needs
- To train horses specially for disabled riders
- To use special equipment to compensate for disabilities
- To be concerned with safety factors unique to persons with disabilities

The horse is unique, in that horsemanship and even the equine setting can be used effectively to treat many types of disabilities by many disciplines. The type of intervention used depends on the client's need and the professional skills of those directing the sessions.

It is important as a therapeutic riding participant to take pride in one's own knowledge and skills and in one's accomplishments. Being placed in the "therapeutic riding setting," however, does not turn us all into therapists, trainers or instructors since each of these functions requires specific knowledge and skill. We remain what we have been trained to be: special education or adaptive physical education teachers, psychologists, recreational therapists, occupational therapists, physical therapists, riding instructors, vaulting coaches, and so on. But, by working with a special population, we do need to acquire specific knowledge about that population and then apply our skills differently. The equine setting also requires special knowledge and additional training to manage the horse and his environment correctly. When a special population is combined with the equine setting, a team is needed to provide the technical medical expertise and the specialized equine training needed to relate to the client's needs. For example, teaching adults requires a different base of knowledge than teaching small children. Teaching an individual who cannot move in the normal way requires particular knowledge, but your professional skills as a teacher or instructor do not change.

A WORD OF CAUTION: DO NOT SAY THAT WHAT YOU OR YOUR PROGRAM IS DOING IS PHYSICAL THERAPY UNLESS, OF COURSE, YOU ARE A PHYSICAL THERAPIST. IN MOST STATES IN THE U.S., IT IS ILLEGAL TO PERFORM PHYSICAL THERAPY UNLESS YOU ARE A LICENSED PHYSICAL THERAPIST. IF NOT QUALIFIED AS A PHYSICAL THERAPIST YOU COULD PUT YOURSELF AND THE PROGRAM IN A POSITION TO BE FINED OR SUED. The term is used in an understandable way. Riding is physical; riding is therapeutic. Therefore it must be physical + therapy = physical therapy. WRONG!

There are many aspects of riding that have brought people to the stable, but it is the horse who is the major focus. The horse has a unique nature and provides a rich assortment of movements which can do wonders for the human mind and body.

Therapeutic effects from riding may include:
EXERCISE. Children and adults with disabilities ordinarily have little access to the quality of exercise that riding provides. Riding involves all of the muscles in the body and in addition stimulates all body systems. A strong cardiovascular system and a strong set of lungs are required to make a person function. Many children and adults with severe physical problems have poorly developed lungs due to their limited ability to challenge their cardio-vascular systems. Exercise can be like giving the system a whole new set of batteries. This author has been impressed with the great changes she sees in clients in her practice even after a month of therapy or riding. This change is due to increased exercise which is imposed on the client as part of the treatment as well as the "therapeutic" intervention.

THE THREE DIMENSIONAL SWINGING GAIT of the horse causes the rider's pelvis, trunk and shoulder girdle to react in ways very similar to those produced by the normal human walk. On a horse, a non-walking person can actually *feel* what walking is like without the need for weight bearing through the legs. A little eight year old client of mine stated, *"the horse is giving me long legs and walking for me."* One frequently hears therapeutic riding instructors mention riders who began to walk more easily after riding. The horse has provided the rider with the upper and lower body sensation and mental images of walking.

BALANCE. The side to side, back and forth, and up and down movements of the horse have the effect of gently shifting the rider off balance to the right, on balance to the center, off balance to the left and back to the center. This constant shifting helps develop balance in the rider. Many people with physical disabilities have difficulty with balance which causes major problems in normal function.

STIMULATION. The undulating movements from the gait of the horse are transferred to the rider providing neuromuscular stimulation while increasing cardiovascular output and respiratory excitation. This offers the rider a rich source of sensation. Rhythmic movement on the horse has been found to be relaxing and soothing to the human mind and body.

BONDING. The horse is a social creature who will readily bond with humans. The horse will accept a rider with no pre-judgement. He will tolerate behavior from a rider that humans find difficult to accept. He immediately returns kindness and affection and will respond to the rider's commands. Bonding has been found to be basic to the development of communication.

RESPIRATION. Exercise increases respiration which in turn increases the ability to vocalize. Speech requires strong lungs. The lungs pass air over the vocal cords to produce sound. Further, the increase in respiration also increases alertness (Oetter, 1989). As a result of both the bonding and the effects of movement on speech, one may see increases in social language and speech.

HAPPINESS AND PLEASURE. Norman Cousins (Cousins, 1989), with his physician, has documented the healing effect of positive emotions and laughter upon the human body. Certainly, the horse brings us pleasure and the environment gives us determination, hope, faith and purpose: all the elements which Cousins feels will heal the mind and body. Most of the clients in a therapeutic riding program are not "sick," but may be recovering from illness or injuries due to accidents. Even the child with cerebral palsy is attempting to gain motor control. Every therapist, and anyone working with children has observed that when the client is happy and motivated, progress comes much more easily. A good attitude does seem to help when one is working to regain the body's functional abilities.

The concept of riding for the disabled person has grown rapidly since the 1970's. For therapeutic riding to gain the full respect of the community, medical and health care professionals, educators and the equine society must be managed in a professional manner. This requires all those involved to take responsibility for their own roles and to represent themselves appropriately. If one takes on the task of head instructor of disabled riders, clients will expect this person to have the knowledge, skills and education to carry out the job. Many countries require each person in this field to pass qualifying tests. Where tests are not required, each person must take on the responsibility to make sure he or she is qualified for the job. One must always remember that when one takes on the responsibility of caring for others, he or she also takes on legal obligations.

RESPECT WHO YOU ARE, THE SKILLS YOU POSSESS, THE PROFESSION YOU REPRESENT AND GIVE YOUR CLIENTS THE MOST YOU CAN <u>WITHIN</u> THE LIMITS OF <u>YOUR</u> TRAINING.

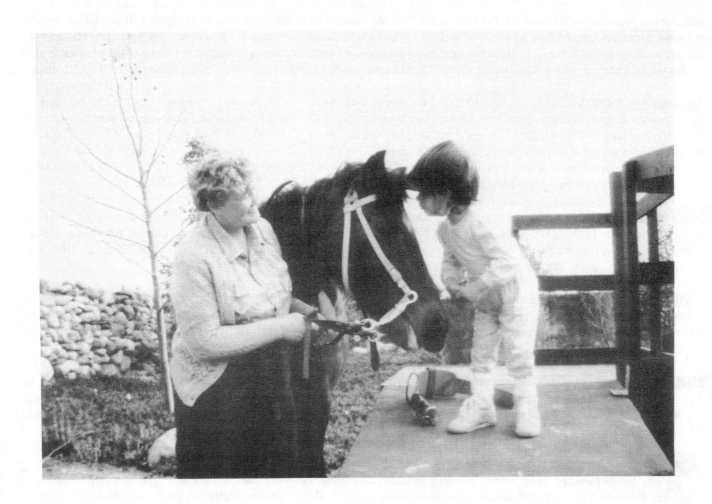

References
Cousins, N. (1989). *Head First*. New York: Penguin Books. 126-27.
Oetter, P. (1987). Course notes. University of New Mexico.

3.08   A MULTIFACETED PROGRAM IN THERAPEUTIC RIDING

Barbara T. Engel MEd, OTR

The hypothetical view of the therapeutic riding center that follows is intended to demonstrate the vast therapeutic possibilities that are available through the use of the horse. Further, it shows the possibilities of programs that are funded and self supporting. This example illustrates the development of a program in the same manner that any business would be established. Therapeutic riding programs encompass all facets of the use of the horse with people for disabilities. The horse is used as the tool to accomplish goals in early childhood education, special education, physical rehabilitation, psychiatric counseling, vocational rehabilitation, socialization, skill development and recreation.

MODEL CENTER
Dr. Fred Samuelson (fictitious name) of Warrenton, Virginia has made contact asking for information to develop a multi-faceted therapeutic riding center. Warrenton is old hunt country within the reach of a large suburban-urban population. Dr. Samuelson is retiring and can no longer care for his country estate but wants to maintain 25 acres as horse property and continue to live in the main house.

RESOURCES AND NEEDS
A survey of the area to be served by a therapeutic riding center could serve showed that there are:
1. Two schools for special needs children
2. A general, full service hospital
3. A rehabilitation center
4. A psychiatric treatment center
5. A center for troubled teens
6. Three large group homes
7. A wheelchair sports group
8. A sports medicine physical therapy clinic

The planning committee determined that there was a need for:
1. A special needs infant development program
2. Job training for mentally retarded teens and adults
3. A recreational program for persons with physical disabilities
4. A therapeutic riding program (the closest one is 50 miles away)
5. PT-OT pediatric therapists
6. An occupational therapy sensory integration clinic
7. A pony club and a 4-H program

The planning committee also surveyed the property assets at the estate which would be available to the therapeutic riding center. These assets consisted of:
1. 25 acres of which 20 are fields and 5 are wooded
2. A 20 stall barn with tack rooms, and a feed room
3. Two smaller open barns with large paddocks
4. A hay barn and an equipment shed
5. A building with an office, storeroom, kitchen, showers and two lounges next to the barn
6. A railed riding arena
7. Two 40 foot turn-out rings
8. Four open paddocks
9. A caretaker's cottage with a kitchen and four rooms downstairs, two rooms upstairs

INITIAL STEPS AND PLANS

A one day conference meeting was held with representatives of all the agencies and individuals who might be served by this center. Physicians, educators, therapists and horse people were invited. The major focus of the meeting was to educate the group in the therapeutic values of the horse. A well-developed presentation was made by a group of specialists in the therapeutic riding field and specialists in hippotherapy. The planning committee then met with Dr. Samuelson to develop the land use plan and other necessary arrangements.

BUILDING PROGRAM

An indoor arena would need to be built to accommodate some programs during fall and winter months, and the therapy program year around. At the far end of the arena, a therapy room would be developed for on site occupational, physical and speech therapy. The therapy facilities would be used by the center staff and by the therapists from the rehabilitation center through an association agreement.

The caretaker cottage would be turned into a center for a special needs pre-school infant stimulation program involving up to 25 children. Infants would be involved daily with the horses and a few small animals. The upstairs rooms of the cottage would service as offices.

One small barn would be used for the vocational rehabilitation, teen psychiatric program and work programs. All horse care, equipment and farm maintenance would be done through these programs. The barn and paddock would allow the group to deal with the horses who would be placed together in their natural herd setting.

One lounge in the office building would be turned into a classroom for instructional work. Here horsemanship would be studied as the basis for reading, sequence skills, spelling and special interest areas.

DEVELOPMENT OF PROGRAMS

Schools could bring out groups of children for adaptive physical education and special education classes. Physical and occupational therapy would be vendored through the school for the physically disabled children. The autistic class could be served by school psychologists using horse-human bonding techniques and the speech/language pathologist for speech therapy.

Group-home clients could be involved in a total horsemanship program including horse care and riding. Some of these could also receive speech, occupational or physical therapy.

Riding classes could be scheduled for both group and individual riders for recreational and therapeutic benefits.

A competitive sport group could be developed for intermediate and advanced riders in dressage, jumping, polo-crosse and vaulting. A trail riders group could evolve for advanced riders to ride through the meadows and woods.

Senior citizen groups might become involved with the infants, children and horses. In addition, a mainstream pony club would be possible. An after-school sensory integration program could be scheduled by the occupational and speech therapists. This would involve tacking, riding, vaulting and more traditional sensory integration activities incorporated within the program.

Finally, student intern programs are proposed, affiliated with nearby colleges offering occupational therapy and physical therapy programs to provide rotating groups of three students at a time for a pediatric clinical affiliation. Adaptive physical education students also could come to the center to fulfill their internship requirements. The students would be exposed to both traditional internship training and specialized training in horsemanship, instructor training and equine-assistive therapy including hippotherapy from the staff in their specialized fields. In addition, students would provide valuable assistance for maintaining a high quality of care and for bringing new ideas to the center.

SUMMARY

Since this text has maintained a focus on the program for the riders, the administrative aspects have not been proposed. There will always be the need for legal aspects, including insurance for both land owner and the center. This proposal might include a bequest to the therapeutic riding center. Other considerations would include the development of a productive board of directors, financial support, needed equipment and the hiring of competent staff.

Centers vary considerably in size and scope of programs. This model is described simply to show possibilities but all are dependent on finding financial support, at least until they can develop an income base for some operating expenses. Centers must also find support for the identification of its populations. In any case, a therapeutic riding center can be a valuable asset to the community it serves and the disabled persons who live there.

4 HOW DOES THERAPEUTIC RIDING WORK?

4.01 REVIEW OF RESEARCH IN THERAPEUTIC RIDING

Karen P. DePauw, PhD

A comprehensive review of the research on therapeutic horseback riding was undertaken and reported by DePauw in 1986. Based upon a review of the literature, she wrote of the need to: "... (a) collect empirical evidence supporting the claimed benefits, (b) develop appropriate evaluation instruments/tools, (c) identify effective intervention techniques, (d) provide for accessibility of publications/information from Europe, and (e) develop printed materials and audiovisuals for the health professional community" (DePauw, 1986).

Less than ten years later, significant progress has been made in each of the five recommendations identified above. Instrumental to the progress made in the last two recommendations are the efforts of the editor (B. Engel[1]) and authors of this book, organizations such as the North American Riding for the Handicapped Association (NARHA) and the Delta Society, national and international conferences on Therapeutic Riding and their published abstracts and proceedings, and the efforts of numerous individuals (e.g., L. McCowan[2], J. Tebay[3], F. Joswick[4]) in disseminating information worldwide.

In addition, progress has been made in establishing the empirical bases for valid, accurate assessment and in effective therapeutic riding intervention programs. This progress is due to the efforts of such individuals as J. Copeland, R. Dismuke-Blakely, B. Glasow, J. Tebay, and V.M. Fox among others. The purpose of this section is to provide the reader with a brief synopsis of current research in North America on therapeutic riding and a suggested framework for future research.

After reviewing published articles, conference presentations/proceedings and other materials on therapeutic riding available since 1986, it appears that a portion of the published information has expanded beyond reports of therapeutic riding intervention programs, training programs for instructors, certification programs, and curriculum innovations. Even though this information still comprises the overwhelming majority of available information, the pertinent literature now contains a variety of studies which support the positive changes or benefits of therapeutic riding programs and the application of such programs to different population groupings (e.g., cerebral palsied, elderly, head injured, mentally retarded).

Relative to the three commonly identified aspects of therapeutic riding (medicine, education, sport), most of the research has been conducted on the medical, or physical, benefits (therapeutic, rehabilitative) especially as applied to those with physical impairments. The research conducted since 1986 has been reported primarily in the following areas: balance, sensory-motor programming (SI--sensory integration, NDT--neurodevelopmental therapy, perceptual-motor training), strength, coordination, posture, and other physical benefits.

Included among the recent findings are the following: (a) improved posture of children with cerebral palsy (Bertoti, 1988), improved balance among children with mental retardation (Biery & Kaufman, 1989), improved arm and leg coordination (Brock, 1988), positive changes in balance, mobility, and posture of physically impaired persons (Copeland, 1986, 1989) and developmentally delayed persons (Walsh, 1989), and increased relaxation of spasticity found among persons with cerebral palsy (Glasow, 1986). In addition, research has brought to light contraindications for those with structural scoliosis of greater than 30-40 degrees and for those with atlantoaxial instability found primarily with Down Syndrome individuals (Tebay & Schlesinger, 1986). Use of sensory integration and NDT techniques have been reported to be effective, as well as "centered" riding (Donahue, 1986).

In addition to the studies identified above, a limited amount of research has been conducted in other areas. The means of assessing performance and measuring change have improved and have become increasingly more sophisticated (Bieber, 1986, Brock, 1987; Fox, 1986). Valid measuring devices remain critical to assessing change accurately.

Dismuke-Blakeley (1981, 1984, 1990) remains the sole pioneer in research on improvement in speech and language as a result of therapeutic riding programs. Increasing interest has been shown in an integrated therapy approach but to date (e.g., Johnson, Elitsky, & Bailey, 1990), very little research has been reported.

In addition, very few research reports were found about other educational or sport benefits of therapeutic riding. Only one author was found to have investigated aspects of therapeutic riding related to sport participation (Bieber, 1986a) whereas two authors reported their findings on the psychosocial aspects of riding (Good, 1986) and psychosocial re-education of "problem children" (Jollinier, 1986).

Early proponents of therapeutic riding "knew" that therapeutic riding was beneficial to participants via their observations but had very little other objective, or empirical data. Current therapeutic riding programs have been designed around, and research data collected on, the a prior determined categories of benefits (e.g., medical, educational, sport) reported by these early proponents. Although the research data seem increasingly to support the claims of the benefits of therapeutic riding, these findings must be published in scholarly journals in order to be more readily accessible to the academic community and other interested persons. Further, a meta-analysis of the existing research could reveal the overall effectiveness of the programs.

That which remains unstudied, or perhaps understudied, are the reasons why therapeutic riding is beneficial. Although the "product" (benefits) is known, an understanding of the process remains relatively unknown. Why does therapeutic riding work? How does therapeutic riding effect change in riders?

Therapeutic riding research must now move from reliance upon descriptive and experimental (quasi-) research designs to more naturalistic inquiry using qualitative research paradigms. This type of research requires direct observation and analysis of the process. Perhaps the answer to why therapeutic riding works lies in understanding the interactions among the rider, the instructor, the horse, and the environment. Among the questions to be posed is the role of the human-animal companion bond (physiological, psychological), the three dimensional movement of the horse, nature and extent of the sensory stimulation received during riding, and the environment (physical, learning, emotional) in a successful therapeutic riding program. Thus, the next phase of therapeutic riding research needs to examine the human-horse-environment interaction. Inasmuch as learning (or change) occurs as a result of the person-environment interaction, it follows that an examination of the role of the horse in this interaction is of paramount importance.

As suggested by Copeland, McGibbon, and Freeman (1990), "... a theoretical framework is imperative in therapeutic riding as we evolve from practicing technicians applying techniques, to professionals basing our programs on a foundation of testable hypotheses and research data." One such framework for future research on therapeutic riding should include an examination of the interaction among (a) the three-dimensional movement of the horse, (b) sensory stimulation and its integrative effects, and (c) the horse-human bond (human-animal companion bond) in the therapeutic riding setting.

[1] Engel, B. (1992). *Therapeutic Riding Programs: Instruction and Rehabilitation*, Durango, CO. 81302.
[2] McCowan, J. The Cheff Center, Augusta, MI 49012.
[3] Tebay, F. Therapeutic Riding Services, PO Box 41, Riderwood, MD 21139.
[4] Joswick, F. Fran Joswick Therapeutic Riding Center, 26282 Oso Road, San Juan Capistrano, CA 92675.

References

Bertoti, (1988). *Effect of Therapeutic Horseback Riding on Posture in Children with Cerebral Palsy*. 6th International Congress of Therapeutic Riding. Toronto, Canada.

Bieber, N. (1986a). Characteristics of physically disabled riders participating in equestrian competition at the national level. In Sherrill, C. (Ed) *Sport and Disabled Athletes*. Champaign, IL: Human Kinetics.

Bieber, N. (1986b). Therapeutic riding: The special educator's perspective. Abstract of paper presented at the *Delta Society International Conference*. Boston, MA.

Brock, B. (1988). *Effect of Therapeutic Horseback Riding on Physically Disabled Adults*. Doctoral Dissertation: U of Indiana.

Copeland, J.C. (1986). A study of four physically disabled riders with twenty-five years of combined riding experience. Abstract of paper presented at the *Delta Society International Conference*. Boston, MA.

Copeland, J.C. (1989). Therapeutic riding as a treatment adjunct after selective posterior lumbar rhizotomy surgery. Abstract of paper presented at Vth *International Conference on the Relationship between Humans and Animals*. Monaco.

Copeland, J.C., McGibbon, N., & Freeman, G. (1990). Theoretical perspectives in therapeutic riding. Abstract of paper presented at *Delta Society Ninth Annual Conference*, October 11-13.

DePauw, K.P. (1986). Horseback riding for individuals with disabilities: Programs, philosophy, and research. *Adapted Physical Activity Quarterly*, 3, 217-226.

Dismuke, R.P. (1981). Therapeutic horsemanship. *The Quarter Horse Journal*. 34-37.

Dismuke, R.P. (1984). Rehabilitative horseback riding for children with language disorders. In R.K. Anderson, B.L. Hart, & L.A. Hart (Eds), *Pet Connection*. 131-140. Minneapolis: University of Minneapolis, Center to Study Human-Animal Relationships and Environment.

Dismuke-Blakely, R.P. (1990). Combined speech/language and occupational therapy through rehabilitative riding. Abstract of paper presented at *Delta Society Ninth Annual Conference*.

Donahue, K. (1986). Centered riding for the physically disabled rider. Abstract of paper presented at *Delta Society International Conference*. Boston MA.

Glasow, B. (1986). Hippotherapy: the horse as a therapeutic modality. *People-Animals-Environment*. 30-31.

Good. C.L. (1986). Psychosocial aspects of riding for adult disabled equestrians. Abstract of paper presented at *Delta Society International Conference*. Boston, MA.

Fox, V.M. (1986 Winter). Measurement device for therapeutic horseback riding. *People-Animals-Environment*. 33

Johnson, L.M., Elitsky, L., Bailey, D. (1990). A holistic approach to therapeutic riding. Abstract of paper presented at *Delta Society Ninth Annual Conference*, October 11-13, 1990.

Jollinier, M. (1989). Horse riding activity and psycho-social re-education in problem children. Abstract of paper presented at *Vth International Conference on the Relationship between Humans and Animals*. Monaco

Joswick, F., Kittredge, M., McCowan, L. et al. (1986). *Aspects and Answers*. Michigan: Cheff Center.

Tebay, J. & Schlesinger, R. (1986 Spring). Riding therapy as a contraindication for Down syndrome individuals with atlantoaxial instability. *People-Animals-Environment*. 31-32.

Walsh, L. (1989). The therapeutic value of horseback riding and the developmental milestones accomplished through horseback riding. Abstract of paper presented at *Vth International Conference on the Relationship between Humans and Animals*, Monaco.

Because of the animal, the excitement the adventure, being outdoors, Air, freedom + the risk of sport

John H. Brough, OTR

Why is horseback riding a valuable tool in helping the child with a disability ? It is recognized that horseback riding aids the handicapped child in neuromuscular and psychological development (Bertoti, 1988; McCowan, 1972; Davis, 1968). A need exists to demonstrate the reasons why and how therapeutic riding techniques benefit the child. This article attempts to present one person's point of view regarding the body's response, especially the response of the autonomic nervous system, to the activities of riding.

The autonomic nervous system is the portion of the central nervous system that controls the automatic functions of the body. It is divided into two parts which work in opposition to each other. The parasympathetic system maintains body function in a normal state. The sympathetic system, commonly called the "fight or flight" system, prepares the body to deal with emergencies. This sympathetic division of the autonomic nervous system takes charge in an emergency. It causes the eyes to dilate, the hair to stand up, goosebumps to appear, and the heart and lungs to work faster. Blood is directed away from the skin and organs of digestion, and is directed to the skeletal muscles. There is an increased urge to empty the bladder. The whole body is in a state of readiness. Functions which are of no particular assistance to defense are slowed down. The bladder wall is relaxed, digestion is slowed, and the activities of the sex organs are inhibited.

In the riding milieu children with disabilities may be ruled by the sympathetic portion of the autonomic nervous system. Think of the probable stress of a child entering the stable for the first time. The instructor may see signs that tell him that this child is being ruled by the sympathetic division. These signs include different degrees of some or all of the following:

SYMPATHETIC NERVOUS SYSTEM STRESS SIGNS. THE CHILD MAY SHOW:
- Wide, dark appearing eyes
- Irregular, rapid, shallow breathing
- Light, jerky, restless movements
- Escalation in strength of movement
- Being easily irritated or distracted by sights, sounds, or smells
- Sensitivity to touching things or being touched
- Increased frequency of swallowing
- Complaint of thirstiness
- Cold, clammy skin
- Voice loud and higher pitched and/or quavering
- Frequent requests to go to the bathroom, or "accidents" occur
- Trembling of the hands, legs, or jaw
- Inability to attend to task--"spaced out"
- Inability to remember what was done
- Reduced efficiency of learning
- After prolonged stimulation by the sympathetic division of the autonomic nervous system, the person may complain of being *weak*, *faint* or *tired*

If control of the sympathetic division decreases, the control by the parasympathetic division increases. The person will demonstrate subsidence in the sympathetic system's behavior and show improved function.

In general, there are three principles for helping a person to change from dominance of the sympathetic system to the parasympathetic system. The person needs:
- WARMTH applied to the muscles
- RHYTHMICAL MASSAGE
- MODULATED SENSORY INPUT

In riding, <u>warmth</u> to the muscles comes from the result of the physical activity. However, increasing the temperature of an area can also enhance the application of the principle. Garments which retain constant body heat are preferable to achieve the desired results.

<u>Rhythmical massage</u>, the second principle for producing faster change to control by the parasympathetic nervous system is accomplished by the horse. After mounting, the rider's body is stimulated by the horse's rhythmic gait. Sufficient time should be allowed for the child to acclimate to the rhythmic pattern of walking before changing to another gait. The gaits enhance rhythmic vestibular and joint receptor stimulation. Muscle spindle and Golgi tendon organs are also stimulated. All of these receptors enhance neuro-integration. The rhythmic movement of the horse further acts on many other sensory receptors thus creating an integrated sensory experience. This experience affects the balance mechanism, position sense, sense of motion, as well as muscle activity, and relaxation.

<u>Modulated sensory input</u> is a necessary concomitant in helping the parasympathetic system to become more dominant. Reducing sensory input to the ears and eyes will enable the rider to cope more successfully with the task at hand. Quick movements or loud yelling should be avoided at all times but especially once the child is mounted. The smaller the arena is the better since it takes less visual stimulation for a person to organize in a confined area. Bright colors and clutter in the arena should also be avoided. Soft, quiet classical music may be added to the arena to aid in relaxation and help concentration. Achieving parasympathetic control of the body will aid the child. He will be more successful as he can attend to the riding lesson. He will then be ready to learn and progress in his riding abilities.

Emotional changes can also be aided by parasympathetic control. When the fragile, explosive child becomes stable, he can tolerate frustration more easily. He will now be easier to handle astride the horse for a longer period of time. The control of the fight or flight mechanism is overridden. The child is better able emotionally to handle the task.

Conclusion:
The <u>elements</u> found in horseback riding are very effective for sensorimotor integration in the child with a disability. These elements augment the transfer of control of the child's responses by the sympathetic to the parasympathetic nervous system. These elements also aid relaxation and learning. One needs to be aware of the effects and power of the autonomic nervous system since it can work for or against the disabled child.

References
Basmajian, J.V. (1964). *Primary Anatomy*. Baltimore: The Williams and Wilkins Co.
Bertoti, D.B.(1988). Effects of therapeutic horseback riding on posture in children with cerebral palsy. *Physical Therapy*. 68.10. Oct. 1505-1512.
Davies, J.A. (1968). *Reins of Life*. London: J A Allen.
Gray, H. (1959). *Anatomy of the Human Body*. Philadelphia: Lea & Feiberger.
Guyton, A. (1964). *Function of the Human Body*. Philadelphia: W.B. Sanders Co.
McCowan, L. (1972). *It is Ability That Counts*. Augusta MI: Cheff Center.

4.03 AN ANALYSIS OF THE EFFECTS OF THERAPEUTIC RIDING ON A STUDENT WITH DISABILITIES: A CASE STUDY AS AN EXAMPLE.

Jean Hoffman, BS

The author, as a volunteer, was an instructor in a therapeutic riding program while completing her bachelors degree in Animal Science. In fulfillment for a senior project, a case study was developed about one of her students. The use of the case study is described here to demonstrate both the steps required to develop a study and how easily one can be accomplished. The method can serve an important place in further validation of therapeutic riding. More of those involved are encouraged to gather information on the results of their riding activities using the case study technique. Ultimately, the purpose of most case studies is to show change in a subject over time. The case study process described as a model here is no different. It was designed and is presented in this instance to show that horseback riding is therapeutic in many ways and can help people having many different kinds of problems.

Preparing to Do a Case Study
This study involved a student relatively new to a therapeutic riding program. Brad had only been riding with the group for a few months when the instructors and parents began to notice many positive changes in him. Immediately, as one of his instructors, I made the decision to document these changes on Brad in case study form. By so doing it was hoped to illustrate that riding was, for him and others, therapeutic.

Since course requirements limited the time in which to complete the project, Brad's riding lessons were documented for three months. This was with written logs of lesson plans and results of each lesson, plus photographs taken during the lessons. Evaluation forms routinely used for all the therapeutic riding students in the group were also completed to record Brad's progress in several mental and physical areas, such as comprehension, balance and coordination.

A literature search was carried out to see what kinds of studies had already been done in this activity with what results. It is best to do the research first, before the case study starts, as this can help one decide what a study needs to examine and how to shape the process. However, one should not be influenced by another person's findings. Those are used later in evaluating one's own findings. The results of a case study must stand alone, based on facts presented. This is more difficult than it sounds since so many "facts" are the subjective observations of instructors, relatives, volunteers and physical or occupational therapists. But observation is a critical research skill, in any qualitative study. A student's lack of improvement or even decline during a study can be caused by many factors, including, in this example, the rider's health and the type of riding being done. All results, positive or negative, when evaluated will help others shape their instructional programs to better benefit their students.

Locating Reports of Relevant Studies
Finding publications on therapeutic riding may be difficult but in general, public libraries have little to no information on this subject. University libraries may be more helpful, but the best hope in therapeutic riding at present usually lies in private sources. Some people involved in therapeutic riding have started their own collections of related books and journal articles. In addition, riding groups/organizations in various countries publish collections of articles from their annual conferences. Thus, networking with those in riding groups to locate materials related to your subject is a good alternative to libraries. In this project, when articles were found relating to Brad's condition and his current program, they were read and highlighted and saved for later citation. Various important points relating to the study and its results were then easy to find later to be used to reinforce the case study findings.

Presenting the Case
When the study period was over, that is, the approximately three-month period of documenting Brad's progress, the handwritten reports of riding plans as well as comments written after each lesson were organized chronologically and typed up. Next, the photographs were developed, duplicated and identified as to activity. A questionnaire was written to give to Brad's mother to complete. It asked for information about his schooling, his disability, his previous riding experience, and other sports in which he was involved. There were also questions concerning his mother's

observation of his progress; had his parents, physician, teachers or others noted any physical, mental or emotional changes in him since he had started riding? The completed questionnaire was included in the finished study along with the uncut written log of lessons. Only clear, representative photos were chosen to be included, four each from five sessions, to illustrate Brad's form and progress.

The photos were presented with captions describing the intent and results of the activity shown, and were, in chronological order. With more time and forethought, a short video of several sessions could have been made. This would have better illustrated points such as coordination, flexibility, and response time to instructions.

Finally, after the photo section, in a summary section, the instructor's overall evaluation of Brad's progress was detailed in the areas of performance mentioned previously, and in areas such as attentiveness, endurance, attitude, and confidence. In a section called conclusion, Brad's experiences were compared to the findings of other studies found in the literature searched.

The appendix included samples of the evaluation forms used, a bibliography of sources (49 in this case), forms for admission to the riding program: consent and release, medical information, physician referral, and occupational/physical therapy assessment. The last form(s) is particularly useful to include in a study, with both pre-and post-study data recorded.

Conclusions

This case study went very smoothly from start to finish; only two make-up sessions were required. The student, instructors, therapist, parent and volunteers were completely cooperative and showed up for each weekly session as scheduled. In addition, the results were uniformly positive, showing slight to major improvement in all areas of performance measured. Thankfully the pictures supported the results. Subsequent studies by this researcher are not expected to always go as well as this first one did, but they will in any case cover a longer period, use more in-depth observations and include better documentation techniques, such as video.

Following the simple steps described can help a person learn not only how to produce a case study, but also to appreciate what is valuable to students in a riding program, and how to observe the changes in students over time. Even with this kind of single case research one can help improve therapeutic riding programs everywhere and thereby ultimately increase the riders' learning and enjoyment.

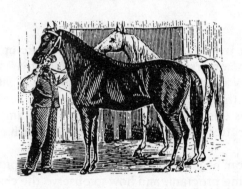

PART III   THE HORSE

The horse is the focus of any equine-assisted activity such as therapeutic riding and hippotherapy. The characteristics and the quality of the horse determines, to a great degree, the quality of services which are provided to the consumer (person with a disability). Instructors and therapists <u>must</u> understand the horse in terms of its anatomy and kinesiology; its nature and trainability; and its effects upon the rider under specific conditions. This chapter directs the reader's attention to areas that are of major concern to all those who are involved in the field of therapeutic riding.

5   CONFORMATION OF THE HORSE AND ITS RELATION TO THERAPEUTIC RIDING

Conformation, according to Webster (1966), is the complete and symmetrical formation and arrangement of parts. The conformation of a horse is a major factor in determine the quality of movement, structural soundness and usefulness with specific riders and appropriateness for individual tasks. Conformation alone will not produce a good balanced and forward moving horse. The horse must also be trained to develop its athletic abilities through cultivating the muscular, cardiovascular, and nervous systems.

Therapeutic riding programs have developed on the concept that the horse influences the rider. Over the years many specialists have studied how the horse influences the rider and what qualities are desirable for specific tasks. Tasks may include dressage training, driving, vaulting, gymkhana, jumping, trail riding, equine-assisted therapy, or developing physical and recreational skills in the rider with a disability. Each of these tasks requires the selection of an appropriate horse. The instructor must have knowledge of conformation and how the horse moves in order to effectively train and direct the horse's influence upon the rider.

The selection and training of a horse to meet a program's needs will be discussed. The appropriateness of the horse will lead to the achievement of both the goals of riders and the program's aims. The horse that is well trained in basic dressage techniques (either through English or Western training), is responsive, supple, and *balanced*. It can be used for therapy and for riders who wish to develop riding skills. The vaulting horse is used for gymnastics on horseback. The carriage horse is used in driving programs. Some horses will have characteristics which will meet several needs while other horses may be used specifically, just for one task. The knowledge of these characteristics is important in developing a program and in the selection of horses appropriate to the task.

It is important to understand conformation components in relation to training and to maintaining the horse in a healthy state. Some defects can be compensated for by other good points or by training the horse to overcome negative factors. One must always keep in mind what it is that the horse is to do.

- What form must the horse take to accomplish the requested task?
- How can the horse be helped to accomplish the task?
- Has the horse been trained to the level essential for a given task?
- Is he presently in condition for the task or has there been a year or so of laps in training?

This section is not intended to be a text on conformation but is to highlight major factors and to instill in the reader the importance of the subject. A full understanding of conformation can be acquired by reading text books on the subject (see the reference section of this text), attending clinics, reading the analysis of horses by experts in the field and to analyzing horses oneself.

Webster's New World Dictionary of the American Language. (1966). Cleveland: The World Publishing Co.

5.01   THE HORSE'S SKELETON

Barbara T. Engel, MEd, OTR

<u>Points of a horse</u> define distinct "parts" of a horse and each horse has these same parts regardless of breed. Collectively the <u>points</u> define conformation. Variations in conformation can be found from breed to breed and horse to horse. For example, the conformation of a Hanoverian is different than that of a Thoroughbred or Iceland ponies.

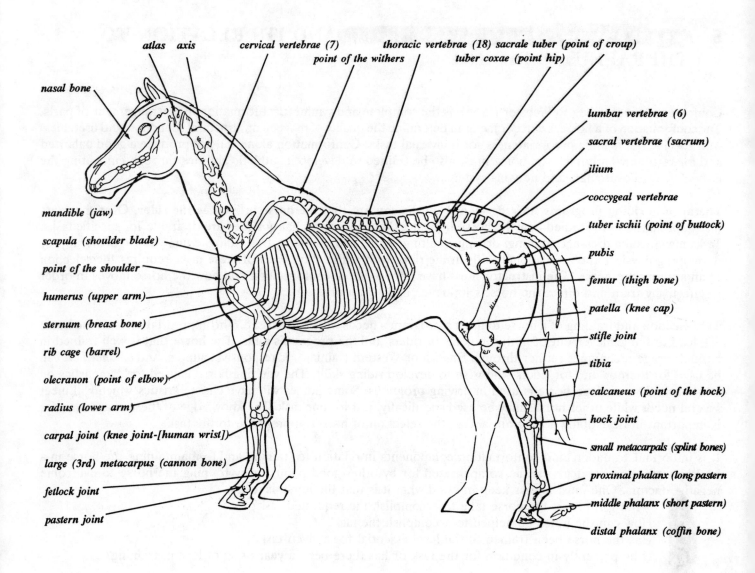

FIGURE 1. THE SKELETON OF THE HORSE

5.02   POINTS OF THE HORSE

Barbara T. Engel, MEd, OTR

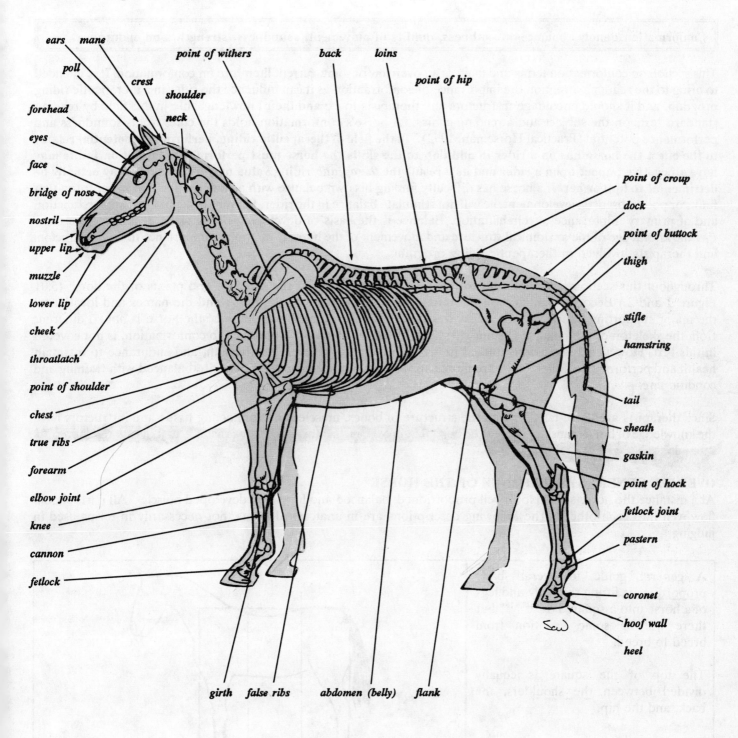

FIGURE 2.   THE POINTS OF THE HORSE

Barbara T. Engel, MEd, OTR

Conformation denotes balance, smoothness, quality of movement, soundness, strength, and endurance

This section on conformation terms and faults is an overview of some current literature on conformation. It is intended to bring to the reader's attention the importance of conformation as it can influence the rider in a therapeutic riding program, and it should encourage instructors and therapists to expand their knowledgeable in this field by reading standard texts on the subject and attending clinics. "A horse's conformation holds the clues to his soundness and performance potential (Practical Horseman, 1992)." **In the field of therapeutic riding, performance potential relates to the effect the horse has on a rider in addition to the skills the horse must perform. Conformation faults may have a negative impact upon a rider and as a result the *therapeutic* riding value may diminish or may actually be detrimental to him or her.** If a horse has difficulty finding his own balance with a rider astride due to conformation faults or poor muscular development, he will not stimulate balance in the rider. Balance is the basis of human function and of primary importance in rehabilitation. Balance is the basis of developing riding skills. It is therefore clear that the knowledge of the anatomical structure and movement of the horse is of primary importance to both instructors and therapists involved in therapeutic riding programs.

Throughout this section it is important to refer to the illustrations of the skeleton and points of the horse (5.01 Figure 1 and 2.) Become familiar with the terminology of the parts of the horse and the names and location of the major supporting bones. For therapists this is an easy task since the skeleton of the horse is not so different from the skeleton of the human. The muscle system, which is of major importance to conformation, is not covered in this text. However, it should be studied in order to understand leverage, strength, and endurance to maintain health and performance. Some faults are more serious than others, some can be counterbalanced with training and conditioning.

Since therapists are more familiar with the structure of bones, muscles and connecting tissue and instructors have the knowledge of horsemanship, it would be beneficial for the instructors and their assistants to join with the therapists to study the subject of conformation.

OVERALL GENERAL APPEARANCE OF THE HORSE
At a distance the horse should look well proportioned, balanced and have well developed muscles. All parts should flow well into each other[16]. The following descriptions are in anatomical terms, not necessarily in terms used in judging.

A general guide to overall <u>body proportions</u> is fitting the body and legs of a horse into a square box [5,20,6,16]* but there will be some variation from breed to breed. The top of the square is equally divided between the shoulders, the back, and the hip.	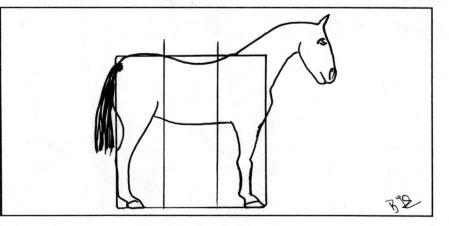

Figure 3.

* numbers will indicate the references listed at the end of the chapter, in this article, due to limitations of space.

The size of the <u>head</u> (from the poll to the muzzle, **1 to 2**) is generally equal to[4,20,6,16]:
1. The point of withers to point of shoulders (**6 to 7**)
2. Point of shoulders to throatlatch (**7 to 3**)
3. Cervical base of the neck (**4 to 5**)
4. Waist (point of hips to flank) (**14 to 11**)
5. Point of stifle joint to point of hock (**15 to 13**)
6. Point of the fetlock to point of elbow (**9 to 8**)
7. Point of hip to point of buttocks (**14 to 12**)
8. Point of buttocks to point of the stifle (**12 to 15**)
9. Point of hocks to the ground (**13 to ground**)

Other body <u>proportions</u> are[20,5,16]
10. The withers to abdomen equal abdomen to ground (**6 to 8 to ground**)
11. Withers to ground equal point of shoulders to point of buttocks (**6 to ground = 7 to 12**)
12. Top of the croup to the ground equals the top withers to the ground (equals 2½ times the size of the head.) (**10 to ground = 6 to ground**)

Figure 4.

The horse's <u>head</u> is composed of the skull and houses the brain, the eyes, the teeth, jaw, and nasal cavity. It is used as an oscillating pendulum to vary distribution of body weight and to effect the center of gravity during movement[7,15,21,22]. The average horse's head weights forty pounds which he uses to effectively mobilize his body[7].
1. The skull should be well structured and proportioned to size of horse[15,21,22]

The head should:
2. Be well set on, with smooth connection to neck[5,16]
3. Have a forehead wide enough to house the brain, sinus, eyes, and upper jaw[16,15]
4. Have good width between eyes, good length between the eyes and nostrils to allow free breathing and air intake to be heated or cooled before entering the lungs[16,15,21,22]
5. Have a jaw proportional to the head[16,15,21,22]
6. Have space between lower jaw and neck to allow for bending at the poll and space for windpipe[5,6,9,10]
7. Have a good expression--expression portrays the horse's emotions, moods, and temperament[5,6,9,10]

Figure 5.

Possible problems with the <u>head</u> include:

1. A head large for the body puts added weight to the forehand
2. A large head on a long neck puts too much weight on the forelegs[9]
3. A large head on a short neck displaces balance less than a large head on a average size neck[11]
4. A small head is better balanced on a long neck[11] but may not provide a balance leverage for a large horse.
5. When head is set on too close upon the neck, breathing maybe restricted[22]
6. When angle of the head to neck is too acute, it compresses the larynx[10]
7. Horses with excessively long heads may have larger blind spots in front of them on the ground[12]

Figure 6.

1. Shape of the horse's <u>face</u> is triangular from the front and generally straight from a side view.
2. Roman nose/Ram-headed (convex) may impair vision[5]. A roman nose is found in some draft horses.
3. Dishfaced (concave) enhances vision[5,20].
   Dishface is characteristic of Welsh and Arabian breeds.

Figure 7.

Eyes should be:
1. Large, round and bright. Increases vision up/down, front/back[22]
2. Wide set to increase the vision field. May indicate good intelligence[15]
3. Warm, friendly, alert, and expressive depicting a good temperament[11]

Negative factors are:
4. Bovine eyes (popeyed)(bug-eyed) may impair vision[4]
5. Pig eyes are small and set far back into head limiting vision and may make the horse nervous because it cannot see the source of sounds[4,5,15]

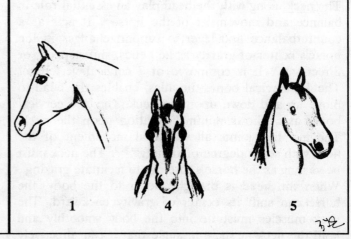

Figure 8.

To enhance hearing the ears should be a good size but not too big. They should be relaxed and mobile to hear well in all directions. Alert ears means the horse is attentive to its surroundings. "Back" ears indicate a sour temperament, and mad and possibly dangerous horse[4,5,15].

Figure 9.

The muzzle includes the nostrils, lips, and covers the front teeth.
The nostrils should be large, sensitive, well-formed, and mobile to allow for adequate flow of air into the respiratory system. Lips should be firm, muscular and oppose each other evenly. They should have good prehension[5] ability since the horse uses his lips, (especially the upper lip) as a 'hand' to feed. The jaws influence the lips and must meet evenly. If they do not meet evenly they will interfere with grazing and chewing[11,15]
Negative factors include:
1. Parrot-mouth--the lower jaw recedes and upper jaw appears buck-toothed[5,8]
2. Monkey-mouth--the lower jaw protrudes and the upper jaw recedes[5,8]

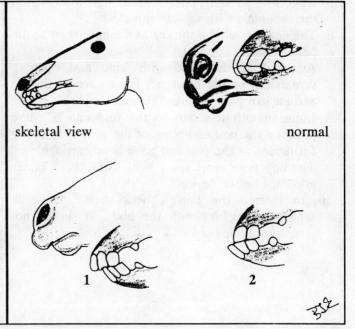

skeletal view   normal

1   2

Figure 10.

The <u>neck</u> along with the head play an essential role in balance and movement of the horse[18]. It acts as a counterbalance and lever to support changes in the horse's center of gravity as he bends, shifts speed, or directions[16]. It is composed of 7 cervical vertebrae. The 1st cervical bone, the atlas, enables the head to move up and down upon the neck. The 2nd cervical bone, axis, allows minimal rotation upon the neck. The last five joints allow lateral movement of the neck with some degree of arching[2a,9,20]. The neck must be as long as the horse's forelegs to facilitate grazing[7]. When the head is brought closer to the body, the horse can shift its center of gravity backward. The neck muscles must tie into the body smoothly and hold the neck at such an angle that it can affectively balance the body and help move the shoulders[7,18].

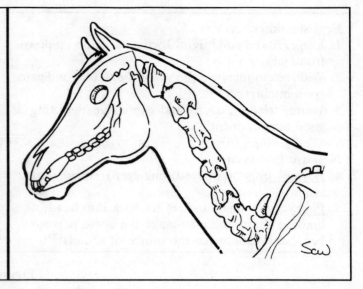

Figure 11.

In order for the <u>neck</u> to function effectively it should have the following characteristics:
1. Well proportioned length to the rest of the body to assist in balance and movement[6,11,15]
2. Set well into the shoulders (equal on both sides) without hollowing at the shoulder line, to aid overall balance[21,9,5]
3. Be convex with a slight arch between the poll and withers[5]
4. Be more muscular on the top than the underline[11,13]
5. Underline should appears as though it slips into the shoulders with smooth muscles[11,21]
6. The neck should be thicker at the base than at the poll[5]
7. Attached at the head with wide and open throatlatch so the head can flex to accept the bit and air can pass through the trachea[4,5,12,20]
8. Long, smooth neck muscles that forms an "S" curve between the poll and point of the withers allowing for flexion at the poll and good head carriage[4,5]
9. Two fingers or more space behind the cheek bones allow for better flexion[11]
10. In motion the horse's neck should move in tandem, gracefully with the body. It should not jerk, wobble or bob[15].

Figure 12.

58

Negative characteristics affecting the <u>neck</u> are:

1. A thick throatlatch, and/or a severe angle of the neck to the head prevents flexion at poll[11]. Therefore the horse may resist the bit, and be less flexible for balance and mobility.
2. Set on too high and straight causes poor balancing ability[21,9]
3. Big neck and large cheek bone decrease the ability to flex at the poll and respond to the bit[15]
4. A short-necked horse will have shorter strides since the neck muscles help the shoulders to move forward[17]. A short-neck decreases its ability to assist in balancing and mobility[7].

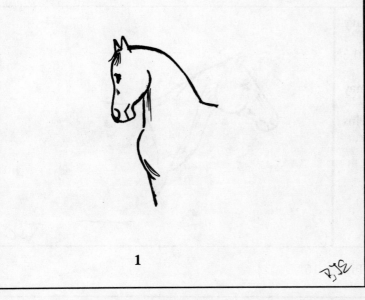

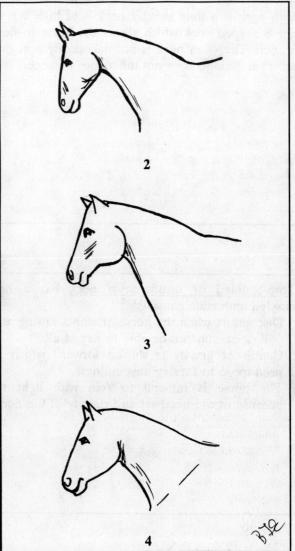

Figure 13.

A <u>Ewe neck</u> is curved like a sheep's neck with no crest and a bulky muscular lower line. The sagging topline makes flexing at the poll difficult. The head tends to go upward and control at the bit is difficult for the rider[11,3]. The horse may also be under muscled which limits its stride[17]. The angle of the head decreases vision[7].

Figure 14.

59

Swan neck is a long slender neck held high[11]. It is a long **S**-shaped neck which allows the horse to flex at the poll. The swan neck is not necessarily a negative factor[6] and alone does not infleuence balance.

Figure 15.

Close-coupled or upside-down neck has a heavy muscled underside causing:[8,10,11]
1) Discomfort when the horse attempts flexing at the poll or he may not be able to flex at all.
2) Center of gravity is shifted forward which may predispose to foreleg unsoundness.
3) The horse is difficult to rein with light reins because of the head set and rigidity of the neck.

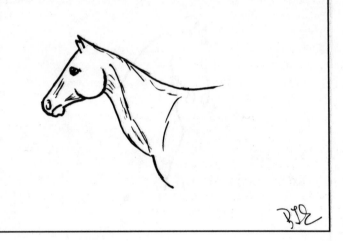

Figure 16.

Low-set on neck causes the horse to go on the forehand and balance and schooling are hindered[9]. This neck shifts the weight forward and may drag down the forehand[8,11,10]. Muscles on the lower neck will lose some of their mechanical effectiveness[18,8,10,11].

Figure 17.

60

The shoulder blade (scapula) rests next to the rib cage and should be flat, long[11], and slope forward 45 to 60 degrees[5]. The length of the scapula determines the degrees of slope. A short scapula is more upright than a long scapula[22]. The shoulders are attached to the body by muscles that allow the shoulder-arm joints to absorb the concussion of the forelegs (sling effect)[5,22]. It is the only joint (not a true joint) that is not held together by ligaments-- instead muscles and tendons move the limbs and hold them together[19]. The deeply defined slope of the shoulders determines the forward angle of movement of the forelimbs. A long shoulder blade causes a longer, springy stride on a longer lever, giving more flow of movement and power[19,13,9,5,2c]. An upright shoulder makes the legs susceptible to greater knee action[2b], but it shortens the forward stride and dispenses jarring movements to the rider[19].

Positive shoulder characteristics include:

1. Shoulder blades should be close together at the top. Wide apart makes the shoulders lumpy, difficult to fit saddle, provides poor movement, and is uncomfortable for the rider[21].
2. A distance of one fist between the ribs and shoulders, at the point of the elbow, allows freedom of movement for the forelimb[11].
3. Long, broad, sloping shoulders, forming a right angle with the humerus, give a springy stride with a longer forward reach and more ground covering[9].
4. Long shoulder bones provide for better muscle attachment (the longer the bone the more acute the angle, the less downward stress is placed on the horse's limbs[16]).
5. The farther back the withers, the more the limbs are capable of straightening, increasing the length of stride[19].
6. The shoulders (point of withers to point shoulders) should not be shorter than the length of the head, to gain the greatest freedom of stride[16].

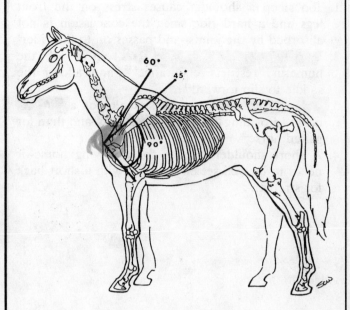

The angle of the shoulder blade (point of withers to the point of the shoulder)*

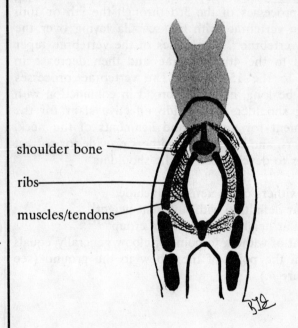

shoulder bone

ribs

muscles/tendons

The "sling" construction of the shoulders and forelegs

Figure 18.

61

Negative Shoulder characteristics:
1. Too steep a shoulder causes stress on the front legs and a hard ride since the concussion is not absorbed by the joints--and passes on to the rider[3]
2. Upright shoulder restricts movement of the humerus, restricts endurance[4,19] and allows the saddle to slip forward[21]
3. Upright shoulder is more suitable for a harness horse--providing good pulling power[21] and than for gaited horse[2b].
4. A short shoulder is poor for a driving horse--it needs to be well set on the neck with a short back for strength[3].

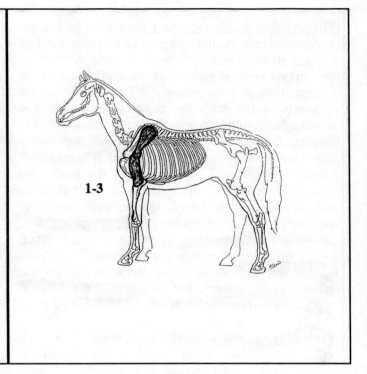

Figure 19.

The withers on the top line are made up of the long spinal processes of the 3rd through the 9th or 10th thoracic vertebrae with the scapula laying over the first 7 vertebrae[22]. The spines of the vertebrae taper upward to the 4th vertebrae and then decrease in height to the 15-16th[19,23.] The vertebrae processes should be long, high, and broad in conjunction with sloping shoulders to provide effective slant for the attachment for muscles and ligaments of the neck, shoulders, and back. Good withers provide for correct muscles to develop behind the shoulders[6,8].

Good withers characteristics include:
1. Clear definition with sufficient height[14].
2. Similar height as that of the croup[13,11,17].
3. Point of withers to point of elbow generally equals from the point of the elbow to the ground (see Figure 4.)

3rd to 10th thoracic vertebrae

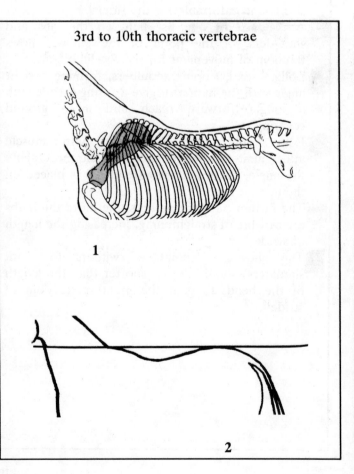

Figure 20.

62

Negative characteristics of the withers include:
4. Withers that are too high cannot accommodate a saddle fit[21];
    a) short steep withers
    b) long steep withers
5. Mutton withers are low and predispose the horse to clumsiness, forging, and restrict rotation at the shoulder causing him to move in a rolling motion[5].

Figure 21.

The topline of the horse runs from the poll to the dock--in line with the spine[2d,7,11] and is supported by the neck, shoulders, back, loins, and croup. It is influenced by the skeletal structure, the spine, and muscular development[22,11]. It should not have protrusion, dips, or hollows, but have smooth flowing curves as viewed from the side--slightly concave behind the withers and convex over the loins[15]. Viewed from behind (from a high platform) the topline should form a straight line[2d].

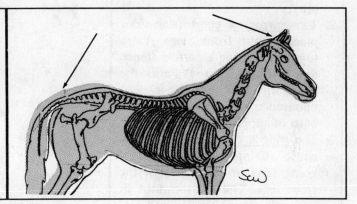

Figure 22.

The trunk is composed of the chest, abdomen, back, loins and croup. It is slung between the forelimbs (Figure 19) in a muscular cradle and attached by a bony union with the hind limbs at the pelvis. It holds the vital organs of the horse[22,9,14]. The spine lies in the upper portion of the trunk and allows for limited movement. The major areas of movement occur in the head-neck region, the cervical-thoracic area, between the last thoracic and 1st lumbar vertebrae, the lumbar-sacral junction and in the tail[22].

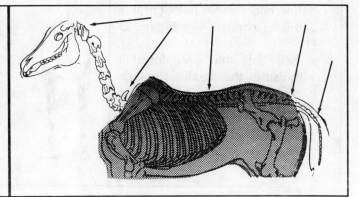

Figure 23.

The <u>internal organs</u> of the horse are housed in the <u>chest</u> formed by the rib-cage and muscles and the <u>abdomen</u> (flank or belly). The chest protects the lungs and heart, and should be of generous depth to provide space for these organs and be in proportion to the rest of the body. Ribs should be curved outward (well sprung), not flat, set apart, carried well back along the body, and not cramped together, to provide good points for attachment of the foreleg and shoulder muscles and tendons[14,10,4,9]. The <u>abdomen</u> lies below the loins and is formed by many layers of muscles which hold up the belly, the internal organs, and help to support the back[2d,23].

1. The chest should be <u>oval</u>, not oblong or round placing the legs straight, providing a good seat (1a) and straight way of going (1b)[6,22].

2. Too <u>narrow a chest</u> (slab-side) places the front legs close together causing a narrow stance and brushing (2a). It limits the space for lungs resulting in poor endurance and provides a poor base of support for the rider.

3. Too <u>wide a chest</u>, rounded, may cause rolling, paddling way of going (3a) or criss-cross of the front legs. The rider cannot sit correctly to use the leg and seat aids (3b).

4. A pendulous belly goes with a hollow back--shows lack of fitness and poor strength--see Figure 25 (1)[2d].

5. A belly line that goes downhill will cause the saddle to slide backward[11].

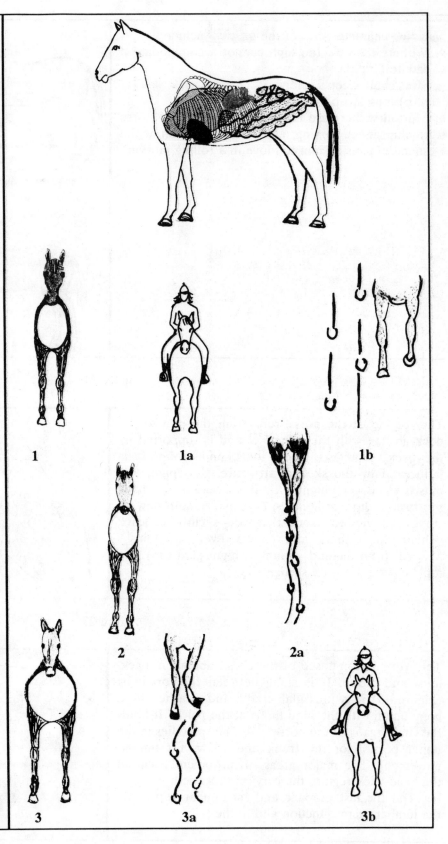

1   1a   1b

2   2a

3   3a   3b

Figure 24.

64

The <u>back</u> is composed of 18 thoracic vertebrae. It should be in proportion to the rest of the body and be well muscled[5,9]. It should be of medium length and almost level. Long backs are comfortable but weak[6,21]. A strong, well proportioned, supple back aids good movement of the rider[11].

1. A <u>hollow back</u> indicate weakness, poor conditioning, causes damage to spine, and is difficult to collect[10,21].

2. A <u>roach back</u> is arched upward, strong but uncomfortable to sit to, and the stride is short[21,5].

3. A <u>long back</u> in proportion to the body but with a weak loin, makes it difficult for the hind legs to come underneath the body (collection)[8,11].

4. A <u>very long back</u> may be weak and makes it difficult to find an effective center of gravity. This horse many have a swinging motion in his stride. These backs must be kept conditioned to avoid weakness[8,11,15].

5. A back that is too <u>short</u> viewed from the side is difficult to supple and uncomfortable to sit to[8,9,10,11].

6. A <u>straight</u> back (top line) restricts the horse's movement and power.

7. A <u>narrow back</u>, especially when long, may be weak and provide a poor base of support for a rider.

8. A back that is <u>too wide</u> is difficult to sit to causing the rider's femur (upper leg bone) to hyper-abduct, preventing the use of the seat bones, "seat aids", leg aids, causing the pelvis to tilt and the back to lose its balance and suppleness.

9. The spine must be straight from the poll to the dock as viewed from above[2d]. A crooked spine (9a) will cause the horse to be off balance and the rider cannot sit straight and in-balance (9b).

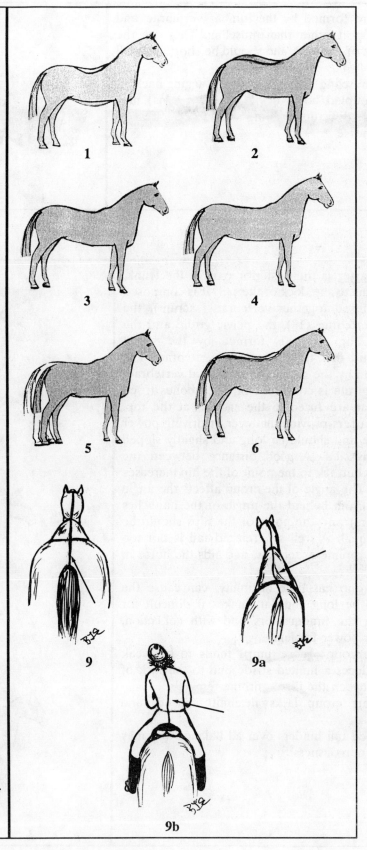

Figure 25.

The loins are formed by the lumbar vertebrae and have no support other than muscling. They are the weakest part of the back and should be short and well muscled.

1. Lack of muscling usually leads to a sagging back[6,11].
2. A long-coupled horse (one with long loins) may have more difficulty carrying weight than a short-coupled horse[5,6,7,11].

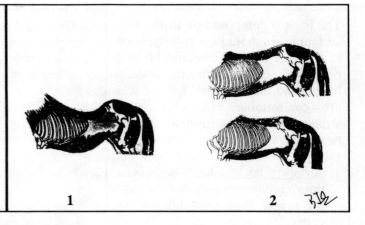

Figure 26.

The hindquarter is the posterior part of the trunk, from the loins to the dock of the tail. It is composed of the (5) fused together vertebrae (sacrum), the coccygeal vertebrae (18), the pelvic girdle and the hind legs. The croup is formed by the sacral vertebrae and first three coccygeal vertebrae. The tail is formed by the remaining coccygeal vertebrae. The pelvic girdle is composed of three bones fused together that are fused to the sacrum at the top. The hindquarters provide the lever or driving power of the horse and should be long and slightly sloped and well muscled. A good distance between the point of the buttock to the point of the hip increases movement. The angle of the croup affects the angle of the leg. From behind the angle of the haunches (hindquarters) and the point of the hips should be level and equal. A well set, relaxed tail is not too high on the topline or too low, and aids the horse in balance[5,6,14,15,21,22].

1. A flat croup has little flexibility, can cause the stride to be long and flat, makes it difficult for rounding the hindquarters and with collection, and poor power for jumping[11].
2. A steep croup (goose-rump) tends to be weak and produces a limited stride due to the lack of angle between the ilium and the femur[13].
3. A short croup lacks flexibility, speed, and power[7,9].
4. A clamped tail hinders over-all balance and may indicate nervousness[9].

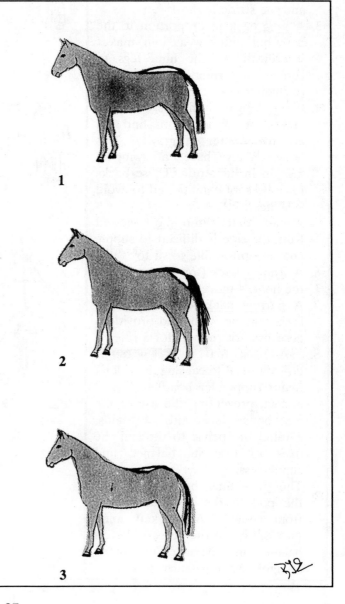

Figure 27.

The <u>hind legs</u> are attached to the pelvic girdle at the hip joint and therefore have a direct influence on the spine. The rear leg is designed to push the horse forward. The stifle should be in line with the body. The part of the leg below the knee or hock has no muscles and movement is influenced by the muscles above the knee and carried through by tendons with ligaments holding the structures together. The hocks and stifle joints coordinate their movements[21,19,22].
1. The leg should be straight as viewed from the rear.
2. Viewed from the side the point of hock should be directly below point of buttock.
3. The hocks (7 bones) should be prominent, wide, deep for attachment of tendons. The hock is a major joint.

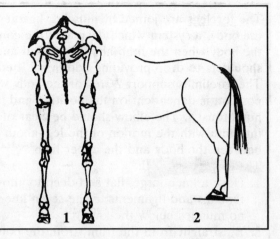

Figure 28.

Negative characteristics of the <u>hind legs</u> are:
1. <u>Bowlegged</u> or <u>bowed hocks</u> viewed from the rear, the hocks turn out with the toes turning in. This tends to cause an uneven load, twisting the hocks outward and causing strains[10,21,9,16].
2. <u>Cow-hocked</u> as viewed from the rear the hocks turn inward and close together with toes turned out. They cause the limb to move outward or rotate instead of forward motion. This tends to strain the hocks, cause brushing[21,9,12,16].
3. <u>Cramped out</u> legs are set out behind the line with the buttock and prevent the horse from stepping under himself or prevents being "strung out". The legs tend to dig into the ground and cannot lift the body--are poor power producers[5,15].
4. <u>Cramped in</u>--legs are under the horse decreasing the base of support and decreasing power[5,15].
5. <u>Post-legged</u> (upright leg) legs are too straight, lacking spring and length to the stride, causing a short hard ride[16,5].
6. <u>Sickle-hocked</u> is an increased angulation of the hock toward the front of the horse which over-stresses the ligaments, predisposing them to injury[10,12,16].
7. <u>Hocks</u>--straight--cause more concussion and are prone to strains. Horse with straight hocks also has straight stifles--difficult for him to sit back on his haunches[21,9].

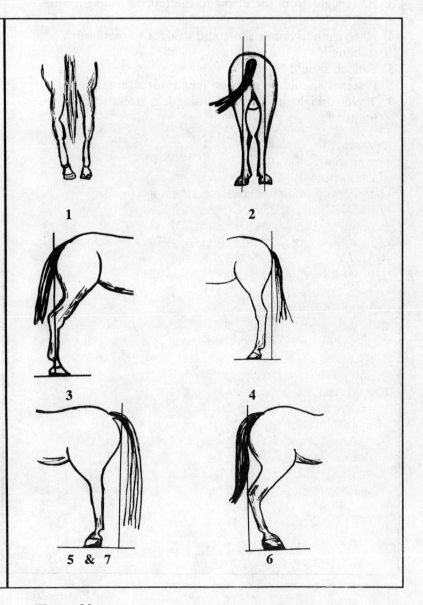

Figure 29.

The <u>forelegs</u> are joined by muscles, ligaments, and fascia to the body, a system which decreases the concussion force to the body when the limb hits the ground and allows the shoulders to drop providing additional "bend" during turns[22]. The forelimbs support 2/3rds of the body weight. The foreleg position is dependent on the position and length of the humorous[10,5]. The elbow should be clear of the body so not to interfere with the motion of the leg--about one fist width between the body and the upper limb[3,4,9,11,12,21,22].

The <u>forelegs</u> should:

1. Have a knee large, flat and deep to allow attachments of tendons and ligaments to the seven knee bones (there are no muscles below the knee)[21].
2. Be straight from the front, from the point of the shoulder to the ground to provide a forward gait[21,5].
3. Be straight from the elbow to the fetlock from the side view[21,5].
4. Have cannon bones short and straight to increase stability[21,3].
5. Fetlock should be flat[21].
6. Pasterns should be medium length for strength[21].
7. Travel straight in balance causing less stress to the joints[11,10].

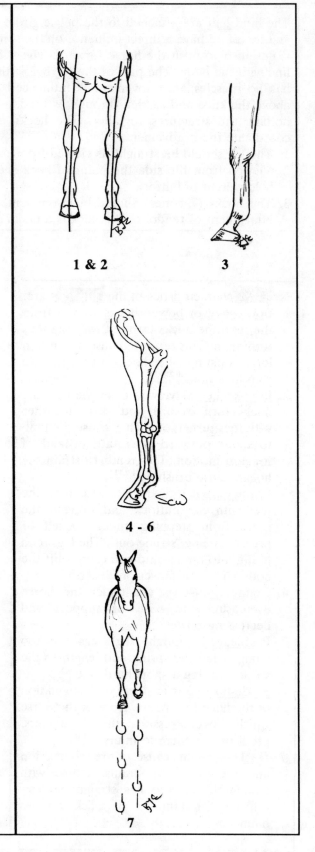

1 & 2   3

4 - 6

7

Figure 30.

68

Negative characteristics of the <u>foreleg</u>:

1. <u>Lack of straightness</u> of the legs from the front will affect motion and put strains on the tendons, ligaments and joints[21,5].
2. <u>Long cannon bones</u> increase weakness and breakdown[22,3,11].
3. Narrow base with <u>toes out</u> make the horse stand on the back of the knee causes winging or dishing[16,5].
4. <u>Buck-kneed</u> (over at the knee) are bent forward and can cause knees to buckle forward and become unstable; dangerous for rider if the leg buckles [12,16].
5. <u>Calf-kneed</u> (back at knees) hyper-extension of the knee joint (concave) in the front, lacks strength and tends to strain ligaments[12,16,5].
6. <u>Pigeon-toed</u>--causes the horse to stand with his toes pointing in toward each other and causes paddling[16].
7. <u>Cramped in</u>--legs are under the horse decreasing the base of support and decrease power[5,15].
8. <u>Spay footed</u>--(toed-out) that cause "winging" to the inside and may hit opposite limb; prone to injury[10,12,16].
9. <u>Knock-kneed</u>--the knees are closer together than at the chest or feet; restricts movement, strains knee[16,5].
10. <u>Bench-kneed</u> (offset) is caused by the cannon bone being offset at the knee joint--not lined up at the center of the joint[12,16].
11. <u>Tied in below the knee</u>--when the cannon bone is narrower below the knee than at the fetlock[21,2,5].

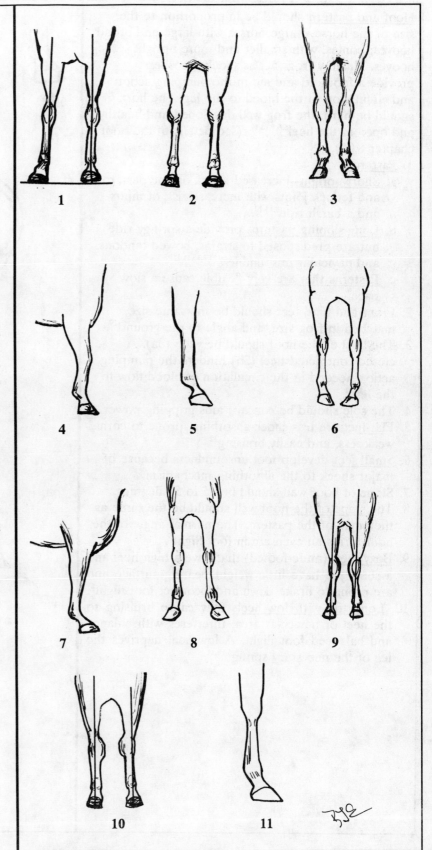

Figure 31.

69

Hoof and pastern should be in proportion to the size of the horse. Large horses with large and broad hooves; ponies, with smaller and more upright hooves. Healthy frogs act as shock absorbers, provide a foothold and aid in the pumping action and circulation of the blood to the leg. The horn should be hard, the frog well developed and healthy and open at the heel[5,6,9,18,14]. (see details of the hoof chapter 8.05).

1. Pasterns:
   a. Short-upright--increased shock on the pastern and fetlock joints with increase risk of injury and a harsh ride[9,11,12].
   b. Long-sloping pasterns provide a springy ride but are predisposed to strains, bowed tendons, and navicular unsoundness[21,3,15,11,12].
   c. Pasterns that are very flexible cause a slow pace[9]

2. Front and hind feet should be the same size, matched in frog size, and angle to the ground[19].

3. The heel of the hoof should be wide (3a). A closed-contracted heel (3b) hinders the pumping action needed in the circulation of blood flow to the leg[12].

4. The sole should be concave aids gripping power.

5. Flat-feet are less shock-absorbing, prone to corns, weakness, and easily bruising[12].

6. Small feet develop foot unsoundness because of major shock to the absorbing mechanism.

7. Slope of hoof wall should be 45 to 50 degrees.

8. The slope of the hoof wall should be the same as the angle of the pastern. The normal angle of the hoof forms an even arc in foot flight[5].

9. Boxy feet, (mule-footed) that have a high heel and a short toe have little weight bearing surface and are prone to brake down and incorrect foot flight[5].

10. Long toe with low heels may cause bruising to the heel or navicular area, interferes with balance and balanced foot flight. A low heal deprives the leg of the necessary spring[5,10,11].

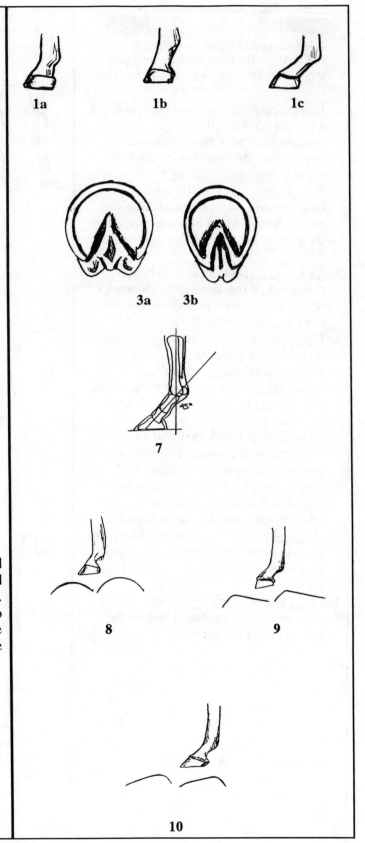

Figure 32.

References cited in Figures

1   Adams, O.R. (1987). *Lameness in Horses*. Philadelphia: Lea and Febiger.

2a Bennett, D. (1990). Clinic, Los Angles.

2b Bennett, D. (1988). *Principles of Conformation Analysis, Vol I*, Gaithersburg: Fleet Street Publishing Corp.

2c Bennett, D. (1988). The right angle on shoulders. 130, 100-105. *Equus*. Gaithersburg: Fleet Street Publishing Corp.

2d Bennett, D. (1989). *Principles of Conformation Analysis, Vol II*, Gaithersburg: Fleet Street Publishing Corp.

3   Bromily, M. (1987). *Equine Injury and Therapy*. New York: Howell Book House Inc.

4   Borton, A. (1990). Selection of the horse. In Evans, Borton, Hintz, & L.D. Van Vleck. *The Horse*. New York: W.H. Freeman and Co.

5   Evans, J.W. (1989). *Horses*. New York: W.H. Freeman and Co.

6   Froissard, J. (1967). *Equitation*. Cranbury: A.S. Barnes and Co.

7   Green, Ben K. (1991 revised). *Horse Conformation*. Northland Publishing.

8   German National Equestrian Federation. (1985). *The Principles of Riding*. New York: Arco Publishing Inc.

9   German National Equestrian Federation. (1987). *Horse Management*. Gaithersburg: Half Halt Press

10 Hadfield, M. (1982). *The Manual of Horsemanship*. New York: Barron's Educational Series Inc.

11 Henriques, P. (1991) *Conformation*. Buckingham, GB:Threshold Books

12 Hill, C. (1988). *From the Center of the Ring*. Pownal: Garden Way Publishing Book

13 Kidd. J. (1984). *The Better Horse*. New York: Arco Publishing Inc.

14 Oliver, R.,Langrish, B. (1991). *A Photographic Guide To Conformation*. London: J.A. Allen & Co. Ltd.

15 Pascoe, E. (1986). *The Horse Owner's Preventive Maintenance Handbook*. New York: Charles Scribner's Sons

16 Practical Horseman, Editors. (March, April, May 1992). *Conformation*. Coatesville: Practical Horseman

17 Practical Horseman, Editors. (1988). *In the Design of a Head, What Really Matters*. Coatesville: Practical Horseman

18 Practical Horseman, Editors. (1988). *What do You Like About a Neck*. Coatesville: Practical Horseman

19 Roomey, J. (1974). *The Lame Horse*. Cranbury: A.S. Barnes

20 Savitt, S. (1981). *Draw Horses*. New York: Bonanza

21 Smallwood, P. (1988). *The Manual of Stable Management: The Horse*. British Horse Society. Gaithersburg: Half Halt Press

22 Smythe, R.H.(1975). *The Horse Structure and Movement*. 2nd Ed. Revised by P.C. Goody. London: J.A. Allen & Co Ltd

23 Way, R.F. (1983). *The Anatomy of the Horse*. Millwood: Breakthrough Publications

5.04   THE VITAL PARTS OF THE HORSE

Barbara T. Engel, MEd, OTR

1 PULSE

2 RESPIRATION

3 ABDOMINAL SOUNDS

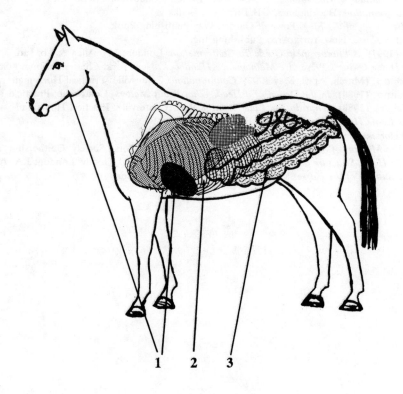

HORSE VITAL PARTS

5.05 MEASUREMENTS OF THE HORSE

Barbara T. Engel, MEd, OTR

SIZE OF THE HORSE IN <u>HANDS</u>: 4 INCHES = ONE HAND

MEASUREMENT FOR A HORSE BLANKET

Barbara T. Engel, MEd, OTR

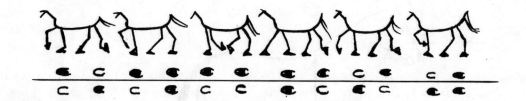

WALK

TROT

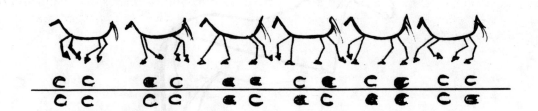

CANTER

5.07   CONFORMATION OF THE DRESSAGE HORSE

Hilda Gurney

Conformation in a dressage horse is important in how it relates to movement. A dressage horse should be built "uphill" so that it moves uphill. The neck should be set fairly high and right side up with a nice arch from the poll to the withers. Low set necks predispose horses to traveling on the forehand and to hanging in the rider's hands.

The hind legs should step well under the body of the horse. This makes engagement and balance easy for the horse. More muscling over the haunches and gaskins makes for power. The loin should also be well muscled, and the spine should not be higher than the back muscles.

Leggy, narrow horses perform better lateral movements. Long legs and a narrow body facilitate the crossing of the horse's legs in the half pass and in leg yields. Wide horses frequently become irregular and labored in movements requiring crossing of their legs.

The author feels that long backs are more supple and softer to sit, but horses with too long backs will have difficulty tracking-up, and in collection. Short backs are often associated with problems in bending and with tight hard backs which make the gaits hard to sit to.

Free shoulders with the front legs carried more forward in front of the horse's body are best for dressage. Front legs carried back under the body make it difficult for the horse to balance itself with the haunches under the body, because the shoulders in this position are already carrying weight. Ideally, forelegs should be about the same length as the hind legs, and the dressage horse's elbow should be about parallel with the stifle. Horses with short front legs in relation to the hind legs look like wheelbarrows and are extremely difficult to balance. Front legs should reach forward. Extravagant knee action is not desirable. The hocks of a dressage horse should bend well at all gaits, even at the canter. Most good dressage horses have fairly well bent hocks. However, any snatching type of action will be severely penalized in competition.

Most dressage horses stay fairly sound if ridden in decent footing. As a result, conformation faults such as calf knees, crooked legs, too short or too long pasterns (though they may affect quality of movement if moderately severe), are usually not as much of a consideration as in horses used for other disciplines. Horses with injured tendons will often stay completely sound when used for dressage.

To conclude, conformation is important only in how it relates to movement and balance. Dressage horses do not have to have legs as straight as necessary for other disciplines, but must carry themselves in an uphill balance with engaged haunches and an elevated forehand with an arched neck. The strides need to be long and reaching with a good overstep at the walk and trot lengthening. Suspension and elasticity are important and the horse should appear to float above the ground in the trot and in the canter.

For further study of the conformation of the dressage horse, see the video by Hilda Gurney, *Selecting Your Dressage Horse*. Available through Dover Saddlery in MA; Millers Harness Co.in NY, equine tack and video companies or your local tack shop.

5.08 CONFORMATION AND MOVEMENT OF THE HIPPOTHERAPY HORSE

Nina Wiger, MA

KEY WORDS
TEMPERMENT
GAIT
TRAINING
CONFORMATION

When selecting a riding horse we keep several general considerations in mind, the main ones being temperament, level of training and experience, gait, soundness and conformation. In many disciplines within disabled riding temperament stands out as being of overriding importance. In the hippotherapy horse we require two main characteristics. These are temperament and quality of gait.

TEMPERAMENT
In addition to being kind, sensible, tolerant and unflappable, the hippotherapy horse has to have energy (to maintain quality of gait), and also be willing to accept constant instructions about position, carriage and stride length. This "rideability through the longreins" is a different temperament characteristic from that of tolerance of equipment, erratic movements, and other unexpected occurrences on his back. An older dressage horse, who has proven through years of training that he can calmly accept endless corrections, is fairly sure to meet the temperament requirements. Horses from other backgrounds might have the required temperament, but often much additional training in carriage, figures and lateral work is needed.

QUALITY OF GAIT
As most hippotherapy horses perform almost exclusively at the walk, faults with the canter or increased gaits in trot are not too important. Two gait requirement are absolute: the walk must be regular and energetic. The natural walk of the most versatile, all-around hippotherapy horse would be rhythmic and elastic, with a stride length and frequency as close to that of a typical adult person as possible. If the walk is very big, it will have too much movement for some clients. The shorter walk that swings freely through the body of the horse can be tolerated by most persons with disabilities, but will still be therapeutic for a less involved client. Ideally several horses, with walks of different frequencies and amplitudes should be available for hippotherapy programs.

TRAINING AND EXPERIENCE
A hippotherapy horse **must** walk on the bit with enough energy to round its back. This is a minimum requirement, and it is the main reason many very nice riding horses do not qualify to be a hippotherapy horse. Horses at second level dressage should be able to do this. Some horses are built to be round and on the bit, and if ridden sensitively previously will have sufficient self-carriage with a swinging back without extensive dressage training. These horses are few and far between; finding one would be pure luck. For maximally effective hippotherapy the horse must also be able to increase the curve of its body (bend), to laterally displace either shoulders or haunches on a straight line, and to move the whole body laterally, all while staying round, impulsive and on the bit.

SOUNDNESS AND FUNCTION
The basis of hippotherapy is the walk, and any unsoundness that interferes with rhythm, stride length and/or the elastic swinging of the back is unacceptable. Unsoundness affecting the quality of the movement, how it is transmitted through the horses back and how it feels to the rider, is not always visible from the ground. A rigid or saggy back is not to hard to detect, but a lack of symmetry in the swinging of the back, or a tendency to slight, constant crookedness are subtler faults. An experienced, feeling rider must try the horse, and on the footing on which he is to perform.

If the normally used footing is soft, many concussion types of unsoundness may be acceptable in the well trained horse, but time is wasted training such an animal. A therapy horse **must** be schooled regularly under saddle, not only at walk, but at all gaits, and therefore must be sound enough for these sessions.

CONFORMATION

Conformation is important only as far as it pertains to soundness and function. Crooked legs and deviate leg movements are of no concern unless severe enough to cause stumbling or interference. The hippotherapy horse needs to move with a round frame at the walk, and it is a definite advantage to have a horse with conformation that allows him to be "naturally on the bit". This would be a strong topline with well muscled back and loin, solid connection between neck and withers, good arch to the neck and an open, supple head/neck connection. If only one horse is available, some compromises must be made. The horse needS to be relatively narrow where the saddle sits, to accommodate spastic riders, but be deep enough in the body to let the whole leg lie on the side of the horse for a secure feeling. He must be stout enough to comfortably carry two people, a client and the back rider, yet be short enough that you do not have to hire a basketball team for sidewalking. Very small horses and ponies seldom have the length and elasticity of stride required in hippotherapy, but if such a gem can be found, life is much easier for therapists and sidewalkers. These horses are especially useful for children, and the shorter gait fit the smaller stride length of the child. The therapist might prescribe a walk with less elasticity and more impact in selected cases, and a horse that hits the ground a little harder can be used. Access to a wide variety of horses is a definite advantage, as long as the therapeutic impact of each horse is known.

Regardless of whether you can have one or several horses for the hippotherapy, remember temperament and the quality of gait are major factors in the success of the program.

5.09   SELECTING A VAULTING HORSE

J. Ashton Moore

I. INTRODUCTION
Describing the "ideal" horse for any activity is relatively easy and can be done with little practical experience by most trainers. However, specific evaluation of strengths and potential weaknesses in terms of relative importance or (severity) takes considerable and practical experience. The following practical hints may help in making a realistic evaluation of real live horses that one is likely to run into in the never-ending search for **vaulting horse prospects**.

II. CONFORMATION
A. Soundness
Soundness considerations in vaulting horses most often involve the back. A sore back is a matter of constant concern and general ignorance as to its causes. In this country where back pads are in general usage, there is not a great deal of direct bruising to the back. Sore backs are mostly caused by *poor way of going* (the wrong way the horse moves)--lack of strength (and therefore lack of springy tension) of the horse's whole topline. This can take two forms:

- ◉ The back must be conformed to carry weight SUPPLELY. A very short back is good for weight carrying, but is usually quite stiff. A longish back with a very strong loin is ideal
- ◉ The generally undesirable quality of "roach back" (convex back), is not necessarily a disadvantage, if the back is long enough, and if it does not adversely affect the quality of the canter (as is usually the case with a roach back)
- ◉ A slack or weak loin connection predisposes to a sore back, as does too deep a back
- ◉ A "disconnect", or dip, in front of the withers may predispose the horse to carry himself badly with insufficient stretch and springy tension in the topline, leading to a sore back
- ◉ The hind legs, big well-angled hocks and broad gaskins must be strong enough to cope with weight and with the stress of working on a circle
- ◉ Inelastic front pasterns predispose to concussion-related lameness

B. Trainability
Certain conformation considerations predispose the horse to react well or badly to the preparatory training and future demands of his work. In the discipline of vaulting, high collection, great extension, speed or jumping ability are not demanded so conformation which precludes those things may not give any problems in vaulting. Conversely, a jumping horse might be forgiven a weak loin connection or snaky unsteady neck which would be a negative attribute for a vaulting horse. The main considerations which might predispose to training difficulties in vaulting most often involve the neck and the back. The first two places to look in evaluating a horse are: the attachment of the neck to the body and the shape of the neck. Conformation that predisposes to a tendency to "disconnect" (dip in front of the withers) can be an extreme drawback in keeping the horse steady in gait and carriage. The shape of the neck in vaulting has more to do with trainability than the length or height of the neck. The topline from the withers to the poll should give the appearance of being about twice the length of the underline from throat to chest. Especially the area of the poll should have sufficient length, otherwise the horse may have difficulty with longitudinal flexion at the poll--causing difficulty or discomfort in accepting contact on the side reins, and difficulty or discomfort in maintaining a good head carriage. The base of the neck should be deep enough from withers to chest, and wide enough just in front of the withers, to give stability to the neck.

- ◉ A long, thin willowy neck, though elegant in some people's eyes, may predispose the horse to unsteadiness in the neck and make resistance and/or evasion a constant threat, as well as making work on the neck difficult

- A low-set-neck that would usually be considered a potential training problem in a riding horse, may be no problem for vaulting if the horse's balance, canter cadence, and shape of the neck are good enough
- A short thick neck (usually considered unattractive and not supple) may be fine for vaulting as it will probably be quite stable, but it must be sufficiently well shaped to allow for comfortable longitudinal flexion at the poll. A very short back, though strong, often adversely affects the horse's balance (conventional wisdom notwithstanding)
- A very flat croup may predispose the horse to a weak canter with insufficient tendency to carry behind, and insufficient "beat"
- Straight hocks which do not articulate well when cantering, as well as "weedy" gaskins (thin), often make the horse disinclined to carry behind, or to keep a clear strong beat in the canter. For work in the trot, it is usually no problem

C. Vaulting Suitability

There are many considerations besides soundness and trainability that make the horse more or less suitable for vaulting.

- A short back gives little room to the vaulters
- A steep croup gives no standing place
- A deep back may make elevation difficult, especially for less experienced vaulters
- A high set-on neck (considered very desirable in a riding horse) may make flight exercises difficult and severely limit work on the neck
- A long neck may be unstable
- High bony withers are hard to fit with a surcingle, and can make some work on the neck uncomfortable for the vaulter
- A bony back may cause discomfort to the vaulters
- A slab-sided horse offers less surface area
- A mutton-withered horse may be difficult in exercises which put greater weight to the one side (tendency to slip)

III. GAITS AND MOVEMENT

If the horse's conformation renders him sound, trainable, and otherwise well suited to vaulting, there is, besides conformation, still the second big consideration in selection, movement. Vaulting is a dynamic gymnastic sport, and therefore, unlike the equipment in the gymnasium, the movement of the horse has everything to do with the performance of the human athlete.

- The correct canter has 3 footfalls, 6 phases, and 1 emphasized beat per stride.
- The canter needs a strong beat in order to provide spring for flight exercises (the vaulter thrusts himself off the horse while the horse is cantering), and to prevent deterioration and improve stability of the gait when the canter is slowed down. (For vaulting at trot a strong beat makes execution of exercises very difficult)
- A 4-beat canter, if stable of rhythm, is not particularly bad for vaulting if it is caused by lack of impulsion rather than by constraint and rigidity. However, in competition, a 4-beat canter is sometimes penalized
- A horse which disconnects in the neck or back (long neck, dip in front of the withers, weak loin connection) may be very difficult to keep stable in pace and balance. A very flat canter, lacking in pronounced beat is "smooth" (if the horse is steady in pace) but will give no assistance to flight exercises; and it is difficult to stabilize the pace if the horse is unsteady in pace or balance.
- A trot with a strong beat is usually not smooth or easy
- A canter which "whips up behind" (causing the croup to raise) will give assistance to flight exercises, often causing difficulties in static balance exercises, especially the flag. However, if the canter whips up behind as an objection, or indication of displeasure (rather than as simply "the way the horse moves all the time,") it may give problems in work on the loin and croup regardless of the quality of training

- A long canter that is bounding or rolling can usually be improved and "collected" with training. A long canter that is flat or sprawling usually becomes flatter, laborious, impure, or unsteady when slowed down
- High action is no problem, provided the beat of the canter is strong

A horse may have all the best qualities of conformation, suitability, and movement - yet still be, when all's said and done, quite useless as a vaulting horse. Conversely, he may have a severe fault, or even several, and still be worth his weight in gold medals. The above hints are meant to be of use particularly when buying a PROSPECT, most particularly one that is not already trained to longe well (the usual situation when horse-shopping for vaulting horses). If the horse is already trained, he will demonstrate whether any faults that he might have do, in fact, generate the expected problems, or whether his promising exterior and movement really do "work". It is also important to learn, or seek expert advice about, what qualities can, hopefully, offset faults (e.g., a too long neck can be offset by a good attachment at the wither, a deep base, a strong back and a very cadenced canter that comes through well behind and has no tendency to "whip up behind").

IV. CHARACTER AND ATTITUDE
No matter how perfect a physical specimen the horse may be, or how ideal the gaits, the bottom line is WHETHER HE AGREES to be a vaulting horse--reliably, constantly, unstintingly, and whether he "has the mind" for it.
- He must not be touchy or ticklish in the least
- He must not have any tendency to kick, buck, or even crow-hop
- He must not rush when something is uncomfortable or unpleasant
- He must not be flighty, nervous, or excitable
- He must not get crotchety when tired, bored, or missing a meal, or working "after hours"
- If a mare, she must not have the tendency to become disagreeable when in season
- He must not have the tendency to shy, or be easily startled into jumping or dashing off
- He must be immune to such things as a slipped surcingle, a vaulter grabbing or hitting the side-reins, and so forth

V. CONCLUSION
The most important considerations in the selection or evaluation of a potential vaulting horse are Character and Attitude. Evaluation (this may require spending some time with the horse) hopefully before buying it, (certainly before letting vaulters near it!) The aspects of suitability of <u>conformation</u> and <u>gait/movement</u> can be determined by observation by an experienced vaulting horseman--outside "expert opinion" can be sought. And finally, familiarization under agreeable circumstances is crucial, acceptance of the side-reins, and training to perform as a vaulting horse will make the animal incomparably valuable in a therapeutic equestrian context, and as a friend and companion to the vaulters.

Selecting and training a vaulting horse requires patience, and EXPERIENCE...and *luck*!

5.10 CONFORMATION OF THE DRIVING HORSE

Liisa Mayo, PT
Andrew Nanaa

The most important characteristic to consider in selecting a driving horse is his <u>temperament</u>. Kind disposition and gentle temperament frequently are indicated quite openly. Such animals rarely get disturbed, enjoy a visit and appear to listen to human conversation. The horse must be calm and trusting and not prone to sudden movements or be easily startled. An even-tempered horse will be able to stand quietly during the extra bumping and movements that accompany harnessing and putting the carriage on as well as during the time people are entering and leaving the vehicle.

The next characteristic to consider is the <u>conformation</u> of the horse. Simply put, conformation is the correct build, proportion and construction of the horse. A good driving horse should have good bone and be solidly built; he should not be overly large nor too small. The shoulders should be long, sloping, flat and smooth and be so constructed as to permit freedom of movement. This will allow the horse to pull the vehicle smoothly and easily and keep the harness from chafing. The withers should be reasonably lean and prominent, free from unnatural bulging of muscular structure. They should extend well into the back. This will allow the saddle of the horse to seat firmly and distribute the weight of the vehicle over the entire back of the horse. The front or forelegs must be built properly, strong and straight, since they receive the first shock as the leg lands in stride, as the movement is transmitted to the leg from the propulsion of the rear. A horse with poor front legs will often stride off balance making for a rough ride. The back should be short and well muscled. It carries not only the weight of the horse but the weight and stress of the vehicle. The back should display a fairly straight top line. The muscles of the shoulders and withers should set well into the back and continue over the loin, croup and hindquarters. The hindquarters should be muscular, broad, and well rounded as the thrust comes from this area. The hind legs should be structurally correct in straightness from both front and side views. Strength itself is not overly important, as a fit horse can pull two thirds of its body weight for extended periods of time.

The <u>gaits</u> generally used in driving are the walk, the slow trot, the working trot, and the extended trot. These are the gaits called for in all pleasure driving classes, are necessary in dressage, and when driving cones and obstacles. The driving horse is trained to respond to both voice and hand cues for changes in gait; the driving horse should display a willingness to listen for quiet, verbal commands from the driver.

In addition to the various gaits the driving horse should be willing to stop and stand quietly at any time until signaled by the driver to move off. He must be willing to back up with quiet voice or rein cues. Generally medium to large ponies, such as Fjords and Hafflingers, make good driving horses as they have both the stature and temperament for the job. Small ponies and miniature horses are too light for work that is required in a disabled driving program. Other breeds, such as Morgans, Welsh Cobs and Quarter horses make good driving prospects as they combine physical ability with even temperaments.

While there are many requirements for a good driving horse there are still many good horses available that lend themselves to driving. Sometimes a poor riding horse makes an excellent driving horse.

6 CONFORMATION--MOVEMENT--TEMPERAMENT OF THE HORSE: AS THEY RELATE TO THE RIDER IN A THERAPEUTIC RIDING PROGRAM

The horse in a therapeutic riding program is the noblest of horses for he has a special mission to fulfill. He will be helping that population with whom some find it awkward and difficult to communicate. He will give of himself, accept the rider without judgement and willingly acknowledge the love bestowed upon him.

6.01   TRAITS OF THE THERAPEUTIC RIDING HORSE

INTRODUCTION

KEY WORDS
- ⊙ Accepting
- ⊙ Trustworthy
- ⊙ Predictable
- ⊙ Focused
- ⊙ Willing to learn
- ⊙ Athletic
- ⊙ Well-balanced forward mover

Conformation of the therapeutic riding horse is important for several reasons. The therapeutic riding horse has a difficult job since he must carry riders with poor balance and delayed reactions to movements. A horse with good conformation can perform this task easily and remain sound more than a horse predisposed to muscle strains and lameness. He will work several hours carrying two to four different riders with varying problems and weights. This requires a strong, well balanced and healthy back with good leg support. The horse must be strong and supple with a forward movement, a rhythmic and balanced gait to provide riders with appropriate stimulation to teach them balance. If a therapeutic riding horse is to be used to facilitate physical changes in riders, both in the general program population and in equine-assisted therapy, then conformation becomes very important. Faults or lameness can affect riders in a negative way instead of encouraging balance, coordination and symmetry. He is a horse whose conformation should not predispose him to lameness.

The horse must be able to perform various skills to meet the needs of many riders. He should accept longeing in both directions. His health and age will allow him to give many years of useful service. His big eyes should show a keen interest in people. He must be is kind, steady and willing to learn. He should be free of disruptive traits, enjoys attention and will not mind being handled by several people at a time.

The selection process of this horse can best begin at the donor's site. Here you will see him in his familiar surroundings. Plan to spend plenty of time with him so you can gain a true picture of his qualities. Check his conformation for areas which may predispose him to lameness. His size and gait must meet the needs of the population he will serve. Lead him with a rider and sidewalkers and hover over him and confine him. Bring crutches and a wheelchair. Remember that not all horses will immediately accept these devices on the first visit, but should show some willingness to accept them readily with further training. Lead him away from his stable mates to see his reactions.

People will say to you, "My children can ride this horse with no difficulty." A child with normal reactions to changes in movement may handle a horse well. This same horse may not be suitable for a person with a disability whose reactions are poor, who presses too hard or whose movements are too uncertain. Once you feel he would be a good candidate for your program the horse can begin his initial training at your center. The most important qualities in a therapeutic riding horse are a trustworthy, predictable and responsive animal. These qualities must be present regardless of who handles him. Safety is always of primary importance, especially when working with people who have disabilities.

The following articles deal with the effect of conformation and soundness on the horse's performance and how that performance influences the rider with disability. Experts from the fields of hippotherapy and dressage give their viewpoints on the effect of different levels of training on both the horse's and the rider's physical performance.

References

Bennett, D. (1988). *Principles of Conformation Analysis, Vol I*. Gaithersburg: Fleet Street Publishing Corp.

Bennett, D. (1989). *Principles of Conformation Analysis, Vol II*. Gaithersburg: Fleet Street Publishing Corp.

C.A.R.D. (1987). *The Therapeutic Application of the Horse's Movement*. Video. C.A.R.D. Toronto, Ontario

Evans, J. W., Borton, A., Hintz, H.F., Van Vleck, L.D. (1977). *The Horse*. New York: W.H Freeman & Co

Green, B.K. (1988). *Horse Conformation as to Soundness and Performance*. Northland Press.

Gonzales, T. (1986). *Proper Balance Movement, A Diary of Lameness*. Manassas, Va. REF Publishing.

Heipertz, W., Heipertz-Hengst, C., Kroger, A, & Kuprian W. (1977). *Therapeutisches Reiten* [Therapeutic Riding]. Stuttgart, Germany: Franckh'sche Verlagshandlung.

Reide, D. (1988). *Physiotherapy on the Horse*. Delta Society. Renton, Washington.

Rooney, J.R. (1974). *The Lame Horse: Causes, Symptoms and Treatment*. Cranbury: A.S. Barnes.

Schusdziarra, H., Schusdziarra, V. (1985). *An Anatomy of Riding*. Briarcliff: Breakthrough Publications.

Smythe, R.H. (1972). *The Horse, Structure and Movement*. Sec. ed. London: J. A. Allen.

Tellington-Jones, L. (1988-1991). *T.E.A.M. News International*.

Eleanor Kellon, VMD

When choosing a horse for beginner lessons, or for handicapped riders, a primary consideration (after disposition) is how the horse will feel under the rider. While there are no hard and fast rules for predicting how easy a horse will be to sit, there are a few identifiable factors that play a role.

First, to be comfortable, level and even, the horse must be sound. Front-end lameness will have the most dramatic effect since a horse with an obvious front-end lameness will be trying to protect the sore (or most sore) leg, resulting in an uneven gait. Shortening of stride is also likely, and gait changes will be rough.

While hind-end lameness will not make the horse particularly rough as a rule, it does lead to uneven impulsion. The rider will feel off balance without knowing why and certainly without being able to correct this feeling by any changes in his own body position.

A common problem with hind-end lameness, and usually one of the most easily felt, is that there will be an obvious difference in how easy it is to post from one diagonal to the other. Exactly how this affects the rider will vary depending upon the precise source of the lameness.

One common problem, however, is that the decreased thrust on the painful side makes it more difficult to leave the saddle. The rider's leg opposite to the lame side may have the sensation of having to "reach" for the stirrup. This will usually happen when the sore hind leg is working to the inside of the ring, which exaggerates most lameness.

Almost everyone has heard it said that a long-pasterned horse will have a smooth and cushion-like ride while the short, upright pastern produces a choppy, rough ride. If this were the only determining factor, it would certainly be true. While pastern length does have an influence, it can be modified profoundly by the slope of the shoulder and how long a stride length the horse has.

The horse with a long, sloping shoulder will naturally have a much longer, freer stride in front than one with an upright shoulder. This is one of the things that to many people makes a horse "comfortable." The reason for the smooth ride is simply that the feet do not contact the ground as often when the stride length is long. Also, the farther out in front of horse the foot is when it contacts the ground the less direct jar the rider will feel.

The angle of the horse's feet is also an important consideration in how comfortably he will ride. Feet that have very short toes and high heels, with the extreme being a club foot, result in shorter stride length regardless of shoulder conformation and poor shock absorption in the fetlock, giving the rider a jolt each time the foot contacts the ground.

The opposite of this, short underrun heels and long toe, contributes greatly to adding length to the stride, reinforcing the effect of the long, sloping shoulder mentioned above and making even a fairly straight shouldered horse more comfortable.

Both extremes, however, place excessive strain on the lower joints of the leg (fetlock and below), which can quickly result in lameness, negating any benefits and making these horses ones to avoid unless the defect can be corrected.

Perhaps the most important consideration, particularly to a beginning or handicapped rider, is how secure the rider feels astride the horse. There are many Thoroughbred types that meet the ideal requirements for front leg conformation and have long, flowing strides. The combination of a long back, prominent spine and relatively narrow body type, however, will still leave the rider feeling perched off balance every time the horse moves.

This is particularly true for riders that have not learned to relax completely through their lower spines, or can't do so for physical reasons. The immediate result is that rider will curl forward, elevating himself further out of the saddle and off balance.

When choosing mounts for beginner or handicapped riders, lean toward the horses with very broad backs, short backs and a generous rib cage. The rider's seat on this type of horse will feel much more secure, encouraging relaxation.

It is also true while horses of this type might lack the "daisy-cutter" stride of fancier horses, they are extremely easy to sit, even at a rapid trot. Their canters, however, may be another story entirely, tending to have a great deal of roll that riders may find a little disconcerting. All in all, however, this type of horse is a good choice since the most important lesson-that of developing a secure, relaxed and independent seat-is easiest obtained on this horse.

Withers can also interfere with a rider's seat and balance, either when too high or too low, pitching the rider back or forward, respectively. This is a fairly minor problem, however, compared to the others mentioned and can be easily corrected by additional, strategically-placed padding.

Finally, while it might seem logical that a rider, particularly a small one, would feel more secure on a small mount that is close to the ground, many ponies are unsuitable simply because their stride length is so short that the ride is too bouncy. Ponies also tend, by their nature, to be a little too quick in their movements for the novice or impaired rider. There are certainly exceptions, either by virtue of the individual pony or by rider preference, however.

Use the guidelines to identify likely candidates for students, then proceed to try them. The most important factor is always to remember how a beginner feels, the things that make him or her comfortable or fearful, and evaluate all potential lesson horses with that important consideration in mind.

Printed by permission - Chronicle of the Horse and Eleanor Kellon

Patricia J. Sayler, MA

When considering the type of horse that is to be used in hippotherapy, it is essential to have a working definition of hippotherapy and an understanding of the requirements of the task to which the horse is to be put. As with other aspects of therapeutic riding the horse must suit the needs of the approach and the intent of the therapist's methodology or of the instructors's lesson. A horse may be quite suitable for work as a remedial vaulting horse, but be unsuitable for hippotherapy and vice versa.

The working definition of hippotherapy, as by the National Hippotherapy Curriculum Committee [1], is as follows: "The term hippotherapy literally means treatment with the help of the horse; from the Greek work 'hippos' meaning horse. Specially trained physical and occupational therapists use this medical treatment for clients with movement dysfunction.

In hippotherapy, the horse influences the client rather than the client controlling the horse. The client is positioned on, and activity responds to the movement of the therapy horse. The therapist directs the movement of the horse, analyzes the client's responses, and adjusts the treatment accordingly. The goals of hippotherapy are to improve the client's posture, balance, mobility and function."

As can be readily seen from the definition and purpose of hippotherapy, the horse's movement is the key to change for the client and the key to therapeutic value for the therapist. Any asymmetries arising from unsoundness or conformation faults, or tension in the back muscles from poor self-carriage will be imparted to the client. The nuances of movement shifts, most often carried out at the walk, are only attainable if the horse is sound, symmetrical, balanced, and equally flexible to both sides. The horse must be able to walk forward with impulsion, with a long free stride that is ground covering and rhythmic. Ideally his training would create for him a relaxation from his jaw to his hindquarters, so that the engagement of his hindquarters would enable him to carry himself with a round top line and a relaxed and swinging back.

While there is not a particular breed or age of horse that is ideal for hippotherapy, the horse must be conformationally sound, gentle and tolerant. The size and width of the horse used will depend on the needs of the particular client. In a "classic" hippotherapy approach, the client faces forward the entire time. This position does not impose the extra stress of weight placement and weight shift on the horse that other positions used in hippotherapy do. For example, sitting backwards is an alternative position used to facilitate increased mobilization of the client's pelvis. The weight shifts and changes to alternate positions create significant demands on the horse, both physically and mentally, and must be taken into consideration and monitored when selecting and using a horse for this type of therapy. The size of the client and the severity of disability is another factor that enters into the tolerance equation.

Backriding is a technique often used in hippotherapy when the client cannot maintain balance or postural control without the assistance of a therapist sitting behind the client. Backriding, while a most valuable and indispensable part of the hippotherapy treatment approach, adds a stressful dimension to the use of the horse. It has been stated that backriding horses are breaking down in two years, both mentally and physically. If this is true, it is imperative that the horses chosen for such a treatment approach have particularly strong backs, be consistently maintained and trained, and be allowed periods of rest and relaxation through turnout and other riding experiences.

In the beginning of this article, I stated that a horse selected for a therapeutic riding activity must be suited to its task. The need for graded movements, changes of pace, and evenness of footfall required in the hippotherapy horse are much greater than the demands on other horses used in therapeutic riding activities. The success of hippotherapy in a program is dependent upon a properly selected and trained horse, and upon the team of therapist and instructor being well trained in hippotherapy skills themselves. The trainer or instructor should be able to train and maintain the hippotherapy horse at first level dressage at a minimum, and through third level dressage preferably. The instructor and horse must be trained in the use of side-reins, longeing and long-lining techniques. The instructor must be proficient in long-lining and therapeutic longeing and leading, and be able to respond immediately and smoothly to the movement requests of the therapist during a hippotherapy session. The therapist, likewise, must be well-versed and trained in hippotherapy techniques and equine movement in order to utilize the technique appropriately and beneficially for the client. Both the instructor and therapist must be alert and sensitive to any signs of stress or discomfort evidenced by the horse. Without the intuitive and trained component of the therapist and instructor team, the horse will be unable to perform its assigned task.

The importance of the team approach of horse, therapist, and instructor to the success of hippotherapy cannot be overestimated. The hippotherapy horse is not "just any horse." He is carefully selected, trained and maintained by a trained therapist/instructor team. As the quality of hippotherapy depends upon the quality of equine movement imparted to the client, the successful performance of the hippotherapy horse is largely dependent upon our judgement and the correct utilization of his attributes and skills. It is our moral and ethical responsibility to judge wisely.

[1] *Hippotherapy Curriculum Development Project.* (1987-1991). Therapeutic Riding Service, Inc., Riderwood, MD. 21139.

6.04   THE VALUE OF THE HORSE'S MOTION TO THE RIDER

Marcee Rosenzweig, PT

For several decades it has been observed that the movement of the horse's pelvis at the walk is similar to the movement of the human pelvis at the walk. A rider sitting astride a horse experiences unimpeded repetitive pelvic motion similar to the pelvic motion of normal human gait.

The well-trained therapy horse which has a symmetrical and rhythmic gait will impart this motion to the rider's pelvis. Therefore, the horse's movement provides an invaluable method of training or retraining pelvic and trunk control.

An understanding of the effects of the three separate components of movement at the walk is the key to comprehending the value of the horse's motion to the rider. First, the acceleration/deceleration of the horse's movement infleuences the anterior/posterior tilt of the rider's pelvis. As the horse's hind leg pushes off and passes through the swing phase of gait (acceleration) the rider's pelvis moves into a posterior tilt. As the hind leg strikes the ground (deceleration) the pelvis becomes anteriorly tilted. The rider's pelvis is at a ninety degree angle to the horse's pelvis. Therefore, as the horse pushes off with his hind leg and thus rotates his pelvis, the second component, lateral flexion of the rider's pelvis, occurs. The third component of the movement occurs as the horse swings his hind leg forward, which laterally flexes his trunk. This motion produces rotation in the rider's trunk and pelvis. All three components of movement are at their peak, i.e., anterior pelvic tilt, forward rotation, and lateral flexion, when the horse's hind leg is directly underneath him.

One other valuable aspect of the horse's movement is the stride length. The stride length of the average horse (14.3 to 15.2 hands) is very similar to the stride length of the human adult. In the reeducation of human gait, a horse is invaluable in producing this feeling of a proper stride length. The horse walks at a rate of 100 - 120 beats per minute, whereas the adult walks at 110-120 beats per minute (Reide, 1988). This provides a rate of movement at which the trunk and pelvis of the rider can learn to accommodate to the motion. A pony which has a choppier gait because of its shorter stride is never appropriate as a hippotherapy horse. (The pony's acceleration along the vertical is too high [Reide, 1988]). The motion of the horse's back and pelvis at the walk is the valuable tool which is essential for the development of trunk control in therapeutic riding and hippotherapy. To date no apparatus has been developed which can replicate this movement.

Summary

- A horse 14.3 to 15.2 hands:
  - has a stride length similar to the stride length of the human adult
  - walks at a rate of 100-120 beats per minute
- An adult human walks at 110-120 beats per minute.
- The rhythm of the forward movement (swing phase of the walking gait) of the horse must synchronize with the rhythm (swing phase of the walking gait) of the human to provide therapeutic motion to the trunk and pelvis of the human.
- A pony cannot approximate the rhythm of an adult's walking gait

References
Glasow, B. (1984), *Hippotherapy: The Horse as a Therapeutic Modality.* New York: Warwick.
Heipertz, W., Heipertz-Hengst, C., Kroger, A, & Kuprian W. (1977). *Therapeutisches Reiten* [Therapeutic Riding]. Stuttgart, Germany: Franckh'che Verlagshandlung.
Hippotherapy Curriculum Development Committee. (1991). *Introduction to Hippotherapy - Module C. Instructor Resource Book.* Maryland: Riderwood.
Reide, D. (1988). *Physiotherapy on the Horse.* Madison: Omnipress.

Marcee Rosenzweig, PT

The horse's movement can be beneficial for a rider; however, it can also be detrimental (Heipertz, 1977). Moving the horse to specifically influence the rider should be supervised and/or performed by a therapist with the knowledge and understanding of the horse's movement and its effect on the rider. However, everyone working in the field of riding for the disabled will benefit from understanding which movements are creating the changes one sees in all our riders.

The first factor to consider when moving the horse to influence the rider is the quality of the horse's movement. A balanced, symmetrical gait is necessary for the rider to perceive symmetrical movement of his or her own pelvis and trunk. The quality of the horse's movement is also affected by the method in which he is engaged into all movements. When driven on long reins, the horse is allowed to maintain a natural freedom of movement. Long reining also provides the opportunity for the therapist or instructor to control the horse as if it is being ridden and make any necessary changes in motion without disturbing the rider.

The first component of the rider's movement which can be influenced by the horse's motion is the anterior/posterior pelvic tilt. All riders should begin to ride on long straight lines at the walk with low impulsion. Gradually the impulsion and/or stride length is increased and this stimulates the anterior/posterior pelvic tilt and also trunk control. To further enhance the rider's trunk control, transitions from low impulsion to a higher impulsion combined with the lengthening and shortening of the stride can be performed by the horse. Transitions from walk to halt to walk will also improve anterior/posterior trunk control. Walking in straight lines, varying impulsion, varying stride length, and acceleration, elicits a flexor/extensor response of the trunk. All upward transitions stimulate a flexor (bending the trunk) dominant response. All downward transitions stimulate an extensor dominant (straightening the trunk) response.

The second component of the rider's movement which can be influenced by the horse's motion is lateral (side to side) trunk control. The horse progresses from walking in straight lines to walking in a large circle, serpentine, and figure eights. Movement through these figures produces increased rotation of the horse's pelvis, facilitating the rider's shift in weight and promotes lateral flexion of the trunk. The therapist must be careful to avoid collapse of the trunk instead of active lateral flexion. School figures should be performed in both directions to encourage symmetry.

The third component of the rider's movement, rotation, can be elicited when the horse's trunk moves laterally through the movements of leg yielding and shoulder in. All three components of movement can be influenced simultaneously with the increase and decrease of impulsion, stride length and acceleration while moving through the school figures and lateral movements. Straight lines can be used to connect the movements as a baseline for the rider to return to before attempting more difficult tasks. The therapist or therapist/instructor team must constantly evaluate and reevaluate the rider's responses to the horse's movement. It is their responsibility to make the necessary changes which will provide a safe and therapeutic program for the rider.

Reference
Glasow, B. (1984). *Hippotherapy: The Horse as a Therapeutic Modality.* New York: Warwick.
Heipertz, W., Heipertz-Hengst, C., Kroger, A, & Kuprian W. (1977). *Therapeutisches Reiten* [Therapeutic Riding]. Stuttgart, Germany: Franckhische Verlagshandlung.
Hippotherapy Curriculum Development Committee. (1991). *Introduction to Hippotherapy - Module C Instructor Resource Book.* Maryland: Riderwood.
Reide, D. (1988). *Physiotherapy on the Horse.* Wisconsin, Madison: Omnipress.

6.06 THE ROLE OF DRESSAGE WITH BOTH DISABLED RIDERS AND THE HORSE

Barbara T. Engel, MEd, OTR
with June Newman, Certified Riding Instructor

A horse trained by the dressage method offers the therapeutic riding program and its riders many advantages. Dressage is work on the flat for the **horse and rider**. The English style dressage methods train the horse to perform the same general skills that a Western reining horse performs. The point of dressage is to make riding more comfortable for both the *horse* and the *rider*. Such training teaches the horse to move in balance which is more pleasant and comfortable for both. Dressage is gymnastic exercise for the horse that develops its natural possibilities and prepares it for all possible purposes. The exercises are performed in a careful, educational, and affectionate way. The horse and rider work together in this method to teach the horse to carry the rider in *balance* thereby increasing his willingness to be obedient and submissive to the rider. It also preserves the horse's physical well-being and longevity. This training develops the horse's suppleness and responsiveness, allowing the rider to control it with light aids. The softness of the horse, its suppleness and flexibility, is transferred to the rider and this helps to normalize the rider's muscle tone and increases his ability to balance. A horse that can be ridden with light aids is a big advantage to the rider with a disability.

Riders at all levels, can gain from a horse trained by the dressage technique. All riders can learn to ride using the principles of dressage. **Dressage and reining techniques train the rider to coordinate his movements with those of the horse. The horse and rider learn to work as one.** For many riders with movement coordination problems, learning to coordinate specific body movement in very subtle ways will be a new experience. Body awareness will develop and selective movements (specific muscle movements) will be refined for increased function of the rider. Though many riders in therapeutic riding programs may not be able to fully "train" their horses, they can perform dressage exercises when their horses are routinely trained by skilled trainers to maintain the horse's flexibility, suppleness, and sensitivity to aids. A well-trained horse accepts the rider's aids and will guide the rider with constant feedback, helping him to stimulate and adjust his movements.

In equine-assisted therapy, the use of horses trained by dressage methods becomes a necessity since the manipulation of the movement of the horse produces the therapeutic effects. The dressage horse is trained to be balanced. Through improving balance, the weight can be shifted to the hindquarters of the horse, thus increasing the collection and engagement of the hindquarters and the proper use of the back. This improves the horse's ability to carry the rider well and move correctly through various gaits. It will also help him to compensate for any imbalance in the rider, an important consideration for this field.

Dressage training encourages:
- The development of a flexible and supple horse which is comfortable for the rider.
- A horse that is obedient and willing, making it easy for the rider and handler to control.
- The horse's acceptance of the rider's aids.
- The rider to "feel" and respond to the horse's movement.
- A deep, mobile, and secure seat which allows the rider to follow the horse's back.
- Balance and security of the rider.
- Body awareness, body control and suppleness of the rider.
- Self improvement with measurement against self.
- The development of timing and rhythm of human movements.
- A systematic method of developing riding techniques.
- Concentration of the rider and the horse.
- Bonding between horse and rider.
- Challenge and confidence.
- Discipline of both rider and horse.

WHAT SKILLS ARE STRESSED IN TRAINING LEVEL, FIRST AND SECOND LEVEL DRESSAGE?

TRAINING LEVEL:
- → The rider encourages willingness, obedience, and responsiveness of the horse to aids and bit
- → The rider asks for free forward movement of the horse and stretching **into** the bit--not on the bit
- → The rider moves the horse from behind with a long and relaxed frame
- → The rider maintains correct hands
- → The rider asks for precision and straightness of the horse on the long side of the ring
- → The rider performs accurate one gait transitions up and down, halt to walk
- → The rider performs correct lead in the canter
- → The rider bends the horse through the corners and on the circle, rhythmically and in balance
- → The rider maintains a true, rhythmical 20 meter circle at a working trot and canter
- → The rider performs a trot, rising
- → The rider performs a working trot, sitting
- → The rider performs a working canter--left and right and trot-to-canter in corners
- → The rider performs a flowing downward transition using seat
- → The rider performs rein changes (changing directions)

Training level does stress a balanced horse, a secure seat but not as deep as higher levels.
It does not stress "on the bit" or collection.

FIRST LEVEL:
- → The rider puts the horse "On the bit"
- → The rider demonstrates a supple, independent seat and quiet hands of the rider
- → The rider supples the horse with increased balance
- → The rider performs a degree of collection
- → The rider brings the horse to a square halt
- → The rider performs a working walk, trot and canter
- → The rider performs lengthening of stride in all three gaits
- → The rider performs 10 and 15 meter circles at a working trot and canter
- → The rider performs beginning lateral work with leg yielding, shoulder-in
- → The rider performs serpentine and preparatory work for the flying change

SECOND LEVEL:
- → The rider deepens his seat to ride "in" the horse rather than "on" the horse
- → The rider rounds the back of the horse and elevates the topline
- → The rider performs collection at the medium gaits, not working gaits
- → The rider performs a precise rein-back
- → The rider performs half-turn on the haunches
- → The rider performs the traverse (haunches-in)
- → The rider performs counter-canter
- → The rider's seat must be so secure that the hands are separate from body influence

References
Burton, R., Sordillo, D. (1985). *How to Ride a Dressage Test*. Boston: Houghton Mufflin Co. 1-89.
Museler, W. (1985). *Riding Logic*. New York: Arco Publishing Inc.
Podhajsky, A. (1965). *The Complete Training of Horse and Rider*. Garden City: Doubleday & Co., Inc.
Swift, S. (1985). *Centered Riding*. North Pomfret: David & Charles.
Traditional Equitation School. (1990). Dressage. Los Angeles.
Wanless, M. (1987). *The Natural Rider*. New York: Summit Books.

6.07 THE SELECTION OF THE CORRECT HORSE FOR A SPECIFIC RIDER

Barbara T. Engel, MEd, OTR

In order for an instructor to select the appropriate mount for a specific person, he or she needs to evaluate the rider to determine the rider's needs. He or she also needs to understand what effects certain attributes of the horse will have on the specific disabilities of a rider, such as movement patterns, size, shape, and strides. For example, a person with poor balance gains more security from a horse with a broader back which provides a larger base of support. A person with spasticity will relax more easily on a horse with good impulsion, long stride, rhythmic gait and smooth transitions. Evaluating a horse's conformation and characteristics, along with one's understanding of a disability and what qualities in the horse best meet the needs of a particular problem, will allow the rider to gain more from the therapeutic riding process (see Figure 1).

Questions one may consider in selecting the horse:
- does the rider need a wide[ ] moderate[ ] or narrow base[ ] of support?
- does the rider need smooth[ ] or rough [ ] transitions?
- does the rider need movement/flexibility from the horse that is strong [ ] moderate [ ] or little [ ]?
- does the rider need a horse with a quiet [ ] moderately loose [ ] or flexible back [ ]?
- does the rider respond best to short [ ] medium [ ] or long strides[ ]?
- does the rider sit best on a short [ ] medium [ ] or tall horse [ ]?
- does the rider need a horse very responsive [ ] moderately responsive [ ] or any responsiveness [ ] to aids?

Many therapeutic riding programs may not have the range of horse selection available to allow this process. Nonetheless, evaluation will point out areas of need and will help to accurately assess the soundness of the horse and determining appropriate training needs. With a few horses, it is still best to select the most suitable mount from those in the program, even if the choice is not ideal. The use of an evaluation process, and understanding its significance can help develop a stable of suitable horses for the program's population and skills. If programs educate the horse society in the type of horses needed for a successful disabled riding program, they are more likely to get these horses donated or at a reasonable price. There are many sound eventing, dressage and reining horses who have out-lived their competitive lives but are ideal for therapeutic riding programs.

6.08 ANALYSIS* OF THE THERAPEUTIC RIDING HORSE FOR PROGRAM RIDERS

Name of Horse: _____   Age: _____   Color: _____

Breed or Breed Type: _____   Height: Hands _____   Weight: _____lbs

Identifying Marks: Draw in White Markings - Or Other.

Front Legs from Front

Hind

Front Legs from Hind

Hind

Physique:

Head Length:	Average/Balanced	Long	Short
Throat Latch:	Average/Clean	Thin/Long	Thick/Short
Neck:	Average/Balanced	Thin/Long	Thick/Short
Neck Set:	Well Set Into Shoulders	Low	High
Shoulders:	Average/45 Degrees_	Steep	Flat

Withers:	Average	High	Low	
Loin:	Average	Very Strong		Weak
Croup:	Well Rounded		Flat	Short	Steep
Belly:	Firm/Muscular		Sagging	
Back (Point of Withers-Point of Croup):	Average	Long	Short	
Topline (Point of Poll to Point of Dock):	Smooth Curve		Wavy	Sagging	Flat
Barrell/Girth - To Point of Rider's Pelvis Span:	Wide	Average	Narrow	
Symmetry-Right to Left (Top View):	Straight	Bend to the Right		Bend to the Left
Angle of Hind Leg - In Line With:	Rump	Behind the Rump		In Front of the Rump

Movement:

Walk:	Rhythm:	Smooth/Flatfooted	Regular	Irregular Beat/Rough	
	Tempo:	Average - 10 Steps/12 Seconds		Fast	Slow
	Stride Length:	Average	Short	Long	
Trot:	Rhythm:	Smooth/Steady	Regular	Stiff	Irregular/Rough
	Tempo:	Average	Fast	Slow	
	Stride Length:	Average	Short	Long	
Canter:	Rhythm:	Smooth/Steady	Regular	Irregular (Changes leads, X Canter)	
	Tempo:	Average	Fast	Slow	
	Stride:	Average	Short	Long	

Gait Transitions:

	Very Smooth	Good	Rough
Walk to Trot to Walk			
Walk to Canter to Walk			
Trot to Walk to Trot			
Trot to Canter to Trot			
Canter to Walk to Canter			
Canter to Trot to Canter			
Walk to Trot to Canter			
Canter to Trot to Walk			
Stand to Canter to Trot			

© B. Engel 1991

93

LEVEL - SKILL OF HORSE'S TRAINING

1. Gait transitions	Neck rein		Backing	
2. Gait Aids: Voice	Good		Moderate	Poor
Leg	Good		Moderate	Poor
Leading	Good		Moderate	Poor
3. Forward Movement/Straightness:	Yes		No	
4. Formal Schooling:	Good		Moderate	Poor
5. Dressage Level:	Training Level	1st	2nd	3rd
6. Ground Driving/Long Reining:	Basic		Intermediate	Advanced
7. Longing:	Basic		Intermediate	Advanced
8. Drive to Cart:	Yes		No	
9. Jumping:	Novice		Intermediate	Open/Advanced
10. Equine Assisted Therapy	Hippotherapy			

TEMPERAMENT - CHARACTERISTICS

Positive:	Kind	Patient	Gentle	People Oriented	Bonds Well	Attentive
	Intelligent	Responsive	Steady Reliable	Does Not Generally Spook		
Negative:	Sometimes Temperamental	Inattentive	Lazy	Stall Bound	May Not Like Other Horses	Other

LEVEL - SKILL OF RIDER FOR THIS HORSE

Adult:	Beginner	Intermediate	Advanced
Child:	Beginner	Intermediate	Advanced

HORSE'S RANGE OF DISCIPLINE

Beginning Skills:	Leadline Riding	Dependent riding w\Assistant		Independent
Intermediate Skills:	Training Level Dressage	1st Level Dressage	Driving To Cart	Backriding
	Longeing Rider	Vaulting	Rail/Equitation	Trail/Equitation
	Equine Assisted Therapy	Stock Jumping		
Advanced Skills:	Hippotherapy	2nd Level Dressage	3rd Level Dressage	Reining
Competition Events:	Driving	Gymkhana	Horse Show	Vaulting
Maximum Weight of Rider for This Horse:	lbs.			
Maximum Weight of Rider and Backrider:	lbs.			

Overall Impression: _____

_____

Recommendations: _____

_____

Evaluator: _____ Title: _____

Date: _____

Figure 1

* This form is intended to assist the instructor in evaluating a horse that has been accepted into the program. Movement and gait transitions should be observed while being ridden by staff & while the horse is free moving. Analysis can then be applied to specific needs of program riders, e.g., Betty needs a horse with smooth transitions and broad back.

© B. Engel 1991

7 TRAINING AND SCHOOLING THE THERAPEUTIC RIDING HORSE

7.01.1   INITIAL TRAINING OF THE THERAPEUTIC RIDING HORSE

INTRODUCTION

> **KEY WORDS**
> TRAINING
> SAFETY

In the average equine environment, there is always concern with the safety of the horse and rider but not to the extent that is required in a therapeutic riding setting. The horse must have additional training to be virtually spook-proof to all elements in his environment and to meet the many obligations required of him in his new venture. The better the horse is trained, the more successful the instructors, the therapists, and the volunteers will be with their riders. The therapeutic riding horse must respond immediately to the voice command of his or her instructor in all gaits. He must learn to stand still upon command for grooming, tacking, mounting, or while being ridden until he is signaled to move forward. This skill can help to avoid many difficult and dangerous situations. Voice command may be necessary for longeing and other riding exercises. When the instructor or handler has verbal control of the horse, a rider may be allowed more independence in the development of his or her riding skills.

One may say that no horse is **spook-proof**. That may be so but under certain circumstances a horse can be *essentially spook-proof*. Initially, the horse is carefully selected (see chapter 6.01). The horse must be well cared for and maintained in a beneficial environment to avoid pressure, stress, and fatigue. The instructor/trainer must be knowledgeable in horse behavior so that vices can be minimized or avoided. Adequate diet, training and exercise is essential and must be planned to meet "this horse's" needs, not just that of the "average" horse. It is important to know if the horse understands what is expected of him and is physically trained and able to carry out these expectations. Saddles must fit well to avoid pain or discomfort. What may be the most important factor, to avoid the possibility of the horse spooking, is to **know** the horse. This must include knowing his likes and dislikes; what disturbs him or makes him uneasy? Does he have some vision problems that cause him to shy at an object or at dusk? Does the wind cause him discomfort or does perfume bother him? Does he need another horse in the arena? Be sure that the horse's likes, dislikes, and needs are both known and met by all leaders or horse handlers. When one really **knows** the horse and works **with him**, one may really have a spook-proof horse. **But** now that one feels the horse is spook-proof, a word of caution is appropriate. A horse reacts when his environment presents something that is unknown to him. This may include a new smell as a perfume he is unfamiliar with or a new horse at the stable. At a horse show away from his stable, he may be exposed to many unknown elements. Always remember that the horse hears and smells things a human cannot. Be alert to his anxiety and ready to calm him.

This chapter focuses on basic and advanced training techniques for the therapeutic riding horse, as well as how to design an ongoing program of schooling to reinforce that training. Section 7.01.2 offers a useful way to record information on a new horse; 7.01.3 is a maintenance record to help keep track of the horse's health and work load. 7.02 is a pre-training checklist for use by donors to use at home to ensure the horse is suitable; or by owners whose animals are "used part time in a therapeutic riding setting.

A willing horse, regardless of age, can be trained in safety methods by a knowledgeable instructor. Ray Hunt (Hunt, 1978), Tom Dorrance (Dorrance, 1987), and John Lyons (Lyons, 1991) give insight to the instructor in handling a horse in a safe manner with good communication and kindness. Linda Tellington-Jones has developed methods to train horses to be handled with safety and ease (see section 7.03). It is important to use training techniques that foster the human-animal bond as bonding is acknowledged as a major therapeutic feature of riding programs. A safe way to groom and tack a horse is while he is ground tied; that is, a horse who has been trained to stand still when the lead rope is dropped to the ground. One will not need to be concerned with tie ropes, cross ties, or pulling back, nor will the horse move about. Ground tying is not difficult to teach a mature horse, but requires patience and time. It is commonly taught to Western style horses but can be taught to any horse. (See 7.01.4.)

Trailering a horse has its own specific training and hauling problems - see section 7.11.

The horse requires an exercise, training, and suppling program to develop cadence and general conditioning to carry out the tasks of therapeutic riding. See section 7.06. A therapeutic riding horse needs to move smoothly from one gait to the other. As most riders with disabilities have difficulty with balance, in order to allow the riders to begin with some sense of stability, the horse needs to move from one transition to the other smoothly. The horse needs to be able to maintain balance under all circumstances. The horse must be physically fit and possess a flexible, strong back and underline. When a horse is used in *equine-assistive therapy* he will be used for his movements in a very specific way. Therefore, his requirements exceed those of the therapeutic riding horse. He must in fact be trained in collection and movement equal to or beyond that required in first level dressage.

The qualities and skills of the therapeutic riding horse will depend on the work he will be required to do. Regardless of his task, he must be in good condition to carry on the strenuous work of a therapeutic riding horse. People may think that carrying disabled riders is an easy job. Though horses seem to enjoy their work with these special people, it is not an easy job working with many different disabled riders; it requires continuous conditioning and training. A way to use volunteers to keep animals fit and happy is discussed in section 7.08.

When the horse has learned all the basics and gained the traits required, he is ready to learn the tasks involved in therapeutic riding. Requirements that are unique to the therapeutic riding horse include being able:
- To tolerate people on each side of him as well as someone leading him
- To tolerate people over him and on each side while confined at the ramp
- To tolerate the 'noise' from several people walking on the ramp above him
- To lead willingly, with balance, from the near or far side
- To stand for long periods of time while he is groomed, tacked, and mounted by unstable and uncoordinated riders
- To walk up to and stand motionless next to the ramp while several people hover over him to assist the rider in mounting
- To learn to tolerate on his back different sizes, and weights of riders
- To imbalanced riders on his back who may jerk or have spasms against his sides
- To walk and trot at varying paces with a handler leading him or next to him
- To tolerate lungeing with a rider and sidewalkers in both directions
- To accept crutches, canes, wheelchairs and other objects against his side

For a discussion of Lungeing and long reining techniques for a therapeutic horse, see section 7.04 and section 7.05.

Prior to being used in an actual therapeutic riding session, the horse may be exposed to many activities and objects he has not previously encountered, such as a ball thrown around him, rings or toys placed on his rump and head or placed on poles or into buckets, walking through obstacles, or stopping facing signs. The horse must also learn to adjust to the special riding tack needed for some riders. After the horse has learned to adjust and accept his new environment, he is ready for a rider from a wheelchair, with crutches or a walker. He needs to learn to expect jerking movements, sudden changes of pressure on his back, or possibly two people riding together. He may experience riders placed in unusual positions on his rump or shoulder. The riders may move from one position to another while the horse is walking. The horse needs to adjust to noises, a possible scream, or music of many kinds.

Three to six weeks of daily training, beyond the initial introduction to program activities, is probably needed to develop a well-trained and safe therapeutic riding horse, a partner in the therapeutic riding team. See section 7.02 for a checklist of training goals. The amount of training time depends on the horse, the skill of the instructor/trainer and the techniques used. Some horses may not be suited for disabled riders and should be returned to their donors or previous owners.

Therapeutic program horses are frequently handled by many people. Because there can be changes in horse managers, it is vitally important to maintain accurate records from the time the horse enters the program to the time the horse is retired. These records serve as a plan for management. A <u>horse history</u> should be initiated when a horse enters the program. Information can be obtained from the previous owner, the vet check, and observations. A <u>maintenance record</u> should be kept continuously, with all pertinent information regarding the horse. The following forms provide the instructor with examples.

References
Dorrance, T. (1987). *True Unity*. Tuscarora: Give-It-A-Go Enterprises.
Hunt, R. (1978). *Thinking Harmony with Horses*. Fresno: Pioneer Publishing Co.
Lyons, John; Browning, S. (1991). *Lyons on Horses*. New York: Doubleday
T.T.E.A.M. News International, Edmonton. 1987-1990.

7.01.2   NEW PROGRAM HORSE RECORD

Margaret L. Galloway, MS, BHSAI

Horse's Name _____ Date of Birth/Age _____

Past Owner _____ Date Obtained _____

Address _____ Phone _____

Breed/Identification marks _____ Hands _____

Sex _____ Past training/work history _____

When last worked _____

History of Injuries _____

Temperament Considerations _____

Vices _____

Likes _____ Dislikes _____

Shoeing Considerations _____

Medications _____

Feeding Considerations _____ Times Daily _____

Drops Weight in Cold _____ Blanketing _____ Clipping _____

Tying problems _____ Trailering _____

Normal weight _____ Temperature _____ Pulse _____ Respiration _____

Vet Check: Date _____ Teeth _____

Soundness _____

Condition _____

Heart _____ Eyes _____ Wind _____

Work Schedule _____

_____

_____

_____

_____

7.01.3 MAINTENANCE RECORD
Margaret L. Galloway, MS, BHSAI

Horse's Name: _____ Year born: _____

Veterinarian: _____ Phone: _____

Farrier: _____ Phone: _____

Bodyweight: _____ Hands: _____ Work Load: Light _____ Medium _____ Heavy _____

Daily Exercise Program: _____

Feed Ration: _____

_____

Medical Problems: _____

Hoof Problems: _____

Special Considerations: _____

Medication: _____ Schedule: _____

Shoeing Date	Worming Date	Immunization	Notes/Medical

7.01.4 HORSE PRE-TRAINING SCHEDULE
FOR OWNERS OF HORSES TO BE USED PART TIME OR DONATED TO A PROGRAM

Jean M. Tebay, MS

KEY WORDS

SUITABLE
TRAINED
SAFE
HEALTHY
SOUND

In therapeutic riding, one may be approached by a well-meaning individual wishing to give a horse, usually for a tax write-off. Perhaps the youngster who owned the horse has gone off to college and the family no longer wishes to keep it, or perhaps the horse is elderly and unable to jump, hunt, or do upper level dressage. It is important to assess immediately if the horse is sound and healthy, before considering it for therapeutic riding. Once this has been determined, then training the animal for specific roles in therapeutic riding can begin.

This training can be conducted by the owner wishing to donate the horse, and the therapeutic riding program can say: "*Here is a training schedule. Once this has been completed, we will be willing to evaluate the horse for the use by our program.*" Or perhaps the horses being used in the therapeutic program are brought by Pony Club or 4-H members. In that case, this training schedule, under the direction of the therapeutic riding program instructor, can be used by owner or rider to ready the horse for participation in the program.

Basically, this form (Figure 1 on the next page) is intended to upgrade the performance quality of the horses used in therapeutic riding programs. Jan Spink, MA, New Harmony Foundation, Charlottesville, Virginia is now in the process of developing an in-depth horse performance program which will be available in 1993. Until that material is finished, this schedule may be useful to improve horse performance in therapeutic riding centers.

HORSE TRAINING SCHEDULE *

Horse's Name:_____

Trainer's Name:_____

Date Training Started:_____   Date Training Completed:_____

Areas completed in training	Completed	Date
1. Accepts Being Led, Both Sides.		
2. Accepts Side-Helpers, Both Sides.		
3. Accepts Rider Movements.		
4. Accepts Rider Noises.		
5. Accepts Ramp.		
6. Accepts Mounting\Dismounting\Ground\Ramp.		
7. Accepts Wheelchair On Ground.		
8. Accepts Wheelchair On Ramp.		
9. Accepts Wheelchair Transfers.		
10. Accepts Crutches, Canes, Walkers.		
11. Accepts Balls, Rings, Games.		
12. Obeys Voice Commands - Halt.		
13. Obeys Voice Commands - Walk.		
14. Obeys Voice Commands - Trot.		
15. Obeys Voice Commands - Canter.		
16. Obeys Voice Commands On Lunge.		
17. Lunges Both Directions - Walk.		
18. Lunges Both Directions - Trot.		
19. Lunges Both Directions - Canter.		
20. Performs Smooth Transitions, Led.		
21. Performs Smooth Transitions, Lunge.		
22. Accepts Special Adapted Equipment.		

This animal has been reviewed and is ready for service in a therapeutic riding program.

_____   _____
Signed - Evaluator   Date Reviewed

Figure 1. Horse Training Schedule

* Printed by Permission - B.T. Batsford LTD, UK., 1991., in Britton., Riding for the Disabled.

Tebay 6\90

7.01.5 CONDITIONING A HORSE FOR A THERAPEUTIC RIDING PROGRAM

Margaret L. Galloway, MS, BHSAI

Let's imagine your therapeutic riding center has been given or acquired a twelve-year old, sound, quarter horse gelding. He had been shown as a four, five and six year old and later was ridden for pleasure and for trail riding. For the last several years, he has been left unworked in the pasture. How would you get this potential "gem" into condition for therapeutic riding and then maintain it?

Every horse is an individual and should be treated as such. If you are in doubt about a horse's capability, you can ask your veterinarian. A suggested schedule for evaluation and training is as follows:

The first step is to have him checked by the veterinarian for soundness and health. He should be wormed and his teeth should be floated as necessary. He should be placed on an appropriate feeding program. If he is fat, he should be placed on a diet; feed should be added if he is too thin. It is also important to establishing a bonding relationship with the animal. Next, strength and muscle should be built up gradually. Walking, with only a little trotting, is the primary gait for very out-of-shape horses. For all out-of-condition horses, the warm-up is very important. A correct warm-up and cooling-down period helps prevent injuries and azoturia, or tying up.

By the second or third week, longer periods at the trot help develop endurance. Work should not last longer than thirty or forty minutes, half of which should be a brisk walk with long strides.

By the fourth week, the horse can be trotted 15 minutes within the 40-minute exercise period. Cantering can begin between the fourth and fifth weeks. For the next several weeks, the work-out should be lengthened, or preferably, long walks (one half hour), ideally on a hilly trail, should be added or alternated with the workouts.

After six to eight weeks, the horse should be fit enough to be used in a busy therapeutic program. To maintain fitness, some trail work, with hills if possible, as well as schooling at all gaits, should be sufficient if carried out once or twice a week. In general, long slow work is better than strenuous short workouts.

7.02 TEACHING THE THERAPEUTIC RIDING HORSE TO GROUND-TIE

Margaret L. Galloway, MS, BHSAI

KEY WORDS

SAFETY
EASY
TRAINING

Ground tying the therapeutic riding horse is a safe, effective way to keep him standing still. Ground tying means you simply take the lead line or reins and drop them to the ground, without tying them to anything. The horse is expected to remain in place.

A well-trained horse can be safely ground tied even in fairly large areas, such as arenas. It is a method with many advantages. Such as one has no ropes to deal with; the horse has nothing to pull against; the horse is obedient to voice command and remains still until the command to move; and there is never a problem finding a place to secure the horse. Some therapeutic riding programs require ground tying, as it makes horse handling much easier.

To train a horse to ground tie, one needs a halter and lead line, possibly a nose chain and a bridle with split reins, such as a western bridle, or reins that can be unbuckled. No gimmicks, such as hobbles, are necessary. To start the training, use a halter and lead line in an area relatively free of distractions. Stand in front of the horse. Take the lead line and give a quick pull toward the ground,saying "Ho," then drop the lead line. Walk several steps away. If the horse moves, walk back and firmly tug again on the lead line, repeating "stay." If there are other horses around who already ground tie, it sometimes helps to have them ground tied nearby, as horses may imitate each other. When walking back to the horse who has successfully stood still, reward him verbally and with patting. Repeat the process of a pull, drop the lead-line, and walk away. Gradually increase the distance moved away while the horse stands. Be sure to reward him if he is successful. *Teaching a horse to ground tie is much like teaching a dog to stay and carries the same type of safety factor.*

The next step is to move the horse to another spot and repeat the performance. Next, repeat the process with reins. Use unbuckled reins to begin with to prevent the horse from getting his leg caught in them. Be aware that a horse can step on the reins and become frightened during his early training. One should practice with a halter and a bridle equally until both are easy for the horse to understand. If, after time, the horse becomes "sloppy" and wanders, he may need to be retrained and reminded to stand. Always emphasize good behavior and use lots of praise.

Advantages: Ground tying is indispensable in controlling the animal. The horse learns to respond to commands. The handlers and riders avoid becoming tangled in ropes. There are no ropes for the horse to "pull back" on or step on. Ground tying is safe for grooming because the horse remains still. The degree of safety is dependent on the degree of training. If the horse is completely submissive to this technique, he will be reliable and safe.

MAKE SURE THE HORSE IS ABSOLUTELY TRAINED IN "GROUND TYING" BEFORE USING THIS TECHNIQUE WITH BEGINNING AND YOUNG PROGRAM RIDERS.

7.03   TT.E.A.M. AND ITS APPLICATION TO THERAPEUTIC RIDING

Linda Tellington-Jones

The Tellington-Jones Equine Awareness Method, (TT.E.A.M.)--the double T stands for Tellington- Touch--is a multi-dimensional method for training and healing horses. The methodology, developed by Linda Tellington-Jones, is divided into three areas: body work, ground exercise, and riding with awareness. The TT.E.A.M. training was inspired by Linda's training with Moshe Feldenkrais, known for his development of *Functional Integration* and *Awareness through Movement* (Feldenkrais, 1984).

TT.E.A.M. methods are applied in a systematic program that promotes learning, aware behavior and wellness in both humans and horses. Therapeutic riding and TT.E.A.M. appear to be working with similar mind-body processes and goals, thereby, TT.E.A.M. provides great value to therapeutic riding. TT.E.A.M. is useful for:
   (1) Preparing, steadying, rewarding and rehabilitating a horse
   (2) Adding safety, order and structure to training sessions
   (3) Educating and empowering staff and volunteers
   (4) Enriching and directing the experience for the rider

DEVELOPMENT OF TT.E.A.M.
A 30 year pursuit of traditional equine training techniques revealed to Linda that those methods did not always provide satisfactory solutions for horses' behavior and physical problems. After studying with Dr. Moshe Feldenkrais for four years (at the Humanistic Psychology Institute in San Francisco) Linda has integrated this education and methodology with her lifetime experience in riding, world-class competition, teaching, training and years of research at the Pacific Coast Equestrian Research Farm. The cumulative result is TT.E.A.M., an internationally renowned organization using these techniques.

Feldenkrais believed fervently that learning is a process which has to occur within the learner (Feldenkrais, 1984). Knowledge cannot be poured into the animal or human like water into a pail, nor can training be injected like some information transfusion. Instead of *"teacher"* or *"trainer,"* the job title should be *"learning facilitator."* Deep insights learned from Feldenkrais are that, in addition to creating an external environment which facilitates learning, the teacher/trainer can alter the learner's inner *"environment"* in ways which radically enhance learning (Feldenkrais, 1984). TT.E.A.M. follows these Feldenkrais principles by using tactile and kinesthetic stimulation to connect the horse with his *"environment"* of mind, nerves, and body (Feldenkrais 1984).

TT.E.A.M. teaching techniques include three areas:
   1. **BODY WORK:**
      Specific body touches (the TTOUCH) and manipulations of head, ears, neck, legs and tail. The horse learns to move his body in a more efficient, pain-free manner. Tension and muscle tightness are lessened. Range of motion, suppleness and flexion are increased.
   2. **GROUND WORK:**
      The horse is led through a prescribed set of positions, non-habitual exercises, exercises, and obstacles. The animal is taught coordination, balance, rhythm and a sense of his own body. He learns to listen to specific signals, and a line of communication is developed between horse and handler. The horse learns to <u>respond</u> to a given set of circumstances, rather than <u>react</u> to them (as in fight, flight or freeze).
   3. **RIDING WITH AWARENESS:**
      While riding in the saddle, TT.E.A.M. ground exercises and body work are carried into the "mounted experience."

CONCEPTUAL MODEL
   Consideration of the following assertions is useful in conceptual modeling when working with TT.E.A.M.
   1. A prerequisite to relating to the horse is to learn his method of communication, mainly body language.

2. Fear, pain, and anxiety block learning. Most equine misbehavior is automatic reflex-like reactions triggered by fear, pain or anxiety. Pain or tension is often a "holding pattern"--a neuromuscular response to present **OR** past experiences.

3. The nervous system organizes habitual patterns for handling inputs, sensations, actions, and behaviors. When the nervous system is functioning below optimum awareness, "unaware" habitual patterns govern the animal's usual responses. These patterns persist until they are changed. TT.E.A.M. allows new patterns to be introduced in a non-threatening, non-painful way.

4. The introduction of appropriate non-habitual touch and movement changes habitual patterns. At this level, the habitual inscriptions tend to be broken and replaced by more effective movement.

5. Non-habitual challenges must also be non-threatening. Failure of a horse to understand creates a threatening, anxious, and confusing situation. Divide tasks into small, sequential components. If the horse is intimidated or balks at a new lesson, return to a level that was easily understood and accomplished.

6. The circular TTOUCH profoundly alters the mental and physical state. The circles effectively activate the nerve connection between the area worked on and corresponding brain centers. Changes include calming, relaxation, focus, and acceptance of humans. Brain wave monitoring suggests activation of both hemispheres into patterns analogous to what is termed the *"Awakened State"* by some biofeedback workers (Wise, 1984; Tellington-Jones 1985). Petting, stroking and massaging DO NOT evoke these changes. The state produced by TTOUCH is a *"learning"* state that connects the experience to the brain, enabling the body to adopt new information such as relaxation, release of pain or tension, and positive behavioral patterns.

7. Aided by TTOUCH and non-habitual TT.E.A.M. exercises, the animal can correct unwanted behavior, enhance performance and amend resting-state body-mind health. Results often occur after one or a few sessions. The modifications are often permanent.

8. Repeated use of TT.E.A.M. to challenge un-aware automatic functioning moves the animal toward operating routinely in the aware mode.

9. The TT.E.A.M. worker experiences changes which mirror the changes in the animal. These include calmness, awareness, openness to learning, connectedness, and changes in brain wave patterns (Wise, 1984; Tellington-Jones, 1985).

10. TT.E.A.M. has positive effects on behavior. This means more than simply adjusting the animal to our human standards of decorum for horses. The term "behavior" in its larger sense refers to "the manner in which a thing acts." With TT.E.A.M., pronounced changes are observed in the mental state and in neural, muscular and cardiovascular behavior. Discoveries in psychoneuroimmunology (the science of dealing with specific neurological and psychological systems) and biofeedback (Newsweek Magazine, 1988; Borysenko, 1987) are providing a paradigm (model) which indicates that changes in neurological and psychological systems result in changed glandular and immunologic behaviors as well. Results observed with horses give the impression that such complex changes are, in fact, occurring.

SOURCES OF INSTRUCTION:
TT.E.A.M. is both simple and capable of seemingly infinite development. Those naive to both horses and TT.E.A.M. can obtain positive results with only a few minutes of instruction; yet, those who have studied for years continue to learn daily.

TECHNIQUES:
A dozen varieties of touch, ten specific leading positions, numerous obstacles and more, are included in the TT.E.A.M. "tool-kit." This variety does not represent capricious elaboration; each technique has been developed to fill a specific need. Selected techniques which have proved most useful to therapeutic riding centers are illustrated.

Touch and leading positions have animal names. In addition to being mnemonic (developing memory), the imagery inspires visualizations which help activate the right brain with its strengths in rhythm, dimension, intuition and creativity. These names often provoke humor which helps in the extremely important task of putting aside ego-driven win--lose thinking. Such thinking loads one's esteem on the animal's behaving "correctly" and diminishes ability to "hear" what he is communicating.

Two training aids are employed extensively in TT.E.A.M., a wand and a chain. They are never used to punish or inflict pain. The wand, to some what might be called a whip, is used to conduct thoughts to the animal. A chain shank is employed as a *chain of communication*. This chain allows the handler to transmit subtle signals between horse and human with the use of light pressure. Such imagery again is to denote function. Through use and testing, a specific model of wand and shank have been selected as most useful for TT.E.A.M..

APPLICATIONS:

The following is a general outline to introduce the horse to TT.E.A.M..(This might be for a horse being adapted to therapeutic riding or a horse who needs to be adapted to new activities). First, begin with two or probably three sessions of complete body work and selected ground work. At the first session use TTOUCH to establish connection; work the body all over to locate tense and sensitive areas. Determine which movements and activities are performed poorly or cause discomfort or fear. Start to establish the TT.E.A.M. leading positions and perhaps start a little obstacle work. Some specific problem solving may be done, but the paramount goal of this initial session is learning. The human learns about this horse; the horse learns to operate in a calm-focused mode with trust in the human and trust in his new way of relating. Start the next session with body work to establish connection and get the horse's mind and body into a relaxed, aware state. Concentrate more on specific problems. Work more on leading positions and introduce more obstacles.

There can never be one set formula because the horse's responses determine the program. Later TT.E.A.M. sessions may become shorter and fit into the daily routine. Subsequently TT.E.A.M. should seep into and color all activities with the horse since the method helps to improve handling in areas such as approaching, catching, touching, leading, grooming, trailering, saddling and riding. Introduction of any experience new to a horse may cause it to react in an unpredictable manner. TT.E.A.M. is extremely gentle but one must be conservative. Introduce any new TT.E.A.M. techniques to the horse before the rider with a disability is aboard or in proximity.

TERMS IN TT.E.A.M.

There are many words used in the teaching of TT.E.A.M.--to define hand movements, leading positions and other training techniques (unfamiliar to those individuals new to the TT.E.A.M. approach). The various Tellington touches and leading positions are named after some of our friends in the animal kingdom and to bring some humor into our lives. We have given each position an animal name which helps attach a visual picture to the technique.

TTOUCH TECHNIQUE

TTouch: Ttouches are single, random clockwise circles with the thumb and little finger resting on the animal and the middle three fingers starting at 6 o'clock and pushing the skin around in a circle and quarter, then pausing and releasing before starting another circle at another spot. The Ttouch method has been expanded into a variation of hand-finger movements to gain specific results.

Wand: A 120 cm (4 ft.) stiff, white whip with a hard plastic "button" on the end. The wand (imported by TT.E.A.M. from Germany) is well balanced and easy to use. It is used as an extension of the arm to stroke, give reassurance and to convey signals.

Half Walk: An exercise that asks the horse to step half the length of the normal stride for 4 or 5 steps, and then to walk on; **repeat** several times. This exercise influence the rider's balance by giving new sensory input. Both rider and horse must focus on the signals, and both learn steadiness and precision.

Lead: A *30 inch chain* sewn to a 6 foot, light, flat and soft nylon lead is attached to the halter in a specific manner so that the **CHAIN GOES OVER THE NOSEBAND** of the halter. The chain is an essential tool of the T.T.E.A.M. work. Purpose: to get the horse's attention, give specific signals, and for control. It is a tool for teaching subtle signals and is **never** used to *shank* the horse. The position of the chain is shown here.

Directions for attaching the chain: From the *outside* in through the lower ring, once *over* the noseband, then from the *inside* of the ring *out*, and hook to the top halter ring.

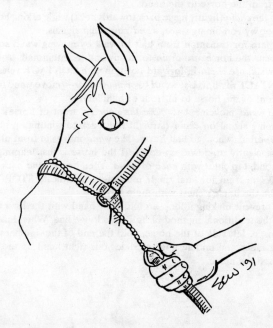
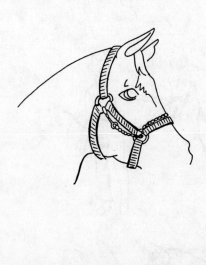

Ribbon Lead: A second loop is added when using the Dingo. Using the folds is safer because line is not wrapped around the hand. It is also much smoother as one slides away from the horse as in the **Dolphins Flickering Through the Waves.**

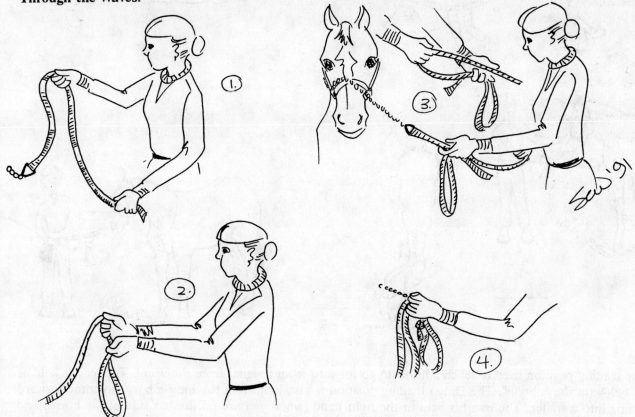

107

Elegant Elephant: The basic T.T.E.A.M. leading position is the safest and strongest way to lead a horse. The leader stays even with the horse's nose and uses the chain for clear signals and the wand as a focus point for the horse.

→Use chain, as well as voice to teach horse to move The chain is held in the other hand (at the triangle of the chain) with a straight line from the horse to the hand.

→Use the chain (lightly jiggle back towards neck) while asking horse to stop by combining voice, wand and chain signals.

→Prepare for transition from halt to walk by moving wand softly to focus the horse..use chain to steady and maintain halt.

→To walk, use chain in forward position with **CONTACT, release, CONTACT** rhythm. Use wand to open the door-- (move wand from in front of the horse to in front of handler).

→Use wand movement to close the door (in front of horse) and stopping signal on chain (straight line back to windpipe), along with verbal "whoa" to halt horse. The wand moves in front of the horse clearly up-down, up-down. If the horse is just learning to respond, **tap** chest with knob of wand. Then bring wand back out to 2½" in front for final single movement to indicate STOP. The stroke the horse's chest with the wand.

→ To prevent making a loop around your hand with the lead line, use the traditional method of holding a longe line. When leading from the left side of the horse, hold the end of the line between your index and middle fingers. Slide your right hand up the line toward the horse.

Dingo: The leading position used to teach a horse to go forward from a signal from the wand. The lead is held as described below in the "ribbon". The Dingo leading position is also helpful in teaching a horse to come forward when loading into a trailer. The wand is held in the right hand (when you are on the left side of the horse) and

108

Dingo: The leading position used to teach a horse to go forward from a signal from the wand. The lead is held as described below in the "ribbon". The Dingo leading position is also helpful in teaching a horse to come forward when loading into a trailer. The wand is held in the right hand (when you are on the left side of the horse) and the lead in the left hand; use the wand in a firm stroke tap motion along the top of the croup following a clear signal to go forward from the chain. The exercise <u>teaches the horse to wait for the signal</u>, <u>overcome nervousness about contact with the back</u>, <u>teaches the horse to come forward from signal on chain</u>, <u>reinforced by wand signal</u> behind.

➔Hold horse still with the left hand on the chain at the triangle while holding hand up.
➔Stroke horse's back from withers to croup 2 times in the same direction, firmly.
➔Tap twice on <u>point of croup</u> (not haunches) <u>while</u> asking asking horse to move forward with chain and voice.
➔*Do not allow horse to move forward before the tap.*

109

Dancing Cobra: A position to improve balance, focus, obedience and self control. It teaches a horse who tends to rush forward, or who pulls back when tied, to move forward when signaled.

→The handler will organize the horse's movement so that he will respond to the signal of the chain and wand **NOT just to follow you**.

→**WAIT.** A light handed connection is kept with the right hand while the wand signals "*wait*". The handler's upper body will be inclined slightly towards the horse with hips and knees bent to stay balanced.

→**GET READY TO MOVE.** The handler's upper body is shifted to upright with about 70% of body weight over the back right foot.

→Bring the wand toward handler to "*open the door*."

→**NOW COME.** Signal **COME** (using smooth flexion of knuckles to tighten line, then release slightly) with the right hand on the lead.

→Step back with left foot **AS** the right hand <u>asks</u> for the forward movements.

→Wand, in the left hand, signal the horse to **COME SLOWLY** by moving wand toward horse's head.

→**WHOA.** Wand forward.

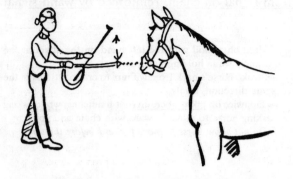

Dolphins Flickering Through The Waves: A method used to teach a horse to stay out away from the handler. It is also used when teaching a horse to longe. This exercise is useful to accustom the horse to signals being applied to different parts of his body. It also helps to overcome sensitivity associated with fear about being touched in these areas.

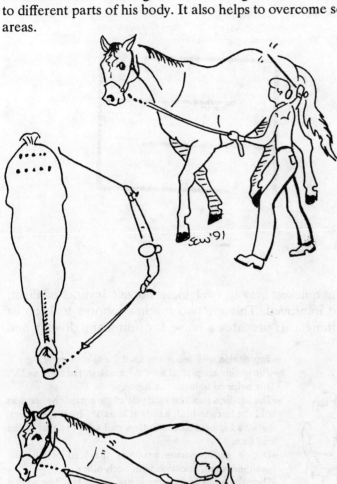

→Begin in <u>Dingo position</u>, ask horse to go forward. Start in a straight line before asking for a circle.

→When horse is moving <u>forward</u>, slide hand down line to knot (end) as you step away from the side of the horse.

→To keep horse moving in a forward motion without drifting into your space, use flicking action, a quick moment of contact; avoid pushing with the tip of the wand.

→As the horse understands staying away from the handler, slide the hand further down the line until reaching the end of the line.

→Specific points signal the horse to do specific movements: on the croup asks the horse to go forward; on top of the scapula signals the horse to bend; tap a few inches behind the ears on the neck indicates the horse should give rather then push in towards the handler.

→The handler stays even with the horse's shoulder.

→If the horse steps in toward the handler, flick him again on the neck while stepping away to maintain the desired distance.

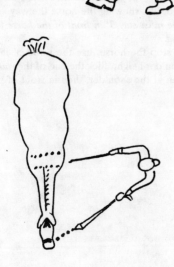

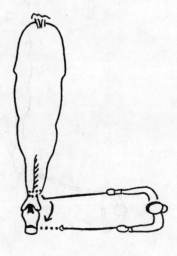

111

Labyrinth: A maze set up with a minimum of 6 poles which is used to teach obedience, balance, self control, focus, patience and precision for horse, horse handler and rider.

→Using **6 poles** that are 12 ft. long.
→For working the horse *in hand*, make the distance between poles about 4 ft. apart.
→For working the horse *under saddle* space poles 5 to 6 ft. apart.
→For a nervous horse the poles can be spread another 2 ft.

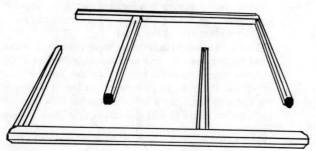

Journey of the Homing Pigeon: A way of leading which is the quickest way to override a horse's instinct of flight. The horse learns to focus. Balance and self-confidence are improved. This method teaches a horse to keep its distance from the handler. It gives a horse a sense of containment. It prepares a horse for riding and driving, and teaches the handler to lead from the right.

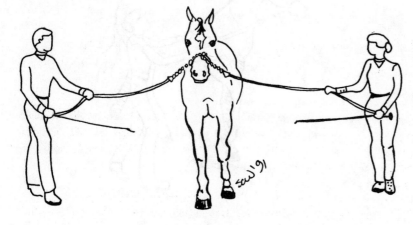

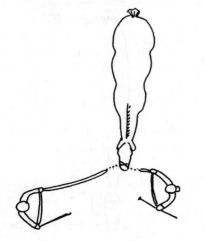

→Two chains with leads are used for this exercise.
→The chains are placed over the noseband to form an "**X**". This helps to balance the horse.
→The handlers stand on each side of the horse. The handlers hold the lines in both hands at least 18" from the chains, the *wand* is held at the button end with the end of the lead line.
→Decide which person becomes the lead person and maintain communication with each other.
→Slide the hand nearest the horse up the lead line so that the space between the hands is slightly wider than the shoulders.
→The handlers should stay far enough in front of the horse so they can always see each other.
→In this position it is not the lead that stops the horse but rather a signal from the *wand*.
→One handler stays in this position while the other moves forward.
→To go forward, stroke the horse's chest with the *wand* and bring the wand forward toward where you want him to go, like showing the horse the way.
→*One must stay 3' in front of the horse for him to see the wand.*
→To stop the horse, use the *wand* 3' in front of him at shoulder height, flick the end of the *wand* twice in front, then at the shoulder, then in front of him to stop.

Star: One end of each of four 12 foot poles is raised onto a straw bale, tire or other object. The other ends of the poles are spaced on the ground about 4 feet apart in fan shape. The height of the poles is gradually raised and the distance between them is changed, depending on the skill of the horse. The idea of this exercise is that the horse can be successful in walking over the poles with full alertness.

STAR
→Use 4 poles that are 12 feet long.
→Place one end of all poles on a tire or bale of straw.
→Space the other ends on the ground about 4 to 5 ft. apart in fan shape.
→If the horse will not step over the poles, reduce the number of poles to two or even one. Add poles as the horse can negotiate them.

THERAPEUTIC RIDING CENTER EXPERIENCES
TT.E.A.M. has been integrated into the care of horses at <u>Winslow Therapeutic Riding</u> in N.Y. All horses have been schooled using TT.E.A.M. leading positions and obstacles. The most frequently used techniques are *Elegant Elephant*, *Dingo* and *Dolphins Flickering Through The Waves*. Even though the horses are led conventionally in sessions, they retain the balance, self control and responsiveness gained in schooling.

<u>Handicapped Equestrian Learning Program</u> in Austin, Texas, is using the TT.E.A.M teaching techniques to achieve the program's desired results. For example the TT.E.A.M. labyrinth and other obstacles have proved to be versatile tools. The process of negotiating a narrow defined area not only benefits the disabled rider, but the horse as well. The labyrinth is extremely adaptable. For the adult the labyrinth is a challenging and difficult task requiring concentration, constant attention to details, changes of speed and direction and constant processing and sequencing of information. "Where the body is in space" and changes in proprioceptive information elicit continuous balancing and coordination adjustment. For the child, the same labyrinth can become a "house" with a little "friend" awaiting the rider. No matter what the disability, its severity, or the age of the rider, that labyrinth now becomes a challenge to conquer and an opportunity for achievement. The labyrinth has become a solid base of learning for all of the program horses and all of the riders: One can be adapted for almost any circumstance or condition. The labyrinth is a multi-effect tool; it forces riders and horses to receive optimum levels of mental, physical and emotional stimuli. The labyrinth can be tailored to provide such a variety of challenges that it seems without limitation.

<u>At C.A.R.D.</u> (Canadian Association Riding for Disabled) the physiotherapist and the TT.E.A.M. practioner worked with a 5 year old boy with cerebral palsy and poor muscle tone who required two side-helpers for him to maintain balance. The TT.E.A.M. practioner worked with the horse while the physiotherapist worked with the child. The physiotherapist wanted slow transitions to help the rider gain balance. The practitioner using the lead rope with a chain shank applied in the usual TT.E.A.M. manner, helped steady the horse's head carriage. This stopped the

Since the rider's head was not staying centered and this was affecting his balance, the physiotherapist walked alongside the rider and at the same time put the wand on the abdominal muscles of the rider to improve front to back and side to side balance. The TT.E.A.M. practitioner switched to the *Dancing Cobra* position. In this way, the horse became very focused and the rider was able to focus on the physiotherapist and gain more control over his balance.

Marci is a 26 year old lady who has multiple sclerosis. She uses a wheelchair and has lost her hearing. She works at R.E.I.N.S.(Riding Emphasizing Individual Needs and Strengths), helping however she can. On a recent visit she noted that one of the aged ponies, who has chronic laminitis, was extremely lame. He was unable to stand without help when one of his feet was lifted. The pony was given TT.E.A.M. work once and a farrier trimmed the feet. A one gram dose of phenylbutazone was given to the pony the following day. Marci has a great affinity for animals. She wanted this pony as a TT.E.A.M. project. She was guided through the TTOUCH and ear and tail work, and began to work on the pony daily. Three days later, the pony was relaxed and free from pain. When the pony was brought to Marci, he lowered his head for her to work on it. Then as she moved to the body and tail he made small movements to make himself accessible to her hands. He even put his hoof on her wheelchair footrest so she could reach him. The pony is now back in the program.

CONCLUSION
TT.E.A.M. is a discipline that can be learned through demonstration and clinics through out the states, and in other countries. Demonstrations provide an observer with simple techniques, while two-to eight- day clinics provide intensive hands-on training. Videos and literature are available for the continuous learning process. TT.E.A.M. techniques provide instructors and the therapeutic riding teams with valuable methods to handle the program horse.

Given the time and manpower demands at therapeutic riding centers, some directors may object that there is not time to learn and do the TT.E.A.M. program. Since time spent on TT.E.A.M. is invested in a systematic program of intense communication with a high rate of success, it is hardly surprising that TT.E.A.M. actually saves time and therefore the investment of time in learning the technique is justified:
1. Less time to adapt horses to the program.
2. Less time wasted circumventing horse's idiosyncratic behavior.
3. Shortened warm-up times.
4. More flexible use of horses for various riders and activities.
5. More flexible assignment of workers to horses.
6. Less time spent training volunteers.
7. Less lay-up time and longer retention of trained horses.
8. A benefit of healthier, sounder and safer horses.

In addition to time-savings and convenience, TT.E.A.M. can add to the quality of a program. Safety margins are increased with aware, connected horses and workers. Horses are more comfortable and involved as real partners. Clients and workers are empowered and enriched by the connection TT.E.A.M. provides. It would seem that from these utility features and from a shared interest in neuromuscular--mind learning, TT.E.A.M. and therapeutic riding are natural partners.

References
Tellington-Jones, L., Hood, R,, *T.E.A.M. News International*, Edmonton, Alberta, Canada.
Humanistic Psychology Institute: Moshe Feldenkrais Center. San Francisco, CA
Newsweek Magazine. (1988). Can Animals Think. May 23,1988. 52.
Pacific Coast Equestrian Research Farm, Badger, CA
Tellington, W., Tellington-Jones, L.(1979) *Endurance and Competitive Trail Riding*. New York: Doubleday.
Wise, A. (1984). Biofeedback. *TTEAM New International*. 4,5, 13-15.

7.04   LONGEING A THERAPEUTIC RIDING HORSE

Margaret L. Galloway, MS, BHSAI

Longeing the horse means that the horse works at various gaits on a longeline in a circle around the handler. It is a training technique that teaches the horse to respond to the handler's commands and balance himself on a circle; it can be used for exercise. *"All tack used when working with a horse on the longe should be light but well made, well cared for and very strong, as it is often subject to sudden strain"* (Inderwick, 1986).

TACK USED IN LONGEING (Figure 1)
- A halter, a bridle with a snaffle bit, or a longeing cavesson
- A longeline of 23 to 33 feet, light-weight but strong. Cotton gives a better grip than nylon
- A longe-whip long enough to *touch* the horse with the lash
- Side-reins
- A saddle, surcingle or a longeing roller
- Brushing boots, bell boots or wraps are used when horses tend to overreach and injure themselves
- Gloves

A halter provides less control than a bridle or longeing cavesson and should only be used on horses well trained to longe. *Use only a snaffle bit* when using a bridle for longeing. A horse that is light in hand, balanced and lets itself be driven forward can have the longeline attached to the inside bit ring. For more control the longeline can be brought through the inside bit ring, over the poll to the outside and attached to the bit ring.

When using a **bridle**, use a regular or drop noseband. The noseband must be at least four fingers above the horse's nostril and not too tight [two fingers between nostril and noseband.] Bring the end of the longeline through the near bit ring and over the horse's poll (Richter, 1986). Snap the longeline to the far side of the bit ring. The reins are removed or secured to the head stall by twisting them and running the throatlatch through them. Be sure to unsnap the longeline and change the direction of the line when longeing in the opposite direction.

The **longeing cavesson** can be used over the snaffle bridle or alone. It provides secure control with a lighter touch, is better fitting than a halter, and with the longeline strapped onto the center nosepiece attachment, the horse may be longed on either rein without further adjustment. The longeing cavesson must be strong and well fitted so there is no shifting. Podhajsky (1968) suggests that longeing should only be performed with a longe cavesson because he feels that attaching the longeline to the bit destroys the soft contact with the horse. Soft contact gives the handler a more obedient and responsive horse. Practice with the cavesson before putting a rider on the longe horse; it affects the horse very differently from a line attached to the bit.

The use of a saddle, a training surcingle, a vaulting surcingle or a longeing roller depends on the purpose of longeing. The saddle is used in preparation for riding or with a rider. The surcingle or a longeing roller is used in training or exercise. The vaulting surcingle is used for sports vaulting, therapeutic riding, or improving a rider's seat. Side-reins are attached to the surcingle, saddle or roller.

PURPOSE AND FIT OF SIDE-REINS
The side-reins attach to the snaffle bit and to the saddle, longeing roller or training surcingle on each side of the horse. The side-reins prevent the horse from turning his head around. They teach him that if he does not pull at the rein, the rein will not pull at him, and they restrain the bit from moving about too much in the mouth. The side-rein should never be so short as to restrict the movement of the horse (Richardson, 1981). When first introducing the horse to longeing, one should not use side-reins, but have all the other equipment in place. Side-reins should not be used until the horse goes forward obediently. When first using side-reins with a horse, they should be longer so that the nose is just beyond the vertical as the horse becomes more supple. Podhajsky (1968) suggests that the side-reins be of equal length on both sides. A German technique teaches that the inside rein is one hole tighter

than the outside rein when going in a circle. It is important to let the horse reach his head down and seek the contact of the bit, shortening his neck by tight side-reins. Lowering the head allows the back to raise (T.T.E.A.M., 1990). The side-reins should be adjusted so that they are comfortable at the halt. As the horse develops a bend, the inside rein might have to be tightened in order to maintain even contact.

AIDS AND POSITION OF HANDLER

The longeing whip is an essential piece of equipment that urges the horse forward with more energy than can be done with other methods. It is used as an aid, for the same reason the rider's legs are used, never as a means of punishment. The handler must learn where to stand in relation to the horse in order to use the whip correctly (Figure 2). The handler, the longeline, and the whip form a triangle with the horse making up one side. The handler stands approximately at the horse's croup, so he or she can drive the horse forward with his or her body position. The whip is held in the hand nearest the horse's hindquarters. The handler moves the horse forward and out and develops a consistent circle. The handler needs to become ambidextrous to manage both the whip and the longeline in a coordinated manner. A horse must not be frightened of the whip, but must learn to respect it. The whip reinforces the voice command and the slight tugs or message on the longeline.

When longeing, "*one of the most important aids is the voice....It may be soothing or exhorting. It is important that the word and sound remain the same for the same commands*" (Podhajsky, 1968). Stand quietly and use a quiet tone. Strengthen the voice command as needed. Avoid shouting. A sharp "no" may occasionally be appropriate, but this sound can easily be confused with "oh," "good," and other exclamations from the student, and should be avoided. The German prrrr, or some reasonable approximation, is better.

The longe session is a good time to teach voice commands. The first command a therapy horse should know is "ho." There may be times when a rider becomes unbalanced and the horse needs to be collected or halted, and a promptly responsive horse is very valuable. To teach the horse "ho," gently give and take with the longeline and say "ho." "Ho" is said in the same tone, usually a deep, drawn-out verbalization. If the horse turns in toward the handler, step back toward his hindquarters and point the whip, saying "walk." "Walk on" is said in a brisk, energetic voice. After a few minutes, repeat the gentle give and take until the horse stops correctly, on the circle facing forward. Walk up to him, gather the longeline in a figure eight while approaching the horse. Praise him heartily, stroking his neck. Reverse and repeat the process.

TECHNIQUE

Most adult horses know the basics of longeing. Those that do not need to be trained. In initial training, an assistant is very helpful. The handler should hold the longeline in his or her near hand and the whip in his or her far hand (Figure 3.) He or she should stand near the horse's head, stepping back toward the horse's hindquarters, keeping a very light contact with the longeline. At the same time, an assistant stands on the horse's far side and begins to lead him forward. The handler stays behind the horse's girth area and uses the whip judiciously to encourage the horse forward. The assistant can step back and away from the horse's head as the horse begins to understand that he must circle the handler (Inderwick, 1977).

It is important to note that, as in leading, the longeline should never be wrapped around your hand, wrist or arm, as this can lead to serious injury. Rather, the line should be folded so that a little can be let out at a time. The longeline should never drag on the ground since the instructor will no longer have direct contact with the horse's mouth. The leadline is held in the same way as one would hold the reins. The upper arm is held next to the body and the lower arm is held in line with the longeline, making a straight line from the elbow to the bit, cavesson or halter (T.T.E.A.M., 1990). The walk and trot are the first gaits in which to work the horse while longeing. Once these gaits are mastered, cantering may begin. Begun too early, the horse may not be balanced or may canter with his hindquarters to the outside (Podhajsky, 1967).

EXERCISING THE HORSE

Exercising the horse can be done on the longeline. The basics of longeing remain the same. Be sure that the horse is warmed up at the walk and then the trot before attempting faster work. If the horse plays by bucking, use a soothing

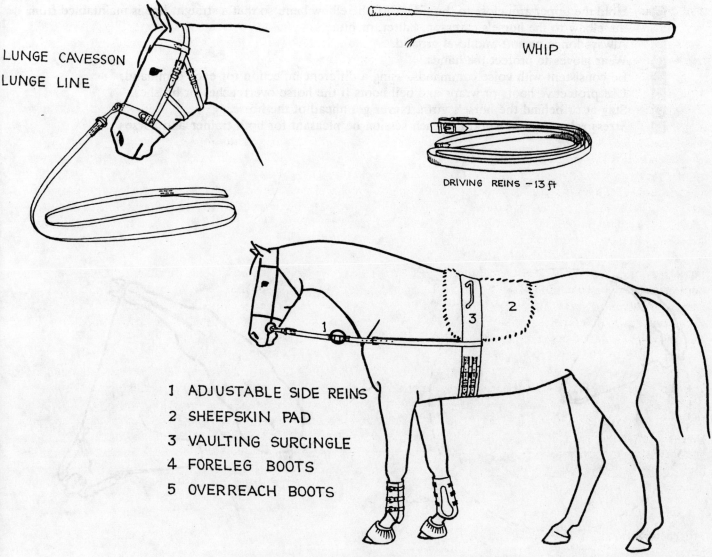

LUNGE CAVESSON
LUNGE LINE

WHIP

DRIVING REINS — 13 ft

1 ADJUSTABLE SIDE REINS
2 SHEEPSKIN PAD
3 VAULTING SURCINGLE
4 FORELEG BOOTS
5 OVERREACH BOOTS

FIGURE 1. LONGEING TACK AND THE HORSE

voice and give and take on the longeline. The horse must learn that longeing requires a working attitude with or without the rider. Play must never be tolerated. Under no circumstance should the horse be allowed to race around the handler as he can injure himself, get loose, or destroy the 'working attitude.' Try long trotting periods for "high" horses. Work in a quiet area so that extraneous stimuli are kept to a minimum. One should work equally in both directions, just as one should ride equally in both directions (Equus, 1989). One should also maintain contact with the longeline; do not let it get slack. Use the whip consistently and effectively as an aid to drive the horse forward and keep him out on the ring. Never use it to punish the horse.

LONGEING BASICS

- The horse must maintain a working attitude at all times.
- Work equally on each side, just as one would ride equally in both directions.
- Keep a sensitive contact with the longeline. It replaces the reins and should be handled accordingly.
- Use a well-fitted longeing cavesson or halter for training and exercise. Longeing with the snaffle bit is hard on the horse's sensitive mouth. The cavesson may be put over the bridle. In vaulting, the snaffle bit is used. The snaffle bit can also be used when longeing with a rider. This, however, requires a very well-trained horse and an experienced longeur.

117

- Hold the upper arm close to the side, with the elbow bent, so that a straight line is maintained from the elbow to the horse's cavesson, halter, or bit.
- Always longe on soft and level ground.
- Wear gloves to protect the hands.
- Be consistent with voice commands, using a different inflection for each command.
- Use protective boots or wraps and bell boots if the horse overreaches or brushes.
- Stay at or behind the horse's girth. Never get ahead of the horse.
- Stress relaxed, calm work. Let each session be pleasant for both trainer and horse

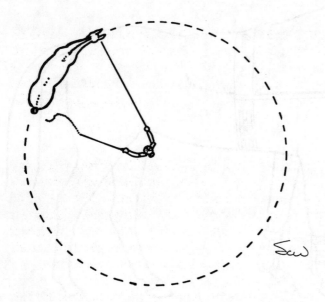

FIGURE 2. POSITION OF THE HANDLER TO THE HORSE.

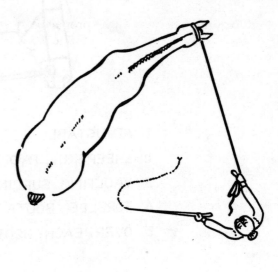

FIGURE 3. POSITION OF THE LONGE LINE AND THE WHIP

References

Equus Magazine, Editorial. (1989). 69. 137.

Hood, R. (1990). *T.T.E.A.M. Clinic.*

Inderwick, S. (1986). *Lungeing the Horse and Rider.* David and Charles Press. 11, 21-23

Podhajsky, A. (1968). *My Horses, My Teachers.*, Garden City: Doubleday and Co. 14, 79

Podhajsky, A. (1967). *The Complete Training of Horse and Rider.* Garden City: Doubleday & Co. 82.

Richardson, J.(1981). *Horse Tack.* New York: William Morrow & Co, Inc. 22-25.

Richter, J.(1986). *The Longeing Book.* New York: Prentice Hall Press. 17

7.05 TECHNIQUES OF LONG-REINING DURING HIPPOTHERAPY AND THERAPEUTIC RIDING SESSIONS

Carolyn D. Jagielski, MS, PT

The use of long reins (sometimes called longe lining) is not a new concept. Man has been working the horse from the ground on long reins for centuries and "work in hand" was part of the training methods used by the European schools of equitation. This technique was found to build the horse's muscles and increase suppleness. Long-reining helped to develop a good mouth and good manners and had the added benefit of allowing the trainer to see what was happening. Although "work in hand" was difficult for even an experienced trainer, the use of the long-reining technique may be modified, and this simplified form may be learned within a few weeks. The purpose of this chapter is to familiarize the reader with the equipment, technique and benefits of long-reining the therapeutic horse.

FITTING THE TACK
Long-reining equipment requires proper fit and should not be "make-shift." The horse should have a snaffle bit and bridle with side-reins adjusted to the same length. Correctly fitted side-reins position the horse's head at least one hand width in front of the vertical. The long reins are approximately 3 meters long and are attached to the bit above the side-reins. For safety, the long reins must <u>not</u> be joined at the ends. The line will thread through a low ring on the surcingle or through a loop (spur strap) attached to the girth. The reins must not be so long that they drag on the ground (Figure 1).

TECHNIQUE
When tracking to the right, the horse handler walks one step behind and just to the inside of the horse's right hind leg. This location allows the handler a less restricted view but facilitates leg yields without interfering with the horse's legs. During a change of rein, the handler should switch position so that he or she is behind and just to the inside of the other hind leg of the horse. This move requires a shortening of the left rein and a lengthening of the right rein as the long-reiner (horse handler) first steps directly behind and then just to the inside of the horse's left hip. The horse handler must be close enough to the horse's hind quarters to avoid the impact of a kick. The horse's movements are controlled through the use of the long reins, the handler's voice commands and the whip.

As the horse walks forward, the handler must match his or her own stride with the tempo of the horse's stride. This technique decreases the likelihood of interfering with the horse's mouth and allows the handler to time his or her rein aids in synchronization with the horse's movement. The handler must be careful not to drop back a step or two as this position will place him or her in a dangerous situation--the center of the kick zone. Side-aid will walk beside the rider next to the rider's legs. The number of necessary side-aids will depend upon the rider's ability. The rider sits on the horse in the normal position. The long reins pass under his or her lower leg so that the reins are not trapped against the horse's flank.

BENEFITS
Therapeutic long-reining has developed as an alternative to leading the horse. Leading is not always an adequate solution for treating a rider's needs. For example, working the horse on long reins allows the horse to move through a variety of school figures, lateral movements, and rein-backs as well as straight lines and circles in a straight and collected position. Unlike in traditional leading, the horse does not need to be pulled forward in an attempt to urge it to walk. When long lining, transitions from walk to halt or halt to walk can be done with precision and with immediate response to a therapist's request.

The quality of the horse's movement is improved when long-reins are used. The horse can move from a collected walk to an extended walk when needed and with more impulsion. The horse carries itself in a better frame when it is long-reined than when it is being led. When performing a curved figure, bending occurs through the entire length of the horse's spine. This bending promotes better weight shifts and more appropriate equilibrium responses in the rider as his or her body accommodates to the horse's bend.

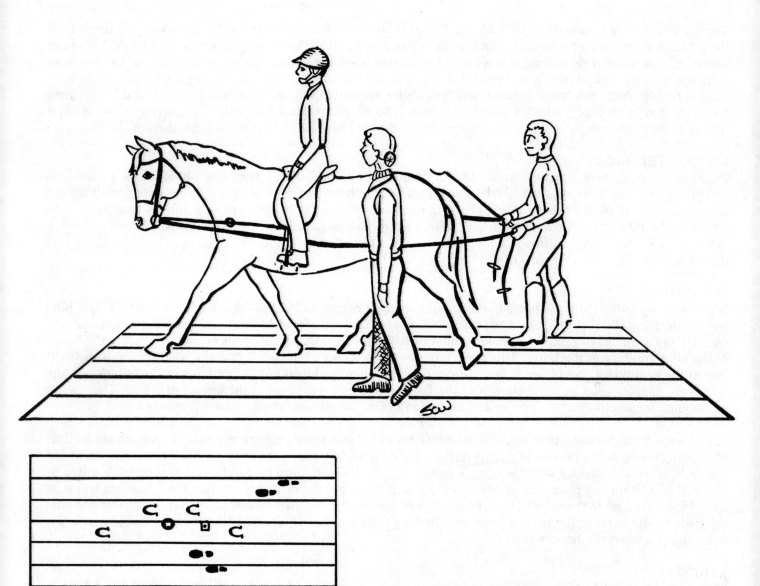

FIGURE 1. THERAPEUTIC LONG REINING HORSE WITH EQUIPMENT AND POSITION OF THE HANDLER

Although used primarily for hippotherapy and equine-assisted therapy, long-reining is an effective tool for the riding instructor in therapeutic riding. Long-reining allows the horse handler to be "invisible" to the rider. The rider feels that he or she alone is in control of the horse. The handler always is present as a back-up should the need arise. The riding instructor may also use long-reining as a way of isolating a task the rider is learning. By having the horse perform a leg yield in long lines, the rider can improve his or her weight shift or coordinate leg aids without needing to concentrate on rein aids.

THE IDEAL HORSE

The horse chosen for long-reining should have a wealth of abilities. As with any therapeutic horse, temperament is foremost. He must be friendly, trusting, responsive and intelligent. A suitable height is between 14.2 and 15.3 hands. This height range allows the rider to be guarded adequately by side aids. The horse must be sound. Asymmetry in the horse's step length will be transmitted to the rider. If the rider already has a postural asymmetry, an uneven stride could increase his or her difficulties rather than improve them. Good conformation is also a requirement for the long-lining horse. Conformation faults in the horse's legs may predispose the horse to injury or progressive lameness; muscle weakness in the animal's back could develop into a sensitive and painful back or progress to a swayed back. As faults in conformation may negate months of training, the horse should be evaluated carefully for weak body structures.

Lastly, the horse's quality of movement is important. The following abilities are necessary to achieve peak performance:
1. To move in straight lines with even strides
2. To track up at the walk with the hind foot stepping into or beyond the imprint of the forefoot
3. To move symmetrically
4. To be able to bend laterally through the whole length of his body in both directions

However, good movement does not come from good conformation alone; the horse also needs good training.

The horse needs specific prerequisites before long reining training begins. Training in longeing or therapeutic longeing makes the horse responsive to voice commands and familiar with a longe line and a whip. The horse should accept the bit with flexion at the poll and a yielding of the jaw. Either ground driving or double longeing will acclimate the horse to contact from an outside line and to the feel of the line behind its hind legs. (Some horses never accept this feeling and therefore cannot be used for long reining). Training the therapy horse to long rein is not within the scope of this article. Information on this procedure can be found in detail in the texts listed in the bibliography.

THE RIDING INSTRUCTOR

With most programs, the person most qualified to long rein is the riding instructor. Long-reining the horse requires more horse expertise than leading. Several weeks of practice are required for the horse handler to learn the technique correctly. He or she must know the equipment and the proper way to fit it on the horse. The horse handler needs a good following hand so that he or she does not interfere with the horse's mouth. Other important abilities for the horse handler are to know the horse's gaits and to have experience working with long reins.

Since the therapeutic riding instructor is knowledgeable about horses and client disabilities, he or she is a good liaison between the physical or occupational therapist and the horse. The riding instructor must be familiar with any ground figures or activities the therapist may request.

THE TEAM

The primary benefit of long-reining is that the effectiveness of the entire team is increased. The horse is capable of better movement patterns and more complex figures. The riding instructor has greater control over the horse's collection, impulsion and direction of movement. The therapist can control the horse's activities through the horse handler and thus can influence the rider's responses with greater precision. All of these benefits are provided to the rider when the horse is long-reined.

References

Heipertz, W., et al. (1981). *Therapeutic Riding.* translated by Marion Takeukchi. Available from Canadian Equestrian Federation, 1600 James Anismith Drive, Gloucester, Ontario, Canada K1G 5M4.

National Hippotherapy Development Project. (1990). *The Horse as a Facilitator* - A Workshop in Hippotherapy. (1990). Warwick, NY.

Stanier, S. (1972). *The Art of Long Reining.* J. A. Allen and Company Limited. London, England.

7.06   SUPPLING THE THERAPEUTIC RIDING HORSE

Judy Rector, BHSI

WHY SUPPLE A HORSE?

Suppling a horse enhances his movement by improving his fluidness, symmetry, rhythm and cadence. The more supple a horse becomes the more willing he is to do what is asked of him. In school, the classes one normally enjoys are the ones that come easily. The same is true with horses. Resistance in a horse is created by discomfort or pain, or by the horse's belief that he is incapable of doing what is asked of him. If the instructor stood behind the student and pushed down on his or her back while he or she was reaching to touch his or her toes, the student would start to push back against the instructor the moment he or she thought it might hurt. Similarly when the rider asks too much of the horse, the horse will tighten and push back.

BITS TO USE IN SUPPLING

Suppling or training is normally done using a snaffle bit, shank snaffle bit or a rawhide bosal. Western horses start in a snaffle bit, and then progress to a shank snaffle bit and later learn to go in a curb bit. English snaffle bits are normally stainless steel and some have a copper mouth piece to encourage saliva. They can also be made of nickel alloy which is a yellow color. Some western bits are made of "sweet iron" and in time will rust. They sometimes have copper inlay on the back side of the mouth piece to encourage saliva. Most horses like "sweet iron." Any time the corners of the horse's mouth are cut, they will become callused and less sensitive after they heal. Loose ring snaffle bits can sometimes pinch the corners of a horse's mouth and therefore he may need bit guards. Full cheek snaffle bits will help give one leverage when turning. The larger the ring, the more leverage one will have. The thinner the mouth piece the more severe the bit. Shank bits give a curb action and the longer the shank the more leverage and severity of the bit. Anytime the curb or port of the bit is two inches or higher, it works on the roof of the mouth. A bosal should have a rawhide core, not a metal cable core. One of the advantages of a bosal is that it does not work on the mouth but applies pressure to the bridge of the nose and under the jaw.

Here is a list of common terms that will be used throughout this section (see FIGURE 1):

1. **INSIDE - The inside is always toward the middle of the circle or ring.**

2. **OUTSIDE - The outside is always toward the rail or on the outside of the circle.**

3. **INDIRECT REIN - This means one's hand moves toward the withers so the rein pressure is against the neck.**

4. **DIRECT REIN - Rein pressure is straight back toward one's jean pocket.**

5. **OPEN REIN - One's hand and arm moves out and away from the horse to guide him.**

6. **COUNTER - This means to the outside. Examples:**
   a) **counter canter - the lead is toward the rail**
   b) **counter arc - bend to the outside**

122

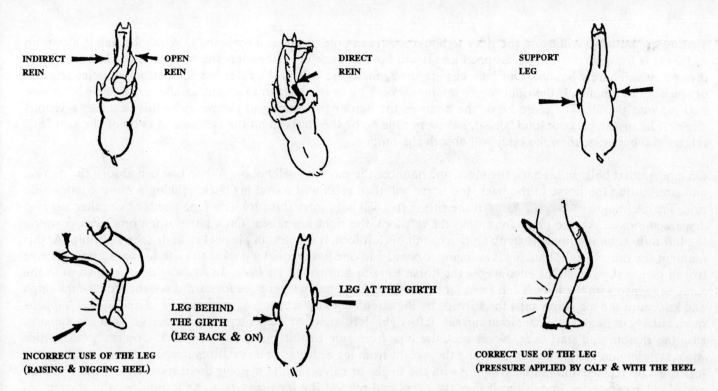

INDIRECT REIN   **OPEN REIN**

DIRECT REIN

SUPPORT LEG

INCORRECT USE OF THE LEG
(RAISING & DIGGING HEEL)

LEG BEHIND THE GIRTH
(LEG BACK & ON)

LEG AT THE GIRTH

CORRECT USE OF THE LEG
(PRESSURE APPLIED BY CALF & WITH THE HEEL

FIGURE 1. COMMON TERMS

HOW THE RIDER'S POSITION AFFECTS THE HORSE

Riders' position affects their horses greatly. Sometimes we give signals that we are not aware of but that our horses pick up on. An example of this is how one's weight affects the horse. When carrying a bucket of water, the weight of the bucket causes one to walk leaning away from the weight. If a person carries the bucket in his or her left hand, he or she will drift to the right, trying to compensate for the weight. This compensation for weight distribution is also true between the horse and rider. We have seen riders lean to the inside as they go by an opening in the fence, anticipating that their horse will try to leave the ring. The result will cause the horse to "bulge out." The rider, not realizing that he or she caused the problem, then disciplines his or her horse. Leaning affects the rider's ability to do a good circle. The aids for circling are: inside rein and leg to bend the horse and outside rein and leg to hold or block him. An example is a horseshoe and an anvil. The horse is the horseshoe, the rider's inside aid is the hammer and his or her outside aid is the anvil. One can hold the horseshoe up in the air and hammer on it, but it will not bend until it is placed on an anvil. The anvil keeps the shoe stationary so that it can then bend. The same applies to the horse. The outside aids must hold the horse so that one's inside aids can bend him. The shoulders also affect the horse. When circling to the left, the outside (right) aids are the holding aids. This author suggests that the rider should have his or her right leg back and on the horse so that his or her weight is going down the outside leg. But if the body twists to the inside of the circle, then the weight has automatically shifted to the inside leg. If the rider puts his or her outside shoulder back and down, the weight shift goes down his or her outside leg. It is very difficult to twist the shoulders to the inside, and at the same time to get the weight to go back and down the outside leg. (Some riders, with specific disabilities, may not be able to perform this maneuver but may need to put the outside shoulder slightly in advance of the inside one in order to weight the inside seatbone and give power to the inside leg that bends the horse and prevents falling to the inside of the circle.)

Believe it or not, even one's breathing affects the horse's behavior. When the rider holds his or her breath, it causes tension throughout the body which the horse can feel. This can cause the horse to become upset. Remember to breath and breath in a rhythm. Some of the following suppling exercises are easier to do at a sitting trot. The sitting trot comes easily to some riders while others find it very difficult. This may partially be due to the horse he or she is riding. If the horse has a straight shoulder and a short straight pastern, then he will be short stride and have very little cushion in the trot (this causes him to be a rough ride). Some horses hollow their backs instead of rounding while carrying the rider; this also makes them difficult to "sit to."

123

Tensing the buttocks will cause the rider to bounce. An example of this is a basketball. When the ball is blown up so that it is firm, then it can be dropped and it will bounce back up. If one lets the air out of the ball when one drops it, it will barely bounce. Our buttocks are the same as the ball. If the rider lets the buttock muscles relax he or she will not bounce. If the rider tenses the buttocks as he or she start to touch the saddle, he or she will bounce back up into the air. The more he or she bounces the harder the tensing of the buttocks this becomes a vicious circle. If he or she says out loud "sit, sit, sit" every time he or she starts to hit the saddle and as he or she says "sit," relaxes the buttocks, then the body will absorb the motion.

On a horse that hollows his back the more one bounces the more he will hollow. When one can absorb the motion and stop hitting the horse in the back, the horse will then relax and round his back, making a more comfortable ride. The technique of *stepping down* at the sitting trot will help solve this problem. One needs to visualize *stepping down* a staircase. As one steps down onto the left foot, the right hip raises. On a horse when one steps down on the left foot while the horse is stepping down with his left foot, it creates an air pocket under the right hip. At this moment the horse's right hind leg is swinging forward and one has created a pocket to raise his back up to (horses trot in diagonal pairs.) This encourages the horse to raise and round his back. In *stepping down* one steps in the same sequence with the horse's left front foot. It will feel like one's weight goes forward down the front of the thigh and knee and the leg gently taps the stirrups by the stretching and relaxing of the ankles and heels. This happens quite quickly. It helps to talk out loud and say "left--right--left--right" or "step, step, step." If one gets out of sequence, stop the rhythm and start over. Never rock the hips from side to side but always forward. One can practice this while standing on the ground and shifting the weight from leg to leg as one visualizes *stepping down*. In riding, the legs must be relaxed and not be gripping with the thighs or calves. While *stepping down* most horses will not need added leg pressure for impulsion; if they do, press and release the leg pressure so as to not lose the rhythm. At first this technique might seem difficult to learn but the rewards are well worth the effort.

SUPPLING EXERCISES

I. BENDING IN AND OUT ON SMALL CIRCLES
This exercise is done on small circles at the walk bending your horse first to the inside and later to the outside. The circles should be twelve to fifteen feet in diameter. If the horse starts to pivot, make the circle larger. This is a very good suppling exercise that the rider can do for five minutes a day or for an hour a day (Figure 2). Start by circling to the right so that the right hand is toward the middle of the circle. Use the inside right rein as an open

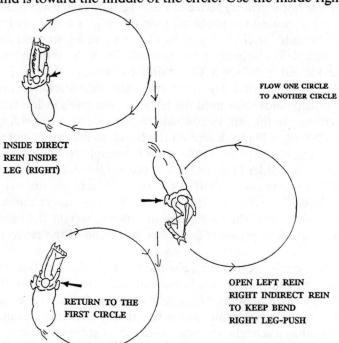

FLOW ONE CIRCLE
TO ANOTHER CIRCLE

INSIDE DIRECT
REIN INSIDE
LEG (RIGHT)

OPEN LEFT REIN
RIGHT INDIRECT REIN
TO KEEP BEND
RIGHT LEG-PUSH

RETURN TO THE
FIRST CIRCLE

FIGURE 2. BENDING IN AND OUT ON SMALL CIRCLES:

124

rein to guide the horse on the circle. Use the inside (right) leg to bend the horse around the circle. The outside rein is passive, resting by the withers. The outside leg is supporting the horse and is ready in case one needs to encourage the horse to walk out. If the horse is cutting to the inside of the circle, increase the inside leg pressure. If he is pushing out, relax the inside leg and, if needed, add outside leg. After doing three to five circles with the horse bent to the right, keep the bend, but change the direction of the circle by walking forward and picking up and opening the left rein to guide the horse on to a new circle (like a figure-eight). Use the right rein as an indirect rein to keep the bend to the outside of the circle. The right leg pushes the horse around the circle. It is not necessary to turn the horse's head way out to achieve good results. After doing one to three circles flow back onto the original circle. A common mistake when circling with the horse's head in is to use inside indirect rein to bend the horse and then he can only bend his neck, not his body. Another mistake that occurs while executing this exercise with his head out is to use the outside rein to pull the horse around. Never allow the outside rein to cross the neck. If the horse will not circle increase the outside leg pressure and use more inside rein and barely turn his head out. The hardest part of this exercise is changing direction from one circle to another. Remember to walk forward and to keep the inside hand up, level with the elbow.

The purpose of turning the horse's head to the inside is to teach the horse to bend his rib cage. His hind feet should follow into the front hoof prints, not cutting to the inside or floating to the outside of the circle. When the horse's head is to the outside, it encourages the horse to shift his weight more to the rear and the rider will learn how to control his shoulders and rib cage. The horse should always crossover in front of his other leg, not behind it. If he crosses behind the leg, the forward momentum is lost. This is a very good warm up exercise and encourages the horse to listen and settle down.

You can vary this exercise, but always work both sides of the horse. To vary the exercise push the horse's shoulders to the outside of the circle. Start with his head to the inside of the circle and then instead of using an open inside rein, use an indirect inside rein by lifting and moving the hand toward the withers. This will cause the horse to push his shoulders to the outside of the circle. Another variation is to push his whole body into the inside of the circle. Start with his head bent to the outside of the circle. Then, increase the outside leg pressure so the horse steps over into the circle with his hind quarters as well as his front end. This is much more difficult. The rider must keep his or her outside shoulder back and down. Remember to start with a part of a circle and as it becomes easier for him, increase the number of circles. Do not exceed five or six circles without rewarding the horse by going to something easier for him to do.

II. PUSHING THE HINDQUARTERS TO THE OUTSIDE OF THE CIRCLE

This is basically a turn on the forehand while walking on a circle (Figure 3). Start by walking a small circle. Put the inside leg back and on to push the horses hindquarters to the outside of the circle. The horse will cross his inside hind leg over the outside hind leg; He or she should never stop or pivot. His front end is always walking on a circle. Guide the horse onto a small circle by opening the inside rein. Make sure that the inside leg (the calf) and heel are used to give pressure. Do not just raise the leg and dig with the heel (Figure 1). Do three to five circles and then change direction. This exercise is very good for a horse that does not obey the leg. Instead of him giving to the leg this horse pushes against it. This will encourage him to yield to leg pressure.

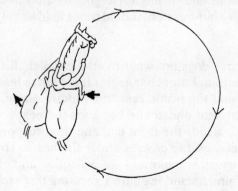

OPEN INSIDE REIN TO GUIDE HORSE. PUT INSIDE LEG WAY BACK TO THE REAR.

FIGURE 3. PUSHING THE HINDQUARTERS TO THE OUTSIDE OF THE CIRCLE

III. LEG YIELDING OR TWO TRACKING

In this exercise the horse is moving forward and sideways at the same time. (Figure 4A). This may be easier at the trot which gives the horse more impulsion than at the walk. It can also be done at the canter. Most horses like to be on the rail, therefore it is easiest to start by being off the rail and pushing toward the rail. Start by coming around the short end of the ring; turn so the horse is four to six feet off the long side of the rail and parallel to it. Do not start to two track (leg yield) while finishing the corner turn or one will teach the horse to float or bulge when cornering. Finish the corner and continue for several strides parallel to the rail making sure the horse is straight before starting to leg yield. To push to the rail, the inside rein is used as an indirect rein so that one can see the inside corner of the horse's eye. The inside leg goes back and on, to push him over. If he does not understand guide him with a direct or open outside rein. As soon as he understands stop opening the outside rein. The outside leg is passive and is only used for impulsion. After the horse has learned what is wanted of him, he will try to get to the rail first with his front end. To correct and control his shoulders, use inside direct rein and outside indirect rein. (The opposite of what one started with). Some riders use too much inside rein which causes the horse to over bend his head and neck, then lead with his outside shoulder which gets to the rail first. Do not over bend the head and neck. One

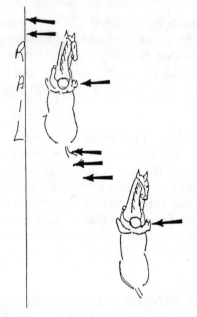

TURN THE HEAD IN THE DIRECTION OPPOSITE OF THE DIRECTION YOU ARE PUSHING TOWARD. USE THE SAME LEG AS THE BEND OF THE HORSE'S HEAD AND NECK. IF NECESSARY, OPEN AND GUIDE WITH THE OTHER REIN. IF THE HORSE TRIES TO LEAD TOO MUCH WITH HIS SHOULDER, STRAIGHTEN HIS HEAD AND NECK.

FIGURE 4A. LEG YIELDING OR TWO TRACKING

should only see the inside eyelashes, not half of his face. Have equal pressure on both reins. If he does not want to "*listen to*" the leg, instead of applying steady leg pressure, think of pushing with the inside leg when his inside hind leg is off the ground, and relax when his leg is on the ground. At the posting trot that would be on the upbeat of the post, assuming one is on the correct diagonal. Eventually, the pushing leg should not need to move back, but be applied at the girth. Technically, the front end of the horse gets to the rail a split second before the rear end, but one needs to think parallel. The horse's hind-quarters should never lead or get to the rail first, or the forward impulsion is lost.

Pushing off the rail is more difficult as the horse does not want to stay parallel. Turn his head toward the rail by using the indirect outside rein and direct inside rein. Later change this if the horse leads too much with his shoulder, by changing the outside rein to a direct rein and the inside rein to an indirect rein. The outside leg pushes back and on. After he has done a few strides, go straight ahead and bend for the next corner; do not allow him to cut across the ring. If his hind quarters lag behind, steady the front end and then reapply leg pressure. In leg yielding, the inside hind leg (the inside of the bend) reaches and crosses under the horse. (It also helps the horse to learn the "diagonal aids" inside leg to outside rein, which is important for collection and engagement). This strengthens his back and hip muscles and helps him better understand leg aids. Executing this exercise at the canter encourages the horse to balance and become lighter on his front end.

126

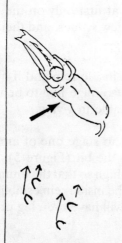

RAISE YOUR OUTSIDE (INDIRECT) REIN
TO TURN THE HEAD INTO THE RAIL. THE
INSIDE REIN IS A DIRECT OR OPEN
REIN. USE OUTSIDE LEG BACK AND ON.
DO NOT OVER BEND THE NECK.

THE HORSE'S LEGS CROSS OVER EACH OTHER.

FIGURE 4B. LEG YIELDING ANGLING DOWN THE RAIL:

A variation of leg yielding (or two tracking) is to do it angling down the rail (Figure 4B). First, with the horse's head facing the rail, and then with his hindquarters toward the rail and his head facing the middle of the ring. Start on the short end of the ring at a trot and turn soon enough so that the horse is several feet off the rail. (Later one can do it right on the rail). As one starts turning, start positioning the horse by turning his head out using outside indirect rein and inside direct and if necessary, open rein. As one approaches the long side of the ring apply outside leg back and on the horse. By allowing several feet between the horse and the rail, it allows him to move forward more easily. (He will eventually reach the rail). He will cross both front and hind legs and will be almost directly facing the rail (but not quite). This can be done at all gaits. It is more difficult than being parallel to the rail. This can be done in reverse so that his hind quarters are at the rail and his front end is now facing the middle of the ring. When coming around the corner, bend the horse by using inside indirect rein, outside direct or open rein and inside leg back and on. As one approaches the rail, turn so that his front end is off the rail, and increase the inside leg pressure. Now, keep enough rein pressure to not allow the horse to go forward to the middle of the ring but to move at an angle down the rail (almost perpendicular to the rail).

IV. ARCING

Arcing is taught in two stages (Figure 5). The first stage is to teach the horse to bend his head and neck. This exercise may be performed at all gaits, but it is easiest to start at the trot. Most horses prefer at first to arc to the outside (counter arc). This means the horse's head is turned towards the rail. Use the outside rein as

STAGE 1 OF ARCING: BRING THE REIN TOWARD THE
NECK (INDIRECT REIN). USE THE LEG ON THE SAME
SIDE. IF NECESSARY, OPEN THE OTHER REIN TO KEEP
THE HORSE ON THE RAIL.

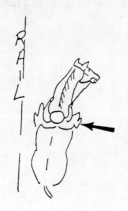

STAGE 2 OF ARCING:
BRING REIN DIRECTLY BACK TOWARD YOUR
THIGH AND BEND THE HORSE'S NECK.
STRAIGHTEN YOUR OPPOSITE ELBOW.
USE THE LEG TO BEND THE HORSE.

FIGURE 5. ARCING

an indirect rein towards the withers. One should not need much, if any, inside rein. Use a slight amount of outside leg so that the horse's body is also bent toward the rail. Do this at first only on the long sides of the ring. When the horse relaxes and gives to the rein pressure, hold for another few strides, and then reward him by allowing him to straighten, move forward and relax.

To arc to the inside, turn the horse's head in by using an indirect inside rein and if he will not stay on the rail use a small amount of outside direct rein. Use inside leg slightly to encourage him to bend. It is not necessary to bend his head back to your knee. Take only what the horse is comfortable in giving.

When the horse becomes very comfortable, with little resistance to stage one of arcing, then stage two of arcing can begin. In stage two, the horse will learn to come down onto the bit (Figure 5). At the trot, start with arcing to the inside by bringing the inside hand back and holding it on the thigh so that the thumb faces to the rear. Straighten the outside arm and apply pressure either outward or backward. The inside rein establishes the bend and the outside rein encourages the horse to come down on the bit. By now one will have even leg pressure, unless the horse does not want to bend.

Arcing to the outside is done by holding the outside hand on the thigh and opening and straightening the inside arm. Remember to ask the horse to go forward so that the hands are holding and the legs are pushing him into the bit. While circling, you can arc to the inside by holding the inside hand on the thigh, open the outside rein and use the inside leg. To make the circle larger, use more pressure on the outside rein and more inside leg. To arc to the outside while circling, use the outside hand on the thigh to position the horses's head (but not to pull him around the circle). Use the inside open rein to guide him and outside leg to push him. *Arcing teaches the horse to give his head from side to side which makes him more willing to go on the bit. It encourages him to round his back and to start to shift his weight to his hindquarters.* While arcing out at the canter, one can definitely feel the horse shift his weight to his hindquarters.

A variation of this exercise is to ask the horse, while arcing out on a circle, to push his rib cage and hindquarters to the inside of the circle. Keep the circle large and do not over bend his head out or he will want to lead with his shoulder. Increase the outside leg and keep it back and on. Also keep your outside shoulder back and down. Doing this exercise at the canter is beneficial to teaching the horse to work off his hocks.

V. TURN ON THE FOREHAND
A turn on the forehand is when the horse's hindquarters walk around his front end, which remains stationary (Figure 6). This is easier to teach with the horse parallel to the rail. His outside front leg (by the rail) is his pivot foot. His outside hind leg crosses over his inside hind leg. One can start teaching this exercise as soon as the horse basically understands leg yielding.

Use an indirect outside rein to turn his head toward the rail, so the outside eyelash can be seen. The inside hand is used as a direct rein to keep the horse from over bending his head and neck. The rider's hands are used to position the horse's head and keep him from walking forward. One's outside leg is back and on to push the horse around. Only use the inside leg if he backs up. When the rider feels resistance, do not use the hands to pull the horse around. Instead increase the leg pressure. Pulling on the reins is the most common fault in executing the turn on the forehand. Start with a couple of steps, then stop and pat your horse. Then, try a couple more steps. Eventually one can move off the rail and work up to a 360 degree turn on the forehand. This teaches the horse to mind the leg aid, and encourages him to reach and stretch his hind leg up under his belly as it crosses over.

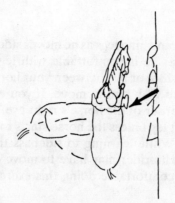

TURN THE HEAD TOWARD
THE RAIL. USE YOUR LEG
CLOSEST TO THE RAIL.
FOREHAND STAYS STILL
WHILE THE HINDQUARTERS
WALK AROUND. RIGHT
TURN ON THE FOREHAND USING
THE RIGHT AIDS, RIGHT FRONT LEG
IS HIS PIVOT FOOT.

FIGURE 6. TURN ON THE FOREHAND

VI. TURN ON THE HAUNCHES

In executing a turn on the haunches, the horse's hindquarters will stay in place while its front end walks around (Figure 7). Like the turn on the forehand, this is easiest to teach the horse while he is parallel to the rail. One can do this exercise from a walk or a standstill. Let us assume one is doing a turn on the haunches to the right. The right rein will be a direct or slightly open rein to guide the horse through the turn. The left rein will be an indirect rein to keep the shoulders in place and to keep the horse from over bending his head and neck. The rider's outside leg is back and on to control the hindquarters and to create energy. Without the leg aid, the horse would swing his rear end out to the left, causing him to swap ends (both front and hind end would move simultaneously). The

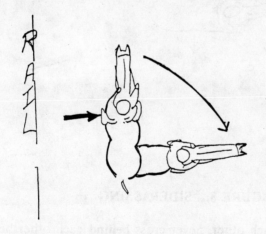

TO TURN ON THE HAUNCHES
TO THE RIGHT, USE BOTH
HANDS TO GUIDE THE FRONT
END (TO THE RIGHT). USE
OPPOSITE LEG (LEFT). THE
HORSE'S RIGHT HIND LEG
IS THE PIVOT FOOT.

FIGURE 7. TURN ON THE HAUNCHES

leg also works like a gas peddle of the car. One can turn the steering wheel, but nothing happens until the driver steps on the gas. In doing a turn on the haunches to the right, the horse's left front leg should cross in front of his right front leg. When doing a turn from the walk, start with a half-halt or a slight hesitation and then proceed.

129

Always walk off after doing a few steps to keep the impulsion. Gradually increase the number of steps until one completes a full circle, at this point one must be off the rail. *This exercise teaches the horse to balance himself over his hindquarters and lighten his front end.*

VII. SIDEPASSING

When sidepassing the horse crosses both his front and hind legs as he moves sideways without walking forward (Figure 8). You can start teaching sidepassing as soon as he is comfortable with leg yielding and turns on the forehand. This is easiest to teach by facing a rail but leave a foot or two between your horse's head and the rail. Start by turning his head in the opposite direction of the way you wish him to move. If you want to move to the left, use the right rein as an indirect rein so that one can see the corner of the horse's right eye. Open the left rein to guide him. Push with the right leg back and on. Do not use the left leg unless the horse starts to backup. At first, he may walk forward a little, but facing the rail will discourage this. While learning to sidepass the horse may find it difficult to move both the front end and the hind end together. The rider may have to move each end individually. Eventually less guiding rein will be needed. Once he becomes comfortable doing this exercise move away from the rail.

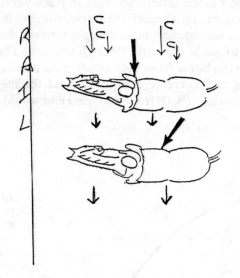

TURN THE HORSE'S HEAD THE OPPOSITE DIRECTION TO THE WAY YOU WISH TO GO. USE THE LEG ON THE SAME SIDE THAT HIS HEAD IS BENT. IF NECESSARY OPEN THE OTHER REIN TO GUIDE THE HORSE.

FIGURE 8.   SIDEPASSING

He should cross his hind legs in front of each other, never cross **behind** each other because he has then lost all impulsion. If this happens ask him to step slightly forward as he crosses over. Crossing his front legs limbers his shoulders by stretching and lengthening those muscles. Crossing the hind legs strengthens the loin and hip muscles.

VIII. SHOULDER-IN

Do not start this exercise until the horse understands leg pressure and is comfortable with leg yielding and arcing. In this exercise the hindquarters stay on the rail, and the front end moves off the rail to the inside (Figure 9). The horse is now traveling on three tracks. His inside front leg is on a track of its own (3), his outside front and inside hind leg are on a second track (2), and his outside hind leg is on its own track (1). In teaching shoulder-in most

130

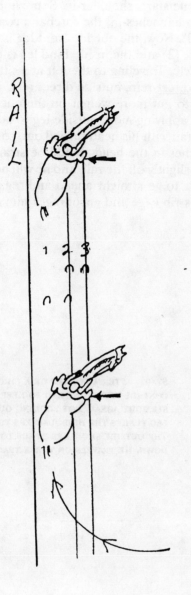

FIGURE 9. SHOULDER-IN

horses do not want to move their shoulders in off the rail. It is easier to start the shoulder-in coming off of a corner or circle at the sitting trot. While using the inside direct rein and the outside indirect rein (slightly higher), move both reins toward the inside hip. The rider will need a lot of inside leg to keep the hindquarters going straight down the rail and not following the front end off the rail. Prepare for shoulder-in on the short side of the ring by doing a sitting trot and bending the horse for the corner by using the inside leg, inside direct rein, outside indirect rein and outside holding leg. The rider drops the inside shoulder back and down; this will put more weight on his or her inside hip and helps push with the inside leg. When over-bending the horse's head and neck, his shoulder will not come off the rail. One should only see the corner of his inside eye. If the horse's shoulders moves too far off the rail, the horse will be leg yielding and his or her hind legs will cross over each other, instead of moving straight down the rail. The outside leg helps keep the impulsion and is used to hold the hind end straight, when doing this without the use of a rail. At first, most horses will want to slow up as they do this exercise, so do only a few steps and then ride forward again. As progress is made, the leg pressure will become more even. *Shoulder-in helps balance the horse and lighten his front end.*

131

IX. HAUNCHES-IN

One can start teaching haunches-in about the same time one starts shoulder-in. Some horses find one of these two easier than the other and this is also true for the rider. In haunches-in, the forehand continues down the rail and the hindquarters move off the rail to the inside (Figure 10). Now, the outside front leg is on a track of its own (1), the inside front leg and the outside hind leg are on a track (2) and the inside hind leg is on its own track (3). This exercise is also easier to do coming off of a corner or a circle. Traveling to the left at a sitting trot, prepare to bend the horse as one approaches the corner by using inside <u>indirect</u> rein, outside direct rein, inside leg and outside leg back and on. Drop the outside shoulder back and down to put more weight on the outside hip. As your horse's front end finishes the corner, relax the inside leg and start applying more outside leg to keep his hindquarters from reaching the rail. The horse would rather angle down the rail with his head turned out, so the rider will need inside indirect rein to insist that he continue straight. In haunches-in the head should be straight or slightly inside the corner of the horse's eye. The horse's hindquarters will be slightly off the rail, and he will be bent around your inside leg. After a few strides, reward the horse by allowing him to go straight ahead and regain any impulsion that he might have lost. Haunches-in helps to stretch your horse's rib cage and encourages him to step up under himself.

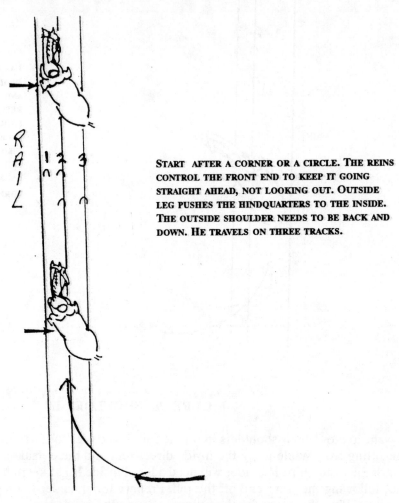

START AFTER A CORNER OR A CIRCLE. THE REINS CONTROL THE FRONT END TO KEEP IT GOING STRAIGHT AHEAD, NOT LOOKING OUT. OUTSIDE LEG PUSHES THE HINDQUARTERS TO THE INSIDE. THE OUTSIDE SHOULDER NEEDS TO BE BACK AND DOWN. HE TRAVELS ON THREE TRACKS.

FIGURE 10.   HAUNCHES-IN

X. C'S OR DOUBLE CINCHING

This is more difficult than haunches-in and should not be attempted until the horse is comfortable with haunches-in. It is very similar to haunches-in, but the rider needs to bend both ends of the horse as though his head and hindquarters were trying to meet one another (Figure 11). On the short end of the ring, prepare the horse by bringing one's outside shoulder back and down. Use the outside direct rein and raise the inside indirect rein to arc the horse to the inside. Use the inside leg to bend the horse. As the rider finishes the corner, he or she relaxes his or her inside leg and

132

increases the outside leg (back and on). If the horse tries to move off the rail or tries to straighten his body, use the inside leg to re-establish the bend and then relax the leg again. Do only three or four steps to begin with. When finishing this exercise relax your rein pressure first, move forward one step and then relax the leg pressure. This exercise is easier at the trot but can be done at the walk and canter. The horse must stretch and bend his rib cage to properly execute this exercise.

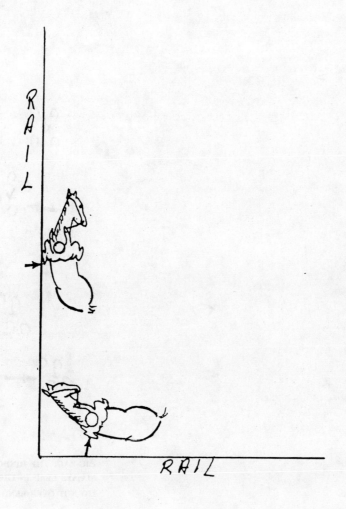

THIS IS SIMILAR TO HAUNCHES-IN. ONE WANTS TO BEND BOTH ENDS OF THE HORSE. USE THE OUTSIDE DIRECT REIN AND INSIDE INDIRECT REIN TO ARC THE HORSE. USE THE OUTSIDE LEG BACK AND ON. THE RIDER'S OUTSIDE SHOULDER NEEDS TO BE BACK AND DOWN.

FIGURE 11. C'S OR DOUBLE CINCHING

XI. BACKING

Backing is an easy maneuver for some horses but for others it is very difficult. Do not start the horse on backing until he can at least do stage one of arcing and a turn on the forehand. Start by gently turning his head and neck to the side that is easiest for him, so the rider can see the corner of his eye. If his head is turned to the left, use left indirect rein, right direct rein, left leg at the girth and right leg behind the girth (Figure 12A). Take a firm hold of the reins to position the horse's head, but do not pull. Use even leg pressure. If he starts to walk forward, increase rein pressure, but do not try to pull him back. Keep in mind one needs to sit straight in the saddle and not lean forward. Keep the leg pressure and normally after a short time he will start to back. The goal is to have the horse give his head as he backs up. The moment he does, reward him and walk forward. Only back three or four steps even if the horse does not give his head. A horse that will not back has locked his shoulders. If he locks up, increase leg pressure on the side his head is bent to. This increased pressure will encourage the horse's hindquarters to step away from your leg (turn on the forehand), then reapply your other leg. If he still will not back, walk forward and

133

try again, but never pull him back. Once he will give and back with his head bent to his easier side, reverse the bend and repeat the exercise. Once he is comfortable with this exercise ask him to back alternating the bend after three or four steps. After he has learned this exercise he will be able to back straight and give his head.

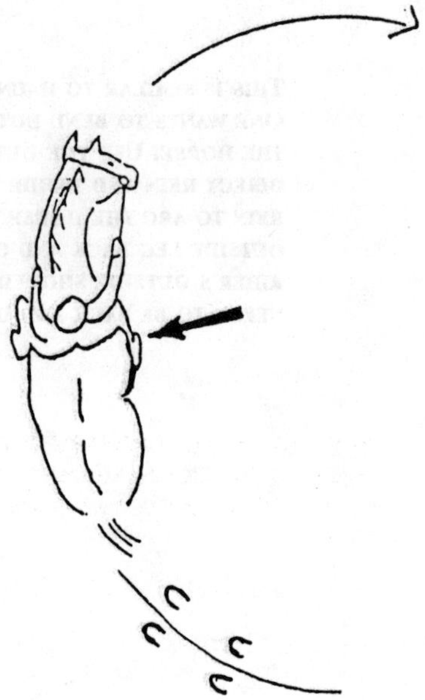

WALK FORWARD ON A CIRCLE. STOP WITH THE HORSE BENT TO THE INSIDE, USE STRONGER INSIDE AIDS.

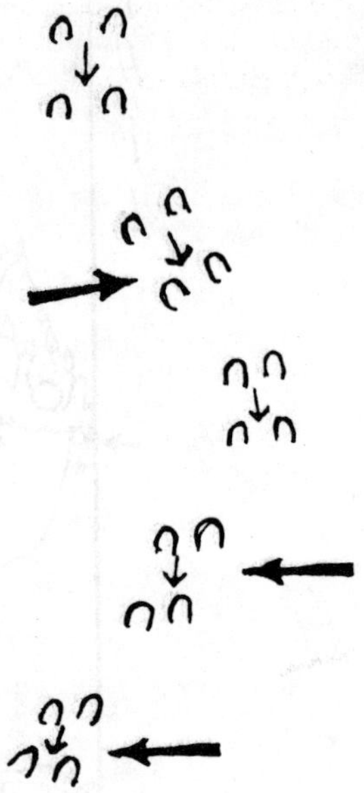

ZIG-ZAG: THE HINDQUARTERS WILL ALWAYS LEAD IN THE BACK DIRECTION. DO NOT OVER BEND HIS HEAD AND NECK.

FIGURE 12A. BACKING

FIGURE 12B. BACKING ZIG-ZAG

Zig-Zag: In this backing exercise the horse backs with his hindquarters leading in the new direction (Figure 12B). Start by slightly turning the horse's head so that one can see the corner of his eye by using an indirect rein on that side. The rider's hands position his head and neck and help keep the horse from walking forward. If the horse's head has been turned to the left, then put the left leg back and on and support with the right leg. The horse will travel to the right as he backs up. After three to six steps of backing, straighten the horse and reposition him using the right hand and the right leg and continue backing. While backing if the horse refuses to mind the leg, stop and ask the horse to do a step or two of turn on the forehand, then continue backing. If all else fails and the horse still refuses to back, take a hold of the reins and gently thump his shoulders with the inside of the feet (using one foot and then the other). The minute he backs one step reward him. *Thumping on the shoulders unlocks the shoulders and allows him to back.* Sometimes vibrating the reins with the fingers will also help but do not start to seesaw or pull. Discontinue this as soon as possible. A horse that will mind the leg and back a zig-zag line, will back straight when asked. *Backing strengthens his loin and gaskin areas while making him more submissive.*

134

XII. CIRCLING

When circling, the horse should be on the same arc as the circle and his hind feet should follow in his front footsteps. The rider's inside aids are the bending aids and normally the inside rein is direct and the outside rein is indirect (see Figure 13).

No A--BEND THE HORSE THE SAME AS THE ARC
OF THE CIRCLE. HIS HIND FEET SHOULD FOLLOW
IN HIS FRONT FOOT STEPS LIKE RAILROAD TRACKS.
INSIDE REIN IS A DIRECT REIN. OUTSIDE REIN
IS AN INDIRECT REIN. USE THE INSIDE LEG AT
THE GIRTH AND THE OUTSIDE LEG BEHIND THE GIRTH.
THE RIDER'S OUTSIDE SHOULDER IS BACK AND DOWN.

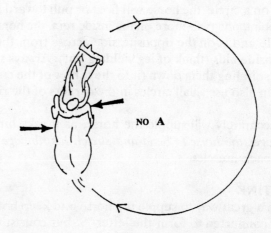

No B - HIS HINDQUARTERS HAVE MOVED TO THE
OF THE CIRCLE. ONE NEEDS MORE WEIGHT DOWN
THE OUTSIDE LEG AND MORE OUTSIDE LEG PRESSURE.

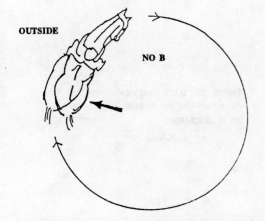

OUTSIDE

No C - HIS HINDQUARTERS HAVE CUT TO THE INSIDE
OF THE CIRCLE. ONE NEEDS MORE INSIDE LEG. HE
ALSO NEEDS MORE WORK TO SUPPLE UP.

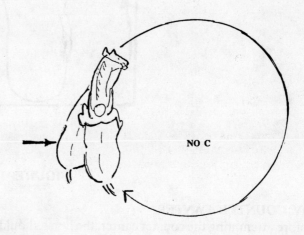

FIGURE 13. CIRCLING

Occasionally, the inside rein may become indirect; if the rider does it all the time, he is probably only bending the horse's head and neck and not his body. The inside leg is used at the girth to bend the horse and the outside leg is back and on, to keep the hindquarters from swinging to the outside of the circle. Remember the horseshoe and the anvil. The outside rein and leg must block or hold, or your horse will go sideways instead of bending. The inside leg bends the horse and causes him to take a "feel" of the outside rein. A common saying is "push the horse from the inside leg to the outside rein."

If nothing is felt in the outside hand, one may be trying to bend using only the inside rein and not enough inside leg. To correct this make sure the inside rein is direct (not indirect) and increase the inside leg. If the rider leans in, the horse will drop his inside shoulder, and at times the rider will need to drop his or her outside shoulder back

135

and down. Some horses like to drop their shoulders in or fall in, and this can be corrected by lifting and raising the inside elbow and shoulder. The hand will only raise an inch or two. Raising the hand without lifting the elbow and shoulder does not give the same results.

In circling, the rider is always having to make minor adjustments to keep the circle round because of "magnets" that are pulling on the horse. Magnets, for example, are other horses, the ring gate or his barn. Riding by the gate (magnet) while on a circle, the horse will float or pull toward the gate and the rider will need to increase the outside aids. If, at that point, one pulls more on the inside rein, the horse will bulge and drift even more. As the horse continues around the circle and is on the opposite side across from the gate, he will try to cut in or cross the circle and will need stronger inside aids (think of leg yielding out). Always start with large circles (sixty feet in diameter) and then vary the size by spiraling them down (into the center of the circle) and then back up to large circles (back out toward the rail). You can also use small circles in the corners of the ring or any time the horse rushes and loses his balance.

Doing circles accurately will supple the horse, as it asks him to reach up under himself with his inside hind leg. *Circling encourages the horse to bend and stretch his rib cage and to go "on the bit."* Going "on the bit" encourages him to use his back muscles.

XIII. SERPENTINE
Serpentines are a great way to supple the horse and keep both the rider and horse from getting bored. Serpentines are half circles connected to form the letter "S" but consist of three or more loops. (Figure 14). In between each half circle straighten the horse and rebend for the next half circle. While doing serpentines one can also practice arcing in and out and adjust the horse's stride from short to long.

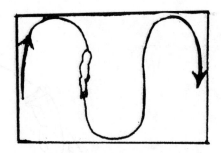

THESE ARE HALF CIRCLES THAT CONSIST OF THREE OR MORE LOOPS

FIGURE 14. SERPENTINE

XIV. COUNTER CANTER
Before attempting the counter canter, the horse should understand the aids for the correct canter departures. Counter canter (cantering on the incorrect lead) is a great stretching and balancing exercise. This is easiest to begin by being several feet off the rail and asking for the wrong lead. If the horse will not pick up the wrong lead start on the correct lead and then cross the diagonal to put the horse on the wrong lead. Be careful, as one approaches the rail, not to make a sharp turn or he might change leads. Once he will counter canter down the long side of the ring, then attempt to continue along the short side of the ring (hold strong with the inside leg). Large circles at the counter canter will help the horse balance up and reach with his front leading leg (left lead, left leg).

XV. TRANSITIONS
Shortening and lengthening the horse's stride works like an accordion and encourages him to shift his weight backward and use his back muscles. The rhythm should not change in lengthening. He should stretch and lengthen his stride and not let the stride get quick and short. In shortening his stride he should become more compressed, not slower, and he should still reach with his hind legs up under himself.

136

Transitions are changes in gaits as in shortening and lengthening or as in trot to canter. Transitions make the horse more responsive, supple, and agile. Before asking for any transition, one needs to rebalance the horse by giving him a half-halt. For a horse to go from a canter to a trot correctly, he must go forward into the trot and not lose his impulsion. In the halt the horse should step under with his hind legs and not fall on his forehand. If he wants to hollow his back as he is stopping, try to stay in a two point position and sink into the front of your thighs, and not hit him in his back which would cause him to hollow.

There are several methods to correct a horse that falls on his forehand as he is stopping. One method is for the rider to lift his or her arms as he or she stops. Do not pull back, just lift. Then hold and have the horse back up a step or two. As one prepares to lift, slump and let all of the air out of the lungs. This puts all of the rider's weight in the seat and keeps one from bracing. Before stopping, one uses the legs to push the horse up to lighten his shoulders and then asks for the halt. Another method is to bury the knuckles into his neck and use a supporting leg to keep his hindquarters under him. Do not hesitate to use voice commands. A horse that is running away with the rider is on his forehand and the rider must first use his legs to push the horse's hindquarters under him, so he can then balance up and slow down. If one uses only hands to pull, the horse will bury himself on his front end and the rider will have a tug-of-war. Continue applying leg pressure and then try a give-and-take of rein pressure. If that does not work, then bury one hand in his neck and use a pulley rein, but always use the leg aid.

CONCLUSION
By doing these exercises, the horse will become more supple and balanced, with less resistance. Suppleness is especially helpful for horses in therapeutic riding programs, as it enhances the quality of their movement. This also enables the older horse to extend his years of performance. After suppling, one will find the horse more enjoyable to ride.

7.07 CAVALLETTI WORK

Judy Rector, Trainer

Cavalletti or gymnastic work is a very good way of suppling a horse. Cavalletti are poles placed on the ground or poles attached to wooden "X"s at both ends so that they can be raised to three different heights. The lowest height is only an inch or two off the ground and the highest is between 18 inches to two feet high. By spacing this equipment at different intervals one can stretch and strengthen the horse's back muscles and encourage him to work more off his hocks. The horse will find the change of work very enjoyable and at times rather stimulating. THE DIAGRAMS TO FOLLOW START WITH THE SIMPLEST EXERCISE AND PROGRESS TO THE MORE CHALLENGING. TO MAKE A TALLER FENCE THE CAVALLETTI MAY BE STACKED ON TOP OF EACH OTHER OR STACKED TO FORM A PYRAMID. Walk the horse over a single pole, then trot the pole. When he is relaxed and not rushing the single pole, advance to trotting three poles (two poles encourages the horse to jump over them). Gradually add poles until he can trot four to six poles quietly. The poles should be placed between four to five feet apart, with four and one half feet being the average. Once he is relaxed with the poles, double the distance from the last pole and add another pole (Figure 1). After one has trotted through this a few times, change the last pole to a cavalletti at its highest or a cross rail; the horse will now jump out over the small jump (Figure 2A). Once the horse is going freely forward, relaxed and fairly straight, then add a second fence 18 feet after the first fence (this makes one canter stride) (Figure 2A).

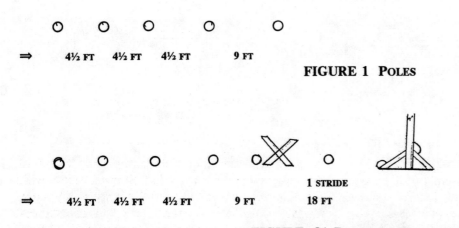

⇒   4½ FT   4½ FT   4½ FT   9 FT

FIGURE 1 POLES

⇒   4½ FT   4½ FT   4½ FT   9 FT   18 FT
                                              1 STRIDE

FIGURE 2A POLES AND CAVALLETTI

If the horse is rushing through the exercise or not rounding his back, place a pole 9 feet after both fences. Later one can place a third fence 21 feet after the second fence (Figure 2B). The second and third fences may be made into oxers or spread fences. By having the front rail lower at first (ramp effect), it gives the horse more time to

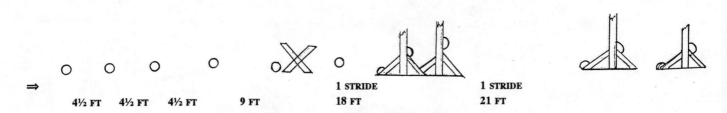

⇒   4½ FT   4½ FT   4½ FT   9 FT   1 STRIDE   1 STRIDE
                                          18 FT   21 FT

FIGURE 2B CAVALLETTI AND FENCE

get his front end up. Parallel rails encourage the horse to become tidier with both ends and round more over the fence. Gradually one can widen the oxers up to 5 to 6 feet, which encourage the horse to use his back and stretch over the fence. Later the second fence can be moved to 29 feet which will give you two strides (not including the landing from the fence). The above exercises are to be approached at the trot and are set accordingly. These fences are small and a horse takes off only 2 to 3 feet in front of a 2 foot fence and lands the same distance away. When one reads or hears that a one stride in and out is 24 feet that is assuming one is cantering in and that the horse lands 6 feet in, canters a 12 foot stride and takes off 6 feet out. Cantering distances for fences 3 feet and higher are:

One stride--24 feet, Two strides--36 feet, Three strides--48 feet, Four strides--60 feet Five strides--72 feet

One may need to shorten the distances between fences if the horse has a short stride or is a pony. By rolling the ground pole out in front of the jump, one will encourage the horse to stand off in front of the fence and not come under it. If one wishes to change the fence to a three stride, add 10 feet for small fences and 11 feet for larger fences. A four stride would be 49 to 50 feet while trotting. This is shown in illustration 2C. The more strides between fences, the more room for error and the more one must help the horse. At one and two strides the horse pretty much just jumps in and out, and the rider just supports and guides his horse. After the horse is comfortable with one and

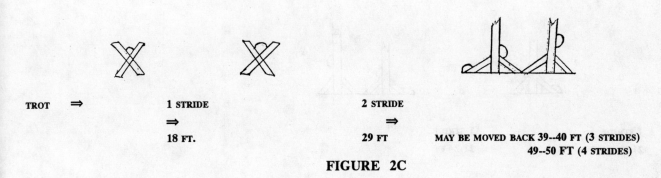

TROT ⇒   1 STRIDE   2 STRIDE
                ⇒   ⇒
                18 FT.   29 FT   MAY BE MOVED BACK 39--40 FT (3 STRIDES)
                                                 49--50 FT (4 STRIDES)

FIGURE 2C

two stride gymnastics, he can begin to learn to do bounces or no strides. Bounces encourage the horse to round his back and spring off his hocks. If the bounces are too long a distance, the horse will get flat. Start as before with trot poles to a cavalletti or cross rail. Ten feet after the cavalletti add a second cavalletti and the horse will bounce in and out. Later add another cavalletti 11 feet after the second one. More cavalletti may be added at 11 feet distances (Figure 3A). With fences higher than 2 feet 6 inches or 3 feet, the distance may need to be adjusted to 11-12 feet. Do not do over six bounces in a row as it makes some horses anxious, which shows up as rushing.

TROT   4½ FT   4½ FT   9 FT   BOUNCE   BOUNCE
⇒   10 FT   11 FT

FIGURE 3A

139

A good exercise is three bounces to a one stride, followed by a one stride to a second fence (Figure 3B). Bounces are normally vertical fences (not oxers or spreads). Another variation is to trot in to a one stride, then to a bounce and then two strides to another fence (Figure 4).

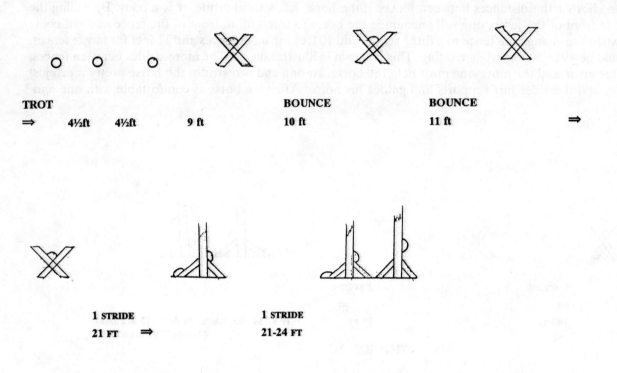

TROT				BOUNCE	BOUNCE	
⇒	4½ft	4½ft	9 ft	10 ft	11 ft	⇒

1 STRIDE   1 STRIDE
21 FT   ⇒   21-24 FT

FIGURE 3B

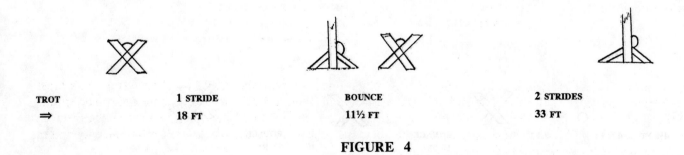

TROT	1 STRIDE	BOUNCE	2 STRIDES
⇒	18 FT	11½ FT	33 FT

FIGURE 4

140

Canter work should start by cantering a single pole, until one can help place the horse so that his front feet are only a foot or so in front of the pole he is cantering over. When he comes in wrong, he straddles the pole with his front legs. After both of you have become comfortable with one pole then add a second pole 9 feet from the first pole. This is a very easy canter stride. Later add a third pole 9 feet from the second pole. Three poles are a good number to use for cantering. If the horse has a good size stride then one will want to come in on a steady stride and if necessary, a backward stride to meet the first pole correctly. This means that as you approach the pole the horse's stride gets shorter and one adds a stride to be able to meet the pole correctly. If one would lengthen and leave out a stride, the horse would be on too long a step (stride) for the other poles. The opposite is true if one is on a pony or a short strided horse. One must ride forward and leave out, not add, a stride if necessary to meet the pole correctly, so that the horse has lengthened his stride to reach through the poles. To add a small jump

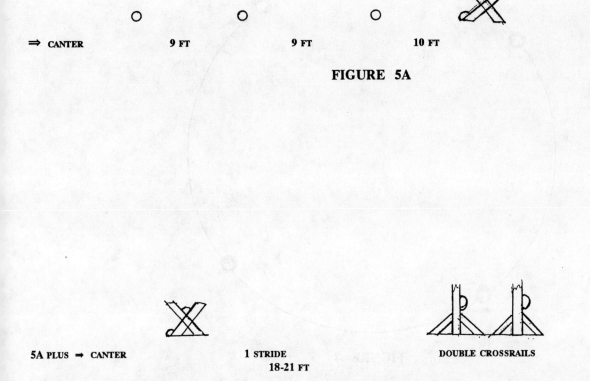

⇒ CANTER   9 FT   9 FT   10 FT

FIGURE 5A

5A PLUS ➡ CANTER   1 STRIDE   DOUBLE CROSSRAILS
                          18-21 FT

FIGURE 5B

go 10 feet after the last pole and build it (Figure 5A). When this is comfortable go 18 to 21 feet and add a cross rail. Then make the cross rail a spread by adding a second cross rail (Figure 5B). The double cross rail can be spread to measure 5 to 6 feet moving the rear cross rail back (this will not change the distance). The shorter the distance between fences and the higher the fences, the more the horse will rock off his hocks. The double cross rail encourages the horse to round his back and look down at the fence.

Canter pole work can be used to lengthen the horse's stride, stretch his back help him and reach with his shoulders. Begin with the three poles set at 9 feet apart. Then lengthen them to 10 feet apart, then to 11 and later to 12 feet apart (Figure 6). At first he will feel like he must gallop and hurry to do 12 foot strides, but he will soon

CANTER   **10 FT**   **10 FT ⟶**   (CHANGE TO 11 FT, THEN TO 12 FT)

FIGURE 6

be able to do them by lengthening his stride and he will not have to hurry. Another exercise is to put four poles on a large circle (60 feet or larger in diameter) (Figure 7). While cantering, practice meeting each pole correctly either by lengthening or shortening his stride. Later one can count the number of strides between the poles and then practice adding or leaving out strides.

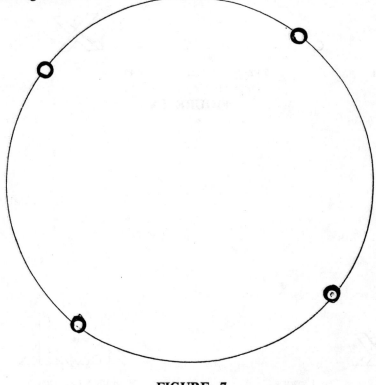

FIGURE 7

Cavalletti work, gymnastics, once or twice a week will keep the horse's attitude positive while it strengthens his back and hindquarters.

TERMS:
Parallel rails--a spread fence consisting of two lines of poles set parallel to each other
Spreading--an obstacle designed to test a horse's ability to jump widths as well as heights
Oxers--any spread fence; an ordinary hedge with a guard rail set about a yard from it on one side. Oxers have 2 or 3 pr of standards
Fence--any obstacle used in jumping
Verticles--straight fences with 1 pr of "standards" or "wings"

142

7.08 SCHOOLING THE THERAPEUTIC RIDING HORSE
HOW TO USE ABLE BODIED RIDERS TO HELP PROGRAM ANIMALS STAY FIT AND HAPPY.

Sunny Pfifferling, BS

> **KEY WORDS**
> ORGANIZATION AND RESPONSIVENESS
> CARE, FITNESS AND ABILITY

Many of us became acquainted with therapeutic riding because of our passion for horses. Often, in the course of carrying out treatment, we become so focused on the progress of our riders that we lose sight of the progress and maintenance of our horses. Those wonderful creatures that originally drew us to this field require ongoing schooling to keep them balanced, fit, responsive and mentally healthy.

How often and how much schooling really depends upon your program, staff, and level of training of each individual horse. The majority of horses in our program (Loveway*) work an average of one to four hours a day, five days a week. Most are in walk/trot classes; in therapeutic riding classes they canter and jump on a limited basis, usually one to three classes a week. Not all of our horses are capable of or are permitted to canter or jump. Be realistic about your horse's physical condition, as well as their ability to carry your students safely. Not all horses who canter and jump make suitable therapeutic riding horses. Conversely, not all suitable therapeutic riding horses need to canter or jump.

We try to keep our horses schooled by competent riders twice a week. Some horses need less. Newer program horses require more. I feel it is most beneficial to alternate a schooling session in the arena with a relaxed hack outdoors. Methods of schooling will vary with your resources and your horse's needs: longeing, long-reining, ground driving and ponying can be utilized as well as work under saddle. This is especially beneficial for ponies too small to be ridden. I will not go into "how" to school the therapy horse, because you know the type of work and needs of all your horses. Each animal will need to be schooled individually. Basically, the purpose of schooling is to maintain the horse's fitness, responsiveness, obedience, balance and mental health. A horse that is properly schooled should be easy to handle by any of your students and volunteers.

Your methods will vary according to your program's goals as well as your horse's individual needs - there is no formula. It is valuable to keep a chart listing each horse's needs and training goals (Figure 1), and to update it annually as these goals are met. Often a horse may develop an inappropriate behavior due to boredom, and you will need to

---

TRAINING SCHEDULE

Sundance--FITNESS GOAL: 20 minutes of trot and canter with normal respiration
SCHOOLING GOALS:
1. Eliminate behavior problems during grooming, tacking and mounting
2. Eliminate head yanking while ridden
3. Maintain steady, slow trot rhythm
4. Developing a slow, balanced canter

Muri - FITNESS GOALS: 30 minutes of trot and canter work with normal respiration.
SCHOOLING GOALS:
1. Softening to rider's hand on turns and transitions
2. Voice response to walk on, whoa, trot and canter
3. Steady and quiet over cavalletti and small jumps

FIGURE 1. HORSE NEEDS AND GOALS

indicate a short term goal of eliminating that behavior. Every schooling rider should be given a chart of "Horse Needs and Goals" (Figure 1); we also post one in the tackroom. Schooling should be done at times when there are no therapeutic riding classes in session, unless it can be accomplished without distracting your program students. If your program is anything like ours, we never have the staff or time to keep our horses schooled adequately. Our first rule is never, never advertise that program volunteers can ride the horses for recreation. Allowing that to occur will undoubtably do damage to your horses. In addition your program's reputation for professionalism, not to mention your liability, may be threatened. You will find "volunteers" crawling out of the woodwork who would do you the great favor of exercising your horses. Usually these volunteers are of the teenage variety, and are not interested in benefitting the horses as much as their own pleasure, and more than likely cannot ride at all. PRINT IN YOUR VOLUNTEER TRAINING MANUAL THAT VOLUNTEERS ARE NOT PERMITTED TO RIDE, AND STATE YOUR REASONS. Make your position clear, and do not make exceptions. Volunteers are more easily replaced than ruined horses (Figure 2). It is most advisable to recruit competent schooling riders from outside your program. Adults are preferable for their reliability, judgement, and understanding of your program's needs. A good source is lesson barns - inquire if there are any intermediate or advanced students who would like additional riding time.

As you get to know your program volunteers, you may discover that some may be competent riders; find out what experience they have, and what their current level of riding is. If you feel confident that a volunteer would be a suitable schooling rider, talk to him or her privately about schooling for you and arrange a try-out session to evaluate his or her riding ability.

You may also submit an article to your local horse publications explaining your need for schooling riders, and the criteria required for acceptance. The more organized you portray your schooling rider program, the more serious and dedicated schooling riders you will attract. Be realistic with yourself: a novice rider, no matter how nice, is not going to be an effective schooling rider. They will usually do damage to your horses that you will need to un-do yourself.

Set up a time for try-outs; we use a combination of riding and written tests not only to weed out the unsuitable candidates, but also to evaluate riding styles so that our schooling assignments assure the best match-ups.

Above all, make it clear to your potential schooling riders that they are doing a job that is vitally important to your program's success. They should be trained and monitored as extensively as your program volunteers. They also need to be understanding of how special your horses are, as well as of the type and amount of work they do.

Another schooling option that has worked for us is to recruit advanced level Pony Clubbers or 4H-ers to ride as a group in a weekly supervised schooling session. We found the advantages to be:
- Many of these children are small enough to school your smaller ponies
- The class will simulate an actual therapeutic class; problems that your program students encounter, such as a horse not staying on the rail while the others are parked in the middle, can be dealt with successfully by competent riders
- You can get a good number of horses/ponies schooled in a small amount of time
- Your program instructor should oversee each schooling session--and stress that it is not a riding lesson

You may find that there are some wonderful and dedicated people who are interested in being schooling riders, yet lack the necessary riding capabilities. As well as encouraging them to obtain riding instruction, you can still use these people in various functions, such as:
1. Ground work with horses:
   a. Body work, such as T.T.E.A.M. work
   b. Schooling on the lead line
   c. Introducing new horses to wheelchairs, games, balls, and so forth
   d. Ground driving, longeing
   e. Grooming, clipping, mane-pulling

2. "Under saddle" work at the walk only, such as:
   a. Teaching the horse to stand immobile while being mounted
   b. Teaching the horse to respond to verbal cues, such as walk on, whoa
   c. Teaching a horse to neck rein
   d. Assisting the instructor when introducing backriding, vaulting positions on the horse

Depending upon the number and types of horses and schooling riders you have, you may want either to assign riders to horses, or post a weekly list of horses to be schooled in priority of needs.

The ideal situation for schooling is to have your program's staff school the program horses. Since most programs do not have the time or staff available to accomplish this, it is vital to your horses' physical and mental health to keep them conditioned, responsive, and happy. Your staff, particularly the instructors, should work more extensively with the newer program horses. This is important for understanding their moods and movement, finding any hidden "holes" in them, and to prepare them specifically for their job as a therapeutic riding horse. Recruit as many schooling riders as you see the need for--realistically look at each horse's age, ability, level of training, fitness and workload and assign your schooling riders accordingly.

SCHOOL RIDING POLICY

1. To help in decreasing Loveway's utility costs, and to give the horses and ponies a break from being ridden
   a. The barn will be closed at 9 pm in the evening
   b. The arena heaters are to be used by Loveway classes only
   c. The barn will be closed on weekends to all volunteers, students, and community service workers --some exceptions with prior board approval

2. Regarding Hartwood Pony Club:
   a. Hartwood PC shall not hold its monthly meetings at Loveway.
   b. Pony Club members shall be considered volunteers at Loveway, and agree.
      - That all schooling be done in supervised lessons under the instruction of Sunny or Marcia
      - That Pony clubbers agree to school Loveway horses/ponies specifically for Loveway's purpose and needs
      - That the supervised lessons be conducted every Monday night from 5:30 to 6:30pm
      - That all members wear boots and Pony Club approved helmets
      - That all members will school only the horses/ponies selected by Marcia and Sunny

3. Regarding Schooling Riders
   Definition: A schooling rider is a competent equestrian chosen by the Loveway staff to school and exercise Loveway horses/ponies selected by the Loveway staff. Schooling riders work to maintain the horses'/ponies' fitness, obedience, responsiveness, and to correct behavior problems:
      - That Loveway utilize Pony Club members as schooling riders on Monday night supervised lessons only.
      - That schooling riders must school, on staff-selected horse/pony each time they school, with the option of working with other horses if they desire in the time following on that day.
      - That schooling riders school at Loveway a minimum of once a week.
      - That Loveway staff increase or decrease the number of riders, depending on the need and subject to prior Board approval.
      - That any schooling rider may be dropped from the program following the disregard for written rules or endangerment to Loveway animals, facility or property.

FIGURE 2. SCHOOLING POLICY

The results of a successful schooling schedule will be evident in your therapeutic riding lessons: your students will be achieving their goals with the help of capable horses that are willingly doing their job. Good luck, and may you always have happy horses!

Figure 1, 2, 3, and 4 are samples of the paperwork use with our schooling riders. You will obviously want to adapt them to fit your individual program's needs.

SCHOOLING RIDER LOG

Week of January 23-29

Horse	Name	Day	Time	Method	Place
Chantel	Marcia	1-23	12:30-2:00	hack	road
Cosby	Kelly	1-23	30 min	schooling	inside
Sundance	Sunny	1-24	7:00-8:00	longe	inside
Choker	Brace	1-24	5:30-6:30	lesson	inside
Ginger	Chris	1-24	5:30-6:00	schooling	inside

FIGURE 3. RIDING LOG

LOVEWAY SCHOOLING RIDER AGREEMENT

1. That the horses/ponies schooled be worked for Loveway's therapeutic riding program, and not for individual recreation.
2. That the schoolers work with the horse(s) listed in order first, and work option horse(s) afterward
3. That all schoolers wear Pony Club approved helmets, boots or shoes with heels at all times when riding.
4. That the horses are not ridden beyond the rider's capabilities unless properly instructed in a lesson.
5. That the priorities in schooling be:
   a. Maintaining safe and appropriate behavior (no nibbling, dragging, pushing leader or walker while being mounted)
   b. Maintaining obedience and responsiveness to voice aids before using physical aids (legs and hands).
   c. Maintaining the horse's responsiveness to turning, keeping steady pace, staying on the rail without using undue force (so that Loveway students can handle them easily).
   d. Correcting any habits or behaviors indicated (neck yanking, aggressiveness, not keeping pace).
   e. Reporting to the Loveway staff any problems, questions, or noted progress.
   f. Horses/ponies shall not be jumped any higher than 2 ft, and then only with prior consent.

I have read above agreement and understand it is my privilege to school the Loveway horses/ponies.

Signed_____

Parent/guardian if under 18_____Date_____

FIGURE 3

146

LOVEWAY SCHOOL RIDING RULES

1. All schooling must be carried out at times when there are no classes in session at Loveway.

2. Schooling must be completed by 8:00 pm.

3. Any schooling rider under age 18 must have a parent present at all times while at Loveway.

4. A commitment of once a week is requested.

5. Schoolers must work horses listed in order of priority.

6. No weekend schooling without prior board (Director's) approval.

7. No solo riding off Loveway premises.

8. No cantering or galloping outside of the arena, i. e., roads.

9. All horses schooled must be logged-in on the clip board.

10. All horses must be ridden in saddles and their own bridles.

11. All horses/ponies schooled must have at least 5 minutes of warm up and cool down at the walk.

12. All horses must be worked according to goals posted.

13. When schooling in the arena, plan on 20-60 minutes per horse.

14. Schooling riders are requested to make note of any lameness or problem discovered.

15. All schooling riders must wear Pony Club approved helmet with harness attached, long pants, boots or shoes with a heel.

16. All schooling riders must leave the barn, arena, and tackroom as they found it. When you are the last to leave the barn, please:
     1. Make sure all doors and gates are latched
     2. All lights are out except entrance floodlight
     3. Tackroom door is locked
     4. Loveway front lobby doors must be kept unlocked

FIGURE 5. SCHOOL RULES

* Loveway Inc, Bristol, IN

7.09   TRAILERING THE PROGRAM HORSE

Jean Hoffman, BS

One of the many skills a horse person needs to know is how to trailer a horse safely. Traveling always has many variables, such as time, weather and road conditions, so planning ahead is key for the horse's safety and the owner's sanity. This guide will cover basic safety tips for trailer maintenance, loading and unloading, and traveling. In addition to these hints, remember to use common sense, obey the traffic laws, and try not to travel alone. It is also wise to belong to an organization such as an auto club that provides emergency roadside assistance. The best way to avoid needing such assistance is to maintain your vehicles.

TRAILER MAINTENANCE
A safety check should be done on a trailer before traveling, whether you own the trailer or are borrowing one, and before buying a used one. Look at the biggest problem areas first, starting with the metal shell. Check for rust everywhere: exterior, wheelwells, floor supports, ramp, hinges, springs, chains, partitions and hooks. While rusting hooks or hinges may not look like a problem, they can stick at the worst possible moment and be dangerous. Next, examine the flooring on the ramp and inside the trailer. The floor is usually made of wooden planks. Look for problems such as dry rot, termites, worn spots and water damage (especially under rubber mats). It may help to seal the floor with a wood preservative.

Lastly, inspect the electrical wiring, lights (bulbs and covers), wheels and bearings, brakes, and tires, including the spare. A professional inspection of these major areas should be done about once a year. In addition, the trailer and towing vehicle should be checked about once a month in the applicable areas: tire wear, air pressure, headlights, brake lights and signals, oil and fluid levels, brake wear, and hitch parts. In other words, all parts that move or slide should do so easily, all stationary parts should be strong and sturdy, and every component should do its job. Finally, make sure all vehicle registration and insurance is up to date, all horses have up-to-date health certificates and Coggins test papers when necessary, and that the horses are not sharing their traveling quarters with hornets or wasps' nests.

LOADING AND UNLOADING
The most important part about loading is this - don't wait until the travel day to try it. Loading horses into a trailer requires practice and patience. The time spent at home quietly teaching a horse to walk in and out of a trailer will pay off. It seems that every horse show has a scene at the end of a long day where a desperate owner and several onlookers spend hours prodding an animal back into the trailer for the ride home. A bad struggle or injury at a time like this is enough to keep a horse from ever going back in a trailer.

In order to protect the horse from injury while traveling, the following pieces of equipment are recommended.
- Head bumper
- Fleece-covered halter, tail wrap or padded tail chain or bar on trailer
- Day sheet or light blanket (optional)
- Non-skid rubber floor mats

There is a fine line between restraining a horse for its protection and releasing it in an emergency. For instance, leather halters, panic snaps or quick-release knots allow a horse to escape when in danger, yet strong lead ropes with sturdy snaps keep the creature from leaving whenever he pleases. Likewise, the animal should be tied loosely enough so he can raise and lower his head enough to eat and maintain balance, but tight enough so that he cannot get himself into trouble or bother his traveling companion. When the horse is properly outfitted for travel, prepare the trailer for him. The trailer should always be hitched to the towing vehicle before the horse is inside, to provide stability. Park the vehicle on level ground and away from possibly dangerous obstructions, such as fence posts and machinery. If possible, try parking the trailer in an aisle so that the horse is more likely to go inside than around

148

it. Since horses do not like dark holes (and who can blame them), turn on the lights inside the trailer and open the windows and escape doors. If the horse is being loaded for the first time, practice without the partition in the trailer. Also, keep onlookers away from the trailer entrance and the horse to keep from scaring him away from the vehicle. When ready lead him in by walking in front of him (for trailers with escape doors) or standing beside him as he enters. Always secure the tail-chain or bar behind the animal before tying his head. Likewise, untie the horse before releasing the tail chain when unloading. Terrible accidents can occur when a horse runs back, finds his head is tied and panics.

Once horses and equipment are loaded safely, the trip begins. To ensure the animals' comfort, drive as if in slow motion. That is, all maneuvers such as braking and turning should be done slowly and smoothly, as if one's self were in the trailer. It may help to pull an empty trailer to practice. Slant load trailers also help the horses to balance themselves. In fact, many experienced horse people claim that horses will most often travel standing diagonally or backward rather than forward when given a choice. In any case, they are safer when tied with a lead rope or in crossties than untied. If a horse is traveling alone in a two-horse trailer, most horse people will load the animal on the left side, since roads tend to slant to the right. As for choosing a ramp-loading or step-up type trailer, personal preference is the only rule. Horses can be trained to load either way. When it comes time to unload, common sense dictates that the same basic rules apply as for loading. Most importantly, <u>always</u> untie the horse's head <u>before</u> undoing the tail bar or chain. Other hints include:

- Back the horse out slowly and toward the center of the ramp, so he does not fall off the side and scare himself.
- Be cautious when unloading the first horse, so the second horse does not try to back out at the same time or panic thinking he will be left behind.
- Walk the horses to help their circulation before putting them back in their stalls.
- Remember to put blocks behind the trailer wheels when the vehicle is disconnected and parked.

Equipment:
Traveling can be made safer and easier by carrying the appropriate equipment. What is actually taken on a trip depends on space allowances and, again, one's belief in Murphy's Law. Each horseman must decide what is best for his situation, but here are some recommendations.

1. Tool kit, including:
    o swiss army knife (to cut lead ropes in an emergency)
    o crowbar
    o screwdriver
    o pliers
    o hammer
    o wrench
    o work gloves
    o flashlight
    o spare batteries
    o WD 40 or grease
2. First aid kit--for horses and humans
3. Jumper cables

4. Bucket
5. Sponges--towels
6. Spare tire--jack for truck and trailer
7. Flares
8. Plastic bottle of water (for car or animals)
9. Extra lead ropes--halters
10. Hay--other feed for trip
11. Maps and phone numbers needed
12. Tools
    o Rake
    o shovel
    o broom
    o plastic bags for cleaning out the trailer

Happy Trails!

8   STABLE MANAGEMENT FOR THERAPEUTIC RIDING HORSES

INTRODUCTION
Stable management is an important consideration of a therapeutic riding program since the health and a good attitude are vital for all horses working with persons with disabilities. This chapter will highlight some important aspects of stable management including the nature of the horse and how he reacts to his environment, hoof care, feeding principals, and basic care.

8.01   NATURE OF THE HORSE

Lita Hughes, BS

WHY IS ONE CONCERNED WITH THE BEHAVIOR OF THE HORSE ?
Humans have an attraction to a horse--a bonding as strong as with a dog. Yet humans want to command this beast that is eight times the size of a human but with a brain that is one-eighth as big as man's brain. The modern horse has had to adapt to our domestic patterns of living. The horse's brain has had little or no change during the past five thousand years (Smythe, 1965). The change that one might recognize in his behavior is the distinction between intelligence untutored and the same degree of intelligence awakened by education (McCall, 1975).

The difficulty in separating intelligence from the tangled skein of characteristics that determine an animal's ability to get along in the world puts a crimp in the human's wish to stereotype.
- If intelligence is the ability to create patterns from the hundreds of stimuli that strike the senses and use this understanding to manipulate the environment--then horses possess a moderate allotment of this ability.
- If intelligence is the ability to solve problems--more than the simple trial and error of getting the gate open--horses are not terribly well-endowed.
- If intelligence is understanding and dealing with new and trying situations, then horses' brains are poorly endowed; their "fight or flight" response (the primitive response to stress) predominates.
- If intelligence is the capacity to think abstractly, then the horse is lacking in this ability.

Horses learn to discriminate very well. Tests were performed to determine the equine abilities in the following areas by providing food rewards (McCall, 1975):
- The equine ear can distinguish between 96 and 100 beats of a metronome; 1000 and 1025 cycles per second; 67-70 decibels.
- The equine eye can distinguish between 87 and 90 watts.

Domestication favors animals that adjust to human lifestyles and needs. Horses and other domestic animals learn from repetition and adjust their behaviors to achieve and avoid (Smythe, 1965). Even adjustments differ within the species. Not all horses are created equal. Fillies may outshine geldings, and geldings may outshine colts in learning quickly. Quarter horses learn faster to discriminate grain in pictures than thoroughbreds, however the thoroughbred shows more fine tuning in initial body response (McCall, 1975). Training has taken advantage of these particular specialties allowing the quarter horse to use his eyes somewhat like a sheep dog, and the quick muscle twitch of the thoroughbred to enable him to race.

Many of the activities that one observes in horses are not acts reflecting intelligence but rather patterns of behavior. All horses exhibit nine behaviors (McCall, 1975):
1. Ingestive behavior (feeding)
2. Eliminative behavior (urination & defecation)
3. Contactual behavior (protective and bonding)
4. Epimeletic behavior (giving care and attention)

5. Et-epimeletic behavior (calling for care and attention)
6. Investigative behavior (sensory environmental inspection)
7. Sexual behavior
8. Allelomimetic behavior (mimicry)
9. Agonistic behavior (fighting or conflict)

INGESTIVE BEHAVIORS

All living creatures need to eat and drink (ingestive behavior) in some manner. This is a strong instinctive behavior. Horses are grazers and their digestive systems are anatomically adapted to accommodate small amounts of food at frequent intervals. Therefore, they must be fed small amounts frequently. Hay is a natural food and should be given before graining, with as much pasture or free foraging as possible. If there is enough balanced nutrition in a pasture the horse will need grain only according to his "work" load. If he eats his food quickly, put large rocks in his tub to help slow him down. Bad feeding habits start from boredom, lack of roughage or nutrients, lack of exercise or can be learned from a companion.

In the horse's natural environment, the leader takes his herd to the best streams and grasses. Food can also be effectively used to train or distract a horse and change his responses in unpleasant or frightening situations. A trainer giving food reward is much appreciated by the horse but not necessarily associated with having done a task correctly. A horse will only associate an immediate prior action to receiving the food. For example if a handler regularly rewards a horse for stopping by going into his pockets and giving his horse a carrot, the horse associates this reward with the sound or motion of going into the pocket, not necessarily the act of stopping. However, a horse that gets treats and plenty of positive attention from his handler is inclined to do new things more quickly than one who receives nothing. Proper reward depends on timing.

ELIMINATIVE BEHAVIORS

Horses will eliminate when they have to or as a result of activity, anxiety or marking their territory. Marking, often exhibited by the "flehmen position" with extended neck, head and a curled upper lip may define territory as well as being a means of communication among equines. Urinating patterns define dominance among a herd; stallions urinate over a mare's fresh urine when she is in heat to diminish her attraction to other stallions. Defecation may also be related to stress. As part of the fight or flight response the body eliminates and shuts down much of the digestive system, directing blood flow to skeletal muscles. Male horses, if slightly alarmed, will stop to smell dung. Their body's response is then to defecate. Horses establish a urination area if enough space is available. Horses will not graze in the elimination area until all other grazing areas are gone. A horse's tendency to be clean rather then dirty is a characteristic learned from the dam. A barn manager can train to preferred elimination areas by cleaning the paddock areas where hay is fed outside, leaving one pile where the elimination areas is wanted. In summer feed the hay in a clean area that has morning sun and may be shaded in the afternoon. Horses will want to stand in the shade in the summer and in the sun in a non-windy spot in the winter. They will move to the periphery of these areas to defecate as long as the areas are otherwise clean.

CONTACTUAL BEHAVIORS

Contactual, also known as herd behavior begins at birth. The mare and foal establish contact immediately after birth. Once the foal is up the mare will touch, nuzzle and attempt to keep herself between the foal and any other horse. The first half hour of imprinting will allow the foal to differentiate between his dam and the other smells and shapes his new systems are receiving. The olfactory system (sense of smell) is quite active immediately after birth and becomes extremely acute. Immediately after birth the new foal will follow any shape until he learns what shape and smell offer him protection and food. His search for food is most immediate and somewhat clumsy, resulting in some nipping or walking off by the mare. Finally the foal suckles, drawing the colostrum and again developing a nurturing reaction from the dam. As the foal develops, his ability and desire to run and play becomes contagious with other foals. This encourages group behavior to develop and the foal learns how to act in a group or alone with his dam. The primary benefit of herd behavior is mutual protection and affection; one herd member may alert others to predators allowing the entire herd to escape.

Contactual behavior can cause training difficulties. Some horses are "sour" about leaving the group.

A trainer can use this behavior by furnishing reassurance that usually comes from other horses. The horse then learns to rely on the trainer for decisions, confidence and ultimately protection in situations where he is unsure.

Riders and trainers must become Alpha (the leader), the number one protector, watching and thinking what the horse needs and a lot of physical and emotional contact must be provided. One must judge how the horse behaves naturally before he is placed in strange and different riding situations.

EPIMELETIC BEHAVIORS
Epimeletic behaviors are nurturing or caring behaviors that encourage a bond to develop between equines. This behavior is also enjoyed by many handlers and disabled persons with their horses. These behaviors start between the mare and foal and are often seen throughout the horse's lifetime. Horses are commonly involved in mutual grooming of the withers or hindquarters. Certain body postures show signs of friendship such as one horse's head over another horse's neck or back.

To create a caring relationship a person may brush the horse at least ½ hour daily. Reward him by scratching and use a soothing tone of voice as a reward immediately after, or if possible during a task well done. Reward the horse after the hardest part of the activity by giving the inside rein or scratching the neck and then finish the exercise. It is important to remember that the reward must be given contingent to the response so that the horse learns by association. This kind of a reward system can be an active part of the any rider's responsibility in keeping his mount interested and responsive.

If one has ever noticed the nurturing between children and ponies, it is no wonder that some ponies will act almost dog-like and bond so easily with children. Older riders should take the time to stand with or just walk beside their horse, putting their arm over his neck or back, scratching his withers to establish a caring relationship. Enjoy him! His responses to nurturing make all the attention worthwhile and he will reward one with better performance.

ET-EPIMELETIC BEHAVIOR
Horses signal their desire for nurturing or call out stress signals. These behaviors are identified with vocalizations and movements. Individual owners have described twelve to thirty individual vocalizations. Think of the basic vocalizations of the horse:

1. The whinny: It is amazing that a foal responds to the dam's whinny when it comes into the world. Horses will call to a handler when returning to the barn to feed or call to another horse that he has been separated from.
2. The nicker: A "come closer" sound. The nicker is often directed towards companions including cats, dogs and goats.
3. The squeal: A sound of introduction between new animals and horses displaying battle and mock battle rituals. It is most often heard while one horse smells another's flanks and is often accompanied by pawing or striking out with the forefoot.
4. The shriek or snort: A sound most often associated with the fight or flight response. It is often directed toward a stranger or intruder by the lead horse.
5. The sigh: A sound associated with contentment, the sigh actually occurs when the horse clears his nostrils.
6. The blow: A sound of alarm created by filling the "false nostril" with air and immediately exhaling emitting an incredibly loud and alarming sound. The snort may be a sound of mock battle to develop the hierarchy or it can be heard when a stallion is smelling dung.
7. The growl: This is a sound made deep in the chest of the stallion. In the wild, stallions growl when near dung. In the human's environment, stallions are heard growling when they enter a quiet barn.

Instructors and handlers are aware that horses respond to human sounds. They must recognize the horse's ability to communicate and their highly developed sense of hearing. One is reminded that talking in a quiet voice is more pleasing to the horse than a loud voice which may disturb him!

INVESTIGATIVE BEHAVIOR

Investigative behaviors are displays of curiosity and inspection of the horse's environment. Horses may be curious because of fear, insecurity or the need for leadership. Horses' sensory systems are very well developed. When they are investigating something new, they may use all of their systems - smell, touch, hearing and sight. The slightest sounds and movements can frighten the horse. Often the display of investigative behavior is a redirection behavior, "An activity that is shifted from the stimulus that elicited a motivational conflict to a more neutral substitute object" (Alcock 1976). While being alerted by one stimulus (a new horse in the arena, for example), a paper blows over the fence and makes an unusual noise. This second stimulus causes the horse to divert his attention from the initial stimulus. Instead of fighting or fleeing from the horse, the activity is directed toward the second problem, the paper.

Dealing with these responses can be unsettling. While being alerted by an unfamiliar object all other sensory systems are distorted to receive the information from the stimulus. If one talks to the horse, he may not "hear" you; touch him and he may perceive that you are hitting him. Punishing a horse at this time may only reinforce his "suspicion" that something was there to hurt him.

The handler should redirect the horse's activity or attention to what is expected of him and stay calm. Investigation can result in mischievous accomplishments which can be misinterpreted as learning. A horse rubbing at a stall latch resulting in the door swinging open is accidental. Some horses can associate getting the door open and getting out with getting a nibble of grass as a reward. Some only get the immediate reinforcement of the handler's attention as reward and go no further.

SEXUAL BEHAVIOR

Sexual behavior of horses include all activities associated with courtship and breeding. Sexual patterns are also displayed by geldings. This is because these behaviors are both neurally and hormonally controlled. Sexual behavior plays a role in the dominance hierarchy. Dominance with horses is determined by the temperament of the animals in the group and their tendencies toward sexual displays. Once a hierarchy has been established, threats rather than harmful acts are likely to occur. Even after the hierarchy has been established, problems and reshuffling can still occur. Geldings as well as mares can become the lead horse, driving the herd to and fro.

Estrus periods of mares may negatively affect their learning patterns. When the mare in a therapeutic riding program has a shorter attention span it may help to change her training schedule to increase her attention.

Flehmen, an olfactory response, is associated with stallions "testing" a female's urine to see if she is in heat. This is the strongest stimulus associated with the flehmen response, although it is also seen at other times. The horse raises his neck, compresses and lifts his lips to direct the air molecules towards the roof of his mouth to the Jacobson's organ. This organ may send information to the brain about the percentage of estrogen in the mare's urine. Foals will also do flehmen smelling of their own afterbirth.

ALLELOMIMETIC BEHAVIORS

Allelomimetic behaviors are mimicking behaviors. Horses do imitate or mimic the behaviors of other horses and other animals. Think about horses that are bored. Some may learn bad habits from their stall or pasture mates. Other horses never pick up bad traits such as chewing, cribbing or weaving because they have never been exposed to these vices. This copying behavior can be used to the riders' advantage. One may want to train with other horses that have accomplished the specific task, even if the task is to stand still! Horses will jump an obstacle more willingly when following another horse. To counteract the mimicking behavior, it is good to teach a horse to stand while another horse is working. Watching this mimicking behavior in the field can relay information about the herd hierarchy. Watch which horse rolls, which one imitates on the outskirts (lower in the hierarchy), and which one waits to roll in the prime spot.

AGONISTIC BEHAVIORS

Agonistic behaviors in the horse are the fight or flight response, threat displays and aggressive or submissive behaviors. Most horses' aggressive tendencies are channelled into non-lethal activities to reinforce the hierarchy. Flight is more important to grazing animals than fight. At first it might seem that nature has drastically erred by introducing aggression into the physiological and psychological make up of the grazing animal. However, aggression is often the basis for motivation and an aggressive animal is normally a better provider for and protector of his subordinates.

Handlers may see the quiet postures: ears laid back, head down, one ear back with head raised and shaking, down curved mouth with twisted muzzle and head. These quiet postures may make humans laugh, yet send another horse a totally different message. These displays can signal peaceful intentions with some minor changes: head up, both ears splayed, eyes squinted with ears at rest or forward, head sideways, teeth clapping with head down. Threat displays include biting, and kicking that can develop into driving, stomping, lunging and running. Eye rolling, a very quick posturing that draws the eye protectively into the eye socket, is accompanied by threats of head swinging.

Aggression has its limits. Personality should affect how individual horses are chosen and the tasks they are directed to do. Stallions and stallion-like tendencies are not appropriate for therapeutic riding programs. Often even herd leaders are not well suited; middle-of-the-hierarchy horses are better suited to this activity. Aggression will also affect the way training proceeds. A young horse that has established a high ranking position among his peers may view training as another dominance struggle and often require a firmer, more demanding training program. This program should include lots of reward and establish the trainer as the leader by keeping the horse busy. Once the dominant horse accepts the supremacy of his trainer, he may show much more brilliance and aptitude in learning.

Be sure, however, not to subdue the aggressive horse; this results in lack of natural boldness. If one uses an aggressive animal, learn to control the flow of energy. A submissive animal, on the other hand needs a calm, perhaps more intermittent program. He may allow himself to be drilled, but beware, he is not often in need of it! Horses learn more quickly if the same lesson is not repeated daily.

CONCLUSION
It is essential to regard all equines as individuals, one never truly fitting into the mold of another.
While they all exhibit the same general characteristics (the above presenting only the major behaviors of adult horses), different combinations of these traits may result in many entirely different types of personalities.

Watch the horse. Take time to get to know him. He is truly remarkable.

References
Alcock, J. (1976). *Animal Behavior, An Evolutionary Approach*. Sunderland: Sinauer Associates, Inc. 199.
Kilby, E. (1981). How Smart is Your Horse. *Equus* 46, 22. Gaithersburg: Fleat Street Corporation, MD.
Hamilton, S. (1978). Man's Impact on Behavior, *Equus* 9, Gaithersburg: Fleat Street Corporation, MD.
Equus Staff. (1981). Attitude: The Winning Edge, *Equus* 49. Gaithersburg: Fleat Street Corporation, MD.
Houpt, K. (1980). Two is a Herd. *Equus*. 35 Gaithersburg: Fleat Street Corporation, MD.
McCall, J. (1975). Horse Management - Course notes. College Park, Univ of Maryland.
Smythe, R.H. (1965). *The Mind of the Horse*. Lexington: Stephen Greene Press.
Vavra, R. (1979). *Such is the Real Nature of Horses*. New York: William Morrow & Company, Inc.

8.02   THE HORSE'S REACTION TO HIS ENVIRONMENT

Barbara T. Engel, MEd, OTR

It is important for handlers, helpers, and riders in therapeutic riding programs to have an understanding of the horse's senses in order to be able to understand and communicate effectively with this large animal. "The instinctive reactions of horses must be known and understood in order to anticipate trouble and then work around horses safely" (Lyles, 1980).

The Ability to Smell: The horse's sense of smell is generally felt to be well-developed. A horse will greet another horse by sniffing. Different emotional states give off different odors (Williamson, 1980). He uses smell to identify food, other horses, people, and places. A horse will remember another horse or a person years later from their smell (Ainslie & Ledbetter, 1980). He can smell things one-half mile away and smell a trail to find his way home (Rees, 1985). At times, a strange smell can cause a horse great anxiety.

The Ability to Hear: A horse's hearing is more highly developed than in humans. It has been an important element in his historical survival. He can hear frequencies higher than man and from distances further away (Evans, 1990). The horse's ears move independently of each other and with the ten muscles that control the ear, they can swivel to pick up environmental vibrations for danger cues or for communication. A horse can judge the distance of an object from the vibrations it receives from sounds. He may snort to hear the vibration returning from a nearby wall. He can hear steps or voices and where they come from before humans can hear them. He can tell the difference between people and individual horses through sound (Kiley-Worthington, 1987).

Soft, soothing sounds help the horse to relax. Playing music helps to wipe out distracting sounds and therefore helps to calm a horse during stabling or during a lesson (Liebermann, 1980). Loud noises can be painful to a horse. When sounds make him apprehensive, he may swing his entire body in the direction of the sound. Sharp, loud commands punish a horse. Low, drawn out commands tend to slow a horse down. A firm, fast command will make the horse go faster. Importantly, the horse can hear and remember words for different exercises (Podhajsky, 1965).

The direction a horse points his ears indicates where he has focused his attention. One ear can point forward to where he is going and the other toward the rider to pick up cues (Williamson, 1974). Ears pricked straight forward indicate interest ahead and when he continues to keep them forward for long periods, it may indicate a sight or hearing problem. Flicking an ear back slightly while being ridden indicates that the horse is attending to the rider. The horse also indicates emotions with his ears. Stiffly pricked ears indicate interest. Drooping ears indicate relaxation, exhaustion, or serious illness. Flattened ears indicate anger, threat, fear or rage. Ears flicking back and forth indicate attentiveness or interest.

The Ability to Feel: A horse can easily feel a very light sensation such as a fly on his body or a leg touching his side. He can respond to the tension in a rider's leg. His muzzle and nostrils are especially delicate and the long whiskers increase sensation for more accurate perception of food sources in his environment. The lips respond to heat, cold, pressure and pain. A horse "processes" tactile sensations with its mouth as humans do with their hands (Williamson, 1980). Some body areas of the horse are more sensitive than others, such as the mouth, the ears, the shoulders, the lower leg, the flank, and the neck. Awareness of pain has protected the horse from danger or injury throughout its evolution. A horse's sense of touch when compared to humans is more acute and sensitive. A horse feels and responds to changes in touch more than to continuous touch, such as steady pressure from the leg or saddle. Susceptibility to touch varies from horse to horse and changes with its emotional state. A drowsy horse is less likely to react to touch than an alert horse and will be less responsive to aids. An anxious or temperamental horse has increased sensitivity. Anger or fear may decrease a horse's awareness or response.

The Ability to See: A horse is probably able to see colors and movement much as humans do (Kiley-Worthington, 1987). He can see quite well both at night and at distances, but his depth perception and focal adjustments appear to be slow and poor. Perhaps this is why a horse may startle or stare at a strange object, especially when seen at the edge of his visual field. Fine focus begins to blur at one and one-half feet from the horse's nose (Liebermann, 1980). His ability to focus both eyes together is poor since the eyes are located at the side of the head and not in front of the face as in man. Although a horse has difficulty seeing at a distance, he can notice the most subtle movement. He may also see a slightly different image with each eye (Williams, 1976). A horse can judge the height of an object such as a jump fairly well but has difficulty with perceiving width (Hedlund, 1988). Horses can learn to recognize patterns and shapes.

A horse has a visual field of about 215 degrees (Evans, 1990), but has several blind spots. He cannot see directly behind his rump and directly in front of his nose. When a person stands directly in front of the horse with the horse's nose at the person's waist, the horse sees two pieces of a person. At four feet away, the horse can see a whole person. When a horse leader stands in front of the horse, the horse sees only a left shoulder and arm and a right shoulder and arm and nothing in between. When the horse has his head forward, he is unable to see underneath himself, between his feet or behind his tail. Sharp, quick movements within his blind spots may frighten him since he can feel but not see the action. (Culbertson, 1969; Williamson, 1974; Hedlund, 1988).

The Ability to Learn and Remember: "It is generally agreed that the memory of a horse is a very remarkable thing" (Williams, 1976). The fact that reward and discipline work so well with the horse points out how strong his memory is. The horse is quick to learn habits and retains them well (Museler, 1984). A horse will *learn* to *learn* (Evans, 1989), and remember certain events for years (Rees, 1985). He has the ability to discriminate and remember patterns and remembers simple tasks longer than difficult ones (Evans, 1989). He will learn the wrong thing as easily as the right thing and therefore it is important to reinforce good behavior and punish incorrect behavior. Evans points out that fear inhibits learning in the horse in the same way that humans cannot learn under threat and fear.

The Horse's Ability to Integrate his Senses: The horse has a sophisticated nervous system which enables him to coordinate and learn in a remarkable way. He integrates his senses to his best advantage for safety and social behavior (Evans,1990). He will point his ears in the direction he looks. He will use his nose to smell and his eyes to look at an unfamiliar object. His sense of balance is influenced by the position of his head with the help of the neck muscles (Hedlund, 1988). A horse's desire to please, his willingness to adapt to human needs, his excellent memory and athletic ability makes him a valuable partner in therapeutic riding programs. As he adapts to these new situations, he has proven to be a good-natured, trusting and reliable friend.

Ainslie, T., & Ledbetter, B. (1980). *The Body Language of Horses*. New York: William Marrow & Co.,Inc. 34.
Culbertson, (1969). 4-H Project
Engel, B.T., et al. (1989). *The Horse, The Handicapped and the Riding Team*. Pasadena, CA 91105. 83-86.
Evans, J.W., et al. (1990). *The Horse*. New York: W. H. Freeman & Co. 119-126.
Evans, J.W. (1989). *Horses*. New York: W. H. Freeman & Co. 43
Hedlund, G. (1988). *This is Riding: Dressage, Jumping, Eventing in Words and Pictures*. Middletown: Half Halt Press. 62-63.
Kiley-Worthington, M. (1987). *The Behavior of Horses: In Relation to Management and Training*. London: J.A. Allen & Co. 24-27,32.
Liebermann, B. (1980). The Sense of It All. *Equus*. Farmingdale: Fleet Street Publishing Corp. 34-39, 57.
Lyles, L.L. (1980). *Horseman's Handbook*. Santa Rosa: California State Horsemen's Assoc. 28.
McBane, S. (1980). *Keeping a Horse Outdoors*. North Pomfret: David & Charles Inc. 13-17.
Museler, W. (1984). *Riding Logic*. Arco Publishing, Inc.
Podhaisky, (1968). *The Complete Training of Horse and Rider*. Garden City: Doubleday. 21, 31, 69.
Rees, L. (1985). *The Horse's Mind*. New York: Prentice Hall Press. 27, 125.
Williams, M. (1976). *Pracical Horse Psychology*. No. Hollywood: Wilshire Book Co.
Williamson, M.B. (1977). *Applied Horse Psychology*. Houston: Cordova Publisher Inc. 2-42.

8.03 BASIC HORSE CARE FOR THE THERAPEUTIC RIDING HORSE--A REVIEW

Margaret L. Galloway, MA, BHSAI

Stable management is based on a combination of sound daily practices, the prevention of problems and accidents, and good routine care of the therapeutic riding horse. The ability to observe any change or difference in a horse's appearance or behavior may mean the difference between a small problem or a crisis. A horse should be examined carefully on a daily basis for cuts, bruises, or any abnormalities. A good time for checking would be during feeding or grooming. *KNOW EACH HORSE*. Note the general signs of his health and investigate any deviations from his normal condition. Hintz and Lowe (Evans, 1977), identify five major areas of horse management that must be addressed in a therapeutic riding program:

1. The ability to identify deviations from a horse's normal condition.
2. The maintenance of a complete record system.
3. Being knowledgeable and up-to-date in equine diseases and their causes.
4. The development and maintenance of a vaccination and worming program.
5. Being knowledgeable about situations that could place the horse at high risk for disease or injury and avoiding such conditions.

It is beyond the scope of this book to provide a <u>complete reference</u> on stable management. Instructors, trainers, and therapists should obtain good reference books on diseases, psychology, conformation, and health care of the horse, (Refer to the bibliography.) In addition, they should keep up with current information by reading and attending short courses in horse management.

THE HEALTHY HORSE SHOULD HAVE:
- Bright eyes without excess tearing
- A shiny coat with hair lying down: in cold climates the hair stands up
- Securely fitting shoes with properly clinched nails--no tenderness in the hooves
- A normal appetite--all feed is eaten
- Normal droppings--droppings must be firm but moist, and break when they hit the ground
- No mucus in the droppings
- Normal weight--one should be able to feel the ribs but not see them
- Adequate hydration--skin that does not "stay up" when pinched but returns immediately to its previous position
- Legs devoid of swelling, tenderness, or heat--the feet should feel cool. Both front and hind legs should appear and feel the same. Many horses have benign swellings, known as wind-puffs or windgall in lower leg joints. Swellings caused by synovial joint fluid are blemishes and are of little concern. Once a horse develops these, they rarely disappear. If they do change, they should be examined (Adams, 1972).
- Good balance at rest. The horse should stand evenly on all four feet. Resting a hind leg is normal but constant advancement of one front foot (pointing) is usually a sign of pain. The weight should be equal on both front legs.
- Sound legs. When walking or trotting, the horse should take strides of even length with equal sound of the footfall. The lame side may have a shorter stride.
- No head bobbing. If a horse is lame in the front, he will raise his head when the lame foot hits the ground.
- Urine--light yellow to yellowish-brown in color and "slimy" (mucous) in texture passed several times a day.
- No signs of sweating at rest except in unusually hot weather.

According to a poll surveying both horse owners and veterinarians, the following were the top ten health problems (in order of the most numerous)(Underhill, 1989):

1. subtle lameness
2. colic
3. wounds requiring sutures
4. puncture wounds
5. breeding/foal matters
6. incapacitating lameness
7. respiratory diseases
8. eye injuries
9. skin diseases and allergies

8.03.1   IDENTIFICATION OF HEALTH SIGNS

Taking measurements of the horse's temperature, pulse, and respiration (vital signs) will provide objective criteria with which to evaluate any change in a horse's bodily functions (King, 1990). It is a good idea to take vital signs when the healthy horse is at rest to determine a baseline for the horse. A record should be kept of these normal readings for future reference. Learning to take the temperature, pulse, and respiration is a simple skill to acquire. It will provide the veterinarian necessary information for acute care and emergencies.

How to Monitor Vital Signs

Temperature: The normal temperature of the horse is 99.5 to 101.4 degrees Fahrenheit (internally). Using a rectal horse thermometer with a string attached, shake the mercury down so that it reads below 98 degrees. Gently raise the tail and insert the thermometer gently into the horse's rectum until one-half inch the thermometer is showing. Tie the string at the end of the thermometer to the horse's tail to prevent the instrument from disappearing into the rectum. Using a clip at the end of the string holds it to the horse's tail and is easier than tying it. Adding petroleum jelly to the bulb end helps it to slide into the rectum. Leave it in the rectum for one and a half to two minutes before reading the temperature.

Pulse: The normal pulse rate is between 26 and 40 beats per minute. The pulse can be taken in several places but there are two common ones are: at the *maxillary artery* where it runs over the underside of the jaw bone on the horse's left side, or on the artery as it curves into *the tail*. Use the first and middle fingers to locate the artery in either place. In the tail there is a groove in the middle of the fleshy underside of the tail bone. Using very light pressure, feel the pulse for several beats before starting to count. Then count for thirty seconds; then multiply your count by two to get the per minute rate. The secret of getting an accurate pulse is not pressing too hard on the artery.

Respiration: Normal respiration is 8 to 16 breaths per minute with the horse at rest. Watch and count for 30 seconds each expansion of the flank as the horse inhales, then multiply that figure by two to get the per minute rate.

8.03.2   HOUSING THE PROGRAM HORSE

A horse needs to be housed in a well-ventilated and dry stall to stay healthy. Good ventilation without drafts reduces the chances of sweating or getting chilled and also helps to remove urine and ammonia odors. A *stabled horse* needs to have his stall cleaned once or twice a day. If urine and manure are not removed, the horse's hooves will become damaged from dampness and toxins. Thrush, the bacterial infection of the frog is likely to develop. The odor of ammonia from urine is unpleasant for horses and humans alike. To clean the stall, remove all manure piles, then begin forking through the bedding to find urine spots. Replace wet spots with dry bedding. Build up bedding material around the edges of the stall to reduce the chance of the horse being cast (rolling in such a way that he cannot move). All stalls must have an adequate supply of fresh water.

Pasturing a horse puts him in a natural environment, in which far less attention is required. "If the pasture is properly managed, many horses thrive on it and there are considerable savings in time and money" (Hadfield, 1989). Horses in pasture need a form of shelter, such as a shed to get out of wind and rain. The pasture needs to be picked clean of manure regularly. Cleaning up the manure is important because it can be a source of worm eggs; if horses are on a well maintained deworming program this should not be a problem. A weekly clean-up may be necessary to avoid flies. Algae needs to be cleaned out of water troughs. Some people keep algae-eating fish in troughs to help keep them clean. Pasturing is the most economical way to keep a horse, as little daily maintenance is needed. It is possible for a pasture to provide a mainstay of a horse's diet, but the area must be big enough to maintain healthy grass. In most cases supplementary feed will be needed.

A major advantage of pasturing horses together is that it places them in their natural herd environment and they can exercise themselves enough for health but not for fitness (Hadfield, 1989). The disadvantage of pasturing horses is that it can cause them to be wet and dirty if the fields are not maintained. There is some possibility of a horse being kicked, but the advantages usually outweigh the disadvantages. Feeding horses separately usually eliminates the problem of kicking.

Horses may be kept in *small corrals or paddocks*, either alone or with other horses. The footing may be of decomposed granite which drains well, eliminating mud. Sand is also used in many areas, as it provides good drainage. However, it may be ingested which can lead to colic. Feed placed in a large container on the ground that cannot be overturned helps reduce this problem. Dirt is often used for footing. It has the disadvantage of turning to mud when it rains. Paddocks should have a shed or at the very least a sturdy tree. Horses kept together in paddocks need to be monitored.

8.03.3 BATHING

In warm weather a horse with a short coat can be bathed by being hosed or sponged off, but it is not necessary to bath the horse completely for his health and this should not be overdone. The main disadvantage of excessive bathing is the loss of natural oils in the hair. Sweat from tack should be removed after riding to prevent sores and infections. The horse can be bathed by running water over all the sweaty areas and then using a sweat scraper to remove the excess water. Be sure to wash between the hind legs and also the poll. When washing the poll, remove the halter and buckle it around the horse's neck first; never tie or leave a horse with a halter around his neck since he can injure himself if he should pull back. Another important factor is to have sufficient traction in the wash area so the horse does not slip. In cool weather or in the evening, rub the coat of a horse with a towel. A heater lamp or a blower can be an asset.

8.03.4 BLANKETING THE HORSE

Blankets are used to keep a horse warm and help to keep a shorter coat in winter. Conversely, a horse left out most of the time develops a long winter coat. If he is blanketed, the hair is flattened, thus actually inhibiting the hair's natural insulating effect. Many horses never need to be blanketed, even in very cold climates. A horse in good condition that is fed properly does not need to be blanketed unless he shows signs of being cold, such as shivering. An older horse that requires extra feed in winter to maintain his body weight may not need as much feed if he is blanketed since the insulation of the blanket conserves his energy. Blanketing with a light sheet may be necessary for white and grey horses, who are more sensitive to the sun, to prevent sunburn and other effects from the sun's rays. When the riding session is over, a blanket can be put over the horses to keep them from catching a chill and allow them to cool down gradually.

Several varieties of blanketing can be used under various conditions. The summer sheet is a cotton or canvas blend with no lining. It offers some protection and may be used alone on cool nights or under a heavier, lined blanket. It is advisable to have two belly straps, which are criss-crossed diagonally underneath to prevent the horse from getting his feet and legs caught in the straps and pulling the blanket off. The most common blanket is the lined or quilted type. It may have an outer shell of cotton, canvas or nylon. Although all lined blankets are efficient, nylon usually lasts somewhat longer. A third kind of blanket is the waterproof type, of which the New Zealand Rug and the Gore-tex are the best known brands. This is made of waterproofed canvas with a sewn-on surcingle and leg straps. It provides the maximum protection. The blanket may rub the shoulders of the horse causing friction burns and hair loss (Kilby, 1987) and lameness. Satin or fleece can be sewn into the blanket at the withers, shoulders and hips to reduce friction. Blankets must fit the horse well in order to stay in place and to avoid injuring the horse.

Blankets must be washed when dirty. A dirty blanket can injure the horse and will not last. To keep a heavy blanket clean on the inside, a light-weight blanket can be used under the heavier blanket. The lighter blanket can be easily washed and kept clean, therefore protecting the horse's skin. If washing is a problem at the program stable, this can be resolved by using three lighter-weight blankets that are layered. Because of their light weight they can easily be washed in standard washing machines and the triple layer provides ample warmth. The other advantage of using a tier of blankets is the ability to adjust to varying temperatures.

8.03.5   CLIPPING AND TRIMMING THE HORSE

Horses should be clipped when their long coat presents a problem. Program horses may need to be clipped to remove long hair for the following reasons:

- ◎ to keep the horse clean and free of dust for riders who are allergic to animal dust
- ◎ to prevent the horse from becoming sweaty after work
- ◎ to keep him cool in warm southern climates
- ◎ to speed drying time after bathing
- ◎ for aesthetic purposes for shows

Clipping should be done before November in North American climates by a person who is knowledgeable and experienced. It should be noted that horses should be clipped only to the extent needed as this removes the horse's warm coat and may necessitate the use of a blanket. Clipping a horse's muzzle and face hair takes away his sensors to feel for food and foreign objects and should be avoided. The style of clipping chosen depends on the workload and the type of stabling of a horse. When horses need to be clipped they should be clipped when they have full coats and become sweaty after a workout. This can be a special problem when it is cold and a long time is needed to dry a horse. Horses can get chilled and this can lead to colds and pneumonia if they are not allowed to cool gradually after working. Because their protection is limited, pastured horses should be clipped minimally, if at all (Watkins, 1986).

TYPES OF CLIPS:

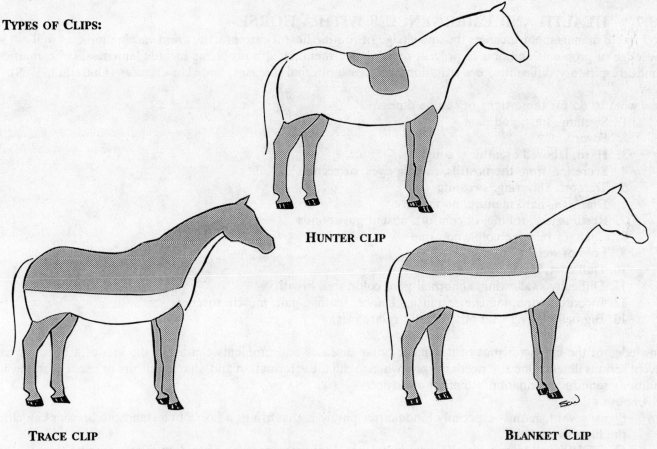

HUNTER CLIP

TRACE CLIP

BLANKET CLIP

8.03.6   HORSE CARE SCHEDULE

A therapeutic riding program relies on healthy, strong, and fit horses. In order to keep a horse strong and healthy, a daily schedule of horse care is necessary.

Daily activities include:

- ☻ Cleaning (mucking) stalls to remove manure and urine-soaked bedding
- ☻ Feeding a minimum of two times daily; three to four is preferred

161

- Checking water supply and condition twice a day
- Grooming and cleaning feet
- Checking for heat, swelling, injury, or changes in vital signs
- Turning-out and an exercise program
- Warming up and cooling down routine
- Blanketing as needed

Periodic scheduled care:
- Shoe or trim every four to eight weeks. A regular schedule should be set up with the farrier
- Worm every two to four months. A schedule should be drawn-up with the veterinarian to meet the program's needs
- Vaccinations given routinely to prevent disease and disease-related physical problems such as colic vaccinations for influenza, rhinopneumonitis, tetanus, rabies, botulism, anthrax, Potomac horse fever, Venezuelan equine encephalomyelitis (VEE, E.E.E., W.E.E.), strangles; equine viral arteritis (EVA) may be included. A schedule should be drawn up with the veterinarian to meet the particular needs of your location, as not all diseases are present in all areas of the country
- Semi-annual dental care--watch for problem teeth in the older horse
- Sheath cleaning for geldings

8.03.7   HEALTH AND EMERGENCIES WITH A HORSE

Good stable management includes the knowledge of routine health care practices and vaccinations, as well as the knowledge of problems and how to prevent or minimize them. Health problems include lameness, colic, injuries, wounds, respiratory difficulties, eye irritations, allergies, internal diseases, and skin diseases (Underhill, 1989).

Know what to do for these signs of equine illness:
1. Swelling, heat, and pain
2. Fever
3. Hard, labored breathing, cough
4. Secretion from the nostrils, mouth, eyes, or rectum
5. Tremors, shivering, sweating
6. Diarrhea, hard manure, no manure
7. Restlessness, rolling, discomfort, absent gut sounds
8. Changes in urine color, no urine
9. Loss of weight
10. Dull coat, loss of hair
11. Difficulty swallowing, abnormal gum color, foul breath
12. Incoordination, lameness, unusual stance, scuffing gait, muscle soreness
13. Big belly, along with other health related signs

Knowledge of the characteristics of the major horse diseases and problems can avoid the loss of a horse or can prevent serious illness. One also needs to know when to call the veterinarian and what to tell him or her. The following conditions require veterinarian attention or advice:

Azoturia
> Signs: severe spasms--especially hindquarter paralysis that brings a horse to a standstill. Spasms can close the blood vessels.
> Cause: believed to be a bio-chemical imbalance. Strenuous exercise after days of rest. Can be threatening!

Colic
> Signs: rolling, horse looks or bites at flank, sweaty flank, kicking, restlessness, not eating, not passing manure, groaning, agitation.
> Cause: pain in the abdomen and gut due to impaction, muscle spasms, gas, blockage of blood vessels. **Can be very serious and life-threatening!**

Laminitis/Founder
> Signs: lameness, stance with weight on heels of front feet, feet hot, body sweats.
> Cause: inflammation (of the laminaein) in the wall of the hoof. The pedal bone in the foot can rotate and cause permanent damage. **Can be very serious.**

Muscle strains
> Signs: pain or stiffness.
> Cause: poor conditioning and exercise habits, asking more from the horse than his condition allows, stepping into a hole or taking a bad step. If not attended to can lead to serious injuries.

Pneumonia
> Signs: fever--102-105 degrees, difficulty breathing, nasal discharge, congestion of the lungs with chest pain and poor appetite. Cause: inflammatory disease of the lungs caused by bacterial or viral infections. Prompt treatment is necessary.

Ringworm--a very contagious skin disease.
> Signs: May cause hair loss. Can be transmitted to riders or handlers. Can be transmitted from grooming tools or other objects used in contact with ringworm.
> Cause: fungi. Veterinarian can provide medication to eradicate it.

Strangles
> Signs: swelling in the lymph glands in the head and neck, cough, nasal discharge, elevated temperature, difficulty in swallowing. An abscess develops and finally bursts.
> Cause: streptococcus infection, which can be carried in the air from horse to horse. **Highly contagious to other horses, so isolation is required.**

Tetanus (lockjaw)
> Signs: muscle spasms or muscle rigidity, "saw-horse" posture, difficulty walking, prolapse of the third eyelid.
> Cause: Bacteria (Clostridium tetani) enters the body through deep wounds. Very serious, fatal if not treated. Potential for death even when treated.

Tying up
> Sign: stiffness that affects the hindquarters during a workout. Similar to Azoturia but less severe.
> Cause: seen after a workout with a horse who stands idle for several days, in out-of-shape horses, or those on heavy grain diets.

Thrush
> Signs: smell and inflammation of the frog of the foot.
> Cause: due to poor care of the foot, degeneration of the frog due to lack of contact with the ground causing decreased circulation, dirty conditions of the stall or pasture areas.

Wounds, punctures or cuts
> Signs; any injury, cut, swelling to any part of the body. Needs to be attended to immediately or can develop into a serious condition.
> Cause: being cut on an object or fence, kicked by another horse, stepping into a hole or on an unsafe object.

EMERGENCY CARE: Wallace (1991) divides emergency care into three categories: crisis care, urgent care, and prompt care.

Crisis care--when life-threatening--is given immediately by the person who is present at the time of the injury or the one first observing the impairment in a life-threatening situation. Care cannot be put off until the veterinarian arrives. Urgent care involves situations that require intervention to prevent a life threatening condition. Prompt care reduces the likelihood of the worsening of an injury.

Crisis care is needed when the horse is:
1) bleeding severely
2) not breathing regularly (obstruction to nostrils or unable to breath)
3) unconscious
4) suffering from shock or trauma to internal organs or to the head
5) colicky

Urgent care is needed when the horse has:
1) heat prostration (severely over-heated) or hypothermia (subnormal body temperature)
2) continuous bleeding
3) fracture/dislocation
4) open joint injuries
5) puncture wounds to vital organs

Prompt care is necessary when the horse has:
1) deep cuts and puncture wounds to non-critical areas
2) sprains or severe swellings
3) eye injuries

Emergency care of humans and horses is similar in many ways (Wallace, 1991). It is certainly similar in the immediate attention required. Instructors, therapists, and horse managers must know how to deal with emergency first aid to both humans and horses in all areas mentioned above.

8.03.8 Measuring the Weight of a Horse: The weight a Horse can Carry

WEIGHT OF THE HORSE: a general measurement of weight can be obtained by: squaring the measure of the girth (W) under the withers (inches); measuring the distance between the point of the hips to the point of the shoulders (S) (inches). Multiply (W x W) x S = T dividing by 225 = body weight in pounds.

CARRYING WEIGHT: Generally a horse who is fit and in athletic condition can carry 20% of his body weight.

For example: Rusty's measurements are 65 x 57 = 240,825 divided by 225 = 1070 pounds of body weight (Perrault, 1987). Rusty is 14 years old, is on a regular training program and has no conformation faults. He should be able to carry a rider weighing 214 lbs. **But always consider:**

◐ The condition, conformation, and age of the horse
◉ The muscle tone and agility of the rider--A rider with low muscle tone will "feel heavier" to the helpers and to the horse because he or she is "dead weight"--(body muscle mass does not resist gravitational pull). A rider with physical involvement, especially if he or she is more involved on one side than the other, will require more work from the horse because he or she must compensate for the rider's lack of balance.

There are a number of good books on horse care, veterinary problems, and preventive medicine. Each program should have one or two books on hand which deal with health care. A good reference book on "First Aid to horses" could be worth its weight in gold, that is, if it is well read.

References
Adams, O.R. (1972). *Lameness in Horses*. 2nd ed. Fort Collins: Lea & Febiger. 340
Blazer, D. (1982). *Horses Seldom Burp*. San Diego: A.S. Barnes & Co, Inc.
Equus. (1980). "Cleaning the Sheath". 32.
Evans, J.W. (1977). *The Horse*. New York: W.H. Freeman and Company. 555
German National Equestrian Federation. (1987). *Horse Management*. Gaithersburg: Half Halt Press.
Hadfield, M. (1989). *The Manual of Horsemanship*. British Horse Society and Pony Club. London: Threshold Books. 108.
Harris, S.E. (1977). *Grooming to Win*. New York: Charles Scribner's Sons.
Kilby, E. (1987). Where Weather is always Front Page News. *Equus*. 110. 40-41, 62.
Kinnish, M.K (1988). *Healthy Hooves Their Care and Balance*. Gaithersburg: Fleet Street Publishing Corp.
King, P.A. (1990). "Your Horse's Vital Signs". *Horseplay*. 18, 26-27.
Lyon, W. (1984) *First Aid Hints for the Horse Owner*. Glasgow: William Collins Sons & Co Ltd.
Pascoe, E. (1986). *The Horse Owner's Preventive Maintenance Handbook*, New York: Charles Scribner's & Sons.
Perrault, G. *The New Horse Owner Illustrated Manual*. Ottawa: Editions Grand Prix Reg'd. 22,
Smallwood, P.(1988). *The Manual of Stable Management: Care of the Horse*. Middletown: Half Halt Press.
Thompson, D. (1979). "They Kill While You Wait". *Equus*.
Watkins, V. (1986). *Trimming and Clipping*. London: Threshold Books.
Summerhays, R.S. (1988).*Summerhays'Encyclopaedia for Horsemen*. Rev. ed. London: Threshold Books. 29, 68, 159, 231, 270, 283.
Underhill, L.J.P. (1989). *The Wellness Movement*. Equus. 145. 44-45.
Wallace, M. (1991). Emergency Care. *Equus*. 166, 52-55 95-97.

8.04 NUTRITION OF THE THERAPEUTIC RIDING HORSE

Robin R. Hall, MS

Basic Anatomy and Function of the Digestive System

The feeding of horses has become more scientific in recent years. Research has enabled horse owners to formulate the best diet for their animals to meet their nutrient requirements at the most economical costs. The old cliche, "we are what we eat," holds true for the horse as well as humans. A good understanding of the horse's digestive system is needed to promote the importance of proper nutrition and to appreciate it in selecting a balanced diet.

Being a nonruminant herbivore, the horse possesses a single stomach and consumes plant material as the bulk of its diet. Through evolution, a continuous eating behavior developed allowing the horse to eat small amounts of food frequently. This explains the small capacity of the stomach compared to the horse's size (2.1 to 4 gallons) and the recommendation to feed confined horses at least twice daily.

Digestion begins in the mouth with the mastication of the feed and the production of saliva by three pairs of glands to moisten it. From the mouth, the food bolus travels to the stomach by way of the esophagus. Because of the stomach's limited capacity, gastric secretions offer little digestive assistance to the food particles. The stomach does, however, provide a constant supply of food to the small intestine where most digestion and absorption of nutrients takes place. The small intestine is the primary site of protein, carbohydrate and lipid digestion and absorption, along with the fat-soluble vitamins (A, D, E and K), dietary B vitamins and some minerals.

From the small intestine, the food passes to the large intestine, which includes the cecum, colon and rectum. Here digestion is dependent on microbes, similar to those found in ruminant animals such as cattle and sheep. The cecum initiates the breakdown of fiber through microbial fermentation producing volatile fatty acids, an important energy source. Significant amounts of the B-vitamin complex are also produced in the cecum by the bacteria. These vitamins contribute to the requirements of the animal. Fiber digestion continues through the colon, along with water absorption. Finally, the remaining waste products are excreted from the rectum.

NUTRIENT REQUIREMENTS

Horses require six nutrients to sustain normal health: carbohydrates, fats, proteins, minerals, vitamins and water. The amount of nutrients vary with the class of horse and depend on age, level of work, reproductive duties and the status of the individual animal.

CARBOHYDRATES AND FATS

Carbohydrates and fats provide the main energy sources. Energy is the fuel of life that enables the horse to perform work. The soluble carbohydrates, such as starch, maltose and sucrose are primarily absorbed in the small intestine. Insoluble carbohydrates, or the fibrous fraction of the diet, are digested in the large intestine and absorbed as volatile fatty acids. These acids are produced in the cecum from microbial fermentation and are used as energy. Dietary lipids are digested and absorbed in the small intestine. The horse does not have a gall bladder, but the absence of one does not appear to hinder the digestion of fat. The requirements for energy vary with each horse and its activity. The maintenance requirement of a nonworking horse is the amount of energy needed to sustain a constant body weight during normal activity. This requirement is based on body weight, and additional energy must be fed to compensate for performance, environmental factors, health and individuality. Energy content of feeds is often expressed as digestible energy (DE) designated in calories. DE is the total energy content of the feed minus the energy lost in the feces. Both forages and concentrates supply energy. The grains such as corn, oats, barley and wheat are the primary energy sources fed to horses. Consuming excess energy makes for a fat horse, whereas symptoms of insufficient energy intake are loss of weight and tiredness.

PROTEIN

Protein is composed of building blocks called amino acids, the major components of lean body tissue, enzymes and several hormones. The amino acids are complex substances, which contain a fairly constant amount of nitrogen. They are divided into essential and nonessential groups. The nonessential ones are synthesized by the body and the essential amino acids must be supplied in the diet. The essential amino acids are arginine, histidine, isoleucine, leucine, lysine, methionine, phenylalanine, threonine, tryptophan and valine. The exact amino acid requirements of the horse are not known. However, the quality of protein and the digestibility of that protein are important to ensure that the horse is getting the proper amino acid compositions. A good quality protein has the same levels of amino acids as are present in the body. Poor quality protein lacks one or more of the required essential amino acids. The feeds most commonly fed are usually of a good quality protein that is readily digested by the horse.

The small intestine is the primary site of protein digestion and absorption in the horse. Protein requirements are referred to as crude protein (CP) or digestible protein (DP). Crude protein is the percentage of nitrogen in the feed, but all nitrogen therein is not available to the horse. Digestible protein is the amount of available protein in the feed. Mature horses have a much lower requirement for proteins than young, growing horses, since their requirement is for maintaining existing tissue, not growing new tissue.

Excess protein in the diet can be used as an energy source, but feeding excess is not recommended due to the costliness of it. Protein-deficient animals exhibit poor growth, weight loss and general lack of thriftiness. Although both forage and grain provide protein, the quality of hay or pasture will determine the amount of protein needed in the concentrate. Hay will supply 7 to 18 percent CP depending on the type and quality, whereas cereal grains range from 8 to 12 percent CP. If additional protein is needed, a protein supplement can be added in the diet. Soybean meal is one such protein supplement commonly used in horse rations.

MINERALS

Minerals serve many functions in the body including skeletal components, muscle contractions and electrolyte balance. Seven macrominerals include: calcium, phosphorus, potassium, sodium, chloride, magnesium and sulfur. The eight microminerals are cobalt, copper, fluoride, iodine, iron, manganese, selenium and zinc.

Calcium and phosphorus make up about 70 percent of the mineral composition of the horse's body. Not only do they need to be supplied in adequate levels, but the proportions of calcium to phosphorus are important for normality of bone development. The ratio should not be less than 1 : 1, but should be fed at 1.2 to 1.6: 1 of calcium to phosphorus, respectively. With either a high level of dietary calcium or a high level of dietary phosphorus relative to the calcium, the digestibility and absorption of calcium are decreased. Salt (sodium chloride) should always be available to the horse. Usually, a trace mineralized salt block or granules are available free choice. The horse procures most of its mineral needs from pasture, roughage, and grain.

VITAMINS

Vitamins are a group of unrelated organic compounds that are necessary in trace amounts for normal metabolic functions of the body. Vitamins are classified as either fat-soluble or water-soluble vitamins. Fat-soluble vitamins include A, D, E and K, while the B-complex groups, vitamin C and others belong to the water-soluble group. Vitamin supplementation is not a recommended practice, if the horse is receiving a balanced diet of good quality ingredients. In fact, vitamins fed in excessive dosages can be harmful to the horse. Most high quality forages contain adequate levels of vitamins. The B-complex vitamins are synthesized by the microflora in the cecum. They are also present in forages, so consequently additional supplementation is not usually needed.

WATER

Water requirements are dependent on several factors, such as air temperature, physical activity, reproduction and diet. Pregnancy, lactating mares, hot weather, high intensity work, and a diet high in dry matter demand increased consumption of water. Fresh, clean water should be available at all times. A horse will drink 10 to 12 gallons per day during normal environmental and working conditions.

FEEDING MANAGEMENT

Horses need long stem forage in their daily diet to maintain normal digestive function. If pasture is not accessible, a hay will need to be fed. It is recommended that a horse consume at least 1 percent of his body weight per day of good quality roughage. Forage quality depends on soil type, climate and harvesting techniques. Stage of maturity at time of harvest is important with respect to nutrient quality. A clean, bright colored forage free of mold, dust, weeds and foreign objects should be fed. Common hays fed to horses include alfalfa, clover, timothy, orchard grass, bermuda grass, brome grass, oat hay and prairie hay.

Concentrates or cereal grains are generally higher in energy and lower in fiber than forages. Oats, barley and corn are the most commonly fed grains. Oats are higher in fiber and lower in DE than the other grains. Corn is higher in energy and lower in protein than oats. After the roughage has been selected, the concentrate can be determined to meet the total daily nutrient requirements of the animal.

Often times, the horse involved with a therapeutic riding program is an older individual. These geriatric horses may require special attention due to the general slowdown of body functions. Additional energy is needed by the older horse to perform physical activity, as compared to the younger or middle-aged horse. Concentrates may be needed to meet the energy needs, if the roughage alone is not adequate. If teeth are in a poor state, a more palatable diet is recommended to help insure proper nutritional requirements. Hay can be chopped and grain can be processed by crimping, rolling or crushing to make consumption easier thereby improving digestibility. When chewing is difficult, a mash can be made by soaking the grain in hot water before feeding. Older horses often by benefit being fed individually, rather than in groups, to reduce feeding competition and to allow them the additional time required to consume the feed that they often need. All horses should be on a routine dental and parasite program to optimize management practices.

Feeding horses successfully is not only the ability to formulate a balanced diet, but also the ability to adjust the diet according to individual needs. Because of variation in production and performance, as well as metabolic and behavioral differences, horses need to be fed as individuals. Experience and good judgement about feeding are key elements to insure the welfare and happiness of the horse.

References

Evans, J.W. (1989). *Horses: A Guide to Selection, Care, and Enjoyment*. New York: W.H. Freeman and Company.

Evans, J.W., A. Borton, H.F. Hintz, and L.D. Van Vleck. (1977). *The Horse*. New York: W.H. Freeman and Company.

Maynard, L.A., J.K. Loosli, H.F. Hintz, and R.G. Warner. (1979) *Animal Nutrition*. Seventh edition. McGraw-Hill Book Co.

Naviaux, J. L. (1985). *Horses in Health and Disease*. Second edition. Philadelphia: Lea and Febiger.

NRC. (1989). *Nutrient Requirements of Horses*. Fifth revised edition. National Academy of Sciences, Washington, DC.

Robinson, D.W., L.M. Slade. (1974). *The Current Status of Knowledge on the Nutrition of Equines*. J. Animal Science. 39:6.

Wood, C.H., S.G. Jackson, (1988). *Basic Horse Nutrition*. Lexington: University of Kentucky Cooperative Extension Service.

Hall, Robin R., BS, MS. Riding Instructor--Equestrian Studies Program at University of Findley, Findley, OH. Certified instructor--Fran Joswick Therapeutic Riding Center; NAHRA instructor training workshop, instructor of Equestrian Challenge Therapeutic Riding Program, Findley OH.

8.05 THE HOOF AND ITS IMPORTANCE TO THE THERAPEUTIC RIDING HORSE

Barbara T. Engel, MEd, OTR

KEY WORDS
  HEALTH
  BALANCE
  POSITIVE EFFECTS

The horse was created to roam over dry grass plains and in his natural environment the hoof served him well without trimming or other special care. In the domestic environment, however, the hoof will need special care because:

- Most horses have limited space to wander. Lack of walking throughout the day decreases circulation because the pumping action of the circulatory system in the foot is not activated, therefore causing weakness of the hoof.
- Even in a well-cleaned stall, bedding harbors acids and solvents from urine and manure which are destructive to the hoof.
- Improper trimming can cause stress at certain points of the hoof. An unbalanced hoof will cause the horse to move unevenly and may lead to hoof problems and lameness.
- Standing in areas too wet or dry contributes to the destruction of the horse's hooves. (Kinnish, 1988)

The hoof is the base on which the horse stands. His four hooves create his points of balance. If the hoof surface is uneven instead of flat, it does not allow the leg to stand straight. One uneven hoof will cause the rest of the horse to be unbalanced. One can compare this to a table with one leg worn off at a corner. The table will not stand evenly. Anthony Gonzales demonstrated how trimming a quarter of an inch off the inside of one hoof can produce balance in the gait of a horse who walked unbalanced prior to the hoof trimming (Gonzales, 1991). (See following section 8.06). A hoof that lands on one edge rather then flat will cause stress at the point of impact and modify the leverage of the total leg with resulting complications and possible lameness. This demonstration showed the subtle changes that can occur due to the shape of hooves and how this can affect the delicate balance of the horse. The balance of the horse influences the rider, as sensation is transmitted through the movements of the horse.

If the horse is not balanced, the rider will not sit straight on the horse, nor will the rider perceive smooth, rhythmic movements which are essential to the therapeutic effects of riding. Healthy, well-balanced hooves are therefore essential to productive therapeutic riding.

THE HOOVES

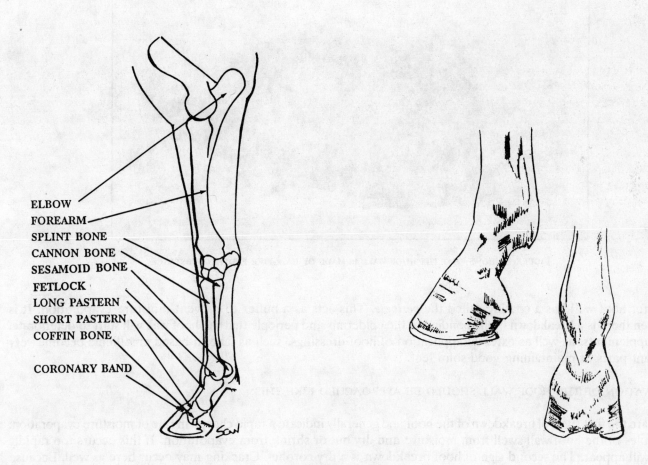

WALL OF FOOT
WHITE LINE
SOLE
POINT OF FROG
CLEFT OF FROG
BAR
WALL - HEEL
BULB OF HEEL

ELBOW
FOREARM
SPLINT BONE
CANNON BONE
SESAMOID BONE
FETLOCK
LONG PASTERN
SHORT PASTERN
COFFIN BONE
CORONARY BAND

THE HORSE'S LEG

References
Kinnish, M.K. (1988). *Healthy Hooves*. Gaithersburg: Fleet Street Publishing Corp. 10-11.
Gonzales, A. (1991). Performance Horse Symposium: Tellington-Jones, Swift, Gonzales. Clinic notes 2-1991, Pleasanton, CA.
Gonzales, A. (1986). *Proper Balance Movement*. Manassas: REF Publishing

169

8.06 THE HOOF: CARE AND RELATION TO BALANCE

Anthony Z. Gonzales

CARE Of THE HOOF

First I would like to introduce you to the technical term for the hoof wall, *epidermis*. Epidermis means skin, and in this case, outer skin. The hoof is an extension of the coronary band and the skin above it. It is made of tubular, hair-like substance, a protein that gets most of its nourishment from the blood supply inside the body (Figure 1). But, like human hair, it needs to be maintained with conditioners and moisturizers from the outside, and nutrients from the inside to stay healthy.

FIGURE 1. SHOWS THAT THE HOOF WALL IS MADE OF HAIR-LIKE PROTEIN SUBSTANCE.

The outer hoof wall has a coating called the *periople*. This acts as a buffer to prevent moisture evaporation. It is only when there is a breakdown in the bonding of the epidermis and periople that the hoof wall will start to deteriorate. Feed supplements, as well as external application of hoof dressings, such as lanolin-based emollients become very important parts of maintaining good solid feet.

OBSERVATION OF THE HOOF WALL SHOULD BE APPROACHED LIKE THIS:

Cracks are the first signs of breakdown of the hoof and generally indicate a rapid change in rate of moisture evaporation: the tubules of the hoof wall swell from moisture and dry out or shrink from evaporation. If this occurs too rapidly cracks will appear. The second sign of hoof breakdown is a dry coronet. Cracking may occur here as well. Because it is in the coronet that most evaporation occurs, hoof dressing should be applied into the hairline of the coronet (coronary band) to keep it moist.

The frog (see 8.05--Figure 1) is very important to the function of the hoof. In inspecting the frog, it is desirable that it be solid tissue but flexible to the push of the thumb. This indicates suppleness as well as the ability to adequate absorption shock from concussion. A wide frog generally indicates that the heels will be wide and flexible. The narrower the frog, the more chances for contraction of the heels, which may lead to lameness.

If a horse is shoeless, inspect the white line located between the sensitive part of the sole and the outer wall. Check to see that there are no crevices in which stones can be wedged since this condition will create a wall separation (Figure 2 & 3). If a stone is found wedged in the wall, a hoof pick can be used to take it out. *If the stone is allowed to stay in, it will move upward due to the weight of the body pushing down on the ground as the horse moves.* If this condition occurs at the toe it is called *seedy toe*. It would be advisable to fill any holes with cotton if deep enough. This will prevent more stones from entering.

REMEMBER THESE THREE WORDS:

- **PROTECT**
- **PREVENT**
- **PRESERVE**

Protection of the horse's hoof is very important. Remember the saying: "*No Hoof, No Horse.*" To help **prevent** damage, use hoof dressings both on the outer hoof and on the coronet band, frog, and sole. **Prevent** thrush, a fungus infestation which develops because of unclean conditions, and treat it if it occurs. **Preserve** the hoof by maintaining a committed series of hoof care procedures all year around.

FIGURE 2. SHOWS WHAT A WALL SEPARATION LOOKS LIKE. THIS IS USUALLY CAUSED BY A GRAIN OF SAND OR STONE MOVING UP THE WHITE LINE

FIGURE 3. SHOWS THE BEGINNING OF A WALL SEPARATION ON THE LEFT HAND OF THE HOOF

HOW THE HOOF RELATES TO BALANCE OF THE LEG

First one must realize that the hoof has but a limited ability to stabilize the leg. The major elements involved with the leg's stability and balance are muscles, ligaments, tendons, and skin. One must not be fooled into thinking that shoeing and trimming alone will give the horse a balanced leg. The hoof is a base and the leg a column. The base must be evenly balanced in order for the column to remain straight and upright.

171

By observation of the horse's leg, one will see that the pastern bones lie below the third metacarpal bone and that the column of short and long pastern bones, forming a straight shaft, will rest in the center of the hoof capsule. The pastern will normally tilt outward at the long pastern/cannon bone connection. When this straightness is not present, and the pastern bones tilt inwardly just above the hoof, the leg will appear pigeon-toed. If the tilt is outward right above the hoof, the pastern is dropped to the inside at the long pastern/cannon bone connection and the leg will appear splay-footed.

One must be aware of some of the conditions that can result from either type of unbalanced hoof:

- ▫ <u>Pigeon-toed feet</u>
- ▫ <u>Sidebone</u> on the outside above the coronary band. This is due to more weight bearing on the outside of the leg.
- ▫ <u>Outside splints</u> due to more pressure on the outside of the knee joint.
- ▫ <u>Sore shoulder muscles</u> on the outside of the leg due to the foot dropping inward toward the body, causing a paddling movement when the horse moves.
- ▫ <u>Splay-footed</u> due to the feet turning outward because of more weight being on the inside of the leg. Side bone may result on the <u>inside</u> of the top of the coronary band and splints. Splints will be due to more pressure on the <u>inside</u> of the knee joint.
- ▫ <u>Sore muscles on the inside of the shoulder</u> due to the body weight of the horse dropping through the chest onto the inside of the front legs instead of being equally balanced front and rear.

These are not the only problems with front legs, but they are the ones you should be readily aware of to make appropriate changes. The hind legs show similar stances to those of the front legs. A *pigeon-toed* condition in the hind leg is called *bow-legged*. A *splay-foot* condition is called *cow-hocked*. However, the hind legs show a totally different set of problems than those of the front legs to produce these anomalies. In the hind legs, both bow legs (hocks turned outward) and cow hocks (hocks turned inward) affect two main joints: the hock and the stifle. Either problem causes a twisting of both the hock and stifle and if this condition persists, it could lead to the stifle catching, arthritis of the hock, or spavin. When the hoof is unbalanced from such conditions, the horse will have a hard time making smooth turns, or may resist taking the correct lead. The hoof must land flat as it strikes the ground for a gait to be correct and true.

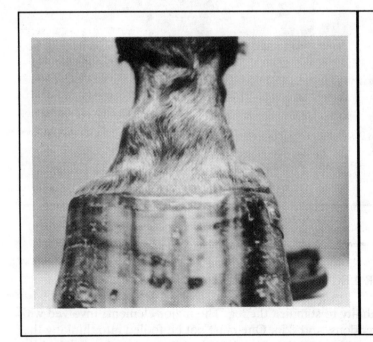

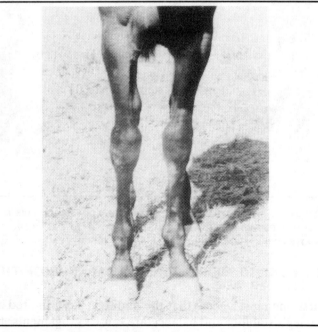

FIGURE 4. SHOWS THAT THE HORSE WILL DEVELOP "SIDEBONE" AS A RESULT OF UNEVEN BALANCE OF THE HOOF AND LEG.

FIGURE 5. SHOWS THE LEFT FRONT FETLOCK TURNED INWARD AND THE HOOF TURNED OUTWARD.

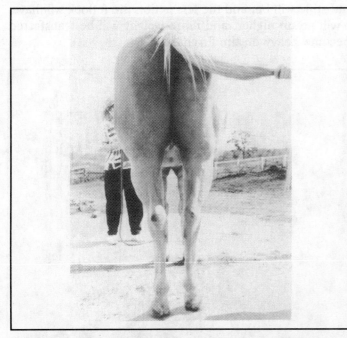

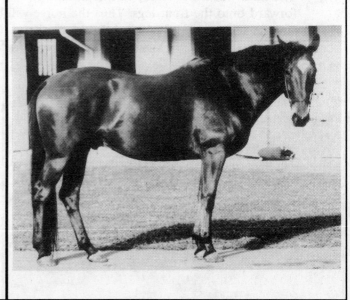

FIGURE 6. SHOWS THE RIGHT HIND LEG OF THE HORSE TURNED OUTWARD MORE THAN THE LEFT HIND LEG. THIS WILL CAUSE THIS HORSE TO PIVOT AT ITS STIFLES.

FIGURE 7. SHOWS HOW LOW HEELS WILL AFFECT A HORSE'S STANCE. THIS HORSE'S KNEES ARE PUSHED BACKWARD AND ITS TOES ARE TOO LONG. THE HIND HEELS ARE LOW AS WELL.

HOW HOOF ANGLES AFFECT THE UPPER BODY

One must remember that the hoof contains a "coffin" bone. The lower coffin bone and the short pastern bones form the first joint in the lower part of the leg. Other joints continue up to the shoulder blade. The first joint, however affects and controls the angle of the hoof. When the hoof angle changes, so will the position of all leg joints change. In other words, if the heels are too low on a horse, not only is the coffin bone joint affected, but also the knee joint and the shoulder. One tends to think only of the lower joints being affected. What is known, however, is that if the heels are low, the short pastern will put a lot of pressure on the navicular bone. But don't rule out that the knee could hyper extend producing possible tendon and ligament pulls. One can tell if a hoof has enough "heel" by looking at the coronary band. If the angle of the coronary band dips from the front of the hoof towards the heel in a sharp manner, (viewing should be done from the side) one sees the "reverse wedge" syndrome. Another way to tell if a hoof has too little heel is to look from the back of the hoof to see if the bulb of the heel is on the ground.

When low heels in the front feet occur, the joints all close with greater backward pressure. When this condition occurs with the hind feet, the joints all close with greater forward pressure. In both case it creates hyperextension of the knees.

Signs to look for to help identify how stance and angle of the hoof affect the upper body are:
1. An unbalanced front hoof is present when:
    a. the knee drops to the inside
    b. one shoulder is lower and more forward than the other
    c. the knee is straight or outward and the shoulder is higher and back
2. An unbalanced hind hoof is present when the leg is "twisted." The more severely the leg is turned out or in, the more twisted it will be. The twist will cause one hip to rise higher than the other.
3. The lower the front heel, the more knee action, and shorter stride of landing the horse will have. By this is meant there is an illusion of having a long stride, but in reality, the landing of the leg is on the backward swing thus shortening the stride. The shoulder will also drop in a downward motion.

173

4. The lower the hind heel, the straighter the hock and stifle will be, and the less action the fetlock will have. The hoof will travel closer to the ground, the hip will go up higher, and more weight will be transferred forward onto the front legs. Thus the horse will become heavy on the forehand.

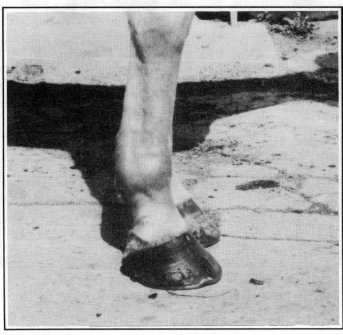

FIGURE 8. SHOWS A HORSE WITH "RUN UNDER" HEELS. IT IS EVIDENT THAT THE WEIGHT IS ON THE HEELS BECAUSE THE HOOF HAS GROWN OVER THE SHOES.

FIGURE 9. SHOWS THE LEFT HIP ON THIS HORSE IS HIGHER THAN ON THE RIGHT.

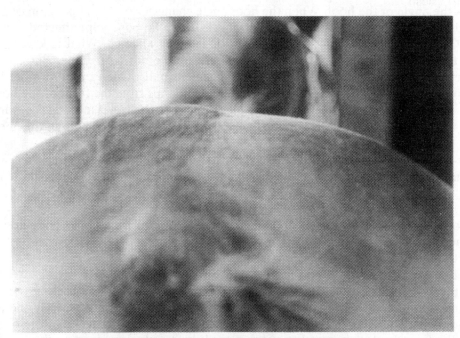

FIGURE 10. SHOW THAT THE LEFT SHOULDER ON THIS HORSE IS WIDER AND HIGHER THAN THE RIGHT SHOULDER

174

8.07   THE OLDER HORSE

Robert R. Johnson, VMD, BS

The vast majority of the equine components of therapeutic riding programs fall into the middle and "older" age ranges. Since the natural life span of the horse is 30 to 35 years, the term "older horse" is given to any horse or pony over ten years old while reserving "geriatric" for those animals over 20 years. The three main areas of special emphasis regarding the older horse are:

(1) Nutrition for the older working horse
(2) Veterinary and health maintenance
(3) Medical and surgical considerations in relation to athletic training and athletic restrictions

Although for these three categories one should be provided with very comprehensive, concise guidelines, the emphasis here is that each animal be approached and considered as an individual first and foremost, and as part of a general category second! So, with this in mind, on to something more informative and interesting.

NUTRITIONAL GUIDELINES FOR THE OLDER WORKING HORSE

The first thing to be considered in nutrition is proper dental care. Horses in their later years should have their teeth examined yearly to avoid rough edges on the lateral, or lip surface of the upper cheek teeth and the medial or tongue surface of the lower cheek teeth. The upper first premolars should be checked for hooks or points. Thorough floating will take care of these problems. In geriatric animals the teeth, both incisors and molars, may be worn down to the gum line, in which case the animal will have problems adequately chewing coarse hay and grains, and consequently lose weight and condition. This can be alleviated by feeding processed feeds such as pellets in a wet mash or alfalfa-molasses as the primary part of their diet.

The weight condition desired in the older working horse is when the ribs are not visible but little or no fat can be felt between the ribs and skin. Trace mineralized salt and plenty of fresh, clean water should be provided. It is highly recommended to put older horses on a broad spectrum vitamin-mineral supplement along with a half to full cup of vegetable oil (peanut, corn or linseed preferably) daily. Most feeds are deficient in fatty acids and fat soluble vitamins, especially if processed by heat or stored for periods of time. Two to three gallons of a soupy bran mash every other day is a good way to help drag sand from the intestinal tract as well as keep manure a little softer, thereby discouraging impaction colic.

Based on the recommendations of the National Research Council, the actual nutrient requirements of the mature working horse are (based on an average 1,000 pound animal):

Daily Feed	Energy	Digestible Protein	Crude Calcium	Phosphorus	Vitamin A
8 kg	15 Mcal	600 gm	20 gm	14 gm	12 iu

In most cases, the ideal diet for most of the therapeutic athletes is half oat/half alfalfa, or half timothy/half oat hay mainstay, with alfalfa-molasses (two pounds per 100 pounds of body weight) added if more weight is needed, along with one-half to one cup of vegetable oil, vitamin-mineral, trace mineralized salt, and fresh water. **Let's not forget a large helping of T.L.C.!**

175

Veterinary HEALTH MAINTENANCE

Routine health programs for the older equine are similar to those for any other adult horse or pony.

I. Vaccinations

1. Yearly "five in one" combination (Eastern, Western, Venezuelan equine encephalitis, tetanus toxoid, influenza)

2. Influenza early Fall and Spring

3. Strangles every six months, Fall and Spring

Note: In our practice we use rhinopneumonitis vaccine only in foals and pregnant mares at five, seven, nine, and ten and a half months gestation.

In areas where Potomac River Fever is endemic (East coast, Illinois and bordering states, and Gulf coast states) twice yearly inoculation with Equine monocytic ehrlichiosis vaccine is highly recommended.

On continents other than North America, other vaccines may be advisable and the owner should consult local veterinary authorities within that region.

II. Parasite Control

1. Worm every two months to be safe, regardless of geographic location
2. Provided Ivermectin (Zimectrim® or Equulan®) is given every four months with any of the following being rotated between the Ivermectin® treatments (Strongid-P®, Benzelmin®, Anthelcide®, Rintal®, Panacur®, Combot®, Negabot®, Equizole-B®), tube worming is not necessary. If the particular horse has a questionable or deficient worming history, then initial tube worming by a veterinarian is suggested.

Note: For pregnant mares, Ivermectin and Strongid-P®, alternating every two months with each, provide a pregnancy-safe, efficacious regimen.

Horses with known parasite damage to the arteries supplying the intestines, or those with a history of chronically poor parasite control, may benefit from a year long, once a month, **Ivermectin only**, regimen due to this compound's excellent Larvicidal abilities.

III. Preventive Dentistry

Have teeth checked yearly; float and trim sharp points and hooks if needed. Verify that each horse's dentition can handle the type and form of feed being provided.

CONSIDERATIONS IN RELATION TO ATHLETIC TRAINING AND ATHLETIC RESTRICTIONS

Many of the horses in therapeutic riding programs are donated and/or retired from other fields of athletic endeavor, many with previous or chronic degenerative orthopedic disorders. Such maladies as osteoarthritis of various joints (spavin in the hocks, ringbone in the pasterns, osselets in the fetlocks, navicular disease in the heels of the forefeet) are very common, as is chronic lower back soreness (coldback) in the lumbar, sacral, and thoracic regions. In spite of these conditions, the majority of these individual animals serve very functionally and enthusiastically.

The best approach to training and conditioning is to start with a long, slow warm up period and finish with the same. Start with ten minutes at a walk and trot, both directions, no matter what kind of work the horse is going to do that day; then, end with ten to fifteen minutes of easy walking followed by five minutes of cold water hosing <u>on the legs only</u>. Most horses with chronic arthritic disorders will warm out of their stiffness and soreness with this approach. There is a definite place among these older equines for warming liniments, braces, and leg washes such as Absorbine®, Bigeloil®, Vetrolin®, isopropyl alcohol, and D.M.S.O., used both before and after workouts. D.M.S.O., especially, is effective for navicular and ringbone; massage it into and around the joints and coronary band before workouts (but always wear quality rubber gloves when touching D.M.S.O. as it is readily absorbed by human hands also.) Be sure to apply standing leg wraps on all four lower limbs when the horses are not working - this protects tendons and keeps warmth and circulation within the lower joints.

(Always check first with your veterinarian to determine the horse's exact problems and appropriate treatment. Do not administer any of the following medications yourself without the specific advise from your vet.) With more progressive or severe degenerative disorders, oral nonsteroidal anti-inflamatories may be in order. Increasing in relative strength (and expense) along with their respective therapeutic doses are: Phenylbutazone®--one to three grams daily until clinically improved, then every other day; Aspirin--ten to thirty-five aspirin (360 mg or 5 grain tablets) given twice, or once daily; Arguel®--one to two packets daily until clinical response, then every 2 to 3 days; Banamine®--one-half to two packets (250 mg packets) daily until response, then every other day.

For chronically sore lower backs, which are usually secondary to hind limb problems, use moist heat therapy, epsom salt soaks, and massage therapy. One of the most effective treatments for back problems and muscle soreness in our practice has been through acupuncture, which works well for many musculo-skeletal problems.

CONCLUSION
Just as the broodmares are a blessed group of our equine population, so are these older, dedicated working horses. Let's face it, most of them have paid their dues to the horse society as runners, jumpers, working stock animals, show horses, and so forth. Now that they have become integral parts of therapeutic riding programs, they deserve some special consideration and human insight. They need a little more time to get warmed up and get that circulation moving, require a little more individualized attention to diet and dentition, but basically they are easy keepers and very rewarding animals with which to work.

To witness the love and respect that occurs between horse and rider as each devotes itself to the other is to understand why this unique therapeutic riding technique works!

8.08   AVOID STABLE VICES IN A THERAPEUTIC PROGRAM HORSE

Margaret L. Galloway, MA, BHSAI

Horses can remember events that are either the first, the most frequent, or most recent. They also remember negative events well (Sumner, 1976) since these pose a threat to them. Bad habits (vices) may develop from bad experiences, fear, boredom, excessive energy, stress, curiosity, nutritional deficiencies, or bad temperament (Borton, 1990). They may be maintained because the horse seeks a way to relieve stress, and thus gets a rewarding response from the vice. Some behaviors are so subtle it is difficult to tell the place and time for a reward to be given. The job of a handler is to prevent negative behavior and reward behavior that is *desirable*. It is important to find ways to keep the horse happy and avoid vices.

"In work with a variety of animals, B.F. Skinner...found that punishment is less effective in behavioral control than positive (rewarding) reinforcement" (Sumner, 1976). This suggests that in correcting problem behavior, ways should be found in which the horse can be rewarded. One should correct a problem when it occurs and then reward the horse for giving the right response.

STABLE VICES
Stable vices are bad habits that horses display while in the stable. Confinement is unnatural for horses and threatens their physical, mental, and emotional well-being. Therapeutic riding program horses need to be attentive, social, and happy to provide the riders with the most beneficial results. Bad habits are easier to prevent than to cure. To help avoid them, turn horses out in paddocks or pastures to allow them more movement and to be around other horses to meet their social needs. They need to see, hear, and smell their peers. Be sure all horses have some form of exercise daily. Feeding them bulky hay instead of pellets or cubes may help alleviate boredom. Change feeding from twice a day to three times a day or more. This will provide them a more natural feeding routine. Adding carrots, potatoes, or other succulent feed can be beneficial. Make sure the horses get enough work and that it is varied. A good daily grooming helps provide for tactile needs. Talking to them while handling also helps alleviate their boredom. Another method of making the confined horse's life more interesting is to provide him toys and music.

Cribbing: Cribbing is the act of a horse grabbing a surface with his mouth, arching his neck, and swallowing air. Swallowing air may lead to colic or gastric upset. It may be copied from other horses. The most effective way to restrain this behavior is the cribbing strap. This is a leather strap at least one or two inches wide, placed around the horse's throat, near his jaw line. It is adjusted tightly enough that the horse cannot suck in mouthfuls of air, but is still able to swallow. The horse needs to be carefully observed with a new cribbing strap to be sure it is effective but also safe and humane.

Weaving: Weaving is a repetitive ritualistic pattern in which the horse stands in one spot but shifts his weight from one side to the other. He almost always does it in the door of his stall. "This suggests that the habit may have its origin in the horse's attempt to find a way out of confinement" (Sumner, 1976) or is copied from a stable mate. Weaving can cause lameness, weight loss, or physical exhaustion (Borton, 1990). Regular exercise and time spent turned out usually help this vice. Smaller feedings given more frequently may decrease the boredom. Some people hang safe objects, such as soft wood or a plastic container, from the top of the stall door so that the horse hits them if he weaves.

Mane and Tail Rubbing: Mane and tail rubbing usually result from itching. Mane itching is often from dirt or an allergy. Tail itching may be from worms. Worming should be performed according to the schedule and method suggested by your veterinarian. Both the mane and tail may be washed with an anti-bacterial or fungicidal soap such as Nolvasan®, or Phisohex®.

Stall Walking: A horse who may be high-strung or does not get enough exercise may develop stall walking. This is a nervous habit that wastes energy (Evans, 1990). Regular exercise will work off excess energy, and companionship, grooming, soft music, and challenges of exercises in the arena and on the trail will help to prevent boredom.

OTHER PROBLEMS AND SOLUTIONS

Aggressive vices: Horses who kick, strike, bite, bolt, buck, rear, or charge their handlers or other horses are unsuitable for therapeutic riding programs as they may cause injury. If the problem cannot be corrected, the horse should not be used in a therapeutic riding program. When a horse with a history of negative behavior causes an injury in a therapeutic riding program, a lawsuit could easily follow. The program "knew" that the horse might be dangerous yet "continued to use it."

Hard to Catch Horses: Horses may become hard to catch because (1) they associate being caught with boring work; (2) they may not want to leave the other horses; (3) they may associate being caught with pain or punishment. The horse needs to associate positive rewards with being caught. Some horses may be cured by being fed carrots or grain every time they are caught or just being given a good rub and attention. The handler may be able to find a way to feed horses their usual ration after catching them. Catching the horse to take him out for grazing or other pleasurable treats is another solution.

Pulling Back: Some horses panic and pull back when tied. These horses should never be tied in the usual way. The best way is to tie them in their stall, where they have a wall behind them and less incentive to pull back. If they must be tied outside, just looping the rope several times around a hitching rail is safe. The best method for handling tying problems is to teach the horse to ground tie or use the T.T.E.A.M. method to retrain this horse from his bad habit (see chapter 7.03 for T.T.E.A.M. techniques).

UNDERSTANDING THE HORSE

There are numerous books which will educate the reader in understanding the horse. When the instructor, trainer, riders, and volunteers understand the horse, they will have more insight into resolving problems and avoiding negative behavior.

Reference

Borton. A. (1990). In Evans, J.W. el al *The Horse*. New York: W.H Freeman & Co.

Blazer, D. (1982). *Horses Seldom Burp! How to Keep Them Happy and Well*. La Jolla: A.S. Barnes & Co. Inc.

Condax, K.D.(1979). *Horse Sense*. Causes and Correction of Horse and Rider Problems. New York: Prentice Hall Press.

Evans, J.W. (1889). *Horses*. 2nd ed. New York: W.H. Freeman & Co. 49.

Schramm, U. (1986). *The Undisciplined Horse*. London: J.A. Allen.

Sumner, D.W. (1976). *Breaking Your Horse's Bad Habits*. Millwood: Breakthrough Publishing.

8.09 THE MEDICINE CHEST FOR THE THERAPEUTIC RIDING HORSE

Barbara T. Engel, MEd, OTR

Horses, like humans, have accidents and become ill. Stable personnel must be able to administer first aid until they can obtain help from a veterinarian. It is important to be prepared for such things as bruises, cuts, puncture wounds, or sprains. Horse handlers should have basic knowledge of horse first aid.

First aid supplies must be kept in a clean chest and tools must be maintained in good condition. The chest should be kept in a central area that is easy to reach by the handlers BUT AWAY FROM THE PROGRAM POPULATION. It should always be kept in the same location and all staff handles the horses should know where it is. These items must be easily available for emergency use. The following list contains the major items that should be included in a horse first aid box:

First aid book for horses
veterinary thermometer
cold packs
adhesive tape
clean towels
bandages
cotton wool or gamgee
cotton leg wraps - 30x36 inches or (diapers)
2 ½ to 3 inch - kling gauze rolls
1 or more rolls of sterile cotton
sterile large surgical pad dressings
surgical sponges
track bandages
triangular bandages
elastic, stretch, crepe, or vetrap bandages.
pads for compression dressing
alcohol surgical soap
eye wash
Epsom salts
glycerine, vaseline
poultice powder
bentadine or iodine
pack of sterile saline solution
melolin, Fucidin Tulle or other dressing
antibiotic or antiseptic wound dressing
plastic bags
latex tubing tourniquet

pill smasher
pail and pan for washing
large bucket for leg soaks/water/ice/ treatment
humane twitch
straight forceps
blunt nose bandage scissors
latex or vinyl examination gloves
50 cc syringe in sterile pack/needles
shoe puller-spreader combination
hoof knife
hack saw
rasp
pliers
flashlight and batteries

8.10 THE GROOMING TOOLS FOR THE THERAPEUTIC RIDING HORSES

Barbara T. Engel, MEd, OTR

Grooming is the daily attention that stabled horses need for the animal's health--to maintain healthy coats, prevent disease, and sustain cleanliness. A daily grooming routine gives the handler the opportunity to check the horse for any problems. The grooming process also provides the contact needed to maintain the human-animal bond.

It is preferable that each horse has his own grooming kit--this prevents the possible spread of disease. Tools must always be kept clean by frequent washing.

The following tools are necessary for proper grooming.

 **BODY BRUSH** is a soft, short bristle brush used after the dandy brush to remove finer dirt.

 **BRUSH CLEANER CURRY COMB** a brush used to clean the brushes while brushing the horse. Hold the metal curry comb in the free hand and run the brush over the metal teeth several times to remove the dirt. A dirty brush cannot clean a horse's coat. A rubber curry comb can also be used if a metal one is not available.

 **CLIPPERS** are used to shear the coat in warm climates, to prevent the horse from over heating and to trim the whiskers for a horse show and possibly when a horse is injured.

 **DANDY BRUSH** is a stiff-bristled brush used to remove the large dirt particles brought up by the rubber curry comb and is used on the large muscle areas of the horse. This brush is used with short wrist strokes; brush in the direction that the hair lays.

 **HOOF BRUSH** is used to paint the hoof with dressing to prevent the hoof from drying out. This is especially important in dry, sandy climates.

 **HOOF PICK** is used on all parts of the hoof to clean off mud and manure; remove stones or foreign objects. Keeping the hoof clean prevents disease, injury, and hoof separation.

 **MANE AND TAIL BRUSH** is used to "lay" the hair down on the neck and to keep the tail hair in order. A human hair brush can be used for the mane and tail. Using small amounts of oil helps make brushing easier and decreases hair loss. The tail is separated into small sections of hair with the fingers and then brushed.

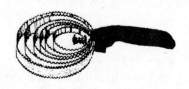

METAL CURRY COMB has a spring action. It is usually used in the winter to remove dirt from heavy coats. Care must be taken not to hurt the horse with the metal edges.

RUBBER CURRY COMB is usually used initially in grooming, to remove dirt from beneath the hair. Using a circular motion and applying pressure helps to bring up dirt and scales. Using a rhythmic motion provides the horse with a relaxing massage. This tool comes in many variations for different effects.

RUBBING CLOTH OR TOWEL is used either damp or dry, to remove the remaining dirt and hair from the horse and to wipe sensitive areas. This is especially important to do for individuals sensitive to dust who will be riding the horse.

SPONGE OR MOIST CLOTH used to clean the eyes, nose, muzzle, rectum and genitals. Always use a clean sponge for the front and another for the rear areas.

SHEDDING SCRAPER OR BLADE is a flexible metal blade with teeth on one side. The teeth are run over the coat in the same direction as the hair grows to loosen and remove hair. This process aids the removal of hair during the shedding season.

SWEAT SCRAPER is a long metal or plastic tool used to remove excess water from a horse after bathing or sponging off.

SPECIAL TOOLS FOR SMALL AND DISABLED HANDS can be adapted from standard tools with straps, velcro, long handles, and wooden blocks. Hand brushes, dog brushes can be used for small hands. Tools can be adapted with splinting material (plastic and rubber materials that hand and leg splints are constructed from--see your occupational therapist for special constructions.)

PART IV. HUMAN BEHAVIOR: NORMAL AND ABNORMAL

9 HUMAN FUNCTIONING AND THERAPEUTIC RIDING

KEY WORDS
NORMAL
FUNCTION
DEVELOPMENT

In order to gain a good perspective of disabilities, one needs to understand normal human function and development. This knowledge provides the background needed to understand the difference between normal and abnormal function. It provides the instructor with the framework required to understand parts of the body involved in a disability and helps the instructor to assist persons with disabilities to work toward normal skills. This section provides the reader with an overview of normal function and development and the terms involved, followed by a brief description of many disabilities seen in therapeutic riding including:

- The skeleton
- Anatomy as it relates to riding
- Growth and development
- The central nervous system
- The psychological systems
- Disabilities
- Indication or contra indication to riding

It is not the intent here to give a course in anatomy and physiology. This is not to say, however, that an understanding of normal human function and movement is not important when working with any rider. Sally Swift (1985) has explained in detail the importance of understanding the human structure and its relationship to riding. It is especially important to understand the anatomy of riders with disabilities so that one can help and not hinder the rider. To provide the instructor and other staff the technical information regarding a particular rider and his specific disability, occupational and/or physical therapists are included as consultants or full time members of therapeutic riding programs.

Areas of the anatomy which relate to riding will be briefly covered. Any instructor must have an understanding of the anatomy of the rider (along with the anatomy of the horse) in order to achieve the harmony of horse and rider. The instructor must be able to "*communicate to the student what should be felt on the horse. It is a problem of recognition and understanding. Accurate and useful images can then be developed*" (H.Schusdziarra, V. Schusdziarra, 1985.) In addition to the general knowledge of the structure of the human body, one must be aware of areas which are directly related to the populations who are "at risk" or physically fragile.

It is also important to have a basic knowledge of those growth and development aspects which relate directly to the learning process, to neurological disorders, and developmental disabilities. This knowledge helps the instructor to relate appropriately to riders with various sorts of psychological or neurological involvement or developmental delays.

References
Swift, S. (1985). *Centered Riding*. North Pomfret: David & Charles. 32-49.
Schusdziarra, H., Schusdziarra, V. (1985) *An Anatomy of Riding* Briarcliff, Breakthrough Publications. ix.

9.01 HUMAN SKELETON

Stephanie C. Woods, BFA

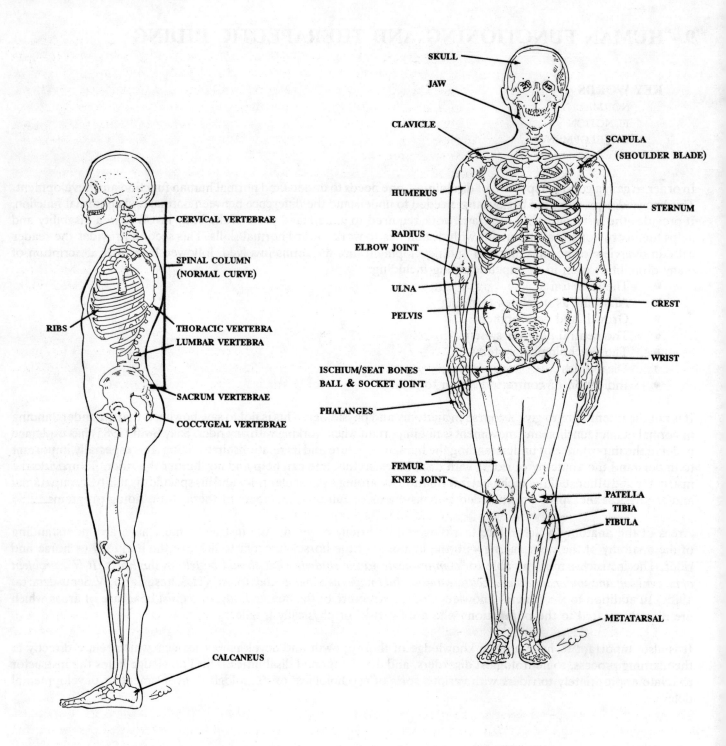

SKULL

JAW

CLAVICLE

SCAPULA
(SHOULDER BLADE)

HUMERUS

STERNUM

RADIUS

ELBOW JOINT

ULNA

CREST

PELVIS

WRIST

ISCHIUM/SEAT BONES
BALL & SOCKET JOINT

PHALANGES

FEMUR
KNEE JOINT

PATELLA

TIBIA

FIBULA

METATARSAL

CERVICAL VERTEBRAE

SPINAL COLUMN
(NORMAL CURVE)

RIBS

THORACIC VERTEBRA
LUMBAR VERTEBRA

SACRUM VERTEBRAE

COCCYGEAL VERTEBRAE

CALCANEUS

Barbara T. Engel, MEd, OTR

The spinal or vertebral column is the major supporting part of the skeleton and is composed of 33 vertebra: 7 cervical form the neck; the chest area has 12 thoracic; the lower back has 5 lumbar; and the sacrum 5 (fused), and 4 (fused) coccygeal vertebra make up the tail bone. Looking at the skeleton from the sideview, the spine curves forward in the neck and waist region where it is more flexible. It curves backward at the upper back and the tail bone or sacrum. In a resting or neutral position, the normal spine does not curve from side to side. Between each vertebra there is a disc which acts as a buffer from jolts received from movement. There is a balance and flexibility to the normal spine which allows for support and a spring reaction (H. Schusdziarra, V. Schusdziarra, 1985). It also allows for stability, mobility and movements in all directions of the torso. Mobility includes rotation, lateral bending, extension, and forward flexion. Muscles are attached to the bones by tendons. Ligaments attach bones to bones, holding the spine together and allowing the spine to move with other parts of the body. Additional stability is provided by the rib cage as ribs are attached to the vertebral bodies by ligaments and muscles. Bones are held together at the joints with ligaments.

The shoulder girdle consists of the clavicle (collar bone), and the scapula (shoulder bone). The humerus (upper bone of the arm) is joined by tendons and ligaments to the scapula. The clavicle attaches to the scapula at one end and the sternum at the level of the 7th vertebra. The shoulder can move up-down, forward-backward, and rotate in a circle.

The sacrum is joined to the pelvis by strong ligaments. The ischial tuberosities (seat bones) of the pelvic bone can be felt through your buttocks and are the bones that carry the body weight when a person is correctly sitting in the saddle or in a chair. The bridge of the pelvis between the spine and seat allows a cushioning, springy effect between the two (Swift, 1985). The top edge of the pelvis can be felt below the waist and is the iliac crest.

On each side of the pelvis, below the iliac crest is a round hollow. The ball-like head of the thigh bone (femur) fits into this hollow. The joint is called a ball and socket joint. The weight of the entire body is distributed into the pelvis through these two joints while a person stands. In sitting, the pelvis can tip to the front or to the back, rocking on the seat bones which are rounded. The seat bones are further apart when rocking backward, allowing for extension of the hip joint and a deeper seat in the saddle. When the seat bones rock forward, the hip joint flexes and the legs come together causing the seat to become shallow. The structure of these bones allow the pelvis to rock side to side or back and forth (H. Schusdziarra & V. Schusdziarra, 1985).

The male and female skeletons are different and this affects how each sits in the saddle (Figure 1 & 2). This difference in anatomy is due to the manner in which humans bear their children. The female pelvis is naturally wider and deeper with a more circular pelvic outlet. Female seat bones (ischia) diverge to the rear and the tailbone (sacrum) also tends to tip toward the back. The position of the seat bones inhibits the female pelvis from rocking back and forth freely. The male pelvis is narrower with the seat bones nearly parallel allowing them to rock back and forth with ease. These differences make it easier for a man to sit with his seat "under" him as his pelvis naturally wants to tilt to the back. The female pelvis naturally wants to tilt to the front causing her to sit more on the pubis rather than the sacrum, making women more likely to sit a "crotch" seat. Due to these differences, men tend to have less and women have more of a lumbar curve (Bennett, 1989; Harris, 1985).

The more the pelvic bones, the spine and other parts of the skeleton are in balance, the more relaxed are the muscles that cover them (Swift, 1985). "With the decreased tension of the muscles, the rider sits more at ease on the moving horse, the pelvis accommodating itself to the swaying up-and-down motion of the horse's back" (Schusdziarra & Schusdziarra, 1985). It can then follow the motion of the horse. Bones come together at the joints. Most joints are sites of movement. The degree of movement is determined by the combined structure of the joint, ligaments, tendons, and muscles. The legs hang from the ball and socket hip joint to the side of the body. The femur (thigh bone) protrudes from the socket joint out to the side (the "neck") like an upside down L, before it drops down toward the knee joint.

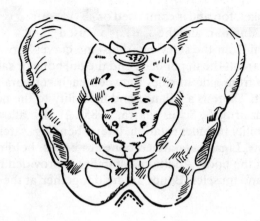

FIGURE 1. MALE PELVIS

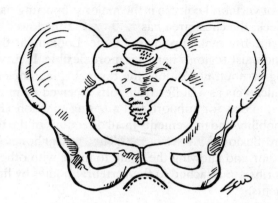

FIGURE 2. FEMALE PELVIS

The neck of the femur forms a 125 degree angle with the shaft in men, less of an angle with the shaft in women (Brunnstrom, 1972). The neck of the femur, which is two to three inches in length, give the legs an increased ability to straddle the horse (Swift, 1985). Because of the different structure of the pelvis and the change in the angle of the neck of the femur, the leg of the female hangs with the knee pointed out more than the male, while the male foot hangs flat and the female foot is angled inward (Goss, 1966, Bennett, 1989).

The spinal or vertebral column houses the spinal cord extending from within the skull bones to the first or second lumbar vertebra. The spinal cord is a part of the central nervous system (CNS). The central nervous system is a communication system that includes the brain as the main computer, the spinal cord as the main trunk line and a system of nerves through which the brain communicates with the muscles and vital organs. The central nervous system relays information through sense organs: receptors of the skin, bones, joints, muscles, eyes, ears, nose, tongue, inner ear and the internal organs. All systems are inter-related to some extent, some more than others. The CNS distributes impulses which activate muscles and cause movement patterns. Movement produces change in the entire organism (Feldenkrais, 1981).

The skeletal system begins to develop as the fetus grows and progresses as the human body gains size. Major maturity begins between 14 and 15 years in girls and 15 and 16 years in boys with complete maturity occurring at about 25 years. Bone formation in the early years is incomplete; it is composed of cartilage and can be fragile (Raney & Brashear, 1971). Normal children under four years may not have joint unions in areas of their body which could be affected by their position on the horse. Children who are affected by problems in development of any kind may have their bone structure delayed (Royer, 1974).

INSTRUCTORS MUST BE AWARE THAT THE ANGLE A JOINT ASSUMES COULD BE AFFECTED BY POSITIONING AND BY STRESS AGAINST THE HORSE AND COULD HAVE A LIFE-LONG INFLUENCE. INSTRUCTORS MUST CONSULT WITH A THERAPIST OR PHYSICIAN WHO IS BOTH KNOWLEDGEABLE IN THE USE OF THE HORSE AND ITS EFFECT ON SMALL CHILDREN PRIOR TO PUTTING A CHILD UNDER FOUR YEARS ON A HORSE. IN ADDITION, THE SIZE AND THE GAIT OF THE HORSE BECOMES AN IMPORTANT CONSIDERATION WITH A VERY YOUNG RIDER, ESPECIALLY ONE WITH ANY KIND OF ORTHOPEDIC DISORDER OR DELAYED DEVELOPMENT WHOSE BONE AGE MAY BE YOUNGER THEN HIS OR HER CHRONOLOGICAL AGE. ONE MUST ALWAYS REMEMBER--HORSEBACK RIDING IS NOT FOR EVERYONE.

Conclusion

When the instructor has a visual image of the skeletal form of his or her student on the horse (Figure 3), he or she will be better able to understand how to manipulate the horse to gain a balanced seat. Remember that bones are connected by ligaments and tendons and that muscles are the movers of the bones. Some preparation is necessary to prepare the ligaments, tendons and muscles for the exercise they receive while horseback riding. Persons who are out of physical condition, getting limited exercise, having more than average high tonal or low tonal qualities are more in need of warm-ups and stretching than the average person. Preparation is always necessary in any athletic endeavor.

FIGURE 3. RIDER ON HORSE

References

Bennett, D. (1989). Who's Built Best to Ride. in *Equus*, 140, June. Equus Magazine. Boulder, Co. 58-63,112-115.

Brunnstrom, S. (1972). *Clinical Kinesiology*. 3rd edition. Philadelphia: F.A. Davis Co. 227-228.

Feldenkrais, M. (1981). *The Elusive Obvious*. Cupertino: Meta Publications.

Goss, C.M. (1966). *Gray's Anatomy of the Human Body*. ed 28. Philadelphia: Lea & Febiger. 222-245.

Harris, C. (1985). *Fundamentals of Riding*. London: A. J. Allen.

Keim, H.A., Hensinger, R.N. Spinal Deformities. in *Clinical Symposia*. West Calwell: Ciba-Geigy. 3-4.

Raney & Brashear. (1971). *Shands' Handbook of Orthopaedic Surgery*. St. Louis: C.V. Mosby Co. 2-7.

Royer, P. (1974). *Scientific Foundation of Paediatrics*. Philadelphia: W.B. Saunders Co. 376-399.

Schusdziarra, H., Schusdziarra, V. (1985) *An Anatomy of Riding* Briarcliff, Breakthrough Publications. 2-35.

Swift, S. (1985). *Centered Riding*. North Pomfret: David & Charles. 32-34.

9.03   HUMAN GROWTH AND DEVELOPMENT

Barbara T. Engel, MEd, OTR

Growth refers to the increase in size of the structure of the human body. This would include the size of the head and body bones, height of the structure, and weight of the body (Banus et al, 1979). Growth can be increased by good nutrition, bonding, stimulation, and exercise or decreased by internal or external causes such as disease, malnutrition, lack of nurturing, trauma, drugs and other factors (Banus et al, 1979).

Progression of growth and development occurs on two basic levels.
1.   <u>Phylogenetic</u> (inherited) development involves structural changes such as cell division to develop into a complex multicell organism, dependent on its genetic pool or species origin as in all more primitive creatures.
2.   <u>Ontogenetic</u> development is the progressive and sequential behavioral change that occurs by the individual's experiences within his or her environment and his or her culture (Banus et al, 1979).

The central nervous system (CNS) receives, assimilates and responds to information it receives. Maturation and myelination of the nervous system increases the speed of messages transmitted and the resulting action of the transmission. The function of the CNS gives the human the ability to move and perform skills while maintaining one's posture and equilibrium against gravity (K.Bobath 1980). "*There is, thus, a continuously changing environment with a continuously changing organism; a closed loop of four elements: skeleton, muscles, nervous system, and environment,*" with feedback and feedforward throughout all systems (Feldenkrais, 1981). The nervous system needs to be stimulated to develop. Development is dependent on the ability to move. "*Only active movement can give the sensation essential for learning voluntary movements and skills*" (K. Bobath, 1980). Movement stimulation needs to be purposeful in order to be registered by the brain for an adaptive response since the brain only *learns* with meaningful activities (Masuda, 1988; Oetter, 1987).

Functional movement stimulation evokes more alertness and provides more comfort to the child than contact without movement. Movement increases motor behavior, visual and auditory alertness (Korner, 1984). Movement increases the respiratory capacity which in turn increases alertness (Oetter, 1987). Movement may be necessary to enable all living things to form their exterior object world (Feldenkrais, 1981). Feldenkrais (1981) points out the need to be *AWARE* of one's movements in order to learn and make choices, "*by shifting our attention to the means of achieving instead of the urge to succeed, the learning process is easier*" and alternative choices can be made.

If the nervous system has not developed to a certain point, a given skill will not develop and cannot be taught. For example, an infant will creep only when his or her nervous system has developed to the point that this can occur. Skills develop in a sequential manner: rolling, sitting with hand support, sitting with hands free to play, kneeling, standing holding on, walking holding on, then standing free with good balance. Though <u>skills can not be taught to an immature nervous system</u>, the nervous system in a fostering environment can be stimulated to help it to adapt and mature (Lawther, 1968).

Early handling of infants and their bodily contact with caregivers are necessary for the development of touch and emotional bonding in children. This give and take interaction between caregivers and infants is also the beginning of language development. Touch and proprioceptive feedback begins four months after conception at which time fetuses sucks their thumbs, touch their bodies and presses against the uterine wall (Almi, 1985). After birth, the babies put their fingers into their mouths and progressively touch all parts of their bodies as mobility increases (K. Bobath, 1980). The infants begins to touch and move, to see and explore their environment as they begin to become more proficient in mobility.

As infants move their arms, their hands come into their visual field and the beginning of *eye-hand connection* begins. As they feel their body parts, they develop a *body perception* or "a feeling of themselves as a unity separate from their environment" (K. Bobath, 1980). As *body perception* is developed, infants begin to relate themselves to the environment around them and *spatial orientation begins. Body image* develops when infants develop a visual image themselves which is separate from the environment.

Development and learning are dependent on maturation of the CNS. Learning and development can be differentiated as follows (Banus et al, 1979):

1a   Development results from genetic endowment with experience in the species milieu

1b   Developmental tasks, such as self feeding, are dependent on the maturation of the CNS in a sequence from simple to complex movements

1c   Development attempts to maintain a stable internal condition (self preservation)

1d   Development requires action on the environment such as maintaining sitting balance when tilted off balance

1e   As development progresses, performance increases to more difficult tasks such as walking rather than creeping

2a   Learning is dependent on environmental influences which guide the individual's potential such as eating with a spoon and fork

2b   Learning involves coping with requirements of the external environment

2c   Learning is knowing that certain surfaces will require balance--learning from past experience

2d   Learning is watching others and copying their actions

2e   Learning can be forgotten. Knowledge is not permanent

Maturation of the Central Nervous System (CNS), influences:

- WHAT INFORMATION THE INDIVIDUAL TAKES IN.
- HOW INFORMATION IS INTEGRATED.
- WHAT OCCURS WITH THE INFORMATION TAKEN IN.
- WHAT ACTIONS THE INDIVIDUAL MAKES ON HIS ENVIRONMENT.

The CNS synthesizes feedback from actions from both internal and external sources and coordinates appropriate data from memory of prior experience. Synthesis and coordination lead to development of perceptual skills and learning. Ayres has noted that input through the touch system increases arousal and the ability to *motor plan* one's actions (the active performance of a skilled task with one's limbs) (Sensory Integration International, 1990). Affolter (1990) states that touch sensation must be felt accurately, registered and interpreted by the brain to be useful in the adaptive process in response to the environment. Feldenkrais cites an experiment in which a group of people used eye-glasses which inverted the image on the brain so all the participants saw everything upside down. Everything they touched began to look normal but what they did not touch continued to be inverted (Feldenkrais, 1981). THERE IS CONSIDERABLE EVIDENCE SUGGESTING THE IMPORTANCE OF TOUCH, AS IT IS FULLY INTERPRETED BY THE BRAIN, IN THE DEVELOPMENT OF MOVEMENT, LEARNING AND INTERRELATIONSHIP OF THE BODY TO THE ENVIRONMENT.

Changes in posture produce changes of the body's relation to gravity. The body must adapt to changes in the environment by making fluid changes of postural tone of groups of body muscles in order to prevent falling. This is called *dynamic equilibrium* since the body is never totally still. There is an interaction of muscle groups which causes one group of muscles to flex and others to extend. This, for example, allows us to walk. There must be enough tension in the muscle tone to allow the body to stand or sit against the pull of gravity of the earth. The tension must fluctuate to allow for intended and controlled movement.

Body postural reflexes and reactions are automatic mechanisms which allow groups of muscles to react together to maintain *equilibrium* in posture. "The reflexes were found to contribute to maintaining the characteristic orientation of the body in space with respect to gravity (labyrinthine reflexes) and with respect to the interrelationship of the body parts (tonic neck and righting reflexes) (Capute, 1978)." These body reactions are present throughout normal life and may be easily observed during physical exertion. These reactions differ in characteristic from "primitive reflexes" which are observed in normal infants' development through the first 6 months of life. "The persistence of <u>primitive reflexes</u> beyond the newborn period has long been a classic sign of central nervous system dysfunction (Capute, 1978)."

Some postural reflexes and reactions which are commonly known are:
1. *Protective reactions:* are active in all directions to protect the body from injury. For example: placing the hands out front of oneself to prevent falling forward after stumbling or losing balance forward
2. *Neck righting reactions*: to maintain head control and an upright body position against gravity. The body follows where the head goes
3. *Tonic neck reflex*--there are two:
   Symmetrical: the head is brought forward, causing the upper extremity to bend and the lower extremity to straighten
   Asymmetrical: the head turns to the side (to look), the arm and leg on the chin side straighten, the arm and leg on the hair side, bend
4. *Body righting on the head:* the body aligns itself with the head against gravity
5. *Optical righting*: upright posture against gravity using the eyes as the main control
6. *Equilibrium reactions:* automatic responses to the change of posture and movement to maintain balance against gravity using any or all of the above reactions to maintain balance

Postural reactions mature and integrate in the normal person though they always remain present. These responses do not interfere with voluntary movements as they can be inhibited at will and support intentional movements. Maturation of the CNS and the consequences of growth in all areas of human development during the infant and childhood ages are a major focus by many investigators, but not so for the older age groups. Assuming normal growth and development continues through adolescence, the body continues to grow and refine its abilities to respond to its environment. It was once thought that growth and maturation of the CNS was completed at the time of adolescence and there was a general deterioration of the nervous system in later years. Evidence indicates that this is not the case. There is reason to believe that constructive changes may occur in the brain into the seventies (Oppenheim, 1981). Man has enormous adaptive capabilities to adjust to injury or illness but one must understand, as an instructor, what the functional implications are that result from such trauma.

References

Affolter, A. (1990). *The Use of Guiding as a Perceptual Cognitive Approach*. Course notes. Santa Barbara.

Almi, C.R. (1985). Normal sequential behavior and physiological changes throughout the development arc: in Banus, B.S.; el al *The Developmental Therapist*. 2nd ed.Thorofare, Charles B. Slack, Inc. 1-163.

Bobath, K. (1980). A Neurophysiological Basis for the Treatment of Cerebral Palsy. In *Clinics in Developmental Medicine No 75*. Philadelphia, J.P. Lippincott Co. vii, 1-2, 5.

Brunnstrom, S. (1972). *Clinical Kinesiology*.3rd edition. Philadelphia, F.A. Davis Co. 242-250.

Capute, A. J.; Accardo, P.J.; et. al., (1978). *Primitive Reflex Profile*. Baltimore: Univ Park Press.

Erhardt, R.P. (1982). *Developmental Hand Dysfunction*. Laurel, Ramsco Publishing Co.

Feldenkrais, M. (1981). *The Elusive Obvious*. Cupertino: Meta Publications.

Knobloch, H, Stevens, F. Malone, M. (1980). *Manual of Developmental Diagnosis* Hagerstown: Harper & Row.

Korner, A.F. (1984). *National Center for Clinical Infants*. "Zero to three". V,1. Sept.1-6.

Lawther, J.D. (1968). *The Learning of Physical Skills*. Englewood Cliff: Prentice-Hall Inc.

Masuda, D.L. (1988). Integrated Approach to Treatment. In *Rehab '88, The Moment of Truth*, Abby Medical Conf. Los Angeles.

Oetter, P. (1988). Las Vegas NM. Sensory System Course Notes.

Oppenheim, R.W. (1981). Ontogenetic Adaptions and Retrogressive Processes in the Development of the Nervous System and Behavior: A Neuroembryological Perspective. in Connolly, K.J. & Prechtl, H.F. ed: *Maturation and Development: Biological and Psychological Perspectives*

Piaget, J. (1963). *The Origins of Intelligence in Children*. New York, W.W. Norton & Co.

Pulaski, M.A.: (1980). *Understanding Piaget*. New York, Harper & Row.

Schusdziarra, H., Schusdziarra, V. (1985). *An Anatomy of Riding* Briarcliff, Breakthrough Publications. 2-35.

Sensory Integration International. (1990). Sensory Integration Treatment Course notes. Los Angeles.

Shortridge, S.D. (1985). The developmental process: prenatal to adolescence. In Clark, P.N.; Allen, A.S. *Occupational Therapy for Children*. St Louis, C.V. Mosby Co. 48-63.

Swift, S. (1985). *Centered Riding*. North Pomfret: David & Charles. 32-34.

Umphred, D.A., editor: *Neurological Rehabilitation*. St. Louis, C.V. Mosby Co. 61-63.

9.04   THE BRAIN

John H. Brough, OTR

KEY WORDS
RIGHT HEMISPHERE
LEFT   HEMISPHERE
INTEGRATION OF HEMISPHERES

A person would find it inconceivable to go to a lawyer who had never studied law; or to a dentist who had never studied teeth. Unfortunately children are sent to school and are taught by people who have never studied the brain or its function in academic learning. It is not necessary for a teacher to be a neurosurgeon. He or she does need to have a basic understanding of the brain's function, such as how integration of fine and gross motor input, perception, long and short term memory is accomplished, and the methods for getting this information back out so that it is useable. This absence of basic understanding of the brain's function is due in part to the schism between the medical and educational communities. The result of the work done in brain research has been reported so technically that teachers and parents are afraid to tackle the task of understanding it. Yet, it is a fundamental need!

The brain is essentially a small but highly sophisticated computer. It responds to stimuli by making choices. These choices are decided by the kind of information being fed in. This information is compared to that already stored and accessible. The information enters the brain through the various sensory channels which include but are not limited to: touch, taste, sight, hearing and smell. In actuality there are eight major pathways to the brain, with at least 23 smaller routes. All of these feed information to the "computer". Most of these paths travel to the brain via the spinal cord, enter the brain stem or enter the brain directly such as visions and sight. As they ascend to the highest levels of the brain, they pass through three basic brain levels. These levels originated as the brain developed through time. The first level is essentially the same as the brain of a reptile, the brain stem. This area is concerned with protecting the organism, maintaining respiration and heart beat. The second level through which the information passes is a filtering mechanism, the medulla oblongata. It decides which information needs to go to the higher brain centers and which information can be dealt with at lower levels. The highest level of brain function is the cortex (cerebellum). This area receives messages from the sense organs, thinks, and among other things sends messages to the muscles. Located here is control of conscious movement, speech, writing, and thoughts and feelings. To learn, the individual needs a small amount of challenge or stress; otherwise he or she would sleep, eat, and only exist. When he or she has a challenge and accepts it as non-threatening, learning takes place. He or she uses the right and left hemispheres of the cerebrum to look at problem-solving possibilities.

At the cortical level, the right and left hemispheres deal with information differently.
The left hemisphere function is believed to be more highly specialized in women. The world of education emphasizes the left hemisphere functions. The left hemisphere is believed to have the following characteristics (Clark, Florey & Clark, 1985)(Sensory Integration International, 1986):
- It is more critical
    - to analytical thinking
    - to logic
    - to skills in the association of verbal and symbolic material involved in auditory-language skills (discrete sound discrimination)
- It is more involved in:
    - abstract thinking
    - task sequencing
    - details
    - concrete thought
    - inhibition

The **right hemisphere** (Clark, Florey & Clark, 1985)(Sensory Integration International, 1986) is believed to be more highly developed in men. Creative and artistic individuals predominantly use the right hemisphere of the brain (Clark, Mailloux, Parham, 1985). It is believed to have the following characteristics:

- deal with math symbols
- be involved in visual-spatial tasks
- be intutive
- be involved in the sensory system
- be involved in the non-verbal areas
- be involved in affective reactions
- be aesthetic
- be uninhibited
- be abstract
- be non-linguistic
- be involved in holistic aspects
- be emotional

For a person to perform adequately, each area of **each** hemisphere must develop fully and there must be effective communication **between** the **two sides**. According to Ayres (1972), this requires brain stem intercommunication. Reading requires the use of both hemispheres, the right hemisphere for visual recognition and perception of the whole and left hemisphere for language skill, and specific details. Some researchers (Umphred, 1985) have found that children with learning disabilities are more "right brained" and seem to have more difficulty with left hemisphere tasks. They have some of the same difficulties seen in persons with left hemisphere injuries. They function more with the right brain. An instructor with right brain tendencies has a great imagination BUT his or her organization and ability to handle specifics are poor.

Let us look at the roles of the two hemisphere of the brain to see which skills or functions required in riding come under the dominance of each:

Right hemisphere:
- Relation of self/horse to environment - holistic relationship
- Visual skills
- Non-verbal responses
- Visualization (Swift's "soft eyes")
- The feeling or awareness of balancing on the horse
- Absorbing the feel of a learned "position on the horse"
- Body image development
- Ability to follow visual demonstration

Left hemisphere:
- Relation of self/horse to instructor - specific focal localization
- Listening to instructions
- Interpreting instructions
- Sequencing given instructions (turn your horse, walk on rail, stop at A, make circle at walk)
- Maintaining rhythm
- Following visual demonstration to verbal meaning (interpretation)
- Learning of aids
- Identification of letters (dressage letters)
- Making a circle or other specific shapes--analyzing shapes
- Stopping or changing transitions at specific points

It must always be remembered that to function adequately--one needs **BOTH hemispheres** to integrate well together.

When any individual is confronted by more stress or challenge than he or she can easily handle, his or her <u>autonomic nervous system</u> function is activated. The more stress applied to the human the more down-shifting in brain level functioning occurs. As stress mounts due to various interfering factors, an individual may not function at a cortical (<u>cerebellum</u>) level, but starts functioning at the next level down, (<u>medulla oblongata</u>). Complex behavioral choices commonly associated with humans are then limited. The mammalian brain is capable only of elementary problem solving such as finding food, nurturing young, and seeking comfort. Additional stress creates further down-shifting so that the reptilian brain (<u>brain-stem</u>) takes over control of internal organs. The <u>autonomic nervous system</u> is centered in the brain-stem and on down the spinal column. Behavioral options are then limited to basically self-protective choices. The individual will choose to fight or leave (fight or flight).

Understanding these brain levels and their importance as to how they alter behavior makes working with people more effective. Those working in therapeutic riding with children who have disabilities need these understandings. An individual who is mentally disabled may appear low functioning due to the stress the environment imposes on him or her. When the stress is eliminated or reduced this individual may function at a much higher level. One must always take into consideration the functional aspects of the CNS before possibly interpreting "that bland look" as a severely defective mind.

Ayres, A.J. (1972) *Sensory Integration and Learning Disabilities*. Los Angeles: Western Psychological Services.

Banus, B.S., et, al. (1979). *The Developmental Therapist*. 2nd ed.Thorofare, Charles B. Slack, Inc. 1-158.

Clark, F., et al. (1985). Sensory Integration and Children with Learning Disabilities. *Occupational Therapy for Children*. St. Louis: C.V. Mosby Co. 365.

Clark, P., et al. (1985). Developmental Principles and Theories. in *Occupational Therapy for Children*. St. Louis: C.V. Mosby Co.34.

Moore, J.C. (1969). *Neuroanatomy Simplified*. Dubuque: Kendall/Hunt Publishing Co.

Moore, J.C. (1973). *Concepts From The Neurobehavioral Sciences*. Dubuque: Kendall/Hunt Publishing Co

Sensory Integration International. (1986). *Sensory Integration Theory and Practice*. Course material.

Sensory Integration International. (1986). *A Neurological Foundation for Sensory Integration*. Course material.

Umphred, D.A. (1985). *Neurological Rehabilitation*. St. Louis: The C.V. Mosby Co.

9.05 A BIRDS EYE VIEW OF PHYSICAL DEVELOPMENT - MILESTONES

Barbara T. Engel, MEd, OTR
Stephanie C. Woods, BFA

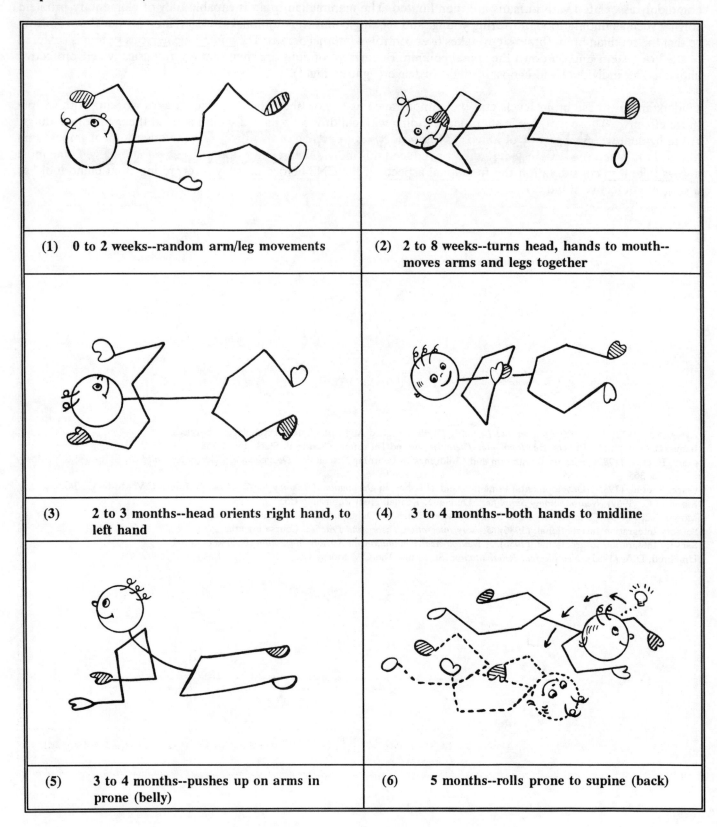

(1)   0 to 2 weeks--random arm/leg movements

(2)   2 to 8 weeks--turns head, hands to mouth--moves arms and legs together

(3)   2 to 3 months--head orients right hand, to left hand

(4)   3 to 4 months--both hands to midline

(5)   3 to 4 months--pushes up on arms in prone (belly)

(6)   5 months--rolls prone to supine (back)

(7)   6 month--sits with support of hands

(8)   7 months--pivots in prone position

(9)   7 months--hand-eye connection develops

(10) 8 months--protective support reaction develops

(11) 7 to 9 months--crawls on belly or hands and knees

(12) 9 months--pulls self to stand holding on

13) **10 months--sits with hands up--crawls on hands and knees**

(14) **10 months--picks up object**

(15) **10-11 months--sit to half kneel**

(16) **11 months--side steps around furniture-- holding-on--"cruising"**

(17) **11 months--walks with hands held**

(18) **12 months--controlled grasp/release of hands**

(19) 12 to 13 months--takes a few steps alone

(20) 15 months--walks well

(21) 18 months--up stairs--holding on

(22) 19 months--get up to stand alone

(23) 23 months - climbs into chair

(24) 2 years - runs well

(25)   2 years - kicks ball

(26)   2½ to 3 years - walks up/down

(27)   3-4 years - jumps well

(28)   5 years - stands on one foot

10   PHYSIOLOGICAL SYSTEMS AFFECTING THE RIDER

INTRODUCTION

When instructors of horseback riding teach able-bodied students, it is to the advantage of both instructor and student to understand how the human body functions; how the nervous system directs the students to understand directions, to coordinate their bodies' movements, to develop balance, or to "feel" the movements of the horse. The rider can then be more skillfully guided through the development of posture, movement and sensitivity in order to learn to manipulate the horse effectively.

However, when instructing horseback riding to a special population this knowledge becomes fundamental! Abnormal behavior cannot be understood unless one understands normal behavior. Certainly it is a big task to place a human on a large, mildly cooperative animal and teach them to work as one coordinated unit in a pleasurable way. When that human has numerous problems with coordination, learning, limbs that do not work well, vision or hearing, the task becomes enormous. For instructors to be successful with disabled clients, it is imperative for them to understand their students' disabilities.

For riders it is frustrating not to be understood. People do not like to be told that if they would only pay attention, they would be able to understand what to do, or to hear that there is nothing wrong except for their negative attitude. How do they "put the heels down" when the muscles are tight or when they cannot "feel" the legs? When an adult does not know right from left, it is certainly degrading to hear "I thought you were smart".

Ayres (1979) describes two vestibular modulation disorders that involve intolerance to movement. First, she describes gravitational insecurity where an individual may experience a sensation of falling when in a stable but threatening position which causes anxiety and distress to movement. The second disorder of vestibular hyper-responsivity describes movement activities unpleasant but not threatening to children except for secondary reactions of nausea and discomfort. The author experiences mild gravitational insecurity and a moderate vestibular hyper-responsivity. After not being able to ride for a year due to knee reconstruction, she is finding that she must begin anew to establish a tolerance to the movement of the horse beneath her. A year ago, she was riding well at the first level dressage with no fear of movement. Now she feels nauseant and discomfort when the horse's gait changes or he makes an unexpected or fast move. An instructor who is unfamiliar with this type of disorder would quickly give up on such a student--"look, she is scared of the horse--she cannot even ride!" Does one need that kind of reinforcement when one is having to struggle with "starting all over again--and I was doing so well"?

Problems that are not visible are difficult to explain, especially to those who have no understanding of human function. An instructor will have more difficulty relating to a person who is physically disabled because that person is visually "different." He or she may ask "what am I going to do with this person? That person cannot learn to ride." On the other hand, with a student with learning disabilities, head injuries or mental problems the instructor may feel socially comfortable because this person is not obviously "different", but understanding this rider may be more difficult.

The following section covers the fundamental systems that humans use to interpret and react to the world around them.

Conclusion: Instructors who have basic knowledge of anatomy and the physiological systems of the human body will be able to gain an understanding of physical, mental and learning disabilities. This will permit them to request assistance from therapists or other professionals and will enable them to adapt their instructions to meet the needs of the rider who is different. They will be more successful instructing and bring out the talents of their students.

Ayres, A.J. (1979). *Sensory Integration and the Child.* Los Angeles: Western Psychological Services.

10.01 THE TACTILE SYSTEM

John H. Brough, OTR

It is touch that provides the child with his or her earliest awareness of who and where he or she is. This tactile system is and remains a primary sensory system. The child touched by his or her mother learns about security, warmth, and love. Early touch and movement responses prepare and strengthen a child's muscles for later stages of normal development. Normal stimulation of this very important sensory system is necessary for the total brain's functioning. When there is a lack of tactile stimulation or some interference to the normal processing of sensory information, the child may not behave as one would expect. Infants deprived of touch crave stimulation. They demonstrate immature, fearful, and even aggressive behaviors. Lack of experience or the inability to process this sensory information interferes with the child's developing awareness and organization of self.

Touch also alerts the child to be aware of threats from the environment. This alarm system can be triggered by touch so light that it barely brushes the hair. Touch that takes the form of deep pressure which cannot be quickly identified, may also trigger the alarm system. The child with learning problems may be under-sensitive or over-sensitive to touch. The individual who is under-sensitive may not respond at all to touch. He or she can cut his or her knee or scrape his or her hand without being aware of it. He or she may not be receiving an important part of the information needed to identify his or her own body. He or she may not receive enough information about objects he or she manipulates to learn his or her tactile characteristics and to match this information with what his or her eyes can show him or her or what his or her ears may hear.

The individual who is over-sensitive to touch lacks the ability to discriminate and determine which touch requires protective responses and which touch gives routine information about him or herself and objects in his or her environment. He or she will be tense and uptight, tactile defensive about being touched and touching. Touch triggers a protective response. Behaviors which interfere with learning will result. Examples of these behaviors may include any or all of the following:

a) Inadequate balance
b) Lack of flexibility of movement
c) Difficulty planning sequences of movements
d) Withdrawal from touch--resistive to touch--pulls away
e) Incorrect interpretation of touch--a light brush or touch may be interpreted as a hit, result in a fight
f) Exhibiting fear reactions to touch--screams in the barber's chair
g) Exhibiting excessive scratching, rubbing, picking, or even self abuse
h) Negative verbal reactions
i) Intolerance of crowds--becomes hyperactive, and whines
j) Dislikes being picked up, holding hands, having someone's arm on his shoulders
k) Makes tactile contact with others only if he initiates it
l) Compulsive cleanliness--avoids getting dirty

Without touch, learning is incomplete from the most elementary developmental step to the formation and organization of multiple concepts. Development of the tactile system and its integration with the other sensory modes contributes to the completeness of the individual. Tactile sensitivity must be an integral part of what every person brings to a learning situation.

References
Ayres, A.J. (1972). *Sensory Integration and Learning Disabilities*. Los Angeles: Western Psychological Society.
Chaney, C. (1980). *The Tactile System*. Columbus: Charles E. Merrill.
Guyton, A.C. (1976). *Structure and Function of the Nervous System*. Philadelphia: W.B. Saunders Co.

10.02　THE VESTIBULAR SYSTEM

John H. Brough, OTR

The vestibular system of the brain (part of the proprioceptive system) is a source of sensory information said to be the second earliest appearing sensory input system (Weeks, 1979). Its prenatal maturation prepares each of us for the effects of gravity from the moment of birth. This special proprioceptive system enables a person to ORIENT HIM OR HERSELF IN SPACE and to make ADAPTIVE OR EXPLORATORY HEAD, LIMB AND EYE MOVEMENTS.

The vestibular system receptors are located in the inner ear on each side of the head and are composed of three connecting tubes called semicircular canals. These canals are filled with fluid that moves as the head moves. The moving fluid stimulates nerves which carry the information about the head position to the central nervous system. Through the semicircular canals the central nervous system learns whether the head is vertical, horizontal, or turned on its side. It also learns whether the head has started to move in any direction or whether it has stopped moving. This directional awareness and movement awareness includes rotation or spinning activities. The vestibular system is considered to be very important to the development of early motor skills such as balance, movement of the head, crawling, creeping, and walking. Information about the position of the head in relation to gravity is continuously being sent to the neck muscles, the muscles of the trunk, and the muscles of the arms and legs where it is matched or integrated with the information being sent by nerves in the muscles and joints (kinesthetic awareness or proprioception). Even the eyes receive information from the vestibular system and match it with what they see.

Adequate vestibular function and opportunity for stimulation of this sensory system has been shown by researchers to aid postural responses, visual attention, and language development (Ayres, 1972)(Norton, 1975)(Gregg, 1976)(deQuiros, 1978). It is known to be directly related to a sense of well being. And absence of stimulation shows a high correlation with emotional disturbance (King, 1978). This system appears to be critical to the integration processes of the brain. Chronic interferences from ear infections, allergy responses, and other internal stress factors appear to result in retarded development of the sensory motor milestones. Adverse behaviors which may result include the following:

    a.   Poor balance--static as well as dynamic
    b.   Abnormal postural adaptations such as head position, spine alignment
    c.   Difficulty with or avoidance of locomotion and movement tasks which require good balancing abilities, such as skipping, jumping, moving sideways or backward
    d.   Very rapid movement patterns--always moves fast, runs, is hyperactive
    e.   Sits in a slouched position--seem to "fold" into a chair
    f.   Fear or avoidance of rotation or spinning
    g.   Seeks out spinning activities with no dizziness resulting from prolonged activity
    h.   Always leans on something--does not stand up

Since everyone must live with the effects of gravity from the moment of birth, this sensory system is extremely important to normal development. Even temporary disturbances can cause disorientation and resulting discomfort. An ear infection can lead to dizziness, and enough dizziness can cause nausea. A moderate degree of interference can reduce learning. Vestibular stimulation is generally a positive stimulation. It can be as calming as the porch swing or as exciting as an amusement park ride. Children will seek out stimulating activities. Adult responses do differ from those of children. They seem to require less intensity and less frequency of stimulation. As one matures, other sensory systems become dominant. In particular, the eyes are used to orient the individual in space and may dominate the vestibular system after the late teen years. This sensory system is primary to survival and does trigger responses of the autonomic nervous system. Because of the individualized nature of our central nervous system, it is difficult to predict how each of us will respond to stimulation of the vestibular system when that system may not be processing information as it should. Therefore, it is wise to be aware of certain behaviors which may occur as a result of spinning, rolling, bouncing, jumping, or even running on uneven surfaces.

Behaviors stimulated by the vestibular system may include the following:

1. Dizziness
    a. reported dizziness
    b. observable unsteadiness while walking
    c. an expressed desire to lie down
    d. an unnatural reaction to movement, unusual tilt of the head
2. Vertigo (severe dizziness)
    a. Unusual pale color about the face and extremities
    b. sweating .. may be a "cold" sweat
    c. Vomiting
    d. Depressed pulse
    e. Nystagmoid (horizonal) movements of the eyes
3. Seizures
    a. any seizure behavior whether normal or abnormal to the child
4. Excitement
    a. increased hyperactivity
    b. destructive behavior
5. Depression
    a. withdrawal from environment

Remember also that these behaviors or symptoms may occur as much as 2 to 3 hours after an experience with vestibular stimulation. It is natural to seek and enjoy stimulation for this extremely important sensory system. Children and adults may need assistance in successfully participating in this area of sensory motor development to facilitate learning at higher developmental levels.

References

Ayres, A.J. (1972) *Sensory Integration and Learning Disabilities*. Los Angeles: Western Psychological Services.

deQuiros, J.B., Scgrager, O.L. (1978). *Neuropsychological Fundamental in Learning Disabilities*. San Rafel: Academic Therapy

Gregg, C., Haffner, M., Korner, M. (1976). The Relative Efficacy of Vestibular-proprioception Stimulation and the Upright Position in Enhancing Visual Pursuit on Neonates. *Child Development*. 47:309-314.

Guyton, A.C. (1976). *Structure and Function of the Nervous System*. Philadelphia: W.B. Saunders Co.

King, L.J. (1978). Occupational Therapy Research in Psychiatry. *Am J Occ Ther*. 32:15-18.

Norton, Y. (1975). Neurodevelopment and Sensory Integration for the Profoundly Retarded Multiply Handicapped Child. *Am J Occup Ther*. 29:93-100.

Weeks, Z.R. (1979). Effects of the Vestibular System on Human Development. AJOT: June-part 1; July-part 2. Rockville: *Am J of Occup Ther*. 376-381, 450-457.

10.03 REFLEXES

John H. Brough, OTR

Neurological reflex: a reaction; an involuntary movement or exercise of function in a part excited in response to a stimulus applied to the periphery or viscera and transmitted to the nervous centers in the brain or spinal cord (Capute, 1978).

- ◘ Primitive reflexes are essential in normal development.

- ◘ The response to reflexes prepares the child for progressive motor development such as rolling over, sitting, crawling, standing

- ◘ In normal development, these primitive reflexes (which are initiated at the spinal and brainstem level) gradually diminish, in order that higher patterns of righting (the body's response against gravity) and equilibrium (balance) may appear.

- ◘ When inhibitory control of higher centers is disrupted or delayed, primitive patterns dominate.

- ◘ Levels of Reflex Development:
  There are different levels of reflexive development.
  a. Spinal level reflexes are the lowest level. These predominate with motor development when the child is lying prone (on the stomach), or supine (on the back) Example: flexor withdrawal. This is the pulling away of the foot when the sole of the foot is touched or stimulated.

  b. Brain stem level reflexes cause changes in muscle tone in the body:
  in response to change of position of the head and body in space (stimulation of the labyrinths).
  in the head in relation to the body (stimulation of the neck proprioceptors).
  Positive or negative reactions to brain stem reflex testing may occur in the normal child within the first 4-6 months of life. Example: The asymmetrical tonic neck reflex (ATNR) can be observed when a child is lying or sitting and turns his or her head to one side resulting in extension of the arm on the chin side and flexion of the opposite arm. This has also been called the fencer's position. The symmetrical tonic neck reflex (STNR) is similar to the ATNR except that the flexion-extension axis changes to upper-lower instead of the right-left side of the body. When the head is extended, the arms will straighten and the legs will bend at the hips and knees; when the head is bent forward, the arms will bend at the shoulders and elbows and the legs will straighten. Both the asymmetrical tonic neck reflex (ATNR) and the tonic neck reflex (STNR) are present up to 6 months of life.

  c. Midbrain level reflexes include the righting reaction. Righting reactions work toward establishing normal head and body relationship in space as well as in relationship to each other. These develop after birth and into 10-12 months. Gradually, they disappear towards the end of 5th year of life. Example: Neck righting reflex occurs when the child is lying on his or her back, rotation of the head results in rotation of the body as a whole in the same direction as the head. This occurs from birth to 6 months and is what permits the baby to roll over. Other righting reactions entail tilting the child and he or she will right him or herself. It is that tendency towards keeping the body upright, the head upright and eyes level with the ground.

d.　The highest level of reflex is that of mature equilibrium reactions. Equilibrium is balance. Development of mature equilibrium responses helps to bring the child to a bipedal stage of motor development. They occur when muscle tone is normalized and they provide body adaptation in response to change of center of gravity in the body. Equilibrium reactions occur from 6 months on and remain throughout life.

Abnormal Reflex Maturation:

- Automatic reactions also reflect maturity of the nervous system. One which stays with us for life is protective extension. This is an automatic thrusting out of the arms when the body is suddenly thrown downward toward the floor. The body is protected from serious injury when one falls, as the first part to touch the surface is the outstretched hand or arm.

- In children with severe nervous system damage one may see a dominance of the early primitive reflexes and the child is "bound" by them. For example, a child with cerebral palsy may be so dominated by these early low level reflexes that the position of his or her head controls and demands a particular position of his or her arms. One can imagine how this may interfere with learning. Achievement of higher level motor patterns will not be possible because the child is rigid and controlled by these reflexes.

- In the learning disabled child, one needs to look at these early brain stem reflexes as well as at equilibrium responses. The ATNR and STNR may cause the child to be "bound" (totally involved) by the reflex or the reflex may appear to be exerting only minimal influence on him or her. If one sees that a child is still being influenced by a reflex, this shows immaturity of the nervous system and one needs to look at how and when that reflex may interfere with his or her movements. Example: ATNR may prevent adequate bilateral use of the arms for coordinated activity. It may prevent complete crossing of the midline of the body and may contribute to decreased flexibility around the midline.

- Good flexibility around the midline is the ability to rotate around the midline and to return to that stable middle point (trunk rotation). If children are being influenced by a primitive reflex when their balance is threatened, that is, when they are pushed off their center or midline, they may be unable to respond normally.

Emotional impact of abnormal reflex integration is significant. If children have not developed normal balance reactions or protective extension, one can easily imagine how fearful they may be as they move through their environment.

In therapy, positioning is utilized to inhibit primitive reflexes so that normal feedback is given to the nervous system. Vestibular stimulation can be also used because this type of information has an integrating, organizing influence on the nervous system. Vestibular input is provided through movement of the head through space (rocking, rolling, spinning are some examples). There is no substitute for integration that occurs at the lowest levels of the nervous system. Normal motor development depends on lower level organization and integration.

Reference:
Capute, A.J. et el. (1978). *Primitive Reflex Profile*. Baltimore: University Park Press.
Fiorentino, M. (1973). *Reflex Testing Methods for Evaluation C.N.S. Development*. Springfield: Charles C Thomas.

10.04   SENSORY INTEGRATION DEVELOPMENT

Jill Standquist, OTR/L, NDT

The infant uses reflexes and information from his senses of:	To develop these sensory motor abilities:	He uses sensory motor abilities to learn more concrete concepts and to develop:	He uses perceptual motor skills to accomplish an automatic level of function in:
TOUCH	BODY SCHEME	EYE HAND COODINATION	ACADEMIC LEARNING
			READING
MOVEMENT	REFLEX MATURATION	OCULO MOTOR CONTROL	WRITING
			NUMBERS
GRAVITY	CAPACITY TO SCREEN	POSTURAL ADJUSTMENTS	SPELLING
	SENSORY INPUT		
HEARING		AUDITORY - LANGUAGE	ACTIVITES OF
	POSTURAL SECURITY	SKILLS	DAILY LIVING
TASTE			
	AWARENESS OF TWO	VISUAL - SPATIAL	ABILITY TO
SMELL	SIDES OF BODY	PERCEPTION	CONCEPTUALIZE
VISION	MOTOR PLANNING	ATTENTION CENTER	INDEPENDENT
		FUNCTIONS	WORK HABITS
		MASTERY OF	BEHAVIOR - ABILITY TO
		ENVIRONMENT	FORM MEANINGFUL
			RELATIONSHIPS

SENSORY MOTOR PHASE 0 - 12 months	PERCEPTUAL MOTOR PHASE 1 - 5 years	LEARNING PHASE (cognitive or intellect)

10.05   SELF-CONCEPT IN CHILDREN AS IT AFFECTS LEARNING

John H. Brough, OTR

One of the most important and least understood areas of development is the affective area or *"the way I feel about myself"* (Piers). Professionals talk about self image, self concept and their importance but little is really known about how such feelings develop. Self concept is a complicated system composed of many sub-systems. The perception of self-worth is elusive and complex. The following breakdown, showing six factors, is taken from the Piers-Harris Children's Self Concept Scale. The six factors give a good view of the important parts of a child's feelings about himself.

The areas measured are:
- Physical appearance and attitudes
- Anxiety
- Intellectual and school status
- Behavior
- Popularity
- Happiness and satisfaction

In the areas of physical appearance and attitudes the child is assessed on his or her feelings related to:
- General looks
- Does he or she see him or herself as strong?
- Is he or she important in class?
- How does he or she feel about his:

    Eyes?
    Hair?
    Face?
    Figure?

What does he or she perceive his or her classmates think about him or her in the areas of:
- Ideas?
- Leadership?
- Popularity?

In the critical area of anxiety, the child is assessed as to:
- Shyness
- Perseverance
- Nervousness
- Amount of worry
- How well does he or she sleep?
- Test taking (how he or she feels about it)
- Feelings of fear

Testing these concepts gives an idea about the degree of anxiety or stress to the body that can be caused by poor self concept, a perception that can radically change performance. A child with a high degree of anxiety is most likely ruled by the sympathetic division of the autonomic nervous system. This means that his or her brain has "downshifted" and he or she is basically working at the most primitive level. Cortical function is repressed and learning may not be possible.

The area of <u>intellectual and school status</u> is evaluated in the following areas:

Does the child feel that he or she is:

- 😊 Smart?
- 😊 Capable of creating good ideas?
- 😊 Liked by the teacher?
- 😊 Good at school work?
- 😊 Important?
- 😊 Popular with peers?

The area of <u>behavior</u> is evaluated in many ways. The child's <u>relationships</u> are rated in the following environments: school, family, home, with peers, with other people. The tester examines how well the child works and what the trouble areas are in the above situations. The behavior the child describes may or may not be the truth, but it is important to remember that the significance is how he or she <u>feels</u> about him or herself and his or her behavior.

<u>Popularity</u> is rated on his relationships in school and peer group--with boys and girls. Popularity can also be looked at in the extended family.

<u>Happiness and satisfaction</u> is rated in all areas. Evaluation is made as to whether or not the individual feels happy, likes the way he or she is, feels lucky and cheerful. Also examined is whether the child wishes that he or she were different, or wants to change. The most important fact to remember is that the relationship of how the child feels and what the truth actually is may be either erroneous or very accurate. The child's self-concept comes from how he or she feels, not necessarily from the truth. The self-concept is very important and may greatly influence the course of therapy. A positive and accurate self-image can speed the learning process. A negative self-image, whether accurate or inaccurate, can slow down or completely hinder the self-concept. To build a good concept, it is necessary to give the individual accurate and concrete feedback; help him or her develop positive attitudes to replace his or her negative ones and tap any or all of his or her sensory avenues as aids in developing the necessary precepts upon which he or she can build his or her self-concept.

References
Piers, E., Harris, D. *The Piers-Harris Children's Self Concept Scale*. (The Way I Feel About Myself). Nashville: Counselor Recordings and Tests.

11 DISABILITIES ENCOUNTERED IN THERAPEUTIC RIDING

The present riding for persons with disabilities was born out of the fact that riding helps to improve a person's physical and mental state. This topic has already been discussed earlier in the text. Why then cannot persons with disabilities seek equestrian skills at any commercial or private training stable? Because any person, whose abilities, skills, and why of functioning, does not fall into the mainstream of average person needs, must work with instructors who not only are skilled in horsemanship but who are knowledgeable about disabilities.

Persons with disabilities need:
- Special understanding that his or her "problem" may need unique considerations. These considerations are obvious with a person who has one leg, is paralyzed on one side, or who can not walk. They are not obvious with persons with language disorders, sensory integration dysfunction, learning disabilities, psycho-social disorders or mental retardation. This problem can be described by a mother of a dyslexic child (learning disabled) with an I.Q. of 130, who cannot find a recreational program that will work with her daughter because she is too difficult, or a mother who relates her daughter's abilities as superior one day and zero another.

- Special equipment allows a person to compensate for a disability, gain physical security, or access to the horse.

- Special handling with well trained helpers encourages progress both in equestrian skills and in the ability to function.

- Special horse provides a rider with a reliable and safe mount.

- Specially trained instructors become an obvious needs since they must be able to deal with all of the above considerations and know that placing the person on the horse will not advance the disability but will rather foster ability. The instructor cannot rely on a physician's recommendation that this person is safe to ride unless the physician is also an equestrian. Though the physician's approval is important it is not enough. The instructor must have a basic understanding of every disability he or she takes into the program.

- Special attitude that dilutes the disability of a person, and emphasizes the person. The riding team is composed of the instructors, volunteers, horse, and client. The team must be a group of "we"; not "us" (the staff/volunteers) and "they" (the client).

The material in this section is specifically directed to the instructor in any therapeutic riding program, not just those programs involved in equine-assisted therapy or hippotherapy.

This section on disabilities is provided to assist the instructor and his or her assistants in gaining some understanding of major disabilities which are commonly seen in therapeutic riding programs. From this information, the instructor can begin to develop a working knowledge of a rider's disability. He or she can also become familiar with terminology used in the health care professions, therefore increasing his or her ability to understand a problem a rider might describe or to carry out recommendations of a therapist. The information should also help the instructor to become aware of precautions such as danger of an increase in a spinal curve, stress signs which may indicate that the person should stop riding, or that the instructor is moving beyond the ability of a rider to integrate information.

Therapeutic horsemanship is a wonderful adventure for most persons with disabilities--BUT--it is NOT suitable for everyone.

11.01 TO RIDE OR NOT TO RIDE: IS THAT REALLY THE QUESTION?

Linda Mitchell, MA, PT

CASE HISTORY--PART 1

It was Matthew's first time on a horse or even near enough to the horse to feel its breath on his hand as he cautiously reached out to pet its nose. The smiling, freckle-faced five year old had been referred to the equine-assisted therapy program by his physical therapist. The therapist was concerned with Matthew's low muscle tone, fear of heights, and decreased postural control. The therapist had obtained a physician's referral for the consulting riding therapist, and shared as much information as possible about her perception of this child and how he might be helped by using the horse in therapy. Based on this information an evaluation on the horse was scheduled and planned.

A short, sturdy horse was selected on the basis of Matthew's fear of heights. Because it was anticipated that he might need a feeling of security, yet should be given an opportunity to feel and respond to as much of the horse's movement as possible, the equipment selected was a bareback pad and anti-cast surcingle. A brief "off horse" assessment was conducted to verify prior information and to establish rapport between Matthew and this new therapist. Matthew was introduced to his horse "Yoda," and was assisted in mounting. He was in an excited, anticipatory state.

It was immediately apparent that Matthew did not include 'midline' in his repertoire of strategies for balance. As Yoda stood quietly and Matthew was encouraged to relax and adjust, he remained tense, gripping the surcingle handle, first with both hands, then one, then the other, in an attempt to find a secure enough posture to request the horse to walk. Matthew's trunk was pulled into collapsed flexion. He was tightly gripping with his legs and moving his pelvis, searching for stability between anterior and posterior tilt, and between right and left weight bearing, but just not able to center and organize.

After a few minutes, it was decided to go ahead and depart at a walk to see if a rhythmical gait in long straight lines would assist Matthew or further disorganize him. The sidehelpers were instructed to give firm tactile support and to reassure him as needed. And, with much encouragement, Matthew finally took a deep breath and shouted out the words "Walk on, 'oda'!"

The ride lasted twelve minutes. The results were disastrous. Throughout the ride Matthew struggled, without success, to feel secure enough to enjoy what he knew was <u>supposed</u> to be fun! With every stride he changed his strategy. With every defeat, he lost a little more control, until he could no longer count on any of his sensory systems to give him a clear message of where he was, let alone what to do about it. He began to attempt a dismount from the moving horse, only he could not find a way, and could not express that he wanted off. The surcingle handle became an obstacle, an intrusion on his space, a distraction from his ability to focus. His chatter increased, but was scattered and full of questions unrelated to his ride. Matthew was asked if he wanted the horse to "whoa," and he immediately shouted "Whoa" to whomever would hear it. He was then assisted to the ground, where he displayed difficulty finding his base of support, and organizing enough balance to walk through the gate to his Mom. He had no desire to further interact with Yoda, and when asked if he'd enjoyed his ride, he responded "That was fun! Are we going home now?"

DISCUSSION

Matthew is a classic example of a five year old child who should be an excellent candidate for equine-assisted therapy. First of all, he does not demonstrate any of the listed "contraindications," has no significant medical or orthopedic problems, and exhibits sensorimotor dysfunction that could be changed through the rhythmical, symmetrical input of the moving horse. A logical "recipe" was followed in the planning and execution of his riding evaluation. Yet Matthew's first ride portrayed a very different picture from the expected outcome, thus illustrating the premise of this paper: the importance of regular, ongoing, individualized assessment of each rider by knowledgeable and skilled professionals in each therapeutic riding program.

INDICATIONS, CONTRAINDICATIONS AND PRECAUTIONS

Lists are available through NARHA[1] and CanTRA[2] publications, and in the training manuals of the Hippotherapy Curriculum Committee[3] that present a summary of the collaborative research efforts, clinical findings, and professional opinions of experts in the field. They are meant to serve as guidelines for decision making, particularly with respect to the medical aspects of various disabilities and their diagnosis. But, without backup knowledge and understanding, no list can serve as a bible or a cookbook. The author is working with populations served by therapeutic riding programs, running the gamut from recreational to medically-oriented, and every decision is essentially a judgement call based on skilled observation and problem solving. The ability to break down the total picture of a client into variable components is the best answer to the questions of accountability, liability, and quality of service.

And so the issue expands from a question of whether or not a person should ride at all to the real "why" or "why not," as well as the "how," "when," "where," and "with whom" should they ride, if at all. The use of the horse in therapy encompasses a rationale which can be as simple or as complex as the level of understanding one has, as well as the scope of the perspective of the whole person with individual needs and abilities. Combine this premise with a sound working knowledge of the tool (the horse) and its potential, and a firm foundation is established for quality practice.

RATIONALE

Above all, the preliminary assessment must rule out that damage or physical harm may be done to the client. This is the basis of any list of contraindications and precautions, compiled in accordance with the actual physical effect of the moving horse on its rider. Prior to the placement of a client in a program, as well as throughout treatment, these questions must be asked:

- What is moving, what is not moving, and WHY?
- Is the effect, or projected effect, a desirable one?
- Is there any reason this interaction of horse and rider should not be allowed to occur?
- And are there any changes that can be made to obtain or improve a desirable result?

Once the absence of contraindications is verified, a reason should be clear for using the horse in some way to uniquely affect an area of dysfunction, and to assist in accomplishing a therapeutic goal. Again, an understanding of the sensorimotor impact in the exchange between horse and rider is critical to the safe, purposeful and appropriate use of the horse in treatment.

VARIABLE

The impact of the horse is strong and powerful; the changes effected are subtle and intense. Fragile, sensitive nervous systems are constantly asked to gather and integrate sensory information and to design a strategy for response. The most minute change in sensory input has immense potential for realizing a desirable difference in the response of the client. Thus, it is the responsibility and ability of the trained clinician to assess and adapt, in both the planning and the treatment stages of every program, utilizing a working knowledge of the changeable components: namely, the horse, the equipment, the position or activities, and, finally, the movement used in order to accomplish change in the rider's response.

CASE HISTORY--PART 2

Matthew returned to the stable with his Mom on the day following his on-horse assessment. He sported a "shiner" of his left eye that Rocky would have been proud of! When asked about it, his Mom reported that he had fallen off the couch the night before, and just seemed to have been "off-balance." This finding was definitely in keeping

---

[1] North American Riding for the Handicapped, Box 33150, Denver, CO 80233 USA
[2] Canadian Therapeutic Riding Association (CanTRA), P.O. Box 1055, Guelph, Ont, N1H 6J6, Canada.
[3] Hippotherapy Curriculum Committee, Therapeutic Riding Services, PO Box 41, Riderwood, MD 21139

---

with the therapist's assessment that some changes needed to be made if Matthew were to ride again. Yesterday's short ride had indeed had devastating results. The new plan had already been formulated. In view of the fact that Yoda's movement had served only to further disorganize a child who apparently struggled with severe inability to organize his posture, a different horse was selected for Matthew to try. Although "Donnie" was taller than Yoda, he was also broader, and had a much shorter, slower stride, thus providing minimal movement input and a larger base of support. The idea was to maximize the ways of addressing Matthew's need for stability and provide it to him in a very different way.

The surcingle had interfered and disoriented Matthew, as it required more motor planning and ability to weight-shift into his arms and hands than Matthew was able to manage on the horse. So the surcingle was eliminated from his visual and tactile field, thus allowing him options for interacting with only one dependable surface, Donnie's back. Matthew was mounted on Donnie on a thick bareback pad, and reminded that he had the power to control Donnie through voice commands of "walk" and "whoa". The sidehelpers were instructed to engage in minimal verbal interaction with Matthew and to give guarding rather than tactile assistance, with the idea of providing him a structured, safe environment, focused and distraction-free, within the boundaries of which he could problem-solve his responses. Using the organization offered by Donnie's movement, Matthew began to find his own strategies for dynamic stability. He demonstrated awareness of being off center, attempts to correct to mid-line, visual attention to his task of staying on this moving horse, a minimum of conversation, and repeated appropriate use of the command to "Whoa" when he needed to reorganize. In addition, Matthew began on his own to tactilely explore Donnie through changing his own position, hugging Donnie's neck, reaching for his tail, and even stopping the horse so he could lie back and touch the horse's rump and "belly". This time, the ride lasted 15 minutes, with Matthew asking if he could stop Donnie and dismount. At the end of the ride, he turned and faced the horse, patted and thanked him, and fed him a carrot, before returning to his mother's side, proud and much more "together" than the day before.

COMMENTARY
For all of us in therapeutic riding, Matthew's experience holds a twofold message: one of caution, flavored with creative encouragement. The instructor's insightful perspective, based on skilled observation, and conclusions based on experience allowed the boy not only to continue the ride but to maximize his potential for a positive and worthwhile learning experience. **Without the benefit of such expertise, despite the best intentions, a child like Matthew would, at best, be prevented from entering a program. Or, in an even more damaging scenario, he might be allowed to continue without recognition of the harm being repeatedly allowed to occur.** It is simply not possible to assure quality and safety through the use of a checklist or a "cookbook" method of client selection and screening. Horses are not generically beneficial to everyone with a disability or even with certain disabilities. But, with the right understanding and the required, trained professional judgement, even the strictest rules can be revised, resulting in a uniquely powerful effect on the quality of the lives that are touched by this unique treatment.

11.02   WHAT ARE THE DISABILITIES RIDERS MIGHT HAVE

Barbara T. Engel, MEd, OTR

Instructors of therapeutic riding programs need to become familiar with the disabilities of clients with whom they will work. Instructors should know what is involved regarding function with each disability and any special considerations in order to guide the team, (along with the physical or occupational therapy program consultant), in appropriate handling of all riders. When team members have this knowledge and understanding, a safer ride can be provided to the client.

11.02.1   AIDS--AIDS (*acquired immunodeficiency syndrome*) or HIV (*human immunodeficiency viruses*)

It is characterized by the lack of helper T-cells and the susceptibility to opportunistic infections; a contagious disease that affects the human's ability to fight infection and disease. It is transferred from person to person directly through infected blood, semen or vaginal fluids. Risky behavior involves sharing drug needles and syringes and oral, anal or vaginal sexual activity. IT CANNOT BE TRANSFERRED BY TOUCHING, HUGGING, COUGHING, SNEEZING, DROOLING, TOILET SEATS, EATING UTENSILS OR THROUGH FOOD CONTACT. IT IS NOT TRANSMITTED FROM SALIVA, SWEAT, TEARS, URINE OR BOWEL MOVEMENT; FROM BED BUGS, LICE, FLIES OR INSECT BITES. It is spread through sharing injection needles with others who have AIDS, through unprotected sexual contact or by an infected mother to her fetus and through her milk in nursing. It is advisable to wear latex gloves when dealing with the possibility of contaminated blood and to wash hands after taking off the gloves. People with AIDS usually die from infections or diseases that their system cannot fight. AIDS itself does not cause death (US Dept of Health & Human Services).

WHAT TO DO WITH A RIDER WITH AIDS
1.   Let the client with AIDS ride in the program as long as he or she feels able to do so. He or she may need healthy exercise and challenges.
2.   Cuts, rashes, abrasions or other injured areas of the AIDS client's skin should be covered with a water proof dressing. Clothing will be sufficient in protecting against any contact.
3.   Avoid sharp instruments with which the client might cut him or herself. Wear latex gloves when attending to a wound of a client with AIDS and wash hands afterward.
4.   Washing hands and any exposed skin with soap and water is a preventive measure also after being in contact with body fluids.
5.   Let the members of the team who are dealing with this client know of his or her condition but remember this information should be kept confidential. Staff members have the choice of not working with this person. (In most states knowledge of a client's AIDS status is unavailable. In such a case, caution should be taken with any person who may be considered at risk).

11.02.2   ARTHRITIC CONDITIONS

ARTHROGRYPOSIS--Arthrogyposis is a congenital condition in which joints are deformed, stiff and weak. The joint may be contracted (a set position) in either a straight or bent position. The upper extremities are most commonly affected.

DEGENERATIVE ARTHRITIS or OSTEOARTHRITIS--Degenerative arthritis or osteoarthritis is caused by trauma or continued stress to joints. Destructive changes to the bones and joints occur which can become painful and cause mild to severe limitations of movement.

213

JUVENILE RHEUMATOID ARTHRITIS--Juvenile rheumatoid arthritis is a chronic disorder which may appear in children between two and four years of age. The disease may involve only a few or many joints. The soft tissue of the joints is inflamed, painful and weak. There may be contractures. The disease has periods of inflammation (active) and periods of remission. In 85% of individuals affected the disease may disappear at puberty. Others continue on with the adult version of rheumatoid arthritis.

OSTEOCHONDRITIS or LEGG-PERTHES DISEASE--Osteochondritis or Legg-Perthes disease is a condition of the femur (thigh bone) which causes destruction due to interruption of circulation to the area where bone and cartilage join.

OSTEOGENESIS IMPERFECTA--Osteogenesis imperfecta is "brittle bone disease". Children with severe cases should not ride, since bones may fracture with little stress. There can be deformities, especially in later years. The skin may be thin and bruise easily. Special instructions in handling these children/adults are needed.

OSTEOPETROSIS--Osteopetrosis is a disease with increased density of the bone. Deformity and fractures are more common than normal.

OSTEOPOROSIS--Osteoporosis involves a decrease in bone tissue causing weakness of the bone and possibility of fractures. The condition usually is seen in older people.

RHEUMATOID ARTHRITIS--Rheumatoid arthritis is a severe crippling condition which involves inflammation and destruction of joints. The joints are progressively destroyed. There are periods of exacerbation and remission. The individual may wear splints to protect the joints. Inflammation of the tendons and muscles accompanies joint inflammation and can be very painful.

WHAT TO DO WITH A PERSON WHO HAS AN ARTHRITIC CONDITION
1. Riding can be an excellent exercise for a person with arthritis. It provides good quality exercise, strengthens muscles, increases circulation and strengthens the respiratory system. The ride should be smooth and not longer than the rider can tolerate. Periods of rest may be needed. A horse with smooth gaits and transitions will be more comfortable.
2. Be gentle when assisting the rider; do not pull on joints that are painful or have contracture. Ask the rider how to help. Most people with arthritis know how to manage their disorder.
3. The rider should be positioned so that there is no pressure on a painful joint. A sheepskin, sponge or gel pad (on the saddle) may protect the rider. A gel saddle pad (under saddle) may make the ride more gentle. Have the therapist give additional advice. A good, balanced posture can help take stress off specific joints.
4. Exercises to relax the rider are helpful. The gentle rocking of the horse helps to stretch tight muscles and gives overall relaxation. The therapist will provide you with exercises.
5. Children may need support. Some may need a therapist to backride with them. The backrider must be careful to provide support without applying pressure or causing the rider to lean to one side.
6. Special equipment may be used to help a crippled hand or arm become useful. Use a horse with a smooth gait and predictable movements.
7. A comfortable saddle that fits the rider is important.
8. Do not ride if the rider is having an exacerbation (worsening of disease) or complains of pain.

11.02.3	BRAIN DISORDERS

Brain disorders have many causes producing varying neurological deficits. Some disorders include:
DAMAGE TO THE BRAIN--Brain damage can occur before birth or at any age in life. Damage can be the result of imperfect development of the brain, stress causing injury at birth or during development, infections, drugs, toxins, disease, abuse, coma, drowning, seizures, accidents or injuries to the head.

BRAIN TUMORS--Tumors are growths which may be benign or malignant. There are many kinds of tumors which may be located in various parts of the brain. Damage to the brain, if any, will depend on the location of the tumor, pressure on surrounding tissue, or damage to other tissue in its removal.

CEREBRAL PALSY--Cerebral Palsy (CP) is caused by damage to the motor (movement) area of the brain. CP is an injury and not a disease, characterized by a lack of ability to control the body. The injury can occur before birth, during birth or during the early developmental years. Cerebral palsy may be accompanied by other brain disorders such as seizures, mental retardation, vision and hearing problems, or learning disabilities. All motor abilities of the body can be affected. The disorder can be very mild or severe, resulting in minimal to extreme movement and coordination difficulties with various body parts moving in unison. When asking the rider to raise his head, his chest and arms may also rise. When bending the arms, the legs may also bend. These actions are not under the rider's control. Types of cerebral palsy include the following:

1. **Spastic:** There is abnormally high "tone" in muscles (hypertonic--stiff arms/legs and trunk) making smooth movement difficult. The feeling is as if the arms are grasping a seventy-pound boulder when picking up the reins. The rider with severe spasticity cannot regulate the amount of movement or tension the arm or leg produces. He or she will also have difficulty with balance and staying upright.

2. **Hypotonic:** There is a lack of "solidness" to a muscle, a lack of "tone". Muscles controlling the joints are weak. A person with hypotonicity (low tone) generally moves more slowly than the average person, may weigh more or "feel" heavier (because low tone muscle mass does not resist against gravity), has difficulty with balance, has trouble keeping his or her back straight and has poor endurance. He or she may have a problem holding his or her arms and legs as instructed since he or she may not "feel" his or her position.

3. **Athetoid:** There is excessive and seemingly purposeless erratic movement. It is as though the limb cannot decide if it will reach or retreat. The muscles alternate between normal and low tone. Posture lacks stability. The body and limbs tend to move at the same time. Speech is also affected.

4. **Ataxia:** There is incoordination of voluntary muscle action. A person with this problem will be clumsy, shaky, may show tremors and walk with a wide based gait. As in the athetoid rider, there is a lack of stability.

5. **Rigid:** There is extreme stiffness. The rider displays constant excessive muscle tightness with little ability to move or bend.

6. **Mixed:** Spasticity and athetosis can be present concurrently in many of those afflicted with cerebral palsy. Some may have spasms in addition to other problems. Spasms are sudden involuntary muscle contractions which cannot be relaxed at will. They usually will last only a brief time, then relax. Spasms are not initiated by movement as is spasticity. Spasms are like a "charlie horse" and may be painful.

CVA (STROKE)--A cerebrovascular accident (CVA, stroke) is caused by an interruption of the brain blood supply, generally affecting one side of the brain, which causes motor impairment (loss of speech or arm and leg movement) to the opposite side of the body. The incidence of stroke rises with age but can occur in infants as well as the aged. A CVA can cause mild to severe neurological damage or death. The dysfunction may improve over time, from months to years, so that the person heals completely. Other individuals may continue to have mild to severe problems. A child will usually recover more quickly than an adult.

DRUG REACTION FROM MATERNAL DRUG ABUSE--Children who have experienced in-utero damage from the drug and alcohol abuse of their mothers, can have a wide variety of problems such as mental retardation, cerebral palsy, attention-deficit behavior, impulsive behavior, learning disabilities or other neurological problems. The drugs in their systems may continue to cause behavioral problems for many years. These children may:

1. Be irritable or get frustrated for unknown reasons.
2. Have a sudden screaming tantrum due to pain or other sensations.
3. Get "stuck" in an action or be unable to resolve a problem such as how to move the arm forward.
4. Daydream, drift, or be unable to attend to the task.
5. Fidget, be hyperactive, or have tremors.
6. Appear to have behavioral problems and poor attention.

EPILEPSY--Epilepsy is a brain disorder which causes recurring seizures. (see Seizures). Today, most people so affected are controlled by medication.

HYDROCEPHALUS--Hydrocephalus ("water on the brain") is due to a blockage of the normal flow of cerebrospinal fluid between the ventricles of the brain and the spinal canal. This blockage causes an increase in the fluid in the brain which in turn causes pressure on the brain tissue. The head may enlarge concomitantly. There may be no damage to the brain or there can be considerable damage. Hydrocephalus can be seen in combination with other disorders. A shunt (drain) is placed to release excess fluid and prevent fluid build up.

SHUNT--A shunt is a tube device inserted surgically which allows the drainage of fluid from the brain to a site of absorption usually in the abdomen. **A child with a SHUNT must have a carefully fitted helmet** which **protects the head and does not slide. There must not be any pressure on the SHUNT or the area of the head holding the shunt.** If the head is especially large, a light weight helmet may be recommended by the therapist. A special helmet may need to be adapted for this rider.

SEIZURES--Seizures are associated with changes in electrical brain activity. Common symptoms may include headaches, pain, fever, nausea, vomiting, dizziness, fainting, sweating, drowsiness, loss of bladder control and mild to violent motor activity. Most riders with histories of seizures are controlled with medication so they do not have seizures or have seizures that are very slight. Seizures can be influenced by such things as fever, hot weather, boredom, stress, or hunger. Some people know when their seizures are about to happen. Seizures can also occur without warning or apparent cause. Riders tend to have seizures before or after riding.

CHARACTERISTICS OF SEIZURES:
1. Minor or petit mal seizures may involve momentary loss of consciousness, sometimes so short that it can hardly be noticed. Some loss of awareness or increased tone can be noted.
2. Motor seizures involve rapid and repeated motor movements or jerking. The jerking can involve the whole body or just a limb. These can be with or without loss of consciousness.
3. There may be a period of restlessness prior to the seizure
4. Seizures can cause pain, pleasure, non specific feelings or brain damage. Severe seizures can also cause incontinence.

WHAT TO DO WHEN A SEIZURE OCCURS
MINOR SEIZURES:
1. A SMALL SEIZURE (lasting a second or two). Stop the horse. Support the rider and check to make sure he or she is normal. Follow the instructions of the therapist. If the rider is not alright after a few seconds, stop the ride for the day.
2. With a seizure that may last "a blink of the eye" without drowsiness or loss of consciousness, the rider may continue to ride if the instructor or therapist makes this decision. If the rider continues to ride, place your arm over his or her legs to steady him or her for awhile.
3. Be aware of loss of balance even after a small seizure.
4. Do not put demands on the rider after a seizure. There may have been only a pause in awareness with a seizure, but there may be some disorientation. Be sure the rider is completely "oriented" before giving any commands.

MODERATE OR MAJOR SEIZURE:
1. Stop the horse. Calmly lower the rider to the ground and lay him or her on his or her side (in case the rider vomits he or she will be able to clear his or her throat). All other horses and riders should carefully leave the arena. Do not try to interfere with the seizure; let it run its course. Do not give the rider anything to drink. After the seizure, take the rider out of the arena and let him or her rest. The instructor must take charge of the rider as soon as possible. DO NOT ATTEMPT TO INSERT ANYTHING INTO THE RIDER'S MOUTH. CALL THE PARAMEDICS FOR SEVERE SEIZURES.
2. Instructors or therapists (unless they are RN or LVN) are not qualified to give seizure medicine--or any medicine--and can put themselves "at risk" if they give any medication to riders/program participants.

TRAUMATIC HEAD INJURIES--Traumatic head injuries are caused by an accident or battering to the head. The individual may recover completely with time and therapy or may have permanent neurological damage in mild, moderate or severe form. The period of recovery may vary from within a year to many years.

216

WHAT TO DO WITH A PERSON WHO HAS A BRAIN DISORDER

1. Respond to the muscle tone problems as suggested. (See muscle tone and handling techniques).
2. A rider will need more time to react to stimuli since the messages from the brain to the limbs may be either imperfect, misdirected or slow.
3. Be supportive. A great deal of effort may be needed to do a simple task.
4. Encourage relaxation. Have fun - laugh and sing. Laughing and singing increases breathing, and in turn, helps relaxation.
5. Help the rider to maintain the best possible posture. This will help him or her to develop muscle balance. Do not give unnecessary help, since this does not encourage strength and independence.
6. A rider tends to lean into support. Discourage this poor habit. Be careful not to lean on the rider with your arms or hand.
7. Encourage the rider to look up. This improves head control, posture and balance.
8. Exercises for stretching and balance are important. Exercises should be done while the horse stands. Later, when the rider can maintain balance, they should be done at a walk. The therapist will help you with the proper exercises.
9. Ataxia and athetosis make the rider appear as though he or she will fall. He or she can maintain his or her balance better than one may think. Be alert for needed support but do not be over-protective; give him or her a chance to be independent.

11.02.4   PROBLEMS POSSIBLY FOUND IN PERSONS WITH BRAIN DAMAGE

BODY PARTS INVOLVED IN DYSFUNCTION
Monoplegia involves disability in one limb.
Hemiplegia involves disability on one side of the body.
Paraplegia involves both of the legs and lower trunk.
Diplegia involves the trunk and 2 arms, or 2 legs with more involvement in the legs.
Quadriplegia involves all four limbs and trunk.
Triplegia involves the trunk and three limbs, usually leaving one good arm.

APRAXIA--Complete or partial loss of memory of how to perform complex muscular movements resulting from damage to an area of the brain. There is not necessarily an obvious physical disorder but rather a problem with motor planning; the rider knows what to do but is slow or uncoordinated in the task. The rider can be very intelligent but unable to perform a simple task such as picking up the reins.

WHAT TO DO WHEN A PERSON HAS APRAXIA

1. The rider may need to use his or her eyes to compensate for poor coordination and to concentrate on tasks. Give the rider instructions for only one task at a time until you can see that he or she can handle more.
2. One may need to help the rider get the "feeling" of the task.
3. Give the rider time and work with him or her. Let him or her do it as best he or she can.
4. Do not consider the rider "dumb" for having difficulty with a simple task.
5. Use a smooth gaited horse with predictable behavior.

ATTENTION-SPAN DEFICIT (attention-deficit disorder [ADD]) - Attention span can be disrupted by brain damage of various kinds. The individual may have difficulty focusing on instructions. Attention may drift or be diverted to something else. Attention span may be shortened due to a related language disorder or poor stress tolerance. Short attention span has nothing to do with intelligence.

WHAT TO DO WITH A PERSON WHO HAS A SHORT ATTENTION SPAN

1. Keep the tasks short. Repeat them if necessary.
2. Make sure you have the rider's attention before giving instructions. He or she may look at you but not be attending. Speak slowly and clearly. Ask if the rider understands you and have him or her repeat the instructions back to you.
3. Make the instructional part of the session short and allow for fun and relaxation at the end of the session.

4. Be aware of signs of stress such as tenseness, twitching or nervousness, not following through with instructions, chatting, showing no interest, changing the subject, having increased muscle tone, sweating, or difficulty with breathing.

FRAGILE EMOTIONS--Emotions can be disturbed by any disability, due to the impact on the system. In turn, when the brain is damaged, the emotions can be affected because the emotional center of the brain is damaged. A rider can get upset for no apparent reason or over-react to simple things. Frustration and depression can be easily caused by fatigue.

WHAT TO DO WITH A PERSON WHO HAS FRAGILE EMOTIONS
1. Understand that the rider may not be able to control his or her emotional reactions, what the rider <u>wants</u> to do may not be what happens.
2. Do not react to the in appropriate behavior but react in a matter-of-fact fashion; go on with the lesson.
3. Give physical and mental support when needed and be patient.
4. Use a calm, slow moving horse.
5. Do not allow outrageous behavior. Take a "time out" for children, and adults also. Tell the rider when he or she is doing well and what is not appropriate. End the session if necessary.
6. Do not get angry with the rider.

HYPERSENSATION--Hypersensation which can occur in a number of disabilities is increased awareness to stimuli. Individuals with sensory-integrative dysfunction or learning disabilities frequently are hypersensitive to touch and may withdraw from contact of surfaces (rough, sharp, furry) that are offensive. Hypersensation can occur when nerves are healing or inflamed, as in traumatic injuries or in nerve disorders. When sensation is disrupted, messages may be sent to different brain areas and can cause unpleasant sensations. Hypersensation can include feelings of pain, burning, tingling, or pinpricks.

WHAT TO DO WITH A PERSON WHO IS HYPERSENSITIVE
1. Touch the rider as little as possible. Firm touch is less offensive than light touch.
2. Do not act as though the rider's behavior is unacceptable if he or she over-reacts to touch.
3. Let the rider initiate touch but do not force this. The deep stimulation from the horse helps to bombard the touch system and desensitization occurs.
4. Long sleeve shirts and long pants help protect against offensive sun, touch and other skin irritations.
5. Do not force the rider to touch things.

HYPOSENSATION--Hyposensation is decreased awareness of stimuli to the body. It is a loss that can be mild or complete. Sensation may be present but distorted. Pressure may seem like light touch but the feedback from affected and unaffected limbs will feel quite different. Loss can be in not knowing the position of a limb, or not being able to coordinate a limb's movements. Temperature and pain may not be perceived accurately. Loss of sensation can affect how one relates to space or interprets movement in sitting and walking. The rider may not sit up straight because of lack of awareness of how he sits. To say "put your heels down" or "tighten your grasp" may be meaningless. Total loss of sensation is present in complete paralysis, for example, when a nerve has been severed, and to a lesser degree in other injuries. Some losses of sensation may also be present in persons with mental retardation, seizure disorders, cerebral palsy, learning disabilities and sensory-integrative disorders.

WHAT TO DO WITH A PERSON WHO HAS HYPOSENSATION
1. Be patient and do not get frustrated as you assist the rider; he or she may not be able to do what is requested of him or her or at least in the <u>way</u> which is requested. Imagine how frustrating it would be not to be able to do a simple task such as holding on <u>tightly</u> to the reins or having difficulty grasping them at all.
2. <u>Show</u> the rider what is meant or how to do it. Have the rider copy what is expected.
3. Do not expect the problem to go away quickly. It may take a long time for sensation to improve or it may never improve.

4. Use techniques to help overcome the problem, such as adaptive reins or textured reins. Using tape on a finger to increase feeling in the hand, or attaching weights onto the limb may help (check with the therapist before using weights with a person with physical problems).

5. A rider may not know right from left if the brain cannot distinguish body parts. The instructor may put a red mark on the left hand and a blue mark on the right hand or use one red rein and one blue rein. Say to the rider, "turn red--left" to help the rider learn directions or be able to follow a course.

6. The therapist will provide exercises to increase sensation, such as putting the hands on the horse's shoulder to feel the movement. The therapist will have additional ideas. Give the rider feedback on his or her actions.

7. The horse provides the rider with stimulation in movement, pressure and skin sensation. Let the horse stimulate the rider with a good walking or trotting pace, when this is appropriate. Sometimes it helps to give several taps to the rider's limb or back to increase the sensation.

8. Remember that poor sensation has nothing to do with intelligence.

9. For a person with little feeling in the legs and buttocks, be aware that pressure sores can develop. A pressure sore happens when there is continuous pressure on skin and muscle tissue without allowing for circulation of blood. Since this person has no feeling, he will not know that damage is occurring. The therapist will instruct you on how to decrease the chances of these sores developing.

10. The rider who is sensitive to pressure should wear pants without seams such as riding britches.

ALTERED MUSCLE TONE (TONUS)--Muscle TONUS is the degree of tension a muscle needs to maintain the limb or body position in a relaxed state. A relaxed muscle normally shows slight resistance when another person tries to stretch it. If there is too much tension, muscles will be stiff or spastic. If there is not enough tension, muscles will be weak or floppy.

WHAT TO DO WITH A PERSON WITH ALTERED MUSCLE TONE

Spastic, tight, stiff muscles:
1. Be gentle handling tight limbs. Pulling on tight muscles will make them tighter. The limb will resist quick change.
2. Give the limb time to relax by itself, if possible.
3. Have the rider breathe deeply. This helps to relax the rider's muscles.
4. The rider should be allowed to maintain his postural control over his body as much as possible. Do not do anything to decrease his control since this will increase his stiffness. Help the rider balance, as necessary.
5. If the altered muscle tone is in the legs, have the rider sit astride a wooden horse or barrel **before** riding for approximately ten minutes to encourage stretch and relaxation.
6. Initially after the rider has mounted, one may need to let the rider relax while the horse stands so that the rider can adjust to sitting on the horse and the horse relax to the rider's weight.
7. Give the rider extra time to mount or do exercises.
8. Let the slow rocking movements and warmth of the horse relax the rider's body and limbs.
9. Use mental image games to help the rider stretch out, such as "pretend to be a rag doll and let everything go", or "imagine that there are strings tied to your legs pulling them down".
10. The therapist may request that the limbs be gently shaken with slow, mild movement to relax the rider. Make sure not to grasp the limb tightly since this pressure will increase muscle tone.
11. Use a horse with a smooth gait and smooth transitions.
12. Use a horse with a narrow barrel.

Weak or floppy muscles:
1. When positioning the rider, be careful not to pull so hard as to dislocate a joint. The muscles may be weak and not able to hold the joints firmly together.
2. Be especially careful with young children whose bones are fragile and developing.
3. Allow the motion of the horse to add "tonus" to the muscles before doing exercises that demand strength.
4. Give support where needed until the rider can balance alone. Backriding by your therapist may be necessary to give good support and avoid damage to the joints.

5. Do not allow the rider's limbs to rest in awkward or abnormal positions.
6. Make sure the rider's head does not "bob" excessively (this can produce a whiplash effect). Stop trotting or slow down the walk. If the rider's head still bobs, discontinue the ride. A rider with a weak head/neck posture must be carefully watched by the therapist.
7. If the rider does not have head control off the horse, he or she should not ride unless a therapist is directly treating him or her.
8. Use a horse that provides a lot of stimulation with gaits energetic enough to increase tone but not so much as to cause imbalance.

PARALYSIS--Paralysis is caused by the interruption in transmission of nerve impulses so that messages or sensations to a particular part of the body do not get through. There is a complete loss of muscle power and possibly sensation as well.

WHAT TO DO WITH A PERSON WHO HAS PARALYSIS
1. Do not expect such a limb to move, for it is not possible. The rider needs to learn other ways to function.
2. The rider will need to work on balance since it will be affected by the paralyzed limb or body parts.
3. The rider may need special adaptive equipment to carry out activities required.
4. Use a horse with smooth transitions and gaits.

PARESIS--Paresis is the incomplete loss of muscle power rather than total paralysis. A limb may appear to be immobilized but may have the potential of gaining function. Any movement possible may be weak, clumsy, or "floppy" with poor control.

WHAT TO DO WITH A PERSON WHO HAS PARESIS
1. The rider may not be able to control the muscle actions of the body part affected with paresis. Help the rider to perform the movement.
2. In some exercises, it may help for the rider to "think" the movements. For example: the rider will visualize squeezing the legs around the horse and say "squeeze" to help do this. The rider is reinforcing with the mind whatever muscle movement there is, to help move the legs.
3. Remember that it will take months or several years for strength and coordination to increase.
4. The therapist will provide exercises to strengthen weak areas. Give assistance and support as needed to provide good body alignment.
5. Let the horse's movements help strengthen the rider's movement patterns. The horse's good symmetrical walk challenges the rider with the balance and stimulation exercises needed to increase strength and endurance.
6. Use special equipment to help balance the rider if needed.

LIMITED RANGE OF MOTION (ROM)--Range of motion is the full swing of a limb up and down, side to side, in or out, or around. Tightness, stiffness, spasticity, and weakness of the muscles can prevent the limb from moving through its full range. Weakened or floppy muscles can allow a limb to move beyond the normal range of the joint and make the joint "loose".

WHAT TO DO WITH A PERSON WHO HAS LIMITED RANGE OF MOTION
1. Move a spastic limb very slowly and gently. Do not pull on a tight muscle to increase the range; this can cause the range to become tighter or possibly tear the muscles/tendons.
2. Encourage the rider to move his or her own spastic limbs and also encourage him to use his voice with the movement, e.g., "I lift my arms up - up - up".
3. Give a loose joint support as you help the rider. A loose joint must be handled carefully so that there is no dislocation or tearing of weak muscles/tendons.
4. Have the therapist show you how to handle the rider.
5. Use a horse with smooth movements.

PROTECTIVE REACTIONS--Reactions are automatic movements which occur to help a person to function effectively. When a person trips, his or her hands come forward to keep him or her from hitting his or her head and body against an object. When a person goes down the steps his or her body stays upright to align his or her body against gravity. These reactions (called righting reactions-against gravity and equilibrium reactions-to maintain balance) occur without thinking about them, but can be controlled at will with a person who has developed normally.

PATHOLOGICAL REFLEXES--Pathological movement patterns or reflexes are seen in people with brain injuries. A person with brain damage may have weak or absent protective reactions, which may result in an inability to stay upright in sitting or standing or to re-balance when thrown off balance. Reflexes are seen in specific patterns.
1. The head is lifted and the total body straightens.
2. The arms bend and the total body bends.
3. The hand is raised to the face while the arm turns inward toward the body.
4. The legs may cross each other (scissoring).

Examples of reflexes that may be triggered (set off) while a rider is mounting, dismounting or performing exercises and riding skills on the horse include:
1. A small rider is raised out of his or her wheelchair by being lifted up under the arms, causing the legs to cross (scissoring).
2. While riding, the rider's head falls forward, causing the arms to bend and the legs to straighten (symmetrical tonic neck reflex).
3. The rider now attempts to raise his or her head and it falls backward, causing his or her total body to straighten (tonic labyrinthine neck reflex).
4. The rider is turned on his or her stomach across the horse, causing his or her entire body to flex or bend (tonic labyrinthine neck reflex).
5. The rider is asked to point his or her toes, causing the hips and legs to straighten and tending to grip the horse around the barrel (scissoring).
6. The rider looks to the right and the arm and leg on the face side straightens while the arm and leg on the skull side bend (asymmetrical tonic neck reflex).
7. The horse blows through his or her nose and the child startles, with the head extending and arms and legs extending (Moro).

The rider cannot control pathological reflexes which are triggered by movement or responses to the environment.

WHAT TO DO WITH A PERSON WHO HAS PATHOLOGICAL REFLEXES
1. A therapist with neurodevelopmental training will show the team how to avoid triggering pathological reflexes.
2. Do not expect the rider to be able to correct his or her posture easily or at all.
3. Ask the therapist how you can help the rider obtain better posture and limb movements.
4. Relaxation will help the rider to control his or her movements with a more normal pattern.
5. Do not expect the rider to relax upon command. He or she is more likely to become tense to this command. Movement, singing, fun or other tactics are more likely to produce the right response.
6. See the section on Helping the Rider Sit Up on the Horse for assistive techniques.
7. Do not expect or encourage the rider to accomplish skills or tasks that increase abnormal movements.
8. When the rider is relaxed and having fun, abnormal reflexes may decrease.
9. Have the rider sit upright on his or her seat bones to create a deep seat. This may encourage a straighter back--but watch out for and prevent a posterior tilt and rounded back.

VESTIBULAR SYSTEM DEFICITS--The vestibular system affects one's body in relation to space, the direction of one's movement or the lack of movement. This system affects muscle tone, body balance, visual perception, and alertness. When there is damage, or this system does not work well, a rider has difficulty with balance and the muscle tone necessary to maintain balance against gravity. Some riders need increased movement to make their systems work. They may "rock back and forth" frequently and show great joy when the horse trots. Others are hypersensitive to movement, especially subtle movements. These riders may be fearful when they start riding. Sudden movements such as a quick turn or the horse shying might cause these riders to panic. The horse provides vibrations, which are produced by the natural side-to-side, back-and-forth, and up-and-down movements: excellent stimulation for both types of riders.

WHAT TO DO WITH A PERSON WHO HAS VESTIBULAR PROBLEMS
1. For riders who need lots of movement, change directions and speed frequently.
2. Riders who are hypersensitive to movement may need to ride for short periods until they can tolerate movement better. A backrider may make them feel more secure at first.
3. The therapist may have you trot the horse for short periods. Make sure the rider does not slip while trotting.
4. Do not say things like "it's OK, it's not so bad". Remember that the problem is <u>disagreeable to the rider</u>; his or her physical system is over-reactive.
5. Most riders who are hypersensitive to movement have fewer problems with a rough gait or trotting. The therapist may mix slow movements with fast movements to increase the rider's tolerance to subtle movements. Ask the rider what feels best and repeat that action. Even a non-verbal rider will indicate what is pleasing.
6. If the rider gets too tense from trotting, trot only for short periods. Help the rider to relax. Have the rider sit on a sheepskin pad and use a vaulting surcingle. The softness of this pad may help to relax him or her and the vaulting surcingle provides good solid handles for security.

11.02.5	EMOTIONAL--BEHAVIORAL DISORDERS

It is important to understand the disorders of people with emotional problems but do not categorize behavior and label any person that you work with. People with behavioral disorders usually do not have a pure disorder as listed below but rather have a mixture of behavioral characteristics. Many riders with emotional problems will take medication to control their behavior. A person with severe behavioral problems can function quite normally in a riding situation. Behavioral or psychiatric problems may have a neurological basis and peculiarities may not be under the control of the individual. Do not expect the person to just "stop doing that". They usually cannot. (See Section 11.03 for more information on these problems.)

ANXIETY DISORDERS--Anxiety disorders are feelings of extreme uncertainty, panic, tension, irritability or crisis. The anxiety may be caused by real or imagined situations. The individual may look fatigued, may sweat, have difficulty breathing or be very apprehensive. Whether the situation is caused by a real or unreal situation, it is <u>real</u> to this person.

DEPRESSIVE DISORDERS--Depressive disorders cause extreme sadness, feelings of rejection, a low self-esteem, feeling constant failure, negative attitudes, feeling let down and feeling guilty. People affected by depression are often quiet and withdrawn. The rider may tell you he did not want to ride or did not enjoy the session even though he actually did.

OBSESSIVE-COMPULSIVE DISORDERS--With an obsessive-compulsive disorder the individual may have isolated, unwanted thoughts or actions which are constantly repeated or performed and cannot be controlled. This person may have to do things in a specific way only and repeat actions many times. Interference with these acts can cause the individual extreme anxiety or distress. The rider may become so concerned with the details of brushing the mane that he or she never gets finished grooming the horse.

PARANOID DISORDERS--People with a paranoid disorder may be suspicious, hypersensitive, rigid, jealous, hostile or have feelings of great and superior self-worth. There is a tendency to feel that many acts by the volunteer, your group or even the public are directed specifically at them. The person may feel you came especially to spy on him or her. In other areas the person functions well.

PSYCHOPATHIC PERSONALITY--People who have psychopathic personalities have a tendency to blame others for their actions and will cause others to suffer rather than themselves. They may be non-conformist, rebellious, have superficial charm, be untruthful, display poor judgment, and not learn from experience. They truly believe in their actions.

PSYCHOSIS--Psychosis is a disturbance of mental function to the extent that it interferes with the daily demands of life. The individual withdraws from the real world into one of fantasy and delusion. This withdrawal may be for a short period or an indefinite time. Individuals with paranoid and schizophrenic disorders can be psychotic. These people do not usually have impairment of orientation, memory or intellect.

SCHIZOPHRENIA--A psychotic person with schizophrenia often displays altered thinking, misconceptions of reality and strange behavior. They may show inappropriate responses and moods, and unpredictable actions. Speech can be symbolic. The person's reactions can swing in and out of states of schizophrenia.

WHAT TO DO WITH A PERSON WHO HAS EMOTIONAL OR BEHAVIORAL PROBLEMS
1. Check with the psychologist or your therapist regarding special handling of any such rider.
2. Listen carefully to your rider, do not argue or challenge a fantasy. Direct the rider's attention to the task.
3. The therapist or psychologist may set definite goals and limits. Be sure you carry them out as instructed. This helps to prevent manipulation and other undesirable behaviors.
4. Remember that you are not there to "treat" the rider but to help him or her with horsemanship skills.
5. If a rider blames you for problems that you have no control over, do not take this personally or respond to it. The rider may be projecting his or her feelings for someone else onto you.
6. Provide the rider with balance and security as needed. Some may need assistance until riding becomes more familiar.
7. Find in each rider something unique and nice. People with long term psychiatric problems may be difficult to like but all have some traits to which you can relate on a personal and friendly basis.
8. Try to develop a relationship between horse and rider. Have the rider spend more time with grooming and touching the horse. Touching brings one in contact with the real world.
9. Encourage completion of the task and successes.

11.02.6	GENETIC DISORDERS

ALZHEIMER'S DISORDER--Alzheimer's is a disease of middle age and older persons showing characteristics of confusion, forgetfulness, and impaired intellectual functions. Recent memory is a major problem with this disorder. The rider will have difficulty remembering anything he is told. As stated by one man with a moderate disability due to Alzheimer's disease, "the task (putting on socks) seems simple as I think about it but when I try to do it that is a whole different story. It seems my body is somewhere else." The disease gets progressively worse.

WHAT TO DO WITH A PERSON WHO HAS ALZHEIMER'S DISORDER
1. Your rider will have some ability to control his actions.
2. Speak slowly and use simple language. Face the rider as you talk. Give only one instruction at a time.
3. Focus on the pleasure and exercise of riding.
4. The instructor will help the rider to improve balance and strength.
5. Give assistance when you see the rider is confused or frustrated.
6. Show understanding and empathy.
7. Expect the unexpected since the rider's attention span may be short.

DOWN SYNDROME--Individuals with Down Syndrome, (chromosome trisomy 21 - 94%, 3.6% translocation, 2.4% mosaic) a birth defect, can have any of the following characteristics which may affect their ability to ride. Intellectual function can be low normal to severely retarded. Muscles tend to be "soft" and floppy. The joints tend to be loose and almost disjointed. Hips may be formed differently than the normal child. Hands and fingers may be small or stunted. The limbs are out of proportion to the trunk which makes it difficult to find a saddle that fits them well.

There may be decreased ability to feel or control movements. Balance may be poor. Other problems can include heart conditions, breathing problems, ear infections, hearing, speech and vision problems. They may also have such disorders as autism and hemiplegia/cerebral palsy. Persons with Down syndrome tend to act younger than their real age but they are usually pleasant and affectionate people who love to ride and to please. **10% of persons with Down Syndrome have Atlanto-axial instability and must be diagnosed by X-ray <u>before riding.</u>** This is a condition of weakness and instability of the neck. **This condition may cause paralysis if the person receives a jolt to the neck such as in a fall or strong thrust.**

<u>WHAT TO DO WITH A PERSON WHO HAS DOWN SYNDROME</u>
1. Follow suggestions under <u>Muscle Tone</u> for weak and floppy muscles. Have your therapist show you how to handle and position this rider.
2. Support the back if it is weak and balance is poor. Encourage good posture so muscles develop in good form.
3. This person may have a fear of heights and movement when he or she first starts riding. Be supportive. Let him or her just get used to being on the horse. The instructor or therapist may backride with him or her.
4. The rider's legs should be in a normal riding position--not spread too far apart--so that the hip joints are not stressed. With small children, use a narrow horse.
5. The instructor should increase riding time slowly to increase strength and endurance.
6. Provide support as needed.
7. Riders that have the strength <u>to steady their heads and bodies</u> will enjoy trotting.
8. Encourage coordination activities, mental development and riding skills that challenge the rider. Riders with Down's may have near normal intellect and can perform all kinds of horsemanship skills successfully.
9. Do not <u>over</u> challenge these riders. They will always try to please you. Some can be very manipulative. Set limits for <u>them</u> to carry out.
10. Many riders with Down Syndrome become skilled in all areas of competitive riding and vaulting.
11. Try to relate to each in a way that is age-appropriate to the rider.
12. Be gentle with corrective criticism.
13. Be careful to avoid dust and to protect sensitive skin from the sun and the wind.
14. Persons with instability at the cervical 1-2 (**Altanlo-Axial Instability**), must not ride.

DWARFISM--People with dwarfism prefer to be called **LITTLE PEOPLE.** Dwarfism is a disproportionately short stature. There are different types of dwarfism. Intelligence, however, is mostly normal. There are characteristics which are of concern to riding programs. Children may have a middle ear infection with balance problems and speech delays. The lungs and breathing patterns may be atypical with less volume because of their small physical structure. There can be hydrocephalus with a shunt or physical problems with hip or elbow contracture, loose joints, and poor muscle tone. Immature motor skills may be seen in children due to delay in structural development, decreased strength, deformed and dislocated joints.

<u>WHAT TO DO WITH A PERSON WITH DWARFISM</u>
1. Check with the therapist for any special directions.
2. Symmetry of movements are important so all limbs are strengthened equally.
3. Make sure the equipment and tack you use fits the rider; select special equipment necessary for some riders.
4. Follow procedures used for persons with arthritic conditions when joint problems are present. Check with the therapist for special handling techniques.
5. Encourage good posture and good joint range.
6. Follow the therapist's advice for persons with spinal curves.
7. In growing children, avoid stress on weight bearing joints (such as trotting while standing in the stirrups). Have the therapist approve new activities.
8. Remember, Little People are generally normal except for their physical structure. Treat them so.

SICKLE-CELL ANEMIA--Sickle-cell anemia is a chronic blood disease most common in black males. There are periods of crisis where the disease worsens. The disease is characterized by pain in the feet, hands and abdomen. It affects the lungs, the liver, spleen and kidney. A CVA (stroke) can occur because of circulatory problems.

WHAT TO DO WITH A PERSON WHO HAS SICKLE-CELL ANEMIA
1. The instructor will request extra help in handling such a person for maximum safety since <u>falls must be avoided</u>.
2. Use protective sheepskin pads or padded supports when necessary. Damage can be caused to the skin rather easily.
3. Beware of complaints of pain and inform the instructor immediately.

11.02.7   HEARING IMPAIRMENT

Impaired hearing or loss of hearing can be caused by problems with the ear structure (<u>conductive hearing loss</u>), by nerve damage (<u>sensorineural hearing loss</u>), or both. Hearing loss can be of varying levels. A hearing impaired person uses the other senses for communication: vision, vibrations, feeling, and residual hearing. The rider will need to use his or her eyes much more to be aware of his or her surroundings.

WHAT TO DO WITH A PERSON WHO IS HEARING IMPAIRED
1. Help riders to develop all their senses.
2. Teach riders to feel the horse's movements and understand what they mean. The horse can provide the riders with much information as they learn to interpret its movements.
3. Know your riders' skills in communication. Some hearing impaired people lip read and others use sign-language and lipreading together, others use sign-language alone. Be prepared and know how you need to interact with them.
4. Become as proficient in sign-language as possible or utilize a sign language interpreter. Also remember that we all use extensive hand and body language. The hearing impaired person can understand this in much the same way that a person with normal hearing can.
5. For riders who lip read, be sure you are face to face with them and have their attention when you give directions. Speak clearly and slowly but use <u>normal</u> pronunciation. Use a pause between sentences. Speak slowly with children. Restate sentences which are not understood after 2 to 3 repetitions.
6. Be certain that you are close enough for the riders to clearly see your hands and face (in order to read your signs/speech.

(All of the following information refers to the rider with impaired hearing as his/her <u>only</u> disability; it does not address the hearing impaired rider with multiple disabilities, although the following information may be helpful in such cases.)

EXPECTED BENEFITS
The same benefits which we <u>all</u> derive from riding - increased physical, mental, and emotional capabilities. Plus - the exposure to <u>lots</u> of new vocabulary and language concepts assists in building of American Sign Language (ASL) and/or English skills. The horse has proven to be a very strong "motivator" for communication with children who had previously been non-communicative. The relationship with the horse, who is non-judgmental about the rider's speech and/or signs, promotes the rider's feelings of self-esteem.

PRECAUTIONS
Some hearing impaired riders also have impaired balance; be sure to check on this area with the rider, parent, doctor, or therapist. Otherwise, proceed with instruction as with an able-bodied rider with normal hearing.

WHERE TO START THE RIDER IN THE PROGRAM
For a child, it is advisable to start with a leader and possibly a sidewalker (for security and communication purposes). The sidewalker can be taken away when the child's confidence has improved and his attention to the instructor or interpreter is <u>consistent</u>. The leader can be taken away when sufficient control of the horse has been established. Independent control of the horse must be <u>excellent</u> before the leader is taken away; remember that the instructor will not be able to relay <u>any</u> instructions when the rider's back is to the instructor! The rider must be able to think and act independently in order to ride safely. Adults may be started with or without a leader, at the discretion of the instructor.

225

SUITABLE RIDING ENVIRONMENT

Any kind of enclosed (fenced) riding area is suitable, either indoor or outdoor. It may be necessary to use only part of the enclosed ring or area by blocking off sections with poles on the ground or orange pylons (highway markers/cones). Starting the riders in a smaller area assists with attention to the instructor and improves visibility of signs/speech. When consistent attention has been established and the rider is familiar with the basic vocabulary/concepts and routine, the instructor may choose to enlarge the riding area. For safety purposes, it may be advisable to utilize leaders or riding volunteers to "pony" hearing impaired riders on the trail, at least in the beginning stages.

THERAPIST

The hearing impaired rider with no other disabilities will probably not require a physical therapist. However, the rider with impaired balance may benefit from the assistance of an occupational therapist with balance/vestibular activities.

TYPE OF HORSE

In the beginning stages, and especially for children with impaired balance, a very "unflappable" horse is a necessity! Horses which tend to spook or move very quickly are probably never suitable for hearing impaired riders, since the riders cannot themselves hear the "scary" sounds, and, therefore, will always be caught off-guard if the horses should shy! However, it is not necessary to use very dull, lethargic horses with hearing impaired riders. An energetic but calm and sensible horse will be greatly appreciated by your hearing impaired riders (and by all of us, for that matter!).

TYPE GAIT/MOVEMENT

Horses with a very distinct 2-beat trot and 3-beat canter will be helpful in teaching posting to the trot and canter leads. Learning to post on a horse with a very smooth, "shuffle-y" kind of trot can be very frustrating for a rider who cannot hear the hoofbeats!

HORSE TACK

The usual English (or Western) saddle with Peacock-safety stirrups is sufficient for this rider. A hand-hold attached to the D-rings on the pommel will be helpful for explaining hand placement.

RIDER EQUIPMENT

No special equipment is necessary for the rider other than the usual ASTM-approved helmet. The instructor may find it helpful to have children wear safety belts when they are learning to post to the trot - the belts make convenient "handles" for hoisting children up and down in unison with the 2 beats of the trot.

LESSON SUGGESTIONS

Treat your hearing impaired riders the same as you would "normal" riders! The following suggestions may be helpful in planning your lessons:

a) Due to the fact that congenitally deaf/hearing impaired persons have never heard the English language (or any other spoken language, for that matter), some concepts may be unfamiliar to them. Do not hesitate to ask for assistance from an experienced classroom teacher or interpreter when one runs into difficulties explaining equestrian concepts to the riders (e.g., diagonals, leads, rein and leg aids, and so forth).

b) If "a picture is worth a thousand words", a live demonstration is worth a million words! Use lots of visual demonstrations by a mounted instructor or other skilled rider, rather than attempting to use lots of lengthy explanations.

c) Ask the rider(s) to ride into the center of the ring and halt so that the instructor can give explanations or complicated directions. Do not attempt to give any but the simplest directions while the riders are circling the arena!

APHASIA--Aphasia is the loss or impairment of speech or ability to understand speech caused by damage to the brain. Intelligence is not generally affected. Aphasia can include one or more of the following problems.

   a. **Expressive aphasia** involves the impairment or the loss of ability to produce or recall spoken words.
   b. **Receptive aphasia** is the impairment or loss of the ability to recognize and understand speech. Words can be heard but not understood-as though the words were a foreign language.
   c. **apraxia of speech** is the loss or impairment of voluntary control of muscles which produce speech sounds. Speech may be slow or slurred.
   d. **Alexia** is word-blindness (failure to recognize written or printed words).
   e. **Agnosia** is the inability to recognize and interpret symbols, shapes, directions, sounds.

WHAT TO DO WITH A PERSON WHO HAS A LANGUAGE DISORDER

Expressive Disorders:
   1. Keep in mind that intelligence is not the problem (although children with mental retardation can have these problems).
   2. It takes lots of patience to understand these riders. If possible, encourage non-verbal language.
   3. Do not be afraid to say you do not understand what the rider says.
   4. Try to encourage the use of single word responses. Say the word, then have them repeat the word, but do not push them if they cannot respond. Not being able to speak is very frustrating!
   5. It is easier to initiate speech than to respond to someone else, so give the person time to try to express him or herself.
   6. Use directions that do not require an answer. When possible, phrase sentences appropriate for a simple verbal or non-verbal yes/no response.
   7. Some people may have only a few words they can say. They may use these words as though they were using full sentences. They may not be aware they cannot be understood. Tell them you do not understand.
   8. Wait a longer time for responses than when talking with people without language disorder.

Receptive Disorders:
   1. Use as much non-verbal language as possible. Show the rider what you want. Often visual demonstrations can preclude the use of language.
   2. Speak slowly and look at the rider when you speak. Use single words for children or adults with severe problems. The rider may be able to understand a little. Give him or her time to process what you say. This can take minutes or more.
   3. Do not treat the rider as though he or she is stupid because he or she cannot understand you. Just do the best you can to communicate meanings, and smile.

Problems with Persons Having Both Expressive and Receptive Disorder:
   1. Communication is very difficult and frustrating with this rider. Try different methods and see what works.
   2. Be patient and relax, for nothing is gained by getting upset.
   3. Use touch, expression and gestures to communicate.

11.02.9   LIMB DEFORMITIES OR LOSS OF A LIMB(S)

Limb deformities or amputations can be caused by disease, drugs, toxins, or accidents. A person may be fitted with an artificial limb. These are becoming increasingly sophisticated and versatile. The rider with an amputation may choose not to wear the artificial limb since motion can cause rubbing on the skin. A rider who is born without a body part is exceptionally capable and does not seem to miss this limb. The major problem faced by this rider is the lack of balance because one side of the body has less weight and less function than the other. A rider who is missing both legs, for example, has less of a balance problem then a rider who is missing one leg.

WHAT TO DO WITH A PERSON WHO HAS A LIMB DEFORMITY OR LOSS OF A LIMB
1. Help to develop balance. Give support when necessary.
2. For a person with a leg missing, it may be necessary to adapt the saddle to help give the rider additional support. The western saddle holds the rider more securely in place. A rider with missing lower limbs may need to have a specially constructed saddle.
3. Give support when a rider lacks balance, security or "feels" off balance.
4. If an artificial limb is worn, care must be taken not to cause rubbing or sores. Watch for redness. Use sheepskins or sponge to protect the limb or stump if this is appropriate. The therapist will advise you on safe methods for seating and supporting these riders.
5. Help to develop strength in other areas.
6. <u>Never</u> tie the rider or the residual limb to the saddle.
7. Add weights to the saddle to give the horse an equal weight on the saddle (if the instructor is unfamiliar the saddle weighing, check with a racing tack shop who are familiar with this technique.)

11.02.10	NERVE INJURIES

BRACHIAL PLEXUS PALSY-ERB'S PALSY--These disorders involve the peripheral nerves and thus the muscles of the shoulder girdle, arm and hand and can cause total or partial limitation. Usually only one side of the body is involved. Damage can occur at any age or during birth. Rehabilitation can assist in recovering function.

WHAT TO DO WITH A PERSON WITH BRACHIAL PLEXUS PALSY-ERB'S PALSY
1. The therapist will move the involved arm through its full range. Exercise both arms with riding exercises.
2. Encourage the use of both arms for riding skills, grooming and tacking activities; use two hands on the reins.
3. The therapist will advise on special exercises or equipment.

11.02.11	NEURODEVELOPMENTAL DISORDERS

AUTISM--Autism is a neurological disorder which produces the following characteristics in those affected:
1. Self-preoccupation--may not relate to people; avoids eye contact; has delayed or no social smile.
2. Communication dysfunction--lack of speech or unusual speech patterns; may repeat what you say ("parrot-like"); difficulty in expressing wishes.
3. Basically normal physical development with abnormal repetitive movement actions, such as moving the fingers continuously.
4. Perseveration or sameness--tends to get "stuck" in an action or obsessed with something such as a possession, spinning an object, rocking or perseverance of an idea, and may be fearful of new things.
5. May appear deaf or blind although he or she can hear and see.
6. May be very smart in specific skills. Generally has excellent memory. Autism may be very mild with near normal functioning to very severe with functional retardation.
7. Function can vary from hour to hour or day to day; for instance a skill can be performed at one time but not at the next try. Autism can exist in combination with other problems created by organic brain disorders.

WHAT TO DO WITH A PERSON WHO IS AUTISTIC
1. Treat the person according to the degree of disability.
2. Approach the individual slowly and without demands.
3. Help make him or her comfortable with tasks that are easy and that bring the most joy. Add new tasks or skills slowly according to his or her ability to accept them. Give praise for accomplishments. Do not create stress, the rider may be stressed already due to his or her inability to communicate.
4. Do not force or expect interaction including eye contact. Be alert to any communication attempts and offer praise for all efforts. Lack of response to your statements does not mean a lack of understanding. Some riders may need to be shown what to do.

5. A person with autism may have low tolerance for stress and may show unusual behavior for no apparent reason. Be ready for actions such as getting off the moving horse or having a tantrum.
6. Do not allow improper actions. Expect good behavior. Be calm, friendly and firm. Discipline much the same as with any other <u>child</u>.

DEVELOPMENTAL DELAY--is an umbrella term used to include most or all functional disabilities that are seen in infants and children. Initially it was used with infants so that they would not be "labeled" until they were older when their condition could be more accurately assessed. It can include infants with true developmental delays due to premature birth, feeding disorders or due to extensive corrective surgery. With good care and therapy, these children recover and are generally normal. Other developmental delays include all children who are delayed or retarded in major areas of their growth patterns which can include any or all of the following: gross motor behavior, fine motor behavior, adaptive and language behavior, and social behavior. Children who are delayed in major growth areas can include those with autism, cerebral palsy, seizure disorders and mental retardation. It is common for the term to be used instead of mental retardation since it is felt by some to be less offensive. A person with a seizure disorder, cerebral palsy or autism may or may not be retarded in the ability to learn, while those who in the past have been termed "retarded" are unable to learn at the normal or near normal rate.

MENTAL RETARDATION--Mental retardation is a disorder due to brain damage, under-development of the brain or genetic disorders. Difficulties that result can be seen in mobility, vision, hearing, speech, understanding, judgment, and behavior. The level of retardation is based on comparison of the level of functioning to the average child or adult of the same age. A <u>mildly</u> retarded person is an individual who has an I.Q. below 70 points. This individual can learn basic reading and math, understand social skills and function independently in self-care skills. A <u>moderately</u> retarded individual functions at 50% of the average ability and is considered "trainable". This means that the individual can usually function independently within the home but needs supervision outside the home due to difficulties with judgment and immaturity in handling social activities. Many people at this level may not understand the concept of money. A <u>severely</u> retarded individual function at 25% or below the average person's ability. These people can learn, but must do so slowly and learning is dependent on various problems within the brain.

A mentally retarded person may seem less retarded as a child than as an adult. The mildly and moderately retarded persons generally do very well with basic riding. The severely retarded person can gain from the exercise and the unique stimulus of riding.

<u>WHAT TO DO WITH A PERSON WHO IS MENTALLY RETARDED</u>
1. Work with the riders on their level of ability and not below it. Have the rider tell you what he or she likes in general. This will give you some idea of the rider's level of function. **All people can learn** but at different rates.
2. Keep the activities simple until you know the rider can do more. Most riders will need time to adjust to the feel of the moving horse before they can do any activities.
3. The rider may need strict guidance to behave in an appropriate way. If this is not necessary, do not provide this structure.
4. Do not give reins to riders until they have been instructed in rein management and you are sure they will not yank at the horse's mouth. It is easier to set good habits than to correct bad ones. Even if the reins are attached to a halter, pulling on the reins develops poor riding skills. Explain to riders that yanking on reins hurts the horse. If they cannot understand this concept, go on to games that are more at their level. The use of *Peggy the Teaching Horse* allows riders to learn the concept of reins without involvement of the horse (see 15.09). The use of reins may be more important to the staff than to the rider.
5. Encourage situations which produce success. Give plenty of praise for a job well done. **Do not praise a poor job,** since this does not give the rider proper feedback.
6. Activities should be challenging and fun.
7. Make sure the rider understands your directions. Speak slowly and use common words and short sentences.

LEARNING DISABILITY--Learning disability is a dysfunction of the brain caused by interference with the normal process of storing, processing and producing information. It can involve any or all of the following areas of brain function: perception, conceptualization, language production and/or reception, control of attention, motor coordination, control of impulses, directional concepts, sensory perception, or visual perception. (Learning disabilities are described by terms such as minimal brain dysfunction, perceptual-motor deficit, dyslexia, attention-deficit disorder or hyperkinetic disorder). A person with learning disabilities has:

1) Average or above average intelligence
2) Basically normal abilities in motor, hearing, vision and emotional areas

The disability may be very subtle and unnoticed by others but the daily performance of tasks may be extremely difficult and take a great deal more energy and effort than others may imagine. The person with this disability can change from day to day or hour to hour, since he is affected by fatigue, stress, environmental influences, the complexity of the task or involvement of multi-deficit areas. Learning disabilities can be associated with head injuries, sensory-integration dysfunction or can be inherited.

Characteristics often seen:

1. Shows self-centered thinking
2. Is distractable and/or impulsive and perhaps unable to tune out distracting stimuli
3. Has poor perception of others' thinking and actions
4. Has difficulty observing facial and body language which may cause misunderstandings in communication
5. May not be able to read or see all symbols or letters of a word. May reverse or displace symbols or letters
6. Auditory perceptual difficulty may cause poor interpretation of comments, not hearing a complete sentence, hearing "slowly" or giving a delayed response
7. May not be able to judge time and space/space relations, or know right from left
8. May have difficulty sequencing tasks. May not function well without structure and may need to organize all tasks
9. May perseverate (get stuck in an action)
10. May be able to handle only one task or action at a time, especially if a new task is presented
11. May have a short attention span and fatigue easily

WHAT TO DO WITH A PERSON WHO HAS A LEARNING DISABILITY

1. Try to develop some understanding of the rider's problem. When appropriate, have the rider tell you what activities are especially difficult and which are the best ways for him to learn and understand.
2. Do not use statements such as "Oh, everyone has some problems like that". "There is nothing wrong with you"; "just pay attention".
3. Problem areas need much practice and patience. They cannot be corrected easily, and some not at all.
4. Try to figure out how the rider can learn best through his or her strong areas. Some learn best visually, others through listening. Do not pressure. Most people with learning disabilities are already under stress since they must put so much effort into concentration and carrying out tasks. *This lack of being able to perform is frustrating and degrading to them since their environment demands more from them. This causes a decrease in self esteem.* Try to keep everything light and happy.
5. Give feedback on what the rider is doing and what the rider should be doing. The rider may also reverse things such as turning left for right. Saying "STOP" may trigger a "GO".
6. Do not get upset at the rider's slow response. The rider needs time to process information without added pressure.
7. Remember that the rider is intelligent and generally understands, but may not be able to perform exactly as desired.
8. Make sessions short when necessary, but always challenge the rider. It is depressing for a person with a learning disability to be treated as though retarded or incapable.
9. End the session with a successful activity and a positive comment.
10. IT IS VERY IMPORTANT THAT THE ACTIVITIES ARE CHALLENGING, NOT DULL. REMEMBER THIS RIDER HAS NORMAL INTELLIGENCE. BEING SLOW IS NOT DUMB!
11. These riders may need structure. DO NOT CONFUSE STRUCTURE WITH REPETITION. Repetition of simple tasks are dull and unchallenging and do not help the rider to progress and resolve his or her disorder.

FRIEDREICH'S ATAXIA--A genetic disorder which begins to appear in late childhood or early adulthood. It is a degenerative (slowly worsening) disease that affects the spinal cord and lower section of the brain. Intelligence is normal but walking becomes unsteady. All muscles can be affected causing incoordination and balance problems. Spinal curves may develop because of muscle weakness and imbalance. Vision and speech may be affected. Symptoms may vary from day to day.

GUILLIAN-BARRE SYNDROME--A disease caused by a virus that affects the peripheral nerves. There is initially a respiratory infection followed by muscle weakness and then paralysis of muscles. Nerve fibers can regenerate and the individual may recover all function over a period of many months to a year. Some people may not recover completely. There may be no feeling in the limbs, but as the nerves regenerate, there may be hypersensitivity or pain to touch or actual pain. Intelligence is not affected.

MULTIPLE SCLEROSIS (MS)--A disease which begins in young adults. There are lesions in the myelin sheaths of nerves in the brain and spinal cord which cause "short outs". There may be inflammation, pain, destruction of tissue and weakness; or there may be distorted sensation, contracture, unsteadiness, double vision or loss of vision, dizziness, and mixed emotional states. Memory and attention can be affected. Intelligence is usually normal. The rider will be sensitive to extreme hot and cold weather which may increase his symptoms. There may be good and bad periods. Some people with MS are without symptoms for years but may react to heat and cold, and fatigue easily.

MUSCULAR DYSTROPHY (MD)--A disorder occurring in several forms, all having a genetic basis. Some forms are very progressive and others develop slowly so the person can expect a nearly normal life span. In one form, there is progressive weakening of certain muscle groups - usually in young males. In another form, the muscle weakness begins in the trunk. Another form involves the muscles of the face, neck, shoulder and arms. In another form the child begins to stumble and fall. The muscles, calves especially, may appear large but are actually weak due to fatty tissue build up. Spinal curves and contracture are common, along with poor posture. Breathing may become difficult in the later stages of the disease. Intelligence is in normal ranges.

NEUROPATHY--This can include any non-inflammatory disease of peripheral nerves with undetermined or unknown cause.

POLIOMYELITIS (POLIO)--Caused by a virus which affects the spinal cord or, if life threatening, the lower part of the brain. It can cause paralysis of the lungs and weakness in muscles supplied by spinal or cranial nerves. The result can be mild to severe weakness or paralysis in any part of the body. Sensation is not usually involved.

WHAT TO DO WITH PERSONS WITH NEUROMUSCULAR DISORDERS

1. Do not let the rider get too <u>tired</u> or stressed. Increase demands in sessions slowly; <u>stop</u> for rest periods. <u>A weak muscle does not strengthen well when tired.</u>
2. Always encourage good, balanced posture , with a level pelvis, so that spinal curvatures and contractures do not develop. Encourage equal strength and full range of the limbs on both sides of the body to prevent deformities. The therapist will advise you on proper seating and exercises.
3. Provide the rider with support when necessary, making sure the sidewalkers do not lean on the rider or pull him or her off balance.
4. Ask the rider how he or she is doing today, since people with these disorders experience changes from day to day. Get the rider involved in decision making. Remember, this person is generally of average or above average intellect.
5. Be careful of tight hip muscles when putting the rider on the horse. This can cause considerable pain from stretching.
6. A good exercise program is important to increase lung capacity and circulation for overall health.
7. Coordination may be poor due to poor sensation, hypersensation or weakness.

8. Watch for pressure sores if the rider has poor sensation in the legs and buttocks. The stirrups should be adjusted to provide adequate support for weak legs with poor sensation. A sheepskin saddle cover can protect sensitive skin. Have the therapist assist you in these areas.
9. Excessive exercise, stress or heat can temporarily increase the symptoms. This can be prevented or decreased by providing rest periods of ten to twenty minutes. A weakened state can be noticed by unsteadiness, slurred speech, cramping, spasms, and/or decreased sensation.
10. Make the lesson stimulating to the rider's intellect. Many riders can develop intermediate to advanced riding skills.
11. In hot weather, have water available for the rider to drink during the lesson and spray the rider's arms and face with a light water mist to cool him or her off. Riders find this light mist cool and refreshing.

11.02.13   ORTHOPEDIC DISORDERS

SPINAL CURVATURE--Spinal curvature which throws the body out of balance is not normal and may be associated with many disorders. A structural spinal curve is caused by diseased or abnormal bone structure. A functional spinal curve is usually flexible and may be due to persistent poor posture. A functional spinal curve can lose its flexibility and the person may develop a contracture after a period of time.
   a. Kyphosis is a "humpback" or rounded upper back.
   b. Lordosis is a hollow back of the lower spine or an abnormal forward curve in the neck area.
   c. Scoliosis is a side to side curve. The vertebrae may deviate to the side but also rotate; scoliosis can cause the hips to tilt and the leg on one side to appear shortened.

WHAT TO DO WITH A PERSON WITH A SPINAL CURVATURE
1. A rider with a spinal curve must be carefully positioned on the horse with the pelvis level. Improper positioning can cause the spinal curve to worsen. It is important for a therapist to supervise this rider.
2. It is important that the person's riding posture keep him balanced and upright.
3. Muscle balance can be increased by:
   a) a well-balanced horse.
   b) a deep seated, balanced saddle properly centered on the horse.
   c) circling the horse in large circles in the direction that tends to straighten the spine.
   These activities will be initiated and supervised by the instructor.
4. Supporting the rider from the back by a backrider will not necessarily straighten the spine. The backrider should be a therapist who knows how to best position the rider's spine.
5. Stirrups should be adjusted to achieve a level pelvis and encourage symmetry.

11.02.14   RESPIRATORY DISORDERS

ASTHMA--A disorder characterized by an increased response of the trachea and bronchi to various stimuli causing narrowing of the airways, producing wheezing. The problem can be mild to severe. A rider with severe asthma should have instructions in his or her file giving information on what to do in case of severe attacks. An asthmatic person can be allergic to horses, dust, pollens, hay and perfume. If the rider becomes much worse in the stable environment, riding is not appropriate.

CYSTIC FIBROSIS--An inherited disorder of the exocrine glands. The major complication is chronic pulmonary disease.

WHAT TO DO WITH PERSONS WHO HAVE RESPIRATORY DISORDERS
1. Exercise is good for this rider as it improves the lung muscles and stimulates general health.
2. Exercise should be carefully increased to tolerance.

3. Dust must be avoided, both the dust from the arena and the dust that comes from the hair of the horse. Wipe the horse with a damp cloth prior to mounting. A surgical or dust mask over the nose of the rider may help decrease dust inhalation.
4. Cold or dampness may trigger an asthmatic attack.
5. Have plenty of water on hand for riders with cystic fibrosis since they sweat more than usual and may get dehydrated.

11.02.15   SPINAL DISORDERS

SPINA BIFIDA--A birth defect to a part of the spinal cord. There is damage to the nerves of the body below the site of cord damage; the degree of dysfunction depends on the level of damage to the spinal cord.

SPINAL CORD INJURIES--These injuries are due to trauma to the spine or less often, from tumors. Damage can lead to complete paralysis when the spinal cord has been severely damaged, or it can be partial, with weakness only, to areas below the injury. Where there is just weakness, there may be improvement with rehabilitation.

Damage in the cervical area of the spine involve the neck, arm muscles and the diaphragm. The thoracic area of the spine involves the chest and abdominal muscles. The lumbar area involves the hips, and knees muscles. The sacral segments involve the bowel, bladder and reproductive organs. The degree of dysfunction is related to the specific spinal cord segment and the type of damage.

WHAT TO DO WITH A PERSON WITH A SPINAL DISORDER
1. The rider's skin may be very prone to pressure problems. There may be a need for a sheepskin or other seating equipment to cover the saddle to avoid pressure areas. Watch for any reddened areas, and inform the instructor immediately.
2. Remember that this person has had structural damage to his or her body and not to the mind.
3. This person may wear braces to protect weak areas.
4. The instructor may select special riding equipment and tack for support and security.
5. The rider should wear pants without seams to prevent skin irritation from friction.
6. Be sure that the rider feels balanced after mounting before you move the horse. Provide adequate support.
7. Include this rider in your team to assist you in understanding his or her specific problems.
8. A therapist shall help to instruct in exercises to develop balance and increase strength.

11.02.16   VISUAL IMPAIRMENT

Most people with vision disorders have low to partial vision. Normal vision is considered 20/20. A person who is legally blind has 20/200 vision or worse with corrective glasses. This means that a legally blind person can see at twenty feet what a normal eye sees at 200 feet. Moderate impairment is 20/100 to 20/200. A mild visual deficit is 20/70 to 20/100. A legally blind person may see a finger in front of his face and general hand movements, and may be able to tell where light comes from or to see light but not know its source. A visual impairment that limits seeing to what is seen in front is called central vision. Central vision can be limited to tunnel vision where only a small area is seen, as though one were looking through a tube. Or, when one looks ahead and can only see to the sides, the condition is peripheral vision. Having good peripheral vision is very important in riding since this is what one uses to see the relationship of the horse to the rest of the arena. Other visual problems include the following:
1. Myopia--near sightedness. Close vision is good, but at a distance objects are blurred.
2. Hyperopia--far sightedness. Objects are clear at a distance but "fuzzy" up close.
3. Strabismus--cross-eyed or squinting. The eyes do not focus together to see an object clearly. The object may "dance", be blurred or move. It may appear as though there are two of everything (double vision). Some people will use one eye for near vision and the other eye for far vision. In such cases it takes more time to focus.

4. <u>Nystagmus</u>--rapid involuntary movements of the eyes. This problem causes difficulty in fixing the eye on an object. The head will often be held at an angle to steady vision.
5. <u>Cortical blindness</u>--there is nothing wrong with the eyes, but the visual parts of the brain do not function. There is no <u>meaning</u> to what one sees.
6. <u>Ptosis</u>--the eyelid droops. This does not affect vision.
7. <u>Amblyopia</u>--lazy eye. One eye may drift. There is difficulty focusing, in depth perception and blurred vision.
8. <u>Cataracts</u> cause blurring of all vision to varying degrees.
9. <u>Photophobia</u>--sensitivity to light, can be painful.

Visual problems can be of varying degrees and in various combinations. Many people are able to compensate well for a deficit. REMEMBER--SOMEONE IS THE RIDER'S EYES AT ALL TIMES. Riders can experience all riding environments with appropriate preparation and leadership.

WHAT TO DO WITH A PERSON WHO IS VISUALLY IMPAIRED
1. Let the rider tell you if his or her vision will cause a problem during riding or other activities.
2. Let the rider help you understand his or her problem, listen carefully. Observe what the rider can see. Some people may deny their problems.
3. Allow the rider time to interpret what he or she sees and to adjust eye focus or feel. Have the rider feel the saddle and reins. Name aloud the parts of the horse, saddle and bridle. Orient the rider well to his or her surroundings.
4. Give a mental picture if the rider cannot see an object or his or her environment.
5. Gently touch or speak to him or her. Do not surprise a blind rider with a heavy grasp or a sudden touch. Tell him or her what you plan to do.
6. Have the rider use other senses such as feel and sound. Encourage him to "feel" the horse and to count the strides to be covered. Use a beeping device to identify distances. Beepers are allowed in competition for the blind. Try using a walkie-talkie that consists of a head set worn under the helmet.
7. Describe the environment. Many completely blind persons can "feel" their environment such as an object coming toward them.
8. Use textured and high contrast colored or white reins. It is difficult to see brown reins on a brown or black horse.
9. Let the rider know that another horse is close by or that he or she is approaching the fence, gate or pole. Use high contrast colored objects to mark the arena's borders and content.
10. Help to develop good posture. Watch for balance problems. Encourage good proprioception in a totally or near blind rider by helping him or her "feel" the correct body position requested by the instructor. Give him or her feedback in what his or her body is doing.
11. Give lots of **VERY SPECIFIC INSTRUCTIONS**. Talk most of the time so that the rider has a reference point.
12. Encourage independence as confidence builds.

Surgeon General; Center for Disease Control; U.S. Department of Health & Human Services. (1991). *Understanding*   *AIDS*. Public Health Service, Center for Disease Control, P.O. BOX 6003, Rockville, MD 20850. USA.

11.03 GUIDELINES FOR WORKING WITH PERSONS HAVING PSYCHIATRIC AND EMOTIONAL DISABILITIES

Philip Tedeschi, MSSW

Increasing numbers of persons with psychological impairments are being referred to therapeutic riding programs and or equine-assisted treatment centers. This section will provide a description of the most commonly seen psychiatric and emotional disorders in clients referred to these programs. Both the risk and potential for these clients will be briefly discussed, and of necessity, much information will be of a general nature. Specific characteristics and differences among these disorders must be understood if these clients are to benefit from the horse and its environment. Instructors and staff working with these clients need to possess a clear understanding about behavioral and psychological conditions, and should seek help from qualified mental health professionals. Further, the ability of the therapeutic riding program to address such problems must be investigated and validated.

The pervasive impact of emotional disabilities can interfere with every aspect of an individual's life. Unfortunately, the emotionally disordered individual frequently is viewed as "less affected" than someone with more observable impairment. Therefore, despite the absence of physical disability, riding center staff must begin to understand how to provide therapeutic riding and animal facilitation services to address the individual needs of these clients. The primary resource to better understand diagnoses common among persons with "mental" disorders is the Diagnostic and Statistical Manual of Mental Disorders III-R (DSM-III-R), prepared periodically by the American Psychiatric Association. It is considered the primary reference for those in the mental health field since it categorizes the symptomatology and manifestations of each separate diagnosis. The material included in this chapter is drawn from DSM-III-R and is presented in a format useful to those in the therapeutic riding community. This is not meant to substitute for consultation with mental health personnel in regard to individual clients. It is recommended that instructors working with an emotionally disturbed clientele receive additional training specific to their needs and work directly with the mental health team. Therapeutic riding programs working with this population should have a mental health therapy consultant (such as an occupational therapist or social worker with a specialty in psychiatry) on their staff.

Throughout this section, several separate and very different categories of emotional impairment will be described. However, it is important to note that several concepts will apply consistently throughout. For example, any rider who is in treatment for his impairment has a therapist or treatment coordinator (**called treatment agent**). It is important for the therapeutic riding instructor and staff mental health therapy consultant to confer with the primary treatment agent. If effective therapeutic riding services are to be provided, then a clear sense of each rider's disability and potential as well as his or her current treatment plan must be gained. Treatment agents involved with the rider may include psychiatrists, psychologists, social workers, counselors, occupational therapists, special education teachers, recreational therapists, and parents. When involved with the rider in the treatment, they will be able to help instructors answer these important questions:

- What are the primary and secondary presenting problems?
- What is it hoped this client will gain from the therapeutic riding experience?
- What are the most debilitating aspects of his or her disorder?
- Are there any special treatment implications or issues that one should be aware of in providing the client therapeutic riding services?
- How will one know if the program is therapeutic for him or her?
- What concerns is this client working on?
- What kinds of medication does this client take? Are there any side effects?
- Can his therapist accompany him or her to the therapeutic riding sessions? If not, why?
- How long will this client participate?
- Does he or she have to earn the right to participate?
- Does this client exhibit any inappropriate/dangerous behavior?

- How should one respond if the client acts out?
- Can one attend Individual Education Plan (IEP) and treatment staffings?

In other words, by raising questions, the therapeutic riding instructor creates the expectation that treatment agents respond to therapeutic riding services with the same type of professionalism that would be expected in any other type of service. Information must be shared if clients are to receive maximum help. The treatment agent must also be aware of the services that the center is able to offer. Centers can be developed to provide:
- Generalized riding lessons for a mixed population
- Generalized riding lesson for persons with psychiatric disorders
- An equine-assisted treatment facility for persons with mental disorders
- An equine-assisted treatment facility for a mixed population
- A general riding program with equine-assisted therapy

Regardless of the diagnoses, it is important for a riding instructor to have an accurate history of each client, including any propensity toward becoming easily agitated or disruptive, assaultive or self-destructive. This information is essential to safeguard the horse, the volunteer, and the student. The riding instructor should have a basic understanding of the medication that clients receive and the potential side-effects. The staff needs to know if the program area accessible to the client is secure from dangerous items (i.e., no razor blades, first-aid kit, medicines, knives) for those with a tendency for self-destructive behavior. Additional volunteers may be needed when close supervision is required, but the referring agent **must provide staff who are familiar with a client who may be at risk for destructive behavior of any kind or for running away.** The therapeutic riding staff cannot be expected to conduct a session and also be responsible for high risk riders. The exception may be centers conducting equine-assisted therapy exclusively with psychiatric clients who have staff especially trained for this work.

Many clients may be referred from group homes or institutional settings where by law strict confidentiality rules prevent unnecessary and inappropriate disclosures regarding treatment issues. However, confidentiality protocols can be established within a riding center to fulfill legal requirements or the riding program can be integrated into a treatment center where the riding modality becomes a part of the client's treatment plan.

Case material must provide pertinent information regarding each individual such as:
- Type of disorder
- Behavior to be expected
- Precautions and contraindications
- Side-effects of medication
- Propensity towards becoming easily agitated
- Disruptive, assaultive or self-destructive behavior toward the horse, staff/volunteers, self
- Need for safe environment--secure from dangerous items (no razor blades, first-aid kit, medicines knives)
- Behavioral objectives
- Expectations from therapeutic riding/equine activities and/or equine-assisted therapy

MAJOR CATEGORIES OF DYSFUNCTION

Developmental Disorders:
The term *developmental disorders* refers to several different diagnostic classifications, the primary ones being mental retardation and pervasive developmental disorders. There is also a classification of specific developmental disorders which are generally considered chronic (ongoing) in nature and have pervasive effects that continue throughout the person's life span. Within these broader categories, however, there are specific labels (changed from earlier DSM labels) defining separate types of each of these disorders.

Mental Retardation might best be described as a problem of sub-average intellect accompanied by impairments in adaptive and social functioning. Most commonly, mental retardation onset is prior to the age of eighteen. The condition of Mental Retardation is broken down into five specific diagnostic categories:
- Mild Mental Retardation, previously labeled educationally mental retardation

- Moderate Mental Retardation previously considered trainable mental retardation
- Severe Mental Retardation
- Profound Mental Retardation
- Unspecified Mental Retardation

Unspecified Mental Retardation is generally used with younger infants and children or individuals who make it difficult to evaluate, and thus to diagnose the degree of retardation present. The Severe and Profound Mentally Retarded make up only a small percentage of the entire population. These individuals generally require constant supervision and frequently are found in group homes, residential or institutional settings. It is important to note that despite the unusual and sometimes abnormal behavior attributed to this diagnosis, most mentally retarded individuals referred for therapeutic riding can learn to prevent or reduce, if not eradicate, inappropriate behaviors and live a worthwhile and productive lifestyle. The primary treatment modality for individuals with mental retardation is behavior modification. The more minor forms of mental retardation can benefit from individual and group psychotherapy.

Pervasive Developmental Disorders

Pervasive developmental disorders refer to disorders in development seen in early childhood and adolescence, primarily referred to as Childhood Schizophrenia, Autism, and Child Psychosis. Of these, the most common condition seen in riding programs is Autism. This is a condition in which a wide variety of intellectual levels are found along with behavioral and motor problems. In order to establish appropriate educational and therapeutic goals, the rider's IQ must be assessed. A therapeutic riding lesson for an autistic rider usually involves breaking down learning tasks into small components, each one separately geared toward success. In addition, behavior modification appears to be the most commonly used and effective means for reducing inappropriate behaviors commonly associated with this particular condition. However, riders with autism frequently are on medication to assist their control of impulsive and inappropriate behaviors and this may ameliorate many of the most difficult patterns of conduct. (Individuals with autism who are seen by occupational therapists may sometimes be treated successfully for both behavioral and motor dysfunctions with the sensory integration approach to treatment).

Specific Developmental Disabilities

These conditions refer to disorders affecting academic skills, language and speech, and motor skills. Generally individuals with these conditions are referred to neurologists and educational specialists, occupational therapists, and speech and language pathologists. These conditions may not be diagnosed until the child has developed other behavioral problems, thus bringing him or her to the attention of school officials or parents. With these students it is important to gear the lessons towards successful outcome and utilization of the students' strengths, minimizing their weaknesses. IEP goals can be integrated into the student's riding lesson plan, thus reinforcing the process of improvement.

Disruptive Behavior Disorders

As the title suggests children with these conditions are seen as being disruptive, having very low self-esteem, and exhibiting temper tantrums. Parents sometimes report that these children have been difficult from early childhood. Under this category there are three separate disorders:

- Oppositional Defiant Disorder describes a child who generally is having difficulty following parental limits or school rules and is getting into frequent conflicts with authority figures, peers, and sometimes the Law. In general the primary form of treatment used with these children in traditional settings has been behavioral modification systems, reinforcing acceptable behaviors and reducing inappropriate behavior through either ignoring or shaping that behavior. Frequently attention-deficit and hyperactivity are associated with this disorder. It is not uncommon to find these children receiving some form of psychotropic medication. In addition, learning disabilities are pervasive as secondary diagnoses with this condition.
- Conduct Disorders. The individuals with this diagnosis demonstrate a fairly severe disturbance in behavior. In residents from group homes serving delinquent populations, this is a common diagnosis. These students have had multiple run-ins with the Law, frequently have failed other out-of-home placements, have tendencies towards aggressive or assaultive behaviors, drug use, gang behavior, suicidal behavior, as well as other delinquent activity. In addition it is not uncommon to find some form of family dysfunction or trauma associated with current or early childhood experiences. These students frequently are on medications. At times, these students are referred with a history of fire-setting, animal abuse or assaultive behavior. It is important for the riding

center staff to be aware of the risk of including these clients in their program. The instructor must set clear, firm, and realistic goals within the setting.

Even though in traditional settings these individuals may have been difficult to treat, animal facilitated therapy has proved to be effective. Recognition of the horse as a living creature that requires nurturing, responsibility, and appropriate care-taking is crucial to the student's ability to learn to care for others. The horse becomes a metaphor for how to treat all people.

Inappropriate behaviors cannot be ignored and consequences should be immediate. If the student is being inappropriate or unsafe around the horses he or she should be removed immediately. Needless to say, there must be good communication between the riding center staff and those mental health professionals who are treating these students concerning any particularly inappropriate behavior.

- <u>Attention-Deficit Hyperactive Disorders</u> (ADHD).
  This diagnosis is frequently associated with learning disabilities and has gone through a multitude of redefinitions. At different times attention-deficit or hyperactivity were considered entirely separate diagnoses. Usually onset of ADHD is during pre-pubescence or early childhood. It might be most appropriate to view this diagnosis as a multiple handicap. The primary forms of treatment are medication, behavioral modification, sensory-integrative therapy, special education services, family therapy, and individual therapy. These various interventions need to be utilized together in order to provide effective treatment. Strategic reinforcement and consequences for behavior are important for the student to learn.

  Students who are unable to sit still and adequately focus in the classroom can begin to learn in the active therapeutic riding setting. Lesson plans need to be broken down into manageable, understandable steps in order for the ADHD student to successfully complete them. For example, first direct the students to go into the barn, secondly, ask the students to find a grooming bucket, thirdly, ask the students to find the curry comb in the bucket, fourth, ask the student to work with a particular horse, and finally ask the student to pick up the curry comb and use it in a particular manner.

Therapeutic riding program staff, who will be using the behavior modification method, must have training before using it with clients. The riding instructor needs to understand the specific behavioral objectives that students are working toward within the equine setting. In order for behavior modification to be effective, timing is everything. Appropriate and inappropriate behaviors need to be addressed immediately and in the same consistent manner as used by the referring agent. Students generally have poor insight into their behaviors and frequently avoid accepting responsibility for their actions. A riding instructor can assist students in looking at their behaviors by demonstrating the way they relate to the impact on the horse and his environment.

Personality Disorders:
Personality disorders are generally considered *Axis II* (see reference) diagnoses. They include three clusters:
- Cluster A -
  paranoid personality disorders
  schizoid personality disorder
  schizotypal personality disorders
- Cluster B -
  anti-social personality disorders
  borderline personality disorders
  hystrionic personality disorders
  narcissistic personality disorders
- Cluster C -
  avoidant personality disorder
  dependent personality disorders
  obsessive/compulsive personality disorders
  passive/aggressive personality disorders

It is well beyond the scope of this section to discuss any of these conditions in detail. However, it is not uncommon for persons with these diagnoses to be referred to therapeutic riding programs which accept emotionally and psychiatrically impaired riders. The functioning of these people can vary greatly, and may fluctuate, but the conditions are usually chronic. In addition, mood disorders can accompany the primary condition. The chief forms of treatment with persons with personality disorders include pharmacological therapy, cognitive restructuring therapies, and behavioral modification. The therapeutic riding program staff can assist in a variety of ways, working jointly with the treatment team. Again, appropriate supervision must accompany these riders and high risk clientele must be identified before being received in the riding center's program. The treatment agent should assist the instructor in setting out behavioral objectives and maintaining communication between all team members so that the approach used with each individual is always consistent.

Psychoactive Substance-Abuse Disorders:

This classification describes persons who engage in pathological use of psychoactive substances. These could include alcohol, opium, amphetamines, heroine, cocaine, inhalants, depressants, hallucinogens, and nicotine. Although new in its application, equine-assisted therapy can serve as an additional treatment service for individuals in substance-abuse treatment programs. Those with addictive behaviors such as drug use need to break a chain of events and be helped to develop other healthy lifestyle activities. Therapeutic riding can provide replacement behaviors and exciting activity for the chemically dependent client. The riding instructor needs to work closely with treatment staff because treatment of a chemically dependent client can often be very difficult, complicated, and dangerous. The staff of the equine-assisted therapy team needs to secure all items such as alcohol, rubbing alcohol, paint thinner, paints, medication for the horses, drugs of any variety, and nicotine in order to assist this rider in not relapsing by having access to these items. In addition, the riding center staff must be aware that the withdrawal process can result in extremely inappropriate behaviors. Some programs without expertise in this field should decline services to chemically dependent persons until they have received "detox" treatment. Following this stage therapeutic riding can be an excellent tool for recovery and maintenance of abstinence.

Eating Disorders:

The two primary eating disorders seen among persons most commonly referred to therapeutic riding programs are anorexia nervosa and bulimia nervosa.

- Anorexia Nervosa is a very serious and complicated psychiatric disorder. The anorexic might be defined as an individual who starves him or herself to the point of poor health or even death. The person with anorexia, through a process of severe cognitive distortions, denies the existence of a problem. Significant problems in working with the anorexic client are body strength and body image.
- Bulimia Nervosa, another diagnosis considered an eating disorder, is difficult to treat and frequently will require in-patient hospitalization in order to control the overeating and purging characteristic of this condition.

Persons with eating disorders must be under the care of experienced mental health professionals and should not be "treated" by a therapeutic riding team without professional guidance. Suicide is the most common form of death for persons with these conditions, reflecting the emotional devastation of the disorders. While working with the anorexic client, the riding instructor should not conspire with the client in denying the severity of the symptoms or the nature of the problem. The cognitive distortions associated with the image, weight and distorted view of him or herself which is carried by the client will be reinforced if volunteers or instructors minimize the seriousness of his or her problem. Discussions related to this problem should be left to the treatment team unless otherwise instructed.

Therapeutic riding can be of significant assistance in the long term treatment and recovery of Anorexia Nervosa and Bulimia Nervosa because it effectively challenges these riders' experience of being out of control of their lives. The riding instructor must understand the behavioral objectives in order to participate actively with the treatment team. A client's therapist should initially attend the riding session in order to frame the effective metaphor* to confront the pervasive, devastating distorted thinking of these disorders.

Schizophrenia:

It is beyond the scope of this section to fully describe the types of manifestations and effective treatment modalities used in the treatment of schizophrenia. The four different types are categorized as: disorganized, catatonic, paranoid,

239

and undifferentiated schizophrenia. For each the treatment varies somewhat. If working with a rider with schizophrenia or a history of the disease, staff should confer especially closely with the referring party or therapist in order to understand the specific behavioral treatment objectives and interventions. The kind of expectations the therapist has from the riding program and its activities need to be well known in advance. Since schizophrenia can be episodic, even though a chronic condition, it is possible to see fluctuating behavior week by week, as well as extreme and bizarre conduct. However, clients with schizophrenia usually are receiving some form of medication which effectively controls or ameliorates their problems. On the other hand, medications can severely affect their functioning ability and cause ticks, sluggishness, inability to focus, lack of concentration, involuntary body movement and loss of balance.

Nevertheless, it is important for the riding program instructor, staff and volunteers to treat these clients as much like their normal clientele as possible. Their style of instruction should provide a sense of security and consistency from week to week, as well as provide predictability and caring attitude for their clients. Firm behavioral guidelines and lesson requirements should be carried out so that the clients understand what is expected and the limits are set for them.

For example, provide the same rider with the same horse each week and always start the lesson with familiar material. Allow time before the lesson for the client to orient to the stable environment. This will allow him or her to attach to the activity of coming to the lesson every week, and to perceive the instructor as not threatening or endangering him or her on any way. Further, be sure to give deserved praise.

Inappropriate behavior should be responded to and not avoided. Such behaviors are actually being taught and reinforced by ignoring them. However, unless working directly on the advice of the therapist, it would be unwise to force a schizophrenic client into activity to which he or she is resistant. If a client becomes agitated it may be appropriate to separate him or her from the other riders and guide him or her to a quiet area for a "time out". Lastly, many schizophrenic clients are housed in residential and institutional settings and have developed "institutionalized behavior". It is important for volunteers and instructors to be familiar with institutionalized behaviors such as repetitive self stimulation or mutilation.

Mood Disorders:
Mood disorders include the following general types, all now considered bi-polar to characterize the mood swings commonly seen:
- with <u>manic</u> features
- with <u>mild</u> features
- with <u>depressed</u> features.

Depression can be categorized as either single episode major depression or recurrent major depression. Some individuals suffer from a manic phase, some with both manic and depressed, and some with simply a depressed phase. The acute features of any of these diagnoses should be treated as very serious emergencies and clients would not likely be seen at the riding center at that time. Yet, for persons in the sub-acute or chronic stages of illness, the therapeutic riding center can become an integral part of assisting them to overcome the debilitating effects of this disorder. Many are on medication which provides sustained relief from symptoms and the affected person can function in a relatively normal way. Like eating disorders, mood disorders continue to perpetuate themselves through cognitive distortions of the world and of the images of themselves which these individuals carry around. It is not uncommon for these individuals to feel helpless or out-of-control.

Cyclothymia is a form of depression considered to be less serious or to have milder manifestations than a major depression; however it refers to an episode or recurring episodes of depression. Many individuals with minor forms of depression such as Cyclothymia are never formally diagnosed as such. Riders with physical disabilities and other limitations, serious life stressors, or emotional or psychiatric illness frequently have cyclothymic disorder in addition to their primary diagnosis. These individuals can have their behavior attributed to being lazy, not being interested

*image, figure of speech where one thing is compared to another in such a way that its likeness throws new light on the subject.

in anything, and unwilling to participate. Individuals with cyclothymic disorder may have some warning that they will be regressing into their depressive mood and may be able to set up therapeutic riding sessions on an as-needed basis to confront and prevent the mood swing, therefore allowing the client to remain in a stabilized fashion.

Dysthymia, another depressive disorder, is similar to cyclothymia and as far as the therapeutic riding staff are concerned, the clients will be treated with the same procedures. Initially, the staff of therapeutic riding centers can become an integral part of assisting these individuals to overcome the debilitating effects of their disorders, working closely with the clients' treatment or treatment agent to offer strategic interventions. When disorders are well into remission these clients can safely participate in a regular therapeutic riding program as a volunteer and benefit from the social approbation associated with volunteering. Research in the area of mood disorders shows that exercise, in particular, can address some of the primary depressive features of bi-polar disorders. Metaphoric therapeutic riding challenges the helplessness, distorted thoughts, and out-of-control feelings that these individuals experience.

This condition primarily refers to major depression with a single episode, with recurring or chronic features, and is a very serious and debilitating diagnosis with self-damaging characteristics and persons affected need to be closely supervised. Persons who are severely depressed will have difficulty finding the motivation to participate or volunteer for any activities. If such a student is asked if he would like to take part in an activity, even if the rider has some interest in it, depressive features frequently will prevail and prevent him from participating. The riding instructor needs to approach these persons with a firm and yet sensitive manner. Thus rather than asking if they should like to participate, they would be given a structured directive to do a specific activity. Volunteers should be made aware by the treatment agent of the client's manipulation methods used to avoid activity and participation. In this way therapeutic riding can be important in assisting, and especially maintaining a client's recovery from depression.

Anxiety Disorders

This label generally refers to a wide range of phobias and panic disorders as well as to post-traumatic stress disorder which can usually be categorized as acute or delayed. There are many different panic disorders and phobias. Anxiety disorders are not uncommon in persons with emotional or psychiatric conditions. In these cases the riding instructor should try to gain understanding of the specific criteria and manifestations of the illness. Some examples of these disorders are obsessive (persistent idea or emotion) compulsive (rituals) behavior, agoraphobia (morbid fear of space), and panic attacks. As with many other psychiatric disorders involving control of impulsive behavior, medication can be used effectively for control. When working with such persons, contact **must** be maintained with the treatment agent in order to understand the overall objectives and strategies of treatment; the instructor and staff <u>may be asked by the treatment agent</u> to reinforce specific expressions of feeling and emotion during the sessions.

Post Traumatic Stress Disorders

This disorder is the result of trauma caused by physical injury, emotional stress or sexual abuse. It can be seen as either the acute or the delayed phase of a traumatic occurrence. Delayed onset usually occurs six months or more following the precipitating event. In some populations, it is not uncommon for a secondary diagnosis, such as substance abuse disorders, depression, or generalized anxiety to accompany the stress condition. These individuals may also have flashbacks (intrusive memories related to all of their senses).

A program which provides equine-assisted therapy, offers the treatment agent/team a setting to deal with a variety of problems. Some of the major goals the <u>treatment team</u> can accomplish for their clients include improving self-image, confronting the impression of being out of control or powerless, helping to re-experience or integrate the trauma into the actual experience, and learning to monitor and manage the intense sensory input of the equine setting. Within the therapeutic riding activities, it is possible to recreate a variety of situations and degrees of stress, to assist the treatment team in reaching the deeply buried emotions of the client. In addition, the pervasive need of these individuals to feel in control, and again be responsible for the events that happened to them in their life can be satisfied.

In working with sexually abused clients it is important to recognize that the process of spreading the rider's legs and sitting on a warm and moving animal can be a trigger for post traumatic stress symptomology related to their own victimization. With riders who have a history of being sexually abused or have dissociated that experience to the point where nobody is aware that they were sexually abused, one must be sensitive to the possibility of triggering a flash-back during the riding lesson. Any event that appears to be a trigger when a rider becomes emotional, frozen, begins to dissociate while in the riding lesson, or starts crying should be addressed by the treatment agent. Through the intentional use of metaphor, post traumatic stress symptomology can be strategically addressed.

Conclusion

This concludes the discussion of emotional and psychiatric disorders to be presented. Those chosen for inclusion are considered to be the most commonly referred diagnoses to therapeutic riding centers. This section's purpose has been to encourage the therapeutic riding community to become more familiar with both the disabling features and the interventions useful in working with persons with emotional and psychiatric disorders. In addition, it is hoped that this section will encourage the therapeutic riding instructor and program staff to more closely align themselves with the mental health treatment teams. If clients with serious psychiatric or emotional disturbances come to your program without a referring agent or from agents who resist sharing diagnostic and treatment information, the staff of the therapeutic riding center must determine whether it is appropriate and safe to all concerned to work with such persons, despite what they feel could be the benefit of therapeutic riding.

One would never accept the responsibility of a bus load of physically involved disabled riders without medical information and contra-indications. The same standard of services should be applied to emotionally and psychiatrically impaired riders.

Diagnostic and Statistical Manual of Mental Disorders III-R (DSM-III-R) is the primary reference for the mental health field prepared by the American Psychiatric Association.

Axis I -   Includes all mental disorders with the exception of Axis II disorders which are considered to be developmental and personality disorders.

Axis II- Refers to developmental disorders and personality disorders generally beginning in childhood or adolescence and continuing into adult life. As an example mental retardation and autism are considered pervasive developmental disorders listed as an Axis II diagnosis.

Axis III- Though not addressed in the DSM-III-R, this category is used to indicate any physical disability relevant to the   understanding of the individual.

Axis IV - Provides a scale to determine the intensity and severity of psychological or social stressors that have occurred over the past year. This allows better understanding of the individual's presenting problems.

Axis V - Is a scale assessment of the overall psychological, social and occupational functioning of the individual. This is usually listed as the global assessment of functioning scale which indicates the highest and lowest level of functioning that can be anticipated from that student.

Reference
DSM III-R
Spitzer, L. R., Et al. (1987). Diagnostic and Statistical Manual of Mental Disorders. (3rd ed, revised).
    Washington, D.C.: American Psychiatric Association.
Spitzer, L. R., Et al. (1989). DSM III-R Casebook: A Learning Companion to the Diagnostic and Statistical Manual Of Mental Disorders (Third ed revised). Washington, D.C.: American Psychiatric Association.

12 IMPROVING THE RIDER'S POSTURE

12.01 INTRODUCTION TO IMPROVING THE RIDER'S POSTURE AND BALANCE

KEY WORDS
BALANCE
CENTERING
GOOD SEAT
STABILITY IN LINE WITH GRAVITY

The basis for becoming a good rider in any equine sport is dependent on the development of a "good" seat. A good seat is one that is "secure" in that the rider can remain in the saddle, move with the horse and perform the skills required in the area of interest such as games, equitation, dressage, pole bending, reining, jumping, eventing, gymkhanas, or rodeo. A good seat requires centering (of ones self and ones self with the horse in line with gravity) and balance; balance not only with oneself but also with the horse and his movements. Balance is defined by Webster (1966) as a state of equilibrium; equality of the two sides or forces of each side toward the center; or mental and emotional equilibrium. In order for a person to be able to balance, he or she must not only have developed the physical reactions and strength to balance, put must have the correct mental (most often unconscious) image of centering oneself. Sally Swift (Swift, 1985) discusses this topic in detail.

Balance in riding is usually developed first at a walk, then jog or trot and finally at a lope or canter. Stability and balance are not only needed for riding but are required in all daily living activities. Without stability and balance, one can not sit and use the hands actively, or walk and perform a task at the same time. This chapter will discuss methods and techniques which can be used to increase a client's balance and stability.

Please note that many of the techniques discussed require special training and many need to be <u>carried out</u> or <u>supervised</u> by an experienced therapist. Performing techniques that one is not adequately trained for can lead to undesirable results which cannot always be visually detected, at least for some years. These techniques may appear very simple but can take a great deal of skill.

The instructor must become familiar with these techniques so that he or she can assist the therapist in developing a client's posture in the best possible way, and will be able to carry through during riding sessions independently or working in conjunction with a therapist.

A rider with poor trunk and/or head control will not be served to his or her best interest by purely being backridden by an instructor or other staff, especially if the instructor has not been trained by a therapist. Posture needs to be developed systematically by a therapist who has been trained to work with persons with neurological/neuromuscular disorders. Trunk and head control may improve over a period of time by riding without trained assistance **but** not as rapidly as with a trained therapist. Secondly, without the knowledge of appropriate facilitation techniques, or contra-indications, the rider **may suffer** negative affects or may not progress adequately or at all. Some clients with poor balance and poor strength may need one-on-one therapy with a therapist, **to be safe on a horse.** Instructors, staff, or volunteers who take on the responsibility of working with persons who have neurological dysfunctions because of developmental disabilities, injury or disease, must take on the responsibility and judgement of providing these individuals with the most appropriate assistance and conditions especially if they are **claiming** to be performing **"therapeutic"** riding activities.

<u>All</u> disciplines in the field of therapeutic riding can work together in order to help each client to progress and discover the joys of riding a horse.

Swift, S. (1985). *Centered Riding.* New York: St Martin's Marek.
Webster. (1966). *Webster New World Dictionary.* Cleveland: The World Publishing Co.

12.02 STABILIZING THE RIDER - HANDLING TECHNIQUES TO IMPROVE THE BASE OF SUPPORT IN SITTING

Jill Strandquist, OTR/L

This article will address methods and assistive handling techniques to be used with the neurologically atypical rider to promote dynamic sitting balance and improve upper body control for more efficient visual-motor (eye-hand) coordination. By activating balance reactions in the pelvis and trunk during assisted riding, dynamic sitting balance is promoted and the upper body, head and arms are freed for more efficient visual motor activity.

Sitting Balance: Stability vs Rigidity

It is well known that sitting balance is achieved through progressive development of the musculature surrounding the lower trunk and pelvis. In a typical child, gross movements needed for one to stay upright (righting reactions) are replaced eventually with minute muscular adjustments (equilibrium reactions) giving the <u>appearance</u> of a rigid, static position. Such a position, while stable, is <u>not</u> rigid, and the normal child learns to constantly monitor and adapt to kinesthetic, vestibular and proprioceptive stimuli with balance reactions.

Dysfunctional Sitting Balance: The Prospective Rider

Normal children, if challenged, will generally be able to sustain or regain their balance without falling. Atypical children lack the ability to adequately control muscle tone for smooth, dynamic balance in sitting/standing/walking. These prospective riders have achieved sitting through rigidly "bracing" their muscles or by relying on external support. They cannot sustain or regain dynamic balance in unsupported sitting.

The prospective rider with inadequate postural control generally also displays impaired visual regard and tracking, impaired visual-motor coordination and poor attention and/or endurance. Common diagnoses of such children include cerebral palsy, head injury, encephalitis, learning disability, developmental delay, Down syndrome, neurological impairment.

The Seated Posture, Corrected Base of Support:

Correct sitting alignment and muscular balance can rarely be achieved or sustained in most chairs/wheelchairs due to their inherent design. In the typical chair the seat is flat or curved up on the sides and tilted toward a concave backrest. Thus a slouched, flexed posture (Figure 1) with the pelvis tipped backwards and the trunk rounded forward is nearly unavoidable. With the center of gravity behind the person's base of support and his or her hips/upper thighs close together with no stabilization (a typical sitter will frequently cross his or her legs in an effort to rigidly stabilize the pelvis), the sitter has little opportunity for dynamic sitting balance. Attempts to perform functional eye-hand activities cause further stress and fatigue.

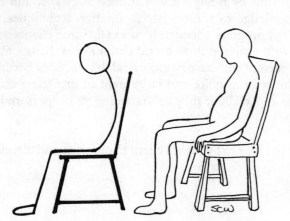

FIGURE 1. A PERSON SITTING IN A SLOUCHED POSITION

FIGURE 2. SITTING ASTRIDE A HORSE

A review of literature (Heipertz, 1977; Reide, 1986) has indicated that the position of a rider astride a horse best promotes correct postural alignment and more evenly activates and strengthens trunk musculature for dynamic balance in sitting (Figure 2). Some innovative chair designs have attempted to improve sitting posture (Scandinavian kneeling or posture chairs and bolster chairs) but cannot provide the 3-D movement of the horse' walk which continuously encourages dynamic sitting balance. The shape of the horse's back and rib cage provides a wide, naturally contoured base of support for the pelvic "seat bones" (ischial tuberosities) and improved stability for the very mobile ball-and-socket joint of the hip and upper thigh. With continuously corrected sitting posture through supportive handling, while astride, muscle tension becomes balanced, endurance and strength for independent sitting is improved and stress is reduced to the shoulders, neck and arms for improved visual-motor activities.

For Those Without Stable, Sitting Balance: Handling and Stabilizing Strategies.

Following medical/therapy evaluations to determine whether therapeutic riding is appropriate, a trained occupational and/or physical therapist should determine initial postural goals for the prospective rider. (Riders requiring backriding support will generally lack trunk and head control or be too difficult to support from the side. The backridden rider is always handled by a trained therapist.)

Handling/supporting techniques following *neurodevelopmental treatment* (NDT) principles, for example, enable the rider to modify muscle tone and posture and respond to a weight shift or movement with a righting or balance reaction. This author feels that NDT training should be strongly recommended for all therapists involved in riding programs. Therapists should then train their instructors/volunteers in these techniques.

The principles of sensory integration affect a rider's response and progress. Occupational therapists are trained in the processing of sensory information by the brain and its effect on behavioral and motor responses. A basic premise of occupational therapy is that active participation in a functional (meaningful) activity always yields the best progress. Riding on horseback is a functional activity which is usually inherently motivating to the prospective client. During riding, strong vestibular and proprioceptive stimuli are produced by the horse. Active participation of the rider means he or she is actively responding to the vestibular and proprioceptive stimulation with an adapted motor response. It is the job of the therapist/instructor/volunteer to assist the rider as he or she responds to these stimuli with improving adapted responses, through handling and activities, in combination with the horse's movement. Repetitive, non-purposeful or stereotypical motor responses are not active participation as they are not modified (adapted) in response to the stimuli.

Facilitating Change: Helping The Rider To Feel A Stable Base Of Support

The initial goal is to achieve a stable, secure base of support from which the rider can learn to better control his or her trunk and upper body. The base of support for the rider is formed by the shape of the horse's back, the pad, or the saddle chosen for the rider to sit on **and the hands-on support provided by the sidewalkers**. Selection of the horse is critical for the entry level rider. A horse which is too narrow or who has an erratic, weaving walk will not provide a stable base of support. A medium sized horse (14.2 to 15.2 hands) with solid bone structure, good conformation, well muscled, and with a straight, smooth movement and a freely swinging back has proven very successful for the average child or smaller adult. It is easier for sidewalkers to reach the rider if the horse is not too tall but the size of the rider must be considered, and occasionally a taller horse is needed to balance a tall or heavier rider. Usually a natural fleece pad is the first choice for the rider to sit on. The fleece allows direct contact with the horse's back for transmission of stimuli and allows unrestricted positioning of the rider's body. A surcingle/vaulting surcingle secures the fleece and provides rigid hand holds for the very unstable rider. If a saddle is used, it should fit the horse and rider and not interfere with efforts to modify the rider's posture and balance.

Supportive Positioning and Handling To Establish Initial Base of Support:

Position and center the rider on the horse as well as possible after he has mounted and before moving the horse away from the mounting device. The rider should be checked from the side as well as from behind. Have someone check during the riding session to maintain the centered position. Stabilize the rider at key points (Figure 3) before moving off. Once walking, adjust supportive handling until the rider accepts and responds to the motion. It is important not to encourage the rider to brace or hold tightly to the hand holds (handles) of the surcingle as this will block

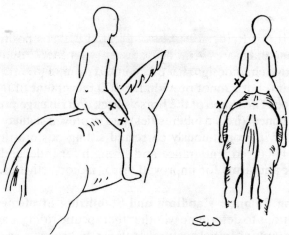

FIGURE 3.   STABILIZING THE RIDER AT KEY POINTS

his or her body from responding to the movement stimulation. Encourage the rider to hold lightly and release hands from the hand holds and move them to his or her thighs, as soon as he or she is comfortable. Sidewalkers should provide enough support to secure the rider, and to allow him or her to feel comfortable without the need to hold on tightly or brace his or her body.

The most secure contact given by the sidewalker is made by walking very close to the horse, next to the rider's side and maintaining contact with the rider's leg with both hands. An insecure rider with poor sitting balance will generally respond to secure and appropriate handling by becoming more relaxed.

Facilitating Changes in Muscle Tone and Pelvic/Trunk Alignment

Frequently the movement of the horse alone will accomplish much of the muscle tone adjustment **if** correct supportive handling is provided. Each session should begin with several minutes of supportive riding without requiring challenging efforts, to allow the rider's body time to organize and respond to the stimuli. As the rider begins to accommodate to the movement of the horse during these initial minutes (changes in muscle tone can be observed or felt by a trained person), handling techniques should continue to offer dynamic support (not static holding) while gradually shaping the pelvis and trunk into correct alignment (Figure 1 & Figure 2). Key points of control help to support the rider and diminish the need for rigid bracing. Be careful not to grab or pinch soft tissue with the fingers but rather to use a widely spread hand to deliver support evenly through palm and fingers while grasping the bony "handles" of the pelvis, shoulders, knees, feet, elbows and hands when moving the rider into position.

Facilitating Change: Helping The Rider To Mobilize The Pelvis

The horse must be able to walk with a smooth, free-flowing, rhythmical gait to stimulate the rider's pelvic movement and help him or her to accept the motion without bracing or resistance. The leader must make every effort to lead or drive the horse in a straight path with a consistent pace which stimulates pelvic movement but does not overly challenge the rider and cause increased bracing or tense holding. **It is extremely important when providing supportive handling that the sidewalker follow the movement of the horse with his or her body and hands to allow the rider's body to move in response to the horse's movements.**

Dynamic balance requires a state of constant muscular activity, and supportive handling must be adjusted continually. However, handling which is too rigid will block the rider from responding to the movement and will not encourage the rider to make balancing efforts. Handling which is erratic or not secure enough will not produce the desired changes in the rider's posture or muscle tone.

Facilitating Change in the Stiff Rider:

Poor sitting posture is frequently accompanied by strong muscle tension (particularly in extremities), making it quite difficult to mold a rider into the correct posture. While the most noted postural defect may be the position and/or abnormal muscle tension of the head and neck, arms and hands or legs, poor control of the pelvic and trunk musculature is generally the cause (Figure 4). If after a reasonable time of 5 to 10 minutes, with appropriate supportive handling in upright sitting position, the rider has not "softened" or has become more rigid it will be necessary to modify the movement of the horse, the position of the rider and/or handling techniques. If the rider needs to use his or her arms to stay upright he should do so by leaning on them with hands open rather than hanging onto the handhold or sidewalkers (Figure 5). Weight bearing on hands (or forearms) increases proprioceptive input into the upper trunk, shoulder girdle and neck, and assists to modify tone. Supportive handling may be necessary to stabilize the shoulder and arm during weight bearing.

FIGURE 4. POOR SITTING POSTURE WITH STRONG MUSCLE TONE **FIGURE 5. WEIGHT BEARING ON HANDS AND ARMS**

It is frequently effective to facilitate increased muscle tone even in a child with extremities too stiff because the muscle tone in the trunk is generally inadequate. Once the trunk has become more active, it is generally easier to maintain corrected posture. The improved trunk control will soon allow the tension in the extremities to relax and they can be molded into corrected positions.

Facilitating Change In The Floppy Rider
Some riders will have too much movement and be difficult to hold in position. Their muscle tone seems too weak and they frequently hold onto or collapse onto available support (Figure 6). It is often easier to mold this rider into position but more difficult to keep him there without strong support. It is particularly important to provide graded supportive handling for this rider (gradually increasing or decreasing in response to rider's control) to develop strength and endurance and reduce reliance on external support. Increasing the sensory input of proprioceptive and vestibular stimuli through strong movement of the horse (active walking, trotting, stop and start) and weight bearing (rider leaning on open hands and extended arms rather than holding on to hand hold) is quite effective in increasing muscle tone.

Facilitating Changes In Alignment And Stability of Shoulder Girdle, Neck and Head.
Once the pelvis and lower trunk have been stabilized and are moving with, rather than braced against the horse's walk, it will be easier to help the rider to unblock his shoulders, neck and extremities. He may show rigidly braced postures such as elevated shoulders, head locked in a chin down position, arms tightly flexed against the body or the upper trunk and head. Weight bearing on extended arms and open hands will help to increase stability in upper trunk, shoulders, and neck. Supportive handling is needed to achieve and maintain corrected alignment. In the forward sitting position, supporting on hands too far to the front will encourage over extension of trunk and neck (Figure 7). Placement of the hands on the thighs encourages more correct alignment. By supporting the rider's arms in extension, (Figure 5) weight bearing is felt in the palm and transmitted to the shoulders, improving muscle tone and head righting. Even a rider with very poor trunk control can be stabilized in this manner and be helped to develop shoulder stability and head control.

FIGURE 6. RIDER COLLAPSES ONTO SUPPORT   **FIGURE 7. HANDS SUPPORTED TOO FAR FORWARD**

Sitting backwards provides a wider base of support for the unstable rider and forearm weight-bearing is a good starting position for those with very poor trunk and shoulder girdle strength (Figure 8). Placement of hands behind the back will encourage trunk extension, chest expansion, neck flexion and opening of the shoulder/arm joints in preparation for reaching (Figure 8). Supporting the rider's upper body is facilitated by stabilizing at the shoulders and elbows, externally rotating the arms to a "thumbs out" position and creating a direct line of weight bearing input from the open hand to the shoulder.

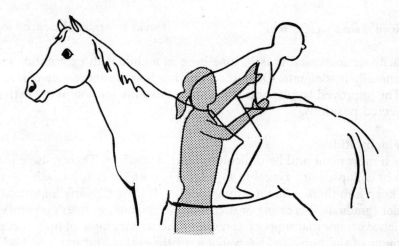

FIGURE 8. SITTING BACKWARD WITH FOREARM WEIGHT BEARING

As the rider's control increases, supportive handling is withdrawn and returned smoothly, as needed, to guide the rider back into correct alignment. Increasing challenges of quick stops and starts, trotting, changes of direction or lateral work can be introduced to improve balance reactions. Riding time can be increased to promote endurance but not so long that the rider fatigues and again requires maximum support or frequent postural corrections.

With each new challenge it may be necessary to return to more supportive handling temporarily until the rider achieves a greater level of control. When the rider is able to maintain a correct sitting posture (Figure 2) with his or her hands resting lightly on his or her thighs and only intermittent or minimal supportive handling or correction, visually-directed reaching should be introduced.

Facilitating Visually-Directed Reaching/Functional Eye-Hand Activity

Dynamic sitting balance is necessary for efficient visual-motor activities. The arms must be freed from supporting the body, and the head must be able to move independently of the upper trunk for tracking of a moving object, visually-directed reaching, and two-handed manipulations. When the rider is able to maintain a corrected upright posture with only light support on his or her hands and minimal support/facilitation/correction from sidewalkers, it is time to begin freeing the hands from supporting and begin visually directed reaching (Figure 2).

It will usually be necessary to increase supportive handling temporarily when introducing reaching in order to promote correct patterns and maintain good alignment of head and trunk. Initially the rider should be directed/assisted to "unweight" one arm at a time by shifting weight to one arm/hand in preparation for lifting the other arm. With prompting as needed to make and maintain visual contact, the rider should be assisted to reach up, forward, and away from the body toward the target. Generally, forward reaching is easiest while reaching out to the side; crossing the body and overhead are more difficult. Reaching behind may be difficult for those with restricted range of motion but is very effective in encouraging rotation of the head and trunk.

When facilitating reaching, support is given to stabilize the shoulder and extend the arm by pushing from behind the elbow, to guide the arm toward the goal, rather than pulling from the hand or forearm. For a rider who is beginning steering control of the horse as a visually-directed reaching activity, it is extremely important that the arms not be held tightly flexed against the body or turned palm down and brought up against the body. Rather the rider should be assisted (as described above) to move the extended arm away from the body in a thumb-up position (direct reining) for turning and to move the arms backward and down along the sides for halting. Reins should be short enough that it is not necessary to over-flex the arms during steering or halting.

Limited ability to stabilize the lower body while turning the upper body and/or head inhibits (discourages) crossing the midline of the body and two-handed visual-motor activities. Stabilization of the pelvis may be needed to assist with body on body rotation (when part of the body turns but the other remains as is). For example, resist the pelvis from following the trunk's movement, and assist the upper trunk to rotate independently. Assist the upper trunk rotation by guiding the shoulders and upper arms across the body while maintaining an upright and stable base of support.

If head alignment and visual regard/tracking are poor during reaching, present objects for grasping at midline and at eye level. When alignment and visual regard are good in midline, move the object to the side gradually, assisting with trunk rotation as needed. Objects grasped in midline can then be released to the side. Be sure to achieve controlled release first with visual regard rather than just dropping or throwing. If necessary, leaning the hand on a support will provide better control for accurate placement. Objects can then be grasped at the side and released in midline. Once reaching to both sides is accomplished with good head alignment and visual regard, reaching across midline can be initiated.

Children with poor postural control will avoid crossing midline and body rotation by transferring objects from hand to hand. Objects which must be held with both hands can be presented in midline and released to the side with gradually increasing rotation as postural control improves. Choosing objects which encourage two handed grasping at shoulder-width apart, as well as presenting them at or near shoulder height and encouraging release at or near shoulder height, will improve postural strength and control.

References

Ayres, A.J. (1972). *Sensory Integration and Learning Disorders*. Los Angeles: Western Psychological.

Boehme, R. (1988). *Improving Upper Body Control*. Tucson: Therapy Skill Builders.

Bobath, B. (1985). *Abnormal Postural Reflex Activity Caused by Brain Lesions*. Rockville: Aspen Systems Corp.

Bly, L. (1983). *The Components of Normal Movement During the First Year of Life and Abnormal Motor Development*. Chicago: NDT Assoc. Inc.

Chakerian, D. (1991).*The Effect of Upper Extremity Weight Bearing on Hand Function in Children with Cerebral Palsy*. NDTA Newsletter 9/7

Dowler, L. (1991). Seated Work Positions. *Occupational Therapy Forum*, August.

Heipertz, W. (1977). *Therapeutic Riding*. Greenbelt Riding Association for the Disabled (Ottawa) Inc. Canadian Equestrian Federation, 333 River Rd., Ottawa, ONT K1L 8B9,

Riede, D. (1986). *Physiotherapy on the Horse*. Delta Society, 321 Burnett Ave. So., Renton WA

Scherzer, A.L.; Tscharnuter, I. (1982). *Early Diagnosis and Therapy in Cerebral Palsy*. New York: Marcel Dekker, Inc.

Swift, S. (1985). *Centered Riding*. New York: St Martin's Marek.

12.03 PERSPECTIVE ON BACKRIDING

Terri Barnes, PT

Cliff Barnes, Art Work and Photography

Backriding is a technique used in many therapeutic riding programs. During backriding, two people are on the horse. The child sits in front of the therapist or riding instructor. The purpose is to provide physical and/or psychological support to the challenged rider. The goal is always that the individual will be able to ride independently as soon as possible. When employed selectively on a limited number of clients, this technique can be valuable.

While being backridden, the rider feels increased security with a trained individual riding behind him or her. For the therapist who wants to give symmetrical input, it is easier to be positioned directly behind the rider rather than trying to reach up to him or her from one side of the horse. Any facilitatory or inhibitory input can easily be performed during backriding. This technique can also decrease effort that would be excessive for some clients.

INDICATIONS/CONTRA-INDICATIONS

It is critical to select an appropriate candidate for backriding. A child who is fearful or posturally insecure may respond well to being backridden in the first couple of riding sessions until some degree of confidence is obtained. If the child does not have the physical requirements to maintain dynamic sitting, backriding might be an option for him or her. For example, if the individual does not have head control, trunk control, or righting and equilibrium reactions, sidewalkers could not easily keep the child safely on the horse. Backriding could then be employed. It can also be used to assist the child to achieve a more symmetrical position, relax and go with the movement of the horse, or decrease the child's fatigue. If the child has severe muscle tone abnormalities, or abnormal movement patterns, backriding may be the best technique. Sometimes, a therapist may choose to backride for part of a session so the client can progress more quickly or achieve the desired response.

Adults are not appropriate for backriding. Because of their size, they pose a risk to the backrider, the horse, and are at risk of injury to themselves. It is essential for the backrider to be able to handle the client with ease should the horse move suddenly. This is impossible if the client's center of gravity is above the backrider's (he or she is taller) or if he or she is close to the same weight as the backrider. Some programs limit the rider's weight to 100 pounds. Tragic accidents have occurred when large clients were backridden.

The child should only be backridden as a transitional phase until he or she is able to ride independently. Individuals who will most likely never have the ability to ride without employing a backrider are not appropriate. Not every challenged person is a candidate for therapeutic riding and backriding is not a tool that should be used on a long-term basis.

BACKRIDER PREREQUISITES:

For backriding to be a successful and safe technique, the backrider needs to be specifically trained. It is appropriate in therapeutic riding programs for the riding instructor to backride a child who may be frightened. However, if the child needs to be backridden because of physical limitations, it should only be done under the direction of the therapist. All backriders must have riding experience. Because it requires excellent balance, backriders should be able to maintain their balance on the lunge line at the walk, trot and canter with their hands resting on their thighs. They should also be competent at tacking up the horse so they can be aware of the equipment, familiar with horse body language and feel comfortable working around horses. The backrider must be able to move correctly with the horse or he or she it will interfere with the benefit the rider receives. The backrider needs to be slight of build. The size and conformation of the horse being used will determine the maximum weight limit. Several programs limit the backrider to 150 pounds and some to even 130 pounds. If the therapist is large or does not have the required riding experience, it is appropriate for the riding instructor to backride the physically challenged child with the therapist giving on-site instruction to the backrider. Backriding for the physically challenged is supervised by a therapist so that abnormal tone or patterns will be diminished rather than reinforced.

HORSE SELECTION AND TRAINING:

Careful selection of the horse used for backriding can prevent injury. As well as having a suitable temperament, the horse should be well nourished and on the upper end of ideal weight range. A short back with the withers sloping evenly into the back and a short loin area are essential. Excessively high withers, a sway back, and horses that are "low in the back" are not suitable. Horses that are heavily muscled in the loin area are ideal. A weak loin appears as a hollow area in front of the point of the hip over the flank area (Figure 1). Looking down on the horse's back while standing on the ramp or mounting block can also help identify weakness. Instead of looking round and full in the loin area, the spine will be prominent and the muscling slopes downward from the spine indicating a lack of strength. Horses legs should have large, flat (rectangular) bones, not round, to be able to bear more weight. Any significant conformation fault predisposes the horse to lameness.

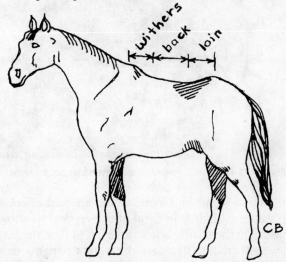

FIGURE 1. THIS HORSE IS "LOW IN THE BACK" AND WEAK IN THE LOIN AREA

Ponies are too small to carry the weight and typically do not have the desired movement to be of therapeutic benefit to the physically challenged. The horse must be of substantial size to carry the adult over the weakest part of their back, the loin. Typically, a horse that is 15 hands to 15 hands 3" is suitable. The horse cannot be so large that the child cannot sit comfortably on it or that the sidewalkers cannot give adequate support. For example, if the child has to sit on a very wide base, his or her pelvis becomes tilted posteriorly due to leg position. Weight bearing is on his or her femur rather than on the rami (bony branches) of the pelvic girdle so the movement is not as beneficial.

The horse must be comfortable with the usual therapeutic riding equipment: balls, mirrors, music, etc. The horse must be able to tolerate two people on his back and be relaxed if the client shifts his or her weight. The horse must be sound and able, to move in a rhythmical, symmetrical manner free of gait abnormalities,. A variety of mounts and dismounts may be used. The horse will need to be specifically trained and have a calm, patient temperament as well.

HORSE HANDLING AND EQUIPMENT:

Many methods of horse handling are used in therapeutic riding programs: bit leading, halter leading, longeing and long-lining. Typically, when a rider is very physically challenged, long-lining can encourage the horse to round up his back, reach further under himself with his hind legs and thus increase the rider's rotation and therapeutic benefits. However, when backriding, it is safer to have the horse bit-led. Most handlers are not as skilled at long-lining as they are at leading. Most horses will not be able to round up their back to any great extent with the backrider over their loins. Bit-leading gives control and a skilled leader can encourage the horse to move forward rhythmically. (Figure 2).

For bit-leading, a German hollow-mouth, loose-ring snaffle with bit guards is ideal. The bit guards keep the bit from pinching the corners of the horse's mouth. Side-reins, with a rubber donut, encourage the horse to reach into the bit, thus resulting in the horse rounding his back and reaching up further under himself with his hind legs. This

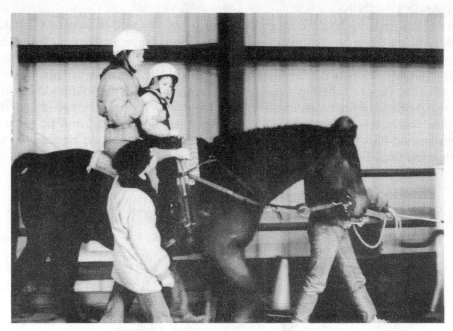

FIGURE 2. THIS HORSE IS MOVING FORWARD IN A RHYTHMICAL MANNER

will improve the rhythmical quality of the horse's gait and increase the amount of rotation the rider receives. The side-reins are adjusted so that the horse's nose is slightly in front of the vertical to allow freedom of head and neck movement while walking. A "joiner" attached to the snaffle allows an even pull on the bit (Figure 3). The lead should be of cotton without a chain and a light-weight snap to decrease the weight hanging from the horse's bit. The wand used in the TTEAM method helps keep the horse's attention and keeps him moving freely. Figure 4 shows the equipment being adjusted to bit-lead the horse.

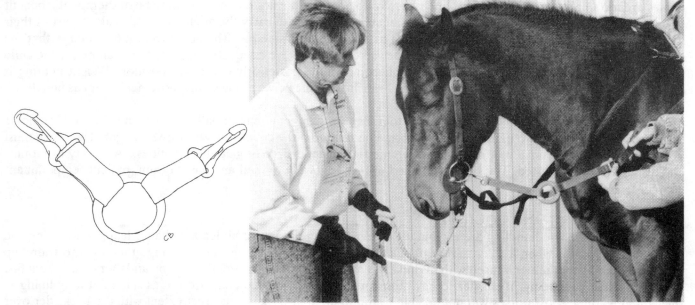

FIGURE 3. THE BIT "JOINER" SHOULD BE MADE OUT OF LIGHT-WEIGHT MATERIAL. IT ALLOWS FOR AN EVEN PULL ON THE SNAFFLE BIT

FIGURE 4. THE RIDING INSTRUCTOR AND THERAPIST ADJUST THE TACK TO PREPARE FOR BIT LEADING

Equipment designed for backriding has to consider therapeutic benefits, safety and minimizing trauma to the horse's back. The child should be able to sit comfortably with the equipment causing no restriction of movement. For safety, it is essential that the backrider be able to have a handle to maintain balance. Should the horse move unexpectedly, the backrider cannot use his or her legs for balance as he or she is positioned near the sensitive flank area. Because the backrider is sitting over the weakest part of the horse's back, it is important that the horse be well padded. Saddles are not appropriate to use because with one the backrider has to sit so far back that it increases the horse's back strain and is ineffective for handling the child.

Typically, thick pads are used with a surcingle to hold them in place. Ideally, the pads are designed to let sweat evaporate and must fit under both riders. A two-handled surcingle can be beneficial to work on upper extremity weight bearing and assist with stability. A one-handled surcingle or anti-cast roller can be used to increase midline awareness and provide security and stability for the rider. Frequently, the problem with either type of surcingle is that the handles interfere with the leg placement of the child, especially if the child has limited abduction. A flat strap-like surcingle can then be used so that this is not a problem; however, the backrider then has nothing to grab during an emergency. A loose-fitting strap can be used. Unfortunately, if the horse should lower its head, the neck strap slides forward leaving the backrider without anything to hold.

Elizabeth Mitchell, President of the Chartered Physiotherapists for the Riding for the Disabled Association, in England, has a design, developed at her program, that has incorporated many good ideas (Figure 5). It has a handle that can be easily grabbed if the horse should move suddenly, it cannot slide forward and it is out of the way of the child. The child does not have any straps that cause discomfort and the horse's movement is not restricted. The foam pad is also covered with a sheepskin. In the United States, Les Watland[1], has developed a backriding tool that will be marketed in 1993. It also employs the forward handle, optimal therapeutic position, as well as tremendous thought to the care of the horse's back.

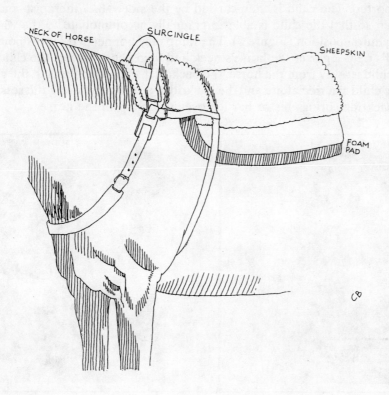

FIGURE 5. THIS IS AN EXCELLENT DESIGN THAT WAS DEVELOPED IN ENGLAND

SAFETY:

Backriding should only be done in an enclosed arena to minimize the possibility of accidents. The client should wear a helmet and belt. While backriding, a light-weight helmet may be used if the child has poor head control. The backrider should <u>wear a belt</u> and <u>brimless helmet</u>. The <u>sidewalkers' responsibility is to the backrider</u>. If they help the backrider to maintain balance during an emergency, the backrider will be able to give more assistance to the child. In most crisis situations there is not time to give the child to a sidewalker. Two sidewalkers are optimal. Some programs use four sidewalkers, two for the backrider and two for the client. The problem is that it becomes very difficult to walk without tripping over-one another. Should an emergency arise, there is no room to move quickly. If the task requires four sidewalkers, the rider should be reevaluated for suitability. Typically, the backrider will grab hold of a handle with one hand and use his or her trunk and other arm to support the child. If the sidewalkers have not maintained at least some physical contact with the backrider (arm resting on his or her leg, or so forth), when an emergency happens, they may be left behind and cannot move in quickly enough to be of real assistance.

THE BACKRIDING SESSION:

The therapist must be able to identify the purpose of treating the client with backriding and identify goals and objectives for the client. The riding session must be active and work toward independence. During each session, main objectives are promoting good postural alignment, balance, and stability.

The riding session should last 20-30 minutes depending upon the endurance of the child. Typically, after 30 minutes, the child is fatigued and the backrider is just holding the child on. Maximum benefits tend to be reached within the first 20 minutes.

Mount/Dismount:

A ramp eases the difficulty for most mounts. When the backrider, child, and sidewalkers are in place, the horse is led in. The backrider mounts the horse first by easing his or her weight down onto the horse's back. The child is never on the horse unsupported. The child is then carried by the sidewalker/therapist and positioned in front of the backrider. Care is given so that the child is able to gradually accommodate to the width of the horse and to bring his or her pelvis to a neutral position (Figure 6). The ramp may not needed for dismounting. The backrider assists with bringing the child's right leg over the horse's neck and then gently lowers the child to the waiting arms of the sidewalker. When the child is away from the horse, the backrider then dismounts to the ground. Occasionally, the therapist may feel that the child can ride alone and the backrider dismounts during the session. The sidewalkers support the child while the backrider brings his or her leg over the rump of the horse.

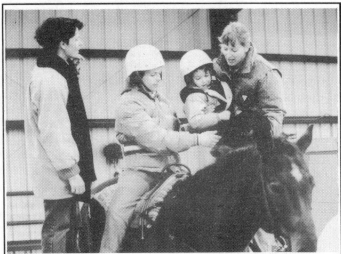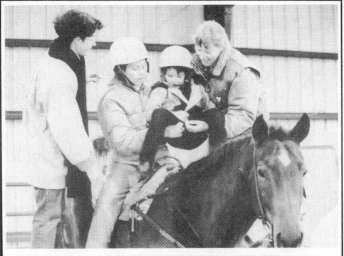

FIGURE 6. THE AUTHOR IS HANDING THE CHILD TO THE BACKRIDER. NOTE THAT THE BACKRIDER MOUNTS FIRST SO THAT THE CHILD IS NEVER UNSUPPORTED WHILE ON THE HORSE. A RAMP AND MOUNTING BLOCK MAKE IT AN EASY TRANSFER.

Therapy Techniques:

The backrider wants to give the minimum amount of support to achieve the desired goal. The child may relax and let the backrider give complete support unless the therapist continually prompts the child to do as much as possible. A cylindrical pillow or towel roll between the child and backrider may be helpful to maintain the child's lumbar curve. The child should be sitting on the level part of the horse's back, just behind the withers, in a neutral pelvic position and thus good posture alignment can be obtained. Sometimes, a slight wedge pad might be helpful to place under the child if he or she remains in a posterior pelvic tilt.

The backriders are in a position where he or she is able to use his or her expertise as if he or she was working with the children on mats. For example, for a child who is hypotonic (low tone), once this child has good postural alignment, the therapist may use approximation (gently pressing down on the child's shoulders or hips) to increase trunk stability. Trotting, another form of approximation, may be tried for a few steps and evaluated to see if head or trunk control is improved. Sometimes riding with the child's trunk behind the vertical can also assist head control.

For a child who is hypertonic (high muscle tone), as the backrider feels the tone decrease, he or she can assist with postural alignment. When asymmetry is noted and the child does not weight-shift evenly, the backrider can position his or her hands to encourage elongation and weight shift when he or she feels the child start to shift to that side. While backriding, reaching, grasping and crossing mid-line can be used. (Figure 7.)

In some programs the child is positioned right on the horse's withers or actually on the horse's neck because the child has extremely limited hip abduction. As well as being uncomfortable, this is an extremely risky practice and very unsafe should the horse not cooperate. From a therapeutic point of view, the replication of the human walk that occurs when a person is on the horse's back does not take place if the child is sitting elsewhere. If the child needs occasional relief from abduction, he or she can be placed in a side-sit position in front of the backrider. This is simply to rest the child, lessening the stretch for a few moments before the session continues.

Another unsafe practice is having the therapist sit backward facing the child rather than behind the child facing forward. It is difficult to keep one's balance sitting backward and should the horse move suddenly, the therapist would not be able to keep his or her own balance let alone the child's.

FIGURE 7. MANY ACTIVITIES CAN TAKE PLACE WHILE BACKRIDING. SHOWN HERE, REACHING FOR RINGS.

HORSE MAINTENANCE:

Maintaining the backriding horse requires conscious effort due to the stress this technique places on the horse's back. During the treatment sessions, the horse should not be scheduled to go immediately from one backriding session to another. If a group of participants is being treated sequentially, alternate horses should be used. Another option is to alternate individuals that need backriding with those who can ride alone. The horse should not be used for more than one hour of backriding a day.

After a heavy treatment session, warm, running water applied to the horse's back will decrease potential muscle soreness. Occasionally, a small amount of Absorbine can be added to the water. (Be careful. Full strength Absorbine™ will blister some horses' backs.)

Training sessions with a skilled rider will enhance the horse's flexibility and muscle strength. The T.T.E.A.M. method of body work in Chapter 7.03 and Rector's Suppling exercises in Chapter 7.06 are excellent for maintaining the backriding horse. Two other exercises are: working in small circles or the use of cavalletti. When circling, the horse's body should be arced to the same degree as the circle to encourage lateral flexion. Cavalletti can stretch a horse's back and increase elasticity. Initially, trotting poles can be set up and the cavalletti added one at a time (Figure 8). The distance will vary depending upon the size and length of stride of the horse. The horse should land and take off between each cavalletti. These are called "no strides".

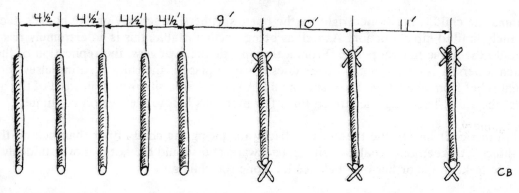

FIGURE 8. THIS CAVALLETTI EXERCISE IS TO INCREASE A HORSE'S FLEXIBILITY. THE HORSE TROTS OVER THE POLES THAT ARE APPROXIMATELY FOUR AND A HALF FEET APART AND THEN "BOUNCES" OVER THE CAVALLETTI THAT ARE 18 INCHES HIGH WITHOUT TAKING A STRIDE IN BETWEEN THEM.

Monitoring the horse for possible signs of soreness can prevent further damage. A change of mood or reluctance to work could be initial signs. Any flinching or uneasiness when the horse is groomed, saddled, or mounted could indicate painful muscles. Short strides with the hind legs or "stubbing" his hind toe may also be noted. The best treatment is complete rest from backriding until all indications of soreness are gone. Light exercise and the hydrotherapy treatment mentioned previously can be helpful.

Careful thought must be given to the backriding horse. Good conformation, appropriate equipment, a manageable weight load, and proper scheduling will prevent damage to the horse. Care of the animals is secondary only to the well-being of the participants in any program.

SUMMARY:

Recognizing the small percentage of clients for whom backriding is appropriate is essential. With proper horse selection and care, the backriding horse will not be overly-taxed as long as the weight load is carefully monitored. Safety guidelines are of utmost importance to follow. However, for selected individuals, backriding can enable them to achieve a greater level of independence and open up the world of therapeutic riding.

[1] Wetland, L. 817-566-2879

12.04 DEVELOPMENTAL SEQUENCE ON HORSEBACK

Colleen Zanin, OTR

DEFINITION OF DEVELOPMENTAL SEQUENCE

Developmental sequence is a term commonly accepted for describing the normal sensorimotor progression of development in the first few years of life. Neuromotor development is concerned with this maturation of the nervous system and the parallel acquisition of control over the muscular system. (Banus et al, 1979). There are four principles concerning the "anatomical directions of development". First, maturation starts in the head region and proceeds toward the feet (the cephalocaudal direction). Control of the joints closest to the central axis of the body occurs before control of the joints farther away from the body (proximal joints develop before distal joints; the shoulder joints develop before hand control). Maturation proceeds from the front surfaces of the body, expanding to the back surfaces (ventral to dorsal). Finally control spreads from near the midline in the anatomical position outward or in the ulnar to radial directions. (Banus, 1971). This neuromotor maturation can be regarded as the acquisition of postural control against gravity and balance which seems to follow a definite sequence relative to the planes of the body, i.e., sagittal, frontal, and transverse. (Scherzer & Tscharnuter, 1982). The normal transition between these stages of neuromotor development occurs in a smooth and overlapping fashion.

As control over the muscular system is achieved, different postures emerge, i.e., front lying, back lying, sitting, crawling, standing, and walking. Again, the anatomical direction of development is repeated in each of these positional levels. In abnormal development (as in a child with cerebral palsy), the sequential development of postural control in the normal anatomical direction is arrested at the initial phase. Therefore, the smooth transition between stages of development is interrupted and faulty movement patterns emerge which prevent control over the muscular system. (Conolly, Montgomery, 1987).

THE DEVELOPMENTAL SEQUENCE ON HORSEBACK

Just as the traditional treatment of clients with movement dysfunctions has been strongly influenced by the work of the Bobaths (1979), the emerging field of *equine-assisted therapy* also draws from the treatment principles of the Bobaths' Neurodevelopmental Treatment (NDT). The scope of this paper is not to compare and contrast the use of these techniques in the clinic to their applicability on the horse. (Refer to Glasow, 1984, 1985 for material on this subject). However it is to discuss how the use of developmental positioning and handling on the horse of the client with movement dysfunction can be an effective form of assessment and treatment. For further information on the use of developmental positions with clients with psycho-social, sensory integrative, or educational impairments, please refer to Chapter 24 in this book by Spink which discusses *Developmental Riding Therapy*. (Tebay, Rowley, 1990).

Throughout the years, several misunderstandings have arisen regarding the use of developmental positions on horseback. Occasionally, these positions are used as a "cookbook approach" and each rider is routinely moved in and out of the designated positions with limited regard to purpose, quality, or individual treatment goal. Stanford, Glasow, and Spink stressed in early seminars the need for an experienced therapist to assess and direct treatment for the client. This principle is reinforced today through the development of the Hippotherapy Competency Guidelines (Tebay, Rowley, 1990).

Therapy goals on horseback are the same as accepted neurodevelopmental techniques (techniques used by physical and occupational therapists to treat clients with movement disorders): the reduction of spasticity and reduction of postural compensations with subsequent facilitation of normal movement skills such as improved posture, balance, trunk control, weight shift, rotation through the body axis, and dissociation at the shoulders and pelvis. (Bertoti, 1988). The use of developmental positions coupled with the movement provided by the horse and the graded handling by the therapist helps to achieve these goals.

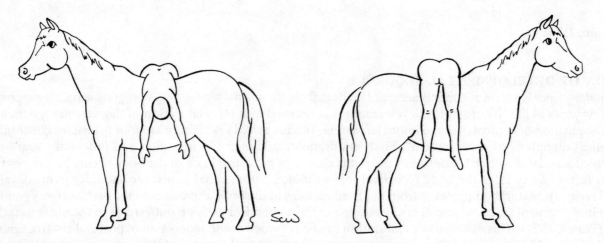

FIGURE 1. PRONE OVER HORSE'S BARREL: POSITION TO NORMALIZE AND DEVELOP EXTENSOR CONTROL (MOBILITY).*

I. CLIENT LYING PRONE OVER THE HORSE'S BARREL

Lying prone over the horse's barrel may be very uncomfortable for the client. The position should be used sparingly (Figure 1). The speed of the horse's walk should be carefully monitored, as well as the length of stride. As long as the client is not experiencing discomfort, this position provides the therapist with an opportunity to mobilize the clients's pelvis and scapulae, to improve symmetry throughout the body, and to promote generalized relaxation throughout the trunk and pelvis. Specific techniques of sensory stimulation such as approximation, tapping, and vibration, can be incorporated into treatment, but need to be applied with good judgement. (Scherzer & Tscharnuter, 1982). The unique demands of the client coupled with the skills of the therapist will determine the precise use of intervention.

PRECAUTIONS: The prone position can cause dizziness in some clients due to the strong vestibular stimulation while the horse is walking. This position should only be used as a preparation for function at a higher level (moving from developmental sequential position to one requiring more maturity). Be aware of a rider with a shunt, with stomach tubes or ileostomies, and use experienced side-aides as the client has a tendency to slip in this position. A properly fitted helmet is a must.

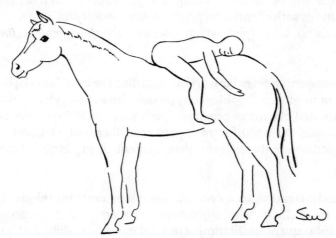

FIGURE 2. PRONE ON THE HORSE'S BACK: POSITION TO INCREASE MUSCLE RELAXATION AND TO DECREASE SPASTICITY

* Horses are drawn without tack and riders without clothes and helmets only to show positions. A rider should never be on a horse without proper attire and a horse is never used without tack.

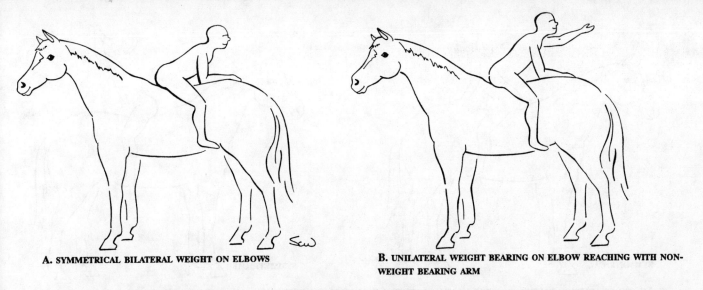

A. SYMMETRICAL BILATERAL WEIGHT ON ELBOWS

B. UNILATERAL WEIGHT BEARING ON ELBOW REACHING WITH NON-WEIGHT BEARING ARM

FIGURE 3. FACING BACKWARD: PRONE ON ELBOWS: POSITION TO DEVELOP HEAD, SHOULDER, AND UPPER TRUNK CONTROL

II. CLIENT LYING PRONE OVER THE HORSE'S BACK AND SITTING BACKWARD ON THE HORSE

This position is usually more comfortable for the client and provides greater opportunity to incorporate relaxation techniques to reduce spasticity (Figure 2). This position can also be used to improve symmetry and upper extremity weight-bearing in bilateral and unilateral prone propped (Figure 3 A & B) positions. Improved trunk control and abdominal/extensor strength may be achieved by facilitating control of upper body flexion/extension, lateral righting, and rotation through the body axis (Figure 4). The position of the client's legs around the horse's barrel promotes abduction and external rotation; also a strong hamstring stretch frequently occurs in this position. When the client can transition to an upright sitting position (Figure 4b) while facing backwards on the horse, trunk extension and a neutral pelvis can be facilitated. By regulating the speed, length of stride, transitions, and direction of the horse, this dynamic treatment surface provides the opportunity to facilitate weight shift, proximal co-contraction (Figure 4a) equilibrium reactions. As in all therapy sessions, emphasis is placed on good bio-mechanical alignment of the client, symmetry, and the reduction of compensatory movements or postures. Occasionally, therapists prefer to ride with the client to achieve greater facilitation of normal movement (See 12.03 for guidelines.)

PRECAUTIONS: Some horses impart a very strong anterior/posterior movement which is transmitted to the client while facing backward. Constant vigilance of head and neck control of the client is required. Some clients fatigue rapidly in this position and some complain of disorientation due to decreased visual input.

A. ASYMMETRICAL

B. ASYMMETRICAL

FIGURE 4A. SITTING BACKWARD--THESE POSITIONS NATURALLY FACILITATE TRUNK EXTENSION AND A NEUTRAL PELVIS - VERY USEFUL FOR RIDER WITH POSTERIOR TILT AND A ROUND BACK.

SYMMETRICAL   **SYMMETRICAL**

FIGURE 4B. SITTING BACKWARD--MORE POSITIONS THAT FACILITATE TRUNK EXTENSION AND A NEUTRAL PELVIS

III. CLIENT LYING SUPINE ON HORSE'S BACK

This position may also cause discomfort to the client (Figure 5) and proper handling/positioning is extremely important, particularly in the client's low back region. (A pillow under the head may help to reduce the strain on the back in this position). The selection of the best modality (horse) is also crucial in this position. When lying in the supine position is used effectively, the therapist can focus on elongation techniques of the neck and trunk, active-passive stretching of upper and lower extremities, shoulder/pelvis dissociation and abdominal strengthening activities. In

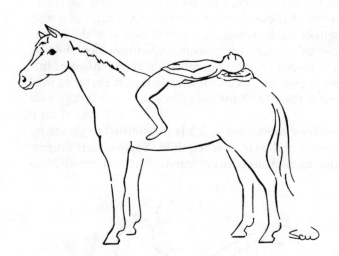

FIGURE 5. SUPINE POSITION ON THE HORSE'S BACK

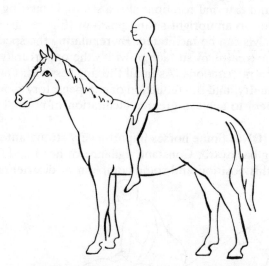

6. SITTING FORWARD--MORE DIFFICULT AS RIDER IS SITTING ON NARROWER BASE AND THE HORSE'S NECK IS A NARROW BASE TO WEIGHT-BEAR ON.

preparation for riding astride, the client can lie supine over the horse's back with legs straddling the horse. Activities to promote neck elongation and head control may be used in this position, with extreme care. Many therapists prefer to assess the effect of this position on the client while the horse is standing still and gradually incorporate movement. A scrutinizing eye and keen observation skills are paramount to discern when the client is becoming over-stressed or when the position is not therapeutic.

PRECAUTIONS: Occasionally, the client becomes fearful in this position due to feelings of vulnerability and the strong effect of gravity on the client in the supine position. Specific treatment goals may be more readily achieved in other positions. A small pillow can be used under the head to decrease the hyperextension of the head/neck region. Monitor the helmet fit carefully when in this position for the helmet has a tendency to slip. The legs of the client should be supported and the lower back of the client should be monitored to avoid strain.

IV. CLIENT SITTING FACING FORWARD

This position is more difficult for many clients as the base of support and weight bearing surface is more narrow (yet more "normal" and easier to integrate for vestibular/visual input) (Figure 6). As with all positions, it is the therapist's role to analyze the client's response to the horse and direct the movement of the horse. (Heipertz, 1981). Treatment goals of improving the client's posture, balance, mobility, and function are continually stressed in this position. Direct intervention by the therapist through "backriding techniques" is most readily used with this position (Glasow, 1984). This position is also used in "classic hippotherapy" to emphasize the influences of the horse on the client. A well-trained dressage horse and a knowledgeable horse trainer with expertise in long-reining will provide the client with a variety of tactile, proprioceptive, and vestibular inputs by performing school figures on one or two tracks.

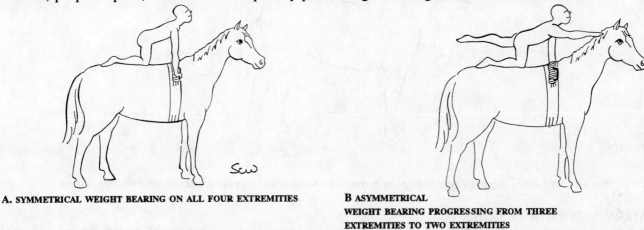

A. SYMMETRICAL WEIGHT BEARING ON ALL FOUR EXTREMITIES

B ASYMMETRICAL
WEIGHT BEARING PROGRESSING FROM THREE
EXTREMITIES TO TWO EXTREMITIES

FIGURE 7. QUADRUPED POSITION (HANDS AND KNEES) DEVELOPS PELVIC AND LEG STABILITY

V. HIGH LEVEL DEVELOPMENTAL SEQUENCES (VARIATIONS OF QUADRUPED, KNEELING, STANDING)

The use of these positions (Figures 7,8,9) in therapeutic riding are similar to some of the exercises used in sports vaulting (flag, free kneel, stand) (Feiedlaender, 1970). Due to the extreme demands on the client's balance, postural control, proximal stability, and motor planning these developmental positions are more suitable for clients with mild movement disorders, sensorimotor disorders, sensory-integrative dysfunction, perceptual-motor disorders, cognitive disorders, behavioral disorders, or language impairments. The emphasis of treatment is usually placed on <u>movement transitions</u> versus postural control within a position. (Tebay & Rowley, HIPPOTHERAPY PROJECT, 1990) For further description and use of these positions, please refer to the chapters on Vaulting, and Developmental Riding Therapy.

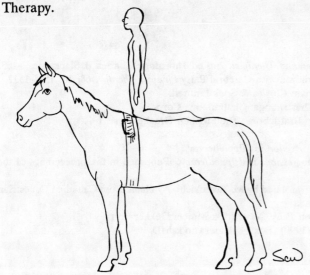

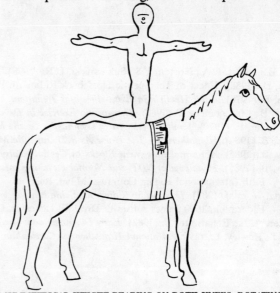

A. SYMMETRICAL WEIGHT BEARING ON BOTH KNEES

B. ASYMMETRICAL WEIGHT BEARING ON BOTH KNEES, ROTATING
AND FLEXING TRUNK AS IN REACHING FOR AN OBJECT

FIGURE 8 KNEELING: REQUIRES GREATER PELVIC AND TRUNK CONTROL

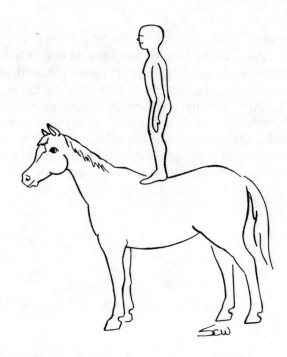

FIGURE 9. STANDING: REQUIRES INTEGRATION OF TOTAL BODY MOBILITY AND STABILITY COMPONENTS OF MOVEMENT

SUMMARY AND CONCLUSIONS

This article provides the reader with an historical perspective and rationale for the use of developmental sequences in therapeutic riding. It is strongly recommended that a therapist receive additional education through seminars on this precise use of the horse for improving the client's posture and balance before experimenting with this dynamic treatment tool.

Editor's note: Instructors should note that these procedures are used as a treatment modality by therapists who have been trained in these techniques with specific work in NDT and a thorough background in the neurological basis for treatment. It is NOT a part of an instructor-rider lesson.

References
Banus, B.S., Kent, C.A., Norton, Y.S., Sukiennicki, D.R. (1979). *The Developmental Therapist.* 2nd ed. Thorofare: Charles B. Slack, Inc. 1-163.
Bertoti, D. (1988). Effect of Therapeutic Horseback Riding on Posture in Children with Cerebral Palsy *Physical Therapy*, 68, 10. 1505-1512.
Bobath, B. (1978). *Adult Hemiplegia Evaluation and Treatment.* London: William Clowes & Sons Limited.
Conolly, B., Montgomery. P. (1987). *Therapeutic Exercise in Developmental.* Chattanooga: Chattanooga Corp.
Friedlaender, E. (1970). *Vaulting: The Art of Gymnastics on the Moving Horse.* Brattleboro: The Stephen Greene Press: I-44.
Glasow, B. (1984). *Hippotherapy - The Horse As a Therapeutic Modality.*
Glasow. B. (1985). *Abnormal Movement Blocks In Cerebral Palsy and Their Correction in Hippotherapy.*
Glasow, B. (1985). *Principals of NDT and Normal Development Applied to Progressions in Hippotherapy.* Published in the proceedings of the Fifth International Riding Congress. Milan, Italy.
Heipertz, W., et al (1981). *Therapeutic Riding: Medicine Education and Sports.* Translated by M. Takeukichi. Available from Canadian Equestrian Federation, 1600 James Anismith Drive Glouchester, Ontario, Canada.
Scherzer, A. L., Tscharnuter, I. (1982). *Early Diagnosis and Therapy in Cerebral Palsy.* New York: Marcel Dekker. Inc.
Tebay, J., Rowley, L., (1990). *National Hippotherapy Curriculum Committee.* (1990). Box 41, Riderwood, MD.

PART V   MASTERY OF INSTRUCTION

13   INSTRUCTION

This section addresses the skills needed in order for a person to instruct: instruct in any area of undertaking--not necessarily instruction in riding. Any person who successfully passes on knowledge needs the skills to "instruct." It is the intent of this section to provide the reader with some basic information regarding the learning process and to arouse an interest in pursuit and development of teaching skills. The section includes information on the learning process, teaching techniques followed by the riding instructor's role, lesson planning and executions of the riding lesson.

Instruction refers to instructing, to knowledge, to education, to teaching (Webster, 1966). Instruction requires an instructor to have a base of knowledge in the field that is to be taught in order to educate others. A person who has competed through the Pony Club and has gone on to compete on the "A" circuit understands the skill involved in dressage or show jumping. But does this make this person an ideal instructor? Not necessarily. Unless this person has learned how to teach, developed instructional strategies and has read the theory behind the development of riding, he or she may be poorly equipped. A riding instructor's purpose is to educate his or her clients in horsemanship skills. This can include any aspect of riding, grooming, horse care, and related subjects. The instructors of therapeutic riding go beyond horsemanship skills. With the assistance of specialists, instructors use the horse as a means to foster bonding, facilitate growth and development, educate or develop work skills. Instructors must have knowledge of the material to be taught and also knowledge of how to teach skills to others. Within the unique setting of therapeutic riding, instructors teach persons who have problems. They therefore need to understand the problems and disabilities, how people learn, and how to teach people with *limitations and learning difficulties*. An instructor once stated that her riding student, who was bright and rode at the intermediate level, manipulated the riding lesson and did not follow through with what she had learned. One day she could remember well, the next day she appeared to remember nothing or lacked motivation. What this instructor did not understand was that the rider was "learning disabled", a condition in which this type of behavior is common. If this instructor had been well informed regarding learning disabilities, she would have been more successful in teaching her student. A teacher must help his or her students to learn how to learn. Piaget felt that children "must be allowed to do their own learning". They need to have the experience in order to learn (Pulaski, 1980). Feldenkrais (1981) feels that for successful learning the individual must proceed at his own pace. He or she points out that having a person *do something* is quite different than *learning how to do it. It must be remembered that all levels and ages of riders MUST BE GIVEN THE OPPORTUNITY TO LEARN*. A teacher or instructor should not and can not determine that this individual will not or cannot learn.

The sidewalker takes the child's hands, then picks up the reins, arranges them in the child's hand and tells him or her to keep them there. This is a different procedure than the child listening to the instructions, making judgements as to what he or she must do to pick up the reins, to motor plan his or her movements, and then judge the correctness of his or her efforts. Is the goal for the student to *hold* the reins or to *learn* how to hold the reins? Moving the child's hand through the process of picking up the reins, as in the first case, may have no carry over effect. The child is learning splinter skills. The child may need to have this process repeated each time he or she is asked to pick up the reins. He or she has not *learned* the process. In the second case, the child is assisted in *learning* the process of picking up the reins. The child perceives what he or she hears and what he or she sees, takes an action in a sensory motor manner to achieve a goal. He or she then will make a judgement to determine if his or her actions are correct and make a correction by him or herself, or with assistance if incorrect. Though he or she may have problems the next time he or she rides, he or she will show progress with each attempt. What is involved in the procedure of instruction? Let us take a look at the learning process to better understand how we take on the task of teaching.

Feldenkrais, M. (1981). *The Elusive Obvious*. Cupertino: Meta Publications. pp 29-37
Pulaski, M.A.S. (1980). *Understanding Piaget*. New York: Harper & Row Publishers. pp 109-110
Webster's New World Dictionary, College Edition. (1966). Cleveland: The World Publishing Co. p 758.

13.01 LEARNING THEORIES
Behavior Modification and Piagetian Theory

Barbara T. Engel, MEd, OTR
Margaret L. Galloway, MA, BHSAI

There are many developmental or learning theories that have evolved over time by psychologists, developmentalists, physicians, and others. Two popular theories, one developed by B. F. Skinner, the other by Jean Piaget, will be discussed here because these theories are frequent bases for developmental approaches used by educators and therapists. B. F. Skinner was an American psychologist who in 1930 identified the operant learning theory, referred to as operant-conditioning, by observing that every response made by an organism has some sort of a consequence, and subsequent actions continue to change the environment (Skinner, 1938). Piaget, a Swiss researcher, is well known as a child psychologist, but he also was a genetic epistemologist and this had a strong influence on the development of his theories in the early 1920s and 1930s (Piaget, 1952). Piaget's theories are concerned with biological organization and with developing structures as they relate to intelligence used in adaptation to the environment. Piaget has shown that his theory of mental <u>structures</u> can be expressed by the symbolism of mathematics and logic, which he refers to as <u>psychologic</u>. Structures are groupings of classes, relationships, and propositions that have rules by which they interrelate (group theory) in an organized and logical way (Richmond, 1971). Piaget is mainly concerned with the structural learning process, but structures are also involved with psycho-social, organizational and psycho-sexual behaviors.

BEHAVIOR MODIFICATION

Behavior modification, based on the theoretical principles of operant-conditioning, were originally developed by B. F. Skinner (Skinner, 1938), a psychologist. This approach attempts to explain causes of human behavior and provide techniques for altering behavior. (Behavior is considered any activity that a person does that can be observed, measured, and analyzed [Marsh, 1983]). The approach uses the assumption that behavior is caused by reactions to stimuli, and that people are motivated by positive reinforcement. Reinforcements can be divided into primary reinforcers (those that fulfill basic needs, such as food, water, or air) and secondary reinforcers (any item, action, or event, that is meaningful to the recipient). Behavior can be altered by changing or modifying the stimulus or consequence. Skinner identifies three types of reinforcements that the environment selects to alter behaviors: reinforcement, the lack of reinforcement and punishment. Students' learning and behavioral characteristics may be systematically altered by manipulating the learning environment. Because motivation is important in learning, positive reinforcement is the prime component in a successful program. Ignoring negative behavior is usually an approach sufficient to stop it, with punishment saved for rare instances of extreme behavior (Schloss & Sedlick, 1986).

A behavior modification program includes an assessment of a person's characteristics and skills, the establishment of goals, systematically planned instruction, and methods that motivate. After assessing the person and defining goals, the instructor plans a sequence of lessons designed to meet these goals. Daily monitoring is used to determine the effectiveness of the approach. If a rider does not make adequate progress, the instructor could try new methods, such as having him or her monitor his or her progress. If the new methods do not work, the instructor can also try different kinds of reinforcement.

Behavior modification is based on the belief that people are social. A typical reinforcement could be an increase in activities that particular individual enjoys, such as longer riding privileges. To obtain the reward or reinforcement, the rider must comply with certain rules. These rules may be made into a contract. This could read, "I, Susan Smith, will not interrupt during instructions. I will put the tack away after use. I will obey safety rules. In turn, at the end of six consecutive weeks, I will be allowed one extra hour with the second class for the remainder of the term." In the contract, the student has agreed to do certain behaviors and, in turn, get a reinforcer or reward. This method/theory is one approach that can be used in teaching and, in general, it produces good results with students of all ages.

PIAGET'S THEORY OF DEVELOPMENT

Professor Jean Piaget is best known as a child psychologist. He was also a mathematician, zoologist, philosopher and genetic epistemologist. These unique skills had a bearing upon the system of child psychology he developed. Piaget's major interest had to do with the nature of intelligence. His research attempts to explain the development of the human being through the stages of growth leading to the development of intelligence. Piaget divided development into four stages of maturation. 1) sensory-motor, 2) preoperational, 3) concrete operational, and 4) formal operational.

The first stage (birth to two years) involves the sensory-motor system where inborn behavior patterns are exercised upon the environment resulting in actions or sensory-motor thinking. The infant learns that any moves he or she makes cause changes as he or she touches his or her environment. He or she learns to coordinate his or her actions to cause change and in this way learns to relate to objects in his or her environment. The infant finds that he or she is separate from his or her environment. Piaget had a strong belief that the sensori-motor stage had a strong influence on perception and learning. In this respect the infant touches and moves objects gaining the sense of texture, two or three dimensions, rotational and spatial awareness. It is from this early exploration of the environment that the sense of object form, distance, right-left discrimination, directionality and other basic concepts develop. It is this stage that is of major concern in horseback riding with physically disabled riders, but also with able bodied, as they learn to deal with their bodies in relation to the horse and its movements. For example, a child with limited use of his or her hands and limbs, who spends his or her day in a wheelchair or lying on a mat, has no experience in the exploration of objects and space. When brought to the stable, he or she can not conceptualize the form and shape of a horse or other objects since he or she has never *experienced them,* nor can he or she perceive distance from the ground to the top of the horse, the spatial relationship of him or her self to the stable environment.

The second stage (two to seven years), with the emergence of language and symbolic representation, is the preoperational period. The third stage, concrete operational (seven to eleven years), is the stage where the child learns simple math and money concepts, begins to understand rules, uses some judgement and is able to begin problem solving. Moderately retarded individuals may never enter this stage or develop it to any extent and therefore always need degrees of supervision. In the last stage, formal operational (11 years to late teens), the child develops mature thinking and cognitive development. The child begins to understand and organize time, begins to see the relationships of objects to things, objects to each other, and events such as social and world events. He or she begins to develop more mature judgements and the concept and consequence of right or wrong. It is during this stage that a child is mentally and physically ready to be a true "riding student", understanding concepts and able to organize and follow through on the processes.

References

Abildness, A. H. (1982). *Biofeedback Strategies*. Rockville: American Occupational Therapy Association. 3-9.
Ginsburg, H., Opper, S. (1969). *Piaget's Theory of Intellectual Development*. New Jersey: Prentice-Hall, Inc.
Marsh, G.E; Barrie, J.P; Tom, E.C. (1983). *Teaching Mildly Handicapped Children*. St. Louis: The C.V. Mosby Co.
Piaget, J. (1952). *The Origins of Intelligence in Children*. New York: W.W. Norton & Company Inc.
Schloss, P. J., Sedlak, R.A. (1986). *Instructional Methods for Student Learning and Behavior Problems*. Boston: Allyn and Becon
Skinner, B. F. (1938). *The Behavior of Organisms*. New York: Appleton-Century Crofts.
Richmond, P. G. (1971). *An Introduction to Piaget*. New York: Basic Books, Inc. Publishers.

13.02   THE LEARNING PROCESS: COGNITION AND PERFORMANCE

Barbara T. Engel MEd, OTR

The human being is endowed with the process of thinking, the ability to acquire knowledge and to use it to perform functional tasks. Human cognition, as this is called, involves all of the processes necessary to take in information, reconstruct it, embellish it, interpret it, store and recover it, and use it to solve simple or complex problems. We use this process in our daily lives either in work or play in the performance of life skills. How successful one is in carrying out these skills is dependent on the ability to fully develop each component of the learning process. In therapeutic riding programs, instructors, educators and therapists are confronted with individuals who have deficits in one or more areas of this process. In order to assist the clientele in overcoming some of these deficits so they are able to carry out horsemanship skills to their maximum abilities, the staff must have a basic concept of the normal process in order to deal with the abnormal mechanisms. When an instructor is able to break down his or her teaching into increments, he or she will be able to assist a rider by stimulating aspects of the learning and performance process. This stimulation will hopefully aid the rider in improving a deficit or weak area. This process is complex. Not only does one as instructor need to be able to identify problem areas but one must also know the stimulation needed to assist in the reduction of dysfunction. Because of this complexity, the instructor will seek the assistance of his or her therapists. In so doing, the instructor will be taking on a truly professional role in therapeutic riding.

LEARNING:
Learning is defined by Webster (1966) as "knowledge of a subject or skill in, by study of, experience in, or by instruction" and defined by Lawther (1968), as "a change due to training and experience. One must learn: to survive and be happy, to progress, and to be socially acceptable." Instructors in therapeutic riding programs want their clients to learn horsemanship skills. In order to be an effective teacher one must have an understanding of the *learning process*. This is especially true when dealing with a population in which many have difficulty learning. "*Learning is something that goes on inside a person and one cannot watch it as it happens. The instructor can only see the results, not the process of learning*" (Ross, 1977). If one cannot see how a child learns, how can he or she be taught? First one must understand how the learning process develops in clients. Then one can better understand how to teach them. de Quiros & Schrager (1978) divide learning into four processes:

- *Primary learning* allows adaptation to the environment. This process deals with survival and the adaptation of a species to changes in its environment. Animals and infants have primary learning mechanisms. They alert or attend to something in their environment; they perceive the smell of food; since they are hungry they are motivated to make adaptations to receive the food. If they do not get any they may be under stress and anxiety because of their hunger.

- The *second process* allows the use of generational (knowledge from other species' members) knowledge. Customs, cultural expectations, and social behaviors are involved in the second process. We perceive through our senses and learn from experience. We interact with others of our species. This process can be seen in young children and some animals. For example: the child attends to his or her environment; he or she perceives his or her mother's voice; he or she is motivated to gain attention; he or she adapts his or her behavior with a social smile and chuckle (since he or she has learned this behavior gains a favorable response).

- The *third process* implies the use of symbols which allow for the transmission and reception of knowledge through language such as writing and speech. This is a process only humans have. One must be able to attend, perceive, adapt, be motivated and use conceptual thinking in this process. A riding lesson would involve the third process when the riders must attend and must be motivated in order to listen to the instructor's directions and must perceive what he says. They must then understand the instructor's concepts and adapt their behavior to carry out the directions.

- The *fourth process* implies the ability to think with verbal symbols and to formulate diverse, different and new patterns of creative communication. This last process is what can be called scholastic learning or cognition and is also restricted to humans only. This process involves all aspects of learning and functioning with increasingly difficult demands to solve complex tasks and problem.

ROLE OF MOTIVATION

Lawther (1968) defines motivation "as a state of *being aroused* to action - aroused from passivity or calmness to restlessness, to a degree of dissatisfaction or disturbance, and then to directed purposeful acts." A person can be motivated to act for reasons of survival, maintenance of basic needs, pleasure, security, social status, praise, achievement, approval, or for exploration. Motivational needs can be divided into physical needs and emotional needs. Scott (1978) questions what can appeal to a person enough to induce him to organize his experiences into concepts and to think out and try solutions. Feldenkrais (1981) and Skinner (1971) feel that choice allows freedom. "When there is no option of choices, a person feels that he or she cannot change even though he or she knows that he or she engenders his or her own misery" (Feldenkrais, 1981). Choice entails self-knowledge, self-control, self-direction and allows one to manipulate his or her environment. This freedom enhances the person's sense of competence and self-worth. Therapeutic riding literature frequently mentions how much riders gain in self-esteem. Here the motivating element is the horse who provides the rider freedom in movement and therefore choice.

Other motivating factors include positive and negative reinforcements. Positive reinforcement includes food, praise, gaining self-worth, fulfilling values, and being given a reward (Lewin, 1935). Skinner (1971) mentions that positive reinforcements can include doing something one is told to do in order to get away from the nagging that occurs when one is not doing it. In this way one is free from attack, the attack of being nagged. This technique is used when training horses. The horse learns "trot" when asked. If he or she does not trot he learns he will be tapped (nagged) with the sound of the whip or the whip itself.

Operant conditioning can also be a motivating factor. One learns that he or she gets hot in the sun but becomes cool in the shade. One therefore seeks the shade for comfort and pleasure. When our actions are followed by a certain kind of positive consequence, it is more likely that we will repeat that action. The instructor uses those methods of motivation which work well for a specific situation and in which the individual feels comfortable. The instructor must believe in the methods he or she uses with students as well as with the horses.

ROLE OF ATTENTION AND FOCUS

Webster (1966) states that "attention is the ability to give heed, carefully observe, notice; give thoughtful consideration to others; or the readiness to respond to stimuli". Attention is an important process for all instructors, for without attention, learning cannot occur. Marsh (1983) states that attention involves:
- positive change in behavior when a stimulus is presented
- the ability to perceive a stimulus and respond to it
- paying attention that includes watching and/or listening to what is happening or to a task
- attending to an appropriate or a specific stimuli
- finding a specific stimulus among many
- sustaining attention in order to complete a task

An infant begins to attend to speech sounds at birth or in utero. A child may attend to a stimulus but may find it too unrewarding to warrant a response (Tjossem, 1976). Children or adults with central nervous system (CNS) impairment may not be able to "tune in" or "tune out" multi-visual, auditory, vestibular and sensory stimuli. Receiving massive input may prevent the individual from attending appropriately to a selected task or to instructions.

Before attention occurs the individual must first be *aroused* in order to orient to or perceive a stimulus. Arousal, referred to as alertness, occurs on a physical and mental level. It prepares a person for some form of action. The stimulus can be perceived through any of the sense organs such as hearing, touch, vestibular/proprioception, sight, taste, or smell. The CNS provides a sensory-filtering mechanism that focuses attention by eliminating irrelevant, trivial input (Heiniger & Randolph, 1981). The information is processed through the CNS and is transmitted to the input-output centers where integration occurs. The next step involves interpretation regarding the relevance and importance of the stimulus. When the CNS has identified a pertinent stimulus, the individual must then have the ability to respond to the information in a meaningful or appropriate way. If there is a time lag in the transmission and reception of the stimulus to integration to response, the individual may have lost the meaning of the original information and be unable, or find it meaningless, to attend or initiate a response.

Duchek (1991) describes four elements of attention:

- Alertness
  Alertness refers to both the physical and mental levels of arousal that are needed at a given time to respond to a stimulus.

- Selection of attention
  Stimuli bombard each of us through any one or all of the sense organs. Once attention has been focused on the selected stimulus, it must be maintained at the exclusion of other information in order for a task to be completed. In a complex task, selective attention may need to be maintained while shifting from one area to another. In riding instruction selective attention will shift from the instructor to the riding aids.

- Allocation of attention.
  When performing a task such as bridling the horse, we must allocate enough attention in order to complete this task. This is referred to as *attentional capacity*. More capacity is needed to bridle the horse than would be needed to return the brush to the basket. A complex task such as controlling and bridling a horse may require the total capacity of attention the person has available. A simple task such as putting the brush back into the basket requires less attention and may allow a reservoir to be carried into another activity such as talking with a friend.

- Automaticity
  More attention is required when a task is unfamiliar. A task that has been learned and performed many times requires less attention since it becomes automatic. When this process occurs a reservoir of attention is created which is then available for additional tasks.

There are a number of theories on the sequential development of the CNS pathways which influence attention and which of these pathways must first be stimulated. Scientists now have methods to study the CNS; future findings will shed light on all areas of human and animal function. **What is of concern to the instructor and staff of therapeutic riding programs is the complexity of a person's ability to attend. It is also important to know that attention can be facilitated by either increasing or decreasing certain stimuli.** Learning how to manipulate stimuli to increase attention is a process that takes both knowledge of and ability to analyze subtle effects on behavior and experience. But with sensitivity and close observation of what responses are caused by which stimuli, one can get a good feel for the situation and how to handle it. For example:

Jimmy does not attend to the instructor in a class of four students. He becomes hyperactive after ten minutes; within fifteen minutes, he becomes a distracting influence to the class. Jimmy is able to attend to two-step directions when he is accompanied by Jane, the side helper, who is very calm and patient. Jimmy's attention is better when his lesson is in the indoor arena with Jason who is organized in the way he functions, since he can copy what Jason does.

The observation of Jimmy's reactions suggests that Jimmy cannot filter out irrelevant information. He attends to all stimuli in his environment--stable noises, other students, instructor and helpers--all this information overloads him and he reacts with hyperactivity. Jane is able to help Jimmy focus better and stay calmer. When most of the environmental stimuli are removed (indoor arena) Jimmy can attend. He can attend even better when visual stimuli supports oral instruction. The instructor asks Jimmy and Jason to walk their horses between the parallel poles. Jimmy could attend to part of the instruction but not all. He looks to see what Jason is doing and copies him. It may be that Jimmy not only has difficulty attending but also has a problem with recall from the memory bank. This reinforcement helps Jimmy to attend to his task.

Attention can be affected by the level of development, alertness, selective attention, motivation, attractiveness of a stimulus or how it is presented, ability to perceive information, dichotic listening, stimuli from internal organs, stress, pain, or fatigue (Ross, 1977). In addition to these common influences, attention is affected by abnormal development, prescribed and illegal drugs, trauma, seizures, inherited deficits, emotional stress, physiological, psychological and metabolic deficiencies (Thomas, 1968). These multiple influences may cause an individual to be very alert and responsive one day and function poorly the next, thus affecting attention. These phenomena are especially observable in learning disabled individuals and in related disorders such as hyperactivity and attention-deficit disorders.

The following description of terms (Cruickshank, 1967) may help one understand the variables which enter into the complexity of attention:

- Distractibility or hyperactivity--inability to refrain from responding to all stimuli
- Motor hyperactivity or hyperkinetic behavior--the inability to refrain from reacting to any stimulus without a motor response (wiggling, poking, twirling, pulling, pushing, talking)
- Perseveration--inability to move from one action to another--fixation or getting "stuck" in any act (repeating a phrase or motor act over and over)
- Disassociation--the condition of seeing parts, not the whole (the head but not the body--the letter but not the word), inability to integrate
- Figure-ground--the inability to separate visually an object from its environment (the tree-barn-horse are all attached) aural figure-ground--to separate a sound from the total environmental sounds (the sound of a word/horse's neigh/airplane are all one sound)

There are other aspects of attention that must be considered. What may appear to the instructor as an inability to attend, may not be a problem of "attention" but rather a problem of responding (Grandin, 1986) which can be seen in people having autistic or learning disability disorders. The author remembers as a child of five, being asked by strangers "does she not talk?" The problem was not the "attention" to the question being asked but the slowness in retrieving the answer. By the time Barbara could respond to a stranger, the stranger had already gotten involved in something else and was no longer paying attention to her. One learns quickly to avoid certain social situations where questions might be asked or to pretend not to "attend" if one cannot **perform as expected**.

Grandin (1986) points out that autistic individuals have difficulty putting order to their world and therefore must be provided an organized and predictable environment. In a predictable and familiar environment, the individual may be able to focus and attend more readily. Grandin also points out that both in autism and in learning disabilities, a person can do only one thing at a time. This may literally mean listening, or thinking, or doing. If pressured to combine these processes, the simplest reaction may be to "phase out" and avoid the stimulation. Affolter (1991) states that the search for information requires a capacity for the amount of information that can be processed (or attended to) in a given time span. We are all familiar with responses such as "that is enough", "that is too much noise", "I can hardly think any more", "I'm too tired to go on" (Affolter 1991). What we mean by these statements is that we cannot process any more stimuli and will no longer attend.

There are other people with a severe inability to focus on anything. They appear as though they are scanning the world with no interest. With very careful stimulation, possibly using touch, movement, or music, they can be trained to attend to simple and appealing tasks. As the ability to attend is expanded through training, riding or therapy, the attention span is lengthened. This refers to the time a particular activity is pursued. The development of attention is followed by the persistence of attention which involves the continued pursuit of an activity in the face of obstacles.

It is important to remember that a lack of attention does not indicate a lack of intelligence. This is demonstrated by very bright individuals with autism, head injuries or those with learning disabilities who may seem "in a world of their own." Treating a person with poor attention as though he or she has limited intelligence giving him or her overly-simplistic tasks is degrading and unproductive. It is best to reserve one's impression and judgements, always focusing and building the students' abilities.

THE ROLE OF ADAPTATION:
Phylogenetic development, called organic learning by Feldenkrais (1981), begins at conception in the womb and continues until all systems have matured. The infant will make changes or adapt his or her responses to his or her environment. During ontogenetic development this learning process continues. Gilfoyle (1981) points out that the environment continuously provides new experiences to which the individual makes adaptive responses, using previously acquired knowledge for further growth. This maturation process requires a continuous spiraling of change and learning.

During this spiraling process of development primitive movements develop into purposeful behaviors. "Purposeful behaviors are the foundations for the development of complex strategies which are adapted to perform purposeful activities and develop skill." Ayres (1979) defines adaptive response as "*an appropriate action in which the individual responds successfully to some environmental demand.*" Piaget states (Pulaski, 1980) "adaptation is the essence of intellectual functioning, just as it is the essence of biological functioning." According to Piaget, *adaptation* consists of two processes:

- *Assimilation--the taking-in* of nourishment, sensation, or experience.
- *Accommodation--the out-going* or reaction to the stimulation of the environment.

These two processes function simultaneously at all levels of development and learning. We say that in the therapeutic riding environment, the client *assimilates* the movement of the horse through his or her central nervous system and *accommodates* with adaptive postural responses. His or her central nervous system is learning to *balance*. The client *assimilates* the instructor's words and *accommodates* by sitting back as instructed. This is a social form of adaptation. Initial changes in the organism occur as a result of pleasurable sensation, or to maintain a balance between assimilation and accommodation, as Piaget would say, to "the on going self-regulating process which he called equilibrium" (Pulaski, 1980). The human organism, as all living things, is never still; so there must always be reaction to change, called adaptation, either in the organism itself or to the environment. Feldenkrais (1981) states that when this process is not allowed to develop naturally by being "PUSHED BY PARENTS OR ANYONE TO REPEAT ANY INITIAL SUCCESS, THE LEARNER MAY REGRESS, AND FURTHER PROGRESS CAN BE DELAYED BY DAYS, EVEN WEEKS, OR NOT OCCUR AT ALL". This is an important point to remember. We can allow our clients to develop balance by allowing adaptive responses to occur when they are sliding off-balance on the horse. Let them regain their own balance with no help or minimal assistance. If the side-walker pushes the rider back to the center of the horse, **the rider can be deprived of learning the concept of balance.** This would also apply to other tasks such as mounting, which requires many postural adjustments and adaptation to movement from ramp to horse. *The organic learning process occurs on a neurological basis and must be allowed to progress in its natural patterns. It cannot be subjected to scholastic methods of learning* (Pulaski, Feldenkrais, Ayres, Bobath).

THE ROLE OF PERCEPTION
De Quiros (1978) defines perception as the recognition of sensory information which is produced by stimuli from the environment. Affolter (1990) feels that perception is a prerequisite for interaction with the environment. The search for information is observed in horses and other animals as well as in humans. We perceive through feeling, hearing, seeing, smelling, and tasting. This allows us to organize information, to memorize, to acquire knowledge, to make judgements and interpretations, to make conscious reactions and interact at progressively higher levels.

Form perception (the ability to assess shapes or objects) is developing long before an infant can explore his or her environment with his or her hands and feet. Many children with severe physical dysfunction rely on form perception for much of their knowledge of objects and their environment. Form perception is innate but also develops with stimulation and maturity. Without physical contact with objects, some dimensions are lost. If we look at a mountain covered with trees, we would not understand the formation/shape of the mountain. If we were to go to the mountain and explore the hills, the trees and rocks, we would have a totally different picture in our mind, the next time we see a mountain. The term perceptual-motor refers to the perception of the stimuli and the motor response. For example: we hear a voice calling our name, we identify the direction of the sound, we understand what the sound is and we make a physical response to what we hear. We made a judgement in responding to what we heard.

THE ROLE OF MEMORY
Memory is a major factor in learning and performance. The child explores his environment to confront new experience. Memory helps the child to build a reservoir of information upon which to build new knowledge. Memory can be short-term, long-term and/or sensory in nature (Duchek, 1991). Sensory memory is momentary, allowing for interpretation and possible pattern recognition. It is then transferred to short term memory. Short term or primary memory has a limited capacity but can be expanded when information is grouped or clustered (Marsh, 1983). The information in short term can last 30 seconds (Duchek, 1991) before it is stored into long-term memory. Deficits in short term memory may actually be a deficit in attention, organization or metamemory [awareness of one's own cognitive processes.] (Marsh, 1983)

Long-term memory is when permanent information is encoded and stored. Encoding refers to those strategies used to levy a type of organization on the facts to be stored so that they will be easier to retrieve. Retrieving information from long term memory appears dependent upon the system of encoding and installing used and the depth of processing which has occurred. Memory processes are those cognitive mechanisms that are under our control when dealing with information. When the rider can attend, clearly hear, is given enough time to <u>attend</u>, <u>absorb</u>, think about, and practice information taken in, he or she is more likely to use "deep processing". With this process he or she will be able to recall the information more readily. Use of visual imagery, verbal associations, key words or cues can aid in recall from permanent memory.

THE ROLE OF CONCEPTION:
Webster (1966) defines concept as "a generalized idea of a class of objects, a thought, a generalized notion." Experiences are developed into concepts which involve abstract thinking. Children use their experiences in perceiving their object world. They begin to see similarities and differences and will categorize or group things together; They begin to develop concepts. The understanding of concepts begins to develop at about age six years and continues to develop into adulthood. A concept is dependent on thought (Pulaski, 1980). A child can see a dog or horse and can name it as an object. This is considered a concrete object. The dog or horse as a "pet" is a concept of animals as companions, protectors or helpers. The child can see the relationship between a dog as a pet and the horse as a pet so he or she can classified these together. You can only describe this. You can not "draw" it or "see" it. As the children's concepts increase they gain additional experiences and knowledge. As they grow mentally, their concepts become more complex and abstract. Later they deal primarily with relationships. Concepts enable children to develop the ability to anticipate and to predict future events.

When instructing a child, especially one who has learning difficulties or is mentally retarded, it is important to understand his or her level of concept development. If this has not developed well, instructions must be such that they can be visualized in simple terms. For example, how would one present the concept of balance to a small child, or to an adolescent mentally retarded girl? Sally Swift (1985) has developed many images which may be useful in getting the point across. A rag doll might be used to show what happens when the doll is not balanced; it falls off.

THE ROLE OF STRESS AND ANXIETY
Anxiety is a state of being uneasy. Feldenkrais (1981) states "anxiety can be a positive, useful phenomenon. It assures our safety from risking what we feel would endanger our very existence. Anxiety appears when deep in ourselves we know that we have no other choice, no alternative way of acting." An example might be: You are warming up a horse, walking slowly around the area when the horse is startled and runs. This startles you, and you become anxious, but you realize you must pull yourself together in order to control your horse. Your anxiety alerts you to this conclusion.

Stress is the result of being under pressure, strained, tense, or fearful. It is the disturbance of the equilibrium in our life. Selye (1976) divides stress into three stages. The first stage is one of alarm, the second is the resistance stage and the third stage is the exhaustion stage. Stress, at a tolerable level, is present in everyone's life and can help a person to become more alert, to heighten awareness, to function and to perform (Heiniger, 1981). It will challenge an adaptive response at a higher level of function.

Stress affects the whole body, the CNS, the endocrine and immune systems, the cardiovascular, and the respiratory systems. The fight-or-flight reaction which is so well known in horses, is also present in humans. Heiniger (1981) points out the three phases of this reaction in humans. First phase is increased arousal or alarm reaction resulting in physical or verbal attack. The second phase is the physical fight reaction. The third phase is the flight reaction. This can involve physical withdrawal, or more damaging, emotional withdrawal. It is important to be aware of signs of stress which indicate that clients are overwhelmed by a situation. Too much stress would indicate that clients are inappropriately placed in a situation, or that too much is being asked of them. When working with non-verbal persons, their visible signs of stress are so very important.

Each person demonstrates his or her stress signs and at his or her own rate. Some people can handle a great deal of stress while others respond to seeming non-stress situations with stress reactions. It is not up to the instructor or the volunteer to make a judgement on the appropriateness of stress since stress is a biological reaction. One can make a judgement on the amount of stress that a person can tolerate without losing the ability to function and learn. Observe the rider and determine which signs of stress he or she may show and under what circumstance this stress appears. Try to stop the activity that produces undesirable stress before it interferes with the activity in process.

Signs of Stress:

muscle stiffness	damp skin	dizziness
unusual hyperactivity	inability to move	upset stomach
vomiting	sudden coughing	unusual decrease in breathing
withdrawal of expression	anger	fatigue for no reason
fear expression	a startled blank look	faster breathing
defensiveness	white face and lips	perspiration increases
drooling		

THE ROLE OF PROBLEM-SOLVING

Problem-solving is involved in all performance tasks that are not immediately accessible. If therapeutic riding instructors and therapists intend to help their clients to become more independent through the acquisition of functional horsemanship skills, they need to assist these clients to develop good problem-solving abilities. Learning the process of problem-solving carries over to all aspects of life's skills and therefore reaches far beyond the equestrian arena. Instructors and therapists will recognize that one cannot assist the client in achieving these goals without possessing good problem-solving skills themselves. Problem-solving occurs when one is trying to accomplish a specific goal. Internal organization comes from quality sensory-integrative function which leads to concrete, sequential classification skills. Furthermore, good development at this level leads to abstract, sequential organizational skills. These abilities are the basics to the progression of developing good problem-solving skills (Knickerbocker, 1980). In addition to these basic elements, all the cognitive-related abilities which have been discussed are involved in problem-solving.

A person approaches a situation which requires him or her to make some decisions. He or she must problem-solve in order to move forward. The steps involved (Umphred, 1985) are:

- The problem must be identified
- There must be an evaluation of the situation
- The components of the problem must be analyzed
- The goal must be selected
- One must choose the best way to achieve each component
- One must select the psychological and physical means to achieve each component

PERFORMANCE

Cognitive and problem-solving skills are necessary in order for performance to occur. Additional areas which are involved include decision-making, the initiation of, carry though with, and completion of the task. For example the task of mounting might include:

Jose is sitting on the bench at the stable. He is <u>aroused</u> by a sound, he <u>attends</u> and identifies a voice. He <u>adapts</u> his behavior to locate the voice and hears the instructor ask him to mount the horse from the mounting block. He <u>interprets</u> the instructions, maintains <u>focus</u>, is <u>motivated</u> to follow the directions. He <u>shifts his focus</u>, <u>initiates</u> action and <u>perceives</u> the location of the horse and mounting block, then walks to the mounting block. Jose must <u>remember</u> how to climb the block and <u>problem-solve</u> the mounting procedure. He then must initiate the action and <u>perform</u> the task of mounting the horse.

Conclusion

Clients who come to a therapeutic riding program have a great deal to learn. Any equestrian knows that the only way to be around horses is the safe way. Safety around horses requires a lot of knowledge. There is so much to learn and the staff of a therapeutic riding program has a wonderful opportunity to teach. Some people have a natural gift of passing on knowledge to others but most people need to understand and develop these skills. Teaching a population who may have difficulty learning requires an indepth knowledge of the total process. By understanding the learning process, the instructor and his or her staff have a better understanding of how to communicate with their clients and teach them all they can about horsemanship and related skills.

References

Affolter, F. (1990). *The Use of Guiding as a Perceptual Cognitive Approach*. Course notes.

Ayres, A.J. (1979). *Sensory Integration and the Child*. Los Angeles: Western Psychological Services.

Bobath, K. (1980). *A Neurophysiological Basis for the Treatment of Cerebral Palsy*. Philadelphia: J.B. Lippincott Co.

Cruickshank, W.M. (1967). *The Brain-injured Child in Home, School, and Community*. Syracuse: Syracuse University Press.

De Quiros, J.B.; Schrager, O.L. (1978). *Neuropsychological Fundamentals in Learning Disabilities*. San Rafael: Academic Therapy Publications, Inc

Duchek, J. (1991). Cognitive Dimensions of Performance in Christiansen, C., Baum, C. *Occupational Therapy Overcoming Human Performance Deficits*. Thorofare: Charles B. Slack Inc.

Feldenkrais, M. (1981). *The Elusive Obvious*. Cupertino: Meta Publications. pp 29-37

Gilfoyle, E.M., Grady, A.P., Moore, J.C. (1981). *Children Adapt*. Thorofare: Charles B.Slack, Inc. pp 47-55, 173-193.

Grandin, T., Scariano, M.M. (1986). *Emergence: Labed Autistic*. Novato, CA: Arena Press.

Heiniger, M.C., Randolph, S.L. (1981). *Neurophysiological Concepts in Human Development*. St. Louis: The C.V. Mosby Co. 6,126, pp 177-208.

Knickerbocker, B. (1980). *A Holistic Approach to the Treatment of Learning Disabilities*. Thorofare: Charles B. Slack, Inc.

Lawther, J.D. (1968). *The Learning of Physical Skills*. Englewood Cliffs: Prentice-Hall,Inc. p 47.

Lewin, K. (1935). *A Dynamic Theory of Personality*. New York: McGraw-Hill Book Co.,Inc.

Marsh, G.E., Price, B.J., Smith, T.E.C. (1983). *Teaching Mildly Handicapped Children*. St. Louis: C.V. Mosby Co.

Pulaski, M.A.S. (1980). *Understanding Piaget*. New York: Harper & Row Publishers. pp 109-110

Ross, A.O. (1977). *Learning Disability*. New York: McGraw-Hill Book Co.

Scott, D.H. (1978). *The Hard-to-teach Child*. Baltimore: University Park Press.

Selye, H. (1976). *The Stress of Life, revised ed.* New York: McGraw-Hill Book Co.

Skinner, B.F. (1938). *The Behavior of Organisms*. New York: Appleton-Century Crofts.

Swift, S. (1985). *Centered Riding*. North Pomfret: David & Charles Inc.

Thomas, A, Chess, S., Birch, H.G. (1968). *Temperament and Behavior Disorders in Children*. New York: New York University Press.

Tjossem, T.D. (1976). *Intervention Strategies for High Risk Infants and Children*. Baltimore: University Park Press. pp 152-53

Umphred, D.A. (1985). *Neurological Rehabilitation*. St. Louis: The C.V. Mosby Co.

Webster's New World Dictionary, College Edition. (1966). Cleveland: The World Publishing Co. pp 302,758,833.

13.03   TEACHING TECHNIQUES

Barbara T. Engel MEd, OTR

To teach or instruct implies that the recipient understands the material being presented. The problem is that all instructors or teachers <u>do not teach</u> in a way from which their students <u>can learn</u>. "A teacher can fill an entire hour with talk but fail to teach anything" (Mandry, 1987).

ATMOSPHERE
Learning requires an atmosphere to induce meaningful information. The session should be relaxed without undue pressure and the instructor must develop a milieu conducive to learning. If the lesson involves more then one rider, group management must also be considered. The attitude of the teacher is very important since he or she is the key influence on the riders' attitudes and their motivation. As learners, people feel most comfortable with a person who is friendly, enthusiastic, receptive, and sincere. A teacher who shows his or her enjoyment in working with the students will create a positive attitude in them. Rewarding the students with a smile, a compliment, and creating laughter can make learning a positive experience. Be sure that the compliments are well earned for even a *child with mental limitation understands the value of an earned compliment*. It is degrading to tell someone that they have done a good job when they know this is not so--this makes one feel of less worth or that the person doing the judging feels this is the most one can do. As a teacher one can always find something that **deserves** a compliment--such as the effort of trying.

CONTENT
A person who is teaching others must show mastery of the material he or she is presenting. If the teaching material is not understood, then it cannot be presented with conviction or depth. Instructors of therapeutic riding programs might consider their students not really ready for "real" instruction and therefore might think that having in-depth understanding of the theory of riding is not necessary. Sivewright (1984) points out that **a correct beginning is absolutely necessary**. Instructors never know how far their students will progress. It is best to develop skills in the normal sequential way, making adaptation only when necessary. In order to do this, a complete understanding of the subject is necessary.

Bobby began riding when he was nine years old. Bobby has cerebral palsy and had limited speech and it was not clear how much he might understand. He needed to be supported on both sides to balance on the horse. The instructor felt it would help his self-esteem if he held the reins and pulled them back hard to stop the horse. Bobby understood well and was able to progress well. He continued to ride for many years. At twenty he could use leg and seat aids and was performing training level dressage. Bobby had one major problem. He had difficulty **unlearning** the original use of the reins--even though mentally he understood the "light" use of the reins, physically the bad habit was difficult to break. "*People with perceptual disorders make errors they often cannot reverse; they must start all over again* (Affolter 1991)."

There are now several new approaches to tackling traditional riding skills. Sally Swift's *Centered Riding* approach is priceless in teaching riders with head injuries and learning disability. Her visualization techniques and explanations provide a new dimension for one who cannot perceive his body in a normal way. Pegotty Henriques's (1987) *Balanced Riding*, Audrey Townley's (1990) *Natural Riding*, and Mary Wanless's (1987) *The Natural Rider* all provide informative material useful in teaching special populations. Of course, these books do not replace, but augment, the standard riding texts.

ORGANIZATION
A good lesson is well organized. The students should be able to focus on the task they are to master without distraction. In a therapeutic riding lesson where there can be many variables with the riders and horses, the teacher must remain flexible, ready to adjust his or her lessons for any reason. There must be continuity from lesson to lesson. This helps the students know what is to be expected. They will feel they are dealing with a familiar topic and will become confident

in the situation. Points to remember when organizing a lesson include:

- Ⓞ Starting a lesson with confidence will encourage a student to do well
- Ⓞ Begin with material from the last lesson
- Ⓞ Increase the challenge of the lesson until you can see that the students are getting too tired or becoming stressed. Lower levels of sensorimotor behavior will emerge when environmental demands (including the instructor's directions) exceed the functional capability of the student (Oetter, 1987)
- Ⓞ End the lesson with a easy and enjoyable experience
- Ⓞ Plan how to make the material meaningful to the student
- Ⓞ Review how to relate the material to the student's life experience

OBSERVATION SKILLS

When assessing the person with retardation, it is important not to put too much weight on reported intelligence levels but to observe what abilities the individual might have. Intelligence tests are known "not to be able to measure an individual's innate intellectual capacity" (Scott, 1978). (Tests are poorly developed for unique disabilities and frequently one finds that a person may have a great deal more potential than was first expected.) Observe what the person can do in various situations. Notice how this person learns best? Visually? By listening? By experience? A combination of which techniques? At what levels does the individual function in each task?

INSTRUCTOR-STUDENT TEAM

Students need to be fully involved in their learning process and in all aspects of their lesson. Therapeutic riding provides a pleasurable environment which offers full involvement on some if not all levels of the lesson. How much involvement depends on the ability and age of the rider; and *the skill, imagination, and adaptation of the instructor*. Adult riders can generally tell you what they want out of the riding experience. They should be encouraged to take part in all aspects of grooming, tacking and planning their horse experience. A teaching relationship should involve team work--the teacher, the student working together. A teacher-student relationship should contain: openness, caring, interdependence, and separateness.

COMMUNICATION

Communication skills between learner and teacher require a link between the two. Communication can involve "talking by means of speech, body language, demonstration, sign language, diagrams, and pictures". The most appropriate kind of communication should be used for a specific situation. Listening is critical in the facilitation of learning. The student must listen to the instructor or helper to be able to follow through on the task. But the instructor must also listen to the student in order to communicate effectively. MAKE SURE WHAT YOU HEAR IS WHAT THE STUDENT MEANT TO SAY. Does the non-verbal language match the words (see section 13.04)? Recognize when the student is bored, turned off, feels put down, disturbed, or misunderstood. **Remember that communication goes from the teacher to the learner; from the learner to the teacher.** Teaching groups of various ages require some differences in approach but the basic principles involved are the same.

METHODS TO ENHANCE LEARNING:

- Ⓞ Help your students learn-to learn
- Ⓞ Challenge the student. If your instructions are below the level of your student's ability, you will not arouse his or her. If the instructions are above his or her level of understanding, the instructor will lose the interest of her rider.
- Ⓞ Relate your teaching to something meaningful to the student
- Ⓞ Use props which aid learning. Dressage letters are aids in developing accurate schooling exercises. With young or retarded students, attach words to the letters or use symbols instead of letters
- Ⓞ Help the student to physically experience the learning process
- Ⓞ Begin with just one or two directions. Begin with a simple principal and use it to build on. Add another direction when one or two can be accomplished. Use pictures to demonstrate. Use toy horses, riders and other objects to show your students what you want them to do and have them show what they are to do. Have the students handle the objects as much as they can. Tactile learning is more effective than just visual learning for many

- Make a contract with a student. For example: Janet decides that she can remember to go through the cones, make a circle at the end, then walk along the rail and stop at "A". She feels that this contract is worth three tokens. If she completes the task without any errors, she receives three tokens. If she makes an error she receives none
- The **effective use of stress** is an important part of instruction
- Set a climate to enhance learning and promote success

TIMING OF INSTRUCTION

It is important to understand the **right time** to give instructions to the students, volunteers and to the staff. For instance:

- When a leader is hurrying to get the horses ready for a lesson, it is not the time to instruct him in handling a rider. The leader's attention is on his task and the rider information may not be completely understood
- When a group of riders is coming into the arena, allow them time to warm up and develop their balance. Instructions can be better understood when the group is warmed up and ready for the next task
- Linda is having a private lesson. She is having difficulty with her balance because of spasms. Is this the time for the instructor to request her to do schooling figures?
- Susie has just learned that her aunt has died. Is this the best time to tell her that her reports must be in tomorrow?

In communication, it is necessary that the person with whom one is communicating is receptive and attending to the message. One may ask if this is the proper time for this message or would it be better received at another time The more sensitive the information, the more critical it is to present it "at the right time."

References

Affolter, F. (1990). *The Use of Guiding as a Perceptual Cognitive Approach*. Course notes.
Affolter, F. (1991). *Perception, Interaction and Language*. New York: Springer-Verlag
Ayres, A.J. (1979). *Sensory Integration and the Child*. Los Angeles: Western Psychological Services.
Bobath, K. (1980). *A Neurophysiological Basis for the Treatment of Cerebral Palsy*. Philadelphia: J.B. Lippincott Co.
Feldenkrais, M. (1981). *The Elusive Obvious*. Cupertino: Meta Publications. pp 29-37
Gilfoyle, E.M., Grady, A.P., Moore, J.C. (1981). *Children Adapt*. Thorofare: Charles B. Slack, Inc.
Heiniger, M.C. (1981). *Neurophysiological Concepts in Human Development*. St. Louis: The C.V. Mosby Co. pp 6,216.
Henriques, P. (1987). *Balanced Riding*. Gaithersburg: Half Halt Press.
Kephart, N.C. (1971). *The Slow Learner in the Classroom*. Columbus: Charles E. Merrill Publishing Co.
Lawther, J.D. (1968). *The Learning of Physical Skills*. Englewood Cliffs: Prentice-Hall, Inc. pp 47.
Mandry, A. (1987). *Effective Teaching*. Saratoga: R&E Publishers.
March, G.E., Price, B.J., Smith, T.E.C. (1983). *Teaching Mildly Handicapped Children*. St. Louis: C.V. Mosby Co.
Oetter, P. (1987). *Sensory integration course notes*. University of New Mexico.
Pulaski,M.A.S. (1980). *Understanding Piaget*. New York: Harper & Row Publishers. pp 109-110
De Quiros, J.B.; Schrager, O.L. (1978). *Neuropsychological Fundamentals in Learning Disabilities*. San Rafael:Academic Therapy
Ross, A.O. (1977). *Learning Disability* New york: McGraw-Hill Book Co.
Scott, D.H. (1978). *The Hard-to-teach Child*. Baltimore: University Park Press.
Selye, H. (1976). *The Stress of Life, revised ed*. New York: McGraw-Hill Book Co.
Schrager, O.L. (1982). *Vestibular-Proprioceptive Syndromes and Other Language/Learning Disorders*. Seminar notes.
Sivewright, M. (1984). *Thinking Riding*. London: J.A. Allen.
Swift.S. (1985). *Centered Riding*. North Pomfret: David & Charles.
Townley, A. (1990). *Natural Riding*: Millwood: Breakthrough Publications.
Wanless, M. (1987). *The Natural Rider*. New York: Summit Books.

13.04 SPEAKING VOLUMES WITHOUT SAYING A WORD

Susan F. Tucker

Nonverbal messages are important and often more believable than verbal communication. (Knapp 1980) Nonverbal communication cannot be isolated from the total communication process, but it is important that we look at it in relation to our work with a challenged population.

Much nonverbal communication goes on at a subconscious level. When interacting with the disabled, these patterns are sometimes violated, causing misunderstanding. Just being aware of the problem can often help us see the messages we are sending and receiving from a different perspective. Obviously, we can't address every situation, but let's consider these seven characteristics and see how they might be affected in interactions with a disabled person.

Knapp lists the following classifications of nonverbal communication:
1. *Kinesics or body motion* typically includes gestures, movements of the body parts, facial expressions, eye behavior and posture.
2. *Physical characteristics* includes characteristics that remain relatively unchanged during the period of interaction such as physique, general attractiveness, body or breath odors, height, weight, hair, and skin color or tone.
3. *Haptic* or touching behavior may include stroking, hitting, holding, guiding another's movements, and other, more specific instances.
4. *Paralanguage* deals with how something is said and not what is said. It considers voice qualities such as pitch, tempo, and control of the voice as well as vocalizers which are sounds other than words.
5. *Proxemics* is the study of our use and perception of personal space.
6. *Artifacts* includes the manipulation of objects with the interacting persons that may act as nonverbal stimuli. These include the use of clothes, glasses, and the whole repertoire of "beauty" aids.
7. *Environmental factors* concern those elements that impinge on the human relationship, but are not directly part of it. These include architectural designs, furniture, lighting, smells, colors, temperature, and additional sounds.

KINESICS
Kinesics is very important in the riding arena. We can tell that an activity is too difficult when the riders "fall apart" or their arms and legs draw up. Self-stimulation also falls into this category. "Stimming" can be as mild as thumb-sucking or rocking or self-abusive like biting or hitting oneself. One will want to identify positive actions on the horse that can disrupt and hopefully help break the pattern of this behavior.

Watch facial expressions to help determine if the instructions have been understood or if the student is uncomfortable. Some riders can express themselves only through facial expressions. Eye contact with autistic riders can give clues as to whether the instructions are getting through to them. However, one should not feel rejected if eye contact can not be obtained. One could be reacting to the subconscious expectation (i.e., eye contact equals paying attention) and not allowing for the disability. The lack of eye contact with a person who is wheelchair-bound can also be misinterpreted. What may be interpreted as a lack of interest may simply be the fact that the person cannot hold his or her head up high enough to look at you. Or, he or she needs to lean back in order to raise his head, which might be unconsciously interpreted as pulling away or rejection.

Kinesics are equally important in the messages one sends. Be theatrical with your instructions. This gets your point across better and makes enthusiasm contagious. Do not let your body say, "I'm bored to tears," while your words are saying the opposite. You will defeat your whole purpose. Riders are often experts at reading approval and rejection on the faces around them, so prepare for an encounter with a particularly disfigured person.

PHYSICAL CHARACTERISTICS

One tends to react more positively to people perceived as attractive. One also tends to view them as more intelligent and capable. Beware of these preconceptions since they may be anything but the truth, especially in our context. It is also important to train ourselves to be unaffected by unusual or unpleasant odors. (You can do it--you tolerate or even enjoy the smell of the stable, don't you? The uninitiated often find it repugnant).

HAPTICS

Touching behavior (haptics) is very important in therapeutic riding. The staff and helpers touch the riders frequently to assist them. Some riders are tactilely defensive, which means they find it unpleasant to touch or be touched. Think of how it would feel if spiders, snakes or leeches crawled all over "your" body; that is what touching may be like for some riders. Other riders will be more accepting of being handled if their permission is first asked. Firm touches are more comfortable than soft, tickling ones. The same is true when getting the students to feel the horses. Hair, especially when barely felt, is not as pleasant as something smooth like leather or a bareback pad. Work into it gradually.

Be very conscious of appropriate touching with children who have been physically and/or sexually abused. This can also be a red flag if a dramatic response is received from a child who has not been reported as having been abused. In many states, sexual abuse must be reported to the authorities.

PARALANGUAGE

Just as the cries and gurgles of babies can be deciphered, one can often interpret the paralanguage of nonverbal riders, Also be aware of changes in pitch or tempo in the speech patterns of all of the riders--increases may signal stress.

Listen for breathing patterns in speaking and singing. A child sitting slumped over may have to breathe after every other word, but when correct posture is achieved, breathing control may increase dramatically. Singing games are great for improving breath control and volume.

One's own paralanguage can have a significant impact on others. Enthusiasm and confidence can be conveyed as well as warning with proper use of the voice. A frightened or angry person can be calmed by consciously lowering the pitch, tempo and volume of your voice. As the voice gets lower and slower, it has a rather mesmerizing affect on everyone around. This is also important to remember, if possible, in case of an emergency.

PROXEMICS

The territoriality that one establishes in everyday life is often abandoned when coming to the riding center. Some people are uncomfortable when someone invades "their space," but are able to forget about it when the demands of a difficult mounting procedure or need for other assistance requires physical closeness. Be aware that closeness may be overwhelming for both new riders and volunteers. The seasoned riders may be accustomed to these activities, but it can be a very difficult adjustment for someone who is just beginning to work with persons with disabilities.

Alert the volunteers to the fact that a person's wheelchair is within "his" or "her" personal space. Another person has no more right to lean on the chair than he or she would to lean on the legs or shoulders of an "able-bodied" acquaintance.

ARTIFACTS

Artifacts refers to how one is groomed and dressed, speaks to the students, parents, and any observers. Is the person a professional therapeutic riding instructor, or is he giving pony rides to the poor little kids? Look the part in neat, clean, suitable attire without any dangling jewelry or excessive makeup. It is better to save the cologne for other occasions since some of the riders (and horses) may be allergic to it, or sometimes horses are attracted by it. Long fingernails are lovely, but they are a detriment when it comes to tightening a cinch; a real hazard during mounting and dismounting procedures. Long hair is beautiful, too, but tie it back so it does not get in the way.

ENVIRONMENTAL FACTORS

Look around. Does the environment of the center give a welcome to the rider with a disability? Are all of the buildings wheelchair accessible? Is the bathroom accessible too? Can the riders get to the mounting ramp without going through a mud hole or over a rocky area that shakes their fillings out? Ask the riders who are wheelchair-bound to give you a critique from time to time. There <u>is</u> no way one can <u>be aware</u> of every detail unless one <u>lives</u> in a chair or asks someone who does. Riders are usually very happy to give constructive suggestions.

Consider the cognitively impaired students. If they are asked to get equipment or to tack their own horses, is everything identified in ways that will help them succeed? Is it possible in the set-up to color code all the items for one horse as well as labelling with names? Or could each saddle and bridle be numbered?

Is the center neat, clean and well-organized? A parent may well be concerned about the quality of the services if there is trash lying around, a heap of dirty tack in the corner, and the helmets are thrown in an old cardboard box with an accumulation of dried mud and straw. Before a prospective client ever meets the instructor, he or she will already have formed an opinion of him or her just by pulling into the driveway. Make sure it is a positive one.

Each area of nonverbal communication is worthy of a study in itself, but hopefully the instructor will be aware of all the messages that are being given and are getting between the lines.

LISTEN TO THE WHOLE PERSON, NOT JUST THE WORDS.

Reference
Knapp, M.L. (1980). *Essentials of Nonverbal Communication*. New York: Holt, Rinehart and Winston. 21.

14. THE INSTRUCTOR

14.01 TEN COMMANDMENTS OF THERAPEUTIC RIDING*

a message from

Jean M. Tebay, MS

As many of you already know, I teach therapeutic riding training courses from time to time. The most recent one I taught was a 4-H sponsored course in Frederick County, Maryland. At the end of our 16 weeks together, I wanted to leave the group with some thoughts to meditate on that might be useful to them at a future time. So I wrote a set of ten commandments, and I would like to share them with you today, hoping that you might find them useful too.

1. Practice Safety First!

This is the most important aspect of any riding-for-the-disabled program, I think. And it does not really matter if you are the instructor, the organizer, a side-walker, a horse-leader--YOU are a member of the safety patrol. Review safety issues from the time the rider arrives until the time that he leaves. Think about everything that he does while he is with you. Not only safety around the horses, but--for example--in the parking lot, in the bathroom, on the ramp or mounting block. Organize a safety search from time to time and walk around the stables looking in every corner for possible problems. Train everyone to be on the lookout!

2. Do No Harm To Any Rider.

All of our disabled riders have the opportunity, when they are with us, to make great strides in their development --physically, psychologically, educationally, and socially. Sometimes we get so involved in helping them take these strides that we lose sight of the small things we might be doing to cause them harm rather than do good. A leg moved incorrectly while mounting. An ill-fitting hard hat causing postural malalignment. Or a volunteer's hand placed incorrectly on a rider's waist belt, pulling the rider off-center. When we do harm, we negate the very therapeutic effect we are working so hard to achieve.

3. Be Professional.

"You do what?" That is a reaction we have all gotten from time to time when we talk about our work. "Therapeutic writing, that must be like art therapy," someone will say. "No, therapeutic **riding** not **writing**." "oh," comes the reply, "Tell me about that. It sounds dangerous." Well, in this business looking and acting like a professional is very important. If you go to a hospital and see a nurse in uniform you unconsciously believe that she is trained to help you. So in the riding setting you need to get the same confidence from your students, their parents, whoever comes to observe you. You want the public to believe what you already know--that it is OK to put disabled people on horseback. If each of us looks the part and acts the part, we have taken a big step toward helping to make therapeutic riding a viable activity. Be PROFESSIONAL.

4. Tune into Your Gut.

Often we know in our guts before we realize in our heads that something is amiss. Something is not going the way we want, and our stomachs are our barometers. Learn to listen to your gut, and to read the signs that your body sends to tell you when you are on shaky ground. Maybe the rider has a disability with which you are not completely familiar, and he is exhibiting odd signs that are puzzling to you and you don't know quite what to do. When you are not comfortable with what is going on, STOP. Take a deep breath. Take a reading of the situation. Proceed on a revised course. You will know things are right when your stomach relaxes again.

5. Recognize Your Strengths and Weaknesses.

All of us who are involved in therapeutic riding wish we knew everything we need to know. Of course to know all of the horsemanship, all of the medical, all of the psychological, all of the educational, and all of the organizational information required to do this job well would require what I call a magnificent miracle. But what are YOUR strengths? We all have areas of expertise, and it is good to know exactly what these are. Similarly, we all have areas where we lack experience. To evaluate yourself realistically is one of the important tasks of each of us involved in therapeutic riding. What do you bring to the therapeutic riding team? Know your strengths, know your weaknesses.

6. Plan for Surprises.

Every therapeutic riding session brings us an unexpected surprise. The relied-on volunteer that cannot come one day. The school bus that arrives with 12 instead of the usual 6 riders. A needed pony that throws a shoe during warm up. Or a rider that has a behavioral problem because of an unexpected medication reaction. Each surprise means quick thinking. Some surprises test our mettle to the limit. In order to give our best to our students, learn to anticipate what might happen, and like a Boy Scout, "Be Prepared". Be Creative. Plan ahead for surprises.

7. Continue Your Education.

None of us is so knowledgeable or so experienced that we know and understand it all. But if the ultimate goal of a therapeutic riding program is to provide that best possible environment for our students, and to ensure the best possible results, then for each of us to continue our own growth and development is one key to reaching the goals we have set for our students. Whether it is attending a regional meeting, taking a continuing education course, learning "basic sign" or maybe visiting another therapeutic riding program to see how they do it--we should all make a commitment to continually seek growth and development.

8. Keep Your Ego Out Of It.

All of us from time to time find ourselves in the situation of vying for the student's attention. We want to be the one to make the difference. We want to find the key to unlock the door for a disabled rider. But, in therapeutic riding, one of the great benefits is the team working together. No one ego standing alone, but rather the team as a whole working together to provide the answer. The horse, the leader, the side walkers, the instructor, the therapist --and of course, the student. Let go of YOUR ego. Pledge to be a member of the team.

9. Enjoy, Have Fun.

There are those days in therapeutic riding when what could go wrong, does go wrong. And when it seems like all of the program tasks, the dirty work, is falling on your shoulders, and yours alone. You wonder if you are suffering from burn-out, and you ask yourself what are you doing in this crazy business anyway. Then you go out in the ring with the riders, and you remember. It is the fun and the joy out there. The creativity. How many different things can students do at the walk? A drill ride, ride to music, a simple dressage test, a trail class, an obstacle course, a map ride, a blind-fold ride, no saddles today, no bridles today, cannot use your voice today. Creativity is a major ingredient of fun and enjoyment. And when you enjoy what you're doing, when you have fun, it is catching. Everyone else around you will too. And we all do BETTER when we enjoy ourselves.

10. Honor The Horse.

Horses are the backbone of our work and the reason for our success. So, I would like to close my talk for today with a short verse to honor our most valued colleague:

The Horse

Oh horse you are a wondrous thing,
No buttons to push, no engine that pings.
You start yourself, no clutch to slip,
No dead battery, no gears to strip.
No license buying every year,
With plates to screw on front and rear.
No gas fumes polluting each day,
Taking the joys of nature away.
No speed cops dashing into view,
Writing a ticket out to you.

Your super-treads all seem OK,
And hoofpick in hand, they should stay that way.
Your spark plugs never miss and fuss,
Your motor never makes us cuss,
Your frame is good for many a mile,
Your body never outdates its style.
Your needs are few, and happily met,
We honor you, we're in your debt!
You serve us well, as our riders you carry,
Making instructors, volunteers - the whole team merry.

Yes, Horse, you are a wondrous thing,
Teacher--Therapist--Friend,
your praises we sing!

Jean M. Tebay

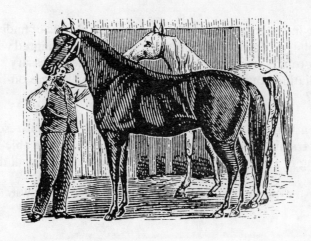

283

Virginia H. Martin, BS

Twenty years ago people who wished to teach persons with disabilities to ride had very little to go on except common sense and the desire to help the person with a disability to enjoy the pleasure of the horse. Some assistance came from the **Riding for the Disabled Association*** in England in the form of pamphlets on special equipment and Do's and Don'ts for volunteers. These <u>were</u> very helpful since they made one realize you were not alone in an activity that everyone said could not be done. *My, how times have changed!*

In the last decade of this century, the U.S. has more than 450 programs recognized by the North American Riding for the Handicapped Association (NARHA), and many other unaffiliated units. Today the field of riding for the disabled encompasses three distinct areas: *medical (health care), educational, and sports*. Each area requires specific methods of teaching or instructing.

The field is so much more sophisticated. We are now aware of the tremendous importance of trained therapists (both occupational and physical) to supervise the **"Equine-Assisted Therapy"** section of our programs (encompassing hippotherapy, developmental riding therapy, riding therapy;) and the inclusion of psychiatrists, psychologists and special education teachers when appropriate in our "remedial" programs and our competitive sports. What about "the instructor?" How does he or she fit in?

The <u>instructor</u> is <u>very</u> important and might be considered the glue that holds the whole operation together! First, and foremost, the instructor must be a real <u>teacher</u>. He or she must be able to impart knowledge or skill to his or her students through words, touch and example. In other words, he or she must have a wide vocabulary to explain one action in many different ways; must be able to assist in positioning the rider through his or her fingers; and, must be able to demonstrate on the horse what he or she wishes the rider to comprehend. Not every <u>fine</u> rider is able to be a <u>real</u> teacher! One has to have the <u>desire</u> to teach, combined with a good eye and a light touch.

Also, the instructor must be wise, patient, knowledgeable of horse abilities and client/rider disabilities so he or she can advise all those professionals mentioned above how the horse/rider team will fit together. (Frequently, the outside professionals do not know about horsemanship and horsemastership and the instructor must be able to advise accordingly). A top-flight therapeutic riding instructor must be able to run the barn, train the horses, recruit and train multitudinous volunteers, and assist diplomatically in solving all the problems of the program! A well-versed instructor is not only <u>indispensable</u> to the program, but also can be the <u>strength</u> of the program.

Now, one begins to see the complexity in the capacity titled "*Chief Therapeutic Riding Instructor*"! This is no longer a job for just any old riding instructor. One has to <u>earn</u> the title through years of experience in the riding arena and the classroom.

The need for therapeutic riding instructors is here today, as are the problems of finding and training suitable candidates. There are very few schools, colleges, universities, or training centers acquainted with the needs of therapeutic riding instructors. Consequently, there are few courses set up to handle the necessary subject matter. Some colleges and universities are presently initiating courses in the field and more will come on-line as the field grows. What does an interested person do **now**?

There are many routes, depending upon one's circumstances: age, financial resources, area of strongest interest, college degree, availability of training sources, number of years teaching the able-bodied, in what mode and at what level, number of years assisting in a therapeutic riding program working with all the disabilities. One does not have

---

* Riding for the Disabled Association. Avenue R, National Agricultural Centre, Kenilworth, Warwickshire CV8 2LY, Great Britian.

to be an Olympic rider but should be able to ride at a relatively decent level. Since, at the national and international competitive level for disabled riders, dressage and jumping are involved, future chief instructors should have participated in these events to some degree. It is much easier to teach the subject if you have experienced it. It is also easier if the rules are known, so join the American Horse Show Association (AHSA) and get the rule book (competitions for the disabled are based on AHSA rules). Keep up-to-date on all information on clinics, workshops, continuing education courses and competitions in the field of therapeutic riding.

In the United States there are thousands of young men and women who, through their teen-aged years, have become superb riders in the fields of dressage, eventing and showing. For a few of them a goal of becoming a "Chief Riding Instructor" (head riding instructor) for a therapeutic riding program might be the perfect choice. The word few is used on purpose since many of these young riders might not have the other required qualities. Those who do would be able to combine their equine involvement and expertise with a college education in the area of their choice, such as psychology, physical or occupational therapy, special education, adaptive physical education, liberal arts or equine studies.

Then there are those who are no longer teenagers or college-bound, whose life experiences may count more than college credits. In other words, the old cliche "experience is the best teacher" may be applicable. These candidates may have been Sally Swift-ed, Tellington-Jones TTEAM-ed, and Lorna Faraldi Alexander Method-ed; they may have taught for years, both able-bodied and disabled; have wonderful vocabularies, excellent brains and good organization skills; they may be chock full of confidence and quite unflappable; all super qualities for a top-flight riding instructor. Best of all, they may be good with people! Sometimes younger instructors have not lived long enough or had enough life experience to understand the complexities of interacting personalities, whether able-bodied or disabled.

In effect, what the above says is that there are many ways of putting together the qualities of the chief riding instructor depending upon where you are in life. There are certain basics that must be part of the picture: teaching ability, ability and knowledge of horses, ability with people, knowledge of disabilities, organizational skills, attendance to safety and enjoyment of work to benefit others. In a country of well over 240,000,000 people one can always find those who have arrived by different routes.

As one can see, the field of riding for the disabled has evolved into a team effort, which is as it should be, since no one person can know everything about medical problems, psychological problems, learning problems; equine conformational differences, temperamental differences, and so forth. In equine-assisted therapy, the therapist is in charge and will ask the instructor for advice or will advise the instructor as to the plan of action. In the area of riding skills, the instructor is in charge and the psychologists and special education teachers may advise. We instructors must remember our constituency--the disabled of the world--will best be served by the team effort of caring professionals and their ability to communicate with one another.

14.03   THE ROLE OF THE THERAPEUTIC RIDING INSTRUCTOR

Margaret L. Galloway, MS, BHSAI

The role of the instructor in a therapeutic riding program is varied and crucial. The therapeutic riding instructor is in charge of:

1. Horse management
2. Developing the instructional team
3. Providing education and development
4. Organizing the instructional program
5. Implementing a riding program
6. Selecting and maintaining equipment
7. Overseeing the center facility
8. Interacting with the center administration

Horse management includes a wide variety of duties. Screening and evaluating potential horses, according to the criteria of a therapeutic riding program, is one aspect of the instructor's management responsibilities. Horses should be monitored for unusual behavior, because anything out of the ordinary is a sign of potential health problems. The instructor must have a familiarity with each horse's habits; knowing the daily norm will allow any deviation to be noticed right away. Any unsoundness or ailments must be noted and acted upon so that the horse's condition is not aggravated and the rider is not at risk with the horse stumbling while riding. The health and maintenance of the horses are extremely important, and so the instructor maintains constant contact with the barn manager. In connection with the maintenance of the horses, he or she must maintain a sound dietary program, veterinary and farrier schedule and records. For emergencies, an equine first aid kit must be kept well stocked and available. Horses must be trained and schooled, while keeping equine stress to a minimum; in other words, the horses must not be under - or overworked, and boredom levels must be monitored.

Developing the instructional team is an important role of the therapeutic riding instructor. He or she will work with all members of the staff, comprised of the volunteers, the professionals, and the office staff. The members of the staff who are involved in teaching students make up the instructional team. The instructional team in a therapeutic riding program consists of the instructor, the leader, and sidewalker. The physical and occupational therapist, special educator, adapted physical education teacher, and psychologist may be consultants to the instructional team or may be active participants. The physical and/or occupational therapist treats clients with physical, developmental and/or emotional disorders--to increase specific areas of physical or cognitive function to improve activities of daily living. The adapted physical education teacher uses therapeutic horseback riding to strengthen the muscles of disabled students and improve their coordination. Special educators may design games and exercises that fit in with the student's school program. The psychologist may work with individuals with behavioral problems, acts as consultant to the instructor, or provide appropriate counseling or intervention to clients and staff. The instructor must formulate instructional team duties and integrate the program. Volunteers must also be recruited and made a part of the program. All staff must be rewarded in some way. As an example, the instructor (or program board) could offer a trophy at the end of the year for the team member who spends the most hours working with students.

Continued education and development are important parts of the leadership role of the chief instructor. All members of the team,--educators, therapists, and instructors--can hold inservice sessions to train each other. Members should also take part in educating the community. By providing continued educational experiences and attending clinics and courses, the instructor builds an educated therapeutic riding team. By frequently evaluating the team status, the instructor is able to help the group prevent team burnout by enrichment and reward.

Organizing the therapeutic riding instructional program is a crucial aspect of the instructor's responsibilities, because the success of the center depends upon the strength of the instructional program. The therapeutic riding instructional program focuses on the students' specific needs. The instructor processes student applications and requests evaluations from consultants. The student is then matched with a horse and with proper equipment, and is assigned to the appropriate team. The instructor helps the student define goals and objectives. He or she also is responsible for overseeing the participation of specialists in the multi-disciplinary teams. With the input of the team, the instructor establishes the developmental lesson plans that form the instructional program. The developmental lesson plan is made up of a progressive series of objectives, beginning with simple skills and proceeding to more complex skills. The instructor must create the instructional environment by determining which relevant tools or educational aids are needed.

Implementing the instructional riding program follows the organization of the program, and this area also requires constant attention to detail. The instructor conducts initial assessments of all students. He or she also develops a rapport with the students during their orientation to the stable grounds and instructs them in safety procedures. This rapport continues throughout their relationship.

The riding instructor begins the teaching process by evaluating the student's preliminary riding skills. He or she takes into consideration the strengths and needs of the student. An occupational or physical therapy consultant with knowledge of neurological disorders may perform an evaluation with persons who have developmental disorders, physical disabilities, or riders with other problems. Throughout the teaching process, the instructor makes sure that the lessons ensure the student's safety.

Beginning with the most basic skills and building to more complex skills, the instructor teaches equestrian techniques by providing challenging and experimental lessons and games. He or she emphasizes correct horsemanship from the very beginning. The student also learns from the horse's actions and reactions and should be trained in the meaning of horse communication. The horse acts as a teacher and the bond between student and animal is strengthened.

The instructor consults with the therapist to <u>determine student and equine equipment needs</u>. The therapy consultant or instructor selects appropriate adaptive equipment and also evaluates donated equipment. All tack and equipment must fit and be in good condition, in order to prevent accidents. *In order to ensure the tack and equipment's good condition, the tack must be cleaned and cared for on a regular basis.* The instructor educates the team in the proper use, maintenance, and care of equipment. Finally, the instructor makes sure that all equipment fits the horse and student rider. *All tack and equipment must be appropriate for each student.*

The instructor should have a pleasant general demeanor and be enthusiastic and positive in his or her associations with students and staff. He or she should be self-confident; should have the power of concentration, with a voice that carries and is pleasant; and must provide an environment that is conducive to enjoyment and learning. At all times, the instructor must be calm, even in stressful situations.

Administrative Duties of Instructors
The instructor's responsibilities may include a variety of administrative duties. The instructor must have a clear understanding of the structure of the organization. When he or she acts as executive director in addition to instructor, he or she may serve as a liaison between the board or governing group and the instructional program and participates in program planning and oversees student placement, scheduling, and class size. On the financial side, the instructor is involved in the budget process and may review operating center insurance. He or she may assist in fund-raising efforts, publicity, and public relations. The riding instructor participates in organizational accrediting process. He or she also monitors compliance with federal, state, and local regulations. The instructor participates in the development and implementation of emergency procedures and also helps develop enrollment and evaluation forms, surveys, and questionnaires.

Overseeing the operating center facility is an integral part of effective, safe instruction. The instructor emphasizes safety in operating the facility. The riding school should be assessed by the instructor in terms of identifying restricted areas and accessibility. The instructor must ensure a safe instructional environment which includes safe mounting areas and proper equipment. The facility requires on-site telephone access and easily accessible human and horse first aid kits, in a secured location. Finally, the instructor must conduct an ongoing evaluation of the riding school to ensure continued safety.

Duty to Keep Informed

A working knowledge of disabilities and equine proficiency can be expanded through continuing education. Instructors should review current literature, maintain professional memberships, pursue instructor certification and network with those in national, regional, state and local groups. An instructor must also review organizational procedures and policies in keeping with an updated profile. The instructor should keep his or her resume current.

Professional Ethics and Expertise

The instructor is responsible for maintaining professional, personal ethics, and expertise. A foremost concern of anybody working in the field is to support ethical practices for both human and animal participants. It is the instructor's responsibilities to carry out all local, state and national regulations as they apply to therapeutic riding. Safety requires that an instructor maintain current First Aid and CPR certification. A self-evaluation and peer review should be ongoing.

In summary, the therapeutic riding instructor must be capable of many widely diverse duties. He or she may perform these diverse duties or delegate them to others. Nevertheless, he or she must be knowledgeable in carrying out these skills. From organization to safety, to meeting the students' needs, the riding instructor's role is of primary importance.

Reference

Rowley, L.L. (1991). The Therapeutic Riding Instructor Profile. Denver: *North American Riding for the Handicapped Association*. P.O. Box 33150, Denver, CO 80233.

14.04 A THERAPEUTIC RIDING INSTRUCTOR'S CHECKLIST

Jean M. Tebay, MS

This checklist was developed as a self-study tool for therapeutic riding instructors. If you have honestly answered YES or USUALLY to each item on the checklist, your therapeutic riding instructor's IQ is quite high. If there are items on the checklist that you have marked NO, these items may identify areas for further development as you gain experience in this profession. Enjoy reviewing this checklist from time to time, in order to refresh your memory about your strengths as a therapeutic riding instructor, as well as those areas needing further attention. Add some of your own items to the checklist in order to tailor it just for you.

Circle Y = Yes, often
Circle U = Yes, usually
Circle N = No, not very

1. I like children and adults, and I have a keen desire to help others.	Y	U	N
2. I have an alert, enthusiastic personality.	Y	U	N
3. I am self-confident and self-assured. People look to me for answers.	Y	U	N
4. I am an observant person. I usually see things others do not.	Y	U	N
5. I am a good communicator. Others listen when I talk.	Y	U	N
6. I am well-groomed. I present a neat, tidy appearance.	Y	U	N
7. I am calm, cool and collected. It takes a lot to get me ruffled.	Y	U	N
8. I like to analyze myself, and identify areas where I can improve.	Y	U	N
9. I am self-disciplined. I like to make a plan and carry it out in an organized fashion.	Y	U	N
10. I like to be prepared. "Winging it" is not my style.	Y	U	N
11. I love animals, and am concerned about their health and general welfare.	Y	U	N
12. I am detail-oriented. I enjoy figuring out how something works, step-by-step.	Y	U	N
13. When I don't know something, I like to search until I've got the answer.	Y	U	N
14. In my work, I like to encourage others to give me feedback about their ideas and concerns.	Y	U	N
15. I like to make things right. Problems are there to be solved, and I like solutions.	Y	U	N
16.			
17.			
18.			
19.			
20.			

Jean Tebay 2/1990

14.05 THERAPEUTIC RIDING INSTRUCTOR TEACHING EVALUATION FORM

Jean M. Tebay, MS

KEY WORDS
RIDING INSTRUCTOR TOOL

As therapeutic riding instructors, upgrading our teaching skills is always important to improve our own professionalism. The evaluation form on page 275 is intended for use by instructors to improve their teaching ability. A therapeutic riding instructor might invite a colleague to visit his or her program for a day, including watching a lesson. The colleague would then be given this evaluation form to use for comments and observations made during that lesson. Other evaluations might include teachers who come with school students to the therapeutic riding lesson, or adjunct professionals who participate when the team approach in therapeutic riding is used. Peer evaluation is an excellent method to gain insight into one's own performance.

In addition to peer evaluation, this form might also be used by the director of a therapeutic riding program to conduct periodic assessment of the therapeutic riding instructor or instructors employed at the operating center. When used in this way, it is helpful to review the written comments and observations with the instructor being evaluated in a one-on-one situation. This will give the instructor a chance to interact with the evaluator for more in-depth understanding of the written information given, and for the opportunity to participate in a dialogue about future performance, education, and other professional development opportunities.

THERAPEUTIC RIDING INSTRUCTOR TEACHING EVALUATION FORM

Name of Instructor: _____ Date: _____

Scoring: Judge each area in the space provided, using a number score, where 1 = unacceptable, progressing to 10 = outstanding.
Besides the number, use the space for any comments you may have.

	Score	Comment
1. Appearance/dress		
2. Voice: quality, audibility, pitch, diction, variability		
3. General teaching attitude/ability		
4. Communication with volunteers: verbal............... non-verbal........		
5. Communication with students: verbal............... non-verbal........		
6. Understanding and use of horses		
7. Understanding and use of special equipment		
8. Organization of lesson: mounting............... warm-up............... exercises................ lesson..................... game/activity.......... cool down............... dismounting...........		
9. Lesson material: knowledge.............. organization........... presentation...........		
10. Overall professionalism		

Teaching Strength: _____

Areas needing improvement: _____

Comments: _____

Safety Issues: _____

Jean Tebay 2/1990

14.06 THE INSTRUCTOR/THERAPIST TREATMENT TEAM

Molly Lingua, LPT

As *therapeutic riding* has grown into a highly developed form of therapy for persons with disabilities, professionals from many specialties are now involved with the client's/rider's program. These professionals include physical and occupational therapists, speech/language pathologists, and psychologists, each bringing their area of expertise to the therapeutic riding program. Each must work with the therapeutic riding instructor to ensure a safe and comprehensive program. It is important to examine and develop ways in which an instructor/therapist treatment team can be effective.

The cooperation required is not as difficult or as overwhelming as it may seem. One often overlooks the fact that although the therapist and instructor may speak different languages, they see similar things. For example, a therapist talks about "postural alignment" while the instructor refers to "conformation." The instructor talks about a horse "being lame", and a therapist discusses its "gait deviations." Another key similarity is that both are interested in the good of the patient/rider (hereafter referred to as "client.") Both strive to uphold the credo *"Do No Harm!,"* which is so important in this litigation-happy world.

There are 5 basic ways the instructor and therapist can interact in the therapeutic riding setting:
1) TOTALLY INTEGRATED; 50/50
Here, both professionals are working with the client, either at the same time or separately. The therapist works on therapeutic goals while the instructor concentrates on riding skills. For example, after the therapist improves muscle tone and postural alignment--therapeutic goals, the instructor can work on steering (a riding goal.) As a team, the therapist works with the instructor to facilitate the success of the session, and vice versa. This type of collaboration must be carefully planned, practiced and executed so as not to bombard the client with too many, or worse, conflicting cues. In the session there may be little or no dialogue, or possibly just a pleasant exchange of ideas between the professionals. Whatever works for the two of them suffices.

2) THERAPIST AS OCCASIONAL CONSULTANT
This situation is called the "program's therapist." The therapist evaluates or screens the clients prior to their first session in order to determine whether the client is an appropriate referral based on his own therapeutic judgment or criteria and the program's guidelines. It is vital to recognize that therapeutic riding is not for everyone. The therapist then assists the instructor in selection of the horse, equipment and appropriate class for the client. During the first session, the therapist assists the instructor on proper mounting, "warm-up" exercises, activities, and dismounting to ensure a safe, FUN and therapeutic ride. Thereafter, the therapist is consulted as needed.

3) CLIENT-SPECIFIC THERAPIST
In this type of interaction, the therapist comes to the program with the client(s) from his or her institutional setting. He or she knows the client(s) well, and can often assist the instructor in the challenging behavioral and/or physical issues which may arise. The therapist may stand along-side the instructor, giving guidance and feedback as needed, or may assist in side-walking a client(s). This is a perfect opportunity for the team members to intertwine their goals--improving attention span, group skills and upper extremity control. The session should be an opportunity for sharing and collaboration, rather than a chance for the therapist to retreat to the lounge for some rest and relaxation.

4) THERAPIST AS AN ADVISOR
In this situation, the therapist may be available for consultation over the telephone, sit on the program's advisory board, or consult only for particularly challenging clients. This type of interaction relies on excellent communication between the team members, even more than in other types of interactions. The therapist is usually not present at the program site. Therefore, the instructor and therapist must communicate outside of the session their needs

and concerns clearly and succinctly without misunderstanding. This interaction is typically found at the well-established therapeutic riding centers, and is not recommended for less-experienced instructors and therapists.

5) INSTRUCTOR AS CONSULTANT TO THE THERAPIST

Equine-assisted therapy has grown tremendously in recent years. Examples such as hippotherapy and developmental equine-assisted therapy have proven to health care and medical professionals just how powerful the movement of the horse can be in the treatment of disabilities. As therapists are learning of this therapeutic technique through journals, seminars, and client case studies, they are becoming anxious to participate.

Despite their enthusiasm, the therapists may not have a good, clear understanding of therapeutic riding. To provide optimal treatment for the client, the therapist must work closely with the instructor. Even someone skilled and experienced in the use of equine movement needs an instructor's expertise to ensure the success of the treatment. After all, how can one person effectively treat the client, closely monitor the horse, and supervise the side-aides at the same time?

The therapist and instructor work together on horse selection, equipment, and school figures to be used to address the client's goals. During the session, the therapist concentrates mainly on the client while the instructor concentrates on the horse and the quality of its movement. The program should be approached as a medical treatment, with the team members working closely and effectively together to provide a safe, therapeutic and fun experience for the client.

For all of the possible types of therapist/instructor treatment teams, there are a few key points to remember:

How to Find a "Good" Therapist

As more and more therapists become interested in therapeutic riding, programs increasingly have the opportunity to involve a therapist to enhance or develop the program. However, not every Polly P.T. or Oliver O.T. is right for a program. The therapist must have clinical experience treating the particular client population for that program. For example, a physical therapist with several years of sports medicine experience is not a choice for cerebral palsy clients. An occupational therapist with experience in the geriatric acute hospital care setting does not have the knowledge required to work with developmentally-delayed children. If the clients are neurologically involved, the therapist should have strong neuro-developmental technique (NDT) background. Otherwise, it may be more work than it is worth to re-educate the orthopedic therapist in neurological disabilities.

Communication

Once the therapist has been selected or has found an appropriate therapeutic riding program, the two professionals must make sure they understand each other's terminology. Although in an optimal case, the therapist would have a strong equine background and the instructor would have a background in health care, this is not always possible. The professionals must teach each other, learn from each other, and in doing so, lay the groundwork for good communication, better understanding and TEAMWORK. This sharing of knowledge can be achieved by reading books, attending courses, and observing one another.

It is very important to agree on similar terminology. When two "experts" team up, they must ensure that they understand each other's professional terms and jargon to be effective, even when it varies from region to region in states and country. The instructor/therapist treatment team is an exciting and vital part of the success of a comprehensive therapeutic riding program. The teamwork may be intense, consultatory, or sporadic depending on the program's and team members' needs. The team members should not be afraid to ask for help, for it may teach both colleagues and clients the spirit of comraderie, all aimed at the goal of using the horse in the bettering of another person's life.

Remember, two heads are better than one. . . . . . .

14.07   WORKING WITH FAMILIES AND CAREGIVERS

Christine Wiegand, MA, RN

An understanding of the family as a system is an essential component for the professional working with children. When working in a therapeutic riding program, an understanding of this approach can be very important. In fact the Education for All Handicapped Children Act, P.L. 94-142, is an attempt to insure the availability of support for children within their family system.

It is important to remember that each family is diverse and has different resources available to it. Each family is made up of individuals and subsystems that have a variety of coping abilities. Consequently by focusing on the needs of the entire family one will enhance their ability to provide for their child (or adult) and his or her special needs.

Parental and spouse adjustment can differ for fathers--mothers, husbands--wives. Current research demonstrates that "fathers show a gradual, steady, adjustment, while mothers described ups and downs with periodic crises (Damrosch, Perry, 1989)." "Health professionals find it difficult to help parents at this challenging time (Mercer, 1990)." Developing an ability to listen and be empathic is essential and genuine responses that are warm and caring help.

The goal in working with parents or caregivers then, is to help them develop the necessary competencies to obtain the best possible for themselves and the child they are involved with. Specifically, this is achieving success in developing their own strengths more fully which enables them to assist the child in accomplishing this too.

A proven approach in family work is to include the family by giving them as much information about their child and his or her condition as possible. This includes what expectations they can have about the benefits of involvement in the therapeutic riding program for their child. "Factual information that provides some hope helps parents make realistic plans (Mercer, 1990)."

It would appear that parents question themselves and all the professionals around them in an attempt to understand all aspects of their situation. This is part of the adjustment process and continues throughout their child's early years with the introduction of anything new or unfamiliar.

Parents are better able to adjust to new situations after a diagnosis is made and they understand what specific difficulties they will be dealing with. When a diagnosis is not made at birth, the parents quite possibly have their own concerns about their child's development. A diagnosis can be a confirmation of their suspicions and can place them in a position of moving ahead and doing what they feel is best for the child.

The next step to assist in resolution is to obtain a prognosis about the child's future. One result of obtaining merely limited information regarding potential is continued worry about the child's future and what to expect. The most essential assistance a family can receive is information. Clear messages regarding what improvements the parents can expect from participation in your program are very helpful. The need for certainty must be stressed to eliminate the possibility of additional disappointment being added to the family's problems. Focusing on ability, instead of a deficit orientation is helpful.

Current research identifies two of the major concerns with which families are confronted. These issues seem to be behavior management and how they will deal with the child's continued dependence. Followed by the financial burden associated with medical costs, and physical barriers in the home and environment.

What can be done as professionals to ensure the continued progress of the differently able child, including promoting caregiver involvement? First one must recognize and acknowledge that families grieve over a disabled child.

One must understand that the grief response produces shock and disorganization to the family system, and also sense the despair that is overtly or covertly evident. Also there is associated anger which can be the most difficult obstacle to confront. Such experiences all have validity for parents, spouses, or children. Each will have his own style as does each individual who works with them. This is a process in which one can become a facilitator for the parents in their personal progression to a place of acceptance and redefining the future for themselves and their child. We as professionals can be most effective if we are able to meet the caregivers-parents where they are in this process and respect them in an empathic way, in their attempts to reorganize and restructure their lives. The respect we must necessarily exhibit for these families cannot be bound by preconceived bias about socioeconomic status, race, ethnicity, or disability. It is important that as a professional, one know precisely where his own limitations are in this regard. Family members should function as their own case manager and have the professionals guide them in obtaining appropriate services. This can be accomplished by enabling them to be comfortable with the role of coordinator and evaluator of available services by increasing their confidence in their own judgment and abilities and by assisting them in being informed. By using this non-directive approach with the parents or caregivers, one lays the ground-work for a future relationship of mutual respect and problem solving within the therapeutic environment.

Through the process of working with parents and caregivers, one can learn to use the capabilities and support that exists within each individual family system. Such an approach enables the family to obtain information and abilities that empower them as advocates for the resources they need to meet their needs as individuals and members of a family. It also ensures the best possibility for success in each program with which the family becomes involved. Good communication is an essential component and as the professional relationship progresses will be a basis for trust and understanding.

References

Bennett, T., Lingerfely, B., Nelson, D. (1990). *Developing Individualized Family Support Plans.* Cambridge: Brookline Books.
Damrosch, S.P., Perry, L.A. (1989). Self Reported Adjustment, Chronic Sorrow, and Coping of Parents of Children with Down Syndrome. *Nursing Research.* 38, 25-30.
Dunst, C., Trivette, C., Deal, A. (1988). *Enabling and empowering families: Principles and Guidelines for Practice.* Cambridge: Brookline Books.
Mercer, R. (1990). Caring for Parents of Infants with Birth Defects. *Nurseweek.* Sept. 17.
Seligman, M., Darling, R.B. (1989). *Ordinary Families, Special Children: A Systems Approach to Childhood Disabilities.* New York: The Guilford Press.

15 LESSON PLANNING

15.01 RAFFERTY * THERAPEUTIC RIDING PROGRAM EVALUATION

Date _____

STUDENT _____

Initial Report _____
End of Year Report _____
Period Covered _____

Student Report

Student: _____ DOB: _____

Instructor: _____ Lesson Type: _____

Years Riding: _____ Diagnosis: _____

Ambulatory ( ) Non-Ambulatory ( ) Appliances Used: _____

Verbal ( ) Non-Verbal ( ) Attentive ( ) Inattentive ( ) _____

Comments: _____

A. BEHAVIOR	Initial (I)	Year End (YE)
1. How does rider come to lessons? (happy, resentful, apathetic, ecstatic)		
2. Is Rider Cooperative?		
3. Does rider follow directions? How? (spontaneously, quickly, with encouragement, detailed explanation, periodically, infrequently, slowly)		
4. Rider's behavior toward: horse/instructor/volunteer: (cooperative, over-affectionate, aggressive, inappropriate, i.e. spitting, ignoring, no interaction, distractability eye contact, touching, defensive)		
5. Does rider exhibit inappropriate behaviors while riding? (spitting, screaming, biting self, moving arms or legs, hyperactive, distractible)		
6. Does rider show allergic response to environment & how?		
7. Medications		
8. Allergies to medications?		
9. What is rider's general affect? (happy, lethargic, cool, over excited, distractable, dull, in & out of realty, appropriately content)		
10. Does rider enjoy lessons?		
B. SENSORY SYSTEM		
1. Can rider hear? (distractable to sounds, deaf-uses sign language, hearing aids, lip reads)		
2. Can rider see? (blind, partially sighted, visually distractible, aids)		
3. Can rider tolerate being touched & touching? (tactilely defensive, seeking, giggles)		
4. Is rider aware of position in space? (follows imitation of postures, positions body without eyes)		
5. Rider's vestibular system function (balance, seeks movement, rigid-won't leave midline)		
6. Can rider keep remember movements (kinesthetic/ synaptic memory, exercises, reining, 2-point, games)		
7. Can rider keep balance against movement & how (walk, trot, halt, falls forward, backward, sideways)		

C. LESSON SKILLS	Initial (I)	Year End (YE)
1. Mounting Procedure: all mounting occurs with a leader steadying the horse and a offside person holding down the stirrup leather on the offside to prevent the saddle from slipping (ground, block, ramp, assist, independent, extend left leg, pull with arm, support with arms)		
2. Behavior once astride (cautious, comfortable, aggressive, non-reactive.		
3. Manner of **communicating** to horse (gesturing, facial movements, vocalizations, verbalization, appropriate, inappropriate, body movements)		
4. Volunteer assistance needed (leader, sidewalkers, full, partial, stand-by, at halt, walk, trot, back rider)		
5. Equipment used (English/Western, pad, hand hold, neck strap, reins)		
6. Can rider **move** horse forward & how (squeezes legs, kicks, moves seat, verbalizes, whip, spurs, gives with hands)		
7. Can rider halt horse & how (says "whoa", closes hands on reins, closes legs, half halts)		
8. After first step, rider (loses balance, holds on, moves with horse, smiles, cries, screams, no affective reaction, posture changes)		
9. Rider holds reins (incorrectly, correctly, consistently, inconsistently)		
10. Manner of steering (direct unilateral, crosses over withers, over hands)		
11. Equestrian/posture (astride, at walk)		
a. Heels (down, parallel to ground, up)		
b. Knees (softly hugging saddle, too tight, clinching saddle, winged outward floppy)		
c. Pelvis (tilted toward ground, held parallel to ground, tilted upward)		
d. Lower back (arched, flat, rounded)		
e. Upper back (straight, rounded, scoliosis)		
f. Shoulders (level & even, one shoulder higher than other, one more forward than other, which one)		
g. Upper arms (too close, squeezed to sides, held too far away from body,/chicken winged)		
h. Elbows & forearms (forearm pointing to sky/upward, forearm in direct line from bit to elbow, forearm pointing downward)		
i. Wrists (cocked backwards/hyperextended, flexed, neutral, correct)		
j. Hands (palms downward, palms facing each other, palms upward, fists too close)		
k. Thumb & fingers (thumb squeezing rein too hard, thumb correctly holding rein, thumb softly holding rein between thumb & index, thumb sticking upwards)		
l. Fingers (loosely holding reins, correctly holding reins, too tightly, holds rein between baby finger & ring finger)		
m. Neck & head (head too far back with chin up in the air, in neutral position with chin parallel to ground, tilted forward chin to chest)		

LESSON SKILLS:	Initial (I)	Year End (YE)
n. Eyes (looking forward in direction of movement, looking downward, looking upward, looking everyplace except in direction of movement)		
12. Can rider assume 2-point position & how (neck strap, mane, hips stabilized in mid-position, too weak, arm drop, trunk too forward, too upright), competency over cavaletti, trotting jumps.		
13. Manner of trotting & how (holding neck strap, mane, saddle, volunteers, arm prop, balance, arms, legs, heels, position)		
14. Manner of cantering		
15. Manner of jumping		
16. Exercises (yes, no, assistance & comments)		
a. Toe touches same side		
b. Toe touches cross over		
c. Touching horse's ears		
d. Touching horse's rump		
e. Trunk rotation		
(1) Putting ring on horse's (cross lateral) ear		
(2) Putting ring on own toes (cross over)		
(3) Putting ring on horse's rump		
(4) Catches ball from front		
(a) 45 degrees - side		
(b) 90 degrees - side		
(c) 75 degrees - rotation to rear		
f. Knows right & left		
g. Throws ball using two hands		
h. Throws ball using one hand		
i. Takes feet out of stirrups		
j. Puts feet in stirrups		
k. Sits sideways on horse		
l. Sits backwards on horse		
m. Sits frontward		
n. Arm swings/airplane wings		
o. Swimmer's motion		
Can rider do the above exercises at walk, which ones?		
17. Games (yes, no assistance, comments, N/A = non-applicable)		
a. Can rider play red flag, green flag		
b. One-step simple relay race (rider goes around barrel or end cone and comes back)		
c. Can rider play two-step relay race (weave cones, go around barrel and come back)		
d. Can rider play three-step relay race (weave cones, pick up an object or place object on barrel and come back)		
e. Can rider pass object to another rider		
f. Can rider slap hand of teammates		
g. Can rider do obstacle course		
h. Play musical cones		
i. Balance nerf balls on tennis racket		

LESSON SKILLS	Initial (I)	Year End (YE)
j. Cone polo (knocking nerf ball off cone with stick)		
k. Nerf basketball		
l. Throwing & catching between teammates		
m. Egg & spoon		
n. Ride a buck		
o. Ride, run, lead relay race		
p. Do a drill team ride		
q. Ride a dressage test		
r. Ride blind-folded		
s. Ride a Caprilli test		
t. Ride a course of jumps		
u. Trail rides		
v. Ride cross country/up & down hills		

w. Does rider ride in special events
    Horse shows for the disabled
    Horse shows for the non-disabled
    Horse-a-thons
    Program Demos		

Summary _____

_____

Date Initial: _____ Riding Instructors _____ Head Instructor _____

Date Year End: _____ Riding Instructor _____ Head Instructor _____

* Sandra L. Rafferty, MA, OTR, RR 1, Box 369, Troy MO 63379

Evaluation is intended to be completed by a riding instructors. It provides a method to determine eligibility and progress.

Barbara T. Engel, MEd, OTR

KEY WORDS
  INDIVIDUAL PROGRAM AND LESSON PLANS
  ORGANIZATION
  GOALS

INDIVIDUAL PROGRAM PLANNING

Program planning provides an organizational design for instructors so that a *comprehensive plan for each individual participant* in the therapeutic riding program can be developed. Within this structure there can be sufficient flexibility for the instructor to adapt and vary the individual lessons within a group setting or on an individual basis, meeting the variables of the equine milieu. Program planning provides a frame of reference by which to appraise performance, determine progress, or lack of progress and to develop further plans (Knickerbocker, 1980).

When a person comes to a therapeutic riding program, he or she is evaluated by head instructor and/or the program therapy consultant/therapist. It is important to establish a personal relationship with a rider and to consider his level of performance, define problems, and establish the reason this individual came to the riding program. An evaluation by a physical or occupational therapist is particularly important with a person who has physical disabilities. The therapists are trained to identify physical and neurological problems and provide recommendations to address them. The collected information allows for appropriate lesson planning and selection of a horse, and may protect the rider as well as the organization against improper handling. A rider can only be appropriately assisted and instructed if the instructor knows both the rider's problems <u>and</u> his abilities.

A therapist's evaluation of a rider without obvious physical disabilities is equally important. For example, a person with multiple sclerosis in remission may not show any physical signs but may well need special considerations. People with learning disabilities have difficulty processing language in some or all areas of communication and may also have difficulty processing motor actions as in motor planning and coordination. Many psychiatric disorders are thought to have a neurological basis. A person with such disorders may have subtle physical dysfunctions as seen in sensory integrative dysfunctions or learning disabilities. Persons with mental delays frequently have problems with coordination and increased or decreased muscle tone. Physical problems are not due to mental delays but are an associated disorder and can generally be improved through careful intervention. Assessment by other professionals may be necessary to identify particular needs.

The purpose of developing a special plan for each rider is to consider a person on an individual basis and not as one of a disability category. For example, all adults with athetoid quadriplegia are not the same nor are all 8 year old boys with Down Syndrome. Program planning helps the instructor to get to know the individual and to formulate a system for action which meets this individual's needs on a physical, psychological and social basis. Since the majority of riders in a therapeutic riding program have a number of problems, a plan helps to organize the problems so they can more easily be addressed. Most riding instructors are used to dealing with riders who have not developed riding skills, have not developed the muscles to balance and carry out aids and may have dealt with mild incoordination problems. They generally have not encountered the severeness and complexity of problems program riders have. The plan helps these instructors **look at** the problem and determine where training should start. Some students might start with (a) equine-assisted therapy or hippotherapy mounted sessions, (b) horse handling and grooming skills, (c) Pony Club horsemanship program, while others will start in a class with other riders with similar problems.

The individual program plan will summarize or list:
- Rider's goals and selection of activities
- Goals that can realistically be achieved (may be similar to rider's goals but more specific and realistic)
- Reflection of rider's real life interests

- Rider's present level (base line) of performance: strengths - limitations
- Problems which can be dealt with, within the equine setting
  - → need for riding helpers
  - → special needs for transfers
  - → special needs in a horse
  - → special equipment/adaptive tack needs
- Step-by-step objectives toward the achievement of goals
- Approach to use to meet success
- Procedures by which the objectives are met

THE DEVELOPMENT OF OBJECTIVES

Goals identify those behaviors and abilities to be achieved on the part of the rider in order to reach the projected outcome. "The goals should reflect the desired changes in [the rider's] behavior and abilities as a result of [the equestrian] activities" (Gilfoyle, 1981).

Objectives describe specific performance behaviors which represent steps toward the achievement of the goals which have been established for a rider. It is useful to write objectives in behavioral terms so that there is a means of measurement (Gilfoyle, 1981). This helps the team identify what the rider will do to demonstrate mastery of the task. Behavioral objectives must be written in <u>concrete</u> rather than <u>abstract</u> terms. For example written in *concrete* terms: <u>John will pick up and hold the reins in his hands</u>. This statement describes an *observable action* which can be observed as correct by numerous people. The words <u>pick up</u> and <u>hold</u> can be observed and will be interpreted in the same way by several people (hold would mean in any way since it has not been described in a specific way). What is being judged here is John will **pick up the reins** (not **how** John will pick up the reins). <u>John will correctly</u> pick up his reins. In this statement, **correctly** is the term being judged. This statement cannot be measured since <u>correctly</u> is a judgement-*abstract* term. What Sue considers correct may not be what Jean considers correct. To make this statement measurable one would need to describe the exact procedure that John must do. In describing measurable objectives, only action verbs can be used that describe observable acts that can easily show a specific measurement. Verbs such as "walking," "placing," "leading," "crying," "stopping," "taking," and so on, are such verbs which several people can judge in the same way. When writing the objective make sure each action which is going to be measured is being described. The measurable action may be simple or complex. For example:

> John will **pick up** the reins
> John will **pick up** the reins with **both** hands
> John will **pick up** the reins and **hold** them **one inch above the saddle**

After writing the objective, one needs to describe the conditions under which the measured behavior will occur. In this example, the condition will be: <u>after mounting his horse and entering the arena</u>. A measurement of proficiency can be added such as: <u>four out of five times that he rides</u> or, <u>for ten minutes at a time</u>.

EXAMPLE OF A PROGRAM PLAN

Background information:
John is a 14 year old adolescent with learning disabilities. He has above-normal intelligence and is enrolled in a regular high school where he attends two special education classes. Mother states he was in a special riding program when in Washington and this "helped him a lot."

Instructor Evaluation:
John was able to lead the horse from the stall to the tacking area but needed reassurance. He held the leadline awkwardly and walked in a jagged pattern. He did not know how to groom the horse. He was unable to mount the horse from the ground but was able to physically mount from the mounting block but did not know the sequence of the procedure. When sitting on the horse, his trunk slumped forward, face was down, his heels were up and he did not want the horse to move fast. Even though his balance seems secure, he wanted sidewalkers. John held the reins by grasping them in his palm and used verbal aids for the walk and halt. John was slow in responding to commands. He spoke very little, only when pressured and then in a soft voice.

Occupational Therapy Evaluation:
John walked with slight flexion in hips and knees with increased tone. His shoulders were forward and internally rotated. He did not walk in a straight line. Sensory evaluation showed a mild problem with auditory processing. He had difficulty hearing all sounds and was slow in processing the information. He had difficulty producing volume. John had trouble judging distances (space relations) but was able to judge the relationship of one object to another (figure ground). He could read well as he reads the dressage letters around the arena (visual acuity and tracking). John had trouble motor planning fine movements. He had a delayed response in identification of body parts. His tactile responses were dull but he did not like to be touched. John did not like subtle movements and his equilibrium responses are delayed and weak. When the therapist discussed her findings with John's mother, she revealed that when John was little, the physician thought he had cerebral palsy.

Rider-parent Goals:
John wants to learn to ride <u>like the other kids</u> and to take care of the horse. Mother wants John to ride <u>better</u> and to help him become more assertive.

INDIVIDUAL PROGRAM PLAN

<u>Summarizing the team findings:</u>
- Learning disabilities with problems in auditory and expressive language, poor respiratory expansion, difficulties with motor planning and space relations
- Increased muscle tone in lower limbs and flexion posture due to tightness of the hip and knee flexors
- Weak extensors. Poor endurance and strength
- Flexion posture prevents mounting from the ground, heels down, a "deep seat", and relaxation on the horse to respond to the horse's movements
- Problems in tactile, proprioceptive, and vestibular reactions resulting in insecurity on the horse, poor equilibrium reactions, and poor identification of body parts
- Difficulty in social interactions
- Poor grooming and riding skills
- Good attitude and well motivated, though shy

The instructor, the riding team and the client/parent determine that the following are realistic long term goals (the time frame may vary from a term to a year--each program will define long term, short term):
- To demonstrate a relaxed posture, with an extended back, deep seat, and secure balance in all gaits
- To demonstrate independence in grooming and tacking skills
- To demonstrate riding skills for Training Level Dressage Test 3
- To demonstrate assertive, social responses, and function "normally" within a group setting (real life goals)

The plan to accomplish the goals is:
- Equine-assisted therapy two times a week for thirty minutes each session

Goals - half year in *equine-assisted therapy*:
- To achieve trunk rotation, relaxed hip and knee flexors, strengthen extensor, and strengthen overall and back extension
- To achieve fine motor responses with good motor planning

Objectives:
    a) At the end of a 20 minute hippotherapy session, John will rotate his trunk while sitting on a saddle, as observed by the therapist
    b) At the end of 12 sessions of hippotherapy, John will sit on the saddle with a straight back for ten minutes of each session, as observed by the therapist
    c) At the end of 12 sessions of equine-assisted therapy, John will hold the reins between his fingers in normal English style while guiding his horse, as observed by the instructor
    d) At the end of 25 sessions John will mount from the ground with leg-up assistance from the therapist, as observed by the therapist

● **Sports riding lessons--individual session, one time a week for 8 weeks followed by small group lessons**
Goals - half year in *sports riding*:
  ● To demonstrate grooming skills to prepare the horse for riding
  ● To demonstrate leg aids at the walk and trot
Objectives:
  a) John will brush his horse with a body brush, then with the dandy brush, from head to tail within ten minutes at the beginning of each session, as observed by the riding assistant
  b) John will use leg aids to make his horse go from stand to walk, and walk to trot four out of five times, when directed by his instructor

The use of measurable objectives in the development of all lesson plans helps the instructor in several ways:
  ● It helps determine the instructor's success in teaching and encourages development of teaching skills in a systematic way
  ● It measures success in a way that can easily be conveyed to others. This is especially important when one may need to show accountability
  ● Accountability provides proof of the influence of therapeutic riding on the rider
  ● It provides data which can be compiled toward a study
  ● It helps the rider see his success in specific areas

When objectives have been developed, one needs to determine the method to be used to achieve the objectives. For example under objective a) above, how will John learn to reach that objective? It was decided that he can best learn by observing others. John will be paired with an assistant. John will observe his partner groom the horse and will learn by observation with some demonstration. The method would read: With a partner John will learn to groom his horse by underlining(observing grooming skills), underlining(copying observed skills), and underlining(by demonstration). Once the individual program plan has been completed, the instructor and the therapist are ready to develop the actual sessions with the rider. The underlining(individual program plan) provides the information one needs to develop the underlining(lesson plan).

LESSON PLANNING

A lesson plan is needed in order to achieve the aims of a lesson or instructional plan. "Teaching without a plan is like building a house without blueprints" (Dierenfield, 1981). A lesson plan provides organization and direction. It helps the instructor to think things through, place ideas in a logical order, and include all points from each individual program plan before working with his students. The lesson plan allows for the selection of the best techniques, the necessary equipment, the appropriate staff and horses.

In addition, it permits one to plan the right amount of time for each task involved in the lesson. Proper planning avoids the lack of being prepared and allows the instructor to deal with unexpected events and situations (Sivewright, 1984). *When one is prepared in all other ways, an added unexpected event is easier to deal with.* In a therapeutic riding session, there are many variables since the rider's condition may change from week to week and not always in a progressive manner. When teaching a class of four riders, there may be a great deal of variety in temperament and physical condition of the riders from one session to the next. General assessments are necessary at the beginning of each session to determine needed changes.

Preparing a written lesson plan, rather than carrying it in one's head, helps the team (leader, side-walker/spotter, consultant) work in a coordinated manner. Each member of the team is prepared well ahead of time when lessons are developed in long term, short term, and session bases. Written lesson plans allow all members of the team to understand the logical sequence of events, to understand the instructor's techniques and method of action and to participate in the plan execution.
Beggs (1971) states the advantages of team teaching as:
  ☐ Using each person's special skills
  ☐ Making the rider assistants feel like full-functioning team members
  ☐ Developing creativity and adaptability
  ☐ Providing a support-backup system
  ☐ Improving the quality of instruction

◎ Gearing to individual needs of the riders
◎ Giving each team member a clear idea of his tasks

Lesson plans are developed on a sequential bases.

1) Long range--for the year
2) Short range--blocks of shorter periods (three months)
3) Divide the short range goals into smaller sections in developing progressive objectives. Each lesson builds on itself and on the one which came before. Smaller segments allow the instructor to handle the material more effectively and to accommodate to the rider's varying condition.

PREPARING A WRITTEN LESSON PLAN

For example: a class is formed for four young women between ages 18 to 26. Individual program plans were completed; each person's major problems were to be addressed. The main interest of these young women was to increase their riding skills, with secondary interest in improving their physical abilities.

They were grouped together because:

- They were interested in the same overall goal
- Their secondary goals were the same
- Their ages were compatible
- They were able to ride without sidewalkers
- They were able to tack up their horses with some assistance

Student	disorder	problem
Judy	closed head injury	difficulty understanding and speaking--ataxia--difficulty judging space--fine motor coordination problems.
Marian	closed head injury	incoordination of trunk and limb movements--poor judgement of space.
Linda	learning disability	bright but slow in (process) understanding--right/left reversals--fine motor incoordination.
Anne	mild cerebral palsy	slow in processing speaking and understanding--fine motor incoordination--difficulty judging space.

Development of long range lesson plan goals:

- Riders will be able to perform all skills required in the Training Level Dressage Test 1. (requires space perception, right/left skills, gross and fine motor coordination)
- Riders will be able to follow the verbally reading, by the instructor, of the Training Level Test 1. (requires hearing processing, understanding and immediate execution of verbal commands)
- Riders will be able to get horses from stalls, groom and tack them for their lesson independently. (requires sequential memory, coordination of limbs, balance, space perception, and fine motor coordination to tack the horse)

In order to make it easier to obtain the long range goals the instructor will sequence the development of these skills and break them down into short term goals. For example, if the instructor takes a look at the first long range goal--to perform all skills required in the training level 1 dressage test and applies it to a rider who is uncoordinated, is slow in getting and executing a command, has poor development of her muscles needed to carry out the aids and does not know where she is in the arena, she would be pretty overwhelmed and not sure where to start or would teach without dealing with the real problems. Short term goals make the teaching process easier.

Short range lesson plan goals:
- Riders will assist each other in grooming and tacking--to encourage communication.
- Riders will learn to saddle their horses with only verbal assistance--understand verbal commands.
- Riders will learn to sit with their weight on their pelvic bones--increase trunk control.
- Riders will learn to use light rein aids--increase fine motor coordination and body awareness.
- Riders will learn to use leg aids for all transitions--to increase leg coordination and strength.
- Riders will learn to ride a perfectly round circle--space perception and integration of sensory-motor functions.

From the short range goals the instructor will develop objectives for specific lessons. Since progress to achieve a specific objective may take a month or two, the objectives may remain the same but the instructor may vary the lessons to make them more interesting. This will depend on the population she or he teaches. Some riders progress faster with a routine they understand and can anticipate what is expected of them. Changes would occur only to increase the difficulty of the lessons to progress toward the objectives. Full description of the objectives as developed from the long range plan do not need to be placed on the daily lesson plan. It is easier for sidewalkers and horse handlers to read instructions specific to the lesson (see Figure 1).

All lesson plans should be divided into five sections: (examples given may be different than those the instructor uses)
- Preparation:
  - Getting the horse groomed and tacked
  - Rider locate helmet, special equipment, and crop (if used) for lesson
- Warm-up"
  - Warming up the horse for the lesson
  - The rider warms up for the lesson--stretches
  - Horse and rider warm up together
- The skill development to meet objectives
  - Instructor goes over basics
  - Introduces new skill
- Wind-down
  - Free riding
  - Walking horse to cool down
  - Rider relaxes
- Put away
  - Run up stirrup irons
  - Loosen girth
  - Horse groomed and returned to stall

At the end of each session, the instructor determines the success of the session and plans for the next one by maintaining or adjusting the stated objectives. Always remember that objectives can be adjusted to meet the needs of the rider and to attain the goals. Situations change to require this. Do not feel that once the objective has been stated it cannot be changed. In a therapy plan or in an IEP, this change must be justified--but it can be made. Important points to consider in evaluating each lesson are (Dierenfield 1981):
- Behavioral changes of the students
- Feedback from the learners
- Learners' responses to the lesson
- What should be taught next

Writing the lesson plan for today, the following must be included:

- ☺ A list of riders
- ☺ A list of staff who will participate in the preparation of the lesson and during the lesson--list jobs.
- ☺ Location of the lesson
- ☺ List of the horses and each horse's possible equipment
- ☺ List of the lesson objectives
- ☺ List of equipment needed and location
- ☺ List of warm-up procedures
- ☺ List of procedures to address the lesson objectives
- ☺ List of the wind-down procedures
- ☺ Review of the results at the end of lesson

DAILY LESSON PLAN

CLASS NAME Tuesday--10 am	DATE 6-09-91	DRESSAGE ARENA X
INSTRUCTOR Sara ASSISTANT Jean--(in training)	class assistants: [2] Pam & Jay leaders [0] sidewalkers [0] spotters [1]	INSTRUCTIONS: Pam--set up letter and cones in arena--see lesson diagram Figure 1. Jay--exercise Princess, Hobo, Jake--Pam exercises Mammie at 9 am, ready for grooming at 10.

RIDER	HORSE	TACK	MOUNTING
Judy	Mammie	brown-multipurpose No 2	assisted--ramp
Mariam	Jake	Wintec dressage--black	assisted from mounting block
Linda	Princess	leather dressage No 4	ground--independent
Anne	Hobo	Wintec--blue	ground--independent

Dressage Ring

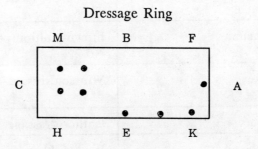

FIGURE 1. LESSON PLAN A

Objectives:

1) *Riders will find the tack for their horse. Riders will tack-up their horses after assistants demonstrate*
2) *Riders will sit on their pelvic bones with straight backs 10% of lesson time*
   Riders will stop their horses at each letter using seat aid 50% of times, as observed by instructor
3) *Riders will ride 2 "round" circles (as judged by the instructor) during the lesson*

Warm-up: *Riders will stretch with Pam before mounting*
After mounting riders will walk around on the rail and perform warm-up exercises as instructed by Jay

Introductory statement: *Class, we will practice the same exercise as last week*
Who can show us this exercise?
Also today we are going to practice circles--develop a mental image in your head of a circle
What does it look like--like an orange

Procedures: *By feeling your seat bones on the saddle, riders will learn to sit back on their seat bones while the horses are at a walk; by applying pressure on your seat bones stop your horses at each cone; riders will increase back extension. Riders ride around the six cones to develop concept of a circle, then ride an independent circle with the cones removed by Jay and Pam*

Wind-down *Riders will walk their horses to music with long reins for 5 minutes changing reins every third time they pass B or E*

Lesson Assessment *Riders are ready to begin grooming. Riders are not doing well with circles--need more cues*

Recommendations *Will try visual diagrams of circles to reinforce going around cones*

A lesson plan can also be set up in different formats (Figure 2) to meet individual needs such as the following: When objectives are placed in columns, they may be easier to follow for the staff who are unfamiliar with them.

DAILY LESSON PLAN

CLASS NAME *Tuesday 10 am*	DATE *6-09-91*	LOCATION *dressage arena*	INSTRUCTOR *Sara* ASSISTANCE *Pam* *Jay*
RIDER	HORSE	TACK	MOUNTING
Judy	Mammie	brown-multipurpose No 2	assisted--ramp
Mariam	Jake	Wintec dressage--black	assisted from mounting block
Linda	Princess	leather dressage No 4	ground--independent
Anne	Hobo	Wintec--blue	ground--independent

OBJECTIVE	PROCEDURES	EXPECTED RESULTS	MEASURE
rider will ride a "round" circle	ride around cones to form circle	develop a visual image of a circle--an orange. maneuver a good circle.	as judged by Sara
rider will sit on pelvic bones	rider will feel her pelvic bones on saddle with each stride	sit on seat bones 10% of the times	as observed by Sara
rider will sit with straight back	by stopping at each cone using seat aids	sit with straight backs 10% of time	as observed by Sara

FIGURE 2. LESSON PLAN B

Conclusion

The use of a written lesson plan can lead to success because it requires the instructor:

To organize him or herself, his or her assistants and to be well prepared

To identify a person's problems

To propose methods of instruction to resolve the problems

To develop analytic observation skills

To assess the results

To propose further instruction toward goals

The lesson plan should be approached as a **helper** not a chore. Any time one uses a new tool, it will take time to learn it. Following the learning process developing objectives is an easy and time-saving task.

Beggs, D. W. III. (1971). *Team Teaching*. Bloomington: Indiana Univ. Press. 13-60.

Bissell, J., Fisher, J., Owens, C., Polcyn, P. (1988). *Sensory Motor Handbook* Torrance: Sensory Integration International.

Dierenfield, R. B. (1981). *Learning to Teach*. Saratoga: Century Twenty-one Publisher. 14-50.

Gilfoyle, E. M. (1981). *Training: Occupational Therapy Educational Management in Schools*. Modules one & four. Rockville, MD. American Occupational Therapy Association.

Knickerbocker, B. M. (1980). *A Holistic Approach to the Treatment of Leaning Disorders*. Thorofare: Charles B. Slack, Inc.

Mager, R. F. (1962). *Preparing Instructional Objectives*. Palo Alto: Fearon Publishers.

Palardy, J. M. (1971). *Elementary School Curriculum*. New York: MacMillan Co. 44, 60-66,104-109,146, 165.

Sivewright, M. (1984). *Thinking Riding*. London: J.A. Allen.

15.03 A LESSON FOR A RIDER WITH LOW VISION

Debi Ruth Parker, MA, NARHA Master Instructor

Development of visually impaired children can differ from sighted children. Sighted infants have good <u>visual grasping</u> of their environment before actual hand-eye connection begins at 20 weeks. Prior to this the infants have already begun <u>visual righting</u> to raise their heads and gain head stability. They are then beginning to fixate their eyes to the environment, aiding in stabilizing themselves in space. Visually impaired infants rely on <u>hear-hand connection</u> to grasp their environment which does not develop until 10 to 12 months. By this time, they are already delayed in the development of the fine motor system. This may influence the lack of the development of smooth dynamic movements and upright posture frequently lacking in persons with low vision. Understanding the major influence vision has on the development of the motor system will help the instructor to understand and work with the person with low vision. The vestibular and anti-gravity stimulation helps the low-vision rider to gain up right posture.

Basics Before Teaching:
1. Determine how much vision exists and any sensitivities or limitations
2. Determine the method of ground travel and review technique with rider (Sighted guide will probably be most common: the blind individual holds the sighted person's arm just above the elbow and can easily follow along).
3. Watch out for parroting language: the rider can repeat everything but really has no true understanding of what he or she is saying. Stress good posture and relaxation with your riders. Poor posture can lead to spinal deviations and back pain. Balance problems may come from an inability to reference their body positions with a visual horizon; slumping and dropped heads are common in blind individuals. Be sensitive to atypical head positioning. This can be caused by poor posture habits, light sensitivity, or perhaps an attempt to utilize any remaining vision to fullest advantage.
4. Give very detailed explanations and use concrete reference points, i.e., "towards me, the rail, the barn, the center of the ring, the horse's head," and so on. Avoid generalities such as "over there, by the yellow one." Remember that the person with low to no vision does not have the <u>visual orientation</u> to places and things. Make sure they understand what you mean by the <u>barn</u>, <u>rail</u>, <u>horse's head</u> or the <u>center of the ring</u>.
5. A slightly shorter outside rein and light inside leg pressure will assist the rider in keeping his or her mount near the rail/wall.
6. Instruct from the middle of the ring and be consistent about it. This will prove to be a strong reference point for the rider and it will have a calming effect, too.
7. Before the lesson remove all props such as poles, barrels, jumps, and so forth, so that the rider will not have unnecessary challenges/obstacles. Walk the rider the length and width of the ring. Discuss the footing in the arena, especially if there are different textures. Let the rider <u>feel</u> the fence/rail. Note any permanent irregularities of the ground such as slopes or dips. Walk out the site of the tack room, the grooming area, the mounting block or ramp, the bathroom and office. Be sure that the rider has a point of orientation to each one of these places and from them to the riding arena. (It can be helpful for the instructor to walk the site, blindfolded, so he or she can gain a better orientation to the **feel** of distances and footing, notice sounds and other things which are normally over-shadowed by sight.)

Note any specific reference points or clues that may be beneficial to the rider such as:
- Consistent sounds such as an office machine, soda machine or wind chimes.
- Wind, especially when riding indoors and there are door and window openings.
- Sun/lights from overhead or through openings such as through windows and doors.
- Highly contrasting colors--a white fence against a dark background or a white stripe painted at an appropriate level around the interior wall of an enclosed ring. Color markers (or electronic beepers) could be placed 15 feet before any corner to assist independent riding.

Re-orient your riders again once they are mounted on their horses; distances will be quite different. Do not encourage your riders to count strides (theirs or their horses's) as this can lead to a false sense of security and potentially dangerous situations. While riding in an enclosed ring some riders may be able to use echo location and thereby sense how near a solid wall is and use this for independent maneuvering.

8. Remember that the rider with no vision has the capability to walk, trot, canter, jump and perform dressage maneuvers. Teamed with a reliable and well-schooled horse, he or she will be able to do almost anything that a sighted rider is capable of doing.

9. Extra available aids include electronic beepers, walkie-talkies, callers, and tactual maps of the site. (*a caller is a person who stands at a letter or center of one side--corner--end, and repeats i.e., corner, corner, corner, corner and so on while the rider is in motion. As the rider comes closer and closer to this caller, he or she hears the word louder and louder. As the rider moves away from this caller--he or she hears the word softer and softer. In a dressage test, a caller will stand at each letter and will repeat the name of the letter in the above mentioned method. In this way the rider knows where he or she is at all times. This method can also be used in a lesson.*)

A Lesson Example

Students: two totally blind riders ages 9 and 14 who have previously ridden four times.

Goal: To be able to turn a horse in either a left or right circle.

I.   Greet the riders and introduce them to their horses. Take about 15 minutes for grooming, pairing up with a volunteer for each rider. Point out different textures like whiskers, mane, body and tail hair and hooves. Discuss the direction of the hair growth. Differentiate between various grooming tools.

II.   Take about 5 minutes to tack up the horses. Discuss the tactile differences between leather, suede, metal, cloth, and so forth. Stress comfort for the horse; buckles not too tight and hair lying in the correct direction under the saddle.

III.   Take about 5 minutes for mounting. Being up high above everyone else might be frightening: keep touching the leg or arm of the rider while he or she is mounting. Reassure the rider that there is a leader at the horse's head.

IV.   Take about 2 minutes to describe the goal of the session ("After reviewing your previously learned skills, today you will learn how to make your horse turn and go in circles".)

V.   Take about 8 minutes for warming up and exercises. Have the riders touch the horse's ears and tail, try toe touches, and hug the horse's neck. Have them listen to the sounds that the hooves make on the riding surface, the saddle creaks, the other riders' horses and any other common sounds. Have them stand up in their stirrups and then try "around-the-world"

VI.   Take about 15 minutes to practice the new skill to be learned. Concise directions with points of reference make learning easier. ("To make a left circle you need to gently bring your left hand back towards your left hip which will bend your horse's head and neck to the left; the body follows which completes the movement of the turn or circle. If you bring your hand back a lot, your horse will bend a lot and you will make a small circle. If you put just a little pressure on the rein your horse will bend just a little and you will make a large circle"). Before doing this at a walk, talk it through at a stand still so that the rider can feel the bend in the horse's neck while a volunteer bends the head to the left and right.

VII.   Take about 5 minutes for a game. Have both riders at the end of the arena. While walking forward blow a whistle once for a left circle and twice for a right circle. See who does the most circles in the correct direction.

VIII.   Take about 5 minutes for dismounting.

Teaching low vision riders is a real challenge. They can perform all skills that able-bodied riders can since vision may be their only deficit. The instructor must learn to present material in such a way that the riders can understand. Blind riders have excelled at the International Dressage Competition for the disabled riders.

15.04   RIDERS WITH HEARING IMPAIRMENT: EFFECTIVE COMMUNICATION IS THE KEY

Robin Hulsey Chickering, MS

Through her years of involvement with therapeutic riding, the author has become aware of a tendency by instructors and other professionals to erroneously downplay or underestimate the impact of hearing impairment, as opposed to other "more visible" handicapping conditions, on a rider. To quote Helen Keller, "...deafness separates people from people." As professionals in the field of therapeutic riding, we are fortunate to have the tremendous communicative potential of the horse at our disposal. In working with hearing-impaired riders, the key word to always keep in mind is not *speech* but *communication*. If the instructor can get his or her message across to his or her riders, and likewise, they can get their message across to the instructor, whether it be through signs, speech, gestures, facial expression, writing, pictures, or mime, he or she is on the right track!

The majority of hearing-impaired riding students in the United States will most probably be enrolled in schools or programs utilizing a *Total Communication philosophy*. In a nutshell, a **total communication philosophy** endorses the use of **all** available means of communication including <u>speech</u>, <u>signs</u>, <u>residual hearing</u>, <u>speechreading</u>, <u>gestures</u>, and <u>printed words</u>.

Depending upon the number of hearing-impaired pupils enrolled in the riding program, the instructor would be wise to consider the following options (to be covered in greater detail in the next section):
  a) Learn to use sign language by enrolling in a manual communication (sign) course--plan to attend regularly and practice frequently!
  b) Use of an interpreter to facilitate communication with student riders

The instructor and/or interpreter will also need to become familiar with signs specifically related to horses and riding, since these signs will not be routinely covered in sign language classes or interpreter-training programs. Although it is not recommended, the interpreter and/or instructor may choose to create their own signs for some of these horse-related concepts, but only if they are native or experienced users of **American Sign Language** (ASL) or working with a native signer of ASL. The instructor or interpreter may also choose to utilize the signs included in the book, *Horseback Riding for the Hearing Impaired* (Hulsey, 1979), which were created for just this purpose.

ENROLLMENT IN A MANUAL COMMUNICATION COURSE
For the sake of brevity (entire books have been written on this very topic), manual communication courses are usually divided into two types:
  1) American Sign Language (ASL)
  2) Signed English

This author strongly recommends enrollment in an ASL course, especially if the instructor is a native signer (deaf or a hearing child of deaf parents). ASL is the language of the Deaf Community, and is a true visual language with its own unique vocabulary, grammar and syntax--it is not based on English. As in any language, there is some variation in vocabulary depending upon region of the country; however, a proficient signer of ASL would be able to easily carry on a conversation with another ASL user in a different part of the country.

Signed English, on the other hand (no pun intended!), is not a "*sign language*", but rather a manual code which has been created to attempt to represent spoken English, an already existing language. There are many varieties of Signed English, and this makes communication with a wide variety of deaf persons potentially difficult, as some persons may be unfamiliar with the type of Signed English learned by the riding instructor. Signed English is generally more easily learned by hearing people; however, ASL is generally more easily acquired and comprehended by deaf people (especially those born deaf or deafened in early childhood). It is well worth the extra effort to acquire at least a fair level of proficiency in ASL--you will find that the "magic" of this visual language makes complicated explanations simple for your deaf riders! Taking a course in ASL will also give you the flexibility to use ASL or Signed English as needed. Simply put the ASL vocabulary/signs in English word order and you will be able to communicate with a Signed English user. Unfortunately, it is not easy or even possible for a user of Signed English to do the reverse--since the linguistic structure of ASL is completely different from that of English. Therefore, the Signed English user has not nearly the flexibility of the ASL user. With the wide variety of hearing-impaired students enrolled in therapeutic riding programs, flexibility in your means of communicating is certainly an important factor to consider!

How does one go about locating a Signed English or ASL class? One of the best sources of information would be the local schools or programs for the hearing impaired; staff there should be able to provide a list of available classes in your community. Classes are often provided by local school districts, colleges, churches with deaf members, and various agencies affiliated with deafness (interpreter agencies.) Once a suitable class has been found, regular attendance and lots of practice are crucial to the development of the proficiency level necessary for teaching riding skills.

USE OF AN INTERPRETER
The other suggested option for the therapeutic riding instructor is to acquire the services of a signing interpreter in order to facilitate communication with the hearing-impaired students. The interpreter should be able to sign spoken instructions to the deaf students, as well as to "voice" their signed communication (if necessary) to the riding instructor. This option may be chosen if:
a) The number of hearing-impaired students in the program is small
b) The riding instructor is unable to devote the time necessary to obtain signing skills or is unable to find a suitable class
c) The riding instructor is currently enrolled in a sign class, but has yet to acquire the skills necessary for successful teaching and communication

An interpreter may be obtained from several possible sources:
1) Local interpreter agency--A professional interpreter may be hired through an agency which specializes in providing interpreters for the community. Fees are usually charged by the hour, and will vary according to the certification and/or skill level of the interpreter
2) Students from local interpreter training programs (college or junior college level)--These students are usually required to complete a certain number of hours of practicum experience. You may be able to find a qualified student who will be willing to use your therapeutic riding program as his practicum; which will, of course, be free of charge for you!
3) Volunteer interpreter--A parent, other relative, or classroom teacher may be willing to serve as an interpreter in your riding program. If this option is chosen, it would be wise to have one or more "back-up" interpreters available in case the original volunteer is unable to attend on a particular day

Since most interpreters will be unfamiliar with horses and riding instructions, it is essential for the riding instructor to familiarize the interpreter with the lesson plan, as well as with safety rules for working around horses. For a class of "normal" hearing-impaired riders (normal intelligence and physical abilities), the best location for the interpreter is in the center of the riding arena, right next to the instructor. This way, the riders will always know where to look for their instructions, and will not need to search for a "wandering" interpreter and/or instructor! In the case of a deaf student with multiple impairments, it may be preferable to have the interpreter walk next to the student's mount, in order to better keep his attention and facilitate communication. The interpreter should not be expected to function as a sidewalker for safety purposes, but should be expected only to serve as a communication facilitator.

The role of an interpreter has frequently been a source of confusion - always keep in mind that the interpreter is present for one purpose only and that is to serve as a communication bridge between the deaf and hearing persons present. The interpreter functions almost as a "non-person" while on the job; he or she is not allowed to interject his or her own words or opinions into the conversation. He or she is also expected to interpret everything that is said during his assignment, regardless of whether the communication is directed to the deaf person(s) present. As a riding instructor you will be expected to speak directly to the deaf person. For example "Susie, you need to shorten your reins," would be the correct way to address a deaf person using an interpreter. The incorrect way to use an interpreter would be to say, "Tell Susie to shorten her reins." When "voicing" (speaking) for the deaf student, the interpreter will speak as if he or she were that person; i. e., "I don't understand how to make the horse trot," rather than, "She says she doesn't understand how to make the horse trot".

Another important factor to keep in mind is that the interpreter should never be asked to function as a volunteer (sidewalker or leader) or be asked to perform any other duties while on the job. It may be tempting (especially when shorthanded), but the interpreter must never be asked to get a helmet for someone or help with a game. To do this would be to take away a vital communication link from your deaf students, if even for just a few seconds. A good interpreter can make a world of difference for both the deaf students and the instructor! Most interpreters also enjoy the variety and exercise provided by a therapeutic riding program.

Class size is another important factor to keep in mind when working with hearing-impaired riders. It may be necessary to limit the size of the class to 4 or less, especially if all the riders are hearing impaired. If a class has more than 4 riders, the horses begin to move further away from the instructor (out of necessity--for safety purposes), making it more difficult for the students to see their instructors in the center of the ring. In the case of the hearing-impaired rider with other impairments, it may be necessary to have a very small class of 2 or 3, each with his or her own sidewalker to reinforce signed instructions. In the case of the deaf/blind student or the deaf student with severe multiple impairments, it will probably be necessary for the instructor or interpreter to walk next to the rider and provide tactile input (signing and/or simply carrying out the desired action) in a private lesson situation.

In conclusion, the single most important factor to keep in mind in working with hearing-impaired riders is COMMUNICATION, which is not limited to signs and speech. Communication encompasses gestures, facial expressions, writing, drawing, mime, and all other facets of body language. The most effective teachers of the deaf are those who are uninhibited in their attempts to get their points across, regardless of their signing skills or the skills of their students. As a constant reminder of this principle, those of us involved in therapeutic riding need only to look as far as our best communicators of all--our horses--and they do not say a word!

Reference

Hulsey, Robin. (1979). *Horseback Riding for the Hearing Impaired: A Practical Guide and Suggested Signs*. From Riding High Inc, 2392 D. Half Moon Dr., St Louis, MO 63114.

15.05   LEARNING DISABILITIES--MANIFESTATION WITHIN THE RIDING ENVIRONMENT

John H. Brough, OTR

People vary in their learning styles. Some need to only hear information and they can remember it. Some need to write things down to remember them. Some never have to look at the notes again to have the ideas etched in their mind. Others need to both hear and see the information before they can retrieve it. Some must write things as they see them and hear them explained, and also look back at their notes to glean the information that they want.

Since people all learn differently, then what is a learning disability? We are all disabled to some extent, in some areas. The term "learning disability" has been defined in different ways depending upon the beliefs of those defining it. The National Advisory Committee for the Handicapped studied this problem and formulated the following now widely accepted definition (Education of Handicapped Children 1968):

> "Children with special (specific) learning disabilities exhibit a disorder in one or more of the basic psychological processes involved in understanding or in using spoken or written language. These may be manifested in disorders of listening, thinking, talking, reading, writing, spelling, or arithmetic. They can include conditions which have been referred to as perceptual handicaps, brain injury, minimal brain dysfunction, dyslexia, developmental aphasia, and others. They do not include learning problems which are due primarily to visual, hearing, motor handicaps, mental retardation, emotional disturbance, or to environmental disadvantage."

It should be reiterated that learning disabled children are not emotionally disturbed, mentally retarded, culturally deprived, or educationally deprived. The areas of their learning behavior that may be affected are:

    I. Motor
    II. Perception
            a. Visual
            b. Auditory
    III. Processing

I. Motor
Children with these difficulties show many problems handling their bodies. The problems are divided into two basic types: the hypotonic--lacking muscle tone; and the hypertonic--having too much muscle tone. Both extremes are difficult for the children. The hypotonic child usually exhibits a protruding stomach, sway-back posture, and is flabby or fat. They move only when they have to. They are called lethargic and lazy. They are neither. They shuffle and scoot as they know no other way. The hypertonic children are the muscle bound children. They have many bulging muscles but no strength. They try to do simple tasks and use massive muscular tension to get them done. For all their bulk and size, they are ineffective.

Both these children are extremes but have trouble with movement. They are clumsy and many times avoid tasks. In a therapeutic riding program they do not interact with the riding environment. They try to avoid it or control it. They may show misbehavior trying to find where the limits are. They structure the milieu and will get their way one way or another. They can be destructive of property, as if asking to be controlled since they cannot control themselves. They need help getting to the tack room, arena, and office. If left alone, they occupy themselves oblivious of the program. They are loners.

Balance also is many times affected. These children are like sacks of potatoes in the saddle. It takes a leader and two sidewalkers to help each of them stay in the saddle at a walk. Another area that can be affected is ocular control. The riders may not be able to use their eyes effectively thus the students may not be able to locate targets in the arena. Their eyes may jump from one bright stimulus to another and not really give the riders valuable information about their environment.

II. Perception

A. *Visual Perception* is the interpretation in the brain of visual images. Visual perception deficits cannot be corrected by glasses. There is nothing wrong with the eyes. Reception of the visual images on the retina is transferred via the optic nerve to the back of the brain. In the child with visual perceptual problems, the interpretation of this information is scrambled by the brain. Visual perceptual problems may be manifested in several different ways--problems of:

    1 - Figure ground
    2 - Perceptual constancy
    3 - Perception of position in space and spatial relations

1. Figure Ground

The problem is the children's inability to perceive objects in a foreground and background relationship and to separate them. With such a loss these children cannot find anything, even when the object is right in front of their nose. The instructor asks them to bring the halters from the trunk and they cannot find them. When the instructor looks for the halter they are the first objects to be seen in the trunk.

These children appear inattentive and unorganized. This is because their attention tends to jump to any stimuli that intrude upon them--to something that moves, glitters, or is brightly colored. No matter how irrelevant it may be to what they should be doing, these children attend to it. These are the riders who are riding but get distracted by the boys going by in their orange jackets. Therefore, they miss what the class is doing

2. Perceptual Constancy

This is the inability to perceive an object as possessing invariant properties such as shape, position, and size despite the variability of the stimuli present to the sense organs. For example, without this skill these are the children who do not recognize the barn when they approach it from the side. It is not the same barn to them as when they stood in front of it. These children do not recognize the trail when they ride out and look back. Therefore they cannot find the same trail again and appear lost. These children oftentimes may become anxious because of the general unreliability of appearance in their world. They become confused because they cannot recognize familiar places or people when the appearance is slightly changed. These children become confused when one changes clothes or removes his or her glasses. To them, the instructor may not be the same person that taught the lesson last week.

3. Perception of Position in Space and Spatial Relations

These children with disabilities in their perception of position in space and spatial relations are disabled in many ways. Their visual world is distorted. They are clumsy and hesitant in their movements. They have difficulty understanding what is meant by the words designating spatial positions, such as in, out, up, down, before, behind, left and right. These children, when told to go to the left, immediately go to the right. These children cannot find the brush in the closet when told it is on the top shelf because they are looking on the bottom shelf. They are lost in space.

B. The second major function for perceptual aberration is *auditory perception*. Auditory indicates the information that is heard. Again as with visual perceptual problems, there is nothing wrong with the ears or hearing mechanism. These children do not need a hearing aid. They receive information through their ears. This is auditory information. These children have perceptual difficulties and can show many different problems. They may have trouble figuring out who is speaking and to them they should be listening. One may tell them to canter; they pay attention to the rider talking behind them instead. This is a problem in auditory figure ground. They may have trouble determining where the sound comes from. They are in the rear of the arena and you call from the front to "come here." They look and look but do nothing. They have trouble with auditory directionality and cannot tell from which direction the sound comes. Some children have <u>no</u> auditory kinesthetic match. This is very frustrating for instructors. The instructor says "go to the tack room." They repeat, "I'll go to the tack room." But nothing happens. They cannot translate the auditory information into motor responses (Wepman, 1973).

III Processing

The highest level of learning behavior possibly to be affected in the learning disabled children is processing. Once information is received in the children's brain, they may lack the ability to use or relate it to other information. This area creates many "unusual" behaviors. These children tend to do what they think they are supposed to do and this usually has no resemblance to what they were told to do. The three areas that affect the children with this problem the most are the areas of association, closure, and sequential memory.

A. Association

Association is the ability of the brain to put materials together that go together, i.e., stop sign, light, red, car. Behavior that is seen: Tell the children to go to the arena. One finds them at the house. Tell them to go to the stable. One finds them at the bathroom. Association affects two channels--visual and auditory. Some children can put together information as long as they see it (visual channel). Some children can put together information as long as they hear it (auditory channel). Some children cannot put any information together. Ask them what a bit is and they say it is a martingale.

B. Closure

Closure is the ability of the brain to recognize a whole from a presentation of the parts. This may be in terms of processing visual or auditory material. One asks the children a question. If you wait, they give the correct answer. It just takes time (auditory channel). They cannot answer quickly. One shows them something, i.e., condition of the saddle with dirt on it, and ask what happened to it--they answer after some delay with the right information (visual closure). In other words, it takes these children longer to "get it together."

C. Sequential Memory

Sequential memory is the automatic ability of the brain to remember the order of things presented to the children and to reproduce this order. This affects behavior in both channels of learning. Children with this type of problem will very carefully put on their shoes and tie them only to discover to their amazement that they have no socks on. One shows them how to saddle the horse. They cannot remember what to do first. One shows them the steps in mounting a horse and they cannot remember how to do it.

Many of these children do not understand time and space. These two items have no apparent meaning for these children. If one tells them to be here at 10, they do not get here until 11:30. They do not understand time. One tells the children to go to the tack room and get their bits. They cannot find the room. They try and try but fail to find it. They are lost in space.

The above material gives some quick idea of the complexity of the problems of the child with a learning disability. The problems can be as severe as described or be rather mild. Remember, these children with a learning disability have normal to above normal intelligence. They cannot understand why they cannot do the things they see everyone else doing. They try and cannot get the same results that everybody else does. As one working in a therapeutic riding program, raise these questions--when working with such children, "why is the child showing this behavior?" "Is he or she actually trying to get back at me?" Is this behavior a "sign-post--signal" that his or her learning disability is keeping him or her from working well? Also, because the child has learning disabilities, please remember that the very same individual has many learning abilities. The real problem is teacher disability. He or she can learn if the instructor learns how to teach him or her and has the patience to endure. Concentrate on what the child can do.

References
Brough, J., Chancy, C. (1983). *Basic Development of Motor Skills.* Kankakee, IL: Brough Learning Center.
Brough, J., Chancy, C., Patton, A. (1982). Camp Manual. Mt. Zion, IL: Camp New Horizon.
Chaney, C., Kephart, N. (1969). *Motoric Aids to Perceptual Training.* Columbus: Charles E. Merrill Publishing Co.
Frostig, M. (1963). *Developmental Test of Visual Perception.* Palo Alto, CA Consulting Psychologist Press.
McCarthy, J., Kirk, S. *The Illinois Test of Psycholinguistic Ability.* Urbana, IL: Institute for Research on Exceptional Children.
United States Congress. (1968). "*Notes and Working Papers. . .,*" Education of Handicapped Children. Prepared for the Subcommittee on Education of the Committee on Labor and Public Welfare, United States Congress (Washington, D.C,: U.S. Gov. Printing Office, May, 1968). 14.
Wepman, J. (1973). *Auditory Discrimination Test.* Chicago: Joseph M. Wepman.

15.06   THE IEP: WHAT IT IS AND WHAT IT MEANS TO YOU

Gigi Sweet, MEd

At an operating center that works with school-age riders, the therapeutic riding staff has probably heard teachers or parents talk about the **IEP (Individual Education Plan)**. Every public school student who qualifies for special services has one. The IEP is a product of the <u>Education for All Handicapped Children Act</u>, passed in 1975. It ensures that the needs of each student will be addressed on an individual basis. Annually, a staffing is held to establish each child's goals and objectives. The staffing team consists of a parent/guardian, teachers, therapists and clinicians with whom the student comes in contact, a special education representative from the school district and the student, if so desired. Support personnel, such as adaptive swim teachers, therapists, and others who have responsibility for many students may not be present at the staffing, but will submit objectives pertinent to their area. The minimum at a staffing will be the special education teacher, parent/guardian and special education representative.

Immediately upon a student's admission to a school, the staffing is held and a written IEP is the product. There should be no lapse time without a current IEP until the student graduates (which will occur on or before the student's 22nd birthday) or is discontinued in the program for other reasons.

The IEP is printed in quadruplicate, with copies given to each of the following: parent, classroom teacher, special education /support personnel, and the student's cumulative record file. Most school districts use three pages for the IEP; the items on each page vary between districts. Information provided includes: the student's pertinent record data, checklist of special services, present levels of performance, consideration of placement options as they relate to <u>least restrictive environment </u>(the student should be mainstreamed into the regular setting as much as possible), date of implementation and signature lines for all those involved in the staffing.

Also in the IEP will be the yearly goals in any or all of the following areas: affective (behavioral), academic, vocational and recreational/physical. Goals are broad general statements summarizing targets for the year. A sample goal in the vocational area for a moderately mentally retarded high school student is, "Harold will function in the sheltered workshop independently on piecemeal tasks contracted to the school."

The remaining portion of the IEP (some districts use an addendum instead) will delineate one or more objectives that support the established goals. Objectives are written in behavioral terms with action verbs, and are measurable in some way, usually through quantitative data. Teachers may work on other objectives not on the IEP, as long as the objectives support the goals. Objectives are updated yearly or more often as they are either totally met (TM) or determined not suitable. Examples of objectives for the previously stated vocational goal are:
   1. Using a template, Harold will package and seal items with 100% accuracy
   2. Harold will clock in and out and deliver his packaged goods to his supervisor on each workday

What is the relationship of the IEP with a therapeutic riding program? Directly, absolutely none. An IEP reflects a contractual agreement within the school setting. An exception to this is the school that includes therapeutic riding on the IEP, either generally listed as a support service, or more specifically with itemized objectives. Indirectly, the IEP goals and objectives will help a riding center integrate and coordinate activities with the classroom.

Often a school district will not wish to include a therapeutic riding program on the IEP because of the difficulty and legality of blending federal regulations with a private industry that is not regulated by the government. It is helpful, nonetheless to have the therapeutic riding program on the IEP, probably as an adjunct to adaptive physical education. One should be very careful, however, having therapeutic riding activities as specific objectives on the IEP. **Remember this is a legal contract that provides documentation of the educational program.** It is subject to continuous monitoring and evaluation. Even though the instructor is monitoring the riding activities, one does not want to lose control of what is happening at the center. What the teacher can include are behavioral and social objectives to be achieved hopefully through their cooperation with therapeutic riding staff. It would be unusual for a teacher to want to include specific riding objectives in the IEP. By doing this, she has made the responsible person (the instructor) someone who is not part of the school staffing team or district personnel.

What are the rights of a therapeutic riding instructor regarding the IEP? She has none. A teacher may wish to share the IEP with the instructor as it benefits both the school and riding programs. Establish with the teacher that each parent has agreed to release the information to the center staff. Respect the school's right not to make such information available, and the confidentiality of the document if it **is** offered. Do not make it available to volunteers, but extract information that is pertinent to the program and summarize it for them. The teacher who is unable to provide the instructor with a copy of the IEP can give him a similar summary. If a teacher does not want to provide him with the IEP, DO NOT go over her head to seek parental permission. This is an excellent way to sabotage all the good will that has been created. For those school-age riders brought to the program by their parents, one may ask them for permission to contact the teacher or, preferably, request an introduction. Even though parents can provide the instructor with a copy of the IEP, it is bad form to accept it without the knowledge of the teacher, the main author of the document. One's primary contact however should be with the person who brings the rider to the center, be it parent, teacher or agency.

What does one do with information provided in the IEP? Working with the teacher the instructor can provide follow-through that is highly motivating on behavior programs, consistency in therapy goals, and practice of educational and vocational skills. Academic objectives from math to social studies may be incorporated into the riding lessons. Vocational objectives are a natural when addressed with unmounted activities. If the instructor cannot gain access to the IEP, one can still do all these things. Provide the cooperating teacher with a form on which she can briefly describe the student's academic functioning level, current behavior plans, particular strengths and areas of interest. Share this information with the volunteers who work with this rider.

In conclusion, the IEP can be a tool that helps the instructor align the therapeutic riding program with goals and objectives developed within the rider's educational setting. Consistency within the child's life maximizes the opportunities for success by providing structure, increasing familiarity and reducing frustration. But do not feel unable to achieve the same benefits without access to the IEP. As a therapeutic riding instructor one has had vast experience adapting equipment to fit the many needs presented by riders within the program. With initiative and expertise, one can create the necessary tools to get every job accomplished!

15.07   ACTIVITY ANALYSIS

Barbara T. Engel, MEd, OTR

KEY WORDS
TEACHING TECHNIQUE
SIMPLIFIED--BREAK DOWN--DECREASE FRUSTRATION

Task analysis is used by occupational therapists to examination the components of a task in order to determine its use as a treatment modality or to teach a client activity of daily living skills (Hopkins & Smith, 1978). Llorens (1978) states in occupational therapy "activity analysis is usable to determine the most utilizable properties of an activity or task to accomplish a specific treatment objective." In this setting the properties to be considered can influence physical, psychological, or cognitive-perceptual-motor deficits. As examples, tasks may be selected to:
- Provide increased range in the shoulder-arms area
- Allow for expression of independence
- Provide an outlet for aggression
- Allow for socialization
- Provide tactile stimulation
- Provide a variety of movement experiences for vestibular stimulation
- Provide fine-motor manipulation of the fingers and hand-eye coordination
- Increase problem solving skills and motor planning.
- Allow for repetitious arm movements

Snow (1985) describes task analysis as breaking down the total task into small components and then forward or backward chaining the steps. Each step is practiced and mastered before the next step is attempted. In forward chaining, the first step is mastered before the second step is attempted and so on. In backward chaining the last step is practiced followed by the prior step. Wallace & Kaufman (1978) state "task analysis may be viewed as a sequence of evaluative activities that pinpoint the child's learning problem and guide the teacher in planning an effective remedial sequence of instructional tasks." This approach uses a step-by-step process of breaking down the activity a child is doing to <u>find</u> the <u>problem</u>. The activity may then be broken down into sub-skills if necessary. Each sub-skill is tackled separately. For example, Christy is have trouble completing her math assignments which are written each day on the blackboard. The teacher does a task analysis which would include:
- Seeing the assignment on the board
- Reading the assignments on the blackboard
- Finding paper and pencil to write them down on
- Transferring what she sees to a motor act
- Writing them down on her paper
- Finding time to complete the problems
- Being able to compute the problems
- Giving the finished paper to the teacher

The teacher examines each step to see which one is causing Christy to fail this task.

Activities are analyzed for the selection of age-appropriate work/play categories in order that the skills involved are meaningful to the client's needs (Clark 1985). Following the suitable selection of the activity, a task may be analyzed to determine if it needs to be adapted in order for Jake (who has cerebral palsy) to do it successfully. If Jake cannot pick up the brush he will not be able to perform the next task, brushing the horse. This example breaks down the activity so that it can be examined for the components of normal physical function. For example--picking up a brush, while standing, from the table requires the following movements:
- Turning around to locate the brush by looking toward it on the table
- Taking several steps toward the table
- Raising the arm at the shoulder

- Activating a arm in extension to reach for the brush
- Lowering the arm toward the brush
- Extending the wrist and fingers to open the hand
- Lowering the arm till the extended hand touches the brush
- Grasping the brush with the hand and closing fingers
- Flexing the elbow and bringing the brush to the midline of the body

This analysis breaks down the physical movements required in this task only. The next step would be to analyze Jake's ability to perform each movement and how he can perform the tasks to gain the best range of motion in body and limbs. In this example the task analysis may help the instructor identify a movement that a rider may have trouble doing, such as reaching with the arm and hand. The task may need to be altered in order for the person to grasp the brush effectively and use it in brushing the horse. For example, the instructor gives Jake a brush with a velcro strap that holds the brush securely in his hand--he does not need to concentrate on clinching the fingers. Jake will be able to extend his arm more easily without tightly flexing his hand and wrist to hold the brush--which in turn may cause his elbow and shoulder to flex. In this way Jake can independently brush the horse with good arm motion.

In a treatment situation, an occupational therapist may use these activities to develop normal motor function while performing a functional task. He or she would stand next to Jake and would assist him to move his hand and arm (using positioning and facilitory techniques) while maintaining a balanced body posture. Jake would learn both balance and function by allowing the therapist to assist when he cannot make the appropriate movement--in essence--Jake and the therapist are working as one--as his body learns new motor behavior. The therapist has used the activity analysis to isolate the areas that need her assistance.

How will the task analysis process help the riding instructor? All instructors break down skills to be taught. In teaching riding, the instructor knows that his or her students must first feel secure on the horse before they can learn to use the "aids" (sending messages to the horse). He or she will do exercises to strengthen their bodies so balance develops. He or she will teach one aid at a time: "use your legs" or "follow the horse's head movements by allowing the arms to move freely." The instructor knows that his or her student will not refine the hand aids until the arms can move independently from the body. Any good riding instructor has broken down the riding skills or informally performed an "activity analysis" without a formal tool. He or she has learned the sequence of skills that are necessary for the rider to learn to ride. He or she can also look at a rider and tell where the rider is in the sequential development of riding skills. In a therapeutic riding program, the instructor needs not only to know the sequential development of riding skills but must also be able (Lamport et al., 1989):

To recognize the physical, mental, and emotional requirements of the task

To recognize the rider's physical, mental and psychological limitations

To recognize the cognitive skills necessary to carry out a task

To recognize the processing skills required in the cognitive area

To recognize the areas where assistance is beneficial

To recognize the areas where the rider needs more practice

To recognize supplies, equipment and environmental requirements

To recognize precautions, contraindications, indications associated with the task

Activity analysis helps the instructor to develop lessons plans and not only to develop a more effective training program for his or her students but also to determine and provide the appropriate training for the program horses. Activity analysis breaks activities into small parts. Remember that small tasks are always easier to deal with than large ones.

References

Clark, P.N. (1985). *Occupational Therapy for Children.* St. Louis: The C.V. Mosby Co.

Hopkins, H.L., Smith, H.D. (1978). *Willard & Spackman's Occupational Therapy.* 5th ed. New York: J.B. Lippincott Co. 102-105.

Lamport, N.K.; Coffey, M.S.; Hersch, G.I. (1989). *Activity Analysis.* Thorofare: Slack Incorporated.

Llorens, L. A. (1973). Activity Analysis for Cognitive-Perceptual-Motor Dysfunction. *AJOT,* 27:8: 453-56.

Snow, B.S. (1985). Children with Visual or Hearing Impairment in Clark, PN & Allen, AS: *Occupational Therapy.*

Wallace, G., & Kaufman, J.M. (1978). *Teaching Children with Learning Problems.* (2nd ed) Columbus: Charles E. Merrill Publishing Co. 105.

15.08   PEGGY - THE TEACHING HORSE AT WORK IN THERAPEUTIC RIDING

Jane C. Copeland, BS, MA,

Almost every riding instructor dreams of a horse so patient it stands quietly while a dozen students learn to mount and dismount. A horse whose mouth cannot be hurt by harsh use of the reins. An easy keeper, an easy shipper, a horse who does not need shoes! *Peggy - The Teaching Horse* is a mechanical horse designed to be used with students learning the basic elements of mounting, reining and behavior around a horse. "*Peggy*", the name given to the first *teaching horse*, is the invention of therapeutic riding volunteer, Seth Armen. Through his years of working with disabled children in a Connecticut therapeutic riding program, Seth witnessed how slipping hands and roving feet could upset a horse. He decided there "has to be a better way to practice basic riding skills." Thinking back to World War II submarine training he asked himself, "why not a riding simulator for equestrians?" Out of his concern came the original plans for a device useful as an adjunct to therapeutic riding. After much consultation with riding instructors and therapists, monetary support from grants, and construction help from numerous volunteers, *Peggy - The Teaching Horse* became a reality in 1987 (Figure 1).

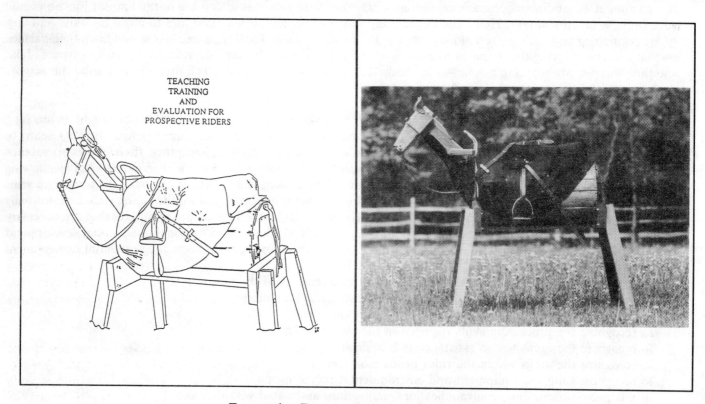

TEACHING
TRAINING
AND
EVALUATION FOR
PROSPECTIVE RIDERS

FIGURE 1.   PEGGY - THE TEACHING HORSE

Machines have long been in use in training for visual motor skills. Electronic advances lend new dimensions of applicability to simulation training especially in the aerospace industry. Simulations which electronically duplicate the movement of the horse have recently been developed in France and the United States for use by jockeys, rodeo bull riders, and experienced equestrians. The *Teaching Horse* does not duplicate the horse's movement. She provides an opportunity for students to master basic riding skills in a controlled, structured environment with a minimum of distractions. Getting on and off, reining, and stirrup adjustment can all be practiced by the hour without fear

DESIGN

A specially designed wooden barrel approximating a horse's body size forms the body of the *Teaching Horse*. The seat area is padded, shaped and covered with suede to resemble a saddle. Removable legs attach to a frame that supports the barrel while a swing away neck and head attach to the front barrel surface. The rear of the barrel sports a leather tail which lifts to reveal a storage area for battery and wiring.

One of the most important aspects of the *Teaching Horse* design is the feedback she provides to the student and instructor. Reins attached to a pressure sensitive bit located in the mouth of the *Teaching Horse* activate a series of lights located on the easily observed neck and head. With a symmetrical pull on both reins, as in a halt, the red light turns on and remains on until rein tension is reduced. If the student reins back unevenly, the red and white lights come on together signaling that the horse is receiving mixed messages. In requesting a turn by increasing tension on a single rein, a white light located behind the ear on the appropriate side comes on and the horse's head turns toward the direction of pull. If both red and white lights appear during an attempted turn, it signals unwanted pressure on one rein, again a mixed message for the horse.

Another pressure-sensitive switch is located in the seat area. This switch activates an amber light on the horse's neck and is used to train the down/up rhythm of posting. A metronome which accompanies the *Teaching Horse* is used to provide a consistent rhythm, adjustable to a wide range of tempos. Practice of the rising, or posting trot, is accomplished through the student rising and sitting rhythmically while keeping time with the metronome and/or observing the rhythmic flashing of the amber light. This pre-trot work is used to develop a sense of timing and helps the student prepare for the unbalancing experience of trotting. The *Teaching Horse* comes with a transportation cart for travel and folds down for storage. Carting the *Teaching Horse* about is designed to be a one person task. For long distance travel a station wagon or Jeep-type vehicle makes a good *Teaching Horse* trailer.

APPLICATION

Peggy, the original *Teaching Horse*, has proven her usefulness in many settings during her therapeutic riding program career. She is at home in a school classroom, at the stable, or in a mobile classroom. Her cart allows her to travel to ringside or she can teach her lessons in the shade of a tree. Today *Teaching Horses* are working in programs throughout the United States, Canada, and England. Preparation for riding is easily addressed with the Teaching Horse. Decisions about mounting procedures and adaptive equipment can be made in a safe, controlled setting with the student given time to try out various positions and equipment alternatives. In an article on motor skill acquisition, skill is referred to as movement appropriate to the task, effective in achieving the goal and executed in a way that is personally economical and least likely to cause undue stress or strain on the body (Higgins, 1991). The ease and value of assessing the skills of prospective students is apparent to instructors during evaluation sessions where impressions can be noted as they occur and not later after time blurs the original impression. A two part evaluation form with a six point rating scale lists assessable skills (Figure 2). Data obtained from initial evaluations is easy to compare to ratings obtained later on.

Students already riding in a program can work on refining skills with the Teaching Horse. One of the very few agreed upon observations in the motor learning literature is that appropriate practice leads to improved motor performance. As obvious as this may seem, it is not always recognized how many movements are required to obtain changes in motor performance. A study by Corcos showed that performance enhancement can take place over at least 1,400 repetitions (Higgins, 1991). Reinforcing motor sequences with the *Teaching Horse* just prior to a riding session adds to the student's rate of success as the reviewed skills are transferred into immediate functional activity. Training sessions also serve as a time to explain concepts such as why riders do not haul on the reins to steady themselves.

The *Teaching Horse* can be used next to the ring with the barn cats, smells and noises of a riding arena or be placed in a quiet, uncluttered room. A one-on-one lesson in a quiet environment away from the sights and sounds of a busy stable may be just the needed atmosphere for success. During training sessions the *Teaching Horse* responds with unlimited patience, standing still indefinitely for a practice session.

Evaluation Form – Part One

Peggy – The Teaching Horse

Name

Age _____ Class

Goals

Relevant Information

Rating Scale:
0 = cannot perform
1 = performs with maximum assistance
2 = performs with moderate assistance
3 = performs with minimal assistance
4 = performs independently with occasional cueing or correction
5 = performs independently

Session Dates	Approach	Mount	Posture	Balance	Whoa!	Half-Seat	Posting	Turn Right	Turn Left	Serpentine	Dismount	Running up Stirrups	Other

Comments

Instructor _____ Location

FIGURE 2.1. PEGGY THE TEACHING HORSE--EVALUATION FORM--PART I

Evaluation Form – Part Two

Peggy – The Teaching Horse

Rating Scale: P = Poor, S = Satisfactory, G = Good, E = Excellent

Session Dates	Effort	Concentration	Following Directions	Verbalization	Attitude	Other

Comments

FIGURE 2.2. PEGGY THE TEACHING HORSE--EVALUATION FORM PART II

In the therapeutic riding ring there is constant competition for the rider's attention. A moving horse, the instructor, a leader and one or two sidewalkers all vie for the student's attention. Add a few birds in the rafters or barking dogs by the outdoor ring and it can border on an overload of sights and sounds,especially for the sensory-sensitive rider. Limiting sensory input during a *Teaching Horse* session can help a student grasp basic riding skills more quickly and with less frustration. Once basic riding skills are learned without distractions and performed a sufficient number of times to establish motor memory, introducing distractions will not have as deleterious an impact on performance.

During her tenure in therapeutic riding, the *Teaching Horse* has added new responsibilities to her job description. In addition to student evaluation and the training of riding skills, the *Teaching Horse* has become an integral part of horse shows, booths at fairs and fund raising events. *Peggy-The Teaching Horse* regularly attends therapeutic riding horse shows at her home program in Connecticut. She helps students review skills during pre-competition warm up. Brothers and sisters of students take turns riding the *Teaching Horse* and learn a little about what their sibling is doing in the show ring. Trotting the *Teaching Horse* out at fairs and local charity events draws people's attention and encourages them to come to the organization's booth to ask questions. Again her patience and ability to stand without tiring make her an ideal spokes-horse in these settings.

LESSON PLANS

A <u>Peggy</u> - <u>The</u> <u>Teaching</u> <u>Horse</u> <u>Manual</u> accompanies each *Teaching Horse* to its new home. In the manual, lesson plans follow a task analysis format covering basics such as: How to approach the horse, and name the *Teaching Horse's* equipment. More detailed task-analyzed lessons are provided on mounting, stirrup adjustment, holding and using the reins, half-seat and posting. These are subdivided into sections for students who need maximal or minimal assistance as well as for students who are approaching independent riding.

Lesson plans are written so that an instructor or designated volunteer can use them to teach skills to students. The lesson for Whoa! is presented as an example. It assumes the student has learned to sit upright, pick up the reins correctly and hold them in alignment. **WHOA!**

- ◉ In calling the halt, ask the student to say, "Whoa!" in a positive voice
- ◉ Ask the student to deepen his or her seat by digging the seat bones into the saddle
- ◉ Ask the student to pull back gently and evenly on the reins by closing his or her fingers, moving the arms back and keeping the hands low
- ◉ To sustain the halt, ask the student to count to five, keeping even pressure on the reins
- ◉ When only the red light goes on, the student is performing a correct halt
- ◉ If a white light also comes on with a red Whoa! signal, the student is pulling on the reins with uneven pressure
- ◉ Use the feedback lights in designing individual programs of practice to equalize the pull on the reins
- ◉ Practice by creating a situation built around whoa/halt/walk on. "You are a policeman riding a horse in stop and go traffic"

FIGURE 3.   PEGGY THE TEACHING HORSE WITH RIDER

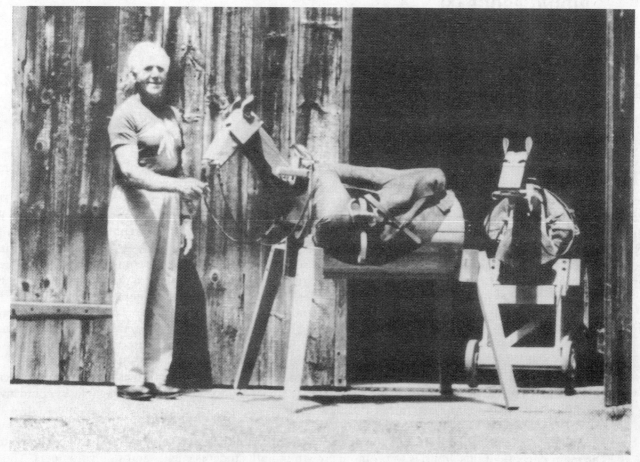

FIGURE 4. PEGGY THE TEACHING HORSE WITH SETH ARMEN

IN CONCLUSION

The Teaching Horse is helping students become better equestrians at a faster pace and with a greater degree of safety. It is designed to be an adjunct to therapeutic riding programs but can assist the beginning rider in developing skills and confidence. The Teaching Horse project attests to the powerful influence of volunteers in the delivery of therapeutic horseback riding to the disabled. Today the Teaching Horse is busy working in over twenty programs. Each simulated horse is hand crafted by Seth Armen, his son Ted, and the Pegasus volunteers who work with them. Proceeds from the sale of the Teaching Horse, as well as the rights to the patent, belong to Pegasus Therapeutic Riding, Inc.

Information on how to obtain a Teaching Horse is available by writing Pegasus Therapeutic Riding, Inc., P.O. Box 2053, Darien, CT O6820-2053.

References
Bartnick, L.M.(1990).*High Tech Horse Gives Feedback With Therapy*. The Chronicle of the Horse, Apr. 20, 5-6.
Carroll, B. (1990). Mechanical Mounts. *Equus.* Dec. 15-20.
Higgins, S. (1991). Motor Skill Acquisition. *Physical Therapy.* Vol 71, Jan, no 1. 48-84.
_____ (1991). Motor Skill Acquisition. *Physical Therapy.* Vol 71, Feb no 2.128-139.
Maar, N.T., Copeland, J.C., (1989) *Peggy - The Teaching Horse: training, and evaluation for prospective riders.*

15.09 GROUP DYNAMICS - GROUP INTERACTIONS IN A THERAPEUTIC RIDING PROGRAM

Barbara T. Engel MEd, OTR

KEY WORDS
SUCCESS
PLEASURE
TEAMWORK

A group consists of two or more people who are motivated to deal with a common goal or task. There are many types of groups and types of leadership styles. A collection of people can become a group. At a social gathering a common goal can be identified such as playing bridge. The group then forms around this common interest. There are social groups, family groups, business groups, like a board of directors. There are horse groups, as the Pony Club, American Horse Show Association (AHSA), 4-H Clubs or therapeutic riding programs. Therapeutic riding programs require a group concept. One cannot work with a disabled rider without a group even if it is just the instructor, the leader, the rider and the horse. Most programs have several types of groups. There is the board of directors for all non-profit programs, the program management, the riding program group and the riding session group. Each of these groups has different tasks to perform and requires different styles of leadership. For example:

- The board of directors main purpose is to secure and control funds, set and carry out policy, and promote the health of the organization. Within the board group, group process is very active and its health can be determined by the fulfillment of the group process. To the organization, its purpose is administrative and therefore collectively has an authoritarian leader role.
- The program management group's main purpose is to carry out the administrative functions of a program. This role may be held by the head instructor or may be a coordinator in a large program. Tasks could involve scheduling, securing appropriate forms, ordering supplies and paying bills. These are administrative tasks and the leadership is authoritarian.
- The riding program group involves all the people that work with the riders and teaching staff and volunteers. The main purpose of this group is to promote growth in both students/clients and staff/volunteers. The task of this group is dynamic and requires dynamic leadership. The healthier the group process, the more productive and cohesive the group will be.
- The riding session group is a sub-section of the riding program group and affects the group process of the parent group. The dynamic group process is active here with the staff/volunteers but not necessarily with the students (the students are always indirectly by affected the dynamics of the staff group).

How well a program functions in spirit, management, and growth depends on the group process.

Why Some Groups Succeed and Others Fail
In order for a group to succeed it must (Hall, 1961):
1. Have stated goals with changing objectives to continue the group's purpose
2. Have leadership
3. Have maintained the group process

Groups fail when (Hall, 1961):
1. The group is composed of the wrong combination of people
2. The organizers have a faulty purpose
3. The atmosphere does not promote organizational growth
4. The members lack skills in playing the necessary group roles
5. All persons are not included in the group, causing subgroups

How a group functions depends a great deal on its purpose and the type of leadership. Therapeutic riding programs have similar goals. Yet they may function quite differently because of their leadership and group process.

328

Basic Leadership Styles

1. An <u>authoritarian</u> <u>leader</u> directs his or her group with little input from its members. This leader takes his or her task and establishes goals and expectations according to his or her perception. If his or her <u>leadership</u> skills are more like a dictator, members will be expected to do as they are told. He or she does not want to give others too much responsibility for fear of losing control of the group. This leader is power-driven and has little if any concern for the members or in the case of a therapeutic riding program, the rider participants and families. Members gain little satisfaction and volunteers do not remain with this type of a group very long. Authoritarian leadership is appropriate to administrative roles but poor for "leading people."

2. A <u>laissez faire</u> <u>leader</u> guides his or her group in such a way as to maintain an equilibrium, avoiding problems with the group and his or her superior at the possible expense of the group goals or its members. A small therapeutic riding program with few changes would suit him or her the best. Whether the riders were gaining from the program would probably be of little concern. His or her focus is on a social and happy environment with no pressures.

3. A <u>democratic</u> <u>leader</u> is group oriented and involves the members in decision making and goal setting. This leader is as concerned in satisfying the needs of the group members as in reaching objectives. The instructor, leader, sidewalker team should be a democratic group with the instructor maintaining the leadership role but involving each member of the team in a fully participatory role with equal responsibility to the rider.

4. A <u>dynamic</u> <u>group</u> (shared leadership) is a participatory group in which members share in the problem solving process and <u>share</u> <u>leadership</u> <u>responsibilities</u>. The leadership role can actually emerge from within the group even when a person initially pulls the group together, or it may be shared by two or more people. The leadership role includes the facilitation of the group process as the group fulfills its purpose. A dynamic group has two major functions. One function is to focus on its major purpose and goals. The second function is to develop group objectives and deal with the group maintenance roles. In a dynamic group, people are willing to listen, understand, consider the merit of a statement from other members, and draw a conclusion based on its evidence. The group thrives from members' different view points. The group members and the group tasks are of equal importance.

Successful leadership is dictated by the group, for one cannot lead if members refuse to follow. The authoritarian and laissez faire groups are not as original or efficient in their work as democratic or dynamic groups. The latter groups will have less deviant members, role conflict or search for sub-leadership. The democratic and dynamic groups put their energy into meeting objectives and group needs. Members are cohesive, gain a feeling of fulfillment and feel responsible for the group productivity. They have an investment in the life of the group, provide support and rewards for each other and therefore prevent "burn out."

A group needs to understand its purpose, focus on its overall goals, and set objectives. It needs to recognize its unhealthy elements, clear them up and move on toward becoming a healthier group. Members need to develop trust in each person in the process. The group process is a movement which passes through various phases. As long as the process moves forward toward its objectives and develops new objectives as old ones are met, the group will become stronger and develop into a mature-function group. A mature group is a self-directing, self-controlling body in which *every member* carries his part of the responsibility for developing and executing the group's plan. (Hall, 1961)."

Your program's group is mature if:
1. Its leader fosters growth of all participants
2. There is intelligent management of its environment
3. It understands the group process and has the ability to make appropriate adjustments
4. It is skilled at problem-solving
5. It has full quality participation of its members

Since therapeutic riding programs have several types of groups who interrelate at different levels, it is important that each group is clear on its purpose and goals. If they overlap in purpose and in control, they can not establish realistic and obtainable objectives and maintain a growth-oriented environment. For example, the lesson group selects teaching methods, matches riders with horses, determines training needs and decides on volunteer and staff tasks. The board of directors sets budgets, selects the program director, makes policies and directs fund raising. Some people may be members of more than one of these groups. When one group interferes with the other's roles and objectives the group growth process breaks down, for the internal control of the group is lost.

Task-Oriented Team Building Groups

The advantages of a functional group are (Rogers, 1970):

- To create an open problem-solving climate
- To increase the knowledge and competence of the people in authority roles
- To build trust among all members
- To recognize achievement and acknowledge it
- To increase the sense of "ownership" of the group project
- To help manage the project toward relevant objectives rather than "historical" practice
- To increase self-control and self-direction of each group member
- To increase success of the group
- To increase the joy of working together toward a common goal

The Group Process, Its Importance

When people get together for the purpose of accomplishing something, they need to become acquainted, to feel each other out. As people within the group test each other, explore their feelings and attitudes toward each other, their facades begin to disappear. Trust increases and the "real" person begins to emerge. At this point one begins to gain a true sense of communication. People may wall themselves off initially, showing their "*public self*". They may feel their *real self* may not be as acceptable because they do not want to get too involved. They may have had difficulty in the past with relationships and thus avoid new ones. Some people will leave the group rather than get *involved* or show *themselves*. As group members become more open they find that their *real self* is more accepted by others and a sense of trust and warmth builds for each member with open communication. Open communication increases group cohesiveness which in turn develops group pride.

During the process of forward movement of the group, there will be times that specific issues regarding each member must be dealt with while still maintaining a focus on group objectives. The group will also establish its own specific goals even though the overall goal of therapeutic riding will be maintained. Each group needs to have the ability to plan for and develop growth. A board of directors which interjects their own ideas or special controls into the program group, may squelch the whole group process and set up a fight or flight process.

Group cohesiveness depends on the willingness of each member to play his role or roles in such a way as to foster the success of **others** (Kemp, 1970). The group develops through building and maintaining roles. These roles must be carried out by a group member. Many times one person will take on numerous roles. Group members will take on these roles as the group develops.

Group roles include:

1.	Initiator--contributor	2.	Information seeker
3.	Opinion seeker--encourager	4.	Information giver
5.	Opinion giver	6.	Elaborator
7.	Coordinator--compromiser	8.	Orienter
9.	Evaluator--critic	10.	Energizer
11.	Procedural technician	12.	Recorder
13.	Harmonizer	14.	Standards and limit setter

Negative behaviors in groups include:
- ◘ Splitting the group by developing opposing methods or not including all members
- ◘ General disagreement
- ◘ Absence of real leadership or a leader who is less skilled than the group members.
- ◘ Lack of interest of members causing their partial or full withdrawal
- ◘ Interpersonal aggressiveness
- ◘ Break-down in overall communication
- ◘ Lack of clear objectives and problem-solving ability
- ◘ Failure to include some members
- ◘ Blocking of the group growth
- ◘ Diverting group direction
- ◘ Focusing attention on self
- ◘ Playboy--diverting attention away from task and group growth

Therapeutic riding groups always begin with a designated leader which is usually the head instructor. The instructor will be the person who must be responsible to carry out the administrative responsibilities and be in charge of the lesson. Administrative tasks are basically determined by policy and are directives or rules which must be followed. On the other hand, leadership roles are related to the development of personnel growth, function and skill. This type of leadership may be shared with other group members. Group roles are shared among members and one person may fulfill several roles. Assigned leader is the initiator of the group process and may begin by giving information and seeking opinions. The leader's ability to communicate and reinforce group problem solving and objectives will have a strong influence on the initial success of the group.

Administrative tasks in therapeutic riding programs may include:
- ◘ Meeting insurance requirements
- ◘ Enforcing North American Riding for the Handicapped Association (NARHA) or other association guidelines
- ◘ Enforcing Board of Directors guidelines
- ◘ Enforcing safety standards
- ◘ Meeting health care standards
- ◘ Reinforcing stable management requirements
- ◘ Meeting state, county or local codes

Groups need time and patience to develop. This does not distract from the program's function since group growth develops best with a task-oriented focus. The growth of the group process is like the growth of any relationship. As it grows, it changes. Change is stressful but necessary for growth. Growth in turn develops strength and a feeling of accomplishment. The process may be stressful at times but its rewards are everlasting--both in the development of meaningful relationships and in the productivity of the group.

Bonner, H. (1959). *Group Dynamics.* New York: The Ronald Press Co.

Hall, D. M. (1961). *The Dynamics of Group Discussion.* Danville: The Interstate Printers & Publishers, Inc.

Kemp, C. G. (1970). *Perspectives on the Group Process.* Boston: Houghton Mifflin Co. 25-26,36,48,62.

Luft, J. (1970). *Group Processes.* Palo Alto: National Press Books.

Rogers, C. R. (1970). *Carl Rogers On Encounter Groups.* New York: Harper & Row.

Reeves, E. T. *The Dynamics of Group Behavior.* American Management Association.

Walport, G. (1955). *Becoming: Basic Consideration for Psychology of Personality.* New Haven: Yale University Press.

15.10 INDIVIDUAL VERSUS GROUP LESSONS IN A THERAPEUTIC RIDING PROGRAM

Barbara T. Engel MEd, OTR

The instructor places the riding student in a class. Should the student be in a group class or in a class by himself or herself? There are a number of considerations which need to be made regarding the best environment for the student and the program's ability to meet the student's need. There are positive and negative considerations for both individual and group sessions. Individuals in groups affect each other in positive and negative ways. One must also remember that therapeutic horseback riding is always a "group" experience. The group is always the rider-horse-instructor, the rider-horse-leader, the rider-leader-sidewalker(s)-instructor. To this core group can be added more assistants and then more horses, riders and helpers. This can produce an overwhelming amount of activity to some people. For persons who have difficulty attending, who are hypersensitive to noise or movement, or who have difficulty making their own nervous systems and bodies perform basic skills, groups can distract from the value of riding a horse. Groups also can add to the experience.

Advantages of Group Lessons:
- More economical than individual lessons
- Can accommodate school and association groups
- More efficient use of the instructor's time
- Staff can reduce the hours they work
- Provide a social environment
- Can use the group for peer pressure or stimulation
- Horses like to work together
- Students can copy or learn from each other
- Students learn social skills
- Games can be incorporated into the session

Disadvantages of Group Lessons:
- Individual analysis and intervention is limited
- Needs may be overlooked
- Less choice of horses
- Students are given stimulation from all the other students--may overwhelm
- May be difficult to understand instructions in group setting
- Independent riding may be less because more horses are in the arena
- Less independent thinking and riding skills - all students do the same task
- Communication is more difficult
- Need for a large staff and volunteer group
- Need for more horses

Group lessons are not <u>functional working groups</u> (where members interact to problem solve); rather it is a <u>parallel interaction group</u>--members copy each other or perform a task at the same time. Lesson students are generally not involved in developing group objectives and maintenance roles. The lesson group meets for shorter periods (the lesson period). The leader is in control of the group in an authoritarian role in order to carry through his or her lesson plan (authoritarian role is used here since the instructor teaches the group without the help of the students (one person leadership). The students may be allowed some decision-making but the instructor will make this determination and set limits.

Any time two or more people get together, even for short periods, dynamics do occur. In a group of children or adults one can observe people who:

- Seek to identify with others
- Copy others' actions
- Please the leader
- Try to be the best in the group
- Get the most attention
- Take over the session
- Avoid being noticed
- Refuse to participate in the group
- Disrupt the session

These acts are the result of social interaction and pressures. All social beings must find their place in the social structure and will react to it in various ways. Peer pressure and group interaction can be used by the leader to foster an individual's progress. One must remember that some people do not tolerate groups well or cannot learn in a group setting.

The instructor in the authority role is able to make his or her students do only what they are already willing to do (Cumming & Cumming, 1963). But instructors can manipulate *groups* to pressure students into actions they would otherwise not take. A social person wants to be accepted by his or her peers and will therefore do something to be accepted which he or she would otherwise not do. This manipulation can be carried out through riding exercises and games which make the experience pleasant and, in turn, productive. The student is not aware of the manipulation and gains a good feeling from a new or improved experience. An example is the use of **Simon Says** with children. They will most often do what the game **Simon Says**, especially when the other children are doing it.

The Need for Individual Sessions

Children or adults who have an attention-deficit disorder, language processing disorder or who have an autistic disorder need to work on a one-to-one basis in a quiet environment. Stimulation needs to be at a minimum in order for them to focus and attend for even short periods. Children and adults with closed head trauma and attention difficulties also profit from a quiet environment. Learning disabled people who must concentrate very hard on instruction and performance work best on a one-to-one basis or in small groups of two to three people.

Is it helpful to "challenge" a rider with attention deficits, some emotional disorders, language processing disorder, autism or head injury (all have degrees of learning disabilities) to be gradually moved into larger group classes? The answer depends on the goal for the rider. If the major purpose of the session is to integrate sensory-motor and communication processes; in turn to increase learning (understanding of riding skills) and to develop a true communication with the horse (execution of riding skills), the answer is no since the additional stimulation would distract from the initial goal. The ability to concentrate to a high degree in a stimulating environment for a person with learning disabilities is not possible. This is so for even an adult with relatively good functional skills (able to hold a professional job). On the other hand if the goal is to increase the rider's social skills and tolerance for environment stimuli then increasing the group size is useful and challenging.

In determining the advantages and disadvantages of individual or group sessions, both on and off the horse, one must consider many factors. What are the rider's most pressing needs? Can these best be carried out in a group or individual setting? Which tasks should be on a group level or on an individual level? What is the best size of the group--two, three, four, six or? Is the instructor skilled as a group leader? Program considerations must also be weighed since time factors and labor are always pressing in a therapeutic riding program.

Cumming, J., Cumming, E. (1963). *Ego & Milieu*. New York: Atherton Press.
Rogers, C. R. (1961). *On Becoming a Person*. Boston: Houghton Mifflin Co.

15.11 TEACHING DISABLED RIDERS TO HANDLE THEIR HORSES WITH SAFE METHODS AND PROCEDURES

Margaret L. Galloway, MS, BHSAI

KEY WORDS:
QUIET AND RELAXED
CONFIDENT
KNOWLEDGEABLE
KIND
SAFETY WITH RIDERS AND HORSES

Knowledge regarding a horse and the methods to be used in handling a horse are primary considerations for staff, volunteers and riders in a therapeutic riding program. This knowledge and these skills are important in order to fulfill the goals of therapeutic riding and to foster the horse/rider bonding process. It is important that all team members, instructors, helpers, consultants, and riders learn effective and correct techniques in all aspects of horsemanship. Without such a knowledge base a program cannot demonstrate the full value of a professionally managed program.

SAFE METHODS AND PROCEDURES:
Safety is crucial when handling horses. Horses are large, potentially fast-moving animals with natural timidity. Correct handling strengthens the understanding between horse and human, and minimizes the possibly of someone getting hurt. When handling horses, it is important to remember that they are instinctively defensive when they feel threatened. They are easily startled, and their first response is flight, or if trapped, fight. However, a solid rapport between horse and human can overcome these instincts. *"The important thing is the mutual confidence which is the basis on which the horse may grow into a cooperative friend"* (Podhajsky, 1968). True horsemen seek to understand their horses and to learn from them. Knowing the horse's nature and individual temperament helps the horseman. The T.T.E.A.M. (1990) method is an approach that specifically helps handlers develop working relationships and overcome any tensions and pain that may influence a horse's behavior.

SAFETY FACTORS TO TEACH AND MODEL TO THERAPEUTIC RIDING STUDENTS:
- Always walk to a horse. Never run around a horse.
- Approach the horse from the side, toward the shoulder.
- Speak to a horse when approaching in the stall or pasture.
- Pat the horse on the shoulder or neck.
- Do not get in front of the horse when he pulls and resists--remember he is stronger than a human.
- Make sure all tack and equipment are in good condition, clean and safe.
- Always lead a horse from the point of the shoulder, never from in front of him.
- Never wrap a lead line, or reins around the wrist or body.
- Never tie a horse by the reins or to posts not intended for that purpose.
-

KNOW YOUR HORSEMANSHIP SKILLS.
- Let the horse know what you intend to do with him.
- Learn the horse's body language.
- Be confident.
- Be firm, consistent, kind, and gentle.
- Do not turn a horse loose at the stall entrance. Walk him into the stall, turn him around to face the door, and then detach his halter.
- Never kneel down beside a horse when grooming; Always maintain a crouch or squatting position.
- Never attach cross ties to a bit.
- When grooming, never walk under cross ties or a lead rope. Walk behind the horse close to his rump or out of kicking distance.

- Protect your head from the horse while working around him
- When tacking-up, check the saddle blanket for foreign objects and spiders.
- Always run-up the stirrups on an English saddle.
- Always wear appropriate clothing when around a horse, and shoes that protect the feet.
- Clean the stable area after the horse is put away.
- Know how to keep the horse happy.
- Teach all staff and students safety measures.
- Never use or teach unsafe short cuts or "tricks."

ALL STAFF, VOLUNTEERS AND STUDENTS SHALL REMEMBER:
- To *become* the horse's leader--he is a social animal and will follow the "herd's" leadership--be in charge
- To be *calm* and quiet whenever working with a horse
- To *reward* the horse with a caress frequently and with peace and quiet for a job well done
- To be *sure* the instructions given to the horse are clear and the horse understands what is wanted of him
- To be *aware* that a horse moves away from pressure or resistance
- Never to *pull* a horse--he will only resist the pull
- To be *consistent* in the program's handling techniques
- To always *maintain* a balanced body position around the horse and let him see, feel, or hear where you are

KNOWING YOUR HORSE:
A global knowledge of the nature of the horse is the backbone of safe horsemanship. Being familiar with each horse's traits and habits is important in establishing trust and response during both care and lesson. Each person handling a horse should know his traits and feel comfortable with him. This is especially important when a client is involved, either in horse care or in riding. It is useful to ride the horse to become familiar with his movements.

APPROACHING A HORSE
A horse always should be approached carefully. Always let a horse know where you are. When walking behind a horse, either walk very close to him so that a kick will not be as damaging should he strike out or walk completely out of the range of his hind feet. Keep a hand on the horse's rump while walking behind him. Never reach out directly towards a horse's face; pat him on the shoulder first. Many horses do not like their heads patted, and some are afraid of having their head touched.

A rider should be taught to let a horse know where you are by calling his name, especially if the horse is approached from the rear. Speak to the horse and touch him while walking around behind him. Teach the rider that horses are more receptive to deliberate and slow movements. Horses should be fed only by permission and by the approved method used by the center. However, teach a rider to offer treats in a bucket or to present the treat in the feed box.

GIVE INSTRUCTIONS IN SIMPLE STATEMENTS. BE SURE THAT THE RIDER UNDERSTANDS THE FOLLOWING:
- Approach a horse slowly
- Speak to the horse softly
- Be gentle and considerate when handling him
- Lead correctly at the horse's side, not from in front
- Never wrap the leadline around the hand or body

HALTERING A HORSE
Instruct the rider to take the halter with the lead rope attached to the center ring and unfasten the buckle. Then stand by the left side of the horse, by his neck facing his face. Place the rope over and around the horse's neck to secure the horse, holding the halter at the near side of the horse in the left hand. Put the right arm over the horse's neck. Grasp the halter strap with the right hand (buckle on the left) and then work the halter over the nose and pull up over the head and buckle. Take the leadline from around the neck to control the horse (Engel et al., 1989).

LEADING A HORSE

Cathy Kuehner (1990) states, *"A horseman can make working with horses seem effortless, but he or she is aware that even leading a horse requires his undivided attention."* Riders should walk near the horse's shoulder so that they can easily observe the horse's ears, eyes and head carriage for signs of behavioral changes. The leadline is held *behind* the chin of the horse. Never lead from in front of a horse nor let the horse drag the leader. The person leading the horse has little control if the horse is behind the leader nor can the horse's reactions be observed. The lead line is held eight to twelve inches below the lead shank snap with the near hand (the hand nearest the horse). The other end of the leadline is held in a figure-eight fashion (Figure 1) or folded across the far hand (the hand away from the horse). Never wrap the lead line around the hand or wrist or let it drag on the ground. If a horse steps on the line, it could startle him.

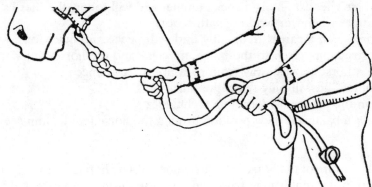

Figure 1. HOLDING THE LEAD LINE

Traditionally, most horses are led from the left. Horses used in therapeutic riding programs are trained to be led from both right and left sides. T.T.E.A.M recommends leading the horse from both sides to help the horse become and stay balanced. To begin, stand at his shoulder, on his left side, with the lead line in the handler's right hand, about eight to twelve inches from the snap. The slack is held folded in the handler's left hand. The safest lead line is a cotton one, rather than a nylon rope, which can cut the hand if pulled quickly. *"The ears and eyes display warning signals that should always be observed"* (Davies, 1988).

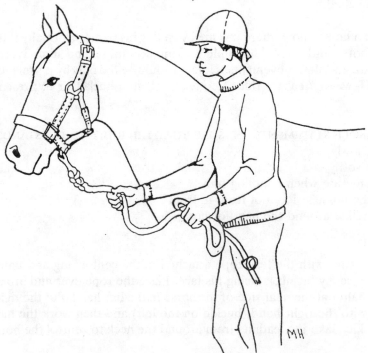

FIGURE 2. LEADING POSITION

T.T.E.A.M. suggests several methods of leading (see section 7.03). Regardless of the type of leading used, the horse moves with or ahead of the handler, never behind the handler. Not only is being ahead of the horse a dangerous position, as the handler has no way of observing the horse, but his gait may be altered by the pull on the horse or the position of the lead line, both of which affect the horse's ability to balance.

Effective horse handling is an achievement of which riders can rightfully feel proud. Even young children can learn to brush and help saddle their horses. **The most important aspects of horse handling are safety rules and precautions for both the rider and the horse.** Rider should not be left unsupervised when handling a horse until they have achieved competency in all handling techniques and safety measures. *Instructors, staff and volunteers must know the proper procedures and use uniform methods of handling to be good role models to their riders. Remember that riders and volunteers, who are keen to pick up on mistakes and short cuts, will be watching you all the time and learn from your behavior.*

Riders should learn that when leading a horse, they can push an elbow into the horse's side to move him over if he gets too close (Engel et al., 1989). A rider confined to a wheelchair may lead a horse by holding the leadline in his or her near hand with the slack end held in his or her lap. He or she may be able to propel his or her chair with the other hand or be pushed in it by another person.

Teach a rider how to walk through a gate safely, with the gate wide open, so neither horse nor rider is hit, also how to release a horse in a turn-out ring. A rider with cognitive impairments can be taught to handle and lead a horse if carefully trained, but the basics must be stressed repeatedly.

TYING A HORSE

Riders should be instructed to tie their horses only to immovable objects intended for that purpose, using a quick release knot (Figure 3). Safe objects for horse hitching may include a hitching rack, a ring in a horse's stall, a cross tie, or a cement-bedded post. A horse can pull back one and one-half times his weight and can injure not only himself but also other horses and people around him if he tries to get loose. Never tie a horse to a car fender, a door of a shed or trailer, a wheel-barrow, the arena rail, or other less solid objects. A cord can be first tied to an immovable object and than the lead rope is attached to it. If a horse does pull back, he will break the cord, not the halter or rope. *A horse who does not tolerate being tied must be trained to stand while ground-tied if he is to be safely used in a therapeutic riding program* (see 7.01.4).

THE QUICK RELEASE KNOT

The quick release knot (Figure 3) is used at all times to tie horses. It is used on an object designed especially for tying, such as a hitching rack or a ring in the horse's stall. It is important to tie correctly. Make the rope that attaches to the horse's halter short enough so that the horse cannot step on it or get a foot caught in it. The knot will release when pulled; one can merely pull the end of the rope to release the horse if this becomes necessary.

GROOMING A HORSE

Knowing how to groom a horse is a satisfying skill to acquire. A rider will feel a bond with the animal and a horse enjoys the attention and the massage he receives. It is important that the rider learn the correct way to clean hooves: how to pick up hooves, and how to use the hoofpick, using it by pulling firmly away from the body. Instruct a rider in how to use a dandy brush and a body brush, brushing in the direction the hair lies (with the hair), and how to use the curry comb in a circular motion. Sponge the eyes, nose, and muzzle with a clean sponge or soft cloth and sponge off the dock. Teach a rider the proper use of grooming tools and why they are used. Using a video on grooming reinforces instruction and makes the lesson more interesting.

TACKING A HORSE

Riders should learn to identify the parts of a saddle. They should be familiar with the pommel, the girth buckles, the cantle, the skirt, and the billet straps. Beginning riders may need to be shown how to carry a saddle if they are able to do so, and should know the direction in which the saddle pad goes on the horse before the saddle is placed on a horse. To correctly saddle a horse takes both strength and attention to details. Are the girth buckles on the first and last billet strap? Is the saddle pad even on both sides? Is the saddle correct, that is, one that fits both the horse and the rider? Are the safety stirrups on correctly, with the rubber bands toward the front when the stirrups are run up?

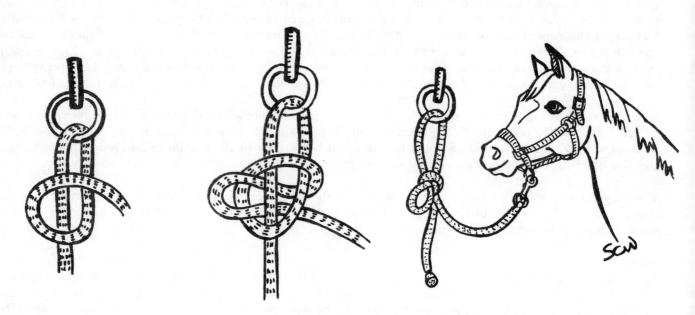

FIGURE 3. QUICK RELEASE KNOT

BRIDLING A HORSE

A riders first unties his horse. Be sure that the lead line is not tied to the post while the halter is attached only around the horse's neck. If the horse should pull back he could be seriously injured. The reins are looped over the horse's neck. The middle of the headpiece is held with the right hand, while cradling the right arm around the horse's neck. Then with the left hand, open the horse's mouth by inserting a finger toward the back of the mouth where there are no teeth. With the left hand, gently insert the bit, while pulling the bridle upward with the right hand so the bit does not fall out of the horse's mouth. Continue to pull the crownpiece over the horse's ears gently, first the right and then the left. The bit should now be in the horse's mouth and the bridle on. Next, straighten the nose piece (cavesson) and the browband. The throatlatch is now buckled tight enough but so that two fingers can be inserted under the throatlatch at the cheek. The rider buckles the cavesson so that it is snug but not tight and takes the reins and loops them over his or her arm, then walks to the front of the horse to see that the bridle is straight and even. Show the rider where the bit should be and that (depending on the bit used) there should be one to two wrinkles at the side of the mouth near the bit ring.

UNTACKING A HORSE

A rider should loosen the girth two to three holes after dismounting and run up the stirrups. He or she will then put the halter around the horse's neck and unbridle the horse by undoing the throat latch and the cavesson and gently pulling the bridle over the horse's ears. Show the rider how he or she should lower the bit without hitting the horse's teeth. The halter is then placed on the horse, after which he is tied and the tack is taken off the horse and put away.

GROOMING AFTER RIDING

Instruct the riders how to feel a horse to see if he is cool and ready for grooming. To check, have them put their hand between the horse's front legs to see if that area has normal body temperature. If the horse is not cool, the rider needs to walk him until he is cool. The hooves must be picked out; this can be done either at the beginning

338

or after grooming is finished. Next remove any visible sweat with a sponge or a towel. Then curry comb him with a rubber curry comb to loosen dead hair and remove sweat marks. The rider will then brush the horse with a dandy brush, to get the heavy dirt off. Finally, a body brush is used all over the horse to get the fine dirt off. Use a body brush to brush the mane and the tail. Instruct the rider to "lay the mane" by slightly moistening the brush when using it on the horse's mane. A towel finishes the polishing of the coat, going in the direction in which the hair lies.

BACK TO THE STABLE OR PASTURE
A horse that is clean and cool can be returned to the stable or pasture. If a horse wears a rug or blanket, it is now put on him. Otherwise simply lead the horse to his stall or take him inside the gate of the pasture. The rider is instructed to face the horse while he or she closes the gate. He or she then removes the halter, moves away from the horse, and leaves the pasture.

References

Davies, J. (1988). *The Reins of Life*. London: J.A. Allen & Co. 43.

Engel, B., Galloway, M., Bull, M. (1989) *The Horse, The Handicapped, and The Riding Team in a Therapeutic Riding Program*. Pasadena, CA. 95-98.

Kuehner, C. (1990). Leading A Horse Safely. *Horse Play*. July. 37.

Podhajsky, A. (1968). *My Horse, My Teacher*. Garden City: Doubleday & Co. 12.

Sayer, A. (1984). *The Young Rider's Handbook*. New York: Arco Publishing, Inc

Tellington-Jones, L. (1988). *The Tellington-Jones Equine Awareness Method*. Millwood: Breakthrough Publications.

T.E.A.M. International. (1990) T.T.E.A.M. Clinics.

16. ADAPTIVE AND STANDARD TACK: EQUIPMENT FOR THE ARENA, FOR LESSON GAMES, AND FOR COMPETITION FOR THERAPEUTIC RIDING PROGRAMS

Athletes know the value of quality equipment needed in order to fulfill their desire to excel in their given sport. Most people who become involved in tennis, skiing, riding, or cycling may initially select basic equipment that is of moderate quality and price. After they have achieved the elementary aspects of the skills involved in their chosen sport, they become aware that better quality equipment selected specifically for the direction they are taking in their sport, will enhance the development of their skills.

In therapeutic horseback riding, not only may the rider be hindered by poor selection of equipment but also the horse is hampered by tack that does not fit. Appropriate tack, in good condition, aids a rider with a disability to develop balance, coordination, and security. For example to develop a correct and balanced seat, the rider's center of gravity must be coordinated with the horse's center of gravity. If a saddle is selected that does not allow for this to occur, then the basics of both riding and balanced posture will not develop. A rider with asymmetrical muscle tone, as seen in persons with stroke or cerebral palsy hemiplegia, may have or be predisposed to spinal deviation. If this rider is placed into a Western saddle that tends to cause a pelvic tilt, the rider will not be encourage to develop balance posture. Special or adapted tack may enable a person to perform skills that might be difficult or impossible do to with their disability. Equipment that fits both rider and horse assists the horse to perform comfortably and without stress.

Safety is always a major factor in any sport and especially horseback riding. Because of the risk factors involved in riding, most sessions are held in an enclosed arena. To make the sessions more fun and to vary the environment within the area, games are often used to challenge the riders and to divert their attention from frustration and fears (Davies, 1988). For more advanced riders competition can be held within the sessions, and trail courses can be constructed.

Susan Lohmann states in "*Riding Lessons for Young Children*" (1990) that attention spans of 15 to 30 minutes, maturity, specific physical coordination, and learning abilities dictate when a child is ready for formal riding lessons-- between the chronological ages of 5 to 8 years. She feels other requirements include some concept of right and left, ability to ride basic shapes, and having a weight of 50 pounds and height of 48 inches to enable a child to control a horse. In therapeutic riding, riders with many types of problems are encountered. Instructors are able to break down skills so that the riding can begin before this criteria is met. But a degree of readiness is necessary.

For the population that is mentally too immature and physically not ready to begin serious riding lessons, games are of great value. Games can be used to teach the rider balance, coordination, and life skills in a fun and challenging way at any level of development or intellectual ability.2

The material in this chapter is intended to assisted the reader is exploring the rationale for specific selection of both tack and equipment used during a riding session.

16.01   SAADLES

Lorraine Renker, BS

Saddles have evolved through the ages and will continue to do so as equestrian needs change. Generally speaking, there are two kinds of saddles--English (Figure 1) and Western (Figure 2). A closer look shows that there are different types of English and Western saddles, each designed for specific purposes. Persons choosing saddles for therapeutic riding programs must have a working knowledge of saddle construction, design, and type in order to best meet the needs of the horse and rider.

Saddles are traditionally made from leather. Leather quality and workmanship vary. Synthetic saddles have gained popularity because they are inexpensive and easy to care for (just hose them off). Riders have complained that the synthetic saddle grips the rider too tightly, not allowing them to move in the saddle. (This may be an advantage to those with poor leg control). Synthetic saddles come in all styles and types just like their leather counterparts. As with leather saddles they vary in quality and workmanship.

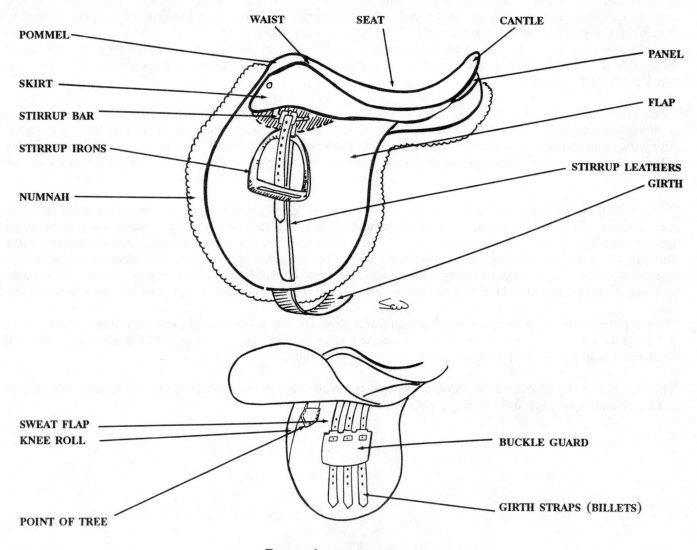

FIGURE 1. AN ENGLISH SADDLE

342

16.01.2 ENGLISH SADDLES

The saddle is built on a frame or tree. The tree is usually made of wood and can be of a rigid construction or a spring tree. A rigid tree is often considered stronger. The spring tree has two pieces of sprung steel from the pommel to the cantle along the tree frame. The spring tree is more comfortable for the rider because the seat of the saddle is more resilient. Some people feel that the movement of the spring tree can cause the horse's back more stress.

The tree can also have different "twists" (Figure 3). A narrow twist allows the rider's legs greater contact with the horse. If the twist of the tree is too narrow, it will cause the panels to be narrower which will decrease the amount of surface that can absorb weight. If the twist of the tree is too wide, the rider's base is spread out causing the loss of leg contact.

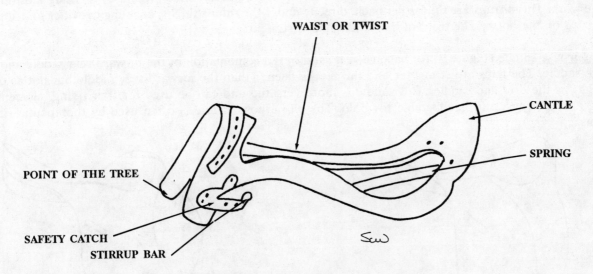

FIGURE 3. ENGLISH SADDLE TREE

The tree can also come in different widths (Figure 4) to accommodate different width horses. The narrow tree for narrow withered horses; the medium tree for normal thoroughbred withers; the wide tree for quarter horses and warmblood withers; and the extra-wide tree for horses where the wide tree still sits too high on the horse's back. Trees can also have a cut back head up to 4 inches. <u>A cut back head often helps eliminate pressure on the horse's withers enabling a saddle to fit a wider range of horses.</u>

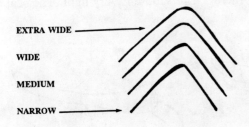

FIGURE 4. ENGLISH TREE WIDTH

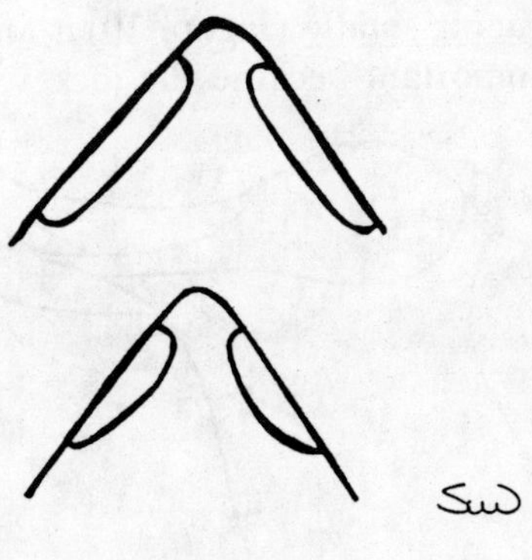

FIGURE 5. PANELS CAN COME IN DIFFERENT SIZES

343

The panel of the saddle distributes the rider's weight over the horse's back. There are two kinds of panels: stuffed and formed. Stuffed panels are made by actually stuffing the saddle. Formed panels are added to the saddle later in construction. Formed panels do not change shape and will either fit or not fit the horse. The panels should fit the horse's back uniformly so the saddle is supported over the greatest area, not just at the withers and rear. Panels come in different sizes (Figure 5).

The **forward-seat saddle** (Figure 8)(jumping saddle or hunt saddle) is primarily used for jumping. It has a shallow seat so that the rider can be free to move into positions required during jumping. The saddle flap is further forward to enable the rider to maintain a shorter leg in order to get up and out of the saddle. This saddle is usually not as comfortable for long trail rides.

The **dressage saddle** (Figure 6) has a deep seat so that the rider will not slide around while using aids during dressage work. The stirrups are set further back, directly under the rider's thighs, enabling the rider to maintain a longer leg on the horse. The front of the saddle flap is straight.

The **all-purpose saddle** (Figure 7) (or balance-seat saddle) is a combination of the forward-seat saddle and the dressage saddle. The flaps are straighter and the seat is deeper than the forward-seat saddle but not as deep or straight as the dressage saddle. This saddle is more versatile and can be used for trail riding, elementary jumping and dressage, and is adaptable for polo. The all-purpose saddle is often used by therapeutic riding programs.

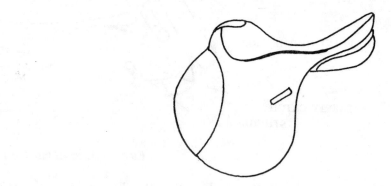

FIGURE 6. DRESSAGE SADDLE

FIGURE 7. ALL-PURPOSE SADDLE

The **saddle-seat saddle** (Figure 9) (show saddle or flat saddle) is designed to show off the action of the gaited horses such as the Saddlebred or Tennessee Walking horse. This saddle is flat to allow the rider to shift his weight further back on the horse. The saddle flaps are straight and the pommel is cut back.

The **racing saddle** (Figure 10) is an extremely forward saddle used for racing. The saddle is very light. The seat is unimportant because the jockey does not use it.

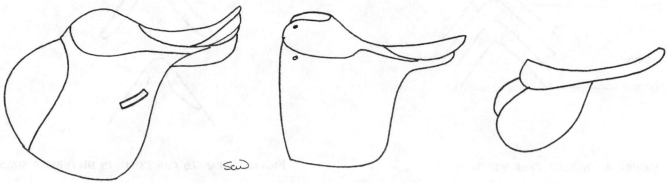

FIGURE 8. FORWARD-SEAT SADDLE   FIGURE 9. SADDLE-SEAT SADDLE   FIGURE 10. RACING SADDLE

WESTERN SADDLES

The foundation of a Western saddle is also the tree. The tree is usually made of wood covered with rawhide although alternative materials are now available, such as a "ralide" plastic tree. The gullet of the Western saddle is measured (Figure 11) vertically and horizontally. The gullet is usually about 6¾ inches to 8 inches high. Horizontally the gullet is measured (Figure 12) at the top of the bars of the saddle (where the saddle strings pass through the saddle skirts). There are several types of Western trees available. The regular tree has bars angled to fit a high-withered horse. The gullet width is 5½ inches, or 5¾ inches. The semi-quarter horse tree has a gullet width of 6 inches. The quarter horse tree has flatter bars for the wide back of the Quarter horse. The gullet width is 6½ inches. The arabian tree designed for the shorter back of the Arabian horse has a gullet width of 6¾ inches. Trees are also available for ponies. The width of the fork is measured from swell to swell and averages from 10 ½ to 14 inches. Large swell forks up to 22 inches were popular at the turn of the century but were discontinued because too many people were hurt by them.

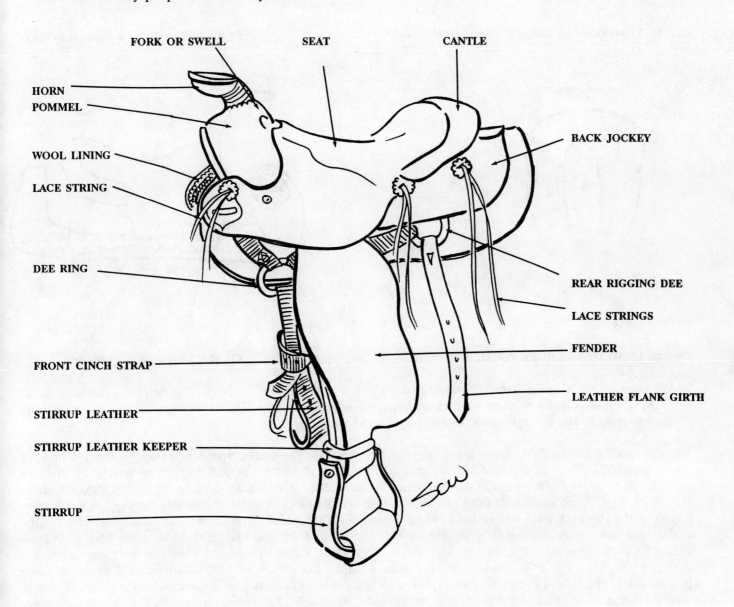

FIGURE 2. A WESTERN SADDLE

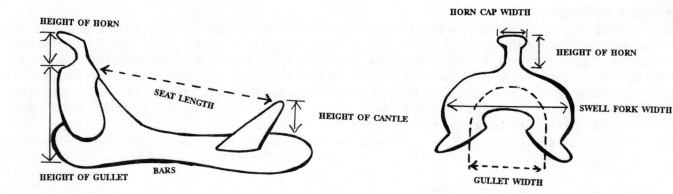

FIGURE 11 MEASURING THE WESTERN SADDLE TREE

FIGURE 12. WESTERN SADDLE HORN

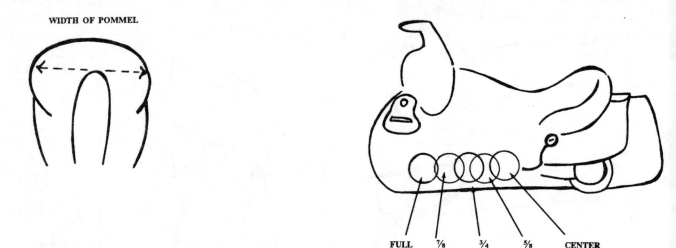

FIGURE 13. WESTERN SADDLE POMMEL

FIGURE 14. RIGGING POSITIONS

Saddle horns come in various shapes and sizes determined by the use of the horn. The height of the horn varies from 2½ to 4 inches. Some Western saddles are being made with no horns. The cantle also can vary in height from 2¾ to 4 ½ inches. The average cantle width is 12½ to 14 inches.

Western saddles are available with various riggings (Figure 14). The full or Spanish, ⅞ inch, ¾ inch, ⅝ inch, or center-fire positions are determined by the location of the front dee-ring. The dee-ring can be attached to the tree or to the skirt (in-skirt). Dee-rings that are attached to the tree are stronger. In-skirt rigging causes less bulk under the rider's legs. These riggings fit in to two basic categories: single or double. The double rigging has a front and a back girth. The back girth was added to keep the cantle of the saddle from coming up which was very helpful when a cow was roped. A short strap should always connect the front and back girth to keep the back girth from sliding back and possibly acting as a bucking strap. With a full double rigging, the center of the front dee-ring is centered under the fork of the saddle (a line can be dropped from the base of the horn) with the back dee-ring located where the side of the cantle joins the bars. A full double still allows for some cantle movement. A ¾ inch double rigging allows for less cantle movement than the full double. The center-fire and ⅝ inch positions are not used in double rigging because the saddle would move too far forward on the horse.

The single rigging has one girth and tends to allow the saddle more up and down movement in the cantle area. The center-fire rigging attaches the girth to the center of the saddle. A wide girth is usually used because the girth sits so far back on the horse's barrel. Center-fire saddles have a tendency to move around on the horse. They will slide forward when going down hill and slide back when going up hill. The rider often has to dismount to reset the saddle. Center-fire saddles have lost popularity. The ¾ inch rigging, the ⅞ inch rigging, ⅝ inch rigging are used for various reasons. By moving the rigging back, the stirrup leathers can move forward more freely. The girth straps also are then moved behind the rider's leg for less bulk. Different rigging positions also allow the saddle to be placed in different positions on the horse.

The **roping saddle** (Figure 15) is designed for roping cattle. It is a heavy saddle. It is built wide with a low fork so that there is less leverage on the saddle horn and the horse's withers when the cow is roped. The cantle is low so that the rider can easily and quickly dismount to get to his cow. A full or ⅞ inch double rigging position keeps the saddle behind the horse's withers for better shock absorption. Because of the heavy, immovable design, it can restrict the rider's seat and leg aids. A roping saddle is not the best choice for pleasure riding.

The **cutting saddle** (Figure 16) is designed for cutting cattle. It is lighter than the heavy roping saddle. The seat is flat with a trend towards a slight built up front. The stirrups are supple and free swinging so the rider's legs can be pushed forward. The horn is taller so that the rider can use it for support during quick turns. Full or ⅞ inch double rigging are usually used with the cutting saddle.

FIGURE 15. ROPING SADDLE

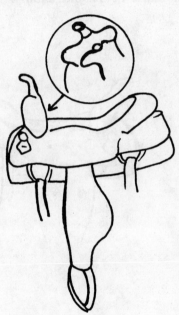

FIGURE 16. CUTTING SADDLE

The **pleasure saddle** (Figure 17) for general Western riding. It is designed smaller and lighter with a higher cantle for comfort. Many modern Western saddles are built up in the front and slope toward the rear of the saddle which positions the rider deeper into the cantle. This often causes the rider's pelvis to be in a posterior tilt. Some saddles are designed without the built up front with a flatter seat which may allow for better alignment of the rider's pelvis (a more neutral position.) These saddles may be called forward, balanced ride, or the old style A-fork saddles (Figure 20). Because of the variety of seats available in Western pleasure saddles, each saddle must be evaluated to determine how the rider will be positioned.

The **equitation saddle** (Figure 18) is designed for young riders competing in equitation classes. It has a deep seat with a high rise in front to attempt to lock the rider into the saddle. This type of construction tends to push the rider too far back in the saddle. The rider is then unable to use his seat and legs effectively. This type of saddle should not be used for general Western riding.

347

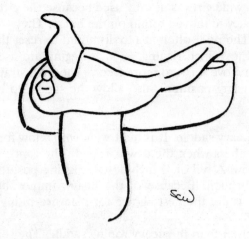

FIGURE 17. PLEASURE SADDLE

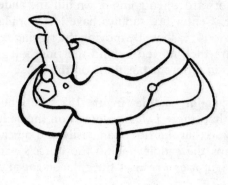

FIGURE 18. EQUITATION SADDLE WITH BUILT UP SEAT

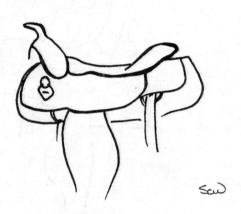

FIGURE 19. WESTERN SADDLE WITH A FLAT SEAT

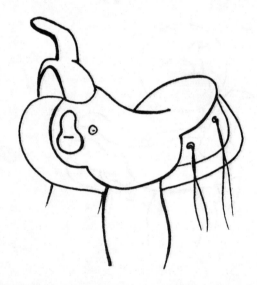

FIGURE 20. OLD STYLE "A" FORK WESTERN SADDLE

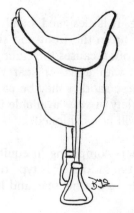
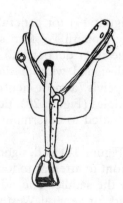

FIGURE 21. McCLELLAN

MISCELLANEOUS SADDLES

The **endurance saddle** is designed for long distance riding. It tries to distribute weight evenly over the horse's back. Extended panels will often be added to provide more area for weight distribution. The added length of the panels varies but some can cause problems for short backed horses because they may put pressure on the weakest part of the horse's back.

The **McClellan** is a single cinch, center-fire rigged saddle. It has a hard wood seat which does not lend to the rider's comfort. The saddle has a high pommel with a deep seat. Adaptations of the McClellan are available as well as seat covers for better comfort.

The **Australian/ New Zealand saddles** have gained popularity in the United States. They can be of either Western or English design. They offer a deep seat.

The **side-saddle** can be either of English or Western design. It is designed for people to ride without sitting astride. The sidesaddle has one stirrup on the left side. There are two horns for the rider to secure the right leg which carries most of the rider's weight.

The **double saddles** are relatively new to the saddle market. These saddles are designed to accommodate two people. These saddles need to be evaluated carefully for fit and function. Many are stuffed poorly or can tilt the rider forward or backward. This can interfere with proper body alignment and position.

Adaptive saddles must be chosen with care. An adaptive saddle is a saddle that has been modified or changed to suit a person with a particular disability. Bars can be added to the front of the saddle for support. Make sure bars are firmly attached to the saddle, preferably into the saddle tree and are sufficiently padded with no sharp edges. Extensions of pommels or cantles must be scrutinized carefully. Any protrusion on a saddle can act as a spear if the horse unseats the rider. Extensions of cantles can cause conflicting movements between the horse, saddle and rider. An adaptive saddle must not attach the rider to the horse.

New saddles can always be found on the market. Some are well received and some are not. If a particular saddle gains popularity and sells, it will continue to be available. Manufacturers listen to what people want and try to fill those needs. Current innovations include saddles designed specifically for women that take into account the differences in shape between the male and female pelvis. Saddles are also available with changeable tree widths. If a new saddle or feature is of interest to a therapeutic riding program, ask questions and talk to people who have tried it. With the wide range of saddle type, design, cost, and quality available, it is imperative to evaluate carefully the therapeutic riding program's needs and resources in order to make appropriate choices.

FITTING THE SADDLE TO THE HORSE AND TO THE RIDER

The ideal is to obtain a saddle specifically to fit the horse and rider combination. Forms of the horse's back can be sent to saddle makers or taken to tack shops to find a saddle that fits the horse. A good tack shop will assist in saddle selection and fit. Many will let saddles be taken and tried on the horse to determine proper fit. Used saddles can be a less expensive option. Therapeutic riding programs have a dilemma in finding saddles that will fit many horse-and-rider combinations. Persons who choose saddles for riding programs must have a working knowledge of saddle construction and design in order to make good saddle choices.

A saddle that does not fit the rider will affect the rider's progress and body alignment.
A saddle that does not fit the horse will affect the horse's comfort and possibly his soundness.
Either are inappropriate for therapeutic riding.

16.01.3 FITTING THE SADDLE TO THE HORSE

A saddle that fits well will reduce the stress put on the horse's back. This is accomplished by providing enough surface through the panel to support the rider's weight. This does not mean that the lighter the saddle the less stress on the horse's back. How the weight is distributed over the horse's back determines how much stress is placed on it. The spine and withers bear no weight at all. The area on the horse's back that can safely carry the saddle is about 15 inches (front to rear) on the average back. Short backed horses can have as little as 12 inches support area while long backed horse's can have as much as 18 inches. The area behind the horse's last thoracic vertebra is the weakest part of the horse's back and can not be expected to support weight for long periods of time. If heavy pressure is continually placed on that area, the horse can have deep muscle damage.

When determining how the saddle fits the horse, there are two general areas to look at: the horse's withers and back. No matter what kind of a saddle, English or Western, is placed on the horse's back it **must never** put pressure on or pinch the withers or spine. Pressure on either of these areas will cause major problems for the horse. The gullet clears the horse's back by at least one finger when the rider is mounted and two when the rider is dismounted. The weight of the rider is distributed onto the horse's back by the panels of the saddle. The panels should lie flat on the horse's back muscles. The panels should not concentrate too much pressure in any one area.

A saddle has to fit in more places than over the withers, so it is not always possible to put a saddle from one horse to the other. Watch for the horse's shoulder movements and pressure on the horse's spine. The weight of the saddle must be evenly distributed over the ribs on the horse's <u>lumbar</u> muscles. No weight must be placed on the loins. This is a problem with some of the **"double saddles"** on the market which are designed to accommodate two people. Many saddles are stuffed poorly and can tilt the rider back or forward. When this happens, a rider may find it impossible to sit in the center of the saddle.

To determine if the saddle fits the horse, place the saddle without a pad on the horse's back. If the saddle fits at the withers, it will clear by two inches. The saddle should be level from the pommel to the cantle (Figure 22) If the tree is too wide the saddle will sit down on the horse's withers (Figure 21). If the tree is too narrow (Figure 23) the front of the saddle will sit high on the withers and the cantle will be lower than the pommel. This will throw the rider's pelvis into a posterior tilt or "sofa seat". Sometimes a horse can have such prominent withers that any saddle put on his back will slope down. This will put too much pressure on the horse's back because the center of balance is destroyed. A bump pad or a built up cantle may be required to obtain the proper fit.

Look down the gullet of the saddle to make sure that no part of the tree touches the horse's spine. Daylight should be seen at the other end of the saddle. If daylight is not seen at the other end of the gullet, then there is too little clearance and the saddle is too wide for the horse. If there is too much daylight, the saddle is too narrow.

Placement of the saddle on the horse's back is important. If a saddle is placed too far forward over the horse's shoulders, it can interfere with the horse's shoulder movement. The rigging on the Western saddle can change the position of the saddle on the horse's back (Figure 14); the rigging places the fork of the saddle further forward on the withers; a ⅞ inch rigging can position the saddle further back.

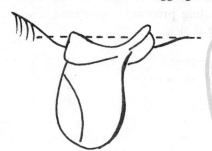

FIGURE 21. INCORRECT TREE TOO WIDE

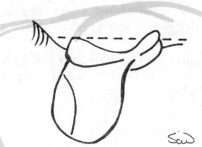

FIGURE 22. CORRECT

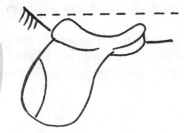

FIGURE 23. INCORRECT TREE TOO NARROW

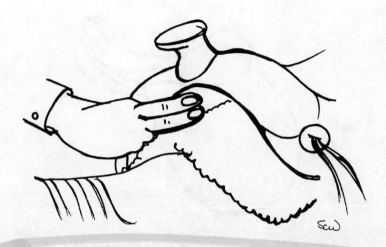

FIGURE 24. THE WESTERN SADDLE SHOULD CLEAR THE WITHERS BY 2 INCHES OR 2 FINGERS

Even if the saddle appears to fit the horse there are several warning signals that should be heeded that point to improper saddle fit:

- If the horse shows any sensitivity during grooming, tacking, or mounting. This can vary from a flinch to a sinking back.
- If the horse has dry spots after removing the saddle. The dry spots are caused by pressure points.
- If any unusual swellings, bumps, wrinkled skin, or bald spots appear on the horse's back or girth area.
- If the horse misbehaves under saddle by jiggling, refusing to stand, or exhibits stiff gaits indicating bracing against pain.

Sore backs from improperly fitted saddles are not new. Historically saddles have been designed with the comfort of the rider in mind. The first saddles had pillows added for rider comfort: stirrups were invented to alleviate pain and swelling of the rider's legs and to give something for Medieval Knights to brace on during combat. The horse does not speak up to give his input on saddle design, so equestrians need to consider the horse's comfort from the silent clues the horse provides.

FITTING THE SADDLE TO THE RIDER

The saddle used is determined by the size of the rider. A small child will not be able to obtain a good riding position in a saddle that is too large for him or her. Or a large person will be uncomfortable in a small saddle that does not support his or her seat.

An English saddle is measured from the head nail to the center of the cantle (Figure 25). Seat sizes range from 13 inches (very small child) to 19 inches (large adult) with 17 inches being the average size. A Western saddle is measured from the center of the base of the fork to the center of the top of the cantle (Figure 11). Seat sizes range from 12 inches (child size) to 16 inches with 14¾ inches to 15¾ inches being average size. The deeper the seat of the saddle, the more crucial the seat size for proper fit.

To determine if the English saddle fits the rider, the rider should sit in the middle of the saddle. There should be a three finger space from the end of the rider's buttocks to the back of the cantle. After the stirrups are adjusted, the rider's knee should be positioned in the center of the knee roll on an English saddle. If the rider's knee is above or below the center point it may be corrected by simply lengthening or shortening the stirrups. However, the rider's legs may be longer or shorter from the thigh to the knee to comfortably fit that saddle.

351

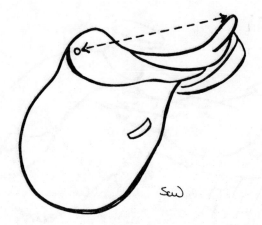

FIGURE 25. MEASURING AN ENGLISH SADDLE

Remember that the type of saddle chosen can affect the rider's leg position in the saddle. The different flap positions of the forward, all-purpose, or dressage saddles dictate the position of the rider's leg and knee angle. If a dressage saddle is chosen and the rider's leg is adjusted for jumping, the rider's knee will extend past the saddle flap. If a forward saddle is chosen and the rider's leg is lengthened, the rider's knee will not come anywhere near the knee roll.

In a Western saddle, the rider's seat should fit comfortably in the saddle. The rider's leg should hang under his seat with the pelvis in a neutral position.

FIGURE 27. CORRECT LEG POSITION

FIGURE 28. LEG ADJUSTED TOO SHORT

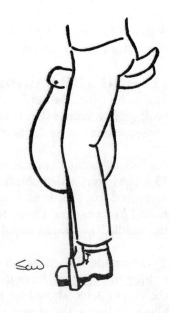

FIGURE 29. LEG ADJUSTED TOO LONG

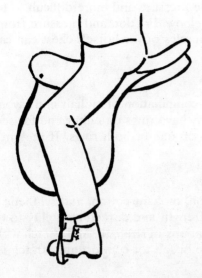

FIGURE 30. SADDLE TOO LARGE FOR RIDER   **FIGURE 31. SADDLE TOO SMALL FOR RIDER**

16.01.4   SADDLE PADS

The purpose of a saddle pad is to protect the horse's back by absorbing shock, wicking sweat, and dispersing heat. Saddle pads are also used by some people to help adjust saddles that do not fit the horse adequately. A saddle pad should not be used as an adjustment for a poorly fitting saddle, only for minor corrections. Some people will pad the withers when the saddle is tight in this area. This is unsatisfactory and only leads to the horse being sore and uncomfortable.

Saddle pads come in a variety of shapes to fit a variety of saddles. Saddle pads are made from a variety of materials. Traditional materials include cotton and wool. Cotton is easy to wash but often not very thick to offer protection. Wool is thicker but difficult to care for. New synthetic materials provide the extra thickness, but may not be as adept at wicking water and can create a build up of heat on the horse's back. There are a lot of hi-tech saddle pads currently on the market. Many of these pads incorporate layers in their design similar to designs used in athletic shoes. Some use open cell foam while others use closed cell foam. Open cell foam tends to compact and loose shape. Closed cell foam does not crush nor does it absorb water. Some pads are incorporating human medical material such as a soft, solid gel that conforms but does not bottom out at pressure points. Some of these pads intend to replace traditional pads and some are used in conjunction with them. Because many are made of synthetic materials, manufacturers often recommend using a cotton, fleece, or other material between the pad and the horse's back. The hi-tech saddle pads often command a high price. Wedges and lollipop pads are often used to help adjust minor saddle fit problems. If the saddle fits the horse very poorly, the saddle must be changed. The pads can be made of a variety of materials. They are often placed under the cantle of the saddle to raise the back end of the saddle up to level. Closed cell foam pads tend to retain their shape better so that when the rider puts weight in the saddle the pad does not compress. If the pad compresses too much, the advantage is lost. Deciding on the best saddle pad can be confusing with all of the choices on the market. Determine what the saddle pad needs to accomplish and then shop around.

16.01.5   GIRTHS OR CINCHES

A girth or cinch passes under the belly of a horse, well behind the elbow, and buckles on each side of the horse to the girth straps of the saddle. The girth or cinch holds the saddle in place. The two most important factors to consider in the selection of a girth is its comfort and fit to the horse and its ability to hold the saddle in place. The selection of either a Western or English girth is dependent on the shape of the horse's chest. Horses with more prominent or rectangular chest shapes are more predisposed to muscle pressure and more difficult to fit. A girth that does not fit the horse can pinch and cause girth galls behind the elbow. Friction and pressure from the girth can cause girth scald. A girth that places excessive pressure on the muscles of the horse's chest can cause tissue damage.

WESTERN GIRTHS
Western girths or cinches are most often made of mohair, cotton, or a combination of mohair and rayon. Western leather girths are now available and gaining popularity. Western girths have rings on either end for securing the girth to the saddle. The rings can be open rings or can have buckles on one or both rings. If the girth has one buckle, the buckle should be attached to the offside of the saddle.

ENGLISH GIRTHS
English girths are made of leather, synthetic leather, fleece-lined nylon, mohair, cotton, and synthetic cord. The girth can be evaluated on the bases of comfort and fit to the horse, strength and durability, ability to breath and wick away sweat. Many girths are now available which provide combinations of strength, and stretch with comfort. For example, a nylon web can be used for strength, padded with fleece or felt for comfort and stretch is provided by elastic inserted at the buckle.

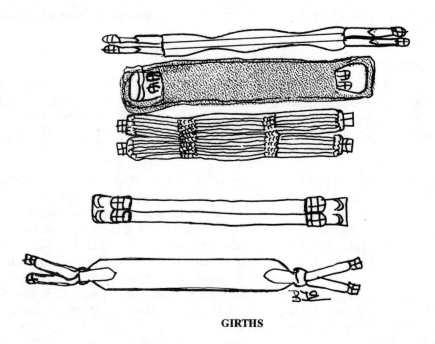

GIRTHS

16.01.6   BRIDLES AND BITS

Taking care of the horse's mouth is as important as taking care of the horse's back. Teaching a rider balance and independent use of the hands is the goal. The reality is that it takes time to learn those skills and in the meantime the horse's mouth often feels all the rider's errors. Use the lightest bit possible for the horse's comfort. Snaffle bits are good choices. Snaps can be attached to the reins so that the reins can be attached to halter rings for those riders with poor arm and hand control. A jumping hackamore is an option. Whenever using a new bit or type of bridle, try it out on the horse before using it with a rider to make sure the horse responds appropriately. Mechanical hackamore should be used with caution. Although they remove the bit from the horse's mouth, they work by using leverage that can restrict the horse's breathing. Unsteady hands can pose a potential problem with a mechanical hackamore.

If a person rides Western, consider using an English bridle and bit. The Western rider can continue to turn with two hands to help maintain symmetry through the rider's body. (One handed neckreining is appropriate for those with <u>no</u> use of one <u>arm</u>). Once control and position are mastered, a switch to a Western bit and neck reining will be easy. Long shank "Western snaffle" bits should be used with care because a curb bit can apply a lot of pressure on the horse's mouth, poll, and chin when in inexperienced hands. A long-shank broken-curb bit or "Western snaffle" can become a severe bit through its nutcracker affect if the hands are unsteady.

The headstall of the bridle should fit the horse. Watch for any pinching. The bridle can be used over the halter during lessons so that the leader can attach the lead rope to the halter The halter can also be removed and the lead rope can be attached to the cavesson or to the bit by using a bit lead. If the lead rope is attached to the cavesson make sure the bridle is checked for wear and tear regularly and any weak stitching is replaced. If the lead rope is attached to the bit, the leader should be experienced and careful not to hang on the horse's mouth or interfere with the rider's control.

<u>Remember that the horse's mouth is worth protecting</u>. Many defense mechanisms exhibited by horses can be caused by improperly fitted bits or bridles and abusive or uneducated hands. Give careful consideration when choosing and fitting bits and bridles.

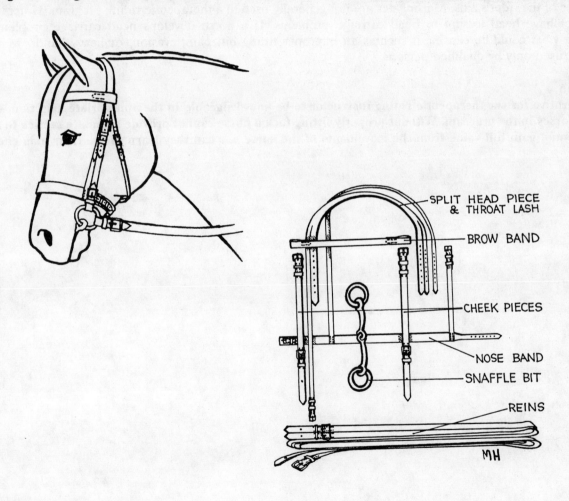

PARTS OF THE ENGLISH BRIDLE

16.01.7 MARTINGALES

Martingales (tie-downs) are equipment used to affect the horse's head position. There are a variety of martingales to choose from. Two of the most common types of martingales are *standing* and *running*.

Standing martingales (or tie-down in Western terms) restricts how high the horse can raise his head. One end of the strap connects to the horse's head. One end of the strap connects to the horse's girth or cinch and the other end to the cavesson or noseband of the bridle. A second strap encircles the horse's neck and maintains the martingale in a safe position. A standing martingale does not usually correct head tossing or high head carriage but rather restricts it. Horses often become dependent on the standing martingale. Once a standing martingale is removed, the problem usually remains.

The *running* martingale affects the horse's head carriage through leverage on the horse's mouth. One end of the strap connects to the horse's girth while the other end of the strap splits in two with rings on the ends. The reins are put through the rings. When the rider pulls on the reins a downward pressure is exerted on the horse's mouth. The running martingale can be strong on the horse's mouth and must be used carefully. Running martingales should be attached to snaffle bits not to curb bits. A running martingale can help correct head problems through correct use of the rider's aids. Martingales are not generally used in a therapeutic riding program. Horses selected should not have head tossing or head carriage problems. If a horse develops head carriage problems try to determine what could be causing it such as an improper fitting bit, pain, evasion, or heavy hands. Martingales should be used only by qualified persons.

Conclusion
It is imperative for the therapeutic riding instructor to be knowledgeable in the appropriate selection and fit of tack for horses in the program. Without properly fitting tack a horse cannot provide adequate service to its rider. Riders cannot gain full value from the movements of the horse nor can they learn to use their aids effectively.

16.02   EVALUATION OF STANDARD SADDLES USED FOR THERAPEUTIC RIDING

Philippa (Pippa) Hodge, PT, CTRI, BHSAI

The types of "saddles" used for therapeutic riding are English, Western, Australian/New Zealand saddles, McClellen, Roho inflatable and sheepskins. Each has definite characteristics and these relate to their purpose. Nevertheless when chosen for use with a disabled rider, additional features must be considered. A review of those follow:

ENGLISH SADDLES
The three major types used in therapeutic riding are: general purpose, jumping, and dressage saddles.
Considerations for English saddles:

- ◉ The rider's sitting balance must be good (sufficient to maintain an upright position as this saddle offers the least support, compared to the Western or Australian/New Zealand saddle
- ◉ It provides more support than a pad.
- ◉ The stirrups are easily adjusted from the saddle by the rider or by someone on the ground adjusting them for the mounted rider.
- ◉ It is lightweight in comparison with other saddles; the synthetics such as the "Wintec" are especially light. This saddle is made from scuba material. It is inexpensive and can easily be scrubbed (for example if a rider becomes incontinent).
- ◉ It is the saddle of preference when doing exercises with clients. By removing the stirrups the base of support can be further reduced, an added value for progressive exercises.
- ◉ It allows freedom of the upper body, allows the arms to cross the midline and provides freedom to perform rotational exercises.
- ◉ It encourages the use of natural balance reactions.
- ◉ It allows for good pelvic movement of the rider and close contact with the horse.
- ◉ The girth is easily accessible and adjusted.

WESTERN SADDLES
There are three major types used: roping, cutting, and pleasure saddles.
Considerations for Western saddles:

- ◉ The Western saddle is good for a nervous rider or one with multiple disabilities who needs a saddle that provides more support or a "deeper seat" and horn to provide good hand support.
- ◉ It is good for use on trail rides and hills as the rider does not tire as quickly as on an English saddle (require less work or body reactions), and it is safer for the rider because of the additional support.
- ◉ The saddle has a deep seat, horn (pommel), and large wooden (plastic) stirrups.
- ◉ Safety stirrups can be used. Western safety stirrups, which are metal with leather covering, are recommended by NARHA).
- ◉ The saddle is higher off the horse's back.
- ◉ Movement of the rider tends to be restricted in the pelvis and even more in the lower spine.
- ◉ Stirrups and cinch (girth) are difficult to adjust once the rider is mounted.
- ◉ Exercises are very difficult for the rider to execute due to the deep seat (restricted movement of the pelvis) and horn.
- ◉ The saddle supports the rider more than the English type and therefore the development of refined balance reactions is not encouraged.
- ◉ The saddle is heavy in comparison to the English saddles and thus more weight to handle (a Western synthetic is now available that is lighter weight).
- ◉ The horn can be dangerous if the rider should fall forward.

AUSTRALIAN/NEW ZEALAND (STOCK) SADDLES

Considerations:

- ◎ It has been successfully used with riders who are afflicted with ataxia who have been unable to progress to a canter in an English saddle. The added support it gives allows the riders to try a faster pace.
- ◎ It provides the combination of advantages of a deep seat as well as thigh support which encourages good leg position, yet allows freedom of pelvic movement (the rider is held at the leg--not at the hip as in the Western saddle).
- ◎ Good for riders with low tone and poor balance. It provides support but allows the riders to develop balance.
- ◎ It has no horn so that the rider has freedom of the upper body to carry out exercises.
- ◎ The stirrups and girth are easily adjustable.
- ◎ Safety stirrups can be used.

McCLELLEN

The McClellen saddle was develop for the US Cavalry and was designed with the comfort of the horse in mind.

- ◎ It has deep seat similar to the English saddle, a high pommel with no horn and a cantle for added support.
- ◎ It forces the rider to sit very upright and to ride light.
- ◎ It encourages the use of natural balance reactions since it does not secure the rider's pelvis.
- ◎ The stirrups are either English or wooden with hoods but with English leathers.
- ◎ It allows freedom of the upper body, allows the arms to cross the midline and provides freedom to perform rotational exercises.
- ◎ The stirrups and girth are easily adjustable.
- ◎ Safety stirrups can be used.
- ◎ It is designed to be comfortable for the horse.
- ◎ The seat is not padded.

INFLATABLE SADDLES

Roho for prevention of pressure sores.

- ◎ The "Roho" saddle is made especially for those who need to reduce pressure on their skin such as individuals with paraplegia or spinal bifida. This saddle will tend to reduce the chance of pressure sores.

SHEEPSKINS

These are used with a surcingle.

- ◎ It is good for riders who have poor sensation and are prone to pressure sores. The softness and pile of the sheepskin exerts less pressure than a bareback pad, leather or the synthetic (Wintec) saddle.
- ◎ It allows the warmth and muscle movement of the horse to comes through the sheepskin which helps reduce spasticity.
- ◎ Due to the close contact with the horse it is the most useful for training natural sitting balance and equilibrium reactions.
- ◎ The sheepskin is ideal for changing a client's position such as lying down on the horse, facing backward astride.
- ◎ It is effective with clients who need a lot of sensory stimulation, both from the horse and from the pad, more so than a bareback pad.
- ◎ It can be used with a vaulting surcingle.
- ◎ It is good for backriding clients who have cerebral palsy, hypotonia, or spina bifida.
- ◎ It is very comfortable.
- ◎ It is very lightweight for the horse.
- ◎ It can be washed in warm water with pure soap flakes (or leather soap) to be free of dust for sensitive clients.

A Review of Advantages and Disadvantages of English and Western Saddles		
Desired action	Western	English
Movement of rider	Causes the lumbar spine to curve	Curve is in pelvis (like walking)
Support	Lots of support--big horn and high back	Minimal support--flatter saddle
Balance	Less balance actions required	More balance actions required
Closeness to horse's back	Lots of padding and leather, rider high off the horse's back	Minimal padding. Rider's seat in closer contact with horse
Adjustment of girth and stirrup.	Difficult to adjust stirrups and girth from saddle or from ground when rider is mounted	Easier to adjust stirrup and girth when mounted, from saddle or ground

CHECK LIST

- **Be sure to attach the sheepskin to the horse with a surcingle. Be sure it is secure.**
- Saddles must fit both the horse and the size of the rider.
- Saddles must allow the shoulders of the horse to move freely with the withers clear of the saddle (pommel) so there is no pinching and the "sling" mechanism of the horse can work effectively (chapter 5, Figure 18).
- The saddle should be clear of the horse's spine.
- The saddle should be balanced to put the rider into level pelvic alignment.
- Check that the tree of the saddle is not broken.
- Check padding in the saddle to make sure it is evenly distributed and well-filled out.
- Stirrup sizes are important and rubber inserts are useful.
- Rubber inserts should not be used with rubber soled shoes.
- Safety stirrups are a *must*.
- Matching stirrup leathers are important and save time for the instructor.
- Watch for wear of the billet (girth) straps (or latigo) and for the stretching of stirrup leathers, especially the left one (from extra use in mounting).
- Leather should be kept clean and supple.
- Make sure daylight can be seen through the gullet both with the rider on the saddle as well as with the rider off the horse.
- Sheepskin should be used on a horse whose back is muscled and level.

Conclusion

To be effective in therapeutic riding, it is important to be knowledgeable regarding the influence of a saddle or pad upon the client. This is even more important when the horse is being used as a therapeutic modality. As any good rider knows, poor or ill-fitted equipment will not allow one to progress to maximum limits but may actually prevent the rider from becoming one with the horse or may in fact cause harm to a person's body alignment.

16.03 TACK AND ADAPTIVE RIDING EQUIPMENT

Barbara T. Engel MEd, OTR

16.03.1 HELMETS

Safety is always the top priority in therapeutic riding with persons with disability. The use of a helmet while working with horse and always when astride a horse is strictly for safety. Helmets are used and are becoming more sophisticated in **all** high-risk sports--horseback riding is considered a high-risk sport. Bikers, football and ice hockey players wear helmets. Even the downhill skiers during the 1992 Olympics wore helmets. A therapist who has worked in a rehabilitation center involved in the treatment of accident cases knows the importance of protective headgear. Persons can function independently without all limbs, difficult but possible, but a moderate head injury can take independence away forever. It does not take a hard fall or a fast horse to receive a head injury. One just needs to hit the head a certain way. It is important that those who are working in therapeutic riding programs respect the need for safety and practice it because of **belief** and not just because it is **required**. When working in a service industry, one MUST be concerned with the safety of one's clients and always set an example for them. *Be smart and safe with foresight--not hindsight.*

All persons astride a horse in any therapeutic riding program, including instructors, staff, and volunteers, should wear helmets. The types of helmets required will change as new material comes on the market and protective headgear is improved. Each country has it own standards and it is the instructor's responsibility to know the requirements and insure that all persons involved with therapeutic riding programs accept these standards. In the USA Pony Club approved helmets are usually the approved head gear for therapeutic riding.

Under controlled circumstances light weight helmets, such as those children use for biking and hockey, may be used with physically disabled riders who are unable to **tolerate** a heavy helmet due to poor muscle strength, and for children whose head size is under size 6½. The need for a light-weight helmet is best determined by a physical or occupational therapist and the individual should ride under the supervision of a therapist. For example, a three year old child who does not have head control due to poor neck strength, would become hindered by the additional weight of a large helmet. Persons with unusual head sizes may need to have specially fitted helmets adapted by a therapist. When a light-weight helmet is used, a sidewalker and leader must accompany the rider.

It is most important that the helmet is in good condition, clean, fits the head, and is comfortable for the rider. A helmet is suitable when it fits snugly to the head but does not cause pressure. It should not slide at all while the rider is moving. Persons who ride regularly should be encouraged to purchase their own headgear. One's own helmet has been chosen to fit and is more sanitary. Any helmet that has been subjected to a fall must be disposed of since a fall can damage the helmet, though not always visible, and make it unsafe.

DETERMINING THE FIT OF THE HELMET:

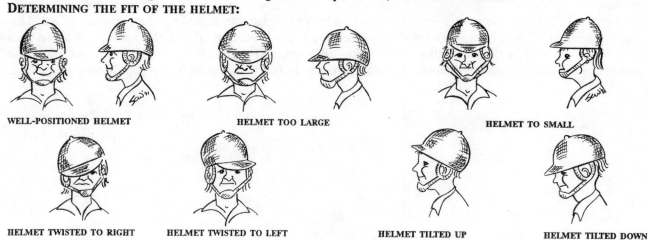

WELL-POSITIONED HELMET   HELMET TOO LARGE   HELMET TO SMALL

HELMET TWISTED TO RIGHT   HELMET TWISTED TO LEFT   HELMET TILTED UP   HELMET TILTED DOWN

360

16.03.2   PADS and NUMNAHS

Pads and numnahs (the Indian word for saddle pad) are designed to provide extra comfort and cushioning for the horse's back. When they are not clean they can cause rubbing and sores. Pads can cause over-heating, sweating and chafing. Quilted pads should be disposed of when the filling "bunches-up". Pads should provide protection, allow circulation, and absorb sweat. See section 16.01 for the use of saddle pads under saddles.

Bare-back pads Bare-back pads are two layers of blanket-type material with foam, felt, or polyester filling, or may have a leather (suede) on one side and fleece on the other. Most pads do not have handles of any sort but a few have a cloth strap at the center front. Bare-back pads provide no support to the rider. Their purpose is to protect the horse's back, to give riders a cushion to sit on and help them to stay clean.	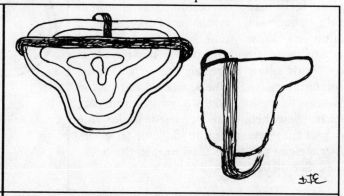
Sheepskin numnahs A sheepskin pad is used with a surcingle to hold it in place. It provides a soft, pleasant-to-touch pad and is preferred by therapists for neurodevelopmental, equine-assisted therapy using Bobath techniques, and sensory-integrative treatments. The pads can be made of (a) alpaca wool that is thick and provides abundance of texture, (b) natural sheepskin, or synthetic fleece. A sheepskin pad can have an under-pad to protect the horse's spine and protect the leather from the horse's sweat.	
Gel pads Gel pads are relatively new to the tack market. The gel pad is made from the same or similar material used in medicine to prevent pressure on the skin after burns, decubiti or during prolonged bed rest. The material does not break down (degenerate) and is protected by a cover. These pads have been developed for eventing and endurance riders to protect their horse's backs. One type has two small packets of gel that fit under each side of the English saddle. Another type is a full saddle pad which is heavy. In therapeutic riding, these pads can be used on top of the saddle to protect a rider's buttocks from pressure sores (consult with your therapist before using with a rider) or under the saddle to protect the horse and make movement more fluid.	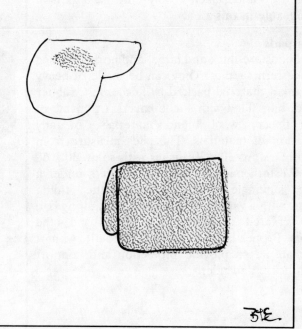

English saddle pads

The English saddle pad is smaller and lighter-weight than the Western pad. The pad can be shaped similar to the shape of the saddle or it can be rectangular. It is made of cotton quilt material, wool, felt, sheepskin, synthetic fleece, or a combination of these materials. Most natural materials are more absorbing of the horse's sweat but fleece pads allow more air flow than some natural material pads. Synthetic fleece and cotton pads are easy to wash. A light-weight cotton pad, that is easily washed, can be used under the standard pad that may be more difficult to clean. This allows a clean pad to be used next to the horse at all times. See 16.01.3.

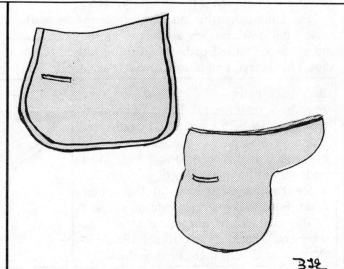

Protective pads

A protective or orthopedic pad is made of rubber or high-tech materials. These pads are light-weight and shock-absorbing and tend to decrease the pressure from the horse's back to avoid or relieve chronic back problems and/or distribute the weight of the saddle and rider. A good quality protective pad, such as those developed by Tony Gonzales (The PBM-Proper-Balance-Movement) can enhance the fluid movements of the horse, especially the older horse. Inexpensive pads can be cut from closed-cell pads used by back-packers for under sleeping bags. Though they are not the quality of a professionally designed pad, they do provide an alternative for tight-budget programs. Creating your own pad should be undertaken only by a person knowledgeable in this area.

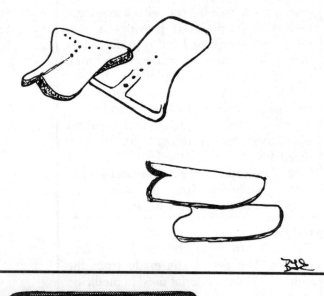

Western pads

Western pads are thick and large, and normally used under Western saddles. They can be made of heavy wool blanket material backed by fleece, felt, rubber centered, hair filled with suede covers, or covers of canvas, fleece, wool blend materials, or any combination of materials. The pads measure from 24 x 24 inches, to 30 x 30 inches with some 30 x 60 inches. Western pads are used by vaulters under a vaulting surcingle and by therapeutic riding programs with a variety of surcingles. A vaulting pad can be created by covering a PBM pad (the Gonzales Proper-Balance-Movement pad) with a fleece material to provide protection and comfort for both horse and rider.

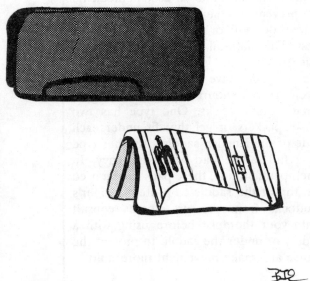

16.03.3 SURCINGLES

A surcingle is a piece of webbing or leather which passes around the horse at the girth line or behind the withers, and is used to secure a blanket, a saddle, or training reins. They are also referred to as rollers. In therapeutic riding programs, a surcingle used to secure a blanket can be used with a pad. A strap can be attached to the center ring to provide a grip for a rider or backrider. This device is useful when a vaulting surcingle is not appropriate, for example, when the rider's legs will not pass over the vaulting surcingle.

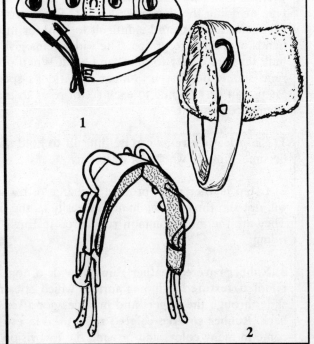

1. Light-weight or the older type vaulting surcingle. These surcingles are constructed with two steel plates, one under each hand. The handles are secured by heavy leather which is continuous from one end of the vaulting surcingle to the other. Because there are two metal plates instead of one, the center of the surcingle remains somewhat flexible. The light-weight vaulting surcingle is appropriate for equine-assisted therapy, developmental riding therapy, and therapeutic riding. It is not appropriate for vaulting especially at the canter since it does not provide the vaulters with two firm and steady handles from which to maneuver. The flexibility, caused by the break in the steel plate, is just enough to cause the loss of balance or control during an exercise.

2. Current competitive vaulting surcingle
These heavy duty vaulting surcingles provide the vaulter with two large handles and a secure surface to move from. Though expensive they are well built and should last many years with good care. They are a must for exercises performed by more than one person, for large vaulters, and kurs (a free style exercise) at the canter.

Anti-cast surcingle or arch rollers
This roller or surcingle was developed to prevent a horse from rolling over and becoming "cast" or caught against a wall. They have a loop on top and are well padded across the withers. In therapeutic riding programs they are used instead of a light-weight vaulting surcingle. They are especially suitable for small children since there is little bulk along the horse's shoulders and a small handle to hold onto.

Natural Rider
The Natural Rider combines the concept of the bareback pad riding with stirrups and with the concept of the anti-cast surcingle for security. It is fairly well secured across the withers to prevent slipping. It is light weight, easy to care for and less expensive than a saddle.

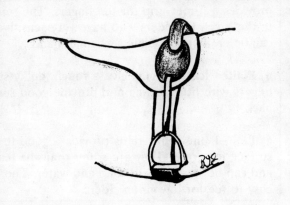

363

16.03.4 COMMERCIAL ENGLISH STYLE REINS

Reins are used as the line of communication between the horse and rider with the reins becoming the extension of the rider's hand. Standard English style reins are appropriate for therapeutic riding programs to assist the rider in the use of reining aids. Reins are made in widths of ½ inch to 1 inch and 4 to 5 feet long. The average width is 5/8 inches. Reins vary in style depending on the type of riding they are intended for. The narrow reins are very sensitive but can be difficult to hold for insensitive hands or immature grasps. The wider reins give added bulk that are easier to "feel" and hold. When possible, reins should be chosen to meet each rider's special needs. Snaps can be attached to each set of reins to make a change convenient.

1) **Plain leather reins** can be difficult to hold and may become slippery when wet or sweaty.

2) **Laced leather reins** provide a degree of texture and will not slip through the hands as easily as the plain reins. They are the most common reins used in English style riding.

3) **Rubber-covered leather reins** provide a non-slip, pimpled, textured, gripping surface which does not easily slide through the fingers and provides good sensory feed-back. **Rubber covered <u>colored</u> reins** used in eventing now come in many colors and provide the low vision rider with contrast between the color of the horse (white or yellow reins against a brown horse). The multi-colored striped variety provide the rider with a cue on where his or her hands should grasp the reins. For example, for an immature or head injured rider, one can say: keep your hands on the yellow stripe or move your hands to the red stripe.

4) **Web eventing reins** are of light-weight canvas material with leather strips sewn across the width of the rein. This provides a firmer grip for the fingers. The rein is gentle to the touch for riders who have very sensitive hands and can be easily manipulated by small hands.

5) **Plaited leather reins** give a rough, bulky surface for fingers with little feeling and provide good sensory feed-back.

6) **Plaited linen cord reins** provide a good textured surface for grasp. They are softer than the leather variety and can be washed with soap and water. The light color is easy to see for low vision riders.

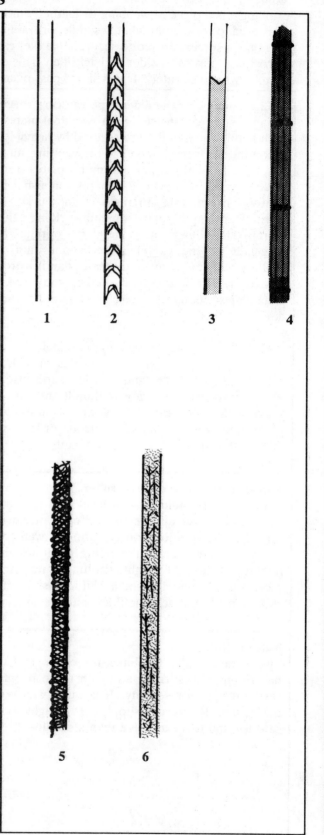

1   2   3   4

5   6

364

7) **German web-looped reins** prevent the hands from slipping yet allow for normal rein handling.

8) **Side-reins**
Side-reins are short adjustable reins made of leather, leather and elastic, or nylon and elastic (8a). Some have a "donut" which provides for additional stretch (8b). They are attached to the roller/surcingle or saddle with buckles or snaps and to the bit by an easy-release clip. Side-reins prevent the horse, to some degree, from gasping or throwing the head around; accustom the horse to the negative control of the reins-if he pulls on them-they pull back; they maintain the bit in a center position; they encourage the horse to stretch into the bit; and they provide the trainer with a means of adjusting the horse's frame (Richardson 1981).

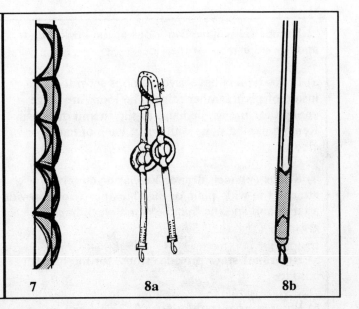

7 **8a** **8b**

16.03.5 COMMERCIAL WESTERN STYLE REINS

Western style reins can be flat or round in plain leather or braided style. They are much longer than English style reins. They can be split reins or closed. The reins that are closed at one end are generally attached to a romal--a long strip of leather. The romal is held in one hand and the horse is turned by neck reining. They can also be used--one in each hand. They can be made from leather, cotton, and nylon and may match the bridle. These reins can be easily knotted for adaptive handling by a person with dysfunctional hands or arms.

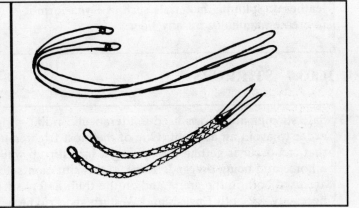

16.03.6 ADAPTIVE REINS FOR SPECIAL NEEDS

Adapted reins are especially constructed reins for rider's with various disabilities. They can be constructed from standard reins which are then altered or they can be constructed from raw materials.

1) **Ladder reins** have three or four "rungs" of leather at intervals of 4 to 6 inches. They provide the rider with a grasp area which will not slip through hands with poor strength or which can be controlled with the wrist or elbow joint if hand grasp is non-functional. To shorten the reins the rider moves up to the next rung. Another advantage is that when dropped, they do not slip down the horse's neck. They can restrict the horse's neck range and should not be used for jumping (Davies, 1988).

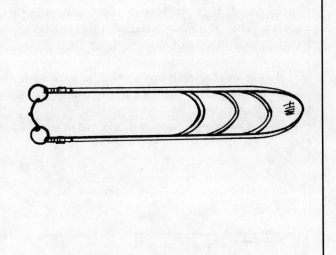

2) **Humes reins** have two loops at the buckle ends and are adjustable at the sides.

3) **Looped reins** have several loops sewn to the inside of plain leather reins. The loops are large enough for the whole hand to slip in and out easily. Reining can be done with wrist, back of hand, or elbow.

4) **Knobs (wooden drawer knobs) or dowels,** attached to wide plain or laced leather reins, provide a large and specific "handle" for a weak hand to grasp.

5) **Horizonal stays** provide "stops" for the hands to hold to.

6) Reins constructed for specific riders can be constructed out of commercial reins adapted with leather or splinting materials such as Dyna-form-it to create handholds for any rider.

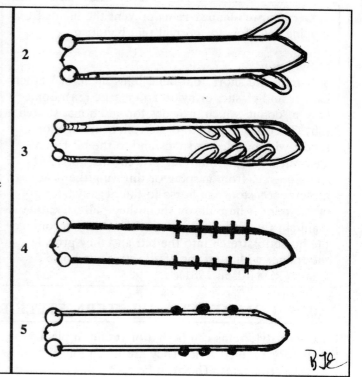

16.03.7 STIRRUPS

Safe stirrups are always used in therapeutic riding programs in order to avoid an accident. One of the most frightening accidents that can occur is getting a foot caught in a stirrup while falling off a horse and being dragged. To avoid this situation safety stirrups are used both in the arena and on the trail. Safety stirrups are necessary for both English and Western style riding.

1) **Peacock stirrups** (English) are commercially available in all tack shops.

2) **Devonshire Boot** (English or Western) is a custom-designed stirrup cover that prevents the foot from going too far into the stirrup. They should be used with riders who are wearing rubber soled shoes or do not have heels on their shoes.

3) **Western safety stirrups** should be used with all western saddles. They allow the foot to slip out of the stirrup easily.

4) **Look Quick release stirrups** come in sizes 4.5 and 4.34 inches.

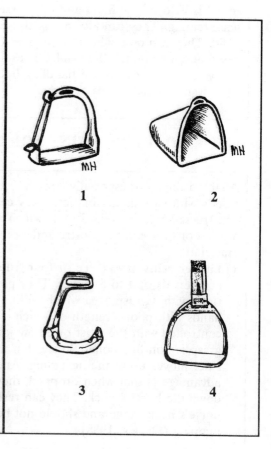

5) **Saferider or Kwik-out stirrups** (made in England) introduced to the US in 1992. They look like regular stirrups but has a strong spring action, designed to open up and let the foot fall out during a fall. They are designed for jumping and polo so are durable. Come in small, medium, and large.

6) **Spring and Swivel Stirrup** is a safety stirrup that has a spring mechanism which gives and absorbs shock while riding. The stirrup rotates 90 degrees and is useful for riders with contracted ankles and knee problems.

7) **Stirrup wedges** (not a safety factor) for English stirrups help to position the foot and can be helpful for riders with leg and ankle problems. Always check with a therapist for this type of adaptation.

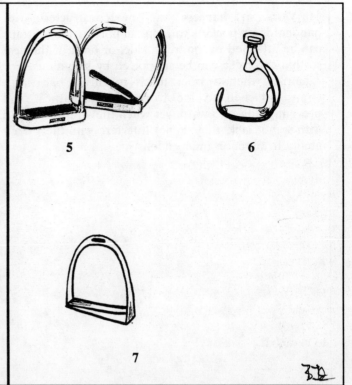

LEATHERS

Leathers hold the stirrups to the saddle. The <u>must</u> be maintained in top condition for cracked or weak leaders can cause accidents. Safety stirrups are of little help in maintaining safe condition when leaders in worn. Leathers must be adjusted to place the rider's leg in good balance with a balanced pelvis.

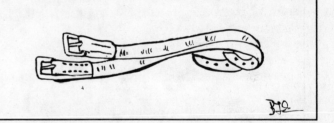

16.03.8   SUPPORT TACK and DEVICES

Supportive devices are used for riders with poor balance. These devices help riders while developing the balance they need to independently sit astride a horse. The supportive devices need to be carefully selected so they will accomplish what is intended. Instructors must always keep in mind that supportive devices are intended to be a temporary aid not a permanent solution (unless used as a safety measure). Supportive devices are generally controlled from the ground by side aides, one on each side, and each must **provide equal support**. The aim of any supportive device is to <u>help</u> balance the rider and to provide maximum <u>safety</u>. Care must always be given not to add to the rider's problem of imbalance. This can easily occur as the side aide's arm gets heavy and he or she rests on the supportive device. The supporting arm must be held up by the side aide without any weight on the device. Since it is very difficult working with a rider who needs so much support, it is best to use persons with strong arms, rotate the task between several people, with each taking turns on one side then the other--for five or so minutes. Programs must evaluate carefully whether they are equipped to accommodate large riders with minimal balance. Enabling a rider while disabling a volunteer with a shoulder strain, should never occur.

1) **Vests or harness** can be constructed with handholds or pockets to help support a rider. Straps can be attached to the front, side, or back of the vest so that the rider can be supported by side-aides. For example, when a rider tends to thrust backward, straps attached to the front of the harness will prevent going backward, yet when the straps are held with some slack, they do not interfere with the rider's ability to function independently.

1

2) **Pelvic hip supports** are used to help the rider to balance from the ground. A hip support provides support next to the pelvic bones, a solid surface, therefore they will not cause soft tissue damage when jerked (when a horse startles). The sideaids (always two) each hold a strap attached to the side of the hip belt to provide <u>equal</u> balance from each side.

2

368

3) **Waist belts** are a heavy duty "walking belt" such as used by physical therapists, or a weight lifter's leather belt with a handle added to each side. For small children a cribbing strap works well. They must be wide and strong. They have been used extensively in the past to help balance a rider and provide safety. They are presently not recommended because of several negative factors, one, they are placed over an area not protected by bone and therefore, can easily cause soft tissue damages if the side aide pulls the rider on or off the horse. Secondly, in observing class videos, it becomes apparent the side aides actually interfere with the rider's and horse's balance by "weighting" the waist belt with their arms and hands.

4) A **weight bearing platform** used by therapists to encourage a rider to extend the arms and shoulders and in turn, straighten the back for a rider who needs to support him or herself. This device is used in contrast to grasping vaulting surcingle handles which encourage flexion of the upper extremity.

5) A **handhold** is a strap which is attached to the front of the saddle. This strap should be attached to all English style saddles used in therapeutic riding programs. The rider will hold on to the hand-hold instead of using the reins for balance when necessary.

6) A **neck (horse) strap or breast plate** can also be used to hold onto instead of a hand-hold.

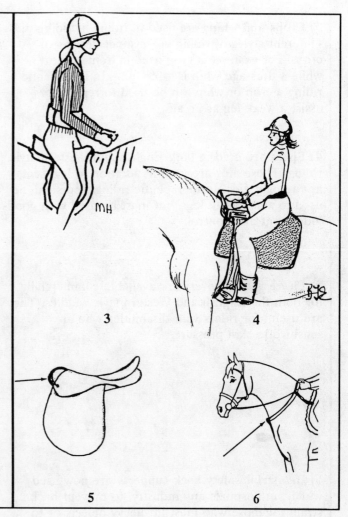

16.03.9 MISCELLANEOUS ADAPTIVE DEVICES

1) **Saddle adaptation** is a cover placed over the saddle that was developed in France. This involves a leather cover over a standard English saddle. The cover has numerous velcro pile strips to which leather covered cushions can be attached. These cushions help to **position and secure**, without strapping, the rider's legs and/or hips.

2) **Bit-leads** attach to the bit rings. These devices are used in therapeutic riding to lead a horse that is tacked with a bridle. The bit-lead allows a horse leader to take control of a horse, when necessary, yet allows a rider to fully control the horse with the reins and seat aids.

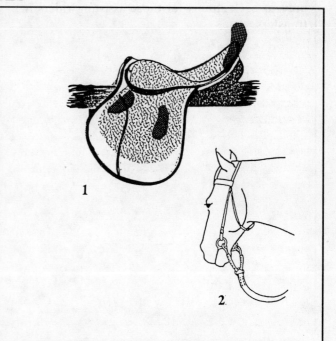

3) **Crops and whips** are used in riding as riding aids. Different styles of riding use distinct designs of crops. For example a crop used in hunt is short while a dressage whip is quite long. In therapeutic riding a crop or whip can be used to replace or assist a weak leg as an aid.

4) **Spurs** are used in both English and Western style riding. These aids are used in addition to leg, seat, and reining aids. In therapeutic riding, spurs can be used to assist weak legs, but must be used with good judgement and control.

5) **Fleece saddle covers** are available commercially for both the English and Western style saddles. They are useful for riders with disabilities who are sensitive to skin pressure.

6) **Industrial safety back supports** are now used widely, in hospitals and industry, to prevent back strain for those who must lift heavy objects or to assist patients. In therapeutic riding they can help prevent back strains for those assisting riders in transfers.

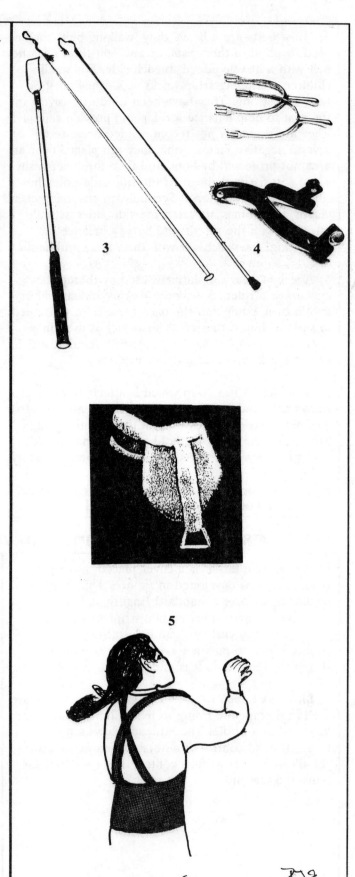

3

4

5

6

370

16.04 THE RIDING RING AND EQUIPMENT

THE RIDING RING OR ARENA

Location:
The riding ring (arena) is an enclosed area in which the lesson takes place. The outdoor ring must be fenced with safe, secure material high enough to discourage the horse from jumping over it. The best material for the rail is metal or plastic pipe, wood, or other safe fencing material. The ring must have one or more gates that can be securely closed. The placement of the outdoor ring should allow for minimal distractions. **Such enclosed area is necessary for safety.** The contained ring provides boundaries for both horse and rider. The horse cannot run away and is less distracted within this barrier.

The riding area can be either an out door or indoor ring. In some parts of the country, an indoor arena is necessary in order to carry out year-round programs. In all parts of the country, an indoor arena is ideal since, it allows for isolation and quietness, an environment that allows for concentration, and easier communication between the instructor-rider and rider-horse. Where this is not possible, an out door arena can certainly be quite adequate. In equine-assisted therapy and hippotherapy, the indoor arena becomes even more important, since the horse must be well-focused and controlled to provide the rider the desired movement facilitation.

Size:
The ring should not be smaller than 20 x 40 meters (66 x 132 feet). This is the size of a small dressage ring and allows one to ride a 20 meter circle, or ride a straight line of 132 feet or 147 feet on the diagonal. A straight line may be necessary for a rider to develop equilibrium, and curves are needed to develop balance and separation of pelvic movements from the spine for an independent seat. In addition, this amount of space is necessary if the instructor is going to teach his or her riders beginning and intermediate riding skills in dressage, equitation, cavalletti work, elementary jumping, or for games and gymkhanas. The size of the arena must not only meet the needs of the lessons or therapy sessions but must also provide the necessary space for suppling, conditioning, and schooling the program horses. A 20 x 40 meter arena also allows adequate space for longeing or a vaulting program. We must remember that for therapeutic riding to cause change, the riders must be challenged to excel in a setting which provides for some demands and is devoid of monotony.

Footing of the ring
The footing is the earth or ground of the ring. The footing is important for the safety of both horse and rider. It should be level with good drainage. There should not be any rocks or obstacles which can cause injuries. The ground should contain peat, sand, sawdust, granulated tires, or other materials which make the ground soft for the horse's footfall and gentler on his legs. Granulated tires provide an excellent footing which not only is soft--slightly spongy, but also is dustless and provides for excellent drainage. Also the softer footing is necessary in case of a fall of a rider. The footing should not be dusty or wet with puddles. Footing that is too wet can be slippery, and too dry a ring causes annoying dust. A dusty ring can cause a person with asthma, dust sensitivity, or sensitive lungs to have difficulty breathing. A dry ring can be sprayed with water to settle the dust. A wet ring can sometimes be dragged or raked to disperse the wetness.

Trail riding--way from the stable or in the country
Trails are enjoyable for both horse and rider. Trails do not provide the security and safety that the riding arena affords but can be used with riders who have developed enough balance to be secure away from the arena in case a horse is startled. The trail must be wide enough for horse and rider plus leader and sidewalker, without hitting brush or having to walk over logs and stumps. Trails should be free from holes and other hazards.

Equipment:

Ring equipment is used to provide training, exercises, challenges, diversity, and games. Since most therapeutic riding programs serve a diverse population, the more variety one has available, the more interesting the lessons can be. Equipment does not need to be expensive. Most of it can be made of wood, concrete, and discarded materials.

To set-up the riding ring for a challenging lesson can be a time-consuming but necessary task. Some equipment such as dressage letters can be permanently secured. Other equipment must be placed according to need. To make the job as easy as possible, a storage shed to hold the equipment should be placed next to the riding ring. The ring should be set up before the lesson and volunteers need to be introduced by the instructor to the correct type, purpose, and placement of equipment to be used during the lesson. The purpose and structure of the lesson will determine the need for ring equipment and props. For example:

- A class involving an obstacle course may include bending poles, barrels, cones, ground poles, and small rings to place over the bending poles.
- A class working on balance and rhythm may need four cavalletti and six ground poles.
- An occupational therapy session for a seven year old may involve bending poles and small rings, six bean-bags and a bucket, a barrel for the child to crawl through, an eight-inch ball to throw and catch, and the four cavalletti and six ground poles.
- A physical therapy--hippotherapy session will not need any ring equipment.
- A class with 10 to 13 year-old riders, beginning to steer independently may need eight cones, and 6 ground poles with which to make an "L"
- A group of three girls--developing balance-- may need eight cones and each have a bag of curlers which they will put in their hair while being lead through the cones.

RIDING RING EQUIPMENT

The equipment listed here provides instructors and therapists with ideas for their sessions. There are many more possibilities that can be explored. The orientation and discipline of the session will influence the equipment used. Occupational therapists, who normally use equipment for activities in their practice will want to incorporate this equipment within the riding session. An educator may incorporate reading, matching, and placing materials within the ring, while a physical therapist working on gait training may need a platform next to the ring for practice after the riding part of the session is over.

Barrels: Hollow metal/plastic "drums" (circular containers). The barrels may be painted different colors or have symbols painted on them and be positioned sideways or upright. They may mark courses for barrel races, support poles for jumping, be used to place objects for games on them, or be used as the center of a circle.	
Beepers: Used for low-vision riders to identify specific spots in the arena to replace cones, dressage letters obstacle-course objects.	

Bridge: A flat wooden platform used in obstacle courses.	
Cavaletti: Poles (usually white) placed on two crossed pieces of wood or on cavaletti plastic blocks. They are adjustable to three different heights for different exercises. They may be stacked for small jumps.	
Cones: Orange (or painted) funnel-shaped plastic road markers, ten inches to two feet tall. These may be used in lessons to mark the rider's course, to show how "deep" a corner should be ridden, to trace an obstacle course, or to mark the center of a circle. Different colors for educational games, communication skill, or developing directionality.	
Dressage Letters: Specific letters of the alphabet, black letters on a white background, placed in a set pattern on a measured field or around the riding arena. The dressage letters for the small arena are A--F--B--M--C--H--E--K on the rail and D--X--G in the center of the arena. The dressage letters for a large arena are A--F--P--B--R--M--C--H--S--E--V--K on the rail and D--l--X--I--G in the center. (See section 18.08)	

Gate: An obstacle used in Gymkhanas and obstacle courses.	
Ground Poles: Long (eight to twelve foot), thick (six to eight inches), octagon in shape or square with the corners shaved off. Round poles of wood may roll and cause the horse to startle. Poles are usually painted white but can be other colors or striped. They may be laid to form a chute or 'L' shape, TT.E.A.M exercises, used for walking or trotting over, or be used as jumping poles. They may also be used to divide the riding ring.	
Jumps: Small jumps for intermediate and advanced riders.	
Mail Box: Used for games or exercises such as reaching and balancing.	
Mirrors: Placed on the wall in a indoor ring or possibly on the equipment shed wall next to the outdoor ring. (Make sure that the sun reflections do not frighten the horse). Helps to provide visual feedback on posture, self-image and eye-contact.	
Megaphones: Used by the instructor to give the riders their directions. It allows the instructor to speak with a soft, more friendly voice rather than shouting from center ring.	

Straw bale: For mounting and dismounting within the ring during gymkhana games where mounting and dismounting is part of the exercise; or during a sensory-integrative therapy session where a client is involved in activities on the ground as well as on the horse.	
Symbols: The symbols can be shapes, colors, or pictures painted on wood, cans or cardboard. They can be used with people who cannot read as a substitute for dressage letters, as educational tools or in games, or as props for speech/language communication sessions.	
Tape recorder: Music can enhance any lesson. Exercises by music show more energy. Marches can be fun to ride to. Singing while riding increases breathing which in turn helps to normalize muscle tone. Riding to music such as a dressage test can be a great exercise and can be used to develop creativity. Music tends to calm horses, especially Classical and Western music.	
Tires, Buckets, Balls: Used for games on horseback.	
Traffic and International Symbols: Used to teach non-readers survival skills. Signs can include: STOP, YIELD, CAUTION, HORSE CROSSING, PEDESTRIAN CROSSING, BIKE PATH, STOP LIGHTS, RAILROAD CROSSING, BUS STOP, HOSPITAL, TELEPHONE, TOILETS, RESTAURANT, WHEELCHAIR ACCESS	

Trampoline: This can be used as a warm-up exercise for **some** riders. It is also used with those vaulters who are learning to <u>vault-on</u> independently.	
Upright poles/bending poles: Six-foot long PVC poles, one inch in diameter, which are set in containers of cement. They can be white or painted in colors. These poles can be placed in various formations to be ridden around. Small cones can be placed on top of the poles to hold rings or hats for games.	
Walkie-talkie: Used with low-vision riders to communicate and direct them during training. Effective with riders with auditory processing difficulty such as individuals with learning disabilities and with riders who have difficulty maintaining attention since the rider can stay focused better with this device, and is not distracted by looking toward the instructor.	

MISCELLANEOUS SUPPLIES

When using any object during a riding lesson, one must always accustom the horse to the object well before using it with a rider. Horses tend to shy away from things that they are unfamiliar with or do not understand. This is just one more step in developing a "spook proof horse." The horse needs to smell and see the object close-up and then see it move several times in the arena. When the horse does not react to the object in the way it will be used during session, it can then be used with a program rider. It is always necessary for the instructor and his or her staff to use any activity with the horse before using it with the program riders.

The following list are examples of items that can be used for exercises and games for therapeutic riding programs:

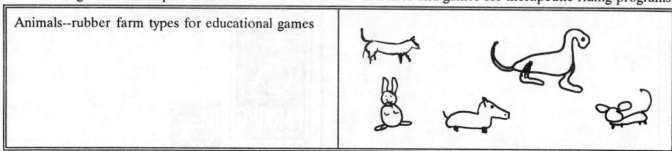

Animals--rubber farm types for educational games	

(photo pictures are courtesy of FlagHouse, Mt Vernon New York)

Balloon--tossing and catch	
Balls--(tennis balls, foam balls, Nerf balls, fleece balls, beeper balls, Koosh Balls, Geodesic balls, and light weight playground balls)	
Bean bags, different sizes and colors--for throwing and catching skills	
Bean bags targets--ball or bean games	
Bats, rubber or nerf--to hit balloons with	
Blocks, cloth or snap-on, can be played with while developing balance on the horse--encourages rider not to hold on to the vaulting girth; to focus on play and react to balance without fear.	
Bubble blowing pipes--expand lungs, visual tracking	

Buckets--small, six inch buckets for carrying items to large buckets, to throw something into	
Catch-balls-- a unique soft rubber "ball" with six spokes for hand-eye coordination	
Clothes pins--placing and pinch skills	
Dolls, Rag types--to "backride", use as example	
Flags--relay games	
Geometric-foam-shapes--can have velcro on one side to attach to signs, place in baskets or mount on wall board.	
Handkerchief--games	
Hair curlers--teaching balance	

Hats of various kinds (Western, fireman, sun-hat, bridesmaid, sailor, army)	
Hula-hoops, large--having horse walk through, using for balance exercises	
Koosh paddle and ball--play Koosh game with partner astride	
Letters--deliver into mail box	
Markers--miscellaneous purposes	
Metronome--can be used to develop rhythm--timing. For example to develop a trot at a specific tempo	
Mitts with velcro--to catch special balls which adhere to velcro	
Money, play--various games	

Mugs--relay games	
Music--for use during any kind of lessons. Music helps to develop rhythm, makes exercises more fun, and enhances games	
Ribbons attached to handles--to play ribbon exercises while riding (with or without music)	
Rings, rubber--toss ring games or placing rings on poles	
Sock-balls--exercises, games, relays	
Spoon, wooden--for relay games- such as carrying eggs	
Stop watches--for races, competition	
Tennis racket--hitting balls	

Thera-Band™ & Thera-Tubing™--color coded resistance rubber band and tubing which can be used for exercises.	
Treasure hunt items--during games	
Vests-- different colors for relay games	
Wands--stretch and balance exercises, relay	
Whistles--for games, blowing while riding increases respiration and normalizes muscle tone.	

Many games have developed through the Pony Club gymkhanas games. They have been adapted for many types riders with disabilities, to be used in therapeutic riding programs. For extensive descriptions of game to be used in therapeutic riding lessons refer to such books as (see the reference section):

- John Davies--*The Reins of Life*
- Joswick, Kittridge, McCowan, McParland, Woods--*Aspects and Answers*
- Mary L. London's--*Teaching Disabled Riders*
- Pony Club's--*Gymkhanas and Rally Games*

DRESSAGE ARENA

SMALL ARENA

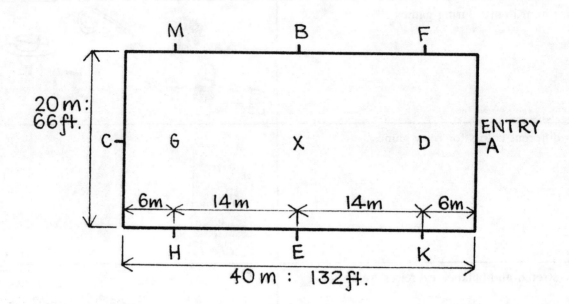

LARGE ARENA

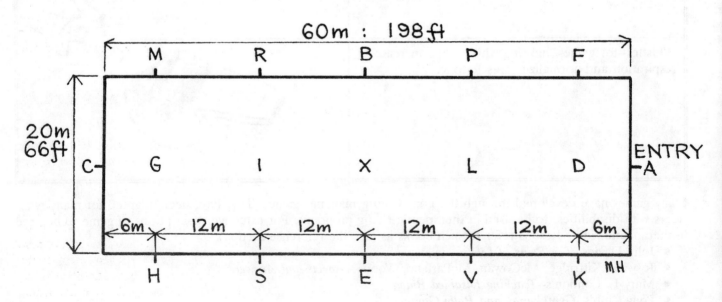

17 THE STAFF AND VOLUNTEERS

17.01 THE ROLE OF THE VOLUNTEER

KEY WORDS
  VALUABLE
  ROLES
  SKILLED

Volunteers are the backbone of most therapeutic riding programs. Such programs may require a large number of workers per rider, and without these people the cost of operating would be prohibitive. Volunteers may work directly with the riders, or they may carry out many jobs which are required to keep the organization going. The type of jobs they carry out depends on the skills these people possess and the structure of the particular program. Some programs may have only one or two paid staff and rely totally on unpaid help. Service personnel not only provide essential work but also bring to the program valuable knowledge, and skills, including support and friendship for the riders. This section will discuss the importance of training volunteers that participate in therapeutic riding programs.

Major jobs performed by volunteers
Horse handlers or leaders handle the horses for inexperienced riders during riding sessions. The horse leader must learn to lead the horse in specific ways that <u>do not interfere with gait or balancing mechanisms</u>. The leader may need to walk next to the horse in case a rider loses control. The handler also manages the horse during mounting of the rider. This may require two to five minutes and the horse must be completely quiet during the mounting process. The handler assists with horse care, grooming and tacking activities.

Sidewalkers, side-aides or side-helpers help with the important job of providing safety for the rider by walking at the side of the horse and rider and giving support. They may walk along watching the rider for loss of balance or they may actually support the rider across the legs to aid in developing sitting balance in the saddle. The sidewalkers also assist the rider in carrying through the instructor's directions by repeating the instruction, guiding the rider's hands or focusing the rider's attention on his or her task.

A spotter helps a rider who rides independently. He or she stands a distance from the rider and <u>watches with full attention</u> for lack of balance or loss of the control of the horse.

The horsemanship teacher may work with individual or small groups of riders in ground activities. Riders learn about the horse and its care. Grooming, care of tack, leading and tacking the horse are some of the skills that are taught.

Those volunteers with teaching skills or extensive equine experience may also assist the instructor in teaching lessons. Other activities include cleaning stalls, feeding horses, preparing the horses for lessons, setting up equipment in the arena as described on the lesson plans, putting horses away after the lesson, cleaning tack, repairs around the facilities, and making special equipment. Preparing for and helping with horse shows also involves the volunteers. Tasks which are necessary in running the program may include setting up a schedule, office tasks, producing a news-letter, and training other volunteers. Without devoted volunteers most therapeutic riding programs would not be able be carry on their valuable services.

17.02 ASSESSING YOUR STAFF AND VOLUNTEERS FOR EFFECTIVE USE

Barbara T. Engel, MEd, OTR

KEY WORDS
ASSESSMENT
EFFECTIVENESS
SAFETY

The program director needs to assess the staff and volunteers to be able to use each person's skills and personality to everyone's maximum and to assist in the development of potential. The utilization of each person's skills and personality helps to develop a strong and lasting team. New staff and volunteers usually fill out an application form which provides some basic information about experience with horses and disabled people, riding ability, interests and reasons for volunteering. This is important information but gives only the basic data one needs to assess the staff and volunteers. In addition one must see volunteers in action.

Areas to be observed:
- How well does this person work with others?
- Does he or she work best in small groups or on a one-to-one basis?
- Does this person work best with the horse, with children or adults? or does he or she work best on self-directed tasks?
- Does this person demonstrate a mature and responsible attitude?
- If this is a teenager, what can he or she handle well, where does he or she need support?
- Where does he or she overestimate or underestimate his or her abilities?
- Is this person able to work as scheduled and is he or she on time regularly?
- Does this person underestimate or overestimate his or her base of knowledge? In what area(s)?
- How well does this person accept instructions or correction?
- Can this person learn different or new methods and techniques?
- Is this person safe and capable around horses?
- Does this person have riding instructional abilities? Is he or she ready to use them?
- Is this person a leader or follower?
- Does this person share or accept the instructor's point of view?
- Does this person receive and follow directions well?
- Does this person follow through a given assignment in the appropriate time allowed?
- Does this person need support and how much?
- Does this person need a lot of praise?
- Does this person know how to instruct others?
- Does this person "listen" and understand what the other is saying?
- Is this person able to observe safety procedures as they are performed by others?
- Does this person take the initiative within his or her area of authority?
- If this person has weaknesses, how can these weakness be minimized and his or her strengths emphasized?

The answers to these questions will help the instructor provide guidance to challenge and assist the staff and volunteers. When people are well placed, feel that their talents are being effectively used and that they are learning new skills, they are more likely to become effective team members and remain with the group. Because therapeutic riding programs require a high ratio of staff/volunteers to riders for a safe program, it is important to value these people and their skills and to use them most effectively.

Therapeutic riding programs require staff and volunteers to acquire unique skills and to become-well trained people who feel fully utilized and appreciated. Well-functioning volunteers and staff produce a safe and challenging riding program.

17.03 THE VALUE OF A WELL-TRAINED VOLUNTEER

Joy E. Ferguson, MAgr.

KEY WORKS
SKILLED
EDUCATED
EXPERIENCED

The most important asset in having a well-trained volunteer in the therapeutic riding program is the safety of those who ride and work in it. Most accidents are preventable; an educated and experienced volunteer can greatly add to the overall safety of riders and other volunteers involved in a program. It is essential that the staff of the therapeutic riding programs invest the time to select, evaluate, communicate with and train appropriate people to help achieve and maintain the goals and standards set forth by the organization. The staff should expect of volunteers nothing less than a professional and serious attitude toward program safety.

If an educated volunteer knows what the job is and how to do it, the organization benefits by smooth daily operations and the volunteer is comfortable and content in that role. The volunteer greatly enhances the quality of the lessons by being enthusiastic and perhaps making helpful suggestions to the staff. The experienced and creative people who are directly involved with the organization and who also know the goals of the program are excellent sources for good ideas.

The valued volunteer contributes to the organization by performing his job effectively; it is important that the person be recognized throughout the year for the outstanding service he is giving. The contented volunteer is perhaps the most important public relations tool of an organization and may be an excellent resource for monetary or equipment contributions, new students, or additional volunteers.

Solicitation and Recruitment:
Good volunteers can be obtained from a variety of sources throughout the community. Suggested places to find interested and committed volunteers may include: a local college or university where students enrolled in related courses may require field experience or practical experience; service organizations such as Optimist, Rotary or Lions Clubs; other community organizations such as Junior League or women's clubs; high school groups such as FFA, 4-H or Honor Society. Alternative sources for volunteers may come from a community's Volunteer Bureau, Job Corps, Retired Senior Volunteer Program or the Juvenile Probation Department. Some Departments of Motor Vehicles have non-criminal offenders who will perform community services.

Selection:
Volunteers who are suitable for a therapeutic riding program should be interested, responsible, committed, flexible and mature people who have displayed these qualities in their associations in the community. Therefore, be aware of the sources and be selective in the solicitation process for the therapeutic riding volunteer.

Communication:
Effective communication with the volunteer will ensure quality in an important aspect of the program. This includes initial contact, maintaining communication throughout the year or course of the program, ongoing support for the job being done, genuine interest in the volunteer and recognition of special occasions such as birthdays, and appreciation letters, as well as events for the volunteers.

Quick response to any volunteer inquiry is recommended. This may include information about the therapeutic riding organization, calendar of events and volunteer registration form. The volunteer should be helped to realize that his time and expertise is needed and desired.

If the volunteer contacts the organization between scheduled orientations or at a time when no volunteers are needed, the volunteer coordinator should communicate to the person that he or she will be needed at a certain date and will be contacted again prior to that date. In the meantime, send him or her pertinent information about the organization, volunteer registration form, and any newsletters or invitations to special events. Try to keep the potential volunteer interested, included and excited about the organization.

Recognition and appreciation are ways volunteers can be thanked for a job well done. It is important for the volunteer coordinator to try to keep up with and acknowledge any important events or special occasions involving the volunteer. He or she should also be formally recognized in the organization or community at least once a year, if not more often. Ways to reward good and consistent service are:
o   Making presentations of certificates of appreciation or hours accumulated
o   Writing articles of interest about the volunteers in local newspapers
o   Giving appreciation dinners or picnics, and so forth
o   Giving the opportunity to contribute to the organization with new ideas or suggestions

An effective avenue for input to the organization is the program evaluation or sent on a timely basis to riders, parents, volunteers, instructors, therapists, and anyone else associated with the riding program.

Job Description:
The person who volunteers should receive an account of the job he or she will be required to do. A good formula for this is a job description. The volunteer has a right to know what is expected of him or her as well as knowing what he or she can expect from the riding program.

Orientation:
Orientation is a time when the volunteer can become acquainted with where the facility is located as well as with the facility, staff, horses, job description, policies of the organization, population seen, and procedures for lessons. Also, if the person has not registered prior to the orientation, the volunteer coordinator should make sure that each has completed the appropriate forms and received the program's volunteer handbook.

At this time, it is important that the staff make the volunteer feel at ease with them as well as with each other. Many new volunteers are unsure of their commitment to the organization or that they really want to help out. Therefore, it is important that the staff make them feel that their expertise is needed and their time is appreciated.

Tour of the facility:
The tour of the facility is important to let the newcomers know the location of rider equipment, tack, rest rooms, first aid equipment, emergency phone, staff area, volunteer area, rider preparation area, horses, and any areas that are off limits to either the riders or the volunteers.

Safety:
The safety rules when working around the horses and within the barn area should be discussed and stressed. It is essential that each volunteer know the methods used by this center and their rules so that he or she may reinforce them with the riders. The safety of the riders, volunteers and staff as well as the quality of the program depends upon education about and reinforcement of the safety regulations.

Emergency procedures:
The staff should explain each of the emergency procedures and the roles of volunteers in the procedures. It is very important that everyone in the program be familiar with the procedures so that in the event of a minor/major emergency everyone knows how to react and then acts quickly and correctly.

Equipment:
This portion of orientation is important because the volunteer is given the opportunity to become acquainted or reacquainted with the equipment that is used around the horses. The newcomer will also appreciate learning the

names of the tack and adaptive equipment that is used in the program. In addition, knowledge of terminology is vital so that people can do their job more efficiently. It also particularly helps those volunteers who are expected to assist riders during lessons.

Role of the Leader/Sidewalker:
Volunteers who are leaders or sidewalkers should know <u>exactly</u> what is expected of them during lessons. This includes:
- The time they are expected to arrive
- Greeting and preparation of the riders and horses for the lesson
- Stable management lesson procedures
- Mounting procedures
- Warm up activities (if appropriate for the riders)
- The lesson in the ring
- Dismounting procedures
- What to do with riders and horses after the lesson
- Clean-up procedures

Also, if volunteers are used in a specific capacity for assistance other than the usual lessons, the roles of that type of volunteering may be discussed.

Mock lesson:
This is another important part of the orientation both for the newcomer and staff. It is useful for the volunteer to go through the mock lesson so that questions can be answered or uncertain situations may be discussed. One can use the mock lesson to get the feel of the lesson and understand better what is expected. The staff can use the lesson to evaluate the effectiveness of the volunteer either as a leader or as a sidewalker.

Review of the Horse:
Parts/Proper Grooming and Tacking Procedures: This portion of the orientation can be optional for volunteers who are very familiar with horses and equipment. However, it is recommended that everyone review this part of orientation so that they are familiar with <u>this</u> program's grooming and tacking procedures, as well as with the horses.

Scheduling:
It is helpful for the <u>volunteer coordinator</u> to have a schedule of lessons and times available for sign-up at orientation, if the schedule has not already been confirmed. The days and times chosen should be convenient for volunteers, and the roles in which they will be serving should be challenging and enjoyable for them. The volunteer must understand that their commitment is essential. A poorly kept schedule can cause problems to the program unless program changes are planned.

Volunteer Handbook:
Each volunteer should receive a handbook at the orientation, if not before. Included in the handbook should be:
- Names and roles of staff
- Pertinent telephone numbers
- Annual program schedule
- Roles and expectations of the volunteer
- Emergency procedure information
- Rider disabilities defined and general information about them
- Program horse information
- Horse parts diagram or other helpful diagrams
- Organizational structure or Board of Directors listing

Conclusion

The therapeutic riding program will be enhanced by the well-trained volunteer. Careful solicitation and recruitment by the organization pays off. Selected persons, through good information, communication and public relations from a calendar of events, job description, volunteer orientation and recognition, will provide that program with support and dedication. Satisfied, safety-conscious persons educated as to the purpose and goals of the therapeutic riding program will be most effective assets to assure the future of the organization.

17.04 "VOLUNTEERING" IN A THERAPEUTIC RIDING PROGRAM

Nancy Hendrickson ** Volunteer in a Program

Having been asked to write about the experience of volunteering at the Institute of Equestrian Therapy*, in Chatsworth, California, I feel compelled to admit that, as a volunteer, I am something of a counterfeit. Allow me to explain...

Some months ago I received a traffic ticket that seemed to pose no more than a mild inconvenience. It required only that I mail in a small fine within six weeks time, so naturally I tucked it away in the dim reaches of my glove compartment and proceeded to forget all about it. What finally jogged my memory was a notice announcing a warrant for my arrest and demanding that I post bail that would seem sufficient to free an axe-murderer.

I went to court, pleading amnesia and hoping for a merciful judge who would let me pay my $35 and go home. But my fine had now escalated to $300. I was informed that, if I was not prepared to pay (I was not) there were two other choices--jail or community service. And so it was that I first came to the Institute of Equestrian Therapy--in much the same "volunteer spirit" with which my son washes the dishes and takes out the garbage. I "volunteered" at IET because, at the time it seemed a better choice than jail.

Until faced with the prospect myself, I had only the sketchiest idea of what community service entailed. Zsa Zsa Gabor notwithstanding (I assumed she had gotten preferential treatment), I imagined myself picking up litter by the side of a freeway in a day-glo vest. What a relief it was when I was offered a choice of assignments near my home. What an unexpected delight when one of the choices turned out to be working with horses.

When asked if I had any experience I answered with an unequivocal resounding "yes!" and only as an afterthought added, "but not very recently." Could it really have been 28 years since I have had regular contact with horses? It could indeed. My first morning at IET attested to that. As I walked to the barn, I had visions of my childhood self, riding, grooming, tacking-up; unfortunately, my memories of how those things were accomplished were somewhat less than vivid and I found myself staring at a halter hoping for a set of instructions or at least a "this end up" sign. Trial and error reminded me that saddles need girths. Brushes and hoofpicks appeared as foreign objects. Words like <u>hackamore</u> and <u>surcingle</u> fell upon my ears like the sounds of a long, lost mother tongue--vaguely familiar but now detached from any former meaning.

Fortunately, not much was expected of me that first day. It was a day to watch, to relearn skills. It was a day of deja-vu in which my mind retrieved many things as deeply buried and thoroughly forgotten as a traffic ticket in a glove compartment. Simple sensations--the smell of horse sweat mingled with leather, my arm, the heat, the dust, the flies--all had the power to send me hurtling backward through time, erasing three decades in an instant flash of recognition.

How ironic it is that I have put off riding and working with horses all these years because it seemed like such a frivolous waste of time and money, and now it is the Los Angeles Municipal Court forced me to pursue it. I feel guilty enjoying myself this much. I feel as though I have been sentenced to enjoy myself--to spend some time doing things I like. I suppose what qualifies the experience as community service, rather than sheer selfishness, is the fact that IET provides a service to disabled people. But from my point of view that merely adds a new dimension of satisfaction to work I already love. It is like being handed a second ice cream sundae--this time with extra cherries on top. At IET I can help some other little girl to have the same experiences I had as a child and to create the

* Institute of Equestrian Therapy, 4241 Valley Fair, Simi Valley, CA 93063.
**Volunteer in a Therapeutic Riding program at the time of preparing this article.

389

kind of memories that life is all about when the world has added one too many complications. Despite disabilities that may deprive her of other childhood pleasures, this is a place where she can be just like any other girl her age. She can fall in love with a horse, make it her own for an hour, and feel its powerful body respond to her commands.

At IET I also help other adults. Some, the victims of accidents or strokes, were in the process of learning the skills of movement and speech they once could take for granted. Here their courageous attempts are made in an atmosphere of pleasure, rather than frustration. And I have the opportunity to help them remember a word, re-experience a familiar sensation, perform again a simple task--even as I help myself do the same.

I am sure the aspect of exercise is an important one and there must be theories behind equestrian therapy that explain why exercise on horseback is both beneficial and effective for the disabled. But I have not read the theories and can go only by my own observation which tells me that its psychological benefits seem far more profound than the physical ones.

For wheelchair clients, riding is a chance to view the world from a lofty place. For the physically limited, it offers a sense of control that is otherwise elusive. Riding offers the disabled a sense of accomplishment, freedom, pleasure, power, dignity. . . etc.

Soon I will finish my court-ordered hours. I know I will be coming back, but even when my community service assignment is complete, it will probably be less than honest to call myself a "volunteer." I'll be back because the old horse-junkie in me has once again reared its head, and because my new experiences here have been equally addictive.

I will be back because there really is no other choice!

17.05 METHODS FOR TRAINING YOUR STAFF

Barbara T. Engel, MEd, OTR

It is important that everyone joining a therapeutic riding program understand the risk factors involved and that safety is of major importance for the rider, the horse, the volunteer, and staff. Accidents can be avoided with well-trained people who are knowledgeable in this field. It is very important to explain that horses are handled differently with special populations and why this is so.

Whether one is instructing a staff member or a volunteer makes little difference in techniques except for the depth of the training. **ALL PERSONS INVOLVED IN THERAPEUTIC HORSEBACK RIDING MUST TAKE THEIR JOB SERIOUSLY, BE WELL TRAINED, RESPONSIBLE AND PROFESSIONAL IN THEIR ATTITUDES AND BEHAVIORS.** Whether or not the person is paid by the organization, job and safety factors are important. The persons who are responsible for training newcomers must be knowledgeable and enthusiastic about the topic they are teaching in order to convey interest to the learners. It is equally important to understand the need for training. *One does not approach a training session with the attitude that this is wasted time which could be spent more productively with the riders. A well-designed training session is educational, interesting, and inspiring.*

<u>Preparing the Training Program</u>
Preparing the training session is similar to preparing lesson plans for riders. The training program is best presented in steps so that it is not so overwhelming. Dividing the material into separate sessions also helps persons new to the field be able to absorb the material in a way that makes sense to them. Begin with basic material, then build on the basics to present more technical information. To develop a training program one needs to identify areas that the staff and volunteers need to know, such as the following basic information:
- ◻ What is your organization?
- ◻ How does your organization work?
- ◻ What is therapeutic horseback riding?
    - ✿ How did it develop, who is it for, how does it work?
    - ✿ How does the program serve the community?
    - ✿ How is the group funded?
- ◻ How does the group use volunteers?
- ◻ Overview of jobs
- ◻ Who rides in your group?
- ◻ Some basics about the disabilities represented

It is useful to develop a training manual which provides a quick reference to the newcomer with all the information needed regarding the therapeutic riding program. One can use the manual when presenting the initial information. Presenting material verbally and visually makes a more lasting impression. The manual can also be helpful in giving the instructor guidelines in presenting the class material. The program manual should contain:
- → History of the specific therapeutic riding group
- → Organizational chart
- → Names of major people in the group and their jobs
- → Accreditation and regulatory requirements (national, state, local)
- → Program procedures
    - ✿ safety
    - ✿ emergency
    - ✿ accident
    - ✿ insurance
    - ✿ attire
    - ✿ responsibilities
    - ✿ horse handling
    - ✿ general stable management

→ Requirements for each job
- ✿ leader
- ✿ sidewalker
- ✿ instructor
- ✿ therapist
- ✿ stable manager
- ✿ mounting

→ Examples of forms (initial information form, emergency release form, treatment form, rider information form, rider/instructor evaluations, other materials)

→ Program schedules

→ Special projects such as ride-a-thon, horse shows

→ Lesson plans
- ✿ teaching techniques
- ✿ exercises
- ✿ games
- ✿ preparing the riding ring
- ✿ special guidelines

Beginning the training session with a video that presents an overall view of therapeutic riding, such as *A New Freedom and A Parent's Story* (NARHA, 1991) or *Aspects and Answers* (Cheff Center) that provides a good introduction to the concept of therapeutic riding. *Partners in Equine Therapy and Education* (Brock, 1987) presents an introduction to a program with adult riders and *Challenged Equestrians* (Glasow, 1988) provides a look at therapeutic riding, equine-assisted therapy, and hippotherapy. The use of videos makes a lesson interesting and is easy to present. Videos can also be obtained on many subjects covering safety, horse care, grooming, T.T.E.A.M. techniques, procedures for riding, vaulting and driving (see reference section). The program can make its own training videos showing procedures that need to be emphasized. Each new volunteer or staff person should read and, better yet, have a copy of a therapeutic riding training manual such as *The Horse, The Handicapped, and the Riding Team in a Therapeutic Riding Program* (Engel el al, 1989), that allows the newcomer to review material after he returns home or at a later date. One might give reading assignments which are followed on another day by hands on training. **THE IMPORTANCE OF TRAINED VOLUNTEERS AND STAFF CANNOT BE EMPHASIZED TOO MUCH. Safety can only be provided by knowledgeable people.**

Training classes should be planned so that they are long enough to cover the subject well but not so long as to lose the interest of the group. By dividing each class session into sections, the group will maintain its interest. One might begin with 20 to 30 minutes of lecture, then a video covering the topic being discussed, and then some demonstrations or hands-on training. Having different staff members lead sessions helps vary the pace and topics. Reading material is always of interest to new staff. A scrapbook of photos and newspaper clippings of riders and events provides an historical record of the program. Books on horses and equestrian activities are useful. For those who have little or no exposure to horses--the book *HAPPY HORSEMANSHIP* (Pinch, 1987) a delightful book that is light reading (written for children), fun for all and provides basic information on "do's" and "do not's" with horses.

In conclusion, make your training sessions a point of importance, make them interesting and informative, and show enthusiasm when teaching your classes. Continue to hold training sessions throughout the year to expand the volunteer/staff knowledge. Encourage your group to read therapeutic riding literature, attend conferences and clinics on related topics. Remember that members of a well-trained group will reward each other and the program with productive work, safe procedures, and enrichment from learning!

References

Brock, B. (1987). *Partners In Equine Therapy and Education.* Eastern Washington University, WA.

Cheff Center, *Aspect and Answers video.* P.O. Box 368, Augusta MI 49012.

Engel, B., Galloway, M., Bull, M. (1989). *The Horse, The Handicapped, The Riding Team.* Pasadena, CA.

Glasow, B. (1988). *Challenged Equestrians.* Winslow, NY.

NARHA. (1991). *A New Freedom and A Parent's Story.* North American Riding for the Handicapped. P.O. Box 33150, Denver, CO 80233.

Pinch, D. H. (1987). *Happy Horsemanship.* New York: Prentice Hall Press.

18. EXECUTION OF THE THERAPEUTIC RIDING LESSON

18.01 WARMING UP A RIDING HORSE

Margaret L. Galloway, MA, BHSAI

Properly warming up a horse is essential in his care, for a careful warming-up procedure prevents injuries, and accidents and makes the horse attentive and responsive to the instructor/trainer's commands. "Neurologically, a warm-up prompts the horse's reflexes and reawakens the automatic response patterns that he'll be using in his sport (Mackay-Smith, 1985)." "Warming up aids the action of the muscles by increasing their efficiency to shorten and thicken (contract) so that an unbalanced response won't hazard a torn muscle or strained tendon (Mackay-Smith," 1985). Warming up the horse benefits his cardiovascular system, as well as his lungs, muscle cells, and joints. It raises the horse's pulse rate to the point at which the trainer can engage him in any activities. "Warm-up redistributes the blood throughout the horse's body. As muscle circulation increases by as much as tenfold, there is a proportionate decrease in circulation to the intestines and other internal organs, fat stores and bones" (Mackay-Smith, 1985).

When warming up a horse, one must consider both the animal's physical and psychological aspects. In terms of the psychological warming up, the trainer tries to guide him into a state of mind characterized by attentiveness, a willingness to work, and a relaxed attitude. First of all, one begins by gaining his attention. If a horse is lethargic, wake him up by upward transitions, or increasing the gaits. If he is tense and overly energetic, use slow, rhythmic work on large circles; for instance, the trainer may make the horse keep a slow, steady trot in a large circle for half an hour. In general, the type of warm-up procedure depends upon the animal. The trainer must remain flexible in his approach to the horse's attitude and needs.

Begin by walking the horse on the rail as well as in large circles for ten minutes. Walking a horse loosens his muscles. For example, if he has arthritis, it may require fifteen minutes or more of walking, because walking loosens inflamed joints and allows the synovial fluid to lubricate the joints. After walking him in large circles, one may progress to guiding him in serpentines, and figure eights.

After the horse and instructor/trainer have completed the walking stage, a posting trot can begin. It is important to post instead of sitting the trot (in English riding), because the horse's back needs time to warm up, and sitting the trot adds pressure to his back. Next, guide him in large circles so as to ensure his balance and to maintain his attention. Circles must be executed correctly, or the circles will not be effective in attaining the trainer's goals. As the horse warms up, guide him into smaller circles and transitions, half circles and changes in direction to keep up his attention and to equalize his workout.

Horses need to be worked in both directions, evenly, for if they work in only one direction, the strength of the muscles becomes unbalanced. Also, horses become more adept at moving in one particular direction. The trainer wants the horse to be able to move equally well in both directions. Cantering work begins next, and cantering may be initiated from the walk or the trot, although it is recommended that cantering begin from the trot. One needs to canter the horse in both directions equally, always making sure that he maintains the correct lead for each direction. The trainer then begins to work according to the specific needs of the horse. This stage ends the warm-up session and begins the actual work period.

Reference: Mackay-Smith, M. (1985). Warm-up and Cool Down Performance Essentials. *Equus*, 12. 96. 12-14.

18.02   WARMING UP THE THERAPEUTIC RIDING HORSE

Kyle Hamilton, MS, PT

The therapeutic riding horse needs a specialized warm-up to ready it for its task in hippotherapy, vaulting, driving or therapeutic riding. The horse used must already be suitable to its specific task and comfortable around adaptive equipment (wheelchairs, walking aids, mounting ramps) and unpredictable behavior (autism, spastic movements of riders, incoordinate movements of handlers.)

The ideal situation is for the therapy horse to be turned out to play before the lesson. In this way it can let off steam, so that subsequently it can go calmly, safely and rhythmically (Heipertz, 1981). A minimum of twenty minutes should be allotted to this turnout. This technique seems to work the best; if the horse is lazy or quiet during the turnout time, an additional ten to fifteen minutes of free or controlled longeing should work out any "kinks." The horse should be worked for a period at all gaits and in both directions.

When settled, the therapeutic riding/therapy horse should be groomed and handled using methods such as the T.T.E.A.M Touch. This will help the horse relax his muscles, balance, focus, and bond with his handler. The horse should then be collected in the stable and equipped with the proper tack for its lesson or clinical duty. At this point, the horse should be calm, relaxed and ready for full attention to his handlers. The horse handler should be aware of the time needed to ready each individual horse for its lesson, and not rush this time, nor allow this preparatory phase to encroach into the lesson or treatment time (ibid.)

The vaulting horse should be longed at all gaits with the side-reins loosely fastened, and the tension gradually increased on the reins until they are of proper length for working a mounted client. Knowing the horse's tolerance for this will dictate the amount of time needed. The vaulting horse needs to be worked in both directions, not just counter-clock-wise.

The hippotherapy horse needs to be collected with side-reins in the same way as the vaulting horse but while being driven from behind. This horse needs work at a walk and with schooling figures (circles, serpentine) to get him on the bit and walking rhythmically in preparation for the rider. Each horse will vary, but it will take anywhere from five to twenty minutes to ready the horse.

The therapeutic riding horse can be loosened up as described by Margaret Galloway in *Warming-up the Riding Horse*, section 18.01). The handler/rider should progress the horse into the work phase or increase the warm-up time to accommodate any rider that may not need such an attentive mount (beginning riders, riders with decreased trunk control or balance.) The riding horse should also be cued with the specific needs of the rider, in that, if an amputee were to be mounted on this horse, the horse should be readied for voice or whip cues, and not leg cues.

The properly warmed-up horse is calm, alert, supple, obedient and ready to work. He is attentive to the rider and not to his stablemates or the hubbub of other barn activity. He will go forward into the proper gait and halt on command. He will willingly bend or circle and submit to the rider's hand. If the horse cannot do these things, he is not properly warmed up and can be a danger or pest.

Reference
Heipertz, W. (1981). Therapeutic Riding. Medicine, Education, Sports. Greenbelt Riding Association for the Disabled Inc., Ottawa.

18.03   GROUND PRE-RIDING EXERCISES

Margaret L. Galloway, MA, BHSAI

Exercises performed before mounting prepare riders for the actual task of riding horses. Ground pre-riding exercises are especially important for disabled persons because they stretch and relax the riders' muscles and help to increase their concentration. There are two forms of pre-riding exercises, namely, psychological and physical exercises. The purpose of psychological exercise is to prepare the riders to attend, to mentally relax, and to build confidence. Therefore, the instructor must first bring the riders to a point of psychological readiness. Secondly, the mind directly affects the body. After the riders are adequately confident and mentally relaxed, the instructor can then introduce physical exercises that will enhance the already established mental preparedness. Physical exercises focus on loosening and stretching the riders' body so that it becomes sufficiently relaxed and supple. Relaxed muscles allow the riders to gain more from their lessons, because a horse reacts negatively to tense bodies.

In order to help riders to relax psychologically, the instructor may allow them to interact with the horses while they are still on the ground. For instance, one may direct riders to groom their horses, an activity that promotes a mental bond between horses and riders. They may also be taught T.T.E.A.M. (Tellington-Jones, 1987) techniques, which not only help to prepare the horses for riding, but also at the same time help the riders to focus mentally and to relax physically. Once the riders learn to assist in the care of their horses, their confidence increases. The instructor may also engage the riders in a game of pretending to be a horse (Swift, 1985). In this game, one asks riders to play the part of both the horses and the riders. For example, rider A pretends to be a horse, while rider B takes the role of the rider. In this exercise, A plays the "horse", acts like a horse, thinks about how the horse would feel under certain conditions, how the horse would treat the rider, and how it would feel to have a human on his back. This game emphasizes the fact that a horse is a feeling, living being that needs to be treated with respect and kindness. Rider B, plays the part of a rider and practices approaching the horse in a quiet and gentle manner, talking to the horse in a soft voice. B also thinks about how to handle the horse, both on and off. The game is purely imaginary and can be played from a chair through speech and sounds. This game would be appropriate for some emotionally disturbed, mentally delayed, learning disabled and physically disabled riders. For those who are not able to participate in the above type game, deep breathing, imagery, t'ai chi concepts, or Feldenkrais exercises are very useful (see reference section.)

After the riders have become relaxed and focused, the instructor then turns to physical warm-up exercises, which limber their bodies and make it easier for them to mount and ride their horses. Depending upon the group, the instructor may use simple exercises, such as stretching or for hyperactive riders, he or she might use stretching exercises along with deep breathing which helps relaxation. If the riders are in wheelchairs, they may be asked to do stretching exercises such as reaching up high and down to the feet with hands held together or bending the head side-to-side, forward and backward. In a group of hyperactive youngsters, the instructor may ask the students to do a slow, rhythmic jog in place with deep breathing (if these activities do not **increase** their hyperactivity). These exercises can be followed by various stretching exercises (see next section 18.04). When everyone is physically and mentally relaxed, the riding lesson can begin.

Reference
Swift, S. (1985). *Centered Riding*. North Pomfret, Vt: David & Charles, Inc. 5.
Tellington-Jones, L. (1987). *The Touch That Teaches*. Gaithersburg: Fleet Street Publishing.

18.04 EQUESTRIAN EXERCISES

Mary Beth Walsh, PT, BHSAI

Equestrians are a unique group of athletes who require a specific regimen of exercises to meet the challenge of all riding including dressage, hunt seat and vaulting. For the physically challenged riders it is especially important that the riders prepare their bodies for riding by performing the appropriate stretches prior to getting into the saddle. Special consideration for each individual's postural reflexes and tonal patterns should be adapted to the stretches performed. Consultation with the riders' physical therapists is encouraged to maximize the quality of stretching. In all forms of riding, flexibility and strength are essential prior to putting their feet in the stirrups.

The following pages describe a comprehensive fitness program for all riders. Special emphasis is placed on the lower abdominal strength and pelvic mobility for dressage riders, and on back extensor muscle strength in order to maintain a solid hunt seat position. Vaulting requires both flexibility and great strength of all muscle groups in order to execute set maneuvers. Daily performance of these exercises is necessary to achieve the best results for flexibility, strength and motor learning. Flexibility exercises should be done prior to riding. Cross training in sports that improve pelvic and low back mobility and improve strength in the legs and abdomen are also beneficial for riders. Some of these sports are swimming, cycling, dancing, gymnastic, cross country skiing and climbing the stairmaster. For dressage riders, practicing the hula hoop (even when sitting on a stool) is highly recommended for improving muscle tone and coordination.

Prior to starting an exercise program within your program, it is important that one understands how to stretch properly. There are a few important points that should be remembered. Remember to relax, to breathe throughout the exercise, to focus on the muscles being stretched, to make the stretch smooth-steady stretch and to avoid pain. Program instructors should request assistance from their physical therapy (or occupational therapy) consultant, to help adapt exercises to special riders with unique needs but remember that everyone, including the staff, profits from proper stretching. Remember, too, that all these exercises are not suitable for every rider.

Please note that although these exercises are designed for the rider, some may not be appropriate for **all riders**. Always contact the rider's physician, physical therapist, or the program's consulting physical or occupational therapist prior to initiating this exercise program.

WHY STRETCH**

Stretching, because it relaxes your mind and tunes up your body, should be part of your daily life. You will find that regular stretching will do the following things:
- Reduce muscle tension and make the body feel more relaxed.
- Help coordination by allowing for freer and easier movement.
- Increase range of motion.
- Prevent injuries such as muscle strains. (A strong, pre-stretched muscle resists stress better than a strong unstretched muscle.)
- Make strenuous activities like running, skiing, tennis, swimming, cycling, and horseback riding easier because it prepares you for activities; it is a way of signaling the muscles that they are about to be used.
- Develop body awareness. As you stretch various parts of the body, you focus and get in touch with them.
- Help loosen the mind's control of the body so that the body moves for "its own sake rather than for competition or ego.
- Promote circulation.
- It feels good.

Reference
Sections and exercises noted with asterisk ** are excerpted from Bob Anderson's book *Stretching* (1980)--reprinted by permission.
Anderson, B., Anderson, J. (1980). *Stretching*. Shelter Publications, Inc., P.O.Box 279, Bolinas, CA 94924.

LOWER EXTREMITY FLEXIBILITY

Quadriceps Stretch

The quadriceps are the muscles in the front of the thigh. Flexibility is necessary for pelvic mobility and to allow legs to be held in proper, aligned position while riding.

Perform standing or kneeling, grab the ankle and relax hip forward. Hold position for 30 seconds. Repeat 5 times. You will feel a stretch in the front part of the thigh and hip.

**

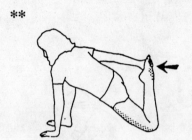

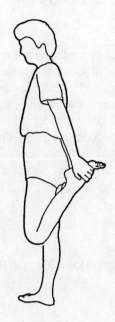

Calf Stretch

The muscles in the back of the calf need to be flexible in order to keep your heels down and your feet in the stirrup. Simply lunge forward and keep your back heel in contact with the floor as in this picture. Hold 30 seconds. Repeat 5 times.

Combination of inner thigh, quadriceps, calf stretch, low back. Hold position for 30 seconds. Repeat 5 times. Nice quick "pre-riding" stretch.

**

Hamstring Stretch

The hamstrings are muscles in the back of the thigh. These muscles will restrict pelvic movement if not flexible.

Start by stretching one leg out in front of you as the picture demonstrates. The calf muscle can be incorporated by using a towel to pull up on the foot. Hold for 30 seconds. Repeat 5 times.

Progress to both legs in front.

Next, sit down with your legs straight and feet upright, heels no more than six inches apart. Bend from the hips to get an easy stretch. Hold for 20 seconds. You will probably feel this just behind the knees, and in the back of the upper legs. You may also feel a stretch in the lower back if your back is tight.

Remember to bend forward from the hip as if it were a hinge.

Think of bending from your hips without rounding your lower back.

If your hamstrings are particularly tight and the above positions put too much strain on the low back, perform the stretch by leaning against a wall. Hold for up to 1 minute. Repeat 2 to 3 times.

398

Inner Thigh Stretch

The inner thigh muscles perform a "gripping" or "squeezing" legs together while contracting. This contraction is necessary to stabilize the lower leg and pelvis while in 2-Point, but must be supple and flexible in Dressage to allow the pelvis to be relaxed in the saddle. If these muscles are not properly stretched prior to riding, the pelvis will not be allowed proper flexibility and a bumpy ride is in store for the rider.

** Remember—no bouncing when you stretch. Find a place that is fairly comfortable that allows you to stretch and relax at the same time.

**

Begin the stretch by sitting with the soles of the feet together. Pull the feet together. Pull the feet close to your body.

** If you have any trouble bending forward, perhaps your heels are too close to your groin area.

If so, keep your feet farther out in front of you. This will allow you to get movement forward.

** Variations:

Then gently press down on the knees. Start by stretching one knee. Hold for 30 seconds. Repeat 2 to 3 times.

** Hold on to your feet with one hand, with your elbow on the inside of the lower leg to hold down and stabilize the leg. Now, with your other hand on the inside of your leg (*not on knee*), gently push your leg downward to isolate and stretch this side of the groin. This is a very good isolation stretch for people who want to limber up a tight groin so that the knees can fall more naturally downward.

To Stretch the Groin Area

**

Then progress to stretching both knees down. This can be done by pressing your elbows into your knees. Hold for 30 seconds. Repeat 2 to 3 times.

Hip and lower back stretches

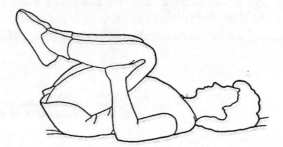

Double Knee to Chest

This exercise helps to stretch out the long broad muscles that surround your spine. Relax and pull your knees up to your chest, and hold for 10 seconds. Repeat 10 times.

Then progress to a **piriformis stretch**. This muscle is deep in your buttocks. Simply pull one leg diagonally across your body, keeping your hips on the mat. Hold up to 30 econds. Repeat 5 times.

Hip Flexor Stretch

The hip flexors are in front of the hip at the top of the thigh. In order to maintain a long leg on the horse and good pelvic mobility, these muscles need to be stretched. Hold position 30 seconds. Repeat 5 times.

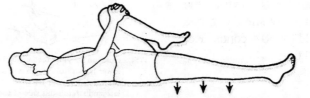

Start by pulling one knee to chest, pushing down on opposite leg.

Again, hold the stretch up to 30 seconds, repeat up to 5 times.

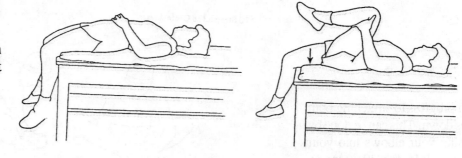

Progress to letting one leg hang over mat.

Pelvic Tilt

The pelvic tilt is performed to increase the mobility of the low back. The exercise utilizes the lower abdominal muscles to pull the seat underneath you. The muscles relax, allowing the low back to gently arch again. Performing the pelvic tilt is similar to the movement necessary to "go with the movement" of the horse, especially in the sitting trot.

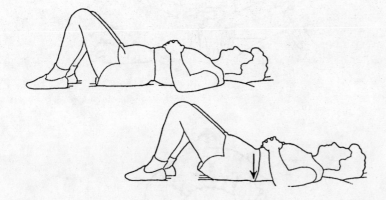

Perform by pulling up with the lower abdominals, pressing the low back into the mat. Perform 10 times.

Pelvic Tilt with Wall Squat

Lean against a wall, squat down to about 45° to 90° and hold. While holding, perform a series of 10 pelvic tilts as shown above. Repeat at different levels of squatting, increasing the time held in the squat position up to one minute.

* This exercise is particularly good to improve strength and mobility for the Two-Point position.

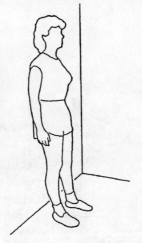

LOW BACK FLEXIBILITY

To improve the mobility of the low back and pelvic tilt, sit and have a friend assist you in rocking your pelvis back and forth while you maintain an upright posture. The movement is the same as a pelvic tilt, perform by tightening and relaxing your lower abdominal muscles. Repeat 10 times.

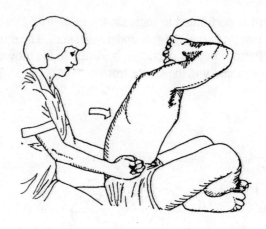

Cat and Camel Exercise

Perform a series of pelvic tilts, rounding your back **as an angry cat** and then **arching your back as a camel**. Repeat in succession up to 20 repetitions.

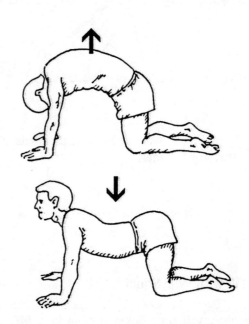

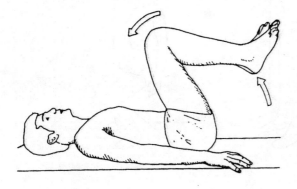

Lower Abdominal Lift

To perform the lower abdominal lift, first perform a pelvic tilt, flattening the low back into the mat. Hold legs up at 90° to the body, then by contracting the lower abdominal muscles, lift and lower the pelvis off the mat. Repeat in 2 to 3 sets of 10 repetitions.

402

Abdominal Strengthening

The best way to strengthen the abdominal muscles is to perform "curls" described below. The muscles are necessary to assist in supporting the back and promoting good posture.

Perform abdominal exercises daily in sets of 10 repetitions. Increase the number of sets performed as the exercise becomes easier and you can maintain good form.

** EXERCISES FOR THE ABDOMINAL MUSCLES:

The abdominal muscles are the strength center of the body. They are essential for endurance. They help keep your back free from pain, assist in proper movement, easy elimination of waste, in rhythmical breathing, and in standing erect. But few of us have ever felt the energy that goes with strong abdominals.

"Sit-ups" are generally considered the best exercise for strengthening abdominal muscles. Yet sit-ups offer little in the way of rhythm and can cause severe strain. Because of this, many people understandably detest sit-ups.

The straight legged sit-up is potentially dangerous for the lower back for this reason: your abdominal muscles can raise your body off the floor to about a 30° angle. To raise any further activates the primary hip flexor muscles, which are attached to the lower back. This puts severe stress on the lower back.

Bending your knees will relieve much of the strain in your lower back. The bent knee sit-up is good, as long as you do each sit-up fluidly and mentally concentrate on the abdominal muscles. Be careful of this exercise because people generally do too many repetitions, and when tired, jerk up quickly, which stresses the lower back.

The developmental exercise I do recommend for strengthening abdominals without straining the lower back is the *ab curl*. Here the upper body is curled forward no more than 30° and the lower back remains flat.

** Here are three exercises and one variation that will work the upper, lower and sides of your abdominals. If your abdominals get tight doing these, just relax and straighten out your legs, put your hands over your head and reach in the opposite direction with a controlled stretch. Hold for 5-8 seconds. This should stretch the abdominals and relieve any tightness that might occur.

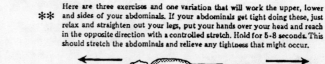

A position to stretch out the abdominals.

The Abdominal Curl (Ab Curl)

fig. 1a   fig. 1b   fig. 1c

Start on your back with knees bent and feet flat on the floor, hands across your chest (fig. 1a). Curl up, bringing your shoulder blades off the floor about 30° (fig. 1b), then lower back down to the floor (fig. 1c). Do not bob your head up and down, as this may strain your neck. Keep your head in a fixed position. Concentrate on the *upper abdominals* (solar plexis area), curling your upper body forward with your chin close to your chest (fig 1b). When you lower, or uncurl your upper body, the back of your head should not touch the floor because you are holding your chin near your chest (fig. 1c).

The Elbow-Knee Ab Curl

fig. 2a   fig. 2b   fig. 2c

This is done from the same starting position as the ab curl, but you interlace your fingers behind your head about ear level and raise your feet off the floor. Using your abdominal muscles, hold your upper body at about a 30° angle off the floor (fig. 2a). Now, bring your elbows forward, touching about 1-2 inches above the knees (fig. 2b). Uncurl as in fig. 2c, then raise your elbows and knees again as in fig. 2b. Your lower back should be flat at all times during these abdominal exercises.

UPPER BACK MUSCLE STRENGTHENING

Pectoral Stretch

The pectoral muscles are located in front of the chest. When these muscles are tight, they prevent you from keeping your shoulders back. Stretch these muscles with hands behind head as in Figure 1 or with arms at side as in Figure 2. Pull back as far as you can. Hold 10 seconds. Repeat 5 times.

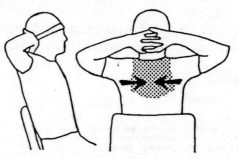

** Figure 1

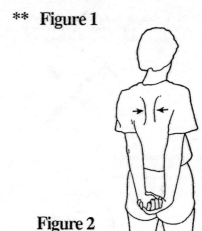

Figure 2

To **strengthen upper back muscles** to promote good posture, start by lying on mat with arms over edge. Raise and lower arms, pulling shoulder blades together with every arm raise. Increase resistance by adding small weights to hands. Repeat 10 times.

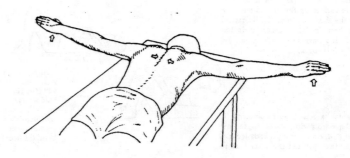

Progress to raising arms and trunk as in this picture. Perform slowly and hold for 5 seconds in the raised position. Repeat in 4 sets of 5 repetitions.

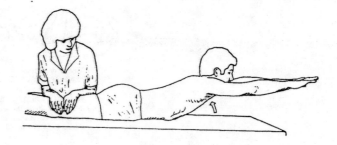

SHOULDER AND BACK FLEXIBILITY

Low Back and Shoulder Stretch

Sit on your heels, bend forward, stretch your arms overhead, hold for 30 seconds. Repeat 2 to 3 times. You'll feel this in the shoulders and low back.

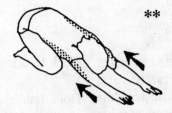

Side Stretch

Stretch as in Figures 1 and 2. Hold for 10 to 30 seconds. Repeat up to 5 times.

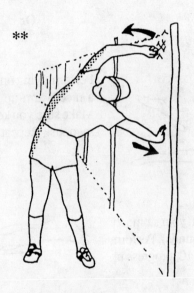

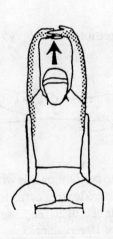

Figure 1   **Figure 2**

Tricep Stretch

Position arm as in the picture and pull elbow as shown. Hold for 10 to 30 seconds. Repeat up to 5 times.

LOW BACK EXTENSION EXERCISES

Leg Extensions

To begin to strengthen the back muscles, perform these leg lifts. Increase the difficulty by adding ankle weights. Repeat 3 sets of 10 repetitions.

Back Bends

Hold hands on hips, gently arch back, hold for 1 to 2 seconds. Repeat 5 times.

Or

Leg Extension

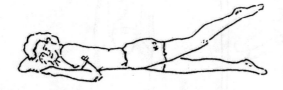

Progress to performing lifts while on your stomach. Again, add ankle weights (up to 5 pounds). Perform in multiple sets of 10 (i.e., 2 sets of 10, progress up to 5 sets of 10 repetitions).

Perform lying on stomach as in a **press-up**. This is a nice warm-up to improve low back flexibility. Make sure you keep your hips on the mat. Hold 10 seconds. Repeat 10 times.

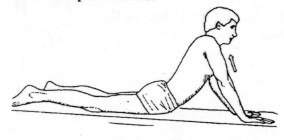

*Total Back Extension (The Swan)

Figure 1

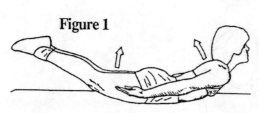

Begin with arms at your side

* These exercises are especially good to prepare for Two-Point and jumping.

Figure 2

When you are really strong, progress to raising all four limbs and your trunk off the floor. Hold position 5 seconds and relax. Progress to arms over head. Repeat 10 times.

18.05   WHEELCHAIR EXERCISES

Barbara T. Engel, MEd, OTR
Stephanie C. Woods

Exercises are not limited to persons who can walk but are just as important and beneficial to those who use wheelchairs. Whether in a wheelchair, on a mat, or standing the same basic stretching and warm-up principles must be practiced. The following exercises are but a few examples which can be safely performed. Many of the stretch exercises by Mary Beth Welsh in section 18.04 can be adapted for wheelchair users.

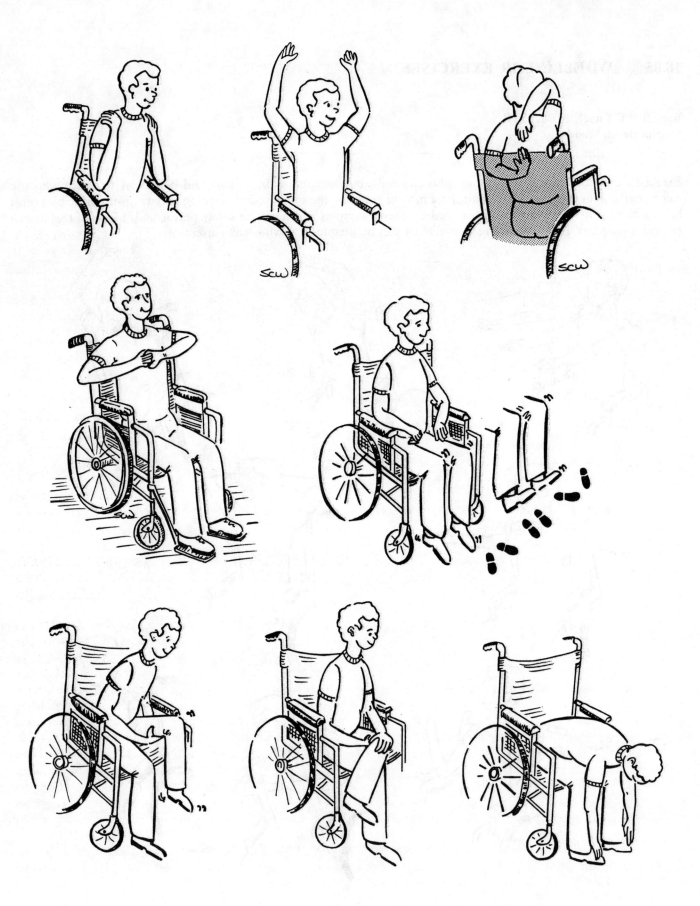

18.06 MOUNTING, TRANSFER, AND DISMOUNTING TECHNIQUES FOR RIDERS WITH DISABILITIES

Barbara T. Engel, MEd, OTR
Joann Benjamin, PT

This section will discuss the process of transferring persons with disabilities onto the horse. The transfers discussed here are the most common transfers encountered. The authors have chosen not to discuss transfers with for those with severe physical disabilities that may need to be tailored specifically to a rider. For example, transferring a adult or a large child who is unable to perform a standing pivot transfer, must be carefully evaluated by a therapist before any transfer is performed. The therapist will determine the most appropriate method to be used. A total lift may be recommended for one person but may not be appropriate for another.

A transfer is a process used by a person to move from one place to another, such as from one chair to another chair. A mounting transfer is the method a rider uses to get onto a horse. The rider with a disability may mount the horse from the ground, from a mounting block, from a platform, or from a ramp. The method of the mounting transfer will depend upon:

1. The rider's skill, strength, and mobility
2. The size and weight of the rider
3. The size of the horse
4. The effect of the transfer on the rider
5. The size, strength and training of the assistant(s)
6. The mounting facilities available
7. The maximum ability of independence for the rider--regardless of age

A mounting transfer that is properly done will encourage the rider to move in a normal manner and will be easier for those assisting the rider in the transfer. **An improper transfer encourages poor posture of rider and helpers, and does not allow the person with a disability to maintain dignity,** and is not safe.

Each rider must be considered on an individual basis. There are general principals involved in transfers but since there are no two people alike each person and his or her transfer must be assessed on an individual basis. Always consider the affect a transfer will have on the horse. Safety and each person's feeling of security are the determining factors.

People with disabilities come to the riding center to learn to ride and also to improve their physical function. In order to increase function, the riders must learn to move in the most efficient way for them and move in this manner consistently. The therapeutic riding center staff are the most helpful when they encourage the riders to transfer as independently as possible. The staff must also help riders to transfer in such a way that they feel secure and relaxed. **To feel secure one must always have contact with a secure surface and *feel* in control. This principle should govern the method of mounting and the method of dismounting.** A rider may use one method for mounting and a different one for dismounting. For a rider who is physically disabled, the method chosen must be determined by the rider's physical needs and the effects the transfer has on the him or her. Otherwise, the lesson time is spent in reducing spasticity and stress from an insecure mounting transfer, and regaining the confidence of the rider rather than gaining the maximum benefit from the horse and lesson. A dismount that increases tone and reflex activity, decreases the rider's control of his or her body, or disorients him or her may undo all the benefits of a lesson. The most normal method is the preferred one BUT may not be the best for all riders. Be sure the selection of the transfer is not chosen strictly for the benefit of the staff, the most "normal", but is the best for each rider.

It is important for staff to be well trained in transfer methods **before** assisting riders to mount a horse. Any time persons are in the process of movement, they are in a position of being off balance. This places them at risk for falling. This applies to both riders and helpers since during the transfer both are moving. In assisting persons with any type of physical dysfunction, one must know the correct method of handling their bodies to avoid injury. Therapeutic riding centers have physical or occupational therapists as consultants to teach the riding center staff how to perform transfers. These therapists have had extensive training in these skills with persons having many types of disabilities.

The program therapist should practice with the staff until they feel comfortable helping with transfers. Transfers are a bit more complicated at the stable since riders will be transferring onto an animal that shifts its body weight in response to the additional weight on its back. Get a feel for a transfer before completing it. **Never try a transfer if you feel unsure of the procedure or of your capabilities.** Seek guidance or more help as the case may be.

POINTS TO REMEMBER:

- ◎ Each rider should mount in the most independent way he or she can, but **SAFETY** must always be the major consideration.
- ◎ Mounting equipment must be appropriate in size and structure, safe and suitable for individual riders.
- ◎ Riders may need to be given extra time to mount independently or with minimal assistance. Give only necessary assistance, do not be overly helpful. Most people with disabilities have been taught a transfer technique by their therapist. Allow the rider to use the familiar transfer unless: it is unsafe for mounting a horse, it is against your program's policy, or you lack the facilities for that type of transfer.
- ◎ Do a transfer only when those involved are well prepared.
- ◎ Make sure the **rider** has been told how the transfer will be executed so he or she is prepared.
- ◎ A rider shall use the mounting technique that is least stressful for him or her, the team, **and the horse.**

CORRECT METHODS USED IN TRANSFERRING AND LIFTING[1]

Whenever transferring or lifting, it is very important to use correct techniques to help prevent injury to the person handling the transfer. Proper body mechanics help one to lift efficiently and safely. One way to learn and remember proper body mechanics is the "APPLAUSE"© system developed by **Paulette Olsen, RPT:***

A *APART*. Keep your feet apart when lifting. A wide base of support keeps the load centered over your base of support.

P *PIVOT*. Be sure to pivot or turn with your feet rather than twisting or turning at the waist. Twisting and turning may increase stress and wear to spinal components.

P *PLAN AND PRACTICE*. If you are unsure about the weight of the load or whether you can handle the weight safely, check the load by doing a practice lift. Simply lift the object and place it back down to judge whether you need help. Planning the lift helps you to be safer.

L *LEGS*. Lift with your legs. The muscles of the legs are power muscles, designed for power activities. So perform the lift by keeping your back erect (normal forward curve at the low back) and bending with the hips and knees. Persons with hip and knee deficiencies may need to modify this.

A *APPROACH*. Approach the lift close to your body. Keep the load as close to your body as you can. A load held at arms' length will make you work harder than a load held close to the body.

U *UP*. Keep the head up while lifting. Keeping the head up (eyes level, head erect, not down) helps keep the spine in its normal curves.

S *STOMACH*. Tighten the stomach muscles as you lift. Just as the weight lifters use belts to protect their backs, we can contract our abdominal muscles when we lift, to add support to our backs.

E *EASY*. Move slow and easy to lift. Quick jerks are harder on the bones, joints and muscles. Slow and easy is kinder to the body.

This simple memory exercise aids in remembering the key principles of lifting.

([1]"APPLAUSE" technique was developed for lifting both objects or people--terms relate to either.

---

* Printed by permission: Paulette J. Olsen is a RPT in the Work Well Program at Mercy Medical Center, Coon Rapids, Minnesota. She specializes in pain management. Paulette is the author of Applause: Body Mechanics For Children.

MOUNTING FROM THE GROUND
Adjusting the Stirrup Leathers
The horse leader stands in front and faces the horse, holds the cheekpiece, lead or the reins of the bridle. The horse leader must keep the horse still.

Check the girth and adjust the stirrups. (The stirrup leathers should be adjusted so that the rider's pelvis is level on the saddle. A rider with tight or spastic legs may need to have his stirrup leathers re-adjusted after five or ten minutes in the ring to allow the leg to lengthen). If peacock stirrups are used, make sure that the **rubber bands are toward the front of the horse.** When using Devonshire boots--the toe hangs toward the horse's side and the opening is outward.

To adjust the stirrup leathers, the rider faces the saddle and takes the stirrup with the right hand. The knuckles of the left hand are placed on the stirrup bar which is under the flap of the saddle while the stirrup is placed under the armpit of the left arm which is fully extended. Adjust both stirrup leathers to this length. Further adjustments may be made after the rider has mounted.

Mounting of the Rider
- A mounting assistant stands on the off side (opposite side from the rider) of the horse and pushes down on that stirrup to prevent the saddle from shifting.
- The rider stands on the near side of the horse facing the rear with the left hip near the horse's shoulder.
- The rider holds the reins in his or her left hand on the horse's withers and the right hand grasps the stirrup iron to steady it.
- The left foot is placed into the near stirrup with the toe into the girth. The rider should place the right hand on the seat or pommel of the saddle, press down, hop on the right foot and lift up, swing the right leg over the saddle and sit down **gently.** The rider should place the right foot into the right stirrup.

If the rider needs assistance, the rider faces the horse even with the girth, bends the left leg, then the helper takes hold of the left leg just below the knee with the left hand and grasps the rider's ankle with the right hand on the ankle. On the count of three, the rider hops up as the helper lifts and the rider swings the right leg over the saddle.

Mounting from the ground promotes independence of the rider because the rider will be able to mount anywhere. This type of mount can be hard on your horse's back, however, so carefully monitor the frequency of using this mount on any one horse.

Dismounting
The horse leader stands in front of and faces the horse and holds the horse still. The helper stands on the near side of the horse and is ready to give assistance when necessary. The rider relaxes the feet and takes **both of them** out of the stirrup irons. The rider holds onto the pommel, bends toward it, brings the right leg back and over the back of the saddle, and lowers himself to the ground without kicking the horse.

MOUNTING FROM THE MOUNTING BLOCK
The horse is led to the mounting block with the near side of the horse next to the mounting block. Using two blocks and leading the horse between the blocks helps to line up the horse correctly. The horse is held still by the horse leader standing in front of him, as above. The rider stands securely on the mounting block. Some riders will need assistance by a helper who stands on the mounting block beside them (the block needs to be of adequate size to accommodate two people comfortably). It is safest to have a spotter to assist on the far side of the horse. The spotter can assist the rider, or hold the stirrup for a heavy rider. The rider takes the reins with the left hand, places his or her left foot into the stirrup and swings the right leg over the horse, sits gently and places the foot into the right stirrup.

411

DISMOUNTING

See the previous section on dismounting. Most riders that mount from a mounting block can dismount to the ground. **Always use the most normal mounting/dismounting method the riders can perform safely for themselves and the horses.** If ground dismounting is not the best dismount for riders then they must dismount to the ramp. It is unsafe to dismount to a mounting block if it is too small.

MOUNTING FROM A WHEELCHAIR RAMP, LIFT OR PLATFORM
General Principles for all Transfers
The rider or assistant moves the wheelchair up the ramp or the person walks up the ramp. If help is needed, assist with the wheelchair from behind. If a person walking up the ramp needs assistance, walk on the his or her weaker side slightly behind the person. Hold at the hips or trunk rather than holding an arm.

Position the wheelchair so that the rider's side will be next to the near side of the horse, facing forward. The front of the chair should be angled approximately 45 degrees toward the near edge of the ramp. Have the rider lock his or her wheelchair brakes or assist him or her if necessary. Remove both footrests and the armrest nearest the horse. If the rider wears a seat belt/chest strap, remove this last. Place all the wheelchair parts away from the working area so the platform is clear.

The horse leader leads the horse to the ramp, lift, or platform and stands the horse as close to the ramp platform as possible. A mounting block should be used parallel to the ramp, lift or platform to allow the horse to move between the two objects. By placing the horse between two objects, he can be placed close enough to the mounting surface to avoid the possibility of a rider (or assistant) sliding between the mounting surface and the horse. (This possibility is the most dangerous part of a transfer of a disabled person onto the horse. It must be avoided!)

The leader then turns around and holds the horse perfectly still. **The horse leader attends to the horse only and does not assist the rider.**

A spotter stands on the far side of the horse opposite the mounting rider. The spotter can be standing on the ground, on a mounting block, or on the other side of a double ramp. Spotters need to position themselves with good balance and in such a way as to provide the necessary assistance to the rider.

Remember the APPLAUSE principals.

Always assist the rider by holding at the trunk or hips. Grabbing an arm can cause damage to the arm or tear the shoulder joint muscles. This is especially dangerous for riders who are either very stiff or whose muscles are extremely loose. A spastic muscle must be moved slowly to avoid increased tension in the muscle. Never pull or force a limb.

Follow the procedure for maximum or moderate assisted-transfers on the following pages.

Once mounted, do not force spastic legs down as you may cause a muscle to tear. Let the legs come down slowly from the crest of the horse with only **light** assistance. Let the rider relax by supporting his back. (Both legs may need to be brought over the crest of the horse and allowed to slowly relax and come down with **very light** guidance.

Both spotter and mounting assistant must see that the rider does not dig his heels into the horse as he mounts. The assistant and spotter may cup their hands over the rider's heels to protect the horse.

The mounting assistant stands on the ramp with the rider. If possible, stand at the rider's weaker side. Explain the transfer to the rider so that the rider knows what to expect and what to do. Moving from chair to chair is different than moving from chair to horse. Check that everyone is ready for the transfer. **Do not rush.**

WHEELCHAIR TRANSFER FROM A DOUBLE OR SINGLE RAMP
Maximum Assistance with a Wheelchair Mounting Transfer.
Position the rider's feet so that they are flat on the platform and will support the rider's weight in a pivot (turn) transfer. The rider's knees should be well over the toes. If not, assist the rider to scoot forward to obtain the correct position (Figure 1).

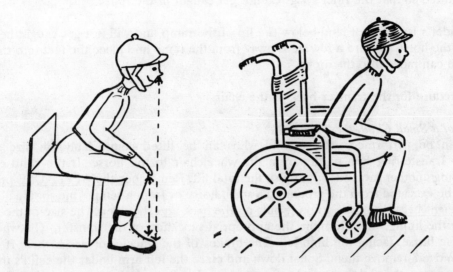

FIGURE 1.   BODY POSITION FOR A TRANSFER

Disabled people with paresis or paralysis who have little or no control of their legs, may have some spasticity in them, and can support some weight using this spasticity. Do not attempt this transfer with persons who cannot support some weight on their legs (regardless of reason).

Bring the horse in, positioned close to the ramp. The assistant stands in front of the rider, have the rider place both hands in his or her lap and lean forward toward his or her toes. The assistant now bends over the rider and grasps the **pelvis** while placing his or her knee against the rider's weakest knee. He or she shifts his or her weight backward to lift the rider forward (Figure 2).

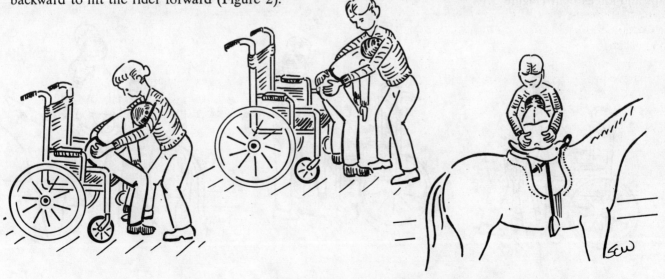

FIGURE 2.   MAXIMUM ASSISTANCE WHEELCHAIR TRANSFER

413

Pivot the rider's buttocks and gently place the buttocks on the saddle so that the rider is sitting sideways. The spotter takes hold of the hips from the rear as the rider is placed into the saddle. Support the rider from both sides of the horse and raise the rider to a sitting position. Pivot the rider and assist the right leg (with minimal pressure if the leg is spastic) over the crest of the horse while supporting the rider's back until the rider is well balanced in the saddle. Both legs may need to be moved together if the rider's legs tend to stay together due to spasticity. In this case allow relaxation and time for the legs to come down. The horse leader should hold the reins until the rider is fully mounted so that the rider's legs do not get caught in the reins.

Make sure the rider's legs do not land below the lip of the ramp and will not get caught between the ramp and the horse. Move the horse forward a few steps away from the ramp and place the feet into the stirrups. When the rider is stable, he can move into the arena.

Reverse the procedure for the transfer back to the chair.

Maximum Assist of a Small Child, the Total Lift

The total lift can be performed with a child who can be lifted comfortably (in size and weight) by the person/instructor transferring him or her from the wheelchair to the horse. If the child can participate more independently using another method, do not use the total lift. Remember the APPLAUSE principals when lifting. The total lift can be executed from the ground to a small horse or from a ramp. One should never lift a child above one's shoulder height because of the strain it puts on the back and shoulder. The size of the horse, the child, and the person doing the lifting will determine the appropriate location of the transfer. The wheelchair is placed on the left side of the horse, facing the hind leg. The brakes of the wheelchair are locked. If the left armrest and legrest can be removed, remove them. Squat down and place the left arm under the child's thighs--near the knees and the right arm across the child's upper back and grasp the chest under the arm, below the arm pit. Straighten the legs to stand, raising the child from the chair. Make a quarter turn and lower the child onto the horse.

Moderate Assistance with a Wheelchair Mounting Transfer

Make sure that the rider's feet are positioned flat on the platform and six to eight inches apart. If the rider's feet do not reach the platform, help him or her to scoot forward to the front edge of the wheelchair. The rider's knees should be well over his or her toes. (Figure 1).

Have the rider lean his or her trunk forward. The assistant **places his or her hands on the rider's back** reaching under the rider's arms. Guide the rider's trunk forward and upward as your weight is shifted backward--keep your hips and knees bent (Figure 3.)

FIGURE 3. PIVOT TRANSFER

414

When the rider is standing balanced, help him or her turn so his or her back is toward the saddle. Seat the rider sideways in the saddle, the rider places his or her left hand on the back of the saddle to assist in lowering his seat to the saddle. The spotter supports the rider on the back or hips. Where to support the rider will depend on the rider's balance and size. Bring the right leg over the crest of the horse. When the rider is secure, move the horse forward a few steps past the ramp and place the feet into the stirrup irons. The horse is now ready to move into the arena.

Reverse the procedure for dismounting.

STANDING MOUNTING TRANSFER FROM A RAMP, PLATFORM, OR LIFT
A standing transfer from the ramp, lift or platform can be accomplished by riders in a wheelchair, on crutches, with a cane, or walker.
- The riders position themselves facing the saddle. If they are in a wheelchair, lock the brakes. They come to a standing position facing the horse.
- The riders places the left hand on the pommel, gives the cane, crutch or walker to the assistant.
- The riders leans forward and swings the right leg over the back of the saddle. The spotter and assistant stabilize the rider only as needed. Since the stirrups are usually below the platform floor, the horse is moved forward beyond the ramp and stopped, where the riders can place their feet in the stirrups.
- A second method of a standing transfer is similar to the moderate-assist transfer: from a standing position, the riders sits sideways on the saddle and swings the right leg over the front of the saddle.

OTHER MOUNTING TRANSFER METHODS
There will be riders who are unable to mount the horse in the traditional ways. Some riders may need to mount from the "off side". Be sure the horse selected is accepting of a rider mounting from the right side.

Some riders who are paraplegic are strong enough to swing themselves into the saddle from their wheelchair by pushing down on the saddle with their arms and then lifting. Others may need to use an overhead bar to swing from wheelchair to the saddle. Some riders can use a sliding board to move from the wheelchair to the saddle. The physical or occupational therapist will assist in teaching how to use these unique transfers.

MOUNTING FOR BACK-RIDING - see section 12.03 on **backriding**.

FIGURE 4. THE TOTAL LIFT

After the rider is mounted, ask him or her if he or she feels secure. Never move the horse until the rider feels on the horse or before the sidewalkers are ready to go.

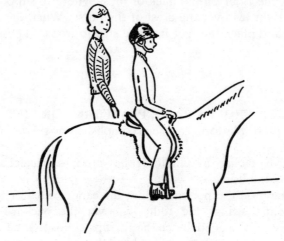

FIGURE 5. WALK OFF

OTHER DISMOUNTING METHODS

Many riders who need to use the ramp for mounting may be able to dismount safely to the ground. If riders use a wheelchair, place the wheelchair next to the rump of the horse facing toward the saddle or pad. Some riders should dismount to the ramp, for example: riders whose leg tone increases when dismounting to the ground may need to dismount to the ramp, or riders may place undue stress on the horse by dismounting to the ground.

Step 1

    Method A - The preferred procedure since it is considered safer then method B.

    A rider holds onto the handhold, neck strap or mane. The sidewalker or spotter on the far side helps the rider's right leg over the rump of the horse. Both sidewalkers or spotter on both sides, help turn the rider so that he or she are now in prone position over the horse.

    Method B - Use only when other methods cannot be used.

    The rider holds onto the handhold, neck strap or mane. The sidewalker or spotter on the far side helps the rider's right leg over the crest of the horse as the rider releases his or her hand grasp and then replaces it. While the right leg is coming over the crest of the horse, the spotter on the near side guides the left leg, allowing the body to rotate. The rider moves his or her hands and again holds on to the hand hold or mane. The sidewalker or spotter on the near side places his or her right arm under the rider's left leg and with his or her left hand, grasps the rider's right lower leg as it comes over the crest of the horse. The sidewalker/spotter on the near side rotates the riders' pelvis and turns them to a prone position over the horse and now assists them to slide to the ground.

Step 2

    The instructor can control (if necessary) the speed of the dismount by putting his or her left hand on the withers of the horse. As the rider begins to slide down toward the ground, the instructor places his or her hip between the legs of the rider. By pulling the rider's body into the horse with the instructor's arm and pushing against the horse with his or her hip, the horse bears the weight of the rider but the instructor can control the speed that the rider moves toward the ground. As the rider reaches the ground, he or she is assisted in a pivot turn which places him or her in front of his or her wheelchair. The rider takes hold of the wheelchair armrest and sit down.

Reference

Cambell, M.,Harris-Ossman,N. (1990). *Adult Positions, Transitions, and Transfers*. Tucson: Therapy Skill Builders.

18.07 MOUNTING DEVICES

Barbara T. Engel, MEd, OTR

Staff of therapeutic riding programs need to assess the population they will serve to determine the type(s) of mounting device(s) that will assist their riders in safe and independent transfers. Most persons with physical disabilities, including children, will need some sort of mounting device to safely mount a horse.

What are Mounting Devices?
Mounting devices are usually blocks, ramps, or platforms which may extend from a building or hill. They are used to assist individuals to get on a horse by placing them closer to the level of the saddle. This allows the rider and the assistants to maneuver a safe transfer without putting strain on the rider, the assistant or the horse. The use of a mounting device is gentler on the horse than mounting from the ground.

Points that must be remembered in the procedure of mounting a horse:
- The procedure of transfer must be <u>safe</u>.
- The procedure must allow for <u>maximum independence</u> and <u>minimal assistance</u>.
- The procedure must <u>not</u> increase the rider's dysfunction such as increasing muscle tone, causing pain, loss of balance or limb control.
- The procedure should not cause undue strain to those assisting in the transfer.
- The procedure must not cause strain to the horse.
- The process must feel safe and comfortable (for the horse--rider--assistants).
- The procedure can be performed in a reasonable amount of time.
- The space allotted for the transfer allows for placement of persons and devices, proper mobility, and balance.
- The procedure is as normal as possible within the skills of the rider.

The type of mounting devices include:
<u>Mounting Blocks:</u>
Mounting platform with several steps
Small one step mounting block
A light weight cavalletti block
<u>Ramps:</u>
A single ramp
A single ramp and a mounting block
A double ramp
<u>Platforms:</u>
From a hill
From a building

Placement
Mounting devices are placed outside of the riding ring on level ground. They should be placed so that there is easy access to the gate of the ring. A person is least secure on a horse just after mounting. Eliminating a turn at this point adds to the safety of the riders and assists them in developing a feeling of security. It is always advisable to have the horse move in between two objects such as a ramp and mounting block, between two ramps, between two mounting blocks. With this method the horse is less likely to shift as riders mount. Secondly, the mounting assistants are in a better position to help to support the riders, providing additional safety for the mounting procedure. Placement of mounting equipment must also take into consideration the needs of those riders who will need to mount from the right side of the horse.

Construction

All mounting devices should be constructed out of heavy duty building material with the frame built of at least 2 x 4's pine or pipe. The surface can be constructed out of <u>exterior</u> 3/4 inch plywood or 1 inch pine. All corners must be securely reinforced. The final product is water-proofed and all walking surfaces are coated with non-skid material such as sand mixed into the final coat of paint, or non-skid strips. Care must be taken not to have any areas of rough wood that can put splinters into the user's hands.

Mounting blocks

Mounting block for assisted mounting

A mounting block is a raised platform of 12 to 32 inches high (Figure 1). The horse is brought next to the block and stands there while the rider mounts from the top of the block to the saddle. The height will be determined by the size of the program horses. The steps should rise 5 to 6 inches with the step depth of 11 to 12 inches to allow for full foot placement and placement of a hemi three-prong cane. The width of the steps should be 3½ feet to allow two adults to walk side-by-side up the steps. There should be a rail on the outside of the mounting block. The top surface of the mounting block should be roughly 3½ x 3½ feet or larger to accommodate two adults comfortably. A small molding around the edge of the top of the platform helps prevent someone from stepping off by providing a boundary.

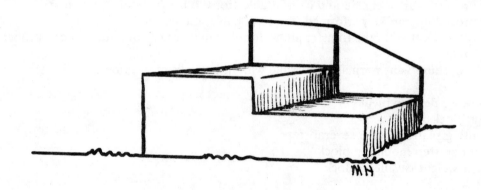

FIGURE 1. MOUNTING BLOCK FOR ASSISTED MOUNTING

Mounting block for independent mounting

A sturdy two to three step block with a platform surface of 18 x 24 (Figure 2) is adequate for a person who is an independent walker and can mount without assistance. The steps can be 6 to 8 inches high. This would provide a height of 12 to 16 inches, allowing the person to reach the stirrup easily.

Independent mounting within the riding ring can be accomplished by the use of one or two plastic cavalletti blocks. They provide a light but sturdy surface and are easily removed after mounting. Mounting devices should never be left within the riding ring.

418

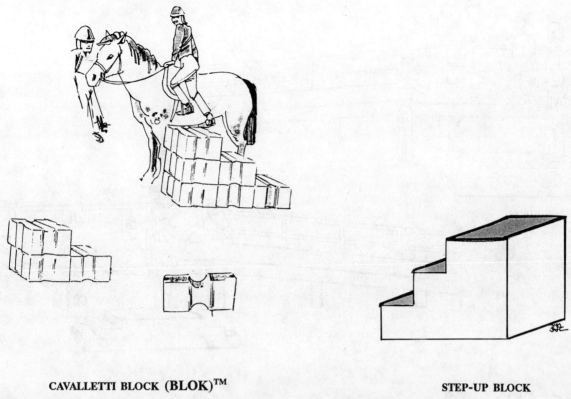

CAVALLETTI BLOCK (BLOK)™   **STEP-UP BLOCK**

FIGURE 2. MOUNTING BLOCK FOR INDEPENDENT MOUNTING

Ramps

Permanent program ramps: A ramp should allow wheelchair users to move their chairs independently up the ramp (Figure 3). The standard measurement for the construction of a ramp for independent mobility is one foot of length to each one inch of height. If, for example, the ramp is to be 3 feet high, it needs to be 36 feet long. Shorter ramps can of course be used where space is not available. A permanent ramp should not be shorter thcn 16 feet. The ramp should be 4 feet wide and the platform section should be at least 4 x 6 feet. There should be a rail on the off-side and the rail should be off-set at the end of the mounting platform to allow for full use of the surface without being hindered by the rail. There should be a small molding around the outside of the ramp and platform surface to prevent a foot from slipping off.

When a rider needs to be supported by sidewalkers, the ramp must be positioned so that the sidewalkers can easily walk down the ramp while supporting the rider. There should be no cause for the sidewalker to stumble with such obstacles as steps. If he or she stumbles it could cause him or her to pull the rider off the horse. When a rider does not need this assistance, the horse can move off the high end of the ramp.

A ramp with a gradual slope provides a surface which can easily be used at any height for mounting, for grooming, or for therapy activities. The most suitable arrangement for a therapeutic riding program is to have two ramps, side-by-side. One ramp can be 42 inches high while the other is 30 inches high. With the two ramps the program has a lot of versatility.

Portable ramps: Portable ramps such as developed in Germany by Dr. Heipertz-Hengst (Figure 3) are much shorter than a permanent ramp and enable a program to move them from one location to another, such as going from one school to another, to a horse show or a trail ride. It will require considerable assistance to help adult wheelchair-users up this steep ramp.

419

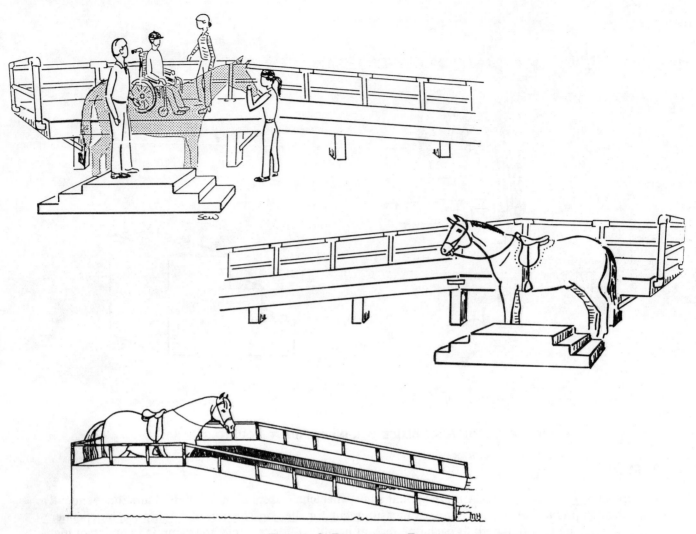

FIGURE 3. PERMANENT RAMPS

MOBILE RAMP

Heipertz-Hengst, Dr.C. **Mobile Ramp**. Rower & Rub GmbH, Hauptstrasse 15, D-2811 Blender, Germany. Phone:04233/1571, FAX: 04233/605

Specific plans for the construction of ramps can be obtained from North American Riding for the Handicapped, P.O. Box 33150, Denver, CO 80233.

18.08 MOUNTED EXERCISES AFTER ENTERING THE ARENA

Barbara T. Engel, MEd, OTR

The rider has finished ground stretching exercises and has mounted his or her horse. Why must he or she now perform more exercises? Mounted exercises are a continuation of the warm-up process and help to adjust oneself to the position on the horse. Molly Sivewright (1984) lists the important objectives of mounted exercises as:

- To improve the rider's position and posture in the saddle or pad
- To supple the rider
- To center the rider on the horse
- To co-ordinate the rider's own feeling for and in harmony with the horse and his co-ordination
- To build confidence

Sivewright, M. (1984). *Thinking Riding*. London: J.A. Allen.

18.09 LEADING THE HORSE TO ENCOURAGE A THERAPEUTIC GAIT

Barbara T. Engel, MEd, OTR

The rhythmic movement of the horse and its influence on the rider is a major factor in the value of therapeutic horseback riding (Heipertz, 1981, Riede, 1988). Physical and occupational therapists study to understand this movement and how it can be enhanced to affect the client to achieve specific changes in function (see section 6.04 and 6.05). Heipertz and Reide have found that the gait of the horse is very similar to the gait of the adult human and therefore the horse can influence the human's walking gait. A good rider knows that the rhythm of the horse must match his or her rhythm to gain the feeling of *being one with the horse.*

Instructors, thought not directly involved with therapy with the horse (unless they are working as part of a therapist-client team), should be concerned with the movement of the horse with <u>every</u> rider. The importance of conformation (chapter 5 and section 6.2), suppling, and exercises (chapter 7) have been discussed. Let us assume that the instructor has the horses in good condition for the lesson with a group of riders who require leaders. The horse leaders need to learn to guide their horses without interfering with the rhythmic movement of their gait. The horse uses his head and neck to assist in balance. If the leader restricts the horse's ability to use his head and neck, he or she will interfere with his ability to move forward with a full rhythmic gait.

How to lead the horse

Cathy Kuehner points out that there is an art to leading a horse safely and it requires undivided attention. Leading a horse during a therapeutic riding lesson requires that the horse be trained to attend to the leader and that the leader use body language and voice aids, and use the lead line with the same lightness as one would use the reins. The horse should be led from the shoulder (Figure 1). This is not only safe since one can observe the horse, but it also allows the horse to move forward freely. The leadline needs to be long enough so that it does not restrict the function of the head and neck. A well-trained horse does not have to be pulled or tugged to move or halt-- rather the leadline is there only as a safety measure. The leader and horse should work together until effective communication and working a relationship is established. The horse and leader should be able to lengthen and shorten stride as needed. It is important when trotting the horse with a rider astride, to synchronize his movements with that of the rider. If the leader moves the horse forward without this consideration, the rider will no doubt bounce and feel out of control, gaining little from the experience. Leading the horse from the front should never be done for not only is this unsafe but it totally destroys the horse's stride and forward movements.

T.E.A.M techniques (see section 7.03) encourage the horse to focus and move with fluid, rhythmic movements. These methods should be learned by each horse leader.

Another leading method which is very effective is using a longe line and whip (the longe line as the rein--the whip as the inside leg.) The longe line is passed through the near bit ring, over the poll and snapped to the far bit ring as in longeing but the line remains short, three to five feet from the bit. The leader can walk in such a way as to observe both horse and rider, yet maintain full control of the horse and encourage a positive, rhythmic gait (Figure 2). This position is effective when working as both leader-sidewalker for a rider who needs minimal help.

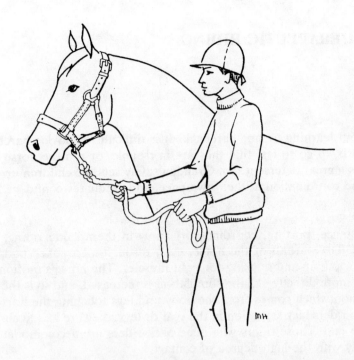

FIGURE 1. THE LEADING POSITION

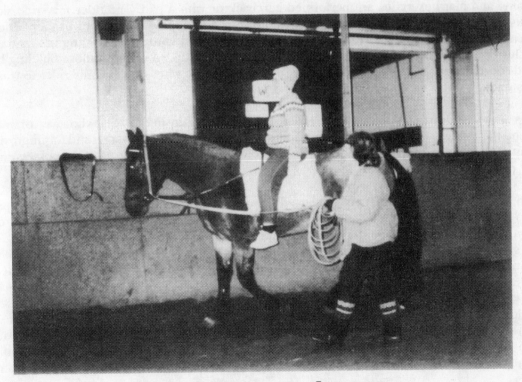

FIGURE 2. LEADING WITH A LONGE LINE

Heipertz, W. (1981). *Therapeutic Riding, Medicine, Education, Sports*. Ottawa: Greenbelt Riding Association for the Disabled Inc.

Kuehner, C. (1990). Leading a Horse Safely. *HorsePlay*. July: 37.

Riede, D. (1988). *Physiotherapy on the Horse*. Madison: Omnipress.

18.10   BAREBACK THERAPEUTIC RIDING

Nancy B. Marshall

Many country children start out learning to ride bareback. It is difficult for novice bareback riders to ride much beyond their capabilities; that is, to go so fast that they are in trouble, or run the horse too much. The potential consequence of such a move is a great deterrent. So, Grandpa safely sets the children up bareback, allowing them to explore balance, posture and coordination at their own pace, and graduates confident, secure riders to a saddle when they are ready.

The same building blocks (balance, posture, coordination) apply in therapeutic riding, but the benefits for the disabled riders are multiplied. The warmth of the horse, even through a bareback pad, can be felt directly and immediately. We know this is soothing and relaxing for tight muscles. The horse's motion, the central modality in this therapeutic activity, is felt more directly. All the stimulation is increased, and so is the feedback between horse and rider. The tactile stimulation which comes from the body and legs touching the horse benefits even the most severely disabled riders. When riders lack sensation in the seat or legs, they are less likely to develop friction sores riding bareback or on a fleece pad. Those riders who need back-riders are accommodated with bareback riding. Bonding also takes place easily with the high degree of contact.

The options for instruction are many. Hippotherapy can be performed bareback or with a fleece for good reason. The mobility the rider has and the ability to change positions is much greater without a saddle. Developmental, sport vaulting, and many exercises are performed bareback or with a pad. The rider may ride sideways, supine, prone, sack-of-potatoes style or backwards with hand or elbow propping (be sure to use a pad for this!) Any of these exercises may be used easily within the lesson when the goal is to improve tone in a certain area, isolate upper and lower body (differentiation), improve laterality and, again, to work on those building blocks, balance, posture and coordination. It is also a real exercise in self-confidence when one asks the rider to trust his horse and sidewalkers enough to try an unusual position.

That brings us to risk-taking. Many at-risk riders (at-risk refers to individuals who may or may not become disabled) find the challenge of bareback riding just the right vehicle for their energy, and for improving self-esteem. While many of their peers may have ridden a "dogged old trail horse," few can say they possess the athletic skills needed for good bareback riding.

Riders with poor attending skills will be challenged enough by a briskly-paced bareback ride to pay a little more attention to the task at hand. Some instructors feel that physically able-bodied riders mounted bareback can learn proper positioning of body, legs and use of hands in preparation for moving on to saddle riding. The finer points of control, such as leg aids and weight shifting, can be explored with this group, and the feedback from the horse is easily felt. Riders can learn the two point position (half seat) or even try posting bareback. When they move to a saddle, these things will be well understood and come easily.

There are lots of good games that work well bareback, such as the Ride-A-Buck, Dress Express Game (Joswick et al, 1986) or any relay. Setting up for a bareback class is quick and easy. Bareback fits just about everyone, as opposed to an ill-fitting saddle which may cause discomfort for horse or rider. A saddle magnifies the upward thrust of the body from the horse, sometimes too much so for some spine-injured riders, for example.

With or without a saddle, special care must be given to the therapeutic riding horse's back. After class, he may need a little therapy himself. Carrying a shifting, off-balance rider is hard work and hard on the back. Sometimes a short ride by an experienced rider may help to work out some of the kinks, the effect of a good rider being somewhat like massage or acupuncture. Reward him with a vigorous rub-down as well, to further relax and stimulate circulation.

There are disabilities for which bareback riding is contraindicated. Tightly adducted limbs may not spread over some horses, where they may rest more easily in an English saddle. Persons with higher level spinal injuries may get not have enough support riding bareback or with a pad and may receive too much motion. Those who tire easily, such as riders with multiple sclerosis or muscular dystrophy, may find bareback riding exacerbates the condition. Adults, who are not in good physical condition may be insecure and so afraid of falling from a bareback horse that they cannot derive the same benefit as someone more relaxed. As always, every person is unique and requires individual assessment.

For all its benefits, bareback riding is not necessarily the ultimate goal of every rider. Most riders will want to go on to English or Western saddles eventually. Nevertheless riding bareback makes an excellent base from which to build skills, serving as a stepping stone to more advanced equitation. It is often helpful to return to bareback riding every so often, to tune up skills or areas of the body that need work. Returning to class after a long break is a good time for bareback review. Instructors whose students have become comfortable with this style of riding often find them choosing it over saddling when they just want to have fun. Ask any rider, and he will tell you that is a very important goal.

References
Brough, J. H., Chaney, C.M. (1990). *Basic Development of Motor Skills.* presentation at Kankakee Area Special Education
    Cooperative and 1990 NARHA National Conference.
Joswick, F., Kittredge, M., McCowen, L., et al. (1986). *Aspects and Answers.* Cheff Center. Agusta, MI. 182,186.
Lingua, M. Clinic at Castle Rock, Colorado, Spring 1989.
Physical Therapy and Hippotherapy Services. The Open Gait. Colorado Springs,Colorado.

18.11   TEACHING BASIC ENGLISH RIDING SKILLS IN THERAPEUTIC RIDING

Loretta Binder-Wheeler

Therapeutic riding programs are directed toward sport, education and/or medicine. Those riders who are not involved with an educator or therapist, come to the program to learn the sport of riding. Some riders are involved at a very basic level; learning to balance while sitting on the horse. Others are ready to begin learning the correct way to ride. It is generally excepted that instructors of therapeutic riding programs have had experience teaching able-bodied riders. Having basic theoretical knowledge of the subject you are teaching is of primary importance and will not be covered in this section. This section will help the instructor make the transition to teaching the disabled rider.

Getting to Know Your Rider:
Teaching a novice to ride is always a challenge. Teaching a novice with a disability to ride becomes a enormous challenge and requires special techniques and knowledge. Instructors will also encounter those riders who were injured after have acquired considerable equestrian skills. These riders will challenge the instructor's knowledge and ability to adapt to unique problems of balance and dysfunction. The instructor must first become familiar with his or her riders' abilities, physical problem areas and needs by gathering information from the referral, the therapists, the riders, and observation of the riders' abilities.

Beginning Instruction:
The place to begin instruction of disabled riders is on the ground. Being near a horse gives a sense of the size and proportion of the animals the riders will deal with when mounted. Learning to groom helps the riders learn the personality of the horses and realize they are working with a living creature, not a machine. Becoming familiar with the equipment will facilitate their understanding of its uses.

It will be helpful to the riders to be able to identify the walk, trot, and canter by sight (or sound) and know the pattern of foot fall for each. This is most easily taught by putting the horse on the longe line with diagonal legs wrapped. It is most effective to put brightly colored wraps on the inside hind and outside fore legs. At the walk, the inside hind foot is designated as 1, the inside fore as 2, the outside hind as 3, and the outside fore as 4. Thus, the pattern is seen as the wrapped inside (1), bare inside (2), bare outside (3), wrapped outside (4). The trot is easily identified as the wrapped diagonal pair move together and the bare diagonal pair move together. At the canter, the pattern is: 3, ¼, 2 or bare outside, the wrapped diagonal pair, and bare outside. The wraps help the eye to see the diagonal pair. Alternately, the other diagonal pair may be wrapped in different colors and the legs then identified by color, i.e., at the walk, the pattern is red, blue, green, red; at the trot, the red legs move together, and the green and blue legs move together. At the canter the green strikes first, then the red pair, and then the blue. The riders may be asked to count out the beats. This might be a good opportunity to give the riders a brief lesson on longeing and allow them, if they are able, to longe the horse themselves and experience the control exerted by the longe line.

Establish the Basic Position on the Longe:
When beginning the rider astride a horse, a sidewalker and leader should always be used. This gives the instructor the opportunity to assess the riders' abilities and needs under safe circumstances. The leader and sidewalker can be dismissed when appropriate. While safety is most important, it is also necessary to allow the rider independence and freedom from over-protection.

The advantage of lessons on the longe is that the rider is able to concentrate on his or her position while the instructor has control of the horse, as covered in section 12.03. If the instructor does not have a dependable longeing horse available, a leader and sidewalkers are necessary. Before the instructor moves to the center of the circle, he or she gives the rider the correct position, that is, he or she assists the rider in achieving a balanced seat on the horse: seat bones in the saddle, legs neither gripping hard nor floppy, head upright, eyes forward and soft. With the rider sitting in the deepest part of the saddle, the instructor asks the rider to bring the knees together over the horse's withers. This should tilt the pelvis slightly under. Then, the instructor helps bring one leg at a time down. This must *always* be done gently and slowly, **NEVER** forcing the leg.(With some riders the sidewalker may need to assist the instructor in achieving these positions.)

Placing the hand nearer the horse's head under the thigh and the other hand on the lower calf, the instructor rocks the leg and gently brings it slightly away from the horse and down to the correct position, guiding the foot into the stirrup. When working with a rider with spasticity in the lower body the instructor should help the rider get his or her seat in the saddle as deeply as possible without discomfort and leave the legs alone; the motion of the horse at the walk will encourage the legs to relax and drop down of their own accord.

Teaching the Use of the Aids
If the rider will be using his or her hands on any assistive or supportive devices now is the time to explain the correct use of them. The instructor also describes, at this time, the sensations the rider is likely to experience when the horse begins to walk, i.e., "When the horse starts to walk you may feel slightly thrown off balance momentarily. The sidewalker is here to help you if you need it." Since the rider has already seen the horse on the longe he or she should be confident in the instructor's ability to control the horse safety. When the rider is ready the instructor moves the horses into the walk. He or she encourages the rider to relax the hips and feel the motion of the horse with his seat. He or she describes again the mechanics of the walk, the 4 beat gait and explains how to feel where each hind foot is stepping forward: "When your left hip drops, the left hind foot is stepping under." He or she may ask the rider to count out loud the beats of the walk: one, two, three, four. While continuing to correct the riders' position, the teacher can also point out the control the use of their seats exerts over the horses. By stiffening the lower back and hips, the rider causes the horse to shorten his stride, then by giving with the hips and lower back the by rider encourages the horse to lengthen the stride. During this exercise, the leader, if any, must remain alert and maintain control without interfering with the horse's movement.

Once the rider feels confident at a walk on the longe, he or she should be taught how to put his horse into the walk himself. That is, sitting in the correct position with the legs in light contact, they give a squeeze with their legs. If this is not effective, more pressure may be applied, increasing up to a gentle kick. If a rider has poor or no control of his or her legs, a verbal command may be substituted. It is never correct to allow a rider to bounce on the horse's back to achieve the walk. To allow this will only encourage a habit which not only causes a horse to throw his head up, but can produce an unhappy, sore-backed horse for the program. For each special case, the instructor must find an alternate method which gives the rider the necessary control.

The instructor may choose to continue on the longe at this point or begin instruction with the rider holding the reins. He or she may want to return to the longe when a rider begins to trot and again when he or she begins to canter. It can also be useful when a rider seems to become dependent on the reins for balance (never appropriate) or simply to encourage continued development of an independent seat. It is important that the instructor end any activity before the rider shows signs of fatigue or boredom. When a rider becomes tired or bored the resulting loss of concentration increases the likelihood of a mishap.

Overcome Fears
Sometimes, even an advanced rider may become fearful of a certain riding activity. This more often results from a near-accident than an actual fall (or from a neurological problem related to the ability to tolerate movement.) It is a case of anticipation being worse than the actual event. When conventional methods fail to alleviate the fear, an instructor might try guiding the rider through the activity in the rider's imagination: that is describing, in detail, the activity, the rider's actions throughout and the behavior of the horse. For example: during a transition from walk to trot the rider lost balance, felt out of control and panicked; the horse (being a good therapeutic riding horse) continued for a few strides, then came to a halt. The rider is now afraid of losing control during the

transition and reluctant to attempt it. Later, with the horse at the halt and in the control of a volunteer, the instructor asks the rider to close his or her eyes and breathe calmly. He or she then gives the rider this visualization: "Imagine yourself walking 'Sandy' around the arena on the rail. Your hips and back are relaxed and moving with him. You and Sandy are enjoying your ride and he is being perfectly responsive to every signal you give."

"You ask him to shorten his stride or lengthen his stride and he does everything you want, because you are giving him clear signals and you are absolutely in control. You decide you would like to trot now, and prepare yourself and him for that transition. When you are ready, give him the aids to trot. He responds perfectly and goes smoothly into the trot. Your seat follows, your balance and control of him are absolutely perfect. Your seat is secure and you feel relaxed and confident." The instructor then sends the rider out to the rail to perform what he or she has just been imagining. This technique can also be used whenever a rider is attempting an activity for the first time. The instructor should speak calmly and confidently, almost as if describing something that is taking place in front of him. He or she should be as detailed as possible about the rider's action and the horse's responses. He or she should probably skip any descriptions of babbling brooks, lush green hillsides, or fairy tale scenery unless these figure largely in the situation at hand.

Observation & Drills as Learning Tools

Observation of good riders is a great learning tool. Riders should be encouraged to watch lessons and training sessions whenever possible. Developing an eye for the correct seat, good use of aids, horse confirmation and movement add to any equestrian's enjoyment of the sport. In addition, since people learn best by imitation, watching a competent rider practice various movements facilitates any rider's learning process. In a group lesson, the instructor may bring one rider at a time into the center of the area with him or her and invite him or her to critique the other riders.

When a group of riders will be having lessons together over a period of months they may enjoy working on a drill pattern, adding movements to it as their skills develop. Simple drill patterns will work well in any group lesson. Example: Dividing the riders into two groups, numbered ones and twos, the instructor asks the group to ride single file down the center line. When all are on the center line, the instructor directs: one's turn left, two's turn right. One's go left at the rail, two's go right. When you meet at A, turn up the center line riding in pairs. At C, one's go left, two's go right on the rail to A and up the center line single file. As riders become more proficient, variations may be added, such as circles, changes of gait, or passing through the center line. Working in teams of two, riders may enjoy developing their own short drills, or pas de deux. Music can also be a pleasant addition but should not be played so loudly as to drown out the instructor's voice.

Conclusion

The therapeutic riding instructor should be thoroughly knowledgeable about riding basics. He or she must know how and why aids work in order to develop good alternatives for the disabled rider: verbal instead of physical commands, alternate methods of holding reins, use of artificial aids for the rider unable to use natural ones. His or her concern in the arena is always safety, but just as important is the development of confident, competent riders. **Never underestimate the ability of a person with disabilities!**

References
Henriques, P.(1987). *Balanced Riding: A Way to Find the Correct Seat*. Gaithersburg: Half Halt Press.
NARHA, (1991). P.O. Box 33150, Denver, Co. 80233.
Podhajsky, A. (1973). *The Riding Teacher*. Garden City: Double Day Co.
Swift, S. (1985). *Centered Riding*. North Pomfret: David and Charles Inc.

18.12 LONGEING THE INDEPENDENT SPORTS RIDER IN A THERAPEUTIC RIDING PROGRAM

Nina Wiger, MA

With proper precautions and a well-trained horse, longeing can be the most successful way to start a rider* with very mild problems. Longeing can correct bad habits and overcome fear. In longeing, the goal of every rider is to develop perfect understanding with his or her horse. To achieve this the beginning rider must learn to coalesce all his or her movements with those of the horse, and later the rider must influence the horse by initiating movement of his or her own. Before this moving with the horse is automatic, some riders are better off on the longeline, where there are no reins with which to contend. With the more advanced rider, new moves can be taught, and problems corrected on the longe line.

The Horse
The longe horse should be trained to respond to the longeur not only through verbal commands, but also to let itself be "ridden" through the longeur's body position, hand and whip. The horse should go in balance at all gaits, execute smooth transitions, not be upset by a rider's stiffness, clutching or loss of balance, and (with help from the longeur) respond to the aids of the rider. An added plus for the beginner would be a horse with elastic gaits but without too much movement. The horse must be kept sharp by regular schooling by a qualified rider.

The Longeur
See chapter 7.04 for longeing technique and equipment. In addition to possessing basic longeing skills, the instructor must have a thorough understanding of the mechanics of a correct seat, and be able to detect underlying causes of faults (often very difficult!). The longeur has to recognize fear and/or fatigue in the rider, keep an eye on the surroundings for potential horse frightening situations, keep the horse going at whatever gait and speed is called for at the moment, and at the same time give the rider appropriate instruction.

Equipment
A vaulting surcingle lets a rider go through a wider range of positions and gives added security through the use of the hand grips (Museler, 1983). Use a Western style saddle pad with the surcingle. Do not longe on a bareback pad; it offers a false sense of security, and gives no more support to the rider (or protection of the horse's back) than riding bareback. If the horse shows signs of discomfort, or the rider is very stiff, extra padding is needed. As the rider progresses he or she may be longed using a saddle. Classic longeing is done in a saddle. (See Chapter 7.04 for further information).

On the Ground
Before mounting the rider, make sure he is given some idea of what is sought. Demonstrate, and then guide him through the different positions and movements. In this way the longeur will get a feeling for the rider's abilities and limitations, not only physically, but also in the areas of following instruction and understanding the instructor's way of communicating. If a large discrepancy is shown between ability on the ground and on the horse, fear is usually the cause, and you must proceed accordingly.

* The "rider" in this context, is a person who has progressed to the point that he or she is ready for formal riding lessons in sports riding and not "therapeutic or adaptive riding" per say. This rider would no longer need a leader or sidewalker.

At the Standstill

If appropriate, initially the instructor should teach the rider two safety dismounts. From sitting in side seat, have the rider slide off the horse while **turning to face forward**. Have him push away and then crumple to the ground and do a sideways roll. In addition, from sitting astride, have the rider **lean forward and then bring both legs together over the croup**, and again slide off while **facing forward**. The exercise can be repeated while the horse is walking. The rider can be placed in the "ideal" seat, but the instructor must make it clear that the rider should be supple and relaxed, and not forced into any one position. Have the rider hold on to the saddle or the grips, proceed at a walk.

Assessment of the Rider on the Horse

While longeing the rider and before starting to give instruction, take some time to watch your student. Let him get comfortable, chat about some theory, name different parts of the horse, wave at friends or anything that lets him relax. Look at the overall picture. Is the rider using too many or too few muscles; in other words is he a soldier or a sack of potatoes? Is he leaning forward or back? Then start at the bottom by looking at the legs. Is he too far forward, too far back, drawn up, clamped on tight or hanging just right? Is the back arched or rounded, or straight and supple? Are the shoulders drawn up, pulled forward, or held rigidly? Does the rider move head, arms and trunk freely? Decide which <u>part</u> is causing the most problems, and work on that first. Keep in the back of your mind a clear picture of the "ideal" seat, as it fits each particular rider. Remember that a good seat cannot be forced into place; along with posture there must be relaxation. When a rider has spasticity this becomes a <u>major focus</u>. Many riders with spasticity benefit from starting their sessions by lying sideways over the horse's back while the horse is walking. This will lower muscle tone and encourage general relaxation. When first sitting astride, proper arm position is facilitated by having the rider place one hand on top at the other on the front of the saddle or surcingle. Twenty minutes in these positions will often reduce spasticity to where a good seat can be achieved.

The Beginner

A good seat is developed by spending hours on the horse. The best way to obtain this seat is while being longed. The horse is the teacher, and the instructor should not award him or herself too much importance by constantly giving instructions. A beginning rider has no preconceived notions. He or she needs to be made aware when something correct is happening, so that he or she can learn to associate that feeling with correctness (Podhajsky, 1965). Good seat and position descriptions can be found in most dressage texts.

Problem Solving

Faults in the rider's seat while being longed and in his or her position are caused by fear, lack of balance, stiffness, and/or misconception about how things should be done. **Fear** is not always easy to recognize, and even the rider might not be aware of being afraid, but his or her body will show it. Start by talking to the rider, discuss possible problems, and then do exercises to overcome trepidation. Start by petting the horse all over, and get the rider to move in the saddle by having him reach for the ears, check the girth, scratch the root of the tail, or for the most timid, fix their own hair and tuck in their shirts. Then proceed to exercises where the arms are held in various positions (use your imagination and keep safety and the riders limitations in mind), the body is bending in different directions, and eventually to where the rider can shift his or her weight and scoot around in the saddle or on the vaulting pad. **Sometimes control over the horse is necessary to instill confidence, and the rider should always be taught to stop the horse either with the body or with the voice.**

Balance or the lack of it, is shown by the rider who is gripping with the legs, leaning forward or back or sitting off to one side. In such cases the rider often does not know or cannot feel which part of his or her seat should touch the saddle. A useful longeing exercise is to have the rider hold the handhold underhand, round the lower back, and lift the knees forward and out to the sides, either one at a time or, if strong, both at once. <u>Hold only momentarily</u>, and let the legs fall loosely back to the horse's side. The exercise can be repeated at any gait, whenever the rider loses track of his seat-bones or balance, or starts gripping with his legs. Once the rider is comfortable on the horse, shifting the seat from side to side without holding on can be practiced, first at the walk, later at the faster gaits. Balance is closely linked to head position. Practice first with the rider looking between the horse's ears. If the horse is going correctly this should be slightly to the inside. As balance improves, different positions and focus points can be practiced, including Sally Swift's "soft eyes" described in her book *Centered Riding (1985)*. Front to back balance can be practiced by having the rider place his or her hands on his or her thighs, close his eyes, and practice staying with the horse as the instructor changes gaits and speeds. A horse that responds to the longeur's body position as well as verbal commands is a real plus here. As the rider improves, he or she can sit sideways and backward during these exercises.

Stiffness is a real problem and occurs in the unskilled and/or disabled rider who has not yet learned which muscles to recruit and which to relax. It can also be the result of lack of balance, discomfort, fear or mental tension. Longeing the rider is a good time to pinpoint and address the underlying causes. In therapeutic riding programs we deal with a population with many and varied problems. It is easy to limit our students by what we expect of them, and assume that their disorders make certain goals impossible to reach. A well-trained longeing horse will react to minute weight shifts and featherlight differences in leg and rein pressure, and will teach even very limited riders how to improve their influence over the horse. Most riders have one particular problem area that will crop up whenever demands are raised, new concepts introduced or the circumstances are intimidating (competitions!). Often problems can be solved by exaggerating movement in the other direction. Tell a rider whose seat does not move enough to wiggle all over, every which way, until the rhythm suddenly is caught. Show a person whose shoulders pull up how to isolate the up, back and down movements, and then practice at all gaits. Rigid arms and hands usually improve as balance and suppleness improve, but often riders have to be reminded to keep their elbows, wrists and fingers from freezing up by consciously moving the joints in rhythm with the horse's gait. A stiffly arched back can be corrected by placing the rider sideways on the horse facing the inside. Have the rider slide the seat to the outside until the arch disappears, and then wrap the legs along the horse's side for safety. Always keep in mind, and remind the student, that stillness on the horse is achieved through movement, not fixation. While longeing, the rider is able to attend to his balance and suppleness and not be concerned with reins and control of the horse.

Continued Education

Longeing can be used to teach riders that most transitions and lateral movements on the horse can be achieved without active use of the hands. The horse must, of course, know the movement, and willingly let itself be ridden into the bridle; also the side-reins must be of correct length. Start with transitions up and down, between gaits and within gaits, proceed to leg yielding the circle smaller and larger, at all gaits, and, when mastered, try shoulder-in and haunches-in.

General Considerations

A longeing session should not last much longer than 30 minutes, depending on how much work is done at the walk. It is advisable to change sides at least four times during that time, more often if much cantering is done. With a "green" rider, it is better to start with much shorter sessions and gradually build up. Get on the horse and demonstrate if necessary. Get somebody else to longe now and then so that you as instructor can check the rider from the outside of the circle. Concentrate on <u>one</u> thing at a time, but not for too long. Come back to a problem area many times during a session. Phase the instructions as "do's", <u>not</u> "don'ts". Give each suggestion time to work. Constantly evaluate during the teaching. Is what you see an error in movement vs. not enough movement? Is the rider's position interfering with his effectiveness, or is his position and style merely aesthetic? **As long as safety is kept the number one priority, one can vary the exercises to suit rider or problem.**

Conclusion:

Longeing can be the most successful way to develop a good seat with the necessary balanced posture. In therapeutic riding this achievement is not only a major goal with any rider but it allows certain types of riders to advance more quickly in the sport.

References
Museller, W. (1987). *Riding Logic*. New York: Prentice Hall Press.
Podhajsky, A. (1965). *The Complete Training of Horse and Rider*. New York: Doubleday & Co.
Swift, S. (1985). *Centered Riding*. North Pomfret: David & Charles.

18.13　School Figures and Dressage.

June Newman, Certified Riding Instructor, Combined--Training--Dressage

KEY WORDS
　STRAIGHT
　RELAXED
　SUPPLE
　BALANCED MANNER

The purpose of dressage is to train a horse to go forward in a straight, relaxed, supple and balanced manner, teaching him to carry his rider in a beautiful and harmonious way, thereby preserving his physical and mental well-being. Through gymnastic exercises made up of work on one and two tracks one works towards this goal. The exercises that strengthen and supple the horse also help the rider to become straighter, more evenly coordinated with better balance and greater trunk control. Due to limited space the purpose of this discussion will be to consider only those school figures consisting of work on one track. These figures are universal and can be practiced by anyone whether they ride "dressage" or not, although anyone training a horse to move in balance under the rider is doing "dressage". These routines can be practiced anywhere from an olympic dressage arena to just an open field. The latter, however, requires a rider with good visualization skills if patterns are to be performed properly.

Before beginning, a few general thoughts should be considered. The horse should always move forward in a straight manner even when bending through the round figures. By straight we mean that the hind legs of the horse should always follow the line of the front legs exactly. The rider should aim to ride in a balanced and upright manner, avoiding as much as possible any deviation from the correct position. The use of these patterns should help decrease, not increase, any unilateral tendencies in both the horse and rider. As a general rule work on straight lines will encourage the horse forward, while any work that is not on a straight line will tend to slow him down. This principle can be used to your advantage in training the horse and rider. With a young green horse that is rushing, work on the round figures will help to slow and relax him. On the other hand, if you have a horse that tends to laziness, forward work on straight lines will help to waken and activate him. The work on straight lines is also a measure of how successful training is and helps to restore forwardness after a demanding bending exercise. Generally one can expect clients to experience a decrease in skill and coordination as the gaits are increased in riding the figures. Work that was good in the walk may need improvement at the trot, although forwardness in all gaits always improves things. Proper visualization of the patterns is important in executing them correctly. To aid the rider, props such as traffic cones may be helpful. They may be used by placing two to form a "gate" that the rider passes through at certain key spots, or single cones may be used as a point around which the rider forms his figure.

To help describe these figures (Figure 1 and Figure 2) they will be seen in relation to a standard 20 X 60 meter dressage arena. The arena is divided lengthwise by three lines into four quarters. The center line runs lengthwise from the letter "A" to the letter "C". The quarter lines run parallel to the center line half way between it and each of the long sides. A rider is considered to be on the right track when his right hand is to the inside of the arena and vice versa for the left rein. The figures are of two types: straight figures and round figures.

432

STRAIGHT FIGURES:

These all incorporate straight lines and often prove to be the most difficult to do correctly. The most common fault, besides crookedness and weaving, is to ride with the haunches to the inside of the shoulders when following a certain track. Any of the figures that are executed away from the fence line will be more difficult for the rider as the fence is no longer there to help guide him. The contact on the reins should be even, light and consistent with no change of pace, rhythm or speed unless asked for by the rider.

Outside track: also known as "going large", this track follows the fence line of the arena all the way around. It should be ridden as four straight lines with four corners. The corners must be ridden with the same attention as with circles (Figure 3).

Inside track: this track parallels the outside track about 1½ meters (four to five feet) to the inside of the arena (Figure 3).

Permanent quarter line: the rider takes each of the quarter lines as his track down the long sides (Figure 4).

Diagonal change of rein: a change of rein using a diagonal line from one corner across to the opposite corner. On the right track these are done from the letters "K" to "X" to "M" or "M" to "X" to "K". On the left track they are done "FXH" or "HXF". They may also be done across the half arena, starting in the corner and ending at "B" or "E" (Figure 5).

Simple turns: a simple turn is a 90 degree turn to the right or left. These turns always end with the same turn they were started with. They can be done across the width of the arena, as in a turn from "B" to "E", or they may be done down the center or quarter lines (Figure 6).

Turns with a change of rein: the same as the above only these end with a change of rein by turning in the other direction as one meets the far side (Figure 7).

Broken lines: in this movement one rides two or more diagonal lines that are joined by a fairly quick turn. For one broken line the rider would ride "M" to "X" then turn and ride to "F"; for two broken line he or she would ride from "K" to "L", turn to "E", turn to "I" and then turn to end at "H". If the rider soften the turns then they are known as "loops" and are more of a round figure. Loops are excellent for helping to soften and relax the horse (Figure 8).

Oblique: this is a 45 degree line from one track to another, or attaching to another figure (Figure 9).

ROUND FIGURES:

These are figures made up of curved lines, ridden with a consistent bending of the horse's spine throughout the entire movement. These are good for improving the lateral suppleness of horse and rider. They increase the rider's torso rotation and can be used to facilitate changes in the way that the rider positions and carries his weight. The aids for riding curves are the same as the aids for the circle, varying slightly in degree with relation to the amount of bend being asked for.

Circles: an excellent movement to flex the horse laterally and loosen and supple him. A novice rider may incorrectly lean inward on the circle, collapsing the inside hip and pushing all the weight to the outside. This may be corrected by encouraging him to ride his inside seat bone forward and push the inside knee towards the ground. These moves may be used to slow rushing horses and as circles become smaller in diameter they demand greater flexibility and control from horse and rider. The aids for the circles involve the inside leg pressing at the girth to encourage the bend and engage the inside hind leg, with the outside leg slightly behind the girth to hold the haunches in; the outside rein controls the bend and speed while the inside rein keeps the horse looking in the direction of the bend. To accurately ride a circle one must maintain an even bend through the entire figure. Circles-may be 20, 15, 10 or 8 meters diameter (Figure 10).

Voltes: these are circles of exactly 6 meters in diameter, the smallest circle that a horse may do. They should be ridden only at the collected gaits (Figure 13,14).

Serpentine: these are a series of alternating half circles that are joined by a short straight line. The longer this connecting line and the larger the half circles the easier the movement is. The constant changes of flexion are beneficial to both the horse and rider (Figure 11).

Figure 8's: this is simply two circles of equal size joined together at the center of the figure (Figure 12).

Half Volte: a half circle ending with an oblique back to the track. Results in a change of rein (Figure 13).

Reverse half volte: an oblique away from the track ending with a half circle back to the track. Results in a change of rein (Figure 14).

Change of rein through the circle: two alternating half circles within a larger circle that result in a change of rein (Figure 15).

These are the basic patterns of dressage and can be combined in infinite ways to aid in the schooling of the horse and rider. One should always keep in mind that their use is to increase the balance and suppleness of horse and rider. Increasing the difficulty of the movement before the horse or rider is ready will only increase stiffness and tension, a most undesirable result.

A final note, when a horse is being ridden often by inexperienced riders special care should be taken to see that it gets regular schooling by an experienced rider to keep it properly "tuned" and in balance.

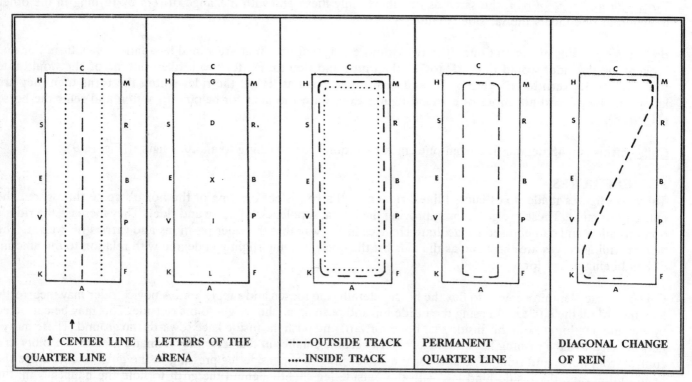

↑ CENTER LINE QUARTER LINE	LETTERS OF THE ARENA	-----OUTSIDE TRACK .....INSIDE TRACK	PERMANENT QUARTER LINE	DIAGONAL CHANGE OF REIN
FIGURE 1.	FIGURE 2	FIGURE 3	FIGURE 4	FIGURE 5

DRESSAGE FIGURES

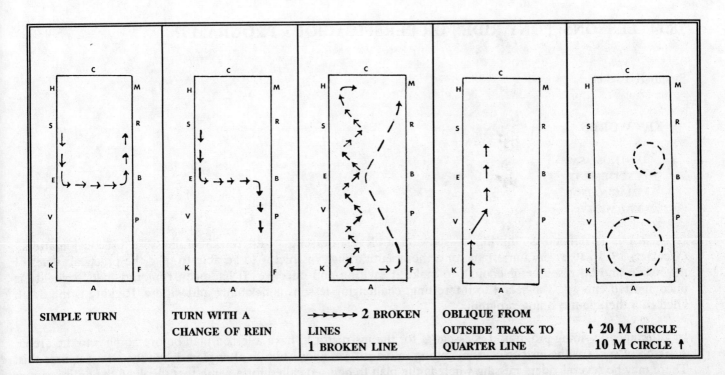

SIMPLE TURN

FIGURE 6

TURN WITH A CHANGE OF REIN

FIGURE 7

➤➤➤➤➤ **2 BROKEN LINES**
1 BROKEN LINE

FIGURE 8

OBLIQUE FROM OUTSIDE TRACK TO QUARTER LINE

FIGURE 9

↑ **20 M CIRCLE**
10 M CIRCLE ↑

FIGURE 10

3 LOOP SERPENTINE

FIGURE 11

FIGURE 8

FIGURE 12

HALF VOLTE

FIGURE 13

REVERSE HALF VOLTE

FIGURE 14

CHANGE OF REIN THROUGH THE CIRCLE

FIGURE 15

DRESSAGE FIGURES

435

18.14 LESSONS: PONY RIDES OR PERSPICACIOUS PROGRAMS?

Susan F. Tucker

KEY WORDS

ENTHUSIASM
EXCITEMENT
IMAGINATION
INGENUITY

Perspicacious is defined as "having or showing a clever awareness and resourcefulness in practical matters." (Webster, 1984). It is very important for a therapeutic riding instructor to be able to take the practical issues of the lesson and be resourceful enough to make it exciting and effective. It has been rumored that 'flexibility is uncommitted energy'. The secret to interesting, challenging lessons is flexibility and variety. Rigidity is the death knell of a therapeutic riding program.

In a therapeutic riding program it is essential for the instructor to have a lesson plan before going into the arena. A lesson plan keeps the instructor from getting into a rut, yet allows him to alter plans when the class requires this. There may be several riders missing whereas the plan to be used called for a game that involved the entire group; the best pony becomes lame; a roaring wind comes up so no one can hear a word the instructor says and the fund-raising committee says it will be at least two years before the program can hope for an indoor arena. What is the instructor going to do? He must be flexible and have enough knowledge of therapeutic riding to give himself options. He must know the resources so that he can keep "Plan B" up his sleeve. Here are some ideas to add variety to a lesson.

Be Inventive. Do not let lessons become boring. The most important element in preventing this is one's own enthusiasm. Each instructor has an individual style, and whether it is high-powered or low key, excitement must be present. Then use your imagination. Select the games and exercises to assure variety. Foster a sense of control by sometimes allowing the riders to have input into the lesson by choosing a favorite game or activity for that day. Look for ways to frame lessons so that the best rider is challenged but the less capable are not frustrated. Alter games so that, for example, different degrees of difficulty are incorporated and assigned appropriately.

Always be on the lookout for new game equipment. Remember the hair curlers called "Benders" that would not stay in the hair? They have a multitude of uses, such as relay batons that will bend rather than stab, or the instructor can direct the student to form them into a chain as a team thus working on developmental motor planning skills. Butterfly hair clips can go in the horse's mane for reaching or color identification exercises, or on the rider's sleeve to help with laterality (left and right) development. Look around garage sales and flea markets while your imagination is working. Those old pieces of plastic fruit could be used in matching games or for tactile discrimination. Empty ice cream containers are great buckets for spatial awareness games. Make balls out of rolled-up socks to toss. Do not limit ideas to just horse-related items. Be resourceful and flexible.

Keep the horse moving. The fun and the therapeutic effect in the class period both come from the motion, not from standing around. As soon as possible, do exercises at a walk (or trot!), or better yet, incorporate exercises into a game so they are fun. Remember to encourage quality movement in classes. When teaching the trot or canter, work with just one rider at a time. Have the entire class keep walking while the one in front trots around to the end of the line. That is more fun than standing and watching, and saves time because the next person is ready to go.

Vary the location if possible. Does the program have a place for people to go on a trail ride? This can be a good alternative on a windy day, provided the horses do not get spooky and the volunteers can handle the terrain. Can an obstacle course be set up in the pasture? Even though the environment is still controlled, the new demands provide a good way to give the feeling of advancement.

Stress different skill areas for riders of different ages and disabilities. Adult riders may enjoy the challenge of dressage and want to work strictly on riding skills. But, it is frustrating for everyone involved to try to teach such skills to a very physically involved child who does not have enough trunk control to sit properly. He should have a lesson implemented and/or designed by a therapist. Developmentally delayed riders may need to focus on learning appropriate social skills and just having fun. Some riders may want to become involved in competition, either in special classes for the disabled or open shows. Training for these competitions can be very challenging and exciting.

It helps to **tell the riders the goals for the day.** Those who are cognitively impaired often understand more than one realizes. They can then all work as a team with a focus. Ask at the end of class what each one felt he did best and what he needs to work on next week. Pointing to the progress and needs can be very enlightening for both rider and instructor.

Always reward good performance. Accustom the horses to cheering and applause and then encourage riders and volunteers to respond that way. Some riders only know the agony of defeat, and the thrill of having people cheering for their success may be the most therapeutic event of the lesson. Ribbons or other prizes may also be awarded at the end of the session. (Have horse show people donate the rosette ribbons they no longer want; just cut off the printing.) They will be cherished by your riders for years.

An interesting lesson depends on the instructor's flexibility, and enthusiasm. Continually seek to expand your base of knowledge and provide yourself options with which to keep challenging the riders.

Reference
Webster's II New Riverside Dictionary. (1984). Boston: Houghton Mifflin Co.

18.15   TRAIL COURSE FOR FUN AND PROFIT

Marci Lawson and Deborah Parker, MS, NARHA Master Instructor

Horses, riders and volunteers enjoy variety and new challenges. Without these, riding can become work and tedious repetition. One way to offer variety and challenges to your riders is to build a trail course. The course can be erected with portable sections when there is minimal space. Or in unlimited space an extensive course can be constructed. The program riders, volunteers and horses will all benefit from a trail course. A lesson on the trail course can be performed once a month as a treat or perhaps a portion of the course can be practiced for ten minutes as part of a lesson. However the instructor ties the course into the program, everyone is sure to benefit.

I. **Why incorporate a trail course into your program?**
   A. As a break for ring-sour horses
   B. As a break for bored riders and volunteers
   C. As a learning tool
      1. Daily living skills such as mail pick-up and delivery awareness; taking a basket off the shelf; taking a stocking cap off the hook, putting it on and hanging it back-up; closing a gate might be new skills for many riders.
      2. New challenges may include maneuvering the horse over a wooden bridge, balancing down and up through a ditch, throwing a ball through a suspended (still or moving) hula hoop--whether sitting on the horse at a stand or walking. The hula hoop can be hung low or high for an extra challenge. Learning and remembering the sequence of various patterns around barrels, poles and other obstacles can be a challenge.

II. **Making up a trail course:**
   A. Use natural terrain and objects to the program's advantage. Scatter the course in between trees in a wooded area or make it more challenging by using a hilly area which has not been used before.
   B. One may be fortunate enough to be able to use a totally separate area for the course or perhaps parts can be set up sporadically outside of the arena.

III. **How to construct a trail course**
   A. A crew will be needed to prepare the terrain for the course but the actual course and props can usually be done in a day
   B. Materials needed are detailed below

IV. **What to do with a trail course**
   A. Daily living skills
      1. Mailbox
      2. Basket off the shelf
      3. Clothing off/on the hook
      4. Gate
   B. New challenges
      1. Bridge
      2. Ditch
      3. Barrels
      4. Poles

V. Who profits from your trail course?
A. Horses
B. Volunteers
C. Riders

TRAIL COURSE - MATERIALS NEEDED
MAILBOX
- 1 post (4 x 4 six feet long) post, 1 mailbox with flag--set into a large coffee can filled with concrete

BASKET AND SHELF
- 1 tree or pole (4 x 4 six feet long), 3 lb coffee can (or other container) filled with concrete for base
- 1 (1 x 8 one foot long) pine or fir for shelf
- 1 6 inch heavy duty shelf bracket
- 1 basket with handle

CLOTHING
- 1 pole (4 x 4 six feet long), concrete and base container (as above)
- 1 stocking cap
- 1 wooden peg 3 inches long (put in a drilled hole near top of post)

GATE
- 2 4 x 4's eight feet long for gate (4 x 4 feet), 2 strong hinges
- 2 posts (4 x 4 six feet long) to which to hinges/latch the gate
- 1 gate latch, container filled with concrete for setting posts

BRIDGE (5 FEET WIDE X 8 FEET LONG)
- 8 2 x 6's 10 feet long P.T. fir
- 2 4 x 6's 8 feet long P.T. fir

ODDS AND ENDS
- 4 barrels, 6 to 8 ground poles, poles to form an "L", 6 to 8 traffic cones, cavaletti or small jump, old tires, traffic signs, nails-screws-bolts, paint or stain.

GAME PROPS
- Bean bags, balls, mail, socks, velcro dart board, basketball hoop, alphabet/number cards.

Figure 1 and Figure 2 show two trail courses that can be constructed with these material to challenge the riders.

THE STUDENT PROFITS
All of the obstacles will challenge the riders' balance and coordination. In addition, posture and control of body position will improve and muscles will strengthen with increased mobility. For example, the obstacles challenge the rider with cerebral palsy to more planning, stretching, grasping, gross and fine motor skills. The rider with spina bifida will, in addition, work on righting reactions. The rider with retardation will increase in the same skills as well as in following directions. Riders with learning disabilities will be offered structured, individualized challenges geared toward success.

Activities can include sequencing (of events), following directions (memory), directionality, orientation and spatial relations. Riders can improve body image, language development, auditory reception and symbol recognition. Games can encourage letter/number/symbol/shape recognition, matching, visual tracking and closure skills.

The riders will build self-confidence and self-image while working as a team; social skills and peer relations will strengthen. All of these skills will be learned without the riders ever knowing that they are "working". A trail course is a perfect learning tool in a fun and challenging setting.

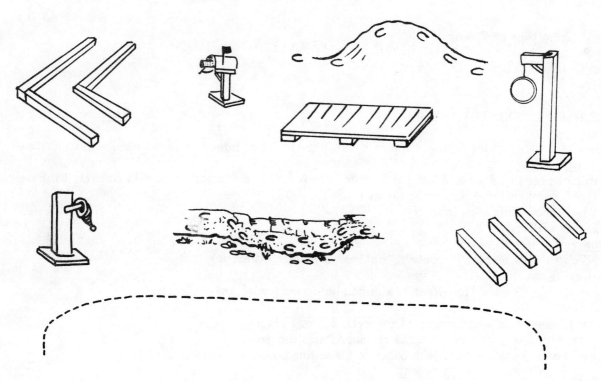

FIGURE 1. TRAIL COURSE

FIGURE 2. TRAIL COURSE

18.16   OBSERVATION SKILLS USED IN THERAPEUTIC RIDING

Barbara T. Engel, MEd, OTR

Observation, as defined by Webster (1966), is the act, <u>practice</u> or power of <u>noticing</u>, <u>recording facts</u> or <u>events</u>. In therapeutic horseback riding programs, observation skills provide the instructor and the therapist with valuable information about the client, the horse and the environment. Observation occurs during every aspect of our interaction with others. One must observe to evaluate, assess, teach, treat, or train others. The ability to perceive also provides feedback on one's capacity to cause change. The talent to hear, to see, to listen provides the instructor and therapist with a volume of information. However, one must also be able to sort through all this perceptual and conceptual data to find the pertinent information with which to deal. What kind of behavior does one focus on? Some of the areas which provide the information needed are:

- ◻ Non-verbal communication which includes:
    - ○ gesture and facial expressions
    - ○ posture, muscle tension, and body movements
    - ○ physiological changes such as blushing or sweating
- ◻ Ability to perform a number of different skills.
- ◻ Inability to perform certain acts or delays in responses.
- ◻ What the person says, how he said it, when he says it.
- ◻ How sensory stimuli affect this person and under what circumstance.
- ◻ How the person perceives others, himself, the horse, or activities.
- ◻ How the person receives information, takes directions or interacts with others.
- ◻ How this person interacts with various aspects of his environment
- ◻ What is the problem, what causes the problem, and what corrects the problem.

Keen observational skills tell one not only what is right or wrong but provides in-depth knowledge of what, how, when, and why something happens. This knowledge allows an instructor to teach skillfully or to determine the conformation of a horse. It allows a therapist to treat proficiently. To know what to observe and increase one's perceptiveness is partially dependent on the base of knowledge one has. But the ability to observe also provides a great deal of knowledge if one can look beyond what he thinks he sees. It is a tool for learning. Make the observations unbiased--do not interpret the information. Interpretations cloud the true information. One sees a child with spastic cerebral palsy with bright red hair--not noticing her soft creamy skin, those expressive green eyes and her ability to communicate with the horse. Identifying a child as "a spastic cerebral palsy" does not identify her as a person with specific abilities.

Take time to observe and then see if there is not more information to be obtained. Watch for the subtle signs. For example: Robert is observing Jason, the little boy on the white horse. Robert sees a clumsy child who is not paying attention and seems to be falling asleep. Linda sees a child with poor muscle tone who cannot sit up straight. She notices the tremors in Jason's arms but sees that they are decreasing as he rides. She also sees that his tone improves when the horse moves a little faster. Margo will be instructing the next class. She notices Maryjane, the volunteer, is in a bad mood. Did she look beyond the obvious? No. She did not notice that Maryjane was alone trying to tack up three horses for the lesson, that she had no help, the tack was misplaced and that there was no lesson plan posted.

Learning to observe in depth brings one into a world most people do not see and provides the ability to make subtle changes in others' behaviors--like an artist molds a figure.

Webster's New World Dictionary. (1966). College Edition. Cleveland: The World Publishing Co.

Hopkins, H.L., Smith, H.D. (1978). *Willard & Spackman's Occupational Therapy.* 5th Ed. Philadelphia: J.B. Lippincott.

18.17 THERAPEUTIC RIDING PROGRAM RIDER OBSERVATION EVALUATION FORM

Jean M. Tebay, MS

This observation form (Figure 2) was developed for use with mentally impaired beginning riders. It is intended to chart progress (or the lack of progress) in an individual rider's ability and mood. The form has been designed for ease in transferring the data to a graph, which could be used to document the rider's in ability and mood over a period of time, such as an eight or ten week session, when the results are noted each week. This evaluation process provides the basis for a simple research study. Figure 1 is a completed survey showing an ideal progression in both ability and mood.

THERAPEUTIC RIDING PROGRAM RIDER OBSERVATION EVALUATION FORM

Name of Rider: _George Hanson_   **Horse:** _Midnight_

Goals for Rider: _Improve self-esteem; improve language skills_

School: _Shady Glen_   **Start Date:** _Sept 16, 1992_

Evaluation Key: ABILITY
1. Cannot perform the task
2. Can perform the task with moderate assistance
3. Can perform the task with minimum assistance
4. Can perform the task unassisted

Evaluation Key: MOOD
A. Unwilling, Unmotivated
B. Somewhat willing, Somewhat motivated
C. Willing, Needs encouragement
D. Willing, Self-motivated

The Lesson	Dates							
	9-16	9-23	9-30	10-7	10-14	10-21	10-28	11-5
1. Putting on Hard Hat	1/A	1/A	2/B	2/B	3/B	3/C	4/D	4/D
2. Mounting the Horse	1/A	1/B	1/B	2/B	2/B	2/D	4/C	4/D
3. Performing the Exercises	1/A	1/A	1/B	1/C	1/C	1/C	3/C	3/D
4. Performing the Lesson Tasks	1/A	1/B	1/B	2/B	2/C	2/C	3/C	4/C
5. Performing the Game Task	1/B	2/B	2/B	2/C	3/C	3/C	4/C	4/D
6. Dismounting the Horse	1/C	3/C	3/C	3/C	3/D	3/D	4/D	4/D
7. Taking Off Hard Hat	1/A	1/A	2/B	2/B	3/C	3/C	3/D	4/D
8. Other	1/A	2/B	3/C	2/C	3/B	3/B	4/D	4/D

Special Remarks: *9-16 no verbal today; 9-23 some language, seemed happier, greeted horse with smile; 9-30 said "hello" to all staff; 10-7 participated vocally in games; 10-14 asked for Midnight, remembered all volunteers names 10-28 smiled and talked the whole lesson.*

Mary Smythe   _Nov. 5, 1992_

Signature of Instructor   Date Completed

FIGURE 2

THERAPEUTIC RIDING PROGRAM RIDER OBSERVATION EVALUATION FORM

Name of Rider: _____ Horse: _____

Goals for Rider: _____

School: _____ Start Date: _____

Evaluation Key: ABILITY
1. Cannot perform the task
2. Can perform the task with moderate assistance
3. Can perform the task with minimum assistance
4. Can perform the task unassisted

Evaluation Key: MOOD
A. Unwilling, Unmotivated
B. Somewhat willing, Somewhat motivated
C. Willing, Needs encouragement
D. Willing, Self-motivated

The Lesson	Dates							
1. Putting on Hard Hat								
2. Mounting the Horse								
3. Performing the Exercises								
4. Performing the Lesson Tasks								
5. Performing the Game Task								
6. Dismounting the Horse								
7. Taking Off Hard Hat								
8. Other								

Special Remarks: _____

_____

_____

_____

_____   _____
Signature of Instructor   Date Completed

Figure 2.

* Printed by Permission: B.T. Batsford Ltd., UK., V. Britton, 1991, *Riding for the Disabled*.

19. HORSEMANSHIP LESSONS

Marty Leff, BA, MA

Therapeutic riding does not begin and end with the mounted lesson. In fact, as every horse person knows, actual riding comprises but a small part of the total experience. Like it or not, for every hour in the saddle, someone, usually the rider, puts in a good two hours of horse and tack care. And while this care may often involve hard, dirty work, it is absolutely critical to the bonding of horse and rider and to the feeling of accomplishment and sense of independence that the student derives from horseback riding--be it "regular" or therapeutic riding. Special populations can and should participate in the many and varied aspects of horsemanship, above and beyond the arena. The barn, for example, offers limitless multisensory input and remedial-psychoeducational opportunities, as well as therapeutic fine-motor and gross-motor activities. In short, the unmounted horsemanship lesson can be every bit as exciting and challenging, and as rich in therapeutic benefits, as the mounted lesson. The instructor can address the same short-term and long-term goals in a horsemanship lesson, that he or she is addressing in the arena, allowing the student to progress from simple to more complex tasks while achieving success in both areas of the lesson. This holds true for every possible therapeutic orientation, be it medical, remedial-psychoeducational, or sport.

The therapeutic riding program that does not operate out of a barn but vans horses into a riding location, can still teach horsemanship by simply bringing along an extra horse or two, some extra tack, and/or any other materials that will enable the students to learn horse care. This type of set-up will probably necessitate some extra planning and creativity, but the added therapeutic benefits are well worth the effort. All the following activities may be adapted to any therapeutic riding setting.

Of course, it will be necessary to tailor therapeutic horsemanship to the particular student, gearing each lesson to his intellectual, emotional, and chronological age, level of physical involvement, and individual abilities and disabilities. But in every case, the bottom line is safety, for the handling of even the most docile paragon of equine virtue is potentially dangerous, especially when the animal is bombarded by unfamiliar behaviors, noises, and equipment. If a lesson is unsafe, it <u>cannot</u> be therapeutic or even enjoyable. Before entering the barn or area where horses are kept, the instructor should discuss safety rules. Students must know which behaviors are acceptable and which are not--and why. Naturally, it is important to avoid frightening the newcomers, but the instructor cannot let them step unwittingly into danger. Probably the best approach is a firm, matter-of-fact presentation of the rules as a way of avoiding possible problems, while stressing the fact that most horses are very gentle and do not want to hurt anyone. The instructor must have adequate volunteer help and must check to see that the stable area is free of traffic and debris. And of course, only well-trained therapeutic horses, accustomed through training to accept odd equipment, behavior, and noises, strangely awkward grooming (unintentional curry-comb jabs) are essential. Within that framework, students should be allowed to achieve the greatest degree of independence that is safely possible. Horsemanship can and should be <u>fun</u>! Even stall-mucking can turn into a game or contest if the instructor is creative. The trick is to enjoy the activities and convey enthusiasm, never to view horsemanship as "a poor relation" to the mounted lesson.

Both organization and flexibility are essential. In order to address progressive goals and to insure educational success, it is necessary to plan ahead. But even the best-planned lesson can go awry; it may turn out to be too difficult or too easy to hold the student's attention--or it may simply not work out as expected. Sometimes the student is simply having a bad day (especially possible when he is going back to school after vacation, when the moon is full, or when medications have changed or fallen by the wayside). At that point the instructor will need to try a new approach--or just toss the lesson out and pull another from his or her well-stocked "bag of tricks." Or maybe he or she should take a break and try again. Sometimes getting physically able students to go for a "walk," "trot," or "canter" on foot will help them to let off steam and return to the task at hand.

Horsemanship lessons should be as active as possible, for fun and activity are the "sugar that makes the medicine go down"--even for adults. The classroom or therapy room is precisely what students are getting away from when they come out to ride or learn about horses and their care. A demonstration on a live horse is worth a thousand blackboard or textbook words, and reaching out to pat an equine friend is far more exciting than doing a therapy exercise. Of course, especially when weather conditions make it impossible for students to be outside (or even in a barn), the classroom-type lesson will be a necessity. But in these cases, creativity can turn learning tasks into games. Sometimes letting students take turns "teaching," assuming other leadership roles, or role-playing will help capture their interest. If they are mature, of average or near-average intelligence, already highly involved in riding and horsemanship, and have serious equestrian goals, of course it is appropriate to introduce more straightforward information on horse care, in-depth reading, writing, and even arithmetic (in the form of equine economics, feed charts, horse heights, or even architectural layouts for ideal barns). But it is important to be aware of each and every student's ability level and best learning modalities before going heavily into equine-related academics. When teaching remedial-psychoeducational riding, the day's lessons, both in the saddle and on the ground, can be the source of creative, fun "homework"--doing crossword or word-find puzzles, recording memories in a journal, keeping lists of horse terms for special bonus spelling tests or spelling bees, drawing and labeling pictures of favorite horses, and so forth.

When teaching horsemanship to special populations, it is wise to make use of every possible resource. Watching a veterinarian, a farrier or groom at work can be a fascinating way to learn about the horse-related concepts. Demonstrations by people expert in various forms of riding--vaulting, Western, show jumping, dressage, and sidesaddle, for example, can show students the wide range of possibilities, create educational discussions, and be very entertaining, as well. Sometimes just watching horses romping and chomping in a pasture or paddock can lead to a new understanding of work versus play and other equine social dynamics.

One fringe benefit of horsemanship lessons is that they can help therapeutic programs address the needs of the students AND the work necessary to maintain tack, program equipment, and the needs of their horses. Every barn, no matter how well run, has chores that need doing. Why not let students help and make a real contribution, according to their abilities? Of course, in the beginning the instructor must always keep watch and be prepared to redo a given task at a later time if students have not quite mastered the lesson. But no student is too "disabled" to help out, and most can learn to be very effective helpers.

Before beginning horsemanship lessons however, students should have the opportunity to explore the facilities - to see, hear, smell, and touch (the sense of taste is the one sense a person probably will not want to indulge!) all the fascinating multisensory stimuli that abound in a barn. A trip to a hay loft (with great care, of course) or play in a (clean) shaving pile can be a truly therapeutic and educational experience. In any event, a tour of the barn and an introduction to a variety of horses will help new students get acquainted with the place and its residents, and overcome any fears. Often just patting a horse for the first time is a major milestone. And for those students who have trouble with transitions--as many do--a chance to observe a new environment in a relatively non-threatening way will help ease the transition from "the real world" of school, hospital, or home, to the often "alien" horse world. This is also an ideal time for the instructor to observe the clients, to begin setting goals and anticipating problems.

The following suggested horsemanship lessons are but a few among many possibilities. Every student-- even a nonverbal, non-ambulatory preschooler with multiple disabilities--can participate in these activities and games with creative adaptation and (only if necessary) a judicious helping hand.

Although most of the following activities are geared toward children, they can and should be adapted to adolescents and adults of average intellect. Even adults can enjoy a game if the instructor presents it in an age-appropriate fashion. The bottom line is to know the population and present the activity accordingly. The "station" concept of moving from one place to another is an excellent way of giving students a sense of order, sequence, diversity, and a sense of independent movement.

HALTERING, LEADING, AND TYING

Becoming independent is a goal that all disabled persons work toward. Learning how to lead and tie a horse is a skill that most persons with disabilities can learn and be very proud of.

Materials:

- ☑ Halters of various colors
- ☑ Leadlines of matching colors (if necessary, dye inexpensive white leadline)
- ☑ Index cards, matching colors (either paint or mark with tape to convert a pastel into a primary color, so that it will more closely match the halter color)
- ☑ Magic markers, matching colors in the same primary shades as the halters
- ☑ "Puffy pens" (optional)
- ☑ Colored construction paper (optional)
- ☑ Glue stick (optional)
- ☑ Chalk (optional)
- ☑ Crepe paper or yarn trail markers (optional)
- ☑ "Boom box" and tape of four-beat "walk" music (optional)
- ☑ Heavy-duty paint buckets or milk crates (for small children who cannot otherwise reach a horse's head)

Volunteer Briefing

Before class the instructor should brief the volunteers carefully, making sure that they understand not only their roles but the individual and group goals for the day's activity. New volunteers should be conditioned not to intervene so students can perform tasks independently, and not to be overly verbal when students should be focused on the instructor. If volunteers have not yet met the students, the instructor should give a brief summary of each student's abilities and disabilities, as well as any of their idiosyncrasies. This pre-class meeting is the time to share information--to hear any of the volunteers' concerns and observations, to convey any special tips or warnings about horse or student behaviors, and to invite questions and comments. Once the volunteers meet the students, the "buddy system" will enhance the volunteers' sense of participation and the students' sense of security. A good instructor will try to pair each volunteer with a particular student for the duration of the session if the program is fortunate enough to have many reliable volunteers! These "buddies" will participate together in both the mounted and horsemanship lessons. Students, too, will benefit from their own pre-class meeting.

Station 1

When the students arrive, the instructor should meet with them in an office, classroom, or other spot outside the barn. If the students are able to understand, this is the time to explain the day's task; finding the correct equipment taking it to a particular stall, then haltering, leading and tying a particular horse. This is also the time to review all safety rules before setting out. Of course, here, as in all aspects of therapeutic lessons, the instructor will have to gear explanations to the students' levels--both mental and chronological ages. If a group of students covers a wide range of abilities, it may be best to have seasoned volunteers work independently one-on-one or with a team of similarly-able students. In any event, it is essential to watch carefully for feedback, to be sure that the explanations and directions are not going over the students' heads or worse yet, that you are talking down to them. As is invariably the case, common sense and carefully thought-out and constantly reevaluated goals should be the instructor's guide in adapting all lessons to the students' particular abilities and needs. And needless to say, every effort by a student, no matter how feeble, should result in sincere praise; there is <u>always</u> something to praise, even if it is just to say a "nice try."

If students are not already familiar with the halter and leadline, the instructor should be sure to have one of each handy and to teach the terms. Then he or she can give each student or team of students one colored index card. If they are able, they should print or write the name of a particular horse on the card with a marker of a matching color. Or they may use the "puffy pens" to add tactile stimulation, or (for those with vision impairment) to create braille. If students cannot yet write, the instructor and/or volunteers may guide their hands, have them trace over lightly penciled names, or write the name for them. If students cannot read, they might instead cut and/or paste onto the card different shaped pieces (such as circles, squares, triangles) of matching construction paper. In any event, make sure that when verbal students say the colors of the particular halter and the names of the particular horses they are to find, that they repeat your instructions. Give only as many directions at one time as the student can assimilate. The number of steps they can cope with can and should progress; in fact, this is in itself a worthwhile goal for many student populations.

Station 2

Next, the instructor should direct the students to the tack room or separate area where the halters are hanging or laid out in a row. The leadlines may be with the halters or in a separate location. It is important to let the students find these items as independently and as safely as possible. The instructor might even want to draw a map or have them follow a marked "trail" (chalk hoofprints or colorful streamers tied to trees or other things along the way), making sure that the route is safe and accessible for all. Another approach is to write clues for a treasure hunt that will eventually lead to the halters and leadlines and ultimately to the horses. When the students find the halters and leadlines, they should select the ones that match the colors of their index cards. (Since index cards come in pastel colors, and halters are generally of bright primary colors, the instructor may need to discuss the relationship of, for example, a pink card to a red halter, or paint the card red, or put a piece of primary color tape on it to more closely approximate the halter color).

Station 3

Now it is time to tell the students how to find "their" horses' stalls, or the place where their horse is being held by volunteers if there are no stalls, or if the stalls are not safely accessible. In any event, the instructor may use similar maps, hoofprints, trail markers or clues to help the students reach the stalls or the area where the horses are being held. The stalls will be marked with index cards that match the ones the students have. If the horses are being held, cards may be affixed to the horses (amazingly, most good therapeutic riding horses do not mind having things taped onto them, but of course it will be necessary to test their reaction in advance!) or to the spot where they are standing (the rail, the ground, or with the volunteer horse holder). If the horses are outside their stalls, they will already be wearing halters. Naturally, these should match the index cards bearing their names or symbols and the halters and leadlines that the students have found.

Before allowing students to go to their horses, however, the instructor should demonstrate--on a different horse-- the correct manner of approach and then the haltering procedure, breaking the task down into its smallest components (task analysis-see Section 15.07), if necessary. Next the students should be shown how to attach the leadlines, then lead and tie the horses with a safety knot or quick-release knot.

The instructor will then ask students to identify their horses' stalls or go to their horse if they are tied at the rail. Naturally, their approach must be safe and orderly, as demonstrated; no one may dash into a stall or rush up to his horse! If students are to enter the stalls, the instructor must make sure that they observe safety rules; the rules should be repeated at this time. Beginning students, however able, must NEVER enter a standing or tie stall. The volunteers should simply make sure that the horses are facing the door, and then have students open the door and approach the horses' shoulder with the halters. Volunteers should of course be ready to help but should do so as little as possible. Next the students should halter their horses, with hands-on help if necessary - **but only if necessary**.

Station 4

When all students have haltered their horses and attached their leadlines, the instructor will have them lead their horses, one at a time, to a designated area. Here, again, it is a good idea to repeat safety rules and if necessary have the volunteers walking as unobtrusively as possible between the leader and the horse or on the off side. Provided that the horses are accustomed to being led from a wheelchair, this is a marvelous activity for a non-ambulatory student. (But just because a horse is accustomed to a regular wheelchair, the instructor should not assume that the normally bomb-prof animal will take a motorized model in stride.)

At this point the instructor will need to direct traffic, making sure that everyone lines up in a safe place, at least one horse's length away from the next horse. A good way to ensure a safe line-up is to make "parking spaces" with parallel jump poles, also labeled with colored index cards that match those of the student--or better yet--marked with tape the same color as the halters and cards.

Next, depending on the age and ability of the student, the instructor may want to have a leading relay --at the walk--to a distant point or around obstacles. Or students may play "red light - green light," getting the horse to "walk on" or "whoa" on command. Or rather than commands, the instructor may use music; when it stops, they should halt their horses. And of course, there's always the perennial favorite game of youngsters, "Simon Says."

Older, more able students might have a "bag race" to music. Weighted burlap bags should be spaced around the arena, one fewer than the number of horses. When the music stops, each should lead his horse to a bag. The student that cannot find a vacant bag is "out." One bag is eliminated on each subsequent round, until only two student-horse teams and one bag is left. The winner is the student who reaches the last bag. It is essential, however, to evaluate the effect of winning and losing on each student. It is often best to save such competition for a time when they are familiar and secure enough to benefit from such dynamics. Many groups of youngsters with learning disabilities and emotional disturbances are easily frustrated and upset if they do not win, and such games do little to help self-esteem, peer interaction, and emotional stability. Adults may simply practice leading, turning, (away from themselves), backing, and so forth. They may also enjoy hand-grazing a not-too-greedy horse.

Station 5
When the leading exercise is over, the instructor should ask students to tie their horses in an appropriate manner in a safe place, designated, of course, by colored index cards. For single-tying one might want to make widely-spaced baling twine loops around a solid fencepost (like a hitching post). The instructor and/or volunteers should teach the safety knot to be used for tying the horses. This will be difficult for many; so it will almost undoubtedly be necessary to use a task-analysis approach and probably even some hands-on help. (Those who have a motor-planning dysfunction or poor memory retention should practice tying the knot at a time when this is the single task that they are dealing with.) When all students have mastered the knot, they will generally be delighted to learn the quick release by simply pulling free the end of the rope.

Alternatively, the instructor may want to teach students how to cross-tie horses in widely spaced, safety-release ties. These may be decorated with tape matching the various halter and index-card colors.

Clean-up and Review
At the end of the lesson, it is important to stress orderly clean-up. Students should always **thank** their **horses** and **helpers**, then retrace their footsteps, taking the horse "home," removing the halter, putting the halter and leadlines away. Children love to tie a "fireman's knot" when stowing the leadline, as it is easy to master and unties in an almost magical fashion. Finally, students should return to the original meeting place for review of the day's lesson. The instructor will want to summarize--or better yet, have the (verbal) students and those using sign language summarize--everything they have learned in the horsemanship activity. This is the time to go over new terms and possibly assign related homework, geared to the students' levels of function. A group with profound mental retardation may just try coloring a drawing of a halter, while a group with greater academic skills may want to write a journal entry or draw "their" horses, with the appropriate colors of the halters and leadlines, labeling both the horse and the colors. Another alternative for students with brain injuries is to pick out parts of a halter, leadline, and horse that have been provided them and put the "puzzle" together. To stress the social aspects of the lesson, the instructor may also want to ask the students to write or say the names of their teammates and helpers. A very mature or adult class may simply want to discuss the experience, what each person liked most or least, how each interacted with a particular horse. Highly intelligent adults may be encouraged to keep a journal and/or to take notes on each day's activity. Such students might also receive reading assignments as homework.

Finally, a formal dismissal, coupled with praise, praise, and more praise is absolutely essential. For the instructor to add, "I really enjoyed working with you" can make a student's day!

GROOMING: THE FIRST STEP IN BONDING

Grooming can easily be used as an activity with riders of all ages. Below is an example for students with many different types of disabilities.

Materials:

- ☐ Colored index cards with the horses' names on them, or color-taped for color-coding grooming tools and kits used when they do not come in a variety of colors
- ☐ Grooming kits, either in a variety of colors to match the index cards or banded in colored tape and labeled with horses' names on index cards; each should include:
  - ▸ Hoof pick, if possible in matching color
  - ▸ Sarvis curry comb, if possible in matching color
  - ▸ Rubber curry comb, labeled with colored tape
  - ▸ Dandy brush, if possible with bristles of a matching color
  - ▸ Body brush, color-coded with tape or (if wooden-backed) painted to match
  - ▸ Sponge or washcloth (optional)
  - ▸ Groom comb or human hair brush
  - ▸ Mane comb (optional)
- ☐ Halter and leadline, color-coded
- ☐ Step-stools, heavy-duty paint-mixing buckets or small milk crates, or cavalletti plastic blocks (for small students)
- ☐ Box or bin containing human grooming tools:
  - ▸ Combs
  - ▸ Brushes
  - ▸ Wash cloths
  - ▸ Toothbrushes
- ☐ 2 empty boxes (paint buckets or milk crates)

Volunteer Briefing

As always, the instructor should meet with volunteers to inform them of the day's activities--not just what, but why and how. This is the time to share information, invite questions and comments, and assign tasks. Whenever possible, it is best to maintain a system of client-volunteer buddies, as this can be a very positive experience for everyone. The instructor must remind helpers of any relevant horse quirks, such as ticklish places, "kick buttons" (i.e., especially sensitive spots), head shyness. If a horse is very thin-skinned or ticklish, it is best to find a less sensitive equine substitute for this lesson.

Station 1

The instructor should always plan a pre-class meeting with the clients at a site apart from the barn or arena. Here he will review the last lesson, taking careful note of what the clients have remembered and forgotten. If there was a homework assignment, this is the time to go over it--and to praise even the tiniest effort.

Next the instructor will introduce the lesson of the day: grooming. If activities of daily living are a goal, the instructor should stress the similarities between human and animal grooming and the reasons why we groom--for hygiene, not just appearance. Demonstrating the ways in which human and animal grooming tools are alike will help the students learn the relevant terms and will reinforce the idea of the functions of the tools. A later demonstration of "what happens if you do not brush your teeth" is invariably a hit. However, the instructor can explain that while we do not ordinarily brush horses' teeth, we do arrange to have a dentist check them every six months.

Students invariably ask the instructor if horses take baths and shampoos. Certainly, the instructor will not want to convey to them that combing and brushing are adequate for human hygiene; so it is best to explain that we do bathe and shampoo horses when the weather permits, and that in winter we do the best we can to keep them clean without jeopardizing their health. Dry shampoos and hot-toweling take the place of baths in cold weather, but of course people have heated homes and apartments and warm clothing and therefore can and should bathe regularly.

For higher-functioning clients an explanation of girth galls, saddle sores, and thrush may be in order. It may also be appropriate to explain that horses have their own grooming tools so that they do not spread any sort of infection, such as lice or ringworm. The instructor may also point out that daily grooming offers the opportunity to check the horse completely for wounds, inflammation, or signs of illness. (Equine health is in itself an excellent horsemanship lesson.)

Next, the instructor should either hand out different-colored index cards with the horses' names and/or symbols on them--or let the clients draw cards from a bag. If the grooming lesson will involve teams, then they can compare cards to find the other members of their teams. Higher-functioning students may make their own cards. It may or may not be appropriate to have students remain with the same horse for every lesson. Probably at first, most students will benefit from such consistency and trust. However, after several weeks, it may be a good idea to change horse assignments, to let students generalize these positive attitudes. Students with learning disabilities and/or emotional disturbances benefit greatly from having their own horse buddies, as well as volunteer buddies. However, depending on the length of the session, the instructor may want to widen the circle of animals and humans for these students to relate to. The instructor can observe the degree of stress that change places on the individual to determine if change is indicated at this time. A word of warning, though: when the instructor decides to switch horses or volunteer helpers, he should be prepared for some heated protests and be able to handle them with firmness. Teamwork with peers is also extremely important for these student populations. The instructor may want to start with small groups, of two or three people, and slowly work up to larger teams.

After assigning horses, whether to individuals or groups, the instructor should direct students to **station 2** - the tack room or other place where grooming kits, halters, and leadlines are color-coded and/or labeled and lined up neatly. The directions may be a game or treasure hunt or a simple statement of one--(or two, or three,) step instructions, depending on the student's level and the instructor's goals.

Station 2
Here students will find a grooming kit, halter, and leadline for each horse. Now that grooming kits and tools come in a large variety of splendid, bright colors, a program may want to invest in a variety, with a different color for each horse. This will not only help students with perceptual skills but will help the program keep its equipment in order. Colored tape is another, less expensive way of obtaining the same effect.

In any event, each kit should be labeled with the individual horse's name or symbol (on the ubiquitous colored index card, of course). The number of tools in each kit must be appropriate for the student population; too many items may bewilder younger or lower-functioning students, while others may quickly become bored with too few tools. Once they have found "their" horses' kits, halters, and leadlines, the instructor will direct the individuals or teams to the next station--the barn or other area where the horses are secured. Naturally, the approach must be safe.

A volunteer should go ahead and recheck the aisle for any hazards, as the area that was free of horses and debris a few minutes before may suddenly contain wheelbarrows, pitchforks, and any number of animals on cross-ties. The instructor may wish to assign a student "scout" to go on ahead with the volunteer. This is one example of a leadership role, a great confidence-builder, just as long as the instructor is careful to let everyone have a chance to play such a role in the course of the lesson.

Station 3

Here each stall or horse will be labeled with a colored index card matching that of each individual or team. Of course, the horses must be at a safe distance from one another (if outside the stall) or have an unobstructed route from the stall to the nearest cross-ties. The students will halter or re-halter their horses, if necessary standing on step-stools, buckets, or crates to reach the horses' heads. Naturally, any experienced school horse can instantly size a rider up, decide exactly how high he can reach, and then raise its head just an inch or two higher! Once, by hook or crook or judicious volunteer help, horses have been haltered they should be led to the grooming site, whether cross-ties or to a space in or near the arena. No student must ever lead a horse past another on cross-ties, and any clients in wheelchairs must have careful supervision--but not unnecessary intervention.

Station 4

Here the actual grooming will take place. Small students may use step-stools, buckets, or crates to reach the horses' faces, necks, and backs. Any student in a wheelchair may groom first from a ramp and then from the ground. Even nonverbal, low-functioning students can learn to select and use the correct tool on command, if the helper says or signs its name and picks it up as often as necessary to help reinforce the association of the name with the object.

The grooming session can illustrate any number of important topics: color, shape (circles with the curry comb), directionality (the brush more or less goes "up" and brushes "down," grooming from "front" to "back"), sequencing, health and hygiene, and even time if the instructor allots a specific period of time for the use of each tool, for students to have their turns, and for the entire activity. Volunteers can warn the students with a count-down--that is, when they have five, then three, then one minute(s) left; when it's almost time to clean up and go on to the next station. Every student should have a chance to use every tool, even--with the utmost caution--the hoof pick. The volunteer may need to pick up and hold the hoof, but all students can have a try at picking. The most important thing is getting the students to communicate and bond with the horses. The students or helper may point out a horse's favorite itchy spot and the places where the student needs to be especially gentle (on the spine, loins, and flank), how the animal shows pleasure or displeasure, how to pat and praise the horse. When the actual grooming is complete, the instructor may want to have the students lead their horses to a separate area for "judging."

Station 5

Here, probably along the centerline of the arena, clients should line up their horses, side by side but with a very generous space between them. Parallel jump poles may delineate "parking spaces." The instructor may award prizes for various aspects of grooming--the shiniest coat, the neatest mane and tail, the cleanest hooves, the fewest muck stains, whatever. In the beginning, at any rate, it seems best to have competitions end in success for everyone. Later, when students have gained confidence, instructors may wish to introduce real competition, but no student should feel that he or she is a "loser." Stickers, gilded or silver-painted horseshoes, or small stick-on gift bows make fine prizes. However, when the students are children, it is best to avoid food treats unless the parents or teachers have specifically okayed them. Some behavior-modification classes do make use of edible reinforcers; the instructor must be well informed as to the correct, appropriate reward.

Clean-up and Review

At the end of the lesson, after thanking the horses and helpers, students must always put everything, including horses and equipment, back where they came from. The grooming tools should be ordered within the kits and the kits, halters, and leadlines put back in the tack room or site where clients found them. If the lead ropes were originally tied in a fireman's knot, then students should learn to retie them at the end of the lesson.

Finally, as after every lesson, students should return to the site of the pre-class meeting for review and homework assignments. The instructor should always try to elicit responses from the students, rather than simply retrace the day's activities. Older and higher-functioning students may be able to tell what they learned, what was fun, what was difficult, how the horse enjoyed the grooming, and so forth. They should be able to name or repeat the name or sign for the various tools, to select from a group of objects the ones that they used for grooming, and to name the colors of their horses' equipment. If the instructor wants to assign homework, work sheets with pictures of the grooming tools may serve a variety of populations. Some students may simply color (scribble on) them; others may

452

label them; still others may wish to write a journal, with an entry for each lesson. The work sheets could illustrate the grooming entry. At the end of the session, students--children and adults alike--will have a wonderful memento of their riding and horse-care experience. And if the program has photo permissions, Polaroid photos of the students both riding and participating in horsemanship lessons add an especially nice touch to the journals, and may also serve to decorate the classroom. Every lesson should end with a formal but friendly dismissal and, of course, praise.

NOTE: Grooming tools can be the basis for any number of matching, categorizing, counting or color-recognition games. Students may put all (or two, three, four) of the blue tools, for example, into one bucket/ milk crate, and the red into another. Or the task could be to separate and sort human and horse grooming tools, to distinguish hard from soft brushes. The instructor may wish to decorate one container with tape and stickers of one color and another container with tape and stickers of another color. Or the decorating could be a project for older students to do to help other classes of "little kids." The possibilities are virtually endless. All it takes is an accurate evaluation of the students' abilities and an active imagination.

Once the students have gotten back to the pre-class meeting site, they should be encouraged to talk about what tasks they have performed and the reasons for different procedures. Lower-functioning persons should try to sign or name the equipment they have used. As always, the instructor should assign any homework and dismiss the students.

TACKING AND UNTACKING

Tacking is a skill that all students should learn, since it is basic to riding. Handling the equipment that goes on a horse is an interesting experience and provides the rider a better understanding of the function of saddles, pads, and other necessary equipment.

Materials:
- Index cards of various colors
- Halters of various colors
- Leadlines of various colors
- Bridles marked with tape of various colors
- Saddles, also color-coded with tape
- Saddle pads (clean, of course), color-coded with tape or labeled with the horse's name in permanent marker of the corresponding colors
- Girths similarly coded
- Safety stirrups if they are not attached to the saddle
- Handholds or neck straps
- Special reins (where needed)
- Horse boots or polo wraps (optional)
- Bump, or bounce, pads, if necessary for correct saddle fit (at best a temporary solution to a serious problem!)
- Step-stools, buckets, milk crates (for small children)

Volunteer Briefing
This meeting will be similar in nature to those accompanying preceding lessons. However, in this case, the instructor must be sure to note which horses, if any, are touchy about too being cinched and which horses resist bridling. If any of the standard pool of horses is too difficult, it is wise to substitute a more reasonable animal. However, a slight challenge--if it ends in success--will make clients feel all the better about completing the task. Volunteers should help as little as absolutely necessary, but of course the instructor and volunteers must structure a successful experience for every client. Sometimes effective holding, coupled with an explanation of why the horse

dislikes having the girth tightened and an assurance that it really does not hurt, can allow a client to meet the challenge of tightening the girth. The student will need careful, easy-to-understand instructions regarding the correct (slow, gentle) manner of girth-tightening. The instructor must make it absolutely clear to volunteers that **it is their job to ensure safety** during this and indeed all other activities. A step-stool or even a wheelchair ramp may solve the problem of the head-lifting, bit-evader.

This is where the instructor's judgment comes into play. He or she must decide which person is capable of which tasks and just how much frustration each individual can handle. Volunteer input can be invaluable in cases like this one. If the buddy system has worked well, the volunteers should have a good idea of whether their students can deal with difficult situations--and whether the individuals have the ability to succeed in harder tasks. A wise instructor will value and make use of the volunteers' ideas and suggestions.

Station 1
As always, the instructor will explain the day's activity and just what is expected from the student and should be accomplished during the lesson. This is an ideal time to go over parts of the saddle and bridle--in as much or as little detail as appropriate for the population.

In any event, the instructor will now direct the students to the tack room or other site where the tack is neatly lined up and labeled. Since students are probably familiar with the route to this site, it is time to vary the directions--either substituting a different game or using two--(or three, or four,) step instructions. Each lesson should be slightly more difficult than the last, but as always, a good instructor will be very sensitive to feedback and will not be afraid to backtrack if students are unable to understand and comply at a given level of difficulty.

Station 2
In the tack room, students will collect their horses' halters, leadlines, saddle pads, saddles, girths, and bridles. Since these items are quite difficult to carry in a single trip, this is an ideal situation for teamwork. Alternatively, the instructor may want to have students make several trips, each of which will provide an opportunity for following directions and sequencing. In either case, the instructor should direct students to the next station, with volunteers providing as little assistance as safely possible.

Station 3
At this site, students should carefully put down the saddle, pad, girth and bridle. The instructor should caution the students to avoid setting the saddle flat on the ground or in any puddles or muck. Ideally, there will be a bridle hook and saddle stand, rack, or fence rail to accommodate the tack. If the students are in wheelchairs or are very small, they should lay the equipment on the wheelchair ramp. Taller, ambulatory clients should put the tack near cross-ties or at safe intervals along the arena rail. Next everyone should proceed, according to the instructor's directions, to the site where horses are waiting.

Station 4
Here, as usual, students should halter their horses and then follow directions back to station 3, where the tack is set out.

Station 3 (revisited)
Here the instructor or volunteers will demonstrate, first bridling, then saddling. This sequence is preferable in instances where the horse is not tied, for it gives the students more control than a halter. If the horse is tied, it is important for students to learn to unfasten the halter, put it around the horse's neck, then refasten it. The instructor must however, stress that a horse should never be left with the halter around the neck, as this might allow the animal to escape or become entangled.

Bridling will be difficult and will almost certainly involve task analysis; so instructors and volunteers should practice the wording to keep directions simple, consistent and clear. Depending on the student population, volunteers may need to lend a judicious, but not overeager, helping hand. The wheelchair ramp, step-stool, bucket, or crate will often be necessary to give students a boost while tacking. After the bridle is in place, the volunteer or one of the students on a team should hold the horse while another puts the saddle on.

Saddling is somewhat easier than bridling, but if the saddles are too heavy for students, another person should help them lift it and set it down on the horse's back. First, of course, the pad should be in place, with the front resting on top of the horse's withers and the center seam on top of the horse's back bone. Next the instructor or volunteers will instruct the students to center the saddle on the pad and to put any tabs over the billet straps or do up the velcro tabs. One cannot over-stress the importance of correct saddle placement (see section 16.01.1), for incorrect placement is (after incorrect fit) the major source of equine back pain and rider imbalance. Far too many experienced horse people fail to slide the saddle back as far as is necessary for it to "fit flat" and not slope downward at an angle. Pads generally fail to correct the problem, for they often make a tight saddle tighter and leave a gap in pressure. Ideally, the saddle should create even pressure at every point of contact with the horse, not just at the pommel and cantle. In any event, the students should learn to slide both saddle and pad back into place, to look for a level fit, and to add a pad if necessary (see 16.01.3).

Students should also learn to pull the saddle pad up into the gullet of the saddle to avoid "crunching" the withers. Next they will learn to attach and slowly, gently, tighten the girth--elastic side, if any, on the left side, and finally, to pull the horse's foreleg slowly forward to smooth the skin and release the muscles under the girth. Some students will be able to accomplish the tacking up with little or no help; others will perhaps only be able to accomplish small parts of the procedure. The important thing is for everyone to participate to the best of his or her ability in readying the horse for riding and to feel a sense of accomplishment, if only by pushing the prong of a buckle into place.

If the horses will go on to the mounted lesson, untacking will have to wait. In any event, students should learn the proper way to cool and untack the animals after the ride. First students will need to "make the horses comfortable" by running up the stirrup irons and loosening the girth. Next the horse should have a little sip of water, then be walked until any sweat has dried and breathing has returned to normal (eight to sixteen respirations per minute). At this point students should learn to remove the saddle, and sponge (in warm weather) the horse or brush off any sweat marks.

Clean-up and Review
Clean-up in this case involves returning all horses to their stalls and all equipment to the tack room. Essentially, this phase of the lesson will be a matter of retracing footsteps and making sure that everything winds up in its correct place. If the saddle pads are dirty, students should relegate them to the dirty laundry pile. Saddles must end up on their own (labeled) racks, as must bridles. Once students have put everything neatly in its place, they should return to the pre-class meeting site to review. The instructor should try to get students to discuss the tacking procedures and remember the terms they have learned. Possible homework could include learning all parts of the saddle and bridle, perhaps in the form of a puzzle or drawings to color and label. Students might also write journal entries, and may include drawings.

TACK CARE

All tack needs good care. Riders and volunteers can take part in its care by learning how to properly clean and handle it.

Materials

- ☒ Colored index cards
- ☒ Leather halters, color-coded with tape, or break-away halters of colors that correspond to the other equipment
- ☒ Snaffle bridles, color-coded with tape
- ☒ Saddles, preferably without suede knee rolls
- ☒ Leather girths
- ☒ Tack cleaning kit
  - ▶ Small beach buckets in colors corresponding to the other equipment
  - ▶ Small sponges, each color-coded with a ribbon threaded through a hole (can be made with a pencil) and tied to form a loop
  - ▶ Individual bars (or half-bars) of glycerine saddle soap
  - ▶ Rags or inexpensive washcloths in colors matching other equipment
  - ▶ Small individual bottles or cans of leather conditioner (to be refilled from more economical large containers)

Volunteer Briefing

As always, the instructor will explain the lesson plan to the volunteers, clearly stating the objective(s) for the day's activity, whether it is learning terminology; following one-step, two-step, three-step, or more-step directions; gaining a greater understanding of activities of daily living; or simply becoming more familiar with horsemanship. Also as always, the instructor should make sure that the volunteers are aware of when to help and when not to help. By this time they should know their student buddies well enough to give some valuable insights and to have some very good ideas. Instructors must always encourage this input; as it may be extremely helpful and will in addition encourage the volunteers by making them understand just how important they are to the program.

Station 1

When the students arrive the instructor will greet them and explain the activity of the day. This is the time to reinforce terms the students already know and to introduce new ones, also of course to go over completed homework assignments. The instructor will have to decide how much new information is appropriate for each particular student population. This lesson lends itself to everything from color recognition to advanced horsemanship. The instructor may want to hold up three halters: a nylon one, a break-away one, and an all-leather one, explaining the relative safety of leather versus nylon and stressing the importance of keeping the break-away crownpiece and leather halter clean and supple. Next, it is a good idea to show a very dirty bridle, get students to name the parts, relating them to parts of equine and human faces (brow band--brow or forehead; cheek piece-- cheek; noseband--nose). Students should see, touch, and smell both clean and dirty, mildewed, dry-rotted tack and in addition should be aware of the relationship of materials-- leather, metal, and nylon, to the students' own footwear, belt, zippers, and clothing. Tack can also relate to care of one's own valuable possessions, not only for the sake of having them look nice but to preserve and protect them. Would they want their shoes to look like the dirty tack? How long would shoes last in that condition?

Depending on the student's level of function, the instructor might also explain that dirty tack can lead to girth galls, saddle sores, and raw places on the horse's face or behind the ears. It is important to stress, however, that even well-cared-for tack may eventually wear out or break. Caring for the tack will help riders discover when things need repair or replacement - and thus help avoid a serious accident. After this discussion, the students, volunteers, and instructor should adjourn to the tack room --**Station 2.**

Station 2

Here the students will find the tack-cleaning kits corresponding to "their" horses (as indicated on the colored index cards). Next they will carefully remove the various items from the pails, lining everything up neatly. When the pails are empty, the students will fill them with warm water.

The instructor must decide how far the tack should be broken down. This will of course depend on the level of function of each student. For some, simply cleaning a one-piece leather halter will provide enough challenge; others may be able to break down and reassemble the entire bridle (a task that often bewilders "able" people). If students seem capable, it is best to start off with removing the crownpiece of a break-away halter. This will not be too difficult, but will encourage fine-motor skills. In any event, all tack should be laid out or accessible, and the leather should be dirty enough to let students see the difference their clean-up work makes.

Once the instructor has taken a sample of tack apart, he or she should ask students to do the same with their equipment. When they have complied, they should continue to follow the instructor's lead. It is essential for students to understand the sequence of steps involved in tack-cleaning. First, the students must dip their sponges into the warm water, wringing them out and then wiping the leather to remove loose dirt. Second, students must rinse and wring out the sponges, then rub them back and forth across the soap to make a thick lather. Third, the students should soap the tack thoroughly, rubbing the soap up and down, back and forth, and around in circles. It might be helpful to explain that, while one should always remove soap from his own body when bathing, the glycerine in saddle soap is like a kind of hair conditioner that one leaves on his hair. Finally, everyone will apply leather conditioner.

If the instructor feels that students can handle breaking down more pieces, they can repeat the procedures. The bridle is a ready-made puzzle, excellent for exercising fine-motor skills, as well as for following directions and sequencing. It may also be a good idea to lay out pieces of tack on top of pictures of those pieces drawn on large sheet of paper. Hands-on help may also be necessary.

Clean-up and Review

Before going back to the original meeting place, students must reassemble any loose parts of tack and put everything back where they found it. All the tack cleaning items must be put back into the pails and the pails put back where they belong. Review may include any of the topics discussed previously, as well as any terminology presented. If students named the parts of tack as they cleaned them, they will be more likely to remember. Any homework (drawings, labeled and unlabeled, of tack; journal entries; original drawings) should help reinforce the concept and terms.

The above are but a few horse-related learning activities. For further ideas and approaches, one may want to refer to the manual *Guide to Therapeutic Groundwork* by Marty Leff and Associates, obtained from:

National Center for Therapeutic Riding
P.O. Box 42501
Washington, D.C. 20015-0501 USA
202-966-8004

PART VI ADVANCED INSTRUCTION

As the field of therapeutic riding has advanced it has developed from leading persons with disabilities around an arena to the challenges that all able-bodied equestrians enjoy. The skilled instructor may take on the challenges of true sports riding/vaulting/driving with his or her clients, to expand their abilities to a truly maximum level. This is a very challenging area for both the riders/drivers/vaulters and instructors for here high level skills can be developed, developed to the level of the able-bodied person, developed to the point of equality. With so many talented equestrians coming up through the therapeutic riding programs, instructors should take note and develop activities which can challenge even Wendy Shugol (see 2.06).

The topics addressed in this chapter, will enlighten the reader to the wide range of equestrian activities that are presently available.

20 EQUESTRIAN ACTIVITIES

20.01.1 VAULTING

Barbara T. Engel, MEd, OTR

Vaulting is *gymnastics on the back of a moving horse*. In vaulting competition the horse is either going at the trot or the canter. When vaulting is used with the special populations of therapeutic riding, it is performed at a walk in the beginning and later at a trot and canter. Vaulting while the horse stands still is discouraged for three reasons:

- ☐ Movement of the vaulters on the back of the horse is stressful to the horse's back at a stand
- ☐ The movement of the horse aids the vaulter in maintaining balance
- ☐ It is the movement of the horse that provides the challenge and therapeutic value

Vaulting in Therapeutic Riding Programs:
Vaulting is adaptable to the three major areas of therapeutic riding - sports, education, and medicine.

Sports vaulting focuses on the <u>development of gymnastic skills on horseback</u> either in the traditional or adaptive approach, using progressively more difficult exercises. It improves <u>general</u> health and coordination. Skills are developed according to the guidelines of the sports vaulting associations. This sport is directed by an instructor skilled in this field. The end product of these sessions is *vaulting skills*. It may include terms such as <u>adaptive vaulting</u> or <u>developmental vaulting</u> which indicate that the exercises have been adapted to meet the needs of a special population.

Educational vaulting focuses on <u>remediation of educational and social problems</u>. Vaulting techniques are used as a means of accomplishing remedial objectives as a part of a total educational plan. It is based on the views of Cratty (1979), and Kephart (1971) who used movement to facilitate the learning process. Vaulting skills are not emphasized and the end product is to improve *learning and psychosocial behavior*. Educational vaulting is directed by educators, psychologists, or by an educator/vaulting instructor.

Vaulting in medicine (including psycho-motoric and remedial vaulting) focuses on <u>increasing specific physical and psycho-social dysfunctions</u> through a treatment process. Vaulting can be used as a modality by physical, occupational, recreational therapists, speech and language pathologists, psychologists or physicians. Gymnastic skills on the horse are not emphasized. Vaulting is used as a means to facilitate <u>specific</u> body functions. The end product is *increased function in specific areas* of concern according to a written treatment plan. Although vaulting techniques are used, the activity is not referred to as "vaulting" but rather "therapy".

Values of Vaulting:

- ◘ It is a goal-directed activity (one with a functional purpose) which is carried out during movement transitions (changes from sit to kneel to stand to lying *by the vaulter*). Vaulting involves both static (still) and dynamic (moving) movement patterns. The movements are dynamic in changing from one position to the other but static as each achieved position is held for a specific count.
- ◘ Vaulting is a strenuous activity which involves "risk". Rosenthal (1975) mentions risk as an important factor for growth.
- ◘ It is group activity which requires cooperation and trust among its members in order for vaulting to be successful, safe and beneficial. The members are the horse, the lunger, the vaulter or vaulters, and the sidehelpers.
- ◘ It is a great ego-developing activity, because the vaulter performs acts which are foreign to most people and develops unique skills.
- ◘ The drills can be adapted to the skill and needs of the individual.
- ◘ It challenges the person to compete against himself as he improves from one session to the next.
- ◘ Movements can be controlled by the vaulter who can create his own kurs (exercises).
- ◘ Vaulting develops strength, balance, coordination, agility, and mobility.
- ◘ Vaulting is an anti-gravity and aerobic activity which helps normalize muscle tone. It helps to increase respiratory speech production and volume. It helps to develop supple limbs, and increases timing, motor planning, and self-esteem. These gains are carried over into activities of daily living.
- ◘ The rhythmic movement of the horse and the transitional movement components of the exercises, the anti-gravity position of the vaulter during the exercises, and the team peer pressure have a sensorimotor-integrative effect on the vaulter.
- ◘ Vaulting develops social bonding, respect and trust.
- ◘ It can be less expensive than riding as the horse can be shared by a group of vaulters at one time and a vaulting barrel can be used to supplement vaulting activities for practice or during unsuitable vaulting weather.
- ◘ *IT IS UNBELIEVABLE FUN!!!*

HOW SAFE IS IT?

"Properly supervised it (vaulting) is far safer than flat riding, certainly much safer than cross-country or stadium jumping" * J. Ashton Moore.

SKILLS INVOLVED IN LEADING A VAULTING GROUP

One must have basic 4-H or Pony Club knowledge of the horse. In addition, good, classic longeing techniques which involve keeping the horse consistently on an even 13 meter circle at an even pace are required. Allowing variations in speed, gait or the shape of the circle can cause the vaulter to lose his balance. The longeur must be able to recognize any problems with the horse such as pain, tiredness or stressed muscles which may influence the horse's responses. The longeur must also be able to longe for extended periods without getting dizzy or losing concentration.

The vaulting instructor should have basic knowledge of the mechanics of vaulting skills or gymnastics and preferably, have experienced the exercises, if not on the horse, then on the barrel. He or she must be able to determine the vaulter's balance abilities and range of skills so that he or she will challenge the individual but will not over tax him or her and cause him or her to fall. Other skills involved include maintaining a supple and well-conditioned horse, maintaining the vaulting arena, maintaining the barrel and exercise surface. The instructor must be knowledgeable about vaulting equipment and its proper fit (particularly the side-reins), how to "spot" the vaulter, (to stand at a distance, observe and respond to a vaulter's difficulty) and be able to guide the sidehelper.

EQUIPMENT FOR THE HORSE:

Vaulting surcingle: The **surcingle** needs to have a metal plate across the inside-top to which the handles are welded. The handles must be securely welded so they are rigid under pressure. The surcingle should have a loop

* USPC Convention speech. 1980.

for the foot on the off side or one on both sides, a top ring to which one can attach a rein for standing; rings on the sides for side-rein attachment are also essential. A competitive vaulting surcingle, which is more expensive but well constructed, will provide all vaulters with a secure base from which to move and is well worth the additional expense (Figure 1).

Side reins: reins, attached to each side of the horse from the bit to the surcingle, that help keep the horse's neck and head in position for vaulting.

Snaffle bridle with cavesson: (preferably dropped noseband), with a plain broken snaffle bit (no more than 2 joints).

Longeing Cavesson may be used according to AVA rules.

Pad: thick western style, (preferably with a **P.B.M. Western** inner pad to protect the horse). It must not be more than 2 inches thick. The pad may not extend more than 8 inches in front of the surcingle nor past the point of the croup.

Longe rein or longe line: a webbed tape 25 feet long, which is used to control the horse.

Long longeing whip: long enough for the thong to reach the horse (for 42.6 foot or 13 meter diameter circle). The whip should be light-weight and well-balanced.

Bandages: (protection boots) to protect the legs of the horse.

Leather gloves: to protect the longeur's hands.

Breast plate or collar: to keep the surcingle from sliding back-ward.

GROUND EQUIPMENT

Longeing area should be 59 to 66 feet [18 to 20 meters] in diameter, allow for a 42.6 foot [13 meter] circle plus eight or more feet around the outside of the circle to allow for movement of the vaulters and sidehelpers. The longeing area must always be separated from the riding areas by a fence.

Ground for longeing and barrel activities **must be soft to land on** and smooth with no holes, stones or other obstructions.

Barrel. Made out of an oil drum (preferably one and a half drums welded together). The drum is raised so that the top is 4 feet off the ground. Handles are welded onto the barrel (See Figure 2.)

Trampoline (small, mini) is a useful piece of equipment for warm-ups and to gain rhythm and height for vaulting-onto the horse or barrel. It can be used next to the barrel for practice "vault-on" exercises. (It is not used next to the horse). The trampoline can be safely used (when tolerated) with persons who have sensory-integrative dysfunction, learning disabilities, emotional disabilities and mentally retardation who do not have physical disabilities. With persons who have physical disabilities the trampoline should not be used without prior approval of their physician and physical/occupational therapist.

Mats for preliminary exercises and to place around the barrel.

VAULTER'S DRESS:

Clothing: Comfortable sweat suits, leotards or gymnastic suits with plenty of stretch are suitable. Jeans do not provide adequate freedom of movement for the vaulter and can be rough on the horse. Some vaulting books recommend shorts but these do not protect the vaulter against rub irritations from the pad or surcingle. Shorts are generally worn (as in Germany) where the horse does not use a pad.

Shoes: Smooth-soled tennis shoes are acceptable but gymnastic or vaulting shoes are the best. Hard-soled shoes, shoes with heels, boots or running shoes with stiff soles are damaging to the horse.

Helmets: Approved (lightweight preferred) ASTM helmets **without brims** are strongly recommended. Peaks are dangerous when moving around on the top of a horse. Heavy helmets can hurt the other vaulter when two vaulters are on the horse at the same time as they can hit each other with their heads. Riding helmets must fit the rider's head securely in all equine activities. The helmet must remain in place while the vaulter moves from one position to another.

(Helmets are not worn during the American Vaulting Association regional or national competitions.) Competition requires exercises such as *shoulder stance*, *roll ups* and exercises with several vaulters on the horse at one time. During these exercises vaulters can cause one another injuries or hurt the horse with helmets. Helmets should be worn during all adaptive or developmental vaulting programs with special vaulters. When these vaulters begin to compete with able bodied vaulters, they would meet AVA standards.

461

EXERCISE TERMS

Preliminary vaulting exercises are to prepare the vaulter's body for gymnastics on the moving horse. Vaulting is a strenuous activity which requires quick and agile body responses. In order for vaulting <u>to be safely performed</u>, the vaulter must <u>first</u> warm up the body and release tension; <u>second</u>, stretch the torso and limbs, and <u>third</u>, condition the body to build strengthen and endurance. This is especially important for a vaulter with abnormal muscle tone and a vaulter who is not symmetrical in the ability to use his or her trunk and limbs.

Warming-up and relaxation exercises are to prepare the vaulter's body, mind and muscle for activity. They are intended to reduce tension, relax the body and warm up the body's muscular system.

Stretching exercises are intended to help the vaulter gain full range of motion at each joint and allow the body to bend to its maximum ability without straining ligaments, tendons, muscles or connective tissue.

Conditioning and strengthening exercises help the vaulter to increase his coordination and ability to move with agility, suppleness and quickness. By increasing the amount and difficulty of these exercises, the vaulter increases his strength and endurance to perform strenuous activity.

Cooling-off exercises are used for stretching after vaulting to reduce soreness. Stretching after a sport has been found, by professional sports teams, to be the most effective time to gain elasticity since the muscle and connective tissue has been well exercised.

VAULTING TERMS (AVA, Pony Club)

Arabesque: the first vaulter sits on the horse and supports the second vaulter by the wrists. The second vaulter stands behind him or her with one leg raised away from the horse; or a vaulter who stands, holding on to the surcingle handles and raises the right leg up away from the horse.

Around the world or mill: sitting forward, then to inside, back-ward, to outside, and forward.

Base vaulter: the one sitting on the horse to support the other vaulter.

Barrel work: the practice "horse."

Basic exercise: compulsory vaulting exercises for competition.

Combination: an exercise involving two or more vaulters.

Compulsories: six required exercises in competitive vaulting: the Riding Seat, the Flag, the Mill, the Flank, the Stand, and the Scissors.

Croup: that part of the horse's back between the point of the hip and the tail.

Dynamic exercise: energetic and active movement.

Fest: competition events.

Flag: in a crawl position with diagonal arm and leg up and straight.

Flank: from basic seat to a scissor kick, to side-sit, to vault-off.

Grip: the handles of the vaulting surcingle.

Half flank: basic seat to scissor kick to a dismount to the inside.

Kneel: kneeling on the horse with arms up and out.

Kur or free style: any exercises which do not include the six required compulsories.

Leg-up: grasping the vaulter's leg to assist in the vault-on from the ground.

Longeing: moving a horse around the longeur in a circle with a 60 meter diameter (in vaulting).

Longeur: person who longes the horse during vaulting.

Mill: same as around the world.

Riding Seat: the basic position on the horse, sitting forward with arms up and to the side.

Roll-up: sitting backward, then somersaulting to land on the neck of the horse.

Scissors: compulsory exercise where the legs cross behind and the vaulter turns around.

Scissors Kick: swing the legs forward and backward to extension in an upward and full extension thrust.

Stand: free standing on the horse with arms up and out.

Static exercise: motionless, maintaining one position.

Surcingle: a girth with handles, secured around the horse behind the withers.

Vaulter: a person who vaults.

Vault-on: to jump or leap onto the horse's back.

Vault-off: to jump or leap off the horse in different forms; a dismount.

Vaulting Seat: the riding seat- the basic seat - the vaulter sits forward on the horse, holding on with the legs and extending the arms outward.

THE VAULTING BARREL

The vaulting barrel is used as a surrogate horse to practice the gymnastic exercises, and is especially useful for warm-up and conditioning workout before getting onto the horse. The use of the barrel has several major advantages:

- Skill can first be developed on the barrel where bumping and clumsy movements will not injure the horse.
- Exercises are more easily performed on a static surface.
- Vaulters can be divided so that one (or a group) work with the horse and the other (or small group) work on the barrel--in this way everyone is kept actively involved in the drills without standing around waiting for a turn.
- Vaulters can work independently on the barrels, with a spotter nearby to assist when needed.
- The barrel can be used indors during inclement weather so that a practice session need not be canceled.
- A vaulter may have his or her own barrel at home to practice on daily.
- Vaulters whose balance on the horse is just developing, may feel more secure and confident on the barrel which provides a steady base (this may be especially true for a special population and with vaulters with gravitational insecurity [poor tolerance to heights] or postural insecurity [inability to control one's body against gravity].)
- The barrel can be lowered (if adjustable) to decrease the fear of heights.
- The barrel allows those with severe physical dysfunctions to try progressive exercises since it is easier to help them on the barrel than on the horse.
- The barrel can be taken into a class room or other location for demonstrations.
- A school with children involved in a horse vaulting program may choose to have their own barrel and incorporate barrel activities into their gym classes.
- Children naturally like to climb and the barrel provides them with a safe climbing device.
- Barrel kurs can be developed for local, regional and national competition.
- The use of a barrel allows competitors to practice without the constant use of a horse.

COMPETITIVE VAULTING IS USUALLY PERFORMED WITH THE HORSE GOING TO THE LEFT. WHEN WORKING WITH PERSONS WHO HAVE DISABILITIES OR WHO HAVE MINIMAL NEUROLOGICAL OR DEVELOPMENTAL PROBLEMS, IT IS IMPORTANT TO VAULT TO THE **LEFT** AND **RIGHT** IN EQUAL AMOUNTS OF TIME IN ORDER TO DEVELOP SYMMETRICAL BALANCE AND STIMULATION IN THE VAULTERS.

THE VAULTING HORSE AND EQUIPMENT

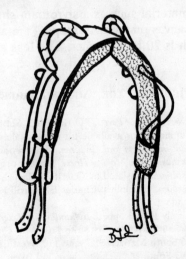

FIGURE 1. COMPETITION SURCINGLE

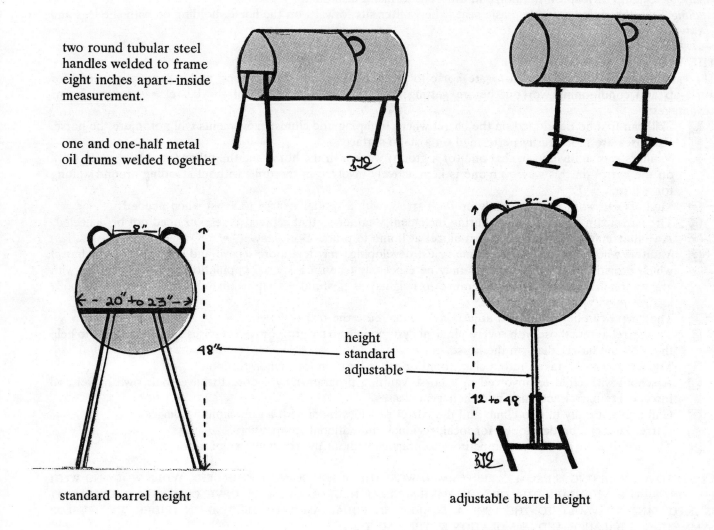

two round tubular steel handles welded to frame eight inches apart--inside measurement.

one and one-half metal oil drums welded together

height standard adjustable

standard barrel height

adjustable barrel height

STANDARD VAULTING BARREL

ADJUSTABLE HEIGHT VAULTING BARREL

The barrel is covered with protective material such as a styrofoam sheet or closed cell foam padding (sleeping bag under pad), then covered with canvas material. Wrapping metal handles with self stick tape makes them more user friendly. The barrel width is 20 to 23 inches. The legs and handles are welded to the barrel. All parts must be totally secure.

FIGURE 2. THE VAULTING BARREL

References and Resources

American Vaulting Association. (1991). *Catch the Exercise Fever Part I.* PO Box 3663. Saratoga, CA 95070-1663.

American Vaulting Association. Extensive list of vaulting videos available for rent or sale. PO Box 3663. Saratoga, CA 95070-1663.

Cratty, B.J. (1979). *Perceptual and Motor Development in Infants and Children.* Englewood: Prentice-Hall Inc.

Friedlaender, E. (1970). Vaulting, *The Art of Gymnastics on the Moving Horse.* Brattleboro: The Stephen Greene Press.

German National Equestrian Federation. (1987). *Vaulting.* translated by C Belton. English ed. London: Threshold Books Limited.

Kephart, N.C. (1971). *The Slow Learner in the Classroom.* Columbus: Charles E. Merrill Publishing Co.

Moore, J. Ashton. (1980). *Vaulting.* Unpublished handout.

Rosenthal, S.R. (1975). Risk Exercise and the Physically Handicapped. *Rehabilitation Literature.* 5. 36. 5. 144-149.

The United States Pony Club. *Vaulting Manual.* 893 South Matlack St., Suite 110, West Chester, PA 19382.

The United States Pony Club. (1982). *Longeing.* 893 South Matlack St., Suite 110, West Chester, PA 19382.

The United States Pony Club. (1982). *Bandaging.* 893 South Matlack St., Suite 110, West Chester, PA 19382.

The United States Pony Club. (1990). *Guide to Successful Longeing.* Videotape. 893 South Matlack St., Suite 110, West Chester, PA 19382.

20.01.2 VAULTING WARM-UPS

Barbara. T. Engel, MEd, OTR

Warm-ups before vaulting are extremely important to prevent muscle strains and injury. Warm-ups should be in the form of stretching (see page 396--section 18.04) and dynamic balance/coordination exercises. The following are some simple and fun active exercises to do before vaulting. For competative vaulters (and those who want to excell) see American Vaulting Association's *Catch the Exercise Fever Part I*. PO Box 3663. Saratoga, CA 95070-1663.

GYMNASTIK BALL EXERCISES

RIBBON EXERCISES

465

20.01.3   COMPULSORY VAULTING EXERCISES AND KURS

Stephanie C. Woods, BFA

VAULT-ON

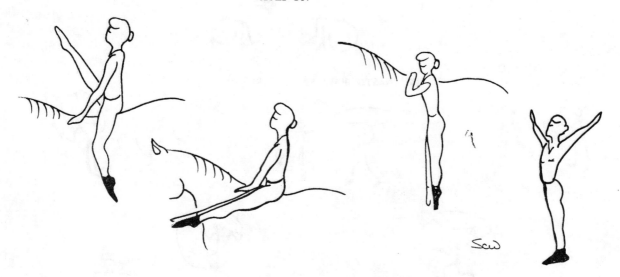

SIMPLE DISMOUNT

COMPULSORY VAULTING EXERCISES

SEAT-COMPULSORY   MILL-COMPULSORY   FLAG-COMPULSORY

FLANK--REVERSE FLAG OFF OUTSIDE--COMPULSORY

467

COMPULSORY VAULTING EXERCISES

FLAG

STAND

SISSORS

COMPULSORY VAULTING EXERCISES

ARABESQUE

FREE KNEEL

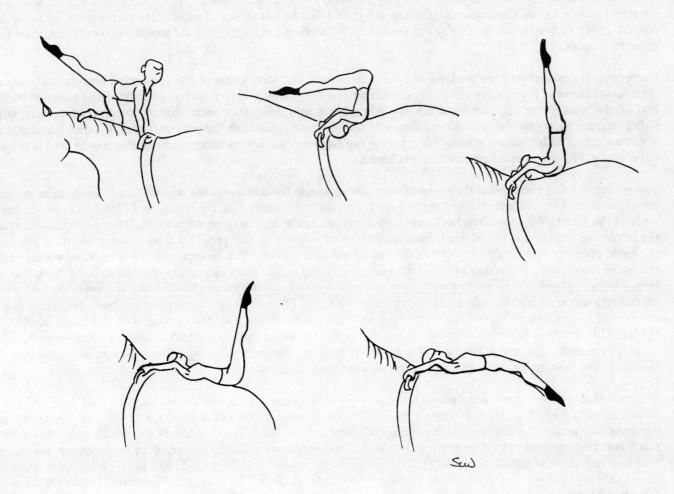

ROLL DOWN FROM REVERSE FLAG ON NECK

469

20.01.4 VAULTING IN A THERAPEUTIC RIDING PROGRAM AS TAUGHT BY A SPORTS VAULTING INSTRUCTOR

Carol Fuller, BA

Whenever the parent of a prospective vaulter calls inquiring about my therapeutic vaulting class, I make it quite clear I am not a physical therapist, that I am a sports vaulting instructor, that I have no special credentials; that vaulting itself may help his or her child, any child, improve his or her balance, coordination, spatial awareness, and other things too numerous to mention. Being able to stand on a moving horse almost always increases confidence and a positive self-image, something many special children lack and all of us need to improve.

I work with the Old Dominion School of Therapeutic Horsemanship*. Colleen Zanin, an occupational therapist and the program director, refers pupils to me. She has talked with their parents, their physical therapists, their teachers, and decides if they can physically do vaulting. She gives me a brief synopsis on the child's disability and special instructions for different problems I may or will encounter. For instance, one young man had muscles like stretched rubber bands. Consequently, Colleen suggested that he not do stretches at all, but strengthening exercises only. A young lady with cerebral palsy did slow stretch exercises only since normal stretching would not allow her muscles to relax.

Currently, all the vaulters I am working with have an autistic disorder. Because their attention span is so short and their muscle tone so low, we are not doing stretching or strengthening exercises, but go right to the horse or barrel and let the work there improve muscle tone. When I run into difficulties with teaching the special vaulter, with either emotional or physical limitations, I consult with Colleen. I also ask the parents for their input if something is not working. With vaulting, whether it is sports vaulting or remedial vaulting, each vaulter can be and is taught individually. His own special promise is developed.

Two volunteers and I work with the three or four young people for one hour. We do our best to keep them moving the entire time. One volunteer works at the barrel, one spots the vaulter on the horse, and I longe. On windy days, we lead the horse. We encourage the vaulter to touch the horse and to learn to pat him. The vaulter has to trust the horse, the coach, and the helpers. Since most special vaulters in this program have low muscle tone, we vary the basic exercises to help develop the vaulter in a balanced fashion. The mount is the only exercise we do while the horse stands still; everything else is done while the horse walks, trots or canters--for the sake of the horse. A helper balances the horse by putting weight on the outside handle of the surcingle while the volunteer on the inside encourages the vaulter to bounce up as high as he or she can. The helper catches him or her halfway up and urges the vaulter to pull him or herself the rest of the way into the seat. The *half flag* is done with the horse moving to the left with weight on the shin of the base leg, the right leg out, then the left, and held for a count of four, then six and then eight. The *mill* is performed in a similar fashion. We then encourage the vaulter to kneel, weight on his shins, first holding on, then freely, as a preliminary step to standing.

The individual vaulter determines his or her own rate of progress. As the vaulter builds trust and confidence, he or she is willing to do more and more exercises, working toward the point at which he or she can do all six compulsories and a one minute *kur* (any free style exercise on the horse that is not a compulsory) routine. We teach kur combinations before we teach the *scissors*, the *stand*, and the *flank* since so many kur exercises are easier than the last three compulsory exercises, and prepare the vaulter for the last three by developing the balance, coordination, strength and confidence necessary to do them. Kur exercises are illustrated in the Federation Equestre Internationale (FEI) rules for vaulting events available through the America Vaulting Association. Kur combinations are fun, and kur routines make the vaulter feel special. They are his own creation. If at all possible with whatever group we have, we do doubles. We sometimes put a vaulter from the sports vaulting group on the

---

* Old Dominion School of Therapeutic Horsemanship, Great Falls, Virginia 22066.

neck to base a child at the stand. Doubles are particularly good for children who do not like to be touched. If they have an opportunity to do something different and more exciting, they will submit to holding another vaulter and to being held. The double kur develops the teamwork that is one of the loveliest results of vaulting. It moves our special people forward toward the social integration so many lack.

Having a vaulter who can role model helps enormously. He or she makes it easier to teach a volunteer how to do an exercise. He or she can then show the special vaulter what to do. He or she can break down the parts of the exercise to manageable sections for the special people as well as show them the goals they are working toward. My volunteer demonstrators have been as young as nine years.

I ask my best "teacher" to help me, not necessarily my best vaulter. He or she almost always can think of a way to explain an exercise to a fellow vaulter that is different from the way I say it. All vaulters have things they can do well. When vaulters grasp a concept, they become the role model for the others; they become the teachers for that one exercise.

I teach the volunteers sports vaulting principles so that they in turn can teach barrel work while I longe the horse. The principles taught include:
1 All exercises are done squarely over the horse's back, that is: shoulders are square over the surcingle handles in the flag and are even when looking from the front; both feet are squarely placed on the horse's back, touching the surcingle in the stand, and shoulders are squarely over the feet.
2 All exercises are done in alignment with the horse, that is: the flag itself and flag type exercises, including arabesques in the cossack loop, are done with the arm and leg extended along the horse's spine. *Roll down* must be done straight down the horse's spine or the vaulter falls off one side or the other.
3 All exercises can be broken down into manageable blocks for the individual vaulter.
4 If the exercise is not secure, start at the bottom, at the feet or the base leg, to fix it. If the base of the vaulter is secure, look at the way he or she is holding the grips. Are his or her shoulders locked? Would it work better with an underhanded grip instead of an overhanded grip?
5 The vaulters must respect the horse. They cannot abuse it by digging the horse with their knees and toes; they must be on their shins. They cannot thump down on the horse's back; they must slide into place. No matter what they weigh or what their disability, they must be <u>soft</u>. They cannot waste the horse, i.e., staying on the horse arguing about what they will or will not do while the horse walks, trots, or canters the circle. If they thump or dig or waste, they do laps, pushups, or simply must get off and miss the rest of their turn. A horse will tolerate behavior other animals will not; therefore, it is up to the coach to protect the horse from abusive vaulters.
6 The vaulter must respect his or her teammates and the coaches. Calling names, throwing things or hitting is not acceptable behavior.
7 Praise the horse. Just as people thrive on praise, so do animals. At the end of the session, everyone pats his horse and thanks him with praise.

In some way, we are all handicapped or dysfunctional. We all carry emotional scars and physical limitations. It is a question of degree. Consequently, I do not feel sorry for my special vaulters, nor do I coddle them. These young people, like all of us, do not deserve pity; they deserve respect. If I feel sorry for them, it leaves me wide open to be manipulated by them, for children are master manipulators. We do not assume that because they are different, they cannot vault. We teach them with a minimum of correction and with lots of positive reinforcement just as we do the sports vaulters. We set basic guidelines and expect that they be followed. I have been told that the program is a success because we regard these vaulters as just plain vaulters, as athletes. We try to determine their native abilities and push them toward their maximum performance.

I believe vaulting helps the special vaulter become the best person he can be.

Reference
America Vaulting Association, P.O. Box 3663, Saratoga, CA 95070-1663.

20.02.1   POLOCROSSE

Susan Rogowski, OTR

The following is an overview of polocrosse. I have included a brief history as well as general information about the game itself. For more information please refer to the reference given at the end of the article.

Polocrosse is one of the fastest growing equestrian sports of the century. It was originally developed in Australia by modifying and expanding an exercise the English used to enhance their equestrian skills. The original interest of the exercise was to teach riders how to effectively supple and control their horses. In 1938, Mr. and Mrs. Hirst, from Sidney, Australia, became intrigued with the exercise during a visit they made to the National School of Equitation at Kinston Vale near London. They knew the game could be adapted to create a perfect outdoor sport which would be suited to Australia's terrain. As a result of the their visit to England, the Hirst's asked Mr. A. Pitty, an experienced horseman and polo player, to help with the creation of the polocrosse game. After many hours, they developed a rule book for polocrosse. Then with the help of Mr. Pitty, the Hirsts performed the first demonstration, and polocrosse was born.

The first polocrosse club was soon formed and its popularity began to grow. Its growth was interrupted as a result of the Second World War when it was almost forgotten. But luckily for us it was not lost and since then its popularity has grown and spread throughout the world. In 1976 the International Polocrosse Association was formed, which recognizes the American and Canadian Polocrosse Associations.

The object of polocrosse is to score as many goals as possible. The thrill of the sport is that one is required not only to put equestrian skills to the test, but also to think and react quickly, in unison with one's horse and teammates. The team who wins is not always the fastest but the one which can control their horses with ease and work well together. To be good riders need to be able to work closely with their teammates, outsmart the other team and control their horses' speed at all times. The rules and regulations of polocrosse are simple and straightforward. Most of the them were developed to protect both the horse and rider. The rules also cover the playing field, the horses, the racquet, the ball, the players, and the umpire.

THE FIELD

The playing field should be flat, 160 yards [146.3 meters] long by 60 yards (54.86 meters) wide. There is a one hundred yard mid-field section, and two thirty yard goal scoring areas, one at either end of the field. The line dividing the goal scoring area from the rest of the field is called the penalty line. Two posts are placed eight feet apart at each end of the field to form the goals. In front of each goal is a semicircle of 11 yards [10.06 meters] in diameter. Players must stay behind this line when scoring a goal. The goal scoring area as well as all boundaries of the field should be well marked (Figure 1).

The rule book does not specify the type of horse which may be used, but mentions types of horse which are <u>not</u> appropriate. In general the horse must be physically fit and must be one that can be controlled at all times by the players so it will not injure another horse or rider during the game. The rule book also specifies that all horses must wear bell boots, polo wraps or galloping boots. A saddle without a horn is used, along with a breastplate, and a bridle and a bit without protruding side bars.

THE EQUIPMENT

Each player needs to have a racquet. A polocrosse racquet consists of a stick three or four feet in length with a loose twisted thread net on one end which is used to carry the ball. The polocrosse ball, four inches in diameter, is made from thick-skinned sponge rubber and weighs about six ounces. All players in a therapeutic riding program must wear Pony Club approved, protective head gear with a full harness and a flexible or snap off brim.

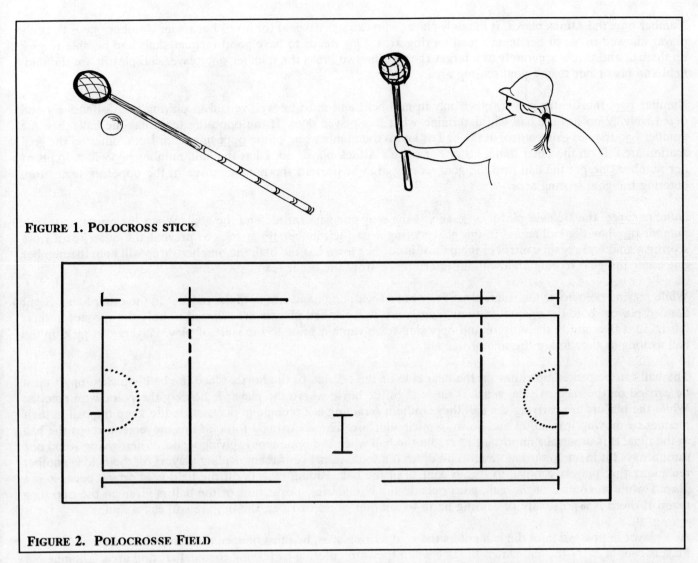

FIGURE 1. POLOCROSS STICK

FIGURE 2. POLOCROSSE FIELD

There can be either one or two umpires who are mounted on horses that can be easily controlled in order to keep up with the players on the field. The umpires should be trained and certified by a national association such as the American Polocrosse Association (APA) in the United States.

THE GAME
The game is divided into as many as eight **chukkas**. Each chukkas is six to eight minutes long. There are six players on each team who are divided into two sections of three players each. Each section alternates playing chukkas to give the horses a chance to rest. This is extremely important since each player can use only one horse during a game. The first section of each team lines up, nose to tail, at mid-field. Players line up in position, number <u>one's</u> first, <u>two's</u> next and <u>three's</u> last, with the opposing team between them and their goal. The umpire faces the players and throws the ball within reach of everyone. The first player to pick the ball up will head toward his or her goal. As the players go for the ball, they need to be able to pick it up and cradle it, give wood (giving wood is when one hits the opponent's racquet and attempts to dislodge the ball from the racquet) and run interference.

POSITIONS
The players are numbered for the position they play and each number has a special job to perform. Number <u>one</u> takes up the **Attack** position, number <u>two</u> is the **Center** and number <u>three</u> is the **Defense**. The rider's position delineates the area of the field in which he can play. It also determines the action the players take and the skills they utilize.

Number <u>one</u>, the **Attack** player, is the only player who can score a goal for his or her team. Number <u>one</u> is the only player allowed in his or her team's goal scoring area. <u>One</u> needs to have good racquet skills and be able to pick up the ball and throw accurately at a target (goal). The two areas the number <u>one</u> player can play in are the mid-field and his or her team's goal scoring area.

Number <u>two</u>, the **Center** player, plays only in mid-field and must be well-versed in playing both offensively and defensively. Who has the ball will determine what this player does. If the opposing team has the ball, then the number <u>two</u> tries to gain control of the ball or keeps the number <u>one</u> of the <u>opposing</u> team from entering the goal scoring area. If on the other hand, his or her team's **Attack** player no. 1 has the ball, number <u>two</u> will help his or her number <u>one</u> get the ball into the goal scoring area or prevent the number three of the opposing team from entering the goal scoring area.

Number <u>three</u>, the **Defense** player or goalie, is the only one who can defend the goal. When the opposing team's number <u>one</u> has the ball and is in the goal scoring area the number <u>three</u> tries to prevent the other team from scoring a goal and regain control of the ball. If his or her team has the ball, the number <u>three</u> will help the number <u>one</u> enter the goal scoring area without interference from the other team.

While playing polocrosse the riders steer their horses with one hand and hold the racquet in the other hand. Right handed players hold the racquet in their right hand. Left handed players are allowed to hold the racquet in their left hand if they notify the umpire and opposing team captain prior to the start of play. Players can pick up the ball as long as they follow the line of the ball.

The ball can be picked up either on the near side or the off side of the horse. Once the ball is picked up, it must be carried on the racquet side, which is the side of the horse where the player is holding the polocrosse racquet. While the players are carrying the ball they cradle it (cradling is a technique players used to keep the ball in their racquet by moving it in an up and down, semicircular arc. The centrifugal force of this movement keeps the ball in the net). It is especially important to cradle the ball when the opponent is giving wood. When giving wood one must always hit in an upward motion; to hit down is a foul against your team. Riding players off the field is another technique that players can use to regain control of the ball. Riding players off the field is effective, because if a player, while in control of the ball, goes outside the boundaries, possession of the ball is given to the opposing team. If there is a possibility of causing harm to another horse or rider, the umpire will call a foul.

As a player in possession of the ball enters the goal scoring area, he must bounce the ball or have it passed to him. Players cannot carry the ball across the line when they are entering or leaving the goal scoring area. The number <u>one</u>only may attempt to make a goal from outside the 11 yard semicircle in front of the goal posts. Once a goal is scored, the players line up as quickly as possible because the clock does not stop. The faster one lines up, the longer one actually gets to play.

SUMMARY

Polocrosse is a sport that involves riding skills and team work. A player must be able to control and steer his or her horse independently. He or she needs to have a horse that can perform with a minimum of effort since the rider/player needs to concentrate on the game and not his horse. He or she must interact with and assist the players on his or her team. While independent effort is important in polocrosse, it is the <u>group</u> that plays as a team that will succeed. By combining the athletic requirements of riding with the social aspects of a team sport, polocrosse is a recreational pursuit with something to offer everyone.

For more information please contact: Equus Outreach; P.O. Box 67, New Milford, N.Y. 10959.
or American Polocrosse Association, 601 Rustic Road, Durango, CO 81301.

References
American Polocrosse Association, (1986). *Polocrosse Rules and Regulations and Information on the Game*. Durango, CO.
Brownson, L. (1990). *Polocrosse Practice for Individuals and Teams*.
Wolfe, F. (1990). *Polocrosse Strategy*. Warwick, NY.

20.02.2   POLOCROSSE AND THERAPEUTIC RIDING PROGRAMS

Susan Rogowski, OTR

*Note: Please read the chapter on polocrosse that precedes this one before continuing, in order
to become familiarized with rules and regulations of the game. It will also give one a general
understanding of how to play the game.*

Polocrosse has some unique qualities which make it especially suitable for therapeutic riding programs as well as programs that are involved in mainstreaming riders. These aspects include:
1) The ability to incorporate all levels of riding skills within the game
2) It can be played by children, teenagers and adults.

The game is not only beneficial for able-bodied riders but has tremendous potential for the disabled rider. Sara Powell, a physical therapist, and Susan Rogowski, an occupational therapist have developed the following concepts on how polocrosse can be incorporated into disabled riding programs. These concepts were developed after the two therapists had the opportunity to play with a recognized polocrosse team and compete in recognized regional matches. The first demonstration of polocrosse for the disabled was held in 1989 at the NARHA annual conference. It was called "Polocrosse for Everyone"[1] and players consisted of both able-bodied and disabled riders.

Just as horseback riding is not the ideal therapeutic medium for everyone, polocrosse is also not for all riders. By looking at the classifications of therapeutic riding, it is easier to understand how polocrosse may be incorporated. The three primary classifications for therapeutic riding: Sport, Education, and Medicine. Each classification has been expanded and divided into a variety of divisions, each designed to achieve specific goals. Where does polocrosse fit within these classifications?

Polocrosse is an equine sport and as such it naturally belongs within the Sports classification. It can be used in one of two ways: 1) in its purity as a sport, or it can be 2) broken down into its elements. It is used in its purity as a sport when disabled individuals join established polocrosse teams or form their own team. Within sports classes, components of polocrosse can be taught to those individuals not ready to join a team.

Principles of polocrosse can be incorporated into some divisions within the Education classification. When using polocrosse within this category, elements of the game are taught so that individuals can learn specific skills. The skill taught may be physical as in eye-hand coordination, or psychosocial as in learning how to work with others.

Polocrosse may not be used within all Medical Classifications. For example, polocrosse could not be incorporated into hippotherapy. It could be used in equine-assisted therapy to increase the range of motion of an arm which sustained an injury.

Which individuals could benefit and in what ways? Generally individuals with the following diagnoses, but not limited to these, could be considered as suitable candidates: mild cerebral palsy, moderate to mild mental retardation, developmental delay, emotional impairment, learning disability, hearing impaired, amputation, and head trauma. The severity of a person's condition and resulting deficits must be taken into account and may prevent the rider from playing in a game since this is a active and strenuous game.

Conditions which are contraindications for riding are also not appropriate for polocrosse and individuals with these conditions should not play: such as uncontrolled seizures, acute herniated-disks, spinal instabilities, acute arthritis, serious heart pathology, fragile bones, poor postural control and detached retina.

VALUE OF POLOCROSSE FOR THE DISABLED RIDER

First of all polocrosse can help develop and improve basic riding skills and the individual's ability to control and guide his horse. The exercises help to develop high level balancing skills and promote agility of both horse and rider. Gross motor skills are improved as well as eye-hand coordination. Sequencing skills are enhanced as riders learn how to play polocrosse. Social skills and the ability to work with others are additional elements which can be improved as individuals work in a group. These are only a few examples of areas of performance which can be improved while playing polocrosse. It is required that the instructor have knowledge of the game as well as have played with a recognized polocrosse team. By having this experience, the instructor will find it easier to teach students the appropriate skills and the proper use of equipment. He or she will be able to explain the strategies required for each position the riders will need to learn. When one knows how to play the game and analyze its components, he or she can teach any suitable rider how to play the game.

TEACHING POLOCROSSE

To analyze what is involved in playing polocrosse one must break the game down into components. In order to play, the riders need to have adequate riding skills on which to build specific maneuvers required in the game. Each rider will also need to learn how to manipulate the polocrosse racquet. When first learning how to use the racquet, however, it is good to start on the ground, without the horse. This has two advantages, first, one can practice almost anywhere at any time. Second, one does not have to worry about controlling the horse while simultaneously learning how to use the racquet. After the basic riding and racquet skills have been mastered, the riders can progress to various aspects of the game. One good test to determine if the riders are ready to be involved in a game is the ability to ride a walk-trot dressage test independently. When the riders are able to complete the test, they are ready to hold both reins in their non-dominant hand while holding the dominant hand on the thigh. While maintaining this position they should walk their horses and practice circling, turning and halting. Riders can perform any number of movements which will help them to learn how to steer with one hand. As the riders' skills improve, challenging them by incorporate trotting and cantering into their exercises. (The canter should only be included in these exercises if they have previously been mastered as part of basic riding skills.) After the riders have learned to steer one-handed at the walk, trot, and through all transitions, they are ready to begin polocrosse.

Next, have the riders hold their racquets in their dominant hand going over the steps previously outlined. The weight of the polocrosse racquet will change the riders' balance on the horse thus making them feel slightly different. When they have become accustomed to the racquet while riding, they can learn to carry the ball in the racquet while repeating the previous exercises. This will require the riders to gain a certain level of skill with the racquet in order to maintain the ball in the net.

While off the horse one can practice picking the ball up, cradling it, catching and throwing it at a target. When the riders feel comfortable with each skill from the ground, they can progress to performing them astride the horse at a walk and later at the trot. The instructor needs to remember that accuracy and controlling the horse is more important than speed.

Elements of polocrosse can be turned into games to facilitate learning. For instance, an obstacle course can be created to help the rider practice steering around barrels or he can pick up a ball with the polocrosse racquet and put it into a basket after completing the barrel portion of the obstacle course. The instructor can plan a competition where individuals throw the balls at a target or complete relay races using the polocrosse racquet. These are only a few examples of games that can be organized to help the riders to learn the required skills while playing a game. In this way polocrosse skills may be incorporated into other classes.

The equipment as well as the rules and regulations of the game should be the same when played by disabled or able-bodied persons. Certain modifications or extra precautions may need to be made when riders are learning the game. For example, polocrosse is a sport which is supposed to be played outside in a very large field. When players are beginning to play, it is perfectly suitable to start in an indoor arena or smaller fenced area. In this way the rider can learn how to (1) control his horse and (2) use his polocrosse racquet in a controlled environment. Once a rider has gained the necessary skills he or she can advance to a larger outdoor field. Please keep in mind that a player who excels in a smaller controlled area may face new problems when playing in a large field. This leads into a second precaution in regard to the horse. The safest horse within a controlled ring situation such as found in usual therapeutic riding programs may not be suitable for polocrosse. The horse must be controllable in a large field where other horses are cantering beside or in front of him. The horse should also be able to stand safely, with no kicking, while very close to a number of other horses. Have an able-bodied rider ride a horse first among other horses in order to make sure it is suitable. Keep in mind how much control this person has over the horse which the disabled rider may <u>not</u> have.

The instructor who has played polocrosse should be able to assess the rider's ability and tell whether he or she is ready to play with an established polocrosse team (or a program team). In general, a person is ready to go into an established team when he can walk, trot, and canter while controlling the horse and carrying a polocrosse racquet. He or she should also be able to pick up the ball and carry it while the horse is walking. A good place for beginners to start is by playing a number <u>two</u> position, the Center. The number <u>two</u> player does not need to have good stick skills but should have the required riding skills. As a rider feels more comfortable he or she can attempt <u>other</u> positions and skills. The beginner polocrosse player also plays at a slower pace as he or she is trying to put all his or her skills together.

Is polocrosse for everyone? Are riders with disabilities ready for polocrosse? Is polocrosse ready for riders with disabilities? Judging from the response received so far the answer is a resounding YES. Riders are no longer satisfied with riding around in a ring for fifteen years. Instructors are looking for ideas to keep their riders interested. Both are attracted to polocrosse because of the challenges the game offers through its ever-changing environment. Besides polocrosse is a game which is fun for everyone!!

[1] Ms. Rogowski of Pine Island, New York, presented "Polocrosse for Everyone", in August 1991, at the 7th International Riding Congress for the Disabled, in Aarhus, Denmark; and in July of 1990, at a conference at Borderland Farm, in New York, Ms. Powell and Ms Rogowski presented the benefits of polocrosse for the disabled.

20.03.1 SWAPPING WHEELCHAIRS FOR A HORSE AND CARRIAGE

. . . even if only for a few hours.

Sandy Dota

In 1986 while schooling a very unhappy horse, I (a paraplegic) was bucked off, resulting in a hip fracture. It took almost a year for my hip to heal properly. Instructions from the doctor included "no riding." Another surgery would be required to take all the "hardware" (as they call it) out. That meant another year of no riding! Needless to say, I was becoming a very ornery person to live with. My husband Louie protested. *"If you don't get out to a barn and roll around in some manure, we're all going to be crazy!"* He was right. I desperately needed a "horse fix" (something I do not have to explain to all of you horse addicts).

So I thought, if I can't get on the back of a horse, I'll get behind one! Desperate but still having reservations, I decided to call on the expertise of Susan Greenall. Susan was instrumental in the establishment of the **National Association of Driving for the Disabled (NADD)** in Pennsylvania; is chairperson of the Driving Committee, **North American Riding for the Handicapped Association (NARHA)**; has 27 years of experience with horses, and is a rated judge for the Eastern Competitive Trail Riding Association and the American Driving Society. Susan's credentials made me feel secure in this new venture.

Prior to calling Susan, I had received many invitations to come drive with her, always responding, "No thanks, driving is not for me!" Carriage driving was an equine sport that did not interest me at all. I felt that true interaction and communication with your horse could only be achieved by sitting astride. You can just forget about friendship and bonding when you have eight feet of reins between you and your horse. Susan (and her pony) proved me wrong (to my delight)!

I started driving in 1988 and I cannot begin to explain the wonderful experience this has been. I drive Susan's pony *Cloudy Skies* (aka Chrissy) and her appaloosa, *Champagne Toast* for recreation and in competition. I use several different carriages (with slight modifications). Communication and interaction with the horse is very similar in driving and riding. In driving, this becomes natural even for me as I have no use of my legs. As far as bonding goes, I am very fond of *Chrissy* and *Champagne* and, they have me trained very well -chilled carrots end every lesson. Driving tandem has been my latest achievement!

I am an officer and director of the NARHA board, and one of my main goals is to promote driving in NARHA operating centers (there are approximately 475 centers in the US, Puerto Rico and Canada). To date, only about 40 operating centers offer driving. Carriage driving in some ways is more suitable than riding for some disabled people. Consider complete spinal quadriplegia for example, in which all four limbs are affected. To balance astride a horse would be impossible. To drive a horse from a carriage would not. The driver could choose a wheelchair-accommodating vehicle or a regular carriage with modifications made to suit his needs. Carriage driving is also more suitable for people with disabilities that require the regular use of an indwelling Foley catheter, since sitting astride would be contra-indicated. Transfers to and from the carriage also would not affect the catheter or wearer. And, let's not forget the fun of carriage driving. I think it's great fun to "toddle on down the road" chatting away with a friend beside me. This is a sport that can be shared by the whole family for years and years. My husband even enjoys driving Chrissy and he has never sat astride a horse in his life. Regarding competition, this is a sport where neither age nor disability is a factor. Everyone in the ring is equally judged on their ability.

Source
North American Riding for the Handicapped Association Driving Committee P.O. Box 33150 Denver, CO 80233.
National Association of Driving for the Disabled (NADD) 87 Main Street, Fort Plain, NY 13339.

20.03.2 DRIVING - AN ASSET TO ANY THERAPEUTIC RIDING PROGRAM

Susan Greenall, BS, Judge

The introduction of driving for the disabled is relatively recent in the United States, but not so in England. Established in England since 1975, driving has expanded to include 565 drivers in 100 programs. The availability of wheelchair-accommodating vehicles has made this progress possible. Such vehicles are not offered in the United States, therefore most programs are faced with the quandary of having to have one built locally or modifying a cart. This problem is not insurmountable and many wonderful innovations have resulted from the trials and errors of many. Several disabled drivers have been able to mainstream into American Driving Society competitions with great success, and more are sure to follow.

WHO BENEFITS FROM DRIVING? ALMOST EVERYONE. Driving can be used to introduce timid students to being around horses. For those who find riding difficult or impossible but have the head and truck stability (either independent or supported), driving is the alternative. Driving can be used to develop confidence in riders when they are experiencing fear of speed or confusion in dressage. The best part of driving is being able to share a drive through the country-side.

SAFETY COMES FIRST. No one should attempt driving before having a complete understanding of the equipment and safety procedures. Three videos, *Drive Safely, Drive Smartly* [1] and *Breaking and Training the Driving Horse* [2] *Driving for the Disabled, Getting Underway* [3] are strongly recommended. The horse, carriage, and harness should be evaluated by an experienced driver before use in a program. Both the able-bodied "whip" and the ground assistant should be completely familiar with harnessing, putting to and driving the horse. Both should be adept at their driving techniques.

CHOOSING THE HORSE. Choosing the horse (or pony) is the most important part of the driving program. A program can choose to have a reliable riding horse trained to drive, or acquire a driving horse. Just like riding horses, they must exhibit certain qualities. The horse should have considerable experience in the type of work for which he is to be used. Therefore, a race horse or a high stepping show horse would not be suitable unless they have been re-trained. The horse *must* stand quietly and for prolonged periods of time, anywhere. The horse should work from voice commands, start and stop smoothly. He should be familiar with ring work, as well as having cross country experience.

CHOOSING THE CART. The two wheeled cart is the least expensive and easiest to obtain, but does not offer the stability of a four wheeled carriage. The Meadowbrook type cart has been used the most, basically because it is of simple design and can be modified quite easily. When installing ramps for loading wheelchairs, weight becomes a factor and must be considered if using a small pony. The seat may be modified to accommodate persons with almost any type of disability without the use of a wheelchair. Four wheeled carriages are by far the easiest to use and provide the best ride. In order to be considered safe, the style of vehicle must be such that the front wheels cut under the body. Drivers can easily transfer from their wheelchairs into modified seats before the horse is put to the cart. Wonderful wheelchair accommodating vehicles are available from England, but still not in the United States, unless one builds his own. Show buggies, racing sulkies and pipe carts do not offer the stability or support that is needed for a disabled driver and should not be used. Regardless of what type of cart is used, it must fit the horse or pony.

IN MODIFYING THE CART TO ACCOMMODATE PERSONS WITH VARIOUS DISABILITIES, versatility is very important. Most wheelchair- accommodating vehicles are designed with a removable seat so that an ambulatory student can use them also. Standard two and four wheeled carriages can be modified easily. Figure 1 shows ways to convert a standard seat. Figure 2 shows how a permanent seat can be specially designed to adjust to the disabled driver's needs. It is very often the case that considerable adjustments must be tried before the ideal situation is achieved.

479

Removable seat cushions allow the driver to use his own wheelchair cushion comfortably. Upper body control can be obtained with a safety harness. Suggested types are the NASCAR racing harness and parachute harness, both of which offer a quick release design. With proper installation, these harnesses can be added and removed as needed.

When securing the wheelchair into the cart, follow the manufactures directions. It is advisable to practice with an empty chair until the assistants become proficient with the procedure of both securing and releasing. Be sure that the method being used not only prevents forward/backward motion, but also side-ward motion. It is here that design of the carriage is most important to be in accordance with the method in which the wheelchair is secured. Should the disabled driver need to be supported in the wheelchair, a quick release harness should be used rather then a method that ties the person to the chair.

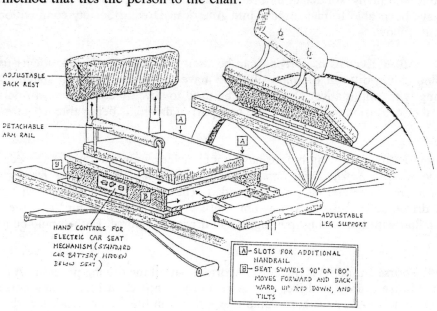

FIGURE 1   CARRIAGE MODIFICATION

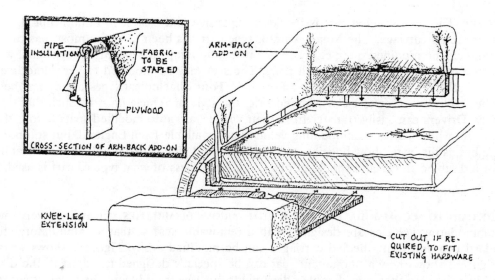

FIGURE 2   ADAPTED PERMANENT SEAT

ACCESSING THE CARRIAGE: Two wheeled carts must be accessed while hooked to the horse. The horse must stand for this exercise. The ground person is to be at the horse's head, the able-bodied driver is to be in the left hand seat, holding a set of auxiliary reins, and the helper is to be with the disabled driver. Loading procedure will vary with every person and every carriage. Four wheeled carriages may be accessed before putting to, giving the advantage of plenty of time to make adjustments. The able bodied driver **MUST** be in the carriage and have the auxiliary reins in hand when putting to. Careful attention should be made to wheelchair-accommodating vehicles. The weight of the wheelchair and two people on the ramp will cause the vehicle to shift or move against the horse. Some carriages have devices to prevent this and attention should be given as to how to use them properly. Electric wheelchairs are too heavy to be used in most carts. The disabled driver should transfer into a light wheelchair.

Regardless of the method chosen by the team of helpers, it is strongly advisable to practice several loading sessions without having the horse hooked. In a four wheeled carriage, this presents no problem; however, with a two wheeled cart, the shafts must be resting on a secure object at the same angle in which they will be on the horse, which is slightly inclined. Two people should be assigned to the shafts in order to prevent the cart from tipping backward during loading. The disabled person should advise the team as to the method with which he or she is most comfortable.

THE LESSON. Basic control of the horse can be achieved through progressive lessons which include the walk, slow trot, working trot and halt. Figure eights and serpentine, as well as schooling dressage movements will develop a feel for the horse and carriage. As the driver's skills advance, additional exercises can be used. Obstacle courses consisting of traffic cones with balls balanced on top can be set up from the simple to the challenging. A 40 meter by 80 meter dressage ring will offer an opportunity to drive both *Training* and *Preliminary American Driving Society* tests. Driving style such as that used in competitions should be encouraged, and can be achieved by many disabled drivers.

MAINSTREAMING. Should driving ability warrant, disabled drivers can consider open driving competition as a goal. It is important to keep in mind that mainstreaming means competing on equal terms with everyone else; therefore, the disabled driver should arrive prepared to do just that.

FOR DRIVERS USING A WHEELCHAIR

Before loading, double check that all harness adjustments to the cart are correct. The cart should move only an inch or two when pushed forward or backward against the horse. *A Header,* using a lead rope attached to the halter, stands at the horse's head. The able-bodied driver takes his or her place in the cart and has control of the horse through the auxiliary reins. He or she also holds the driver's reins. The header remains at the horse's head. *Helper #1* prepares the cart for loading. This header should make sure that 1) tailgate/ramp are in proper position and secured. 2) devices used to secure the wheelchair are in position to receive the chair.

SPECIAL NOTE: In a two wheeled cart, loading will cause the shafts to raise when the weight of the wheelchair and two people get on the ramp. Care must he taken to hold down the shafts. In a four wheeled cart, the movement on the ramp will often cause the carriage to move forward, causing the horse to have to brace through the breeching. If the carriage has one, apply the brake during loading to prevent this. Some carriages have special devices to correct these problems and care should be made as to how to properly use them. Wheel blocks can also be used.

Helper #2 pushes the wheelchair up the tailgate/ramp, and with the assistance of *helper #1,* secures the wheelchair. The tailgate/ramp is then put into driving position or removed. The disabled driver is handed the reins and adjustments are made if needed. Upon direction of the able-bodied driver or the disabled driver, *the header* releases the horse and the session begins.

FOR DRIVERS WHO TRANSFER FROM A WHEELCHAIR

IN A TWO WHEELED CART. Care must be taken that the wheels of the cart do not move; therefore, blocking the wheels with wheel blocks, both front and behind, is important.

<u>For front entry carts</u>: The wheelchair is brought to the front of the cart and adjusted so that the disabled driver can transfer to the floor of the cart. *Helper #1* assists the disabled driver in the transfer, while *Helper #2* removes the wheelchair. Both helpers may assist in raising the disabled driver to the seat, or the driver may be able to do so himself. Once the driver is secure, the blocks are removed from the wheels.

<u>For rear entry cart</u>: The wheelchair is brought as close as possible to the back of the cart. The cart wheels are blocked. Under the direction of the disabled driver the transfer may be made with one or two helpers. It may be made directly to the seat, or to the floor of the cart and then to the seat. The disabled driver should be secure in the seat before removing the wheel blocks.

IN A FOUR WHEELED CARRIAGE. The carriage may already be hooked to the horse before transfer, or hooked after the disabled driver is in the carriage. The decision as to which method is used depends upon the team of helpers and with which procedure they are comfortable. The transfer should be made under direction of the disabled driver. Only a carriage in which the front wheels cut under the body should be used. The front wheels of the carriage should be turned in order to allow for the most room for the wheelchair. However, the wheels should never be turned to the extent that they rest against the *reach* (the support that connects the front axle to the rear axle).

The wheelchair is brought into position by *Helper #1*. *Helper #2* blocks one of the carriage wheels, both front and back, and may assist in the transfer, then remove the wheelchair. Depending on his disability, the driver may be able to transfer to the floor of the carriage himself. Raising the disabled driver to the seat may or may not require assistance. When the driver is secure in the seat, the wheel blocks are removed. The *Header* should carefully step the horse forward until the carriage is straight.

If the horse is not hooked at this point, the following procedure should be followed. If the carriage has a brake, it should be applied during this process. With a *Header* at the front of the horse and the able-bodied driver in the carriage with the disabled driver, the two *Helpers* pull the carriage to the horse. The able-bodied driver and the driver are given their respective reins. Traces are attached, then the over-girth, then the breeching. Upon direction of the able-bodied driver or the disabled driver, the header releases the horse and the session begins.

NARHA Driving Guidelines For Open Competition
- ☐ The disabled driver **MUST** always be accompanied by an able-bodied person.
- ☐ A ground person **MUST** always be available.
- ☐ The vehicle **MUST** be suitable for the type of competition entered.
- ☐ Auxiliary reins are strongly recommended
- ☐ (Both disabled and able-bodied drivers must wear approved hard hats with full harness when NARHA insurance is used.)

Rules for competitions may be obtained through:

American Driving Society	American Horse Show Association
Box 160	220 East 42nd street
Metamora, MI 48455	New York, NY 10017

Pleasure Shows
Pleasure driving competitions offer a variety of classes, all of which are considered suitable for a disabled driver. Adherence to the rules as set down by the American Driving Society (ADS) and the American Horse Show Association (AHSA) is mandatory. Should a competitor feel that, for safety purposes only, he needs special consideration, he must approach the acting technical delegate and/or management. It is up to these individuals whether or not the consideration will be allowed. Regardless, NARHA safety guidelines should be upheld.

Combined Driving Events

Combined driving events offer a higher level of competition for both the horse and driver. Due to the complexity of such events, only training and preliminary level competitions are considered suitable for a disabled driver. It is strongly suggested that a disabled driver have extensive experience before considering such an event, as the marathon offers a cross country challenge often not dealt with in programs. However, disabled drivers have competed both safely and successfully in such events and participation is encouraged. Adherence to the rules as set down by the American Driving Society (ADS) and the American Horse Show Association (AHSA) is mandatory. <u>Special note</u> should be made that the able-bodied assistant must be dressed as a groom when sitting next to the disabled driver in phase A, dressage, and phase C, obstacles. In phase B (cross country) it is strongly recommended that both able-bodied and disabled drivers use hard hats secured with a properly fitting chin strap. Only two seater vehicles should be used, as a back seat or groom's seat would necessitate the groom to sit behind the driver which is not in accordance with NARHA safety guidelines. Also note that auxiliary reins are not allowed in any phase of competition.

When I'm driving, no one knows I've temporarily swapped my wheelchair for a horse and carriage. That's true mainstreaming . . . Even if only for a few hours, I'm just like everyone else.

Sandy Dota

Driving references and resources

References
1. *Driving Smartly, Driving Safely.* The Carriage Association, R.D. Box 115, Salem, NJ 08079.
2. *Breaking & Training the Driving Horse* video by Farnham, available from NARHA.
3. Driving for the Disabled, Getting Underway--available from NARHA.

Bibliography:
Canadian Equestrian Federation Manual of Basic Driving. Canadian Horse Council.
The Horse in Sport-Driving. Equestrian video Library. The Gladstone Equestrian Assoc. Library. GE, PO Box 119, Gladstone, NJ. 07934.

Advanced Classic Driving with Larry Poulin. The Morgan Horse Club. PO Box 960, Shelburne, VT 05482-0960.
The Carriage Association, R.D. Box 115, Salem, NJ 08079, has information on the following:
Kellog, C. *Driving the Horse in Carriage.*
Walrond, S. *A Guide to Driving Horses*
Ganton, D. *Drive On.*
Norris, A. *Harnessing Up.*
Norris, A. *Driving.*

20.03.3 DRIVING IN A THERAPEUTIC RIDING PROGRAM: PROPER HARNESSING PROCEDURE

Liisa Mayo, PT
Andrew Nanaa

Harnessing is critical in any driving. It must be done correctly and in a timely fashion. In anticipation of harnessing, the horse has been groomed and remains tied by the halter and lead rope to a secure point, or fastened to the cross ties. The first piece of harness to go on is always the saddle and crupper set. These consist of the saddle, backstrap, crupper, hip strap and breeching. After placing the saddle on the horse's back in the proper position, close to and just behind the withers, buckle the girth loosely to keep it from falling off the horse. Pass the crupper under the tail making sure that no hair is caught in it. Buckle the crupper to the backstrap. The girth is now fastened so that it is snug but comfortable (able to slide two finger between horse and girth). A fleece pad can be used under the saddle to help cushion the harness, absorb moisture and prevent the harness irritating the horse's back. The breeching should be adjusted so it is just below the round of the horse's buttock.

The second part to go on is the breastplate and traces. The neckstrap should be unbuckled and passed around the horse's neck so that it will not be necessary to untie the halter. With the breastplate in place the traces should be crossed over the horse's back to prevent them from being stepped on. The reins are put on by running the buckle ends through the saddle terrets. If the neck strap does not have rein dees, the reins should be slipped under the neck strap to keep them from getting caught under the shaft points. The end of the reins that go to the driver's hands are then run through the saddle terret or around the backstrap, to keep them from dragging on the ground or under foot. The reins should be placed on the side of the carriage from which the driver will be entering. If auxiliary reins are to be used they should be put on the same way as the primary set of reins and hung from the opposite side of the horse to prevent them from getting entangled with the driver's reins. A second set of terret rings can be added to the saddle for the auxiliary reins. This is done by using a double ended snap with one end fastened to the existing terret and the other end fastened to a ring through which the auxiliary reins can pass.

The bridle can now be put on over the halter by holding it by the crown piece with the right hand while standing on the left side of the horse. In the open palm of the left hand cradle the mouthpiece of the bit and pull up on the bridle with the right hand. Use the left hand to make the horse open his mouth and take the bit. Next slide the crown piece carefully over the horse's ears and smooth the hair of the mane as the bridle is seated into position. The forelock should be smoothed down underneath the browband. The throatlatch should then be fastened comfortably but snug enough so that the bridle cannot be shaken off. Fasten the noseband comfortably snug and check the adjustment of the blinkers. See that the eyes are centered and that they are clear of anything that could rub against them. Check the height of the bit in the horse's mouth to see that he cannot get his tongue over the bit. Fit the buckle end of the reins, both the driver's and auxiliary reins, if used, onto the proper position on either side of the bit. (Occasionally the auxiliary reins can be fastened to the halter in the case of a light-mouthed horse **and** when sidewalkers are employed, to make the horse more comfortable). After thoroughly rechecking all parts of the harness for proper fit the horse is ready to be led up to the carriage.

The horse should be led to the carriage by the lead rope fastened to the halter, not by pulling on the reins or other parts of the bridle. A carriage should never be brought up to a horse that is still tied to the wall or cross-ties. One person remains at the horse's head while another brings the carriage up from behind the horse. Hold the shafts close to the point of the shoulder, raise them above the horse's back; pull the carriage forward, speaking quietly to the horse so as not to startle him. Remember that he cannot see all that is going on behind him. Lower the shafts and slip them through the shaft tugs (Figure 1). Attach the traces to the evener making certain that they are adjusted to the right length by pushing the shafts back to tighten them and then check to see that the shaft tugs line up with the middle of the saddle and the shaft tips are even with the point of the shoulder of the horse.

Next, secure the belly band which can be fastened in several ways depending on the type of tugs found on the harness. With open tugs, the type most commonly found, wrap the end of the belly band around the shaft, first in front of the tug and then behind the tug, forming a figure eight on the shaft with the shaft tug in the middle of the eight, and buckle securely. This method will prevent the shaft from sliding out of the tug. With a running backband, a type of harness which permits up and down movements of the shaft by allowing the shaft tugs to slide on the saddle, the belly band (with buckles on each end) is fastened to a strap end on the tugs. With this type of harness the belly band should not be tied as tightly as with open tugs. A wrap-around belly band allows for slight movement necessary with this type of harness.

Next the breeching straps are fastened to the shafts by passing them through the loops on the outside or bottom of the shafts and then wrapping them securely around the shafts several times as necessary. Be sure to take all the slack out of the harnessing; then buckle securely. When properly adjusted the harness should fit just snug when the horse is at rest. One should be able to place a hand flat between the horse's hind end and the breeching. This adjustment will allow free movement of the horse's hindquarters when trotting or walking but will also prevent the vehicle from running up onto the horse when going downhill or coming to a sudden stop.

The last part of the harness to be fastened is the check or bearing rein. This is attached to the fly terret on top of the saddle. It should be adjusted so that the horse has free use of his head and neck but is prevented from putting his head down while at rest and/or tugging at the reins. The correct adjustment of the check requires a little practice with each horse. When a horse is standing still the check always appears to be much tighter than it actually is.

It should be noted here that a wide variety of bits can be employed for driving, the most common being the snaffle bit or the smooth bar bit. A Liverpool bit, which has lever arms on either side, can give more sensitive control of the horse to a driver who has limited muscle use. It is sometimes necessary to try several bits to see which one will work best and with which one the horse will feel most comfortable. Bits should be tried during training sessions; a new bit should not be used without the driver's knowledge and understanding of the difference of the bits.

Before taking the reins and getting into the carriage, the driver must carefully look at both sides of the horse to see to it that all parts of the harness are properly adjusted and that all straps are "done up" and ends are in their keepers. The first person to get into the vehicle is the driver assistant. The driver assistant takes up both the auxiliary reins and the driver's reins. He then positions himself in the vehicle on the left side. Once in the vehicle the driving assistant's primary duty is to pay attention to the horse and be prepared to take control of the horse. Once the driver has entered the vehicle, the driving assistant passes the driver's reins over to him and when the driver signals that all is ready, then the horse is prepared to move off by the ground helpers who check to see that the horse has been freed from the cross ties and/or other fastenings. After the driver or driving assistant has checked with each member of the team to be sure that no problems exist, the horse can then be asked to move on.

To unharness, follow the above procedure **IN REVERSE; NEVER REMOVE THE BRIDLE WHILE THE HORSE IS STILL HOOKED TO THE CARRIAGE.** Be sure to look over the horse after he is unharnessed for any rubbed places which indicate the need for adjustment of the harness or the inclusion of a fleece pad to protect a particular spot. Be sure to reward the horse for a job well done. When putting the harness away, look over all straps and hardware for cuts, tears and breaks. Take all the strap ends out of the keepers and check closely at the buckles for wear and damage. If the harness needs to be taken apart for repair or cleaning, the straps can be marked with tape or bits of colored wool tied into the holes used so that the harness can be reassembled with the same adjustment.

1. **BRIDLE WITH A SNAFFLE BIT**
2. **REINS**
3. **SIDE-CHECK**
4. **BREASTPLATE**
5. **SADDLE**
6. **TERRETS (RINGS)**
7. **SHAFT STRAPS**
8. **BELLY BAND OR GIRTH**
9. **TRACE**
10. **CRUPPER**
11. **SHAFT TUG**
12. **BREECHING**
13. **BREECHING RINGS TO HOLD REINS**
14. **BACKSTRAP**
15. **HIP STRAP**
16. **NECK STRAP**
17. **BLINKERS**

FIGURE 1

20.04   STARTING A DRILL TEAM

Lorraine (Frosty) Kaiser, MA

The following overview of drill team activities is designed to allow instructors of therapeutic riding and Special Olympic programs a simple activity that will stimulate students and horses used in such programs. There are many instructors who can expand on the information presented. Those interested in doing more advanced drill work should pursue further information on the subject *.

WHY DRILL?
Drills! Horses love it, students love it, and the audience is impressed.

Riding in or on a drill team promotes horsemanship, teamwork, and concentration, all of which are especially beneficial for the disabled riders. Besides being challenging both mentally and physically, the activity develops a sense of camaraderie and cooperation between horse, rider and other team members. It stretches the students' memory capacity, making them responsible not only for knowing where their horses need to be, but what signals need to be given to get the horse there.

The music used in drills helps the horses and the riders maintain a forward motion and adds to the overall fun involved. Choose music with a good beat; Sousa marches are always good for a beginning drill. Later other music can be added for themes or occasions. Most horses enjoy working to music and will pick up the cadence.

SELECTION OF HORSES
Horses should be paired by the following criteria:
1. *Temperament*
   Horses need to be able to work together as a pair. The horses will be asked to work in close contact at times and they need to be able to do so without getting irritable.
2. *Gait*
   Horses used in the drill need to have similar strides. It will not only look more uniform but allows the outside horse the ability to keep up on turns. Horses with longer strides should be placed toward the front of the group. Since most drills with disabled riders are done at the sitting trot or jog, having horses with gaits that allow the rider to sit comfortably are recommended but not mandatory.
3. *Size and color* (optional)
   Size and color are a luxury that most programs do not have available to them. So, these are suggestions only. Horses of approximately the same size are more eye appealing and allow the riders to appear equal in height. Color coordinated pairs (bays, blacks, chestnuts) are effective for audience appeal and general overall visual impact. It will also help the rider locate his partner easily.

BEGINNING DRILL WORK
A dressage size arena, 20 x 40m or 20 x 60m, is recommended using dressage letters or cones as markers. This allows riders guidelines or points of reference when doing drills. Using 6-8 riders, begin working in pairs at the walk using both directions of the arena. As the riders become capable of keeping good lines, then begin having them do small circles in pairs, going both directions. This can be made easier by placing cones inside the arena at the same letters **K, E, H,** and **F, B, M.** Allow enough room for the pair to circle the cones and return to the rail. Riders will soon learn that the outside horse needs to move more quickly in order to keep up. Having riders practice half-halts will help them learn how to vary the horse's pace while working with a partner.

* There are books available on quadrille such as, Riding to Music, by Werner Strol

Once riders are able to execute these movements and are riding into the corners and not taking short cuts, then introduce the next maneuver. Color code the riders or horses with ribbons (i.e., red & blue) to allow the riders a clue or prompt as to which direction they are to go.

1. blue - right
2. red - left
3. blue - right
4. red - left

Riders ride in single file from **A** to **C**. At **C** they split, red goes left and blue goes right keeping their partners in view across the arena. They pair up with their partners at **A** and ride in pairs down the center line to **C**. Using different riders as leaders, practice doing the split and riding in pairs until everyone has had a chance to be leader. Later on a captain can be chosen. This person will then be the main leader.

MANEUVERS

Threading the needle (Figure 1) requires concentration, timing, and horsemanship. It requires the riders to speed up or slow down, as well as to demonstrate patience while it is being learned. Once it is accomplished it looks exquisite and the riders feel that they have accomplished a great deal. ***They have!*** Riding in pairs, riders go up the center line to **C**. They split at **C** and ride into the corners (between **C & H - C & M**). They turn and change the rein across **X** (center) to opposite corners and pair at **A**. They repeat this pattern and should be with their original partners after the repeat.

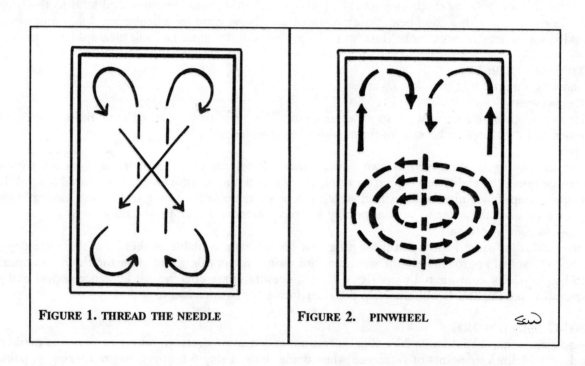

FIGURE 1. THREAD THE NEEDLE   FIGURE 2.   PINWHEEL

The drill ending can be done in various ways. After threading the needle twice, and riders are returning to **A**; instead of pairing they alternate into a single line again--red, blue, red, blue--. Riding down the center line, they halt mid-way down the arena. The first three riders turn left and the next three turn right. A *pinwheel* (Figure 2) or other pattern can be used at this time when the riders are accomplished enough to do so. Each group, at the captain's signal, does a dressage salute. The captain calls for a forward motion and the group returns to single file line and trots out of the arena.

488

When these maneuvers have been learned at the walk, try them at the trot and add music. The horses and riders quickly get into the cadence.

Included are drawings of other drill patterns (Figures 3, the *Crossover* and 4, the circle *Serpentine*) that can be used as the riders progress. Choreography and imagination are unlimited when it comes to drill work. Just keep your drill under 15 minutes. This keeps the horses, the riders, and the audience interested.

MOST OF ALL - HAVE FUN!

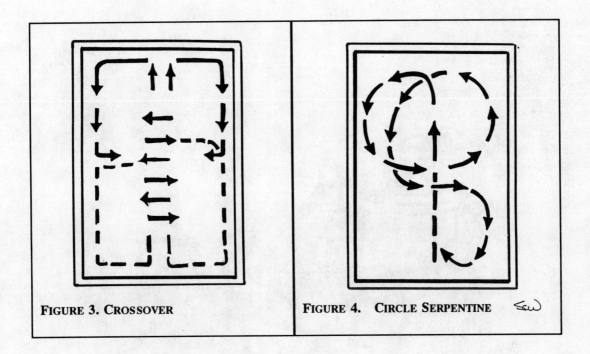

FIGURE 3. CROSSOVER   FIGURE 4.   CIRCLE SERPENTINE

Bibliography:
Strorl, W. (1986). *Riding to Music*. English translated by Sandra Newkirk. Millwood: Breakthrough Publications. (lists over 40 different formations in addition to Dressage to music.
Bruno, H.J. (1976). *Riding in Formation*. Germany: Albert Muller.
Hanke, C.M. (1980). *The Book of Quadrille*. Dusseldorf, Germany: Sankt Georg.

Lorraine (Frosty) Kaiser has taken her drill team, <u>American Riding Club for the Handicapped</u>, to participate in the internationally known **TOURNAMENT OF ROSES PARADE** (1988 to 1992) held each year on New Years day in Pasadena, California, USA. This has been the only representation of a Therapeutic Riding Program in the history of this parade.

21 COMPETITION WITH RIDERS WITH DISABILITIES

21.01 COMPETITION AND HORSE SHOWS FOR THE DISABLED RIDERS

Sandra L. Rafferty, MA, OTR

KEY WORDS:

FUN
CHALLENGE
SELF WORTH
GROWTH
ACCOMPLISHMENT

Competition is defined in the Random
House Dictionary (1966) as:
1. The act of competing; struggle or rivalry for supremacy, a prize;
2. A contest for some prize, honor, or advantage;
3. Rivalry between two or more persons or groups for an object desired in common, usually resulting in a victor and a loser.

Competition occurs every day in everything we do from earning grades in school and seeking praise from superiors, to sibling rivalry at home, and even rivalry between parents to win the affections of children. Whether we like it or not we live in a competitive society.

The basic premise in the field of rehabilitation is for the health care professional to assist the clients in reaching their maximum potential. Reaching this potential includes becoming a functional and competitive member of society. The clients need to be able to work, play, and live as they choose. Therapeutic horseback riding takes a person one step further--offering clients the <u>opportunity to compete</u> in organized events. This chapter will address this opportunity. The levels of competition available will be discussed along with what is expected at each level.

One word of caution. The concept of competition should be introduced carefully to those riders who have worked hard to develop a controlled posture, especially if they are still quite young. The stresses and strains of competition can lead to the undoing of all the good relaxing work that has been accomplished during therapeutic riding or equine-assisted therapy. At times when riders are asked to function beyond their ability, something must give way. With physically disabled riders it is usually their muscle tone and posture. With the mentally disabled riders their cognitive functions may suffer. For example: a young boy with cerebral palsy is competing in a class relay race. Three boys are lined up at one end of the arena each holding a spoon with egg. As the relay proceeds, the boy with cerebral palsy is so involved in maintaining the egg on the spoon that his posture deteriorates and spasticity increases. The question must be asked--does the value of the competition outweigh the deterioration of physical posture? For an adult, competition may be more challenging and of greater value.

The author apologizes for using the phrase **disabled rider** instead of saying **riders with disabilities**. We must keep in mind these are riders who **happen** to have a disability.

Riders should be introduced to the concept of competition at an appropriate time. All riders, able-bodied or not, need to have a foundation of skills before taking on the additional stress of competing at any level. For horsemen this foundation usually includes being seated securely on their horses and learning to control their mounts. With riders with disabilities, it is also important that they do not lose the physical and psychological gains they have made on their horses. A person with cerebral palsy for example, should be able to maintain his or her best posture during the challenge of competition and not be allowed to regress into reflexive behavior.

Instructors and staff in therapeutic riding programs frequently include in their lessons games which are fun but have some elements of competition. When the games are kept at a level where riders can excel both physically and mentally, riders are prepared (especially the young) for future challenges. On the other hand adults may be challenged to improve all aspects of their riding when given the chance to compete early in their riding experience. They may be more motivated to work on relaxation, posture, use of aids and making gains in overall riding skills when being judged against a peer. Peer pressure can be great medicine, but also remember, it can be destructive.

I. Self-contained competitions for disabled riders against other disabled riders:

A. On-Premises Horse Shows:

As part of the group sports riding lesson, games are usually included. Riders compete against each other in team competitions, in relay races or as individuals. Often riders may compete against themselves in a race against the clock. At the end of the semester, a fun show such as a Schooling Show may be held as the last lesson to give students a goal to work toward. A person unfamiliar with the students, such as a local trainer or horse person, may be asked to judge the show. The judging may be, candidly, "fixed" so all students win a blue ribbon and trophy; or a 4-H system of judging may be used where each rider gets 2 ribbons - a first place and then a judgement placing, or impartial judging according to how the judge sees each rider based on his equestrian background.

Types of classes* offered at this level would incorporate skills taught during the semester such as <u>grooming</u>, <u>name-that-horse-part</u>, <u>relay race</u>, <u>brush race</u>, <u>equitation class</u>, <u>obstacle or working trail course</u>, <u>red flag-green flag</u>. **Expectations**: At this level the competition is usually used to reinforce the skills which have been taught in lessons.

B. Off-Premises Horse Shows:

1. <u>Special horse shows</u> can be arranged where competition is between disabled riders from different programs at the local, regional, state, national and international levels. These competitions require more organization and can include many of the same types of classes as the on-premises horse shows along with conventional horse show classes, such as, pleasure, gymkhana, dressage and jumping.

Generally, for non-lesson competitions, riders need to be divided into categories for greater equality in judging. The most frequently used divisions are:
Level 1: Riders requiring 2-4 assistants.
Level 2: Riders requiring 1-2 assistants.
Level 3: Riders requiring 0-1 assistants.

Each level can then be further divided into physically disabled riders and non-physically disabled riders.

Types of classes offered at these levels are determined by the show committee. For example, the show can offer *walk only* classes at every level. For more information on "*How to Organize a Horse Show*" contact the office of North American Riding for the Handicapped Association (NARHA) for their manual. Dixie Morrow is developing a new "handicapping" system (see resources) which would eliminate the need for the above levels.

* A class in a horse show is a group of riders competing against each other.

a. Local shows can be an "invitational" show in which riders within a certain geographic area are invited to compete in a "Fun Show", "Play Day" or "Schooling Show". The expectations of this show may be the same as for riders competing at a lesson show. Or riders may be preparing to compete at the next level. In this case, some advanced classes will be offered.

b. Regional shows prepare riders for national competition and may also be for those competing for a spot on a state team. Classes offered at a regional show include equitation, obstacle course or working trail, relay race, dressage, jumping, vaulting and driving. Competition is more advanced than at local levels.

c. National shows allow riders to compete with riders from all over the nation. There may also be state teams competing against each other for high point awards. Depending on where they occur, the national shows may serve as the selection trials for choosing a National Team to compete at the International Games. Competition at this level provides riders with types of classes found at regional meets but also will give them the opportunity to experience classes found at the international level. Competition at the national level usually involves a higher level of skill than at the regional level.

Previous Competitions in the USA at the National Level Include:
United States Cerebral Palsy Athletic--Cerebral Palsy/Les Autre Sports:
  1979: New Haven, CT
  1981: North Kingston, RI
  1983: Fort Worth, TX
  1985: Cheff Center, Augusta, MI
  1989: Mankato, MN
  1991: Long Island, NY

d. International shows are the highest level of attainment for competition. The rider is a member of a national team, representing his nation in competing with the best disabled equestrians in the world. He has had years of experience in showing, from beginning level up through the National level and may have experience competing in shows for able-bodied riders.

Previous International Competitions and U.S. placement:
Cerebral Palsy/Les Autre Sports:
  1982: Greve, Denmark Demonstration before International committee to introduce riding as a
                        competitive sport in CP Games.
  1984: Long Island, NY, USA
  1987: Orust, Sweden   USA--3rd place
  1990: Assen, Holland   USA--3rd place
  1991: Aarhus, Denmark USA--7th place

e. Special Olympics: According to the Director of Equestrian Sports for Special Olympics in the United States, equestrian competition is held on chapter (state) and International bases. There is no national competition.

International Special Olympics Games:
  1983: Baton Rouge, LA   Demonstration sport with medals awarded
  1987: South Bend, ID   Demonstration sport with medals awarded
  1991: Minneapolis-St.Paul, MN Official sport

2. Horse shows for able-bodied riders may include special classes for disabled riders. The show organizers can offer classes for disabled riders in all categories but usually have classes in equitation at all levels of disability. The coach of disabled riders needs to consult with the judge to explain basic procedures of judging riders with disabilities. The judge needs to disregard the assistants used and evaluate the rider according to basic equitation rules allowing some latitude for effort. After judging a class of disabled riders, the majority of judges have said they really enjoyed the classes but found judging very difficult because of such individual differences represented among the riders.

II. Mainstream competition for disabled riders against able-bodied riders

Disabled riders in these competitions have now advanced to a new arena of competition and are judged in the same manner as their able-bodied counterparts. To encourage more disabled riders to enter this stage of competition, the NARHA's Competition Committee has developed a letter for disabled riders to submit to a show organizing committee "requesting special-needs permission" for adaptive equipment necessary for this rider to compete. Special equipment may include carrying two dressage whips, using an adapted saddle with either a higher pommel or cantle, using special reins (ladder reins, finger loops on the reins), wearing special boots. The letter is intended to gain approval from the organizing committee, technical delegate and/or judges to allow the rider to compete. It was felt that a letter addressing the adaptive needs of the rider would be more practical than attempting to add a rule chapter for disabled riders to the American Horse Show Association Rules Manual. In some areas of the country, disabled riders have the opportunity to compete in any type of horse show. However, education of the able-bodied equestrian community is necessary before a disabled rider may compete in an open show. The NARHA Competition Committee and the ASPIRE organization (see below) may be helpful in planning the education process.

CONCLUSION:

Therapeutic riding continues to grow. More programs are providing the opportunity to riders with disabilities for competition at horse shows at all levels as a part of sports riding programs. With the increase in public awareness of the capabilities of disabled riders through the publicity in national journals (RDA, NARHA News, Chronicle of the Horse, United States Dressage Federation Bulletin, Cerebral Palsy Update, Special Olympic News) there has been an escalation of interest among riders to compete. Riding instructors are identifying students capable of competing on a broad level, as well as including competition in their lessons. After all, competing is a lot of fun, a lot of hard work with some tears of joy and disappointment, but competing is another excuse to spend more time with your horse!

Organizations that can help Riders with Disabilities Compete:

North American Riding for the Handicapped Association Competition Committee
Committee Chairperson, NARHA, PO Box 33150, Denver, CO 80233, USA. phone 303-452-1212

Information available: **Outline of Special Needs Request Letter**; a pamphlet - *How to Manage a Horse Show*; **Judges List** - listing judges who have judged disabled riders in the US.

United States Cerebral Palsy Athletic Association (USCPAA)
Equestrian Technical Advisor, USCPAA, 34518 Warren Rd.,Suite 264,
Westland, MI 48185, USA. phone 313-425-8961.

Information available: USCPAA organizes the National Games for the Physically Challenged which include an Equestrian Competition for all riders with a physical disability. Classification of Disabilities.

The Equestrian Committee of USCPAA selects the United States Disabled Equestrian Team to compete at the Cerebral Palsy- International Sports and Recreation Associations Games conducted by the International Para-Olympic Committee. This event includes all physically disabled athletes (multiple sclerosis, muscular dystrophy, amputees, visually impaired, brain injured, cerebral palsy, spinal injuries, polio, strokes).

Coaches Seminars:.
Seminars are held by organizations to increase instructors' ability to prepare and coach riders through competition. The following organizations will provide information and/or seminars on coaching.

<u>Special Olympics</u>, International Headquarters, Director of Equestrian Sport, 1350 New York Ave.N.W., Suite 500, Washington, D.C. 20005-4709, USA

Information available:
Equestrian competitions at the local, regional, and international levels for riders with mental retardation including those riders with both physical disabilities and mental retardation. *Equestrian Venue Management Guide.*

<u>ASPIRE</u>, Association for Special People Inspired to Riding Excellence
R.D. 4, Box 115, Malvern, PA 19355
Information available:
Judges List -list of judges who have judged disabled riders
Forums on How to Judge Disabled Riders
Coaches seminars

Other Resources

Booklet: *Mainstreaming Into The Horse Show World: A Guide for the Handicapped Equestrian*
by Robin Minden. The Handicapped High Riders Club, Inc., RR #3 Box 2760, Allenton, NJ 01501, USA

Proposed "Handicap system to equalize degrees and types of disabilities in riding competitions".
Source: Dixie Morrow, VARHA, Inc., P.O.Box 226, Franklin, PA 16323

Reference
Morrow, D. *Handicap System to Equalize Degrees and Types of Disabilities in Riding Competitions.* VARHA, Inc., P.O.Box 226, Franklin, PA 16323.
Special Olymics International, Inc. (1989). *Special Olympics Equestrian Sports Skills Program.* 1350 New York Ave., Suite 500. Washington D.C. 20005.
Bonte, M.L. (1991). *Equestrian Sports Program History.* Special Olymics International, Inc. 1350 New York Avew., Suite 500., Washington D.C. 20005.

The Random House Dictionary of the English Language. (1966). New York: Random House Publishers. 300.
₁ *Driving Smartly, Driving Safely.* A video from the Carriage Association of America, Inc. R.D. 1 Box 115. Salem, NJ 08079

21.02   GYMKHANAS FOR THERAPEUTIC RIDING PROGRAMS

Celine Green, BS

Gymkhana is defined by Webster (1964) as:
a.   A place where athletic contests are held.
b.   A sports meet.

The Gymkhana Division allows special equestrians a place where horse and rider teams can compete against equally matched teams. This division of riding for persons with disabilities is enjoyable and may be performed safely by all classifications of riders. Riders who need leaders and/or side-walkers can compete as well as those who are capable of loping the entire event. The ability of riders to negotiate a course safely is the main criterion. Riders can ride either English or Western style.

PREPARATION
ATTIRE:
Attire at local shows is less formal that at national shows but generally riders are encouraged to dress according to show standards. All riders must wear U.S. Pony Club approved helmets with full chin straps. Riders may wear English or Western attire; long pants and a clean, neat shirt are suggested. They may wear boots, but are not required to at local or national shows. However, if tennis shoes are worn, Western safety stirrups, peacock stirrups, Devonshire boots (see 21.03.2), or other approved stirrups must be used. Riders may wear spurs (only for advanced riders) and may carry a crop.

TACK
The type of tack used should conform to the needs of the rider and comfort of the horse. Riders may use either English or Western tack (tack should match the style of attire). The rider may use adaptive equipment such as a handhold, Devonshire boots, a horse neck strap, a saddle cover, ladder reins, when these items are necessary. Equipment that would in any way strap riders to their saddles is not allowed. All riders must be able to fall free from the horse when an accident occurs.

ASSISTANCE
Assistance may be given riders by leaders and/or sidewalkers. A leader must walk beside the horse and is not allowed in front of the horse's nose. He or she is in charge and responsible for the horse at all times. A leader needs to be aware that he or she should not take control of the horse away from a rider during competition. Sidewalkers may assist only as a safety aid to help a rider maintain his or her balance.

TYPES OF EVENTS
POLE BENDING
Pole bending is a timed event. Riders will begin from the starting line at whatever speed is safe for each individual. Classes may be broken down into walk only, trot only, or canter. The time starts when the horse's nose crosses over the starting line and ends when the horse's nose crosses the finish line. (A clearly visible starting line shall be provided). An electric timer or at least two stop watches shall be used with the time indicated by the electric timer, or the average time of the watches used by official timers, to be the official time.

A pole bending pattern is to be executed around six poles. The poles are placed with each twenty-one feet from the next. The first pole is placed twenty-one feet from the starting line. Poles shall be set on top of the ground, six (6) feet in height, with no base more than fourteen (14) inches in diameter. Riders may start from either the left or right of the first pole and then work the remainder of the pattern accordingly (Figure 1). Knocking over a pole shall carry a <u>five second</u> penalty. Failure to follow the course will disqualify a rider. Riders may not touch a pole with their hands in pole bending.

For novice riders, the course may be simplified. The riders will weave a line of poles (cones, or barrels may be used for training). This shortens the time required for each rider. Poles may be made from PVC pipe set into 3 lb coffee cans filled with concrete.

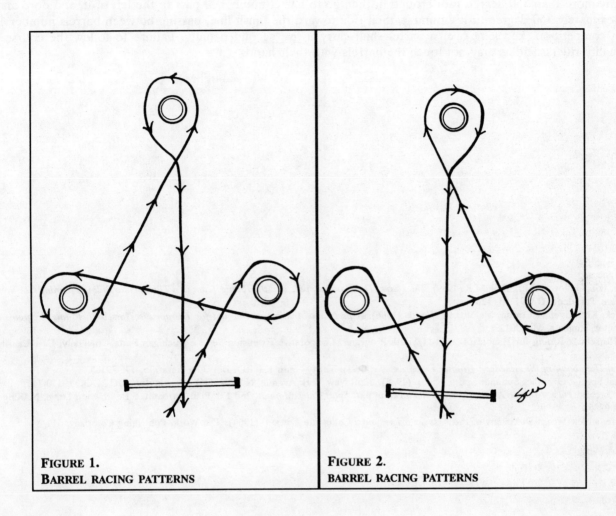

FIGURE 1.
BARREL RACING PATTERNS

FIGURE 2.
BARREL RACING PATTERNS

BARREL RACE

Barrel racing is a timed event. The barrel racing course must be measured exactly. If the course is too large for the available space, the pattern should be reduced <u>five yards</u> at a time until the pattern fits the arena. Remember to leave adequate space between barrels and walls. The distance from barrel <u>number three</u>, (Figure 2) to the finish line does not need be reduced <u>five yards</u> if there is sufficient room for the horse to stop. This class may be divided into divisions by age and disability. A class for walk-only riders with leaders and side-walkers can have just as much fun by being cheered on as those capable of loping. Safety is always a major consideration. Riders should not be entered into classes above their ability to control their horses. Barrels may be painted bright colors. Plastic barrels are not recommended unless they are well weighted.

Starting line markers or electric timers shall be placed against the arena fence. The electric timer or two or more stop watches shall be used to time the event. The time indicated by the electric timer, or the average time of the watches used by official timers will be the official time for the event.

The riders will start at the gait indicated. Timing will begin as soon as the horse's nose crosses the starting line and will stop when the horse's nose passes over the finish line. The course may be ridden from the left or right (Figure 2). At the signal from the starter, a contestant will ride toward barrel number 1, pass to the left of it, and complete an approximately 360 degree turn around it; then go to barrel number 2, pass to the right of it, and complete a slightly more than 360 degree turn around it, then go to barrel number 3, pass to the left of it, and does another approximately 360 degree turn around it, then ride toward the finish line, passing between barrels number 1 and 2. In competition, knocking over a barrel shall carry a <u>five second</u> penalty. Failure to follow the course shall disqualify riders. Riders may not touch the barrels with their hands.

References

Engel, B.T., Galloway, M.L, Bull, M.P. (1989). *The Horse, The Handicapped, and the Riding Team in a Therapeutic Riding Program.* 621 Westover Place, Pasadena, CA 91105. 125.

Joswick, Kittredge, McCowan, McParland, Woods (1986). *Aspects and Answers, A Manual for Therapeutic Horseback Riding Programs.* Cheff Center, Augusta, Mi 49012.

4-H Horseback Riding for Handicappers. 4-H Youth Programs: Cooperative Extension Service Michigan State University, East Lansing, MI 48824. 2.

Official Handbook of the American Quarter Horse Assoc. (1991). Thirty-Ninth Ed. P.O. Box 200, Amarillo, TX 79168.

Official Special Olympics Summer Sports Rules. (1988). 1250 New York Avenue, N,W. #5OO, Washington. DC 2OOO5. 110-111.

U.S. Cerebral Palsy Athletic Assoc. (1988). *Classification and Sport Rules Manual.* 2nd Ed. Paul Tetreault. 5 Beachwood Drive, N. Kingstown, RI 02852.

Webster's New World Dictionary of the American Language Collegiate Edition. (1964). The World Publishing Company. 647.

21.03 STANDARDS FOR COMPETITION FOR THERAPEUTIC PROGRAM RIDING

Standards for competition for disabled riders are based on the American Horse Show Association official rules. Deviations are made to accommodate the disability. The level of the competition, that is, local, state, national or international, may determine the degree of deviation allowed. For example, riders at local shows may wear any suitable riding attire and have assistance from the ground. At international horse shows for the disabled riders, standard riding attire is required and no ground assistance is allowed. (See 21.05.1 Judging Guidelines).

21.03.1 ENGLISH DIVISION

Margaret L. Galloway, MA, BHSAI

DRESSAGE

Purpose
"The object of <u>dressage</u> is the harmonious development of the physique and ability of the horse. As a result it makes the horse calm, supple, loose and flexible but confident, attentive and keen, thus achieving perfect understanding with the rider" (AHSA 1989).

Equipment and Attire
Horses should have a plain snaffle bit only (absolutely no twisted bits are allowed), a cavesson and one set of reins. Any English saddle is allowed. Absolutely no gimmicks, such as martingales, side reins, or similar articles are allowed. Riders should wear breeches and boots, or jodhpurs and jodhpur boots, and a hunt coat of dark material. An approved Pony Club hard hat with a full harness is mandatory. The whip should not be longer than 4 feet, if used. <u>Spurs are allowed in competition</u> **but should only be used with riders who understand their use and who have control of their legs so that the horse is not accidentlly spurred.**

Position
The dressage seat is defined as a more vertical seat than the hunt seat. The upper body is upright. The rider should sit erect, without undue stiffness, evenly on both "seat bones" with supple hips and thighs and the legs should hang naturally, steady and long. The head should be held so that the eyes are looking directly ahead. There should be a contact with the saddle and horse's side. Ideally, the aids are as subtle as possible.

Test
Dressage tests range from training to international levels. Some shows may include Swedish tests, Pony Club or other tests that are more basic than training-level tests. All tests may be read aloud during competition. Tests are scored on a range from one to ten, with ten being nearly perfect. The rider is scored and remarks are made on general impressions, purity of gait, rhythm, suppleness, and obedience.

HUNT SEAT EQUITATION

Equipment and Attire

Hunt Seat riders ride in an English saddle, either all-purpose or forward seat. The bridle must have a cavesson. The bit may be any snaffle, a pelham or a double bridle. Martingales are permitted in jumping classes, but not on the flat. Protective boots may not be worn by the horse, except in jumper classes. Horses should have their manes braided, although it is required only in large "rated" shows. It is optional to have the tail braided, although recommended. Riders should be neat and workmanlike, dressed in breeches or jodhpurs and jodhpur boots or hunt boots. Hunt boots should be plain black or brown, field or regular. They should not have a patent leather or rust colored top, such as members of the hunt wear. It is mandatory that riders use a Pony Club-approved hunt cap with chin strap in place. Spurs and a crop are optional. A hunt coat, of a traditional dark color, should be worn. The saddle should fit the rider and the horse. The pommel should not press on the horse's withers. The rider should be able to get about one hand's width to the cantle, behind his seat. The stirrups should be adjusted long enough to hit the rider's ankle bone when the legs hang free out of the stirrups.

Position

The riders are judged on seat and hands, and ability rather than tack and apparel. The hands in repose should be ahead of the saddle with the knuckles thirty degrees inside the vertical, with the fingers closed, one rein in each hand, little fingers on the outside of the rein with the thumb on top. The arms should follow a straight line from the hand to the horse's mouth. A light contact should be maintained at all working gaits. All reins should be picked up at the same time. The hands should follow the horse's mouth at the walk and canter but be as still as possible at the trot. The rider should sit in the deepest part (the center) of the saddle, evenly on both "seat bones" with his or her legs relaxed into the stirrups. The legs should hang closely to the saddle and the horse with no space between. The torso should be lifted so that the rider sits erect without undue stiffness. The seat should follow at the walk, sitting trot and canter. The rider should post on the outside diagonal, that is, when the horse's outside shoulder comes forward, the rider should be out of the saddle. Unless told otherwise, the rider should post the trot (unless the disability prevents this). At the hand gallop, the rider should bring his or her body slightly forward and out of the saddle.

Equitation

The rider may be asked, in addition to the walk, trot, and canter, to do individual work. This may be: a sitting trot, a figure eight at the trot, and canter to halt. Equitation, accuracy of figures, and smoothness of transitions will be judged.

Hunter classes

Hunter classes are to consist of jumps over a course, with two changes of direction. They may be no more than two feet high for novice or maiden classes. Regular AHSA classes are three feet, six inches high, consisting of six jumps over a course with two changes of directions.

Reference

The American Horse Show Association 1990-91 Rule Book. (1989). New York: *The American Horse Show Association Inc.* 132-145, 208-214.

Celine Green, BS, NARHA Master Instructor

STOCK SEAT EQUITATION

EQUITATION is defined in Webster (1964) as "The art of riding on horseback; horsemanship". Stock seat equitation is the art of riding in western attire and tack according to the AHSA stock seat regulations. Figures 1 and 2 are illustrations of the proper posture and balance in a western saddle.

Equitation should be taught using the standard riding aids, the hands, the legs, and the voice. Horses must be suitable for their riders, considering size, gaits and disposition. Riders must be able to control their horses and meet all safety conditions. Riders may carry crops, wear spurs, and give voice commands to their horses. (Note, spurs should be used only with an advanced rider or a rider who can control his or her legs and have the judgement to use spurs appropriately so that the horse is not accidentally spurred.)

FIGURE 1.
BASIC POSTURE AND POSITIONING FROM THE OFF SIDE (RIGHT)

FIGURE 2
BASIC POSTURE AND POSITION FROM NEAR SIDE (LEFT).
SHOWS TRADITIONAL WESTERN STIRRUPS AND ROMEL.

POSITION

Basic Position: A rider should work toward sitting in the saddle as shown in Figure 1. The stirrups should be short enough to allow the heels to be lower than the toes with the weight of the legs on the ball of the feet. The rider's body should always appear comfortable, relaxed and flexible. One hand is to be used with split reins or a romel. Two hands on the reins with a Bosal (Figure 10).

POSITION IN MOTION

At the walk a rider should sit comfortably, *with his or her back as straight as the person's disability allows*. If he or she is riding with the reins in the left hand (reins are held in the left hand if right handed, and just the opposite if left handed, if possible). Adaptive reins are permissible. A rider should sit to the jog and not post. At the lope, he or she should be close to the saddle (Figures 3, 4, 5 and 6.)

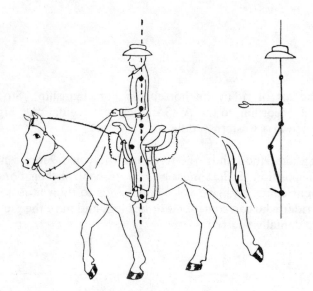

FIGURE 3.   POSITION AT THE WALK

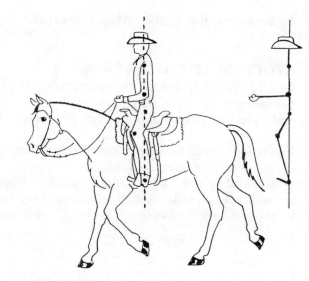

FIGURE 4.   POSITION AT THE JOG/TROT

FIGURE 5.   POSITION AT THE LOPE

FIGURE 6.   POSITION AT THE STOP

ATTIRE

In stock seat classes the riders must wear long pants, a clean shirt with a collar and cuffs, a belt under loops, a western hat and boots. In AHSA classes riders will be penalized for not wearing the suggested attire. In classes for disabled riders, appropriate attire is encouraged but riders will not be penalized when wearing other clothing. If riders do not wear riding boots they should wear shoes with heels if the disability does not prevent it. When tennis shoes are worn safety stirrups (Figure 7) or *Devonshire boots* (Figure 8) are mandatory. **AN APPROVED PONY CLUB HELMET IS MANDATORY.** Chaps (leather seatless "overalls") worn on the legs of the rider) are worn for protection of the riders' legs.

TACK

The type of Western saddle (see Section 16.01, page 318-322) (side-saddles are permitted for those riders who cannot ride astride) should conform to both horse and rider. Special adaptive equipment (Engel, et al, 1989) such as handhold, Devonshire boots (English stirrups covered with leather so that the foot cannot slip through the stirrups), neck straps, saddle covers, and ladder reins may be used where appropriate (Engel, et al, 1989). No equipment is allowed that would in any way strap the rider to the saddle so that he would be unable to fall free from the horse if this became necessary.

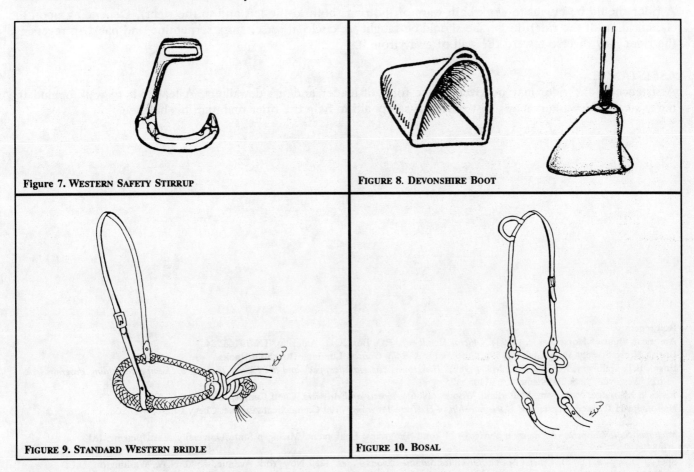

Figure 7. WESTERN SAFETY STIRRUP

FIGURE 8. DEVONSHIRE BOOT

FIGURE 9. STANDARD WESTERN BRIDLE

FIGURE 10. BOSAL

Western bridle, bosal, mechanical hackamore and snaffle bit are acceptable. (Figures 9, 10, 11, 12) for various styles of bridles that are acceptable. The important thing is that the rider has control of the horse with the <u>least amount</u> of wear and tear on the horse's mouth.

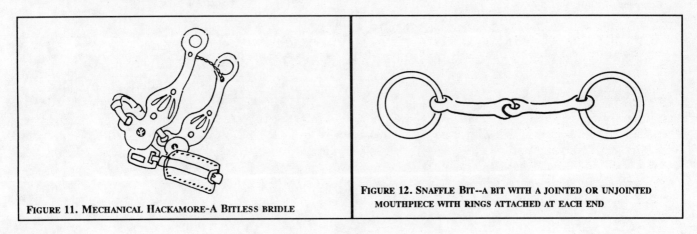

FIGURE 11. MECHANICAL HACKAMORE-A BITLESS BRIDLE

FIGURE 12. SNAFFLE BIT--A BIT WITH A JOINTED OR UNJOINTED MOUTHPIECE WITH RINGS ATTACHED AT EACH END

QUALIFYING GAITS

The <u>walk</u>: true, flat-footed, four beat gait. Special emphasis shall be placed on the walk. The <u>jog</u>: free, square, two beat gait, slow and easy. The <u>lope</u>: smooth, slow, three beat gait, easy and straight on both leads.

Gaits used in classes shall be determined by the age and ability of the rider,and the rider's disability. Safety is the number one rule.

A rider should be taught to work both ways of the ring (both to the left and to the right). Depending upon the classification of the rider, he or she should be taught to: circle, reverse, stop, serpentine and back. In reversing, the rider may reverse toward the wall or away from it.

ASSISTANCE

Assistance to the rider may be given in the form of leader and/or sidewalkers. A leader is to walk behind the horse's ear. Sidewalkers may assist only as a safety aid to help the rider maintain his balance.

References

American Quarter Horse Assoc. (1991). *Official Handbook*. P.O. Box 2OO. Amarillo. TX 79168. 84.

British Horse Society, Pony Club. (1989). *Gymkhanas & Rally Games*. London: Threshold Books.

Engel, B.T, Galloway, M.L., & Bull, M.P. (1989). *The Horse, The Handicapped, and the Riding Team in a Therapeutic Riding Program*. 621 Westover Place, Pasadena, CA 91105. 125.

Joswick, Kittredge, McCowan, McParland, Woods. (1986). *Aspects and Answers*. Cheff Center, Augusta, MI 49012.

National 4-H Council. *Horses and Horsemanship, 4-H Horse Program*. 7100 Connecticut Avenue, Chevy Chase, MD 20815. 20,21,25,26.

Michigan State Cooperative Extension Service. 4-H Youth Programs: Equipment. Michigan State University, East Lansing. MI 48824. 2.

Special Olympics. (1988). *Official Special Olympics Summer Sports Rules*. 1250 New York Avenue, #500, N.W., Washington, D.C. 20005. 108.

Tetreault, P. *U.S. Cerebral Palsy Athletic Assoc, Classification and Rules Sports Rules Manual*. (Jan, 1988, 2nd Ed,) 5 Beachwood Drive N. Kingston, RI O2852.

Webster's New World Dictionary of the American Language Collegiate Edition (1964). Cleveland: The World Publishing Company.

21.04 TRAIL COURSES FOR THERAPEUTIC RIDING

Stephanie C. Woods, BFA

FOR BEGINNERS, INTERMEDIATE, AND ADVANCED RIDERS

A trail course can be an oasis in the middle of dry ring work. This oasis, if designed and built thoughtfully with the needs and safety of horses and riders foremost in mind, presents a myriad of opportunities for enhancing therapeutic riding sessions.

In general, trail courses, whether used in a top "A" rated American Horse Show Association (AHSA) show, or in the private single horse owners' backyard rings, have a basic goal in common: to provide reasonable, fair tests of skill levels. In addition, trail courses challenge and activate minds to "think and plan ahead," stimulate alertness while helping to prevent boredom, and build confidence through obstacle completion. Also, these courses encourage attentiveness of riders to their horses' needs and the horse to its riders' "aids". For riders with disabilities, therapeutic riding horses, and the teams of support personnel, a trail course can add still another dimension to the basic goals and objectives as specific therapeutic goals are successfully integrated.

This article presents three examples of courses designed for the average, able-bodied rider at the beginning, intermediate, and advanced horse and rider levels. These courses should be viewed only as prototypes, and as such, should be modified to fit individual program and their participants. For simplification, side-passing and backing are not shown, and jumps and tires are excluded for reasons of safety. Forward movement is emphasized in conjunction with reining and change of direction exercises. To provide greater course flexibility, many of the obstacles can be entered from either the right or left side. The choice of route may be dictated by the rider's special needs.

AHSA requires a course to contain a minimum of six and a maximum of eight obstacles with the exception of "Classics" or "Stake" classes. For a non-competitive course, distances between these obstacles can be determined by the size of the working arena or ring with the primary consideration being safety or rider and horse.
As the following three courses are designed for horses <u>at the walk</u>, a relatively small area can suffice, 60 by 60 feet. As in all course designs, when judging the inclusion of an obstacle, the words <u>reasonable, fair, and safe</u> must be paramount.

Basic Trail Course Equipment:

Miscellaneous equipment
    Lime (marking)
    100 foot cloth measuring tape--to measure the distance between obstacles.
    Steel measuring tape for measuring obstacle height

    AHSA height--spacing regulations:
        walkovers: single pole maximum height--16 inches
            multiple poles maximum height--10 inches
            Spacing between poles--20 to 24 inches.

When possible, obstacles should be painted white. Poles should be sanded before painting, to remove splinters. Choose wood that is light in weight for the poles.

EQUIPMENT	SIZE	USE
16 poles	4 x 4 x 10 square, hexagon, octagon	walkovers, "T"s and "L"s labyrinth, star/wheel spokes
6 standards	base--14 inches maximum height--6 feet	pole beding, weave, serpentine, pass-through, start-finish markers
3 fifty gallon drums	height--36 inches width--24 inches	weave, circles, pass-through, flat top for picking-up/carry (pails, baskets) equipment
3 to 6 polyethylene or rubber cones	standard road construction cones	markers, weave, circle, pass-through
truck/tractor tires	tread width and diameter vary	support for star/wheel spokes
pails or baskets	1 to 2 gallons	transport items from one place to another
bridge	height--4 to 6 inches width--3 to 4 feet	to walk over
gate*	height (latch)--5 feet width--4 to 5 feet	to pass through
mailbox*	height--5 feet	to get or place item

* Denotes obstacles that are not included in the illustrated trail courses.

TRAIL COURSES--courses are designed with a minimum of obstacle changes.

BEGINNER:

1. Walk over 4 ground poles

2. Enter "T" stem; turn right

3. Weave poles

4. Walk across bridge

5. Pick up pail on barrel "A" and move pail to barrel "B"

6. Walk around tractor tire pass through cones circle barrel "C" cross finish line

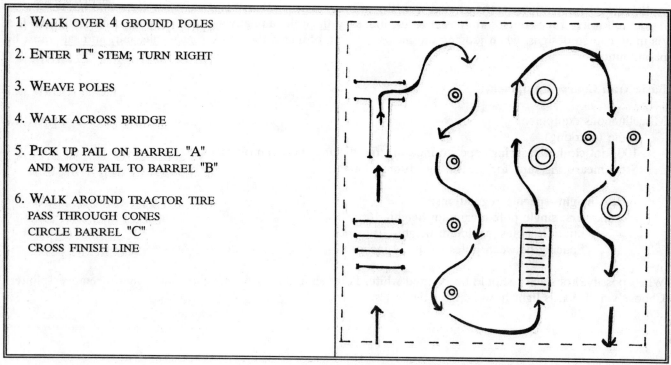

INTERMEDIATE

1. Walk over 6 ground poles

2. Enter "T" stem
   Turn right, circle "T" top
   Re-enter "T" top, turn right
   Exit stem

3. Poles bending (AHSA table I)
   Weave poles 1 to 6
   Circle pole 6
   Weave back to pole 1

4. Walk around tractor tire
   Pick up pail on
   Barrel "A"

5. Walk across bridge

6. Place pail on barrel "C"
   Walk through cones across finish line

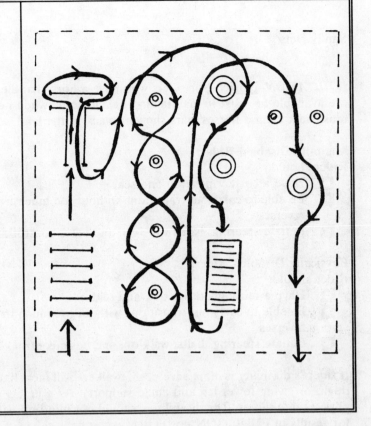

ADVANCED

1. Walk across 2 ground poles, turn right,
   walk over 2 ground poles

2. Enter labyrinth, turn right, left, right,
   left

3. Weave pole 1, circle pole 2
   Weave pole 3, circle pole 4
   Weave pole 5, circle pole 6

4. Walk across bridge

5. Walk to tractor tire
   Walk over wheel spokes

6. Pick up pail on the barrel "A" or "B"
   Weave 3 cones
   Place pail on barrel "C"
   Cross finish line

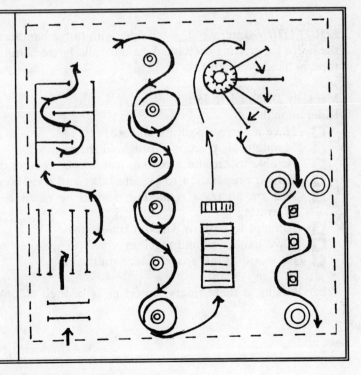

Intermediate and advanced riders may jog or trot portions of the course

507

21.05 JUDGING GUIDELINES FOR RIDERS WITH DISABILITIES

Sandy Dota

EQUITATION--<u>Novice</u> (for riders who have a horse handler and one or two sidewalkers). Walk only. Sidewalkers are available to assist in maintaining balance only when necessary. Horse handler holds lead for safety only and must walk behind horses' ears showing slack in the lead.

Mentally Disabled Rider:
Rider should:
- ◻ Have a correct position and seat
- ◻ Be able to carry out transitions without too much irregularity or roughness, e.g., halts, walk-on, circles and reverses
- ◻ Initiate steering, halts, walk-on, and basic control of the horse

Physically Disabled Rider:
Rider should:
- ◻ Have a fairly good position and seat
- ◻ Be able to carry out transitions without too much irregularity or roughness, e.g., halts, walk-on, circles and reverses
- ◻ Initiate steering, halts, walk-on, and basic control of the horse

If riders's disability is more severe, sidewalkers will most likely be giving physical support (i.e., by locking arm over thigh, or giving lower leg and ankle support). As a judge, one must be able to look past the limitation of these physical disabilities. The disabilities should not interfere with the riders' ability to exhibit their riding skills. Look for results in FUNCTION not FORM.

EQUITATION--<u>Intermediate</u> for rider with horse handler for trot only. (Horse handler may attach a lead rope to the horse for trotting exercises.) At the walk, horse handler walks behind the horse's ears with an unattached lead rope in hand. Walk/trot.

Mentally Disabled Rider:
Rider should:
- ◻ Have a correct position and seat
- ◻ Maintain his position throughout the class
- ◻ Be able to execute a posting trot, on the correct diagonal and in rhythm
- ◻ Exhibit preparation to execute tasks and good control of the horse
- ◻ Perform all tasks requested; should be carried out independent of horse handler with the exception of trotting
- ◻ Attempt to perform smooth transitions
- ◻ Have hands low and together
- ◻ Be aware of his "space"/"place" in the ring

When looking at these riders, expect more of their abilities than in the novice level

Physically Disabled Rider:
Rider should:
- Have a correct seat and position
- Maintain his position throughout the class
- Be able to execute a posting trot, on the correct diagonal and in rhythm
- Exhibit preparation to execute tasks and good control of the horse
- Perform all tasks requested independent of horse handler with the exception of trotting
- Attempt to perform smooth transitions
- Keep hands low and together
- Be aware of his "space"/"place" in the ring
- Attempt to perform smooth transitions
- (May) hold the reins in one hand while holding the pommel with the other

Again, if the rider's disability is more severe, one must try to look past the limitation (spasticity), and look more for unity of the rider with the horse. Results are by function not form. If the horse responds to the rider's aids, no matter how awkward they may appear, the end result is what must be judged. General impression plays a very important role in judging this class.

EQUITATION--<u>Advanced</u> (rider with no horse handler or sidewalkers). Walk/trot & walk/trot/canter

Mentally Disabled Rider:
Rider should:
- Have a secure/independent seat
- Use correct natural aids
- Post on the correct diagonal
- Execute walk/trot transitions smoothly (canter may be a bit erratic)
- Do all task requests smoothly and with preparation, e.g., figure eight should be two nice "round" and even circles with an execution of a change of diagonal in between
- Be able to avoid "bunching up" or "traffic jams"

One should expect good coordination, attention, control and attitude. These are the riders that can go on to regional, national and eventually "open" competition. Also expect emotions to be under control at all times.

Physically Disabled Rider:
Rider should:
- Have a secure/independent seat
- Use correct natural aids
- Post on the correct diagonal
- Execute walk/trot transitions smoothly (canter may be a bit erratic)
- Perform all task requests smoothly with preparation, e.g., figure eight should be two nice "round" even circles with an execution of a change of diagonal in between (as possible) with preparation; expect posting on the correct diagonal
- Be able to avoid "bunching up" or "traffic jams"

These riders will be judged on use of aids, control of the horse, and position of the rider (as much as disability will allow--keeping in mind necessary modifications). Those riders with physical limitations preventing posting at the trot should be able to explain and understand posting on the correct diagonal. One should expect good coordination (as can be), attention, control and attitude. These athletes also are ready for regional, national and "open" competition. But, again, keep in mind, results by function not form. One may have an independent rider, moderately involved with cerebral palsy, mixed in with those with mild cerebral palsy and spinal cord injury. The latter will present much more quiet riders--look past the disability to the end result. This is very difficult, but one must have an obligation as a judge to separate emotions from intellect. Riders want to be judged by their abilities, not disability.

DRESSAGE--<u>Novice</u> (only for rider <u>with</u> a horse handler and one or two sidewalkers) Walk only.

Mentally Disabled Rider:
Rider should:
- Make round circles, straight diagonals, staying on center line
- Emphasis is on accuracy
- Have fairly good transitions (halt, salute, walk on)
- Show that he or she is initiating all steering and basic control of the horse

Physically Disabled Rider:
Rider should:
- Make round circles, straight diagonals, staying on center line
- Emphasis is on accuracy
- Perform fairly good transitions (halt, salute, walk on)
- Show that he or she is initiating all steering and basic control of the horse

Exception in that the physically disabled rider may need support from the sidewalker. This should not interfere with rider's skills.

DRESSAGE--<u>Intermediate</u>: (for rider with horse handler for trot only: horse handler may attach a lead rope to the horse for trotting exercises). At the walk, horse handler walks behind the horse's ears with an unattached lead rope in hand. Walk/trot.

Mentally Disabled Rider:
Rider should:
- Perform accurately--movements required must happen at specific letters
- Be going deep into the corners

Emphasis is still on accuracy of the specific movements required in a dressage test. If one gets a square halt, some bending, impulsion or even tracking up, this should be considered "icing on the cake" for this group.

Physically Disabled Rider:
Rider should:
- Perform accurately--movements/ transitions required must happen at specific letters
- Be going deep into the corners

Emphasis still on accuracy of transitions, general appearance may not be as smooth as with the mentally disabled rider. Again, results are judged by function not form.

510

DRESSAGE--<u>Advanced</u> (for riders with <u>no</u> horse handler or sidewalkers). Walk/trot and walk/trot/canter.

Mentally Disabled Rider:
Rider should
- ◘ Emphasize accuracy of the specific movements required in the dressage test
- ◘ Attempt square halts, bending, impulsion, leg yielding
- ◘ Understand the basics of dressage with the horse
- ◘ Be able to show a very good position

These riders are advanced and should understand the basics of dressage with the horse and not just try to complete a series of movements and figures. **Do not** be patronizing with the scoring.

Physically Disabled Rider:
Rider should
- ◘ Emphasize accuracy of the specific movements required in the dressage test
- ◘ Attempt square halts, bending, impulsion, leg yielding
- ◘ Understand the basics of dressage with the horse
- ◘ Be able to show a very good position

Limitations of some disabilities make smooth transitions and impulsion very difficult, e.g., paraplegia because of no use of the lower extremities. Here again, as a judge, try to look through the awkward and/or modified aids needed to perform the end result. One should still be seeing some bending, square halts, and accuracy of required movements (e.g., 20 meter circles, straight diagonals, etc.). Judge the horse and rider as a team.

TRAIL (or OBSTACLE)--**Novice** (for rider who must have a horse handler and one or two sidewalkers). Walk only.

Mentally Disabled Rider:
Rider should:
- ◘ Go over ground poles in a forward position
- ◘ Show that he is initiating all steering and basic control of the horse

Novice course usually consists of at least four obstacles. Skills include sequencing (performing the course in the exact manner that is posted), i.e., starting a serpentine of cones on a particular side.

Physically Disabled Rider:
Rider should:
- ◘ Go over ground poles in a forward position
- ◘ Show that he is initiating all steering and basic control of the horse

Novice course usually consists of at least four obstacles. Skills include sequencing (performing the course in the exact manner that is posted), i.e., starting a serpentine of cones on a particular side. May need some physical assistance for support & may not be able to go into a forward position.

TRAIL (or OBSTACLE)--<u>Intermediate</u> (for rider with horse handler for trot only: Horse handler may attach a lead rope to the horse for trotting exercises). At the walk, horse handler walks behind the horse's ears with an unattached lead rope in hand. Walk/trot.

Mentally Disabled Rider:
Rider should:
- ☐ Go over ground poles in a forward position
- ☐ Show that he is initiating all steering and basic control of the horse

Intermediate course usually consists of at least five obstacles. Trotting/jog is added and should be performed (English) posting. To be judged on preparation, accuracy and obedience of the horse to perform the tasks asked.

Physically Disabled Rider:
Rider should:
- ☐ Go over ground poles in a forward position (English)
- ☐ Show that he is initiating all steering and basic control of the horse
- ☐ Perform trot in posting (English), Western jog

Intermediate course usually consists of at least five obstacles. To be judged on preparation, accuracy and obedience of the horse to perform the tasks asked. Some riders may not be able to go into a forward position or do a posting trot.

TRAIL (or OBSTACLE)--<u>Advanced</u> (no horse handler or sidewalker). Walk/trot.

Mentally Disabled Rider:
Rider should:
- ☐ Go over ground poles in a forward position (English)
- ☐ Show that he is initiating all steering and basic control of the horse
- ☐ Perform trot in posting (English), Western--jog

Advanced course usually consists of at least 6 obstacles. To be judged on preparation, accuracy and obedience of the horse to perform the tasks asked.

Physically Disabled Rider:
Rider should:
- ☐ Go over ground poles in a forward position (English)
- ☐ Show that he is initiating all steering and basic control of the horse
- ☐ Perform trot in posting (English)

Riders to be judged on preparation, accuracy and obedience of the horse to perform the tasks asked. Riders may not be able to go into a forward position or do a posting trot.

21.05.1   GUIDE TO RESPONSIBILITIES OF A JUDGE

Sandy Dota

1. Ask for the prize list--you want to be sure that you are qualified to judge the class.

2. Knowledge of the rules--use the prize list, know the show steward.

3. Your knowledge:
    - ◎ Keep up with rule changes
    - ◎ Observe
    - ◎ Try not to be dull, e.g., equitation classes, use ground poles, figure of 8, or other ring equipment
    - ◎ You should know a little bit about all the disciplines
    - ◎ You should be aware of some of the restrictions of riders because of their specific disabilities, e.g., persons with spinal cord injuries cannot post

4. Integrity--you serve 3 people:
    a. Yourself. Do not be intimidated by anyone. Do not let emotions cloud your judgement. Remember, these riders want to be judged on their abilities. Results by _function_ not form.
    b. The rider. Explain what he did or did not do right.
    c. Spectators. Again, do not be intimidated. Also, your first impression is usually the best.

5. Secretarial Skills--Develop a system of symbols, numbers, and so on to identify the riders.

6. Help to keep the show moving.

7. Get to know your ringmaster and announcer.

8. If you are using any kind of equipment (e.g., walkie-talkie), make sure it works.

9. Attire - The horse and rider enter your class well-groomed; it is only proper and respectful that the judge be dressed suitably also. It is very difficult to command respect from the exhibitors when one appears in shorts and a tank top.

10. Acknowledge the riders--can be done with a smile to the whole group at the end of each class. Let them know you are absolutely interested in their performance and truly enjoy judging that class.

It is not a responsibility, but it is good to ask the announcer to remind horse handlers and sidewalkers that improper assistance will result _in rider penalty_.

22.01 "SPECIAL OLYMPICS EQUESTRIAN SPORTS:

Mary-Lu Bonte, SOI DIRECTOR

The mission of Special Olympics International, Inc. is to provide year-round sports training and athletic competition in a variety of olympic-type sports for all individuals with mental retardation. Participation in Special Olympics sports gives athletes continuing opportunities to develop physical fitness, demonstrate courage, experience joy and participate in the sharing of gifts, skills and friendship with their families, other Special Olympics athletes and the community.

As one of the official sports of the Special Olympics movement, the equestrian sports program certainly meets the criteria stated in the mission of the movement. That it is all done with the companionship of the wonderful furry and fuzzy creature known as the horse only intensifies the experience. However, the future of the equestrian sports program will be very much influenced by the nature of the equestrian sports industry and its very competitive atmosphere. Coaches and participants alike must examine their personal philosophies about competition before entering into this most complex of all sports activities.

HISTORY
A brief history of the equestrian program begins in 1968 with its inclusion as one of the activities offered in the backyard of Mrs. Eunice Kennedy Shriver, the founder of the movement. It was included as a demonstration in the 1975 and 1979 ISSOG (International Summer Special Olympics Games) and was first officially recognized as a demonstration sport in the 1983 ISSOG in Baton Rouge, LA. Increased recognition and participation came with the 1987 ISSOG in South Bend, IN as 36 athletes from 2 countries and 17 chapters (states) competed in four equestrian events. Elevation to official sport status was achieved in June 1988 and the 1991 ISSOG was the debut of equestrian events into official international competition status. Competition is offered in: dressage, equitation in English and Western style, prix caprilli, showmanship at halter/bridle, and working trails.

To date, competition opportunities exist in barrel racing, dressage, English equitation on the flat & stock seat equitation, pole bending, prix caprilli, showmanship at halter & bridle, team relays and working trails. Special Olympics has created its own athlete-specific dressage tests of increasing difficulty to prepare its riders for open competition should they desire to mainstream into open competition during their equestrian sports careers. Time constraints have prevented the creation of rules for drill teams of two's and drill teams of four's but they are also considered official events in the equestrian sports program.

GETTING INVOLVED
For those readers who have already decided to become involved as volunteers or coaches, contact should be made with the national/chapter program office in your country or state. If you are not sure of its location, contact the Special Olympics International Headquarters, 1350 New York Avenue, NW., suite 500, Washington, DC, USA, 20005-4079 and you will be provided the address. It should be remembered that not all national/chapter programs offer equestrian sports to their athletes and that decision is determined by those groups. There were 20 countries (national programs) and 38 US chapters represented at the 1991 International Summer Special Olympics Games so the reader need not feel discouraged.

COACHING PHILOSOPHY
At the beginning of each sports skills guide published by Special Olympics, Mrs. Shriver states, "in the Special Olympics programs, coaches play a unique and indispensable role. It is they who impart to Special Olympians the sports skill and competitive spirit that define the true athlete. To be a coach in Special Olympics demands qualities

that transcend knowledge of specific games or events. The foundation of good coaching is competence and solid grounding in the fundamentals. I cannot emphasize enough that sound training of coaches and athletes alike is the basis for everything we do at Special Olympics."

A solid grounding in the fundamentals goes beyond physical abilities and skills. Reflect on the following questions whether or not you are already coaching:

1. Are the equestrian sports of Special Olympics appropriate for each of the athletes in this program?
2. Has the athlete been included in decisions in the same way anyone would want to be consulted?
3. Did the coaches select the sports that their athletes will compete in or were the athletes allowed to make their own choices (within safety limits) of the number and type(s) of sports in which they would like to compete?
4. Are instructors' decisions based upon their teaching strengths and skills or upon their athletes' desires and abilities?
5. Are instructors competent in their equestrian knowledge to be working with these riders? Are they able to be consistent role models?
6. Can the instructors impart that same attitude to those who may be assisting them?
7. Are instructors willing to commit the necessary time to the development of the riders' skills and able to adapt activities to their strengths and weaknesses? Are they willing to say "I do not know" and seek assistance to help their riders progress?

The selection of the sport(s) for competition, pre-ride and post-ride dismounted exercises, off-season exercises, astride activities, visits to other equestrian activities and competitions for observation and lesson reinforcement, visits by outside coaches and instructors and participation in open competitions (where available) are all factors which should be considered in instituting a Special Olympic program. Last but certainly not least, discuss the plan with your riders (particularly your adult riders) and be prepared to make adjustments (within safety limits) to best suit the needs of your riders.

As the date for a competition draws closer, what do the riders need and are they ready for this competition? Is the instructor succumbing to pressure from outside sources, i.e., parents, program volunteers, others? Is the instructor pushing for progress when the athletes are competing or is he or she pushing for the medals and losing his or her perspective on sportsmanship?

The excitement and enthusiasm of competition must always be tempered by the qualities of sportsmanship. Let 'Sportsman's Charter' of the American Horse Shows Association be your guide; "... that sport is something done for the fun of doing it and that it ceases to be sport when it becomes a business only, something done for what there is in it;... that amateurism is something of the heart and spirit--not a matter of exact technical qualifications; --that the exploitation of sport for profit alone kills the spirit and retains only the husk and semblance of the thing."

The equestrian sports athletes may not be completely aware that they are riding at inconvenient times in loaned/borrowed facilities, on donated horses and ponies and in second-hand attire. What they can demonstrate with great poise and confidence is their desire to compete and their wish to do their best in front of others, for some, for the first time in their lives. They are demonstrating the courage of their convictions in their skills with their horses. And they are there because you as their coach have shown them part of the way to the self-esteem deep within their characters.

Many coaches have been involved with some form of equestrian sports competition in the past and it is the memories of these experiences which will influence coaching styles. When personal memories are combined with discussions with athlete's parents/guardians, teachers, physicians and physical therapists (each where applicable), it will be possible to formulate the best individual mental and physical training plan for athletes headed for competition. It is nurturance of this competitive spirit which will determine the course of the equestrian sports program of Special Olympics.

22.02   THE RESIDENTIAL FARM SCHOOL APPROACH

Samuel B. Ross, Jr., PhD

Imagine a tough, troubled young teen from the mean streets of New York City patiently soothing a frightened pheasant or gingerly setting a rabbit's broken foot. Watch another child work with a gentle team of Percherons or drive a young Haflinger gelding as part of the horse's schooling. These are some of the many small daily miracles at Green Chimneys' farm and wildlife center where animals help troubled urban youngsters heal and blossom.

Near Brewster, New York, on 150 acres purchased in 1947 by the Ross Family, Green Chimneys, a residential treatment center with a special education school, has become home to 102 inner-city youngsters who share its rolling campus with a host of rare and common barnyard animals. Here for the past 40 years staff have pioneered the use of the healing power of human-animal interaction as the cornerstone of our work with youngsters.

Many of the Green Chimneys children arrive with histories of neglect or sexual, physical or emotional abuse. Many are also learning disabled and have never experienced success at school. They have had a rocky existence at home, in school and in the community. They come defeated because they have failed in those things by which children get judged. They must learn that there never has been an animal which asked a child his achievement test score. Children here learn self-worth. They begin to excel and are given a chance to share their new found skills with others.

Green Chimneys has inspired child care specialists and others here and abroad. Unlike many programs for children with special needs that become magnets for community protest, Green Chimneys attracts local residents to a broad range of recreational and educational activities. On any given day the young residents join visitors for classes in nature, horticulture and horse care as well as riding lessons. The rewards are great. The funds acquired through programs offered to the community help to support the entire agency.

Recently certified by the state and federal government as a "disabled wildlife rehabilitation center", the barn and pens now shelter mending turkeys, geese, owls and falcons. Here again the community becomes tied in to the children and the program.

Thanks to a special interest of the farm staff, modern breeds graze alongside rare breeds. Under the leadership of the farm director, Green Chimneys residents and local visitors learn to care for these and the hundreds of other animals on the grounds. On evenings and weekends, Green Chimneys' youngsters gently help community children out of their wheelchairs onto horses as part of the farm's therapeutic riding program.

Taking year-round care of animals, including over 20 horses and ponies, teaches children responsibility. Caring for animals can be the first step in developing the human ethic: a concern for other people that comes from the opportunity to love and be loved. The farm draws the children who are upset, sullen, depressed and frustrated. The animals serve as catalysts--linking child to child, child to staff, child to family.

The following letter, written from one student to another whose horse had died, illustrates what the horse care program means:

> *Dear R.D.,*
> *I am sorry about Jagger. He was a special horse. We all loved him. If there is anything I can do*
> *to make you feel better, I will do it because I know how you feel. I am upset myself. I know you*
> *will miss him for I will miss him too.*
> > *Your Friend,*
> > *M.P.*

Jagger's death was an emotional time for many children. Many had family or friends who had died or were killed. It gave them a chance to mourn old friends and ask many questions, along with coming together to support one another. For children who might have trouble expressing themselves in verbal therapy in an office, animal-assisted therapy becomes a vital link in the child's treatment.

The program was originally founded to house a private school where children could interact with farm animals. From the very beginning ponies and horses were the biggest attraction. Seemingly, they reduced the anxiety of being away from home. The school, which is in session year-round--223 days per year, evolved into specializing in the care of children with special needs, and in 1974 expanded its scope and became a social service agency. The agency now serves children with handicapping conditions as well as local children and adults from New York City, Westchester, Putnam and Fairfield (CT) Counties who participate in the variety of programs being offered.

Therapeutic riding instructors provide classes indoors and out for 102 residents and 35 mentally retarded and/or physically disabled youth, a summer riding clinic, the agency's 100 day campers and 50 pre-school children, as well as hunt seat lessons for children and adults in the community. The program is staffed throughout each day--seven days a week. The children in residence serve as aides for the instructors. The main emphasis remains the 102 resident children and is designed to provide an opportunity for social, emotional, academic and physical growth and progression through the medium of therapeutic riding and horse care. This is achieved through a variety of equine events including 4-H, Learn and Earn, "adopt a horse" program, various contests, skill team, vaulting team, field trips, trail rides, horse shows and, of course, riding during program time.

Each child at Green Chimneys adopts a horse as a project. The child may ride the horse during the program times and during special programs. The student is responsible for care of the horse, with supervision in event of injury to or sickness of the horse. Some children are reluctant to ride but are still involved in horse care and equine studies. Children can be found at the farm throughout the day. Top riders within each class are united into a team that performs patterns and maneuvers. Teams perform for Green Chimneys events including times when families are on campus and for the public.

An extensive Learn and Earn program is provided. A number of hours are regularly scheduled for residents to learn the responsibilities of holding and keeping a job. The students are able to earn some money which, in turn, they bank in a savings account. Other residents have experience working at the Horse Center. During an average week, in addition to riding, 30 residents work at the Horse Center. Job experiences range from:
- Unsupervised morning student workers who arrive at 7:15 A.M., measure and feed the correct types and amounts of feed to the horses
- Supervised barn management where students sweep, hay, water, lead horses, mucks stalls and do whatever is necessary to maintain the barn and a healthy herd
- Advanced riders work as one-on-one peer tutors with new or young students teaching them horse science, grooming techniques and walking beside them to insure their safety

Young students get first job experiences as part of a clean-up team, one-on-one, with an instructor. They learn to put equipment away, rake, sweep or do within their ability whatever is needed. Emphasis is on learning and job responsibility.

Residents are trained to work with riders with disabling conditions either as a therapeutic riding leader or sidewalker. Children learn to care for others and become more service-oriented as a result of this experience.

Some residents are selected to join the vaulting team because of ability or need. They learn cooperation and team work as they work in pairs to do "tricks" and gymnastic exercises atop a moving horse. It is a great confidence builder. Teams perform at many annual events. Students create written and visual reports of these activities. All of this is considered part of the student's school program. An extensive 4-H program overlaps with the adopt-a-horse program. Children participate in the Putnam County 4-H Fair Horse Show. Well over 50 residents earned the honor of representing Green Chimneys. 4-H members enter the local record book contest. The 4-H quiz bowl team competes in the NY State Regional Horse Bowl. Children learn to ride English, Western and bareback. They participate in vaulting, learn to harness and drive the pony cart and draft team.

College students of many majors (psychology, agriculture, science (pre-med), animal behavior, liberal arts) are recruited and assigned to the Horse Center. They expand the program by doing special projects related to their fields, with the animals and children. One instructor is assigned responsibility for training, supervision and evaluation of college students.

The Farm Center also includes a staff person who serves as a liaison to the treatment teams and who represents the program at all reviews of a child's progress. The availability of such a person has increased the effectiveness of the program. Everything the child does is included in the child's academic program and documentation is absolutely essential. Specific skill cards have been designed for every activity.

Many people have spent their lifetimes searching for means for humans to better understand and accept the responsibility of environmental stewardship. Green Chimneys sees itself as part of that effort. When one learns to nurture, he or she is able to accept responsibility and learn to be patient; then he or she has the attributes which will serve him or her well for years to come. These are some of the major goals of the program at Green Chimneys.

Children are our future. <u>Every</u> child therefore is important. Children need to be able to take their places in society and society has to be prepared to let them.

Samuel B. Ross, Jr., Ph.D., Executive Director, Green Chimneys Children's Services, Brewster, NY 10509

22.03 THERAPEUTIC HORSEBACK RIDING: A SCHOOL DISTRICT PROGRAM

Chris McParland, BS

BACKGROUND

The excitement and success enjoyed by therapeutic riding programs in the United States throughout the past thirty-plus years can realistically be achieved within a school district. Special education students are served in a variety of ways including pull-out programs (students are seen individually or in small groups outside of classroom), partial integration into their regular class, full inclusion in regular education program, and in special day-classes.

Educationally, therapeutic riding can provide a wide spectrum of learning opportunities for special education students. It enhances existing services by complementing and extending other special learning programs such as speech and language, adapted physical education, occupational or physical therapy, and psychological services.

An example of a school district's success in utilizing a therapeutic riding program to provide expanded learning opportunities for special education students can be found in Elk Grove, California. The Elk Grove Unified School District (EGUSD) has integrated such a riding program into its curriculum--Project RIDE (Riding Instruction Designed for Education). Modeled after the nationally and internationally recognized Cheff Center for the Disabled (founded in 1970) in Augusta, Michigan, EGUSD's therapeutic riding program combines the background of an established center with the stability of a progressive school district to create a firm foundation for lasting success.

Project RIDE began in 1979 and served thirty students at Jessie Baker School once a week as part of their adapted physical education program. Soon after those modest beginnings, other special education classes throughout the District expressed an interest in adding horseback riding to their curriculums. Consequently, the case load of riders at Project RIDE increased considerably from one session a week to three times a week. After ten years and continued growth, Project RIDE became a full time teaching position staffed by an EGUSD adapted physical education specialist and an instructional assistant. And, in direct response to the program's acceptance and expansion, the District has included Project RIDE in its master plan for education. Underscoring the program's importance is the inclusion in the master plan of a fully enclosed riding arena scheduled for construction at Jessie Baker School in the very near future.

Professionally, the riding program has benefitted from the beginning as well. The credentialed, district teacher, an adapted physical education specialist, became the riding instructor. As Project RIDE'S instructor, she not only brought current knowledge of classroom and physical education curricula, but also a formal background in English and Western horsemanship. In addition, she accepted responsibility for program organization and coordination.

COMMUNITY INVOLVEMENT/VOLUNTEERS

From the onset, the history of Project RIDE represents one of America's finest traditions, community members coming together to help a worthwhile organization develop and become a solid and integral part of their community. It was in 1979 that EGUSD and the Jessie Baker School, a school for students with severe disabilities, became the core around which community involvement could form and flourish. Adult volunteers provide the manpower to haul the horses to Jessie Baker for classes. (An outdoor arena was built on the Jessie Baker campus for the riding program.) They also feed and care for the horses at the ranch leased to house the horses, as they cannot stay at the school. Other volunteers assist with the daily classes as program volunteers, fund raising events, demonstrations, competitions, and other special activities.

In 1980 the scope of volunteer involvement broadened as Project RIDE became an incorporated, non-profit organization (501(c)(3). With this legal status, the board of directors (comprised solely of volunteers) assumed additional responsibilities. Project RIDE, Inc. relieved EGUSD of financial support for horses, tack, truck, trailer, and other equipment. The District continues its educational support, however, by monetarily sustaining the instructor's salary and benefits. Also, EGUSD provids in-kind support by maintaining the campus arena, utilities in the tack room (lights and phone), processing student forms, and coordinating Project RIDE with other special education support services included on the students' Individual Education Programs (IEP'S).

There are two secondary schools within walking distance of Jessie Baker School. These secondary schools provide student volunteers to Project RIDE during school hours as well as after school. The Project RIDE Club is comprised of students from Joseph Kerr Junior High and Elk Grove High Schools whose parents, administrators, and instructors have given permission for the students to be released from a minimum of three classes one day a week to volunteer for the program at Jessie Baker School.

The integration of regular education students into this special riding program has had positive results for all students. The regular education students gain disability awareness and an understanding of special education students, in addition to receiving instruction in equine safety and equestrian skills. The riders are given a tremendous opportunity to interact educationally and socially with regular education students; thus the riders and student volunteers learn from each other and the educational opportunities for all students are expanded considerably. Related equine activities such as riding demonstrations, field trips, competitions (horse shows), and fund raising events provide other ways to integrate special education and regular education students.

DISTRICT COMPONENTS/FEDERAL LAW
Components of a program within a school district can be described by recapping the federal law which set the stage for developing adapted physical education programs. The definition of Adaptive Physical Education is: a diversified program that incorporates a variety of individual programs including developmental activities, games, sports, and rhythms. All the activities are considered to be suited to the interests, capacities, and the limitations of the students with disabilities who cannot safely or successfully participate actively in a regular physical education program.

In 1975, physical education was included in the Education for All Handicapped Children Act (Public Law (PL 94-142). This was the first piece of legislation to recognize physical education as an important component in the education of children with disabilities. The federal law defines handicapped children as those who are mentally retarded, hard-of-hearing, speech and language impaired, deaf, blind, and multi-handicapped. The law helped to regulate what was previously defined by AAHPERD* that physical education is to include adapted physical education, special physical education, motor development, and movement education.

CHRONOLOGICAL PLAN FOR PROGRAM ORGANIZATION
The steps taken to develop a therapeutic riding program within a public or private school system are quite similar in many respects to the creation of a program through a privately funded group, public agency, horse-related group, or riding stable. The development of a program within a school district must be coordinated administratively first. The individual or group who has the best chance to sell the idea of a therapeutic riding program would probably come from within district staff. The idea might develop through the adapted physical education staff, special education teachers, occupational or physical therapists, speech and language specialists, or other district individuals knowledgeable about riding for the disabled programs.

Planning a therapeutic riding program for a school district contains so many factors that make it unique, thus the proposal should be written by someone with an extensive background in horsemanship, stable management, veterinary care and hopefully, special education or disability awareness training. It would be quite difficult to develop a thorough proposal without a solid background in the previously mentioned areas.

Community support for the program will demonstrate to the district administration that financial responsibilities will not totally rest with the district. If the district allows one of their credentialed employees to teach the program, then the district's responsibility will probably be very significant in terms of salary and financial demands. Bussing

AAHPERD: American Association of Health, Physical Education, Recreation, and Dance.
AAPHERD (1952) defines adapted physical education as "diversified program of developmental activities, games, sports, and rhythms, suited to the interests, capacities, and limitations of students with disabilities who may not safely or successfully engage in unrestricted participation in the vigorous activities of the general physical education program.

the riders to a center will have a definite financial impact on the school district; therefore, the coordinators of the riding program may have to consider trucking the horses and ponies to a school site.

The next step, once an individual or small group has developed a proposal, is to seek support for the idea from the director or coordinator of special services for the district. That special education administrator will play a key role in presenting a therapeutic riding proposal to the superintendent, other district administrators and the school board. The proposal should include a brief history of riding for the disabled, information on the North American Riding for the Handicapped Association, in addition to state and local riding-for-the-disabled programs.

When developing a proposal, qualifications of instructional personnel, target population of students, entrance and exit criteria for service, funding sources, location of facility, bussing considerations, sources for volunteers and board of directors, accident insurance and liability coverage, and sources for locating mounts and riding equipment are all areas to be researched and included in the proposal.

The proposal must be well-planned, concise and complete with funding alternatives. Those alternatives can be researched in the special projects office in the district. The funding options may include grant possibilities, public agencies, private funding sources, sponsorships, service groups, and perhaps, third party insurance reimbursement for occupational or physical therapy.

An information-sharing session with invitations sent to all support agencies, parent groups, horse organizations, school district administrative personnel, and others from the community who may become involved with the therapeutic riding program should be held prior to submitting the proposal. It is important to have a support group organized before the proposal is formally presented to the district administration.

There should be many private schools or public school districts in the United States who would endorse or support, as much as possible, a therapeutic horseback riding program just as the Elk Grove Unified School District has for the past ten years. It takes leadership, coordination, cooperation, pride in services and staff, and community support to create and sustain a quality program. Let's hope that other school districts will give therapeutic riding a place in their curriculum for special education students.

References

Seaman, J.A., DePauw, K.P. (1982). *The New Adaptive Physical Education*. Mayfield Publishing Co.
U.S. Congress. Education for All Handicapped Children Act, PL 94-142, 1975.

22.04   SPECIAL EDUCATION WITHIN THERAPEUTIC RIDING

Virginia G. Mazza, MS

Special education is charged with providing education to children with special needs and with bringing them into the mainstream of life as much as humanly possible. Children of all disabilities of varying intensities are served. Special education can take place in a variety of settings ranging from the normal classroom setting to special schools. Therapeutic riding is a natural partner in special education.

It is important for the riding instructor to understand thoroughly the particular problems facing the children in a given class, as the more severely disabled are often grouped by disability as well as age. In particular, he or she must understand the problems of each individual child as well. Therefore, a good professional relationship needs to be established between the special education classroom teacher and the riding instructor so that together they can review the mandated IEP for each child and develop appropriate riding goals. It is vital that the director of the riding program develop the necessary pathways to access this confidential material and, of course, this confidentiality must be respected. Parental authorization can be a very speedy and effective means of obtaining this important information. One of the critical roles of the riding instructor, as well as the special education teacher, who are both generalists, is to interface with the other professionals as they deem necessary, e.g., physical therapists, occupational therapists or speech/language pathologist. The whole child needs to be observed and appropriate teaching goals and strategies developed. These plans should include specific lessons for carry-over to the classroom as well.

Depending upon the age of the child and the disability he or she faces, a wide variety of activities exist that use the horse educationally. Reading, writing and arithmetic can be incorporated into riding lessons painlessly. The critical talents needed for professionals working in this field are an understanding of disability, a solid knowledge and experience in teaching riding to "able-bodied" riders and the ability to be creative. A sense of humor and tireless energy also helps. The classroom teacher can often help in adapting academic material. It also falls to the riding program to let the many teachers out there know that remedial riding exists and to help them access this field on behalf of their students. Most teachers make wonderful volunteers and are very much interested in anything that can make a difference in the lives of their students.

Conclusion:
Good planning, specific goals, incorporating happy times can give the riders a new look at life that is both therapeutic and exhilarating. It is a demonstrated fact that well-developed lessons do remediate. Remediation in a way that is enjoyable--is powerful. Fun is healing. Success breeds confidence. Having something to look forward to and talk about is a positive influence. Riding can provide all of this. Using the horse incorporates all of the senses, all of the modalities and that helps learning to take place. Riders should learn all there is to know about the horse world and be helped to aspire to be their best. To understand the many areas that can be integrated into a special education program in an equine setting, an information list has been provided.

SOME SPECIFIC ACTIVITIES FOR THE RIDING LESSON AND CLASSROOM

These activities can be adapted to fit the appropriate level from beginner to advanced student riders. The activities can incorporate special education skills that are needed in daily living:

- Balance exercises (the flag, bear stand, riding backward)
- Coordination exercises (all of the above activities in addition to ring tossing and other games)
- Concepts such as under, over, behind, in front
- Language development (group story telling, singing songs)
- Creating a horse story. Putting it on tape and finally writing it out
- Creating a trail course and acting out a horse adventure
- Scavenger hunts on horseback

- ☐ Learning relays using letters or sentences
- ☐ Grooming skills and learning to identify, read, spell and write the names of tools
- ☐ Learning riding skills by taking direction, sequencing tasks and maintaining attention
- ☐ Beginning trail class
- ☐ Advanced trail class
- ☐ Learning to canter
- ☐ Finding out what a horse show is
- ☐ Taking part in a horse show for physically disabled, 4-H club members or Special Olympics
- ☐ Planning a horse show
- ☐ Helping to develop a horse show
- ☐ Gymkhana games
- ☐ Joining a 4-H or Pony Club
- ☐ Scout Badge

This list is just the beginning--it is endless, so begin with your program ...to develop the education experience!

22.05   EQUINE WORKABILITY PROGRAM

Pegi Ryan, Director HWAC

One purpose of the Helen Woodward Animal Center in San Diego, California is to bring animals and people together in a cooperative work/learning environment to enrich both man and animal. With this principle in mind the Center staff set out to explore the environment in and around the barn to see what programs could be offered and for whom to develop this cooperative learning concept.

Three high schools in the San Diego area contacted the Helen Woodward Animal Center regarding their "*workability*" programs (work training) to see if students could be trained in marketable job skills. The workability program, sponsored by the vocational education division, is a state-wide cooperative solution to assist students with disabilities to enter the work world. Schools screen applicants to work and be trained at particular job sites. The schools also pay the students a wage. This seemed like a viable program for the Center so for the past five years four students have been in training here each semester. Southern California is an area rich with horses, from backyard stables to public facilities to multimillion dollar race track training sites. It seemed there was a sure market needing properly prepared applicants.

In the Center's program students are trained primarily in barn skills so that they may enter the job market with good, safe, competitive skills. Each student is introduced to the barn animals, the equipment and safety procedures. They start out learning the skills of cleaning stalls since this is a major barn job. Every two students have a job coach, either a trained volunteer or one of our staff. The coach verbally goes over each task to be completed with the student. The coach then physically performs the task for the students. Next the coach and the students do the task together. Finally the coach watches the students and is there to answer questions that arise or to assist the student should a problem develop. Once basic skills are learned the coach then works on performance quality; finally he or she emphasizes quality work within a reasonable time frame. Students learn not to chat on the job, not to interrupt lessons, to ask questions when they need help, to put tools away correctly and to conform, as required by the job, in dress and attitude.

In the program, students come for 2 to 2½ hours at a time. Within that time frame they are given one fifteen minute break. Approximately one third of the time is spent on actual animal hands-on exploration. What is a horse, goat, sheep, burro? How are they alike? different? We discuss how to safely move around the animals, to lead and handle them. Students practice these skills weekly. Grooming skills are learned and practiced. Weather permitting, students also may assist in bathing a horse. If the hot walker is working, students learn how to place the horse on it. In the last ½ hour of the student's stay things taught are reviewed and how and why they are done at the center. During the semester appropriate behaviors are taught, and employment applications, forms, interviews, dress codes are discussed. The program has worked well for the Center. Two to three times a week, four extra workers come. Many of the students have gone on to other "real" jobs from here. One, in fact, went on to work at Charlie Whittinghams race training facility.

In evaluating the program it was felt that exposing the students to the various animals--burros, goats, sheep--along with the horses was good because many farms have a variety of animals. In fact, when the Center's equine hospital gets an occasional llama in for observation the students are exposed to the llamas as well. Continuing the evaluation it was found many students had the interest and desire to learn and work with horses, but many were extremely fearful and unsure around larger animals. They had very little prior exposure to horses, and farm animals. The very size and movement of the animals was intimidating and confusing. Therefore, it was decided that perhaps a prevocational class was necessary to expose students to various animals and their movements and behavior before the student reaches the "workability" age of junior and senior in high school. With such a class students would (hopefully) better understand and know for themselves if they would want to work in such an environment and if they would feel safe and comfortable. Also such a class would cut down on ultimate training time.

At present the Center is working with a middle school for children with severe learning handicaps. Five students come two times a month with three assistants to work for two hours with one of the staff in just such a prevocational program. The students are shown all the animals at the center, barn animals as well as rabbits, guinea pigs, birds, ferrets, dogs, cats. In each visit they are to introduced to work with a new animal--touching, feeling, leading (if applicable). If students show an interest but are frightened, then they work with the same animal for several visits to establish a comfort zone. Once a comfort zone is reached, related job skill is introduced. At first the task tends to be very removed from the animal, i.e., cleaning out the automatic watering troughs for the horses. This can be done through the pipe corrals without having to get near the horse, raking shed rows, or helping to mix a bran mash are other examples. The vocational skills, however, are not the main intent of this prevocational class, rather developing an interest level is sought.

The prevocational program for younger riders with learning disabilities has begun, during holidays and vacations. Not only do they receive more exposure to the horses but they can see and do jobs with the other animals as well. With such an overall exposure one student went on to volunteer at a pet store. For students working in this prevocational atmosphere it was found they have developed more confidence, and are more apt to approach and interact with people. Their communication skills have improved. At the same time, The Center receives extra help in regular maintenance chores. Eventually some of the riders have gone on to assist as big brother or sister with other youngsters during our summer camps. Others are now volunteers in the riding program. As for the children of the middle school, the same group of children are now coming for the second year. They too are more confident, much less fearful and take a much more active role in working with the animals.

The results of these vocational programs have encouraged the Center to work with Partnership With Industries (PWI), made up of clients from San Diego Regional Center and funded by the Department of Rehabilitation and Habilitation. There is now a contract with PWI to hire five disabled workers for year-round full-time employment. They clean stalls, watering troughs, keep the grounds raked and neat, level stalls, clean the goats' and burros' pens, the chicken coop, and duck pond. They feed the chickens, ducks and horses. They walk the horses, groom and bathe horses and in general perform all the duties a barn worker would. They have a PWI job coach (trained by the center to direct the workers) to assist them should they run into problems. They do the work well and always within the required safety standards.

In this arrangement both parties have benefited. The Center has competent help paid at a rate that does not overly tax its budget, and a group of people who did not work before are gainfully employed. Before PWI clients are hired they must go through an interview with the director of the Center's therapeutic programs. If they "pass" the interview they must call in to the office to let the department know they have passed the interview and are ready for their jobs. Then they receive on-the-job training. If they repeatedly practice unsafe techniques that are dangerous to themselves, others, or the animals, they are subject to termination. Happily, however, many of these workers have gone on to placement in individual jobs in a competitive market.

The Center feels its vocational and prevocational programs definitely fulfill the stated goal of bringing animals and people together in a cooperative work/learning environment. The staff have learned how to be creative and flexible in their teaching. The Center has received assistance at a fraction of usual cost while students learn job skills, giving them confidence to compete in the job market. All parties have been enriched.

Helen Woodward Animal Center, P.O. Box 64, Rancho Sante Fe, CA 92067

22.06   RECREATIONAL RIDING

Barbara J. Brock, PhD

Lance, disabled from a parachute jump six years ago, had not been involved in <u>any</u> physically challenging activity since the accident. He rode for six months in a therapeutic riding program. After gaining the skills to ride, he then quit the program, began to attend weight-lifting classes and signed up for white-water rafting trips. For Lance the riding had been a means to another end .

Chin, disabled with polio, was told by many doctors that he would lose his ability to walk. To conclude his six months of riding, Chin led his horse to the arena, mounted, and with only a small amount of assistance, galloped away. He did not continue to ride with the next program. He had proven something to himself, and walked away with a grin on his face.

Pat, Chip, Diana, Lori, Steve, Lonnie, Jay, and many others also needed exercise, therapy, and confidence, but continued to harbor an interest in riding. The most important reason they continued to ride was "just for the fun of it." They enjoyed horses and the freedom felt from being in command, having the wind in their hair and the dust in their boots. They always arrived a little early to watch and assist with preparation and stayed a little longer to pet and groom their horses.

There are no statistics in the literature on the number of disabled persons who are recreational riders, "just for the fun of it," however participation statistics have been extrapolated from the records of outcomes with disabled winter skiers with some agreement among equestrians. Approximately 2% to 5% of disabled skiers choose to enter into some form of competition, 25% drop out of the program, and 70% continue to ski for a variety of reasons (Cogley, 1989). Similar estimates might be made among disabled riders. Of one hundred riders, five may go on to seriously compete, 25 may go on to other recreational pursuits, and about 70 may continue to ride, if the opportunity exists, "just for the fun of it."

The beauty and benefits of **recreational riding** for disabled persons should not be taken lightly nor overlooked. In teaching an activity, i.e., riding, cooking, camping, swimming, sewing, or reading, if one teacher becomes caught up in the singular goal of "accomplishment", students may miss out on a wealth of positive side effects from the activity. For example, to teach cooking, aside from basics of measuring, heating, and combining ingredients, one should also teach how to arrange a plate, how to combine colors, how to use textures, how much fun it is to sneak a taste, and how great one will feel when others benefit from the learned skill. Likewise, to teach a fitness activity such as running or swimming, one must be aware of not just teaching the skill, but also the dozens of benefits associated with that skill.

Benefits in therapeutic riding may not only be mastery of riding and fitness, but also freedom, weight loss, relaxation, social skills, fresh air, a change of pace, competition, self-confidence, stress relief, or many others. The positive side effects of learning to ride are many and varied. Some of those "other" benefits from horseback riding are documented from as far back as 5th century B.C. It is written that Greek athletes would place those with disabling conditions on the backs of champion horses following the Olympic Games. It was reported to cheer their spirits, and improve mental and physical well-being. (Encyclopedia of the Horse, 1973). Physical, intellectual, and emotional benefits have been reported and documented by riding therapists. Speech, sensory integration, social skills, strength, coordination, verbal skills, and self-esteem have improved as a result of riding programs (Brock, 1987).

After the skills of riding a horse are gained, after strength and coordination improves, after self-esteem and confidence have grown, and after many doors have been opened for the rider to expand his talents, the singular motive that keeps most participants riding is not the benefit of therapy or the ecstasy of successful competition, but simply the joy of riding.

"Those who continue to ride, win...even if ribbons are not the reward, something greater is. One thing that all disabled riders will attest to is this: any limitation experienced in daily living is lost in the thrill of commanding the movements of a 1,000 pound (plus) animal of grace, beauty, and power" (Williams, 1985).

Aside from gaining strength, coordination, and muscle control from use of the horse purely as a therapeutic tool, and aside from the keen confidence developed in advanced levels of horsemanship and competition, there is something more that attracts most of the disabled riders. The lack of limitations and barriers, development of friends among fellow riders and volunteers alike, feelings of control, love and warmth of the friendly beast underneath, and the powerful sense of freedom of direction and movement are usually enough incentive for most disabled persons to continue to ride.

There are many wonderful and "right" ways to teach and offer therapeutic horseback riding programs. The beauty of creativity and the fun of spontaneity need to play a part in each class as well as expert instruction and therapy. <u>Don't forget, ALL riders need to have fun!</u>

"Sometimes the best thing for us to do is to "get them out there" and let the horse take over!"

Reference

Encyclopedia of the Horse. (1973). New York: Viking Press. 130-131.

Brock, B. (1978). *Effects of Therapeutic Horseback Riding on Physically Disabled* Adults. Dissertation. Indiana University.

Cogley, J. (1989). Personal Communication. October 20.

Williams, M. (1985). Personal Communication. June 30.

22.07   ADAPTIVE HORSEBACK RIDING
TRAINING HORSES SPECIALLY FOR PHYSICALLY DISABLED INDIVIDUALS
WHO DESIRE TO RIDE INDEPENDENTLY IN WILDERNESS AREAS

Kerrill Knaus

H.O.R.S.E.S for the Physically Challenged.   H.O.R.S.E.S. stands for Horseback Outdoors Recreation, Scenic Experiences and Services. H.O.R.S.E.S. For The Physically Challenged is a non-profit organization established to offer people with disabilities a family-oriented, integrated program that provides a wide variety of services adapted to the disabled individual.

The goal of the organization is to provide the support services needed by disabled individuals who wish to become independent riders. This is accomplished primarily in three ways:
1.   Custom training of specially selected horses
2.   Providing adaptive saddles and other riding and safety equipment
3.   Training the rider to understand and control his or her mount in spite of physical limitations

The organization owns a number of specially trained horses which are used by disabled riders for both skill building and wilderness exploration. Guidelines are being developed to assist other people in the selection and training of equines for this special field. H.O.R.S.E.S has also begun a breeding and foal training program in order to produce equines with the intelligence, temperament, and physical characteristics needed for adaptive riding. In addition to these services, H.O.R.S.E.S. also locates and trains horses and other equines for disabled individuals who prefer to own their own mounts. In order to avoid confusing this type of riding with other forms of therapeutic and recreational horseback riding and driving for people with disabilities, H.O.R.S.E.S. For The Physically Challenged refers to itself as an "adaptive riding program".

Adapting the mind of the horse to the needs of riders with severe physical disabilities requires a philosophy of training that is detailed and highly versatile. Beginning with the selection of the right horse, the trainers then create a specific training program tailored to the abilities and intended use of that particular animal. He or she must however be constantly willing to deviate from traditional training techniques and expectations while at the same time building as much as possible on a strong foundation of knowledge and experience of tried, proven methods. The goal must always remain to create a working harmony between the horse and rider, not merely a list of skills which the horse can perform. Training clinics, workshops, and consultation services are offered to individuals and organizations seeking detailed information on adaptive equine training and equipment.

ACCESS EQUINES
An Access Equine is a horse, pony, or mule that is specially selected and/or trained to the individual requirements of a disabled person for their use in recreation, sport, employment, or wilderness exploration. These are not intended to be therapy horses. The purpose of these equines is to provide a means by which the individual with disabilities may gain access to these activities. The Access Equine's duties may include but are not limited to, providing access and mobility by carrying or pulling the individual, packing a wheelchair, crutches or other needed equipment, and performing specific tasks related to the person's disability such as lying down so the rider can mount.

SELECTION OF TRAINING RECRUITS --AGE birth to 12 years
Animals selected by H.O.R.S.E.S. for specialized training must be physically sound, with a calm and gentle temperament, and an obvious affection for and interest in people. The horse should tolerate changes of environment and routine without exhibiting signs of anxiety or stress. The horse should also demonstrate caution and curiosity, but not fear, of new and unusual objects, such as a metallic helium balloon. He must never threaten aggression toward people even if harassed. Breed and size will vary according to the needs of the person with a disability.

Access Equines are trained to four levels depending on the disabilities of persons they are intended to serve. The following is a summary of those levels. Whenever possible, training information has been included. However, a complete and detailed review of this training would require an entire manual devoted solely to that subject and is far too lengthy to be adequately addressed here.

Level I

Basic training of Access Equines begins in the training corral. The horse is taught to free lunge, follow the handler without halter or lead, and to come when called by name. Additional training includes:

A. Attitude training

1. Training the horse to cope with fearful situations without risk of harm to the handler or horse by focusing on the "spook" reflex. The horse is taught to turn and face the situation, rather than run from the things it fears.
2. Basic desensitizing to loud noises such as chain saws, motorcycles, gun shots, sudden movements, i.e., dogs darting past, birds breaking suddenly from the brush, mechanical aids such as wheelchairs, crutches, and an extensive list of frightening stimuli which might be encountered in an uncontrolled environment.
3. Teaching the horse to focus, and maintain its attention and alertness whenever in use, without becoming nervous or tense. This concept begins in the training corral where the horse is taught to maintain eye contact with the trainer when being worked. The requirement to pay attention is continued and expanded through the training process.
4. Teaching the horse to relax on cue. The horse is taught to drop its head and assume relaxed physical posture, which in turn causes the horse to emotionally relax. This is first taught with a physical cue, tightening the reins. This cue is very useful as most riders subconsciously pull back when startled or tense. The result of this training is that a tense rider will have a relaxed horse instead of an uptight one. Horses that are trained to the advanced levels are trained with verbal cue which is later added for riders who are unable to use the reins.

B. Ground training

Ground training includes those skills needed to enable the rider with disabilities to handle and care for his horse as much as possible without assistance. Ground training includes:

1. <u>Leading without resistance in all three gaits and backwards</u>. This avoids the common problem of the horse allowing itself to be towed around the practice arena. Such a habit alters the natural movement and therapeutic rhythm of the horse by allowing him to become stiff, rigid, or hollow backed. Being pulled along also fosters resistance to pressure, rather than the more desirable behavior of yielding to pressure. Allowing habits of resistance to form can have serious implications on other areas of training and behavior.
2. <u>Leading from a wheelchair</u>. The horse is taught to remain beside the wheelchair, never in front or behind, and to walk with its head lowered to the leader's level. This keeps the leader within the horse's field of vision. The horse is also taught never to touch or rub against a person while standing or using a wheelchair, preventing the person from being knocked off balance, or the horse's halter becoming tangled in the chair causing a serious accident.
3. <u>Grooming and Tacking</u>. The horse is trained to assist in the grooming and tacking process by changing position when requested on verbal cue, lowering its head and picking up the bit (see Figure 1.), standing without fidgeting, and other skills as needed. This benefits both the rider who wishes to participate in this activity, and serves to make maximum use of volunteer time in horse preparation.
4. <u>Mounting/Dismounting</u>. All methods are taught from both sides including from the ground, leg up, lifted on, mounting from a platform, and mounting with a slide board.

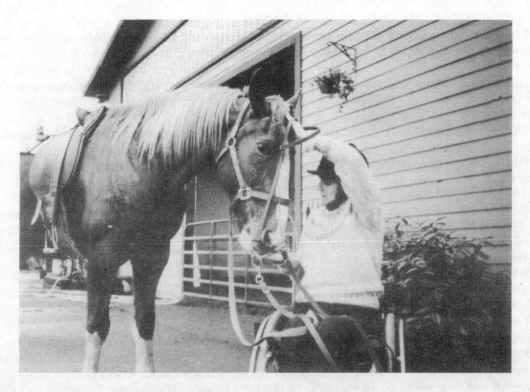

FIGURE 1. LOWERING HEAD FOR BRIDLING

In addition to attitude and ground training, a Level I horse is trained to be:
- ⊙ Responsive to traditional leg and hand aids
- ⊙ Proficient at neck reining
- ⊙ Able to yield to bit pressure
- ⊙ Skilled in collection and lead changes
- ⊙ Accepting of back riding
- ⊙ Safe for a novice or a child rider

Equines' intended use:
- ⊙ Used by able bodied rider solo in the practice arena and/or trail
- ⊙ Used by novice physically challenged rider for introductory riding or equipment evaluation and development while on lead, or with a back rider in the practice arena and/or on the trail
- ⊙ Used by experienced physically challenged riders (with minimal lower extremity impairment) independently, if rider does not need a mount with higher level, more detailed skills

LEVEL II

A level II horse must be proficient at level I activities plus:
- ⊙ Leg cues replaced with verbal cues for walk, trot, and canter

Equines' Intended Use:
- ⊙ Used by the novice physically challenged rider (with only lower extremity impairment) solo in the practice arena
- ⊙ Used by experienced physically challenged rider (with lower extremity impairment) solo on the trail

531

LEVEL III

Horse must be proficient at levels 1 and 2 activities plus:

◎ Traditional leg and hand aids are replaced by verbal cues including asking the horse for upward and downward transitions, in all three gaits, side passing, backing, and right and left turn The horse that has been trained to this level can be moved through varying patterns and obstacles without a rider or any tack, whips, or other equipment. The horse should be able to perform any desired moves solely by the verbal directions of a handler seated or standing anywhere in the arena or training area.

Equines' intended use:

◎ Used by novice physically challenged rider (with all four extremities partially or fully impaired) solo in the practice arena

◎ Used by experienced physically challenged rider (with all four extremities partially or fully impaired) solo on the trail

LEVEL IV

Level 4 involves customizing a horse's training for one specific rider. The horse must be proficient at level I activities. He may or may not be proficient at levels 2 or 3 activities depending on the needs of the rider. Custom training includes, but is not limited to the following:

◎ Lowering the head for haltering and bridling (usually included in level 1)

◎ Opening and closing gates on cue

◎ Lying down for mounting

◎ Ground tying

◎ Hobble training

Whatever the goal, be it recreation, sport, employment, or wilderness access and exploration, the horse's training is tailored to the needs and abilities of the individual disabled rider. With this foundation the horse becomes an aid to the rider in his or her independence and mobility, in much the same way that an Assistance Dog aids in the mobility and independence of its blind or disabled master. The Access Equine is one of the newest members of the <u>service animal industry</u>.

For more information on Access Equines contact: H.O.R.S.E.S. No portion of this article may be reproduced without the express written consent of H.O.R.S.E.S. For the Physically Challenged and editor of the text. PO Box 5, Scotts Mills, Oregon 97375

22.08 STUDENT INTERNSHIPS

Barbara T. Engel MEd, OTR

Incorporating student training within the therapeutic riding setting can have many advantages. Internship programs can add to the overall educational quality of the therapeutic riding program. Along with the fulfillment of course requirements student programs help to keep standards high.

Advantages of internships:
1. Provide extra staff with definite time commitments
2. Help to keep standards high to be in accord with the requirements of the student training program and with the association or the affiliating institution
3. Help to bring fresh ideas into the program at a professional level
4. Promote a community-based association with an institution of higher learning
5. Educate future professionals in the value of therapeutic riding

Student internships are set up for specific months or numbers of work hours. Different types of affiliation have different requirements. Some college courses require their students to perform pre-course volunteer requirements. Other programs incorporate internships within the class structure. Training of therapists usually requires internships at the end of the academic course work. Types of student programs which could fit within the framework of therapeutic riding include:
1. Adaptive Physical Education
2. Occupational Therapy
3. Physical Therapy
4. Speech and Language Therapy
5. Psychology
6. Psychotherapy and Counseling
7. Recreation
8. Recreational Therapy
9. Special Education

Internship programs each set forth specific requirements. Most will require a formalized teaching program in addition to specific time requirements for hands-on participation. The teaching program must be either directly or indirectly taught by a qualified professional in the specific field being offered. For example: a rehabilitation center has a student training program for physical and occupational therapists. As a part of their training, each student spends four hours a week treating rehabilitation center patients at the therapeutic riding center. The physical therapy students are supervised by a physical therapist and the occupational therapy students are supervised by an occupational therapist in *equine-assisted therapy*. Adaptive physical education students would be supervised and trained by an adaptive physical education teacher involved in the program. It is important that those who are involved in training students in therapeutic riding settings be trained and knowledgeable in the application of principles of their profession as they relate to the use of the horse.

Despite the extra work for the staff, especially at the beginning of an affiliation period, students do contribute a great deal in working with clients. In addition they enrich the overall therapeutic riding program.

534

PART VII   EQUINE-ASSISTED THERAPY

This section involving equine-assisted therapy is included in this text to provide instructors with an overview of the field. It will also give a therapist, new to the field, an idea of what equine-assisted therapy involves.

As programs in therapeutic riding have grown during the last forty five years, an increasing focus has been directed toward the use of the horse as a modality used by health care professionals for the treatment of specific disorders resulting from a variety of disabilities. The health care practioner can make use of the same "therapeutic" elements that have advanced the therapeutic sports riding field. Through their special knowledge and training in a multitude of therapy techniques, therapists can manipulate the horse as a modality in addition, they can stimulate the client using more traditional methods in order to gain exceptional results.

In order for the field to advance several processes must occur:

- <u>Information must be disbursed</u> to health care professionals and physicians; to professional horse trainers interested in the field of therapeutic riding, to the general community interested in therapeutic riding, and to the population it serves.

- <u>Advancement of trained equine-assisted therapy teams</u>. Equine-assisted therapy is a **team undertaking** involving:
    1. A therapist specifically trained in the use of a horse as a modality.
    2. An instructor who has been trained in at least first, and preferably second level dressage.
    3. A horse who is sound, trained to first/second level dressage and who meets the conformation and qualities necessary in a therapy horse.

- <u>Sharing of information</u> of all those who are involved in the field of equine-assisted therapy.

- <u>Continued education</u> available to equine-assisted therapy teams, or available through national and international organizations such as the American Hippotherapy Association, practioner-specialists in the field of equine-assisted therapy who have gained the special knowledge in their own professional field in addition to specific knowledge on equine-assisted therapy--necessary to further train others in the field.

- Pursuit of individual and group <u>research projects</u> and the publication of the results of these projects.

This section includes the disciplines of occupational and physical therapy, speech/language therapy, psycho-social therapy, and recreational therapy. The articles include different treatment approaches used by a few therapists in the field. This section is not intended to provide the reader with in depth knowledge of equine-assisted therapy but only to present the contributing author's points of view and to stimulate interest in the field.

23 DEFINING EQUINE-ASSISTED THERAPY

23.01 THERAPEUTIC USE OF THE HORSE IN HEALTH CARE

"The rhythmic movement of the horse's back, together with the physical contact and the motivation created through use of a living exercise apparatus, meets all the requirements of modern kinesitherapy techniques: increased flow of impulses from the periphery through proprioceptive, tactile, and vestibular stimulation; and improved activation of the voluntary motor control loop (periphery-cerebellum-parietal lobe-frontal lobe-periphery" (Riede, 1988; ie.). As early as the 1500's, physicians found that riding was beneficial to health. The Greeks used horseback riding with people who were found to have incurable problems in order to improve their spirits (Mayberry, 1978). In 1750 Francisco Fuller, in the first sports medicine text, mentioned equitation and its implications for maintenance of physical exercise and the effects it has on the mind and body.

Benefits which have been attributed to riding during the 1600-1800's are stimulation of the digestive system, alleviating gout, relieving tuberculosis, influencing body metabolism, increasing strength in weak bodies, helping psychological problems, improving general wellness of body and soul (De Pauw, 1986). Riders who were seriously injured were reported as making remarkable recoveries after they began to ride again; also in helping to relieve their psychological stress (Riede, 1988). The movement of the horse at a walking gait and the resulting swinging motions of its back are transferred to the rider; these actions duplicate the same movement impulses or sequences that occur when a person walks normally (Heipertz, 1981).

The current use of the horse in medical care has developed since the late 1950's, mainly by German physicians and therapists. In 1965 Joseph J. Bauer and Dr. R.E. Renaud began using riding to rehabilitate patients. Clients involved in rehabilitation have included those with such disorders as multiple sclerosis, closed head injuries, orthopedic disorders, cerebral palsy, behavioral disorders and developmental disabilities. In the late 1970's, a few therapists, including physical therapist Barbara Glasow, who studied hippotherapy in Germany, began to spearhead the development of hippotherapy in the United States. International Congresses for Therapeutic Riding began in 1964 in Paris; 1976 in Basle, 1979 in Warwick, 1982 in Hamburg, 1985 in Milan, 1988 in Toronto and 1991 in Aarhus. These Congresses have been especially helpful in the exchange of information leading toward the development of the treatment applications of the horse.

Heipertz (1981) points out that the type, degree and quality of the horse's movement are important since these movements provide the therapeutic effects sought for the rider. In addition, the facilities where activities occur must be appropriate for treatment purposes. A third essential element is a therapy team of qualified specialists. The treatment team consists of a therapist who is well trained in *equine-assisted therapeutic methods and in the theory of Hippotherapy*, a skilled riding instructor who influences the horse's movements at the first/second level dressage maneuvers, and trained support assistants or helpers. The use of the horse for therapeutic purposes combines the ability to produce specific movement in the horse with traditional therapy techniques used by physical therapists, occupational therapists, speech pathologists, and other health care practitioners.

References
Bauer, J.J. (1972). *Riding for Rehabilitation*. Toronto: Canadian Stage and Arts Publications Ltd.
DePauw, K.P. Horsebackriding for Individual with Disabilities: Program, Philosophy and Research. *Adaptive Physical Activity Quarterly*. 3,3, 217-226.
Heipertz, W. (1981). *Therapeutic Riding*. English Ed. Ottawa: National Printers Inc..
Mayberry, R. (1978). The mystique of the horse is strong medicine: Riding as therapeutic recreation. *Rehabilitation Literature*.
Riede, D. (1988). *Physiotherapy on the Horse*. Renton: The Delta Society.

23.02 THOUGHTS FOR THERAPISTS

Nancy H. McGibbon, PT

The rider's smiling face, proud look of achievement, new-found freedom of mobility, and renewed energy and purpose are enough to satisfy the interest of many a therapist interested in new treatment strategies. Perhaps, a therapist, one who has been working in the field for a number of years is looking for new motivational treatment options, or is just out of school and sees equine-assisted therapy (E.A.T.) as a natural integration of the techniques and theory learned in class. On the surface, equine-assisted therapy looks like the ideal holistic treatment as it incorporates psychological and motivational as well as sensorimotor goals. It is hard to think of many clients who would not benefit from it. Is it too good to be true? Not really, but the therapeutic use of the horse, which looks deceptively easy, requires a great deal of knowledge, experience, and good sound judgement.

Extensive horse knowledge is a prerequisite for any therapist considering equine-assisted therapy. The steady, kind, patient and obedient therapy horse is in reality a complex and variable creature, which the therapist must understand better than any modality used in the clinic. Unlike the ultrasound or Cybex, no two horses are alike, and even a seasoned "therapy horse" is not necessarily safe or appropriate for all clients. For a therapist who does not have extensive horse experience, an introductory hippotherapy workshop provides an excellent overview but does not give a therapist the depth and range of knowledge necessary to immediately use this treatment as part of a client's therapeutic program. The use of the horse presents a greater safety risk to the client than traditional clinical treatment. Thus it is the obligation of the therapist to become thoroughly familiar with the horse's temperament, basic instincts, body language, and movement characteristics before even considering incorporating equine activities into a treatment plan. Lectures and workshops are no substitute for experience: regular riding, handling, grooming, and "hanging out" with all sizes, types, and breeds of horses is necessary to gain this experience. The more hours spent with horses, the better the judgement the therapist will use in enhancing treatment efficacy and safety.

The work environment in equine-assisted therapy is ideal for a therapist who enjoys the outdoors, who likes working with animals as well as people, and who enjoys creative, non-traditional treatment approaches. However, there are some drawbacks. One-on-one therapy requires much walking on soft and sometimes uneven ground, and the therapist must tolerate dust, horse hair and outdoor temperature variations. It is physically impossible to treat, hands-on, the same number of clients per week that one would see in the clinic, and a single therapist-client session requires a minimum of 1-2 trained staff. In order to proceed with a safe, effective therapy session, many factors must be coordinated: the horse, horse and rider equipment, team members, facility, and weather. Clearly, the logistics are more complicated than in the clinic.

A horse professional, other than the therapist, in whom the therapist has complete confidence, is an essential member of the treatment team. The therapist cannot handle, simultaneously, both the horse and the client and must rely on the expertise of a horse handler to produce the desired equine movement and behavior. In spite of this, the therapist is still ultimately responsible for the entire treatment team, for monitoring both client and horse, and for making key decisions regarding horse-client interaction.

Considering backriding? What could be more fun than riding a horse and treating a client at the same time! Well, the therapist may want to reconsider, unless she is a very experienced, competent rider. Though backriding seems to get the most publicity of all the techniques used in E.A.T., backriding is not equine therapy. It is a technique for client handling. The advantage of allowing the therapist to be at the same level as the client and to be able to provide bilateral facilitation is certainly a consideration. However, before proceeding with this technique, ask yourself the following questions: *If the horse should spook or buck, can I maintain an independent seat?* (maintaining balance and security on the horse without holding on) *Is my horse's back strong enough to carry the combined weight of me and my client? Is backriding truly necessary, or could I effectively assist this client from the ground?* The therapist must be aware that backriding presents an increased risk to the client and therefore, should consider carefully before choosing this particular technique.

<u>Insurance and liability issues</u> that arise in any treatment situation are even more critical when a horse is involved. What is one's personal liability? Will your malpractice insurance cover this particular activity since it is somewhat out of the ordinary? Will these therapy sessions be adequately reimbursed or can one afford to donate these services? Do not automatically assume that by volunteering your services your liability is reduced.

<u>Professionalism</u> must be maintained in spite of the outdoor, non-medical, recreational atmosphere. If one is considering affiliation with a center which offers riding therapy, check its credentials. Is it accredited by a national organization? Does it operate under the strictest safety guidelines? One needs to critique it in the same way one would any facility which offers professional services. Do the staff and volunteers dress professionally and appropriately? Are they mature and responsible? Will they inspire confidence in the clients and client families? Do they work well together as a team? Is the facility maintained well with regard to both horses and equipment? Can one carry out the treatment in a quiet, controlled environment without concern for unexpected trail riders, neighborhood dogs, or ATV's (all terrain vehicles) paying a surprise visit?

<u>Getting started</u> in equine assisted therapy is best done by volunteering to be a therapeutic riding consultant a few hours per week at an established program. The therapist advises the therapeutic riding instructor on rider posture and positioning, appropriate exercises, and special equipment and, at the same time, gains knowledge and experience in assessing horse-rider interaction. Assisting a rider as a side-walker also gives the therapist helpful information on tone and postural response changes due to equine movement. In addition, experience working in close proximity to the horse increases the therapist's confidence and general rapport with the animal. Equine therapy workshops in combination with increasing hands-on experience provide the groundwork for an exciting and rewarding therapeutic experience.

23.03 TYPES OF THERAPISTS INVOLVED IN EQUINE-ASSISTED THERAPY AND THERAPEUTIC RIDING PROGRAMS

Barbara T. Engel, MEd, OTR

Therapeutic riding programs normally seek the services of a physical or occupational therapists as the programs major consultants. Depending on the types of clients, therapists may include a speech and language pathologist, clinical psychologist or recreational therapist. As a consultant, the therapist provides information to the program staff regarding the needs and disabilities of the clients. The physical or occupational therapist should have both training and experience with the specific populations that the program serves. Medicine has developed into highly specialized areas. The same is true in both physical therapy and occupational therapy. Specialization has become necessary in order for one to develop a complete understanding of groups of disabilities and methods of dealing with them. The basic educational preparation provides the graduate therapist with fundamental knowledge of human function, disease, disabilities and of their professional concepts. Specialized training is necessary, for example if one is to work with children and adults with cerebral palsy or other neurological and developmental disorders.

An *Occupational Therapist* (OTR) is a bachelor's or master's degree level college graduate with a major in occupational therapy. In addition to the academic training, the therapist will have completed internships in such areas as pediatrics, psychiatry, and physical disabilities. The therapist must pass an examination at the end of his or her training before he or she is certified to practice as registered occupational therapist. Post graduate education may be in such areas as hand therapy, sensory integration treatment, geriatric care, neonatal care, arthritis, general rehabilitation, developmental disabilities, community mental health, work hardening and other highly specialized areas. Most states require therapists to be licensed as well as certified. The occupational therapist treats clients with the use of activities with the aim of returning them to their useful "occupation." "Occupational" can mean activities of daily living, work, or play/leisure.

A *Physical Therapist* (PT) is a graduate of a four year college with a major in physical therapy. In addition to the academic courses, a physical therapist also completed internships in various specialty areas. The physical therapist must pass a state examination to be licensed by a state in which he practices. He may seek additional post-graduate training in neurodevelopmental treatment, various sub-specialties in orthopedics, pediatrics, sports science and medicine, and other areas of acute or chronic care. The physical therapist treats clients with the use of modalities such as light, heat, water, electricity, and with movement activities such as exercises and neurological stimulation. The aim is of gaining maximum mobility in the client.

A *Speech and Language Pathologist* is a graduate of at least a masters' degree level or doctoral degree. He is certified by a national association (ASHA) and is licensed by some states to practice. He also may specialize in specific areas as do physical and occupational therapists. The speech and language pathologist facilitates the development of the oral-motor area and provides language focused treatment with persons of all ages who have communication problems.

A *Clinical Psychologist* is a graduate of doctoral level university programs. He usually specializes in distinct areas of human behavior, normal or aberrant, and offers counseling and support to individuals with problems of adjustment to their social environment.

Recreational Therapist (RTR) is a person who has graduated from a four year college with a major in recreational therapy: The academic requirements include internships with various special population groups such as developmentally delayed, emotionally, and physically disabled persons. A national competency exam and state certification in some states, are required. The recreational therapist uses participation in leisure activities to improve functional behavior and physical condition in clients while giving them the opportunity to acquire skills, knowledge, and effective use of leisure time.

23.04 DEFINING STRATEGIES FOR REMEDIATION IN REHABILITATION

Barbara T. Engel, MEd, OTR

Instructors of therapeutic riding programs are becoming more involved with a variety of professionals in the medical, educational and equine fields. Practitioners in these fields may have studied and developed special strategies and remediation techniques which they are able to apply to the therapeutic riding and/or equine-assisted therapy situation. A review of techniques is presented here to give the reader a brief understanding of the terms.

Affolter Method
Dr. Felicie Affolter, a Swiss language pathologist, has developed a treatment approach involving *Guiding as a Perceptual Cognitive Approach* to functional development of persons with motor disorders. This approach is based on Piagetian theories of development. It assumes that perception is a prerequisite for interaction, tactile-kinesthetic information is necessary for interaction to occur and interaction is always goal-directed. The technique, as described by Affolter, requires a hands-on approach in which the therapist assists the client in performing a task. The therapist puts her arms and hands over the client's arms and hands and guides the client through the performance of a task. The client learns to <u>register sensation</u> of touch and movement in the process of performing the task. The client learns to register information regarding his environment and his ability to a interact on tactile- kinesthetic basis with his environment as he becomes aware of himself and his actions within his surroundings (Affolter, 1991).

Alexander Method
Gerda Alexander, a German, calls her method *Eutony*. "Eu" in Greek means good, well, harmonious, and "tonus" means tension. This method involves focusing on the unity of the total person. This "feeling of unity and integrity liberates the creative forces and develops the capacity of contact with others without losing one's own individuality." Her method increases one's awareness of his bodily systems and influences the way he functions (Alexander, 1985).

Centered Riding
An approach developed by Sally Swift of Brattleboro, Vermont, which increases the mental and physical images resulting in perfect body balance and an increased inner awareness of both oneself and one's horse. The approach is not a method to teach riding but a way to teach how one breathes, balances and how one moves one's body and limbs. By using the Centered Riding approach, any person may improve his ability to control his body while learning to ride a horse. The technique is used by instructors with their students and by therapists with their clients to improve functions.

Conductive Education System
Also known as the Peto System, Dr. Andras Peto from Budapest developed conductive education in 1950's. This is a method of learning called "rhythmic intention". In it each task to be learned is broken down into component parts; each part is practiced separately until success is reached. This aspect is the intent. Meanwhile, the client counts while practicing the tasks providing the rhythmic component and stimulus which guides the movement. Rhythmic intent as a method of learning claims to involve the client's motor, linguistic, perceptual and cognitive abilities. When several clients are working together the group provides further motivation (Cotton, E.).

CranioSacral Therapy
John Upledger, an osteopathic physician, developed *CranioSacral Therapy* (Upledger, Vredevoogd, 1983). It involves the understanding of the cranio-sacral system and the specific techniques used by those who have been trained in this method. The technique uses gentle and non-invasive palpatory skills to detect subtle biological movements, and to perform fascial and soft tissue releases. This modality is used with persons with neuromuscular dysfunction and helps to identify and reduce accumulated pain and stress, calm down the autonomic system, lower blood pressure and fevers, remove transient and minor restrictions, relax muscles, improve fluid exchange and blood flow, lengthen the spine, and promote general relaxation and a balancing of the body system.

Developmental Stimulation

Developmental stimulation includes all types of facilitation and stimulation techniques based upon the normal growth process. Techniques arise from different theories as they are developed by various professions. For example, the techniques used by early childhood specialists to encourage movement and play will vary from techniques used by pediatric occupational and physical therapists treating children with cerebral palsy. Nevertheless, such techniques can be incorporated into therapeutic riding.

Feldenkrais Method

The Feldenkrais method is an educational, neuromuscular approach to improve function. It strives toward ease of movement and improved coordination. This is accomplished through increased awareness, sensitivity and coordination (Feldenkrais, 1981). The entire sensory-motor system is involved in order to unravel habitual patterns and replace them with better motor function through changing the person's perception of movement. Dr. Moshe Feldenkrais developed the techniques of *Functional Integration* and *Awareness through Movement*.

Functional Integration uses touch, the feelings of pressure and pull, the warmth of the hands and their caressing stroke. This technique is based on neurological milestones in development. Feldenkrais felt that a "crucial point of the learning was the arrival of the impulses sent by the nervous system in patterns such that all the intricate movements can be performed" (Feldenkrais, 1981). When the nervous system is damaged, *Functional Integration* techniques help the nervous system to respond to establish impulses which facilitate normal movements.

Feldenkrais *Awareness through Movement* is based on several concepts: that one needs to learn at one's own rate, that movement is the vehicle for learning and that one need to have alternative ways of moving. Learning must be pleasurable and it must be easy. These two elements increase relaxed breathing. He felt that emphasis should be on the action of learning the movement, not the goal to be obtained; one needs to be aware of the learning process.

Handling Techniques

Any hands-on technique which can be used to manipulate the posture or limbs of a client for therapeutic reasons is called a "handling technique." Bobath methods involve many techniques for handling children and adults with spastic disorders. Facilitory techniques are special handling techniques used by the therapist to increase the ease in carrying out a functional action or to inhibit neural responses. They assist the client by enhancing function. Handling techniques are used by caregivers and therapists to handle a person at key points in such a way as to maintain *normal* or near normal posture and are used when moving a person from one position to another (Finnie, 1975). Inhibitory techniques are also handling techniques which inhibit (restrain or interfere with) an action or a process. Therapists use inhibitory techniques to reduce spasticity, or to relax or slow down undesirable actions.

Holistic Treatment

Holistic refers to treatment of the whole or consideration of all functional aspects of a person. Holistic treatment deals with all aspects of a person's function and dysfunction and usually encompasses many different approaches. A holistic occupational therapy approach to learning disorders was developed by Barbara Knickerbocker, OTR (Knickerbocker, 1980) which incorporates sensory interaction theory but uses a different treatment approach.

Myofacial Release

This technique was developed by John F. Barnes, a physical therapist. Myofascial release is designed to be utilized with appropriate modalities, mobilization, exercise and flexibility programs, neurodevelopmental treatment (NDT), sensory integration and movement therapy. Myofascial release relates to the fascia of the body. The facia is a three-dimensional connective tissue which runs from the head to the foot throughout the body. Its purpose is to support structures by holding tissues together as well as separating structures so that they can move without friction (Barnes, 1989). Myofascial Release is the lengthening of superficial and deep body tissue through a gentle and sustained stretch (Boehme, 1988)(Barnes, 1991).

Neuro-developmental Treatment (NDT)

NDT, also referred to as the Bobath Technique, was developed by Berta Bobath, a British physiotherapist, and her husband, physician Karel Bobath. This method is based on the recognition of the interference of normal maturation of the brain leading to arrest of motor development and the presence of abnormal postural reflex activity (Bobath, 1970). The aim of this handling technique is to inhibit abnormal movement patterns while facilitating normal reactions and movement.

Perceptual-Motor-Stimulation

Perception refers to the interpretation in the brain of sensations one takes in. Motor is a movement response. Perceptual-motor stimulation refers to activities what increase when the brain interprets, feels or senses and the motor responses as the result.

Proprioceptive Neuromuscular Facilitation (PNF)

Herman Kabat, MD, and two physical therapists, Margaret Knott and Dorothy Voss, developed *Proprioceptive Neuromuscular Facilitation* techniques for the treatment of neuromuscular problems. PNF is "a method of promoting or hastening the response of the neuromuscular mechanism through stimulation of the proprioceptor" (Hopkins & Smith, 1978). The PNF patterns and techniques are used both independently and with exercises, gait training and self-care activities to develop strength, balance and motor learning.

Rood: Neurophysiological Approach

Margaret Rood, an occupational and physical therapist, developed a treatment approach which involves activation, facilitation, and inhibition of muscle actions, voluntary and involuntary, through the reflex arc. This approach assumes that an exercise is a treatment only when the response is correct and the feedback results in enhanced learning of that response (Hopkins, Smith, 1978).

Sensorimotor Stimulation

There are many therapeutic treatment applications of sensorimotor stimulation which have developed during the last 50 years. They are based largely on the work of Sherrington and others, and include approaches of the Bobaths, Fay, Doman-Delacato, Rood, Kabat, Pavlov, Brunnstrom, Fuchs, Ayres, Cratty, Kephart and others. Most have emerged as current knowledge of the nervous system has progressed. Sensorimotor stimulation techniques are applied according to the theoretical base of the professional using them - i.e., physical, occupational, speech therapists; physical educators, movement therapists, child development specialists and so on. There is a great deal of change occurring in the approaches being used in treatment because of the growth in the knowledge of how the central nervous system actually functions. Many of the "old" techniques are outmoded since the reasoning behind their development has been found to be inaccurate and the techniques have been either "revised" or discarded in order to apply to the current base of knowledge about function.

Sensory Integration or (SI)

Sensory Integration is a system of treatment techniques, based on theories of evaluation and treatment developed by A.J. Ayres, an occupational therapist. It involves active participation by the client in purposeful activities which are always initiated and directed by him. It requires the client to make an adaptive response to his environment. In this process, activities which are rich in proprioceptive, vestibular and tactile input are not repeated but are done as a continuous series of events. After careful evaluation using Ayres tests, the therapist manipulates the environment to obtain the desired results for the dysfunction and to facilitate or inhibit neurological functions or stated goals of improving the processing and organization of sensation. Sensory integration does not include the teaching of skills or the arousal of specific sensations such as applying tactile stimulation to a client or placing the client in an activity which provides him with vestibular stimulation. Sensory integration methods must be administered by an occupational or physical therapist who is specifically trained in the techniques. (Sensory Integration International, 1990). A Sensory Integration Certified therapist (occupational or physical therapist) is recognized by SII (Sensory Integration International) as qualified for testing purposes only.

Tactile Stimulation

Tactile refers to the sense of touch. Tactile stimulation can include any type of arousal of the touch system; it may include direct excitation to the skin or having the client engage in tactically arousing activities. (Sensory Integration International, 1990)

Vestibular Stimulation

Vestibular refers to the vestibular apparatus of the inner ear which includes those parts innervated by the eighth cranial nerve: the saccule, utricle, semicircular canals, vestibular nerve and vestibular nuclei, and those parts of the brain which are directly affected by this system. The vestibular system responds to type, direction, angle, and speed of movement and head position enabling a person's to orient in space and time and maintain a sense of equilibrium or balance (Dunn, 1991). Vestibular stimulation can include any excitation which arouses the vestibular system (Sensory Integration International, 1990).

References:
Affolter, F.D. (1991). *Perception, Interaction, and Language*. Berlin: Springer-Verlag.
Alexander, G. (1985). *Eutony*. Great Neck: Felix Morrow
Barnes, J.F. (1991) Myofascial Release Techniques. *Occupational Therapy Forum*. July 19, 1991.
Blakiston's Gould Medical Dictionary 4th Ed. (1979). New York: McGraw-Hill Book & Co.
Bobath, B. (1972). *The Concept of Neuro-developmental Treatment*. Lecture notes Western Cerebral Palsy Centre, London Cermak, S. (1989).
Boehme, R. (1988). *Improving Upper Body Control*. Tucson: Therapy Skill Builders.
The Efficacy of Sensory Integration Procedures in *Sensory Integration Quarterly*. Torrance: Sensory Integration International.
Cotton, E. (no date given). *The Hand as a Guide to Learning*. London: The Spastics Society.
Dunn, W. (1991). In Christiansen-Baum (ed) *Occupational Therapy, Overcoming Human Performance Deficits*. Thorofare: Slack Inc.
Feldenkrais, M. (1981) *The Elusive Obvious*. Cupertino: Meta Publications.
Finnie, N.R. (1975). New York: E.P.Dutton & Co., Inc.
Hopkins, H., Smith, H. *Willard & Spackman's Occupational Therapy*, 5th Ed. New York: Lippincott Co. p 127-28
Knickerbocker, B.M. (1980). *A Holistic Approach to the Treatment of Learning Disorders*. Thorofare, Charles B. Slack,Inc.
Sensory Integration International (1990). Course notes.
Swift, S. (1985). *Centered Riding*. North Pomfret: David & Charles Inc.
Upledger, D.O.; Vredevoogd, J.D. (1983). *CranioSacral Therapy*. Seattle: Eastland Press.

24 OCCUPATIONAL AND PHYSICAL THERAPY WITH THE USE OF THE HORSE

24.01 AN INTRODUCTION TO TREATMENT WITH THE USE OF THE HORSE

Kyle Hamilton, MS, PT

The traditional treatment setting in hospitals has no modality to match the versatility of the horse. This alive and moving "apparatus" provides a multitude of stimuli to treat a variety of diagnoses. The horse can assist the client in attaining motor skills that would be difficult or slow in coming in the clinic.

Any therapist trained in movement dysfunctions can design a workable treatment plan using the horse as the primary modality but the therapist should be well-versed in horse handling skills. It takes many months of working with horses to be able to "read" them, just as it takes many months of hands-on treatment to properly evaluate and treat patients. Programs that use a therapist to draw up lesson plans, yet the therapist never participates in the treatment of the rider, miss a vital ingredient in their approach. Only by instantaneous feedback will the therapist realize the benefits or short coming of the exercise.

The therapist working as a "hippotherapist" or equine-assisted therapist should have at least attended a hands-on clinic taught by a reputable specialist in the field. In 1991, there was no certification for "hippotherapists" except in Germany, Switzerland and Italy. A group of therapists in the United States under the direction of Jean Tebay* began working toward this end, but until this exists, care must be taken how riding programs are presented.

To work in equine-assisted therapy, the therapist must be a competent rider. To make this more objective, the therapist should at least be able to ride a horse in a training level dressage test. Germany is more specific, requiring more of a second level riding test which includes lateral movements. This level of competency is certainly wonderful to have, but in our fledgling programs it is a bit too much to ask. Many programs would not be in existence if this level of riding ability were a requirement; so, it is better to do a lot of "beginning" work than to have so few served by a handful of "experts."

The horse must be well-chosen and properly cared for, both mentally and physically. Ideally, a variety of horses to choose from for different diagnoses would be wonderful. A horse of 14.2 to 15.3 hands high seems to be a good height to provide that lovely, swinging gait so necessary for proper client treatment.

The horse and therapist must be a team. One cannot stress this too strongly. Hacking out in the fields/mountains will develop a strong bond between the horse and the rider, and ring work will make both responsive to subtle cues. A good working knowledge of dressage school figures will help add variety to your program, while maintaining an objective measurement (i.e., three 20 meter circles to the left at "A", followed by a three loop serpentine the length of the dressage arena).

The evaluation of the client should determine the treatment plan. This simple statement is often neglected and the treatment team goes around and around like a pony ride, leading to boredom and insubordination on the part of the horse. Critically evaluate the client's weaknesses, choose the mount to remediate those weaknesses, and provide proper school figures to challenge the client to strengthen those weak areas. Keeping the treatment objective in this way can benefit documentation and reimbursement by third party payers.

The horse must be a "happy camper" to fully participate in the program. He does not understand that he must provide an even, rhythmic pace to best benefit his rider. A sour horse is a dangerous horse; it will not provide the rhythmic, elastic stride so desired, and will cause one to lose volunteers not happy about working with a disgruntled team member. To avoid a sour horse, provide lots of turnout time, trail riding and short treatment sessions. Horses enjoy routines, but not drudgery. Do not overwork the poor beast!

More and more good articles are being written about therapeutic riding; take the time to read these to add to your repertoire. Be sure you understand the difference between riding for sport, therapeutic riding, and equine-assisted therapy/hippotherapy so that you can represent your program properly.

Enjoy working with clients, your staff, and your horse - an amazing living "apparatus."

Jean Tebay, Therapeutic Riding Services, Riderwood, MD 21139, USA

24.02 ASSESSMENT AND EVALUATION OF THE CLIENT IN A THERAPEUTIC RIDING PROGRAM BY A PHYSICAL OR OCCUPATIONAL THERAPIST

Gertrude Freeman, MA, PT

During recent years a holistic approach both to life and to the study of the human body has found wide acceptance. In most cases the attention is concentrated on one system; however the influence of all systems are considered. A therapeutic riding session may offer an example of input from the sensory, musculoskeletal and perceptual-motor systems combining together for function. For example, a riding session is aimed at the over all goal of trunk control while specific work is being directed to the development of the musculo-skeletal system. However, this session would also include the creation of an intensive contact between the horse and rider, setting up a sensory relationship. In addition, having the client pronounce the order to walk not only encourages speech, but when the horse responds, the rider has realized a cooperative behavior (Hauser, 1988).

Whatever the goal for the riding program, one is evaluating the ability of the student to perform a motor act which requires planning (feeding information forward) and preparation (predictive set). Having an explanation of the theories which attempt to describe the mechanism that allows the central nervous system (CNS) to control movement will enhance the instructor's ability to identify problems and develop treatment strategies.

When discussing control of movement great emphasis used to be placed on how the CNS produces movement. Currently there is a shift in emphasis from studying how the brain produces movement to how it controls movement or behaviors in order to achieve specific tasks, thus the term motor control. Motor control stresses the importance of all the body's systems interacting in a balanced way to enable an individual to perform an act. This is explained by the systems model of motor control. Examples of systems which are important to establishing motor control are the perceptual-motor and musculo-skeletal systems.

EVALUATION PROCESS

A thorough evaluation based upon the systems model of motor control is of critical importance in order to select the most appropriate therapeutic riding program for the rider. The evaluation should be divided into two parts: measurement and assessment. Measurement is a process of reducing behaviors to numbers; these numbers provide objective data of change. Assessment combines these measurements with judgment, considers all systems influencing the client arrives at decisions regarding the needs to be addressed in the client's riding program. It is of the utmost importance that specific, standardized, and normative based measurements be employed when evaluating clients for therapeutic riding (Krebs, 1980).

Evaluation is a continuing process involving a series of interrelated steps which enable the evaluator to design and continually alter the riding program. During each step of the process the evaluator must employ effective decision-making as well as knowledge of and skill in therapeutic riding. Also critical to an evaluation process are change and effective communication with the client and other members of the riding team. The program chosen should be compatible with the goals of the client and interrelated with the client's other therapy programs.

The first step of the evaluation process is the preliminary measurement which includes measurement of the client's present level of function and dysfunction, organization, analysis and interpretation of the assessment data and establishment of long term and short term goals. The evaluation is ongoing during riding sessions. The instructor must constantly assess what is occurring and know how to alter the program to accomplish the established goals. Immediately following each individual session it is important to assess the outcome. Lastly, a long term reassessment of the treatment outcome is necessary to determine which goals have been met and what will be transferred to other activities in order to provide long term results.

The preliminary evaluation includes the gathering of both subjective and objective information. The medical or school record can be an important source of objective information regarding history, precautions and present status.

An interview with the client or parents is a subjective measure which can reveal information regarding the client's lifestyle, personal goals and expectations. It can assist the evaluator in determining goals and the appropriate means of motivation for this individual. In some instances, therapeutic riding can serve as an extension of physical, occupational, speech therapy, psychotherapy or of programs in special education centers. It is not expected that the therapeutic riding instructor will obtain nor analyze the objective data. It is the task of the therapists/psychologist/teachers to formally assess the rider and to clearly transmit relevant information for riding instructors to incorporate into treatment plans (Longden, 1988).

A client is first assessed by the therapist in terms of program offerings and the tabulated limitations of his particular disability. Record such things as sight, hearing, communication, comprehension, intelligence, confidence, balance (in sitting, standing, and walking), coordination, skin sensation, attention span, behavior and social skills, mobility, deformities, aids and appliances and gait. Such an assessment reveals the potential client's capabilities on the ground, reveals any area of potential danger and highlights areas of particular need (McNab, Poplawski, 1988). Together the therapist and instructor should analyze the data to develop a problem list. Identify which of the problems can be addressed effectively through the riding program; those which cannot be helped but must be accommodated; and those which do not have an impact on the program and can be ignored. Based upon these decisions, goals for that particular client and the barriers to achieving the goals will be identified and incorporated into a plan for therapeutic riding. The determination may be made at this time whether the client can participate in therapeutic riding or if he may need to be involved with the therapist in treatment sessions.

Long term goals should integrate functional outcomes into an interdisciplinary treatment plan. They should describe a functional outcome of riding in terms of activities of daily living, mobility within the environment, and communication or interaction within the environment. Once long-term goals have been established, the next step is to determine the component skills that will be needed to attain these goals. Each component skill then becomes the objective of a short-term goal. The short term goal should identify a task in which the rider is actively able to participate and is difficult enough to be a challenge. The final step of evaluation is ongoing and involves continuous reassessment of the rider and the efficacy of the program. Compare the effectiveness of the session to the established goals and modify the plan as needed. Long-term goals may be revised if the client progresses more rapidly or more slowly than expected. The lesson plan therefore becomes a fluid statement of progress.

EXAMPLES OF AREAS TO EVALUATE
An evaluation based on the systems approach will assume that many systems interact to produce the outcome of intervention. To design an effective riding program one needs to evaluate all of the systems or subsystems that participate in or should participate in the riding session. It is important to know which of the client's systems are intact and how one can best stimulate those which are faulty. Examples of areas to evaluate are the environment, the perceptual-motor system, the musculoskeletal system and other functional systems which may be affected by riding, and learning (Barnes, el al 1990).

Environment
Consider the physical environment: is it motivating, appropriately challenging, what spatial and temporal demands does it make on the rider? Examples are what effect the level of noise, lighting and presence of other riders in the arena are having. Consider, is the rider distracted by this external input, or is it appropriate to add external input to the session in order that he may be prepared to ride in varied environments?

Perceptual-Motor System
In evaluating the perceptual-motor system, one is determining how the rider sees him or herself and his or her environment. Perception is a process which integrates past experiences, memory and judgment with the sensations one is currently experiencing preparatory to movement. Think of perception as programming from the inside out as compared to sensation as programming from the outside in (Montgomery, 1990). The rider's ability to extract information from the stimuli present in the environment must be measured, as well as his or her capacity to develop an appropriate motor response. Examples of subsystems of the perceptual-motor system to be evaluated include visual-motor coordination, auditory-motor responses, cognition, body image, gross and fine coordination and motor planning. During an interview, try to perceive the attitude of the client and his family toward the riding program.

547

What is their motivation for riding? What do they hope to accomplish? Evaluate how these characteristics (e.g., fear) may affect the goals of the riding program. To determine cognitive impairment, evaluate such areas as attention to task, memory, sequencing and organization of information. Is the rider able to organize the sensory input and perceive the requirements of the activity he or she is being asking to perform? Can he or she remember the parts of the horse? The process of mounting may be a means of assessing sequence. Examine how the rider learns. Is immediate feedback appropriate? If someone with poor short-term memory, for example, is provided some delay between tasks so he or she can process what he or she has accomplished, will he or she be more successful with the riding program (Barnes, el al 1990) (Riolo-Quinn, 1989)? Body image refers to the client's perception of his or her body, its parts, movement abilities and the limitations. Evaluation of motor planning involves determining the rider's perception of the need to move, and initiating or modifying movement as needed in response to environmental demands. Determine the perceptual areas of need and the guidance required in order for him to successfully carry out the riding program. As the client progresses, the program should be modified to maintain a challenge.

Musculoskeletal System
Examples of subsystems of the musculoskeletal system include joint motion, muscle strength and sensation. If the joints required for riding are restricted due to limitation of joint motion, alterations in muscle length or strength, the client will have limited ability to assume certain postures and respond correctly to the movements of the horse. Pain will also affect the riding program since normal movement cannot occur in the presence of pain. A thorough history should detect the level of pain and indicate its effect upon the quality of movement, and therefore the potential success of the riding program (Barnes, et al, 1990).

Functional Skills
The horse represents a multisensory medium for the improvement of antigravity trunk control. This improvement is often reflected through gains in functional skills. Therefore it is important to evaluate those skills which may be affected by the program. Examples of skills to measure include sitting balance, reach and gait.

Riding is an excellent method for balance disorders. Effective means of measuring balance available to most therapeutic riding programs are cameras, timed video-cameras and posture grids. A camera and posture grid can evaluate the rider's ability to maintain a stable trunk both on and off the horse. Employing a timed video camera, one can evaluate how far the rider is able to move in each direction in response to the horse's movement and still maintain balance (boundaries of stability). Another important component of balance which can be evaluated is the appropriateness of the strategies employed by the rider to regain the sitting position following displacement, including his perception of this control. Weight shifts are automatically imposed upon the rider in response to the movements of the horse; assess how well the disabled rider responds in comparison to normal riders. Does the weight shift come in automatically as anticipatory postural adjustment? If so it is incorporated as part of the predictive set (Barnes, 1990; Calveley, 1988; Donahue, 1988; O'Sullivan, 1988). The rider has incorporated preparation for weight shift into his predictive set.

Improved reach is often an indirect result of improved sitting balance. One may also observe improvement in gait resulting from improved trunk control. Gait may be evaluated by measuring foot prints or by video recordings. Measured footprints can evaluate changes in step width or length; base of support or the degree of toeing out can also be determined. With the addition of a stop watch, measurements of velocity and cadence can be included (Nelson, 1974; Shores, 1974).

Learning Medium
Riding is an ideal learning medium for children with disabilities. In order to progress with academic learning a child must first master the abilities of language, cognition and perception. Realizing the value of horseback riding as a learning medium reinforces the necessity of including in the evaluation process activities which occur both during and outside of the riding or treatment session, i.e., concentration and retention in the classroom (Krebs, 1980).

Conclusion

According to recent rehabilitation literature, an individual needs to perform activities which are functional, challenging and related to the real environment in order for lasting improvement in motor capabilities to occur (Barton, 1989). Therapeutic riding is an activity which meets these requirements. To improve the credibility of therapeutic riding in the United States, further research to document its value is of critical importance (McGibbon, 1990). Many claims are made concerning the benefits of the rhythmic movement of the horse in respect to the physiological improvement of the client's balance and coordination. In addition the rider's friendship with and understanding of the animal and the horse's acceptance of the rider are said to improve self esteem. The social occasion is thought to be beneficial in modifying behavior. However, very little empirical research is available in this country which can adequately substantiate the benefits of therapeutic riding (Armstrong-Esther, 1985). Well structured, carefully documented evaluations of clients and their individual programs can form the basis for this much-needed research. These evaluations need to be as objective as possible; simple descriptions are not reliable for base line measures or as the basis for treatment progression.

Development of a quantitative research methodology requires that scientific principles be applied to therapeutic riding including basing results on normal values and applying standardized tests for measuring outcome. There is a need to develop methods of systematic observation and devices for measuring the effect of riding programs. The instruments currently accepted by the individual disciplines involved in therapeutic riding need to be applied. Reports of studies which may serve as guides for further research are published in the proceedings of the 5th and 6th Congresses on Therapeutic Riding.

Only by performing quantitative studies will we realize the value of the horse. Through systematic evaluation and planning, members of therapeutic riding teams together should strive to apply stricter standards and methods in order to develop a concrete data base through which the validity of therapeutic riding can be substantiated. Only when this data base has been achieved will the barriers which currently exist in the areas of recognition and financial support be overcome.

References

Armstrong-Esther, C.A.. Myco. F., Sandelands, M.L. (1985). An Examination of the Therapeutic Benefits of the Horseback Riding Technique Used by the Lethbridge Handicapped Riding Association. *Proceedings of the 5th International Congress on Therapeutic Riding.*

Barnes, M., Crutchfield, C., Heriza, C., Hardman, S. (1990). *Reflex and Vestibular Aspects of Motor Control, Motor Development and Motor Learning.* Atlanta: Shakesville Publishing Co.

Barton, L., Black, K. (1989). Setting Functional Outcomes for Inpatient Rehabilitation. Measurement and Assessment Problems in Physical Therapy. *Proceedings from the Forum on Neurological Physical Therapy Assessment.* Neurological Section of the American Physical Therapy Association.

Calveley, J. (1988). The Effect of Horse Riding Upon Sitting Balance in People with Cerebral Palsy. *Proceedings of the 6th International Therapeutic Congress.* Toronto, Canada.

Donahue, K. (1988). The Use of Hippotherapy as an Adjunct Treatment for Traumatic Brain Injured Clients. *Proceedings of the 6th International Therapeutic Congress.* Toronto, Canada

Hauser, G. (1988). Hippotherapy Under the Aspect of Therapeutic Pedagogics. *Proceedings of the 6th International Therapeutic Congress.* Toronto, Canada.

Krebs, D. (1980). Measurement and Assessment Problems in Physical Therapy. *Proceedings of the Forum on Neurological Physical Therapy Assessment: Neurology Section of the American Physical Therapy Association.*

Longden, M., Lane, B. (1988) Riding Instructors: the Vital Link. *Proceedings of the 6th International Therapeutic Congress.* Toronto, Canada.

McGibbon, N. (1990). Theories of Motor Control, A Historical Perspective. Presented at the *National Meeting of the Delta Society.* Renton, WA

McNab, J.R., Poplawski, V. (1988). Sharing the Experience of the World if the Horse. *Proceedings of the 6th International Therapeutic Congress.* Toronto, Canada.

Montgomery, P. (1990). *Presentation II Step Conference,* Norman, OK. July.

Nelson, A. J. (1974). Functional Ambulation Profile. *Physical Therapy.* 54:1059.

O'Sullivan, S. (1988). Chapter 1 Clinical Decision Making in *Physical Rehabilitation Assessment and Treatment.* O'Sullivan & Schmitz ed. 2nd ed. Philadelphia: F.A. Davis & Co.

Riolo-Quinn, L. (1989). Motor Learning Considerations in Treatment Neurologically Impaired Patients. *Proceedings of the Forum on Neurological Physical Therapy Assessment: Neurology Section of the American Physical Therapy Association.*

Shores, M. (1974). Footprint Analysis in Gait Documentation. *Physical Therapy.* 60:1163-1167.

24.03 STABLE MANAGEMENT PROGRAM: AN ADJUNCT TO EQUESTRIAN THERAPY

Ellen Adolphson, PT
Gillian Forth, PT

The concept of therapeutic stable management used at Bryn Mawr Rehabilitation Hospital by the therapists was originally developed to make good use of the time the clients spent while waiting for their therapeutic riding sessions. As the clientele is comprised primarily of young adults with head injuries, the program quickly expanded to address the range of cognitive and physical impairments found in this population.

The primary goals are to improve a client's:

1. Attention span
2. Recognition and recall
3. Sequencing skills
4. Right/left discrimination
5. Laterality
6. Ability to follow directions
7. Eye/hand coordination
8. Visual-spatial awareness
9. Motor planning skills
10. Fine and gross motor skills
11. Appropriate social interaction/communication skills

The first lesson is a tour of the barn. This allows the clients to acclimate to this novel environment and appease some of their curiosity. As they become familiarized with the setting (tack room, feed room, where the helmets are kept, etc.), safety is emphasized as the primary concern. Much care and time is spent demonstrating and reinforcing safe movement around a horse, proper and safe handling of equipment, and the attention to and understanding of horse "body language." These basic skills are then incorporated into all horse-related activities. Clients are encouraged to move around the horses, touching and interacting with them. This interaction reduces the anxiety level of clients and provides them with multi-sensory stimulation. At the same time, it allows the staff to become familiar with the behaviors of clients in this environment. Ground rules and expectations are communicated.

Subsequent lessons can include, but are not limited to: horse safety, feeding, grooming, tack, tacking/untacking the horse, parts of the horse, and colors and markings. Throughout these sessions, the therapist is constantly evaluating and cuing the client as needed, tailoring these one to one "treatment" times to address individual needs. Is the client attending to the task? Is he incorporating prior knowledge? Is body awareness (both of horse and client) demonstrated? If an answer is "no," the problem must be identified and dealt with accordingly.

The therapist can increase or decrease the challenge of a situation for the client by controlling the environment, but the number of available choices can be limited. Visual, verbal, or written cues can be provided as needed. A task can be made less difficult by decreasing the number or complexity of choices involved. On the other hand, for example, balance can be challenged by increasing the range of motion or rotation involved in a task. Grooming and tacking are excellent high level balance activities!

Do not let yourself fall into the rut of limiting clients in wheelchairs to interaction with a book. From grooming to tacking to feeding, the properly and well trained horse in the correct situation with an attentive therapist will allow full participation of just about anyone, not the least of whom are those in wheelchairs. Get all clients actively involved!

Stable management can be a successful experience for all. However, keep a few things in mind as the program evolves.

- This aspect is an adjunct to riding. Do not encourage a "You must learn, you will be tested" environment. Clients are here to ride.

- If you do not know the client's cognitive abilities, start simply, stay on the subject, and gradually increase the complexity of the task.

- Always allow for success but without insulting the client's intelligence.

- Have a basic plan for each session, but be flexible.

- Health, attention span and mood of both client and therapist, as well as unexpected happenings seem to play a role in the mechanics of a session. Allow the clients to assist in these problem-solving tasks.

Finally, make it fun. We owe it to our clients, ourselves, and our horses.

Reference:
Bryn Mawr Rehabilitation Hospital, 414 Paoli Pike, Malvern, Pennsylvania 19355 USA.

24.04   A COMPARISON OF CHANGE IN FLEXIBLE KYPHOSIS PRE- AND POST- HIPPOTHERAPY--A RESEARCH APPROACH

Elizabeth A. Baker, PT

Hippotherapy has achieved a tremendous popularity which continues to grow in many countries. As clinicians we see the benefits and improvements achieved through the use of hippotherapy. As clinicians it is our responsibility to know what changes hippotherapy can facilitate in what client populations. Only then can we say with confidence that it is the treatment of choice. But this means research, which means time, effort, and usually money. Our challenge then is not only to do the research that validates hippotherapy as a treatment technique, but to find ways to make doing that research possible. Research at the level of the individual clinician can be made significantly easier by the use of single system research.

Single system research design looks at small groups or a single subject. The intervention, as well as the outcome, is studied and may be modified as one would do during treatment. The emphasis is on knowledge for immediate practical use; the costs are small, and the procedures can be easily included as part of the clinical routine. This method of research relies on variations within the individual or small group to make inferences about the performance of an individual or small group. It appears ideally suited to therapeutic riding, as it is to physical therapy, because it allows one to study small client groups or individuals such as are seen in treatment every day. But it also allows one to legitimately document findings, so that this information becomes retrievable from the professional literature.

In hippotherapy, the three dimensional movement pattern imparted to the rider by the walking horse is thought to improve the proximal motor control of clients with disorders of movement, such as cerebral palsy. Many such clients demonstrate low muscle tone in the trunk accompanied by increased muscle tone in the extremities. They often show a sitting posture on and off the horse that includes an exaggerated but flexible kyphosis or rounding of the entire trunk, with forward head, rounded shoulders and a posteriorly tilted pelvis. The stabilizing extensor muscles of the posterior trunk will be weakened and difficult to activate when allowed to remain in the lengthened state that exists in the kyphotic, flexed trunk; they must be placed in a shortened range and activated there to be strengthened. The movement of the horse coupled with other facilitation techniques is thought to be effective in correcting this posture and allowing this strengthening to occur. The constant, precise and rhythmic movement of the horse is also thought to provide the additional sensory input needed to maintain the well-aligned posture, allowing the client to experience and practice normal balance and movement skills. The therapist should see an improvement in the client's alignment off the horse, but more importantly, the improved posture should result in functional and noticeable gains in everyday life, such as better balance and extremity use.

From 1985 to 1990, the author was the physical therapist for a therapeutic riding program at a residential facility for adults with developmental disabilities. Since many of the clients with motor deficits showed the flexible kyphosis previously described, hippotherapy was used as a part of the physical therapy program to activate their trunk musculature and improve alignment and trunk control, so that normal trunk equilibrium reactions and extremity use could follow. It was difficult to assess the change in trunk posture in the sagittal plane by observation alone, as the changes were often subtle. A review of the available literature in English indicated that measurement of posture immediately pre- and post-hippotherapy sessions was relatively unexplored. However clinicians support the belief that hippotherapy improves posture based on treatment observations. The author decided to investigate changes in trunk posture as viewed from the sagittal plane. Specifically the research problem addressed was to determine whether hippotherapy would change the flexible rounded or kyphotic posture while on the horse; how did static sitting affect the same postural problem; and how would this be measured.

Methodology
The hypothesis was that a decrease in flexible kyphosis as measured while still on the horse, in those with this postural problem associated with neuromotor dysfunction, would result from hippotherapy. Four clients were selected to participate. Three were already involved in a physical therapy program on and off the horse to improve some aspect

of ambulation: one was in a hippotherapy program to develop preliminary skills on the horse prior to progressing to therapeutic riding. Each participant was an adult with developmental delay; they had varying degrees of retardation; their motor deficits also varied. All demonstrated poor alignment in the trunk from the sagittal view, specifically an increased rounding or kyphosis that was flexible.

The research design used was alternating treatment, with the subjects serving as their own controls. The treatment sessions consisted of the subject mounting the horse followed by immediate use of a measurement tool to record the initial degree of kyphosis. The subject was then treated in an individualized hippotherapy session. When the therapist felt that the optimum benefit from the session had been achieved which was typically after about 15 to 25 minutes, the treatment was stopped and the measurement tool was used again prior to the dismount. In the controlled, or non-treatment sessions, the client sat on a bolster in an approximation of the mounted position for fifteen minutes. The measurement tool was used at the beginning and at the end of the fifteen minutes while the client was seated on the bolster.

The measurement system consisted of a tool worn by the client. The tool was a somewhat flexible plastic strip with three-inch screws projecting from it. The tool was worn on the back and secured by straps which were elasticized for comfort and to accommodate movement. It was applied from the seventh cervical vertebrae down and aligned with the posterior midline of the trunk. The plastic strip itself was broken in one place with an elastic insert to accommodate the elongating and shortening of the spine associated with movement. During all sessions it was closely monitored for position and adjusted if needed. Immediately before and after hippotherapy, but while the client was still on the horse, a slide photograph was taken of the client wearing the tool. The slide was later developed and projected onto white paper using a straightedge, the screws at the approximate upper and lower thoracic spine were traced onto the paper and extended until an angle was formed. Angles were then measured and compared. It had been previously established that when a normal subject was sitting more erect, the angle would be more acute, such as 45 degrees, and when the spine was rounded the angle was larger such as 70 degrees. Reliability was partially addressed by having one person, the expert, consistently apply the tool and complete all measurement procedures. To be recorded as a positive or negative change, the difference in angle measurements had to be greater than five degrees.

Results
Consistent with single system research, the angle measurements before and after treatment were compared. Each subject was treated as an individual; the clients' results were not treated as group results. One client, JS, achieved a more upright posture in 8 out of 10 treatment sessions: during the other two sessions there was no change. The second client, ST, achieved a more upright posture in 6 out of ten sessions. The third client, JS, achieved a more upright posture in 6 out of ten sessions. The fourth client, RW, achieved a more upright posture in two out of ten sessions. In the non-treatment sessions, there was no improvement in posture seen; rather there was a tendency for the posture to worsen to become more rounded.

Conclusions:
Three of the four clients showed the desired result from the treatment sessions, and thus supported the hypothesis; all were either the same or worse in the non-treatment sessions, as expected. The client who showed the least improvement while on the horse did demonstrate pelvic rotation and has progressed to assisted ambulation, a new skill for him. It may thus be said that in three of the clients studied, hippotherapy did produce the desired changes in posture. It is suggested that the client who showed less improvement in posture did so because his kyphosis was less flexible than the other clients, and was accompanied by a structural scoliosis. This project sparked great interest for this author and others working with me in the research, because the single system design was simple and appropriate for very small numbers of clients, and was relevant to the individual client. It is acknowledged that changes in posture occurring while on the horse are difficult to assess objectively but is nonetheless necessary. Further research in this area is needed to enable clinicians to predict that hippotherapy is the treatment of choice.

Presented at the VII International Congress on Therapeutic Riding, August 1991, Denmark

24.05 GROOMING AND TACKING-UP AS AN ACTIVITY USED FOR TREATMENT IN OCCUPATIONAL THERAPY

Judy Hilburn, OTR

A Therapy Experience

Max, tall for his age, was a handsome 4 year-old, with big brown eyes and coppery hair. Blessed with high intelligence and advanced verbal skills, he would talk excitedly and incessantly about his many super heroes and their grand and varied adventures. But ask HIM to climb the tower or leap even a small building in a single bound, he would fail miserably. Max's big brother was excelling in school. His little brother was running circles around him. Max's parents were baffled. Then the bi-monthly children's clinic came to town. During the clinic it was discovered that this gifted child had a learning disability. Max was hypotonic and afraid of heights. He shuffled rather than ran. When he did try running, he did so with arms pinned at his sides, his shoulders fixed for extra control; even then with this extra control, Max appeared to be on the verge of tumbling forward.

Max was unable to enjoy the playground like the other boys. In the classroom, things were no different. Manipulating a crayon was beyond his capabilities, since his eyes and hands had offered little help in developing visual-motor skills. But being a bright boy, Max was able to cover up most of his short comings---but not for long. His gravitational insecurity would soon win out. Max was admitted to a pre-school program where he received occupational therapy with a sensory integrative emphasis, for several months.

When a small hippotherapy program was established in town, Max's parents requested that he be considered for it. Indeed, he was. Combined with clinical occupational therapy, hippotherapy filled in the gaps, and his treatment program was enriched. Max was first involved with grooming the horse to improve his tactile responses and motor planning skills. He also began to use the mounting block to reach the top of the horse. First he could only tolerate the lower step because of his gravity insecurity. Max then began to assist in the leading the horse from the stall. His interest in the horse helped him challenge his fear of movement and soon he had the courage to mount the horse with help. Max continued to progress over the months to come and soon was able to ride alone in the ring. Everyone stood back and watched Max's failures slowly turn into successes. Before a horse can be used in a hippotherapy program or in a therapeutic riding program, it must be regularly groomed and tacked. Many hours are spent by stable staff providing these needs. Why not use these as treatment activities for selected riders in a therapeutic riding program? Occupational therapists will find that horse grooming and tacking-up are easily adapted for the treatment needs of disabled clients.

Before a horse can be used in a hippotherapy program or in a therapeutic riding program, it must be regularly groomed and tacked. Many hours are spent by stable staff providing these needs. Why not use these as treatment activities for selected riders in a therapeutic riding program? Occupational therapists will find that horse-grooming and tacking-up are easily adapted for the treatment needs of disabled clients.

To begin, equipment required for such activities would be combs, brushes of varying sizes and textures, hoof-pick, halter, ropes, saddle blanket, saddle or surcingle, and bridle. The horse to be groomed must be under the control of a riding assistant at all times, but can be positioned so that riders of all sizes, either ambulatory or in wheelchairs, can participate.

There are several factors inherent to the activity of grooming and tacking that address frequent needs in persons whom occupational therapists treat, namely occupational role development and occupational performance. These functions involve activities that require one to involve himself in setting realistic goals and making decisions. Grooming and tacking-up require these skills. He will also develop safety awareness, recognize established routines while working around a horse and caring for him.

Due to the fact that these activities integrate the demand for various senses and skills, there is a continuous overlap in therapeutic effects. For example, the areas of gross motor function, muscle tone and co-contraction of muscles can be influenced by heavy work patterns while a client carries a grooming kit, saddle blanket or saddle. Or, if a platform or mounting block is used during these activities, a client may have the opportunity to "practice" climbing or jumping skills (jumping off the block). If a client is advanced enough in his horse skills to begin leading the horse to the grooming area, then ambulatory skills could be influenced. A client may need to walk over uneven terrain or execute stops, starts and turns. A client must match his own rate, rhythm and sequence of movement to that of the horse. The author has noted that most of the time, her mare changes her way of walking, to accommodate her "challenged" handler's gait.

A client's upper extremity strength and range of motion can be facilitated by brushing a horse, since anti-gravity, resistive movement patterns are inherent in this activity. Tightening cinch/girth straps will also affect strength of the upper extremity. Bilateral upper extremity integration and coordination can be facilitated by using two grooming implements at a time. For example, a client may hold a curry comb in one hand and a body brush in the other, alternating the use of each tool as it is appropriate. While assisting with lacing/adjusting a cinch-strap, reciprocal, hand-over-hand movement patterns are involved.

Similarly, fine-motor development can be affected in many ways. For example, activities of daily living (ADL) skills are improved by the ability gained while manipulating buckles on halter, bridle or girth; or rein and lead-rope snaps; or while brushing mane/tail. Pincer grasp is increased while picking a horse's loose hair out of curry comb or body brush. During combing of a mane, a client may use his fingers as the comb. Such an action is effective as an active-resistive exercise for strengthening the hands. Establishment of dominant /non-dominant hand patterns can be affected by these brushing/combing activities since they are rich in spacial sequencing patterns. One can see this as a client may handle the brush with his dominant hand while being encouraged to use the non-dominant hand as a support/assist by resting it on the horse's body. The same situation can also be duplicated while a client is helping to tighten a latigo cinch.

Establishment of hand dominance can be facilitated while a client is leading a horse, carrying the lead rope properly (i.e., one hand holding excess rope folded, while the other hand holds rope near snap end). This activity can be adapted for the right or left-handed client. For such adaptations to occur it is obvious that the therapy horse must be accustomed to being led from either side. Tactile perception for fine-motor control is enhanced because the lead-rope is being held on the diagonal against resistance. Hypotonicity of oral musculature can be improved during highly resistive activity using the hands, such as pulling on latigo girth during cinching of saddle, or while using hoof pick to dig out debris imbedded in hoof (oral musculature and hand function have an associated reaction).

Postural responses are facilitated whenever a client must reach high spots, either during grooming or tacking-up, when needing to get up on tip-toes to brushes horse's back, or to help adjust saddle or blanket. Equilibrium responses are elicited when a client bends over to brush horse's belly or legs, or to reach for the cinch. When appropriate, a client may assist with picking out horse's hooves and in so doing, the vestibular system is again stimulated because of the bending position he must assume. Leading the horse also affects postural control. Such an activity requires the client to use trunk rotation, and separation of head, eyes, and upper extremities.

Grooming and tacking are activities which lend themselves well to a high level of tactile input. Grooming implements are made of varying textures. For example, brushes are stiff or soft, combs are made of plastic or metal. As far as tack goes, there are ropes of nylon or cotton; ropes are braided, round or flat; reins that are of cotton webbing or leather. The horse, himself, has a myriad of varying textures. The mane and tail are coarse; body hair can be furry or smooth; the muzzle area is velvety; hooves are hard and rough. A groomer comes in touch with all these areas.

Development of cognitive perceptual skills is also easily worked into the grooming/tacking activity. Spatial terms are an integral part of these activities, such as brushing the horse on top of his back, or under the girth area. The individual can start brushing from front (neck area) to back (hind quarters). He can learn that saddle blankets go on under the saddle. Body scheme concepts are continually used as the person brushes softly on horse's face and carefully around his eyes and ears. He will learn to be sure to brush the "off" or right side of horse also. Comparison of human body parts to horse's parts can also be easily done. The horse has a scrape on his knee, just like a child sometimes gets on his knees. While leading the horse, a client is faced with such "body-map" dilemmas as where to stand (right or left side, or in front of the horse), how close to stand to the horse, how fast to walk, and how to get both the horse and himself safely through a gate, or barn doors.

During grooming, enhancement of tool use and motor planning is seen. The client will realize how the rubber curry comb is to be used in order to remove dried mud, or during tacking-up, how is one going to get the awkwardly shaped saddle or vaulting surcingle onto the horse properly-positioned. The activity of grooming and tacking-up easily lends itself to developing direction-following and problem-solving skills. Tacking-up requires that specific sequences be followed; that is, the saddle blanket must be placed under the saddle, or the girth must be tightened before mounting. Such questions as how does the horse pick up its hoof for cleaning, or how does one keep the reins from dragging on the ground, facilitates the use of problem-solving skills. Other cognitive areas such as ideation, sequencing, and programming are enhanced when various questions arise. "In which corral is my horse?" "How will I get him out of the corral?" "Will the horse come willingly?" "What equipment will I need?"

Opportunities to use communication skills are many, both verbal and non-verbal, when dealing with the horse. Simply looking for and greeting the horse encourage communication. Communication is facilitated when various verbal and body cues are used for leading/halting the horse, finding ways to praise the horse either by patting or verbalizing "good girl". Some horses will actually seek out the client with a look or movement which might suggest: "rub-me-here" or "who are you, brushing me so nicely?" And each of us has seen every horse non-verbally (or verbally!) say "where's my carrot?". Such demonstrative body language by the horse is hard to miss and the client usually has no choice but to respond.

Benefits in the area of social-emotional development are many and inherent in the activity. There is the arousal of nurturing instincts of the client toward the horse. Several needs of the horse may be met such as, brushing away a bothersome fly, cleaning off dried mud from girth area to prevent chaffing, or removing twigs from mane or tail. The client finds he must be attentive to the horse's likes and dislikes, such as ticklish spots to be avoided during grooming, or taking care of that itchy spot behind the ear. The client is made aware of his own behavior and how it might affect the horse, such as learning that running and jumping around could startle the horse or that, jerking on the lead rope or hitting the horse may scare him. The client learns to understand "others'" behavior (the horse's) when he had to deal with a horse that momentarily balks, or veers off course while being led. The client learns what pleases the horse (grain, hay or carrots) and how the horse acts to get that treat. Self-esteem is enhanced when the he was successful in controlling such a large animal as the horse. He receives approval and leads it himself when he sees the horse properly prepared for riding. Finally, the caregiver of the client sees the positive effect. The treatment setting has usually been the clinic or hospital, with clients surrounded by wheelchairs, crutches, and walkers, but is now the great outdoors where one is surrounded by fresh air, trees, birds, horses, viewing people busy, working with their horses. The caregiver happily sees his son (or daughter, husband or wife) as a part of this active, bustling environment.

Conclusion
A frame of reference is a body of hypothetical assumptions and principles that give unity and direction to practice and research. It provides the basis for treatment - in this case the treatment used by occupational therapists. The major frames of reference used by occupational therapists include (Christiansen & Baum, 1991):
- Cognition & Activities
- Sensory Integration
- Spatio-temporal Adaptation
- Human Occupation
- Adaptive Responses
- Facilitating Growth & Development
- Role Acquisition
- Occupational Behavior

The approach to treatment involved in all of these frames of reference can be applied within the equine setting. Using the focus of the horse and the manipulation of the environment to meet the specific treatment needs, the occupational therapist has at her disposal many functional and meaningful activities. These therapists carefully select activities to allow clients to adapt behavior as they confront disabilities and to organize sensorimotor systems for function and skills.

Reference
Christiansen, C.. Baum, C. (1991). *Occupational Therapy, Overcoming Human Performance Deficits*. Thorofare: Slack Inc.

24.06 BACKRIDING TECHNIQUES IN THERAPY

Elizabeth A. Baker, PT

Within the past decade and a half, backriding has attracted a level of acclaim shared by few other teaching or therapy techniques in the field of therapeutic horseback riding. A simplistic description of backriding is riding double on horseback. Backriding is used in therapeutic riding to improve the quality of the individual riding session. The acclaim that backriding has received, and deservedly so, results from observations of the rapid progress made by riders with whom this technique has been successful. In these instances, backriding has provided the initial physical facilitation and/or emotional support needed to allow the development of skills for more independent riding, and for improved balance and movement skills off the horse. Presumably, the same support or facilitation could not be adequately provided from staff on the ground. However, some areas of concern have also surfaced. These have included safety practices; the use of appropriate equipment; horse size, conformation, maintenance and training; and other ethical concerns related to both horse and client. It appears that while backriding can be a tremendously effective technique, it must be carefully and judiciously used.

Backriding is a technique in which two people sit astride a horse. One is the client, who is physically, emotionally or mentally disabled, and who cannot be adequately supported or assisted from the ground by sidewalkers or the therapist. The other is a specially trained individual, usually a therapist or riding instructor (the backrider may also be a designed of the instructor or therapist, under that person's direct supervision). For the physically disabled client, the backrider should be an experienced physical or occupational therapist; for a client with an emotional or mental impairment, the backrider should be a therapeutic riding instructor. When the backrider is a physical or occupational therapist, the choice of backriding as a therapeutic technique has been made because the therapist can skillfully provide the physical handling and facilitation required to maximize the physically disabled rider's balance and posture during the therapy session. If the backrider is a riding instructor, backriding has been chosen as the best possible means to further the development of riding skills in that person. For example, the close physical contact of the backrider may alleviate the initial fear of riding found in the mentally or emotionally disabled student. In any instance, the choice of backriding should be a timely one; that is, backriding is used as a therapy or teaching technique at the appropriate time in the development of the client's skills, when it will do the most good, and with the expectation of progressing beyond backriding toward his or her optimal level of independence.

Whatever his educational background, the backrider must be a skill led rider and knowledgeable "horse person." The backrider must be able to ride independently at a walk, trot, and canter; and to ride on a lunge line without "holding on," on a pad with a surcingle, at the walk and trot. Good riding skills are extremely important, because the backrider is responsible for maintaining the safety of the client should the horse shy or stumble. However, the backrider is seated behind--rather than over--the center of gravity of the horse, Figure 1. In this position it is more difficult to remain balanced and to follow the movement of the horse. Thus, the backrider with inadequate riding skills will have difficulty maintaining his own balance, impairing his or her ability to provide skilled assistance to the client. The backrider should be able to correctly groom and prepare the horse for a backriding session, as well as recognize and anticipate signs of emotional and physical stress in the horse which would indicate that backriding may be inappropriate. The backrider should be familiar with effective equine training methods which improve the horse's suppleness, strength, and overall mental health. While the backrider may not be capable of providing the training, he or she should be knowledgeable enough of such methods to recognize their necessity and advocate for them. Other considerations are weight and height. Previous unpublished writings have indicated that the backrider's weight should not exceed 150 pounds, and that this is also true for the client. The combined weight of the client and backrider should be a factor in selecting a horse of suitable size and conformation.

Backriding may be chosen by a physical or occupational therapist as an equine-assisted therapy technique. The client who will benefit from this therapy technique usually presents with a movement dysfunction, and as noted cannot be adequately supported or facilitated from the ground. This may include a variety of diagnoses, such as cerebral palsy, multiple sclerosis, spina bifida, spinal cord injury, and others. Backriding is never prescribed on the basis of the diagnosis alone; it is the accompanying deficits in muscle tone, strength, balance, postural stability and symmetry which provide the indicators for the use of this technique. These indicators include the following: poor head/trunk control, poor balance, significantly asymmetric position and movement patterns, increased tone as a result of the position of horse's movement, severe tone and movement abnormalities, rapid fatigue, and lack of progress due to the effort required to ride. All these problems, in certain instances, can be effectively treated without backriding. Backriding thus should be the chosen approach because the therapist on the ground cannot provide the client with the input needed to allow progression in treatment.

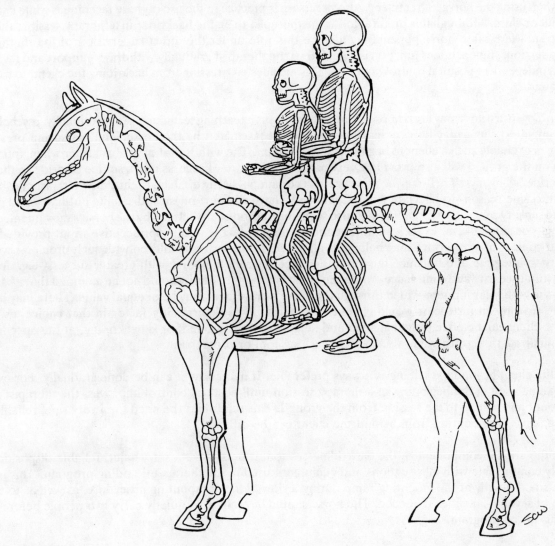

FIGURE 1. BACKRIDER IS SEATED BEHIND RATHER THAN OVER THE CENTER OF GRAVITY OF THE HORSE

Backriding allows the therapist to provide facilitation and support in a symmetrical, precise manner because the backrider is at the same level as the client. This in turn allows the motorically impaired client to relax, to achieve a balanced and symmetrical position, and to follow the movement of the horse without excessive effort, spasticity and fear. What input the therapist provides depends on the specific needs of the client at that point in the treatment program. Very often, the client for whom backriding is utilized is one whose head and body postural control is so impaired that sitting balance is poor or virtually nonexistent. The therapist's hands can provide assistance to maintain the correct spine and pelvic alignment until the horse's movement facilitates control there; they may gently emphasize the pelvic rotation caused by the horse's movement to enhance normalization of muscle tone and postural control. Manual facilitation of oblique abdominal flexor musculature or hip extensor, and approximation through the shoulders

559

or pelvis, may also be used. This input facilitates the development of proximal stability needed to support upper extremity use such as weightbearing on hands, patting the horse, and reaching for objects. When very small adults or children are treated, the therapist may also choose to utilize developmental positions and movement transitions during the backriding session. This might include positioning the client in prone inversion, in front of the backrider. The backrider may also sit facing backwards on the horse, positioning the client in supine or prone, or in upper or tower extremity weightbearing positions to develop proximal stability, midline control, and weight-shifting skills. Experience in neurodevelopmental treatment and handling techniques off the horse is necessary for their correct application when using the horse in treatment. Also necessary is practice in the use of these techniques while backriding a normal adult or child. Although it is preferable for the therapist to be the backrider in a therapy session, the riding instructor or knowledgeable horse person may assume this role under the direct supervision of the therapist. As in all therapy sessions, independent function is a goal; thus the therapist gradually withdraws support and facilitation as the client's independent postural control improves. This includes progressing from backriding the client, to treatment from the ground.

Therapeutic riding instructors may also choose to use backriding as a teaching technique. An emotionally, psychologically or mentally impaired client may be very fearful of riding yet fascinated by the horse. The reassuring presence of the backrider may enable such a client to begin a riding program. The withdrawal of the backrider when appropriate to a position on the ground will also provide a very concrete measure of success and a source of pride to the client, who can now ride "all by myself." (It may be said that with certain physically disabled clients, the therapist may backride initially for the same reason--to alleviate fear). Clients who have no overt physical disability but have mild postural insecurity and sensory processing problems may also seem fearful and overwhelmed by the horse's movement, clinging to the surcingle or sidewalkers. In such situations the additional tactile and proprioceptive input provided by the close physical contact of a backrider may help. It is also true, however, that children with such problems will show greater ability to integrate and organize the input they receive from the horse with greater success--e.g., less fear, improved postural security and confidence--while the horse is <u>moving</u>. Thus it should not be assumed that a backrider is necessary; the vestibular input provided through the horse's movement may be of equal value. There may be other client-specific reasons an instructor would choose to backride. The determining factor in that choice, as always, is whether the client can be effectively managed and taught from the ground; or is backriding, at this specific point in the individualized riding program, a necessary teaching tool or progression.

Progressing the client beyond backriding is always preferable. If necessary, it can be done gradually. For example, backriding can be used in the beginning of a therapy session until postural control improves; the therapist may be able to dismount and complete the session from the ground. This reinforces the need for a very safe, reliable, well-trained horse, since dismounting from behind the client can be difficult.

The horse is the critical component of the backriding session. It must have a safe, quiet, reliable disposition, and be completely comfortable with all situations and equipment used in the therapeutic riding program. This includes the ability to stand quietly at the mounting ramp during a slow, difficult mounting procedure, as well as to tolerate the presence of several sideaides if needed. The horse should be trained to quietly carry two people before it used for backriding in the program.

The horse's conformation will also dictate whether it is appropriate for backriding. The horse should have good basic conformation and be sound, because backriding will impose additional weight and stress on any structural abnormality present. This stress is compounded by placing a good deal of that weight over the horse's loin area, the weakest part of the back. Thus, an older horse that has a mild unsoundness or structural problem, suitable for light work (a common description of the donated program horse) may become unsound and unusable if backriding is attempted. The horse's back should be muscular, strong and supple, with a "level topline," i. e., without high withers, high rump, swayback deformity, or prominent backbone. The length of the back should be short to average; a horse with a long back is inappropriate for, and likely to be injured by, backriding since a long back is bio-mechanically weak before the addition of the backrider's weight. A short back with the withers sloping evenly into the back and a short loin area are ideal. In assessing the horse's back, looking down at it from a high point such as the mounting ramp can help identify weakness. If the loin area is weak, the spine will be prominent and the muscling will slope downward; it is strong, the area will appear round and full. The ideal height has been described as 14.2 to 15.2 hands, but a safe larger horse with well-trained taller sideaides may be appropriate. If a smaller horse is used, the previously mentioned weight limits for the backrider and client begin to seem excessive. A smaller horse may also be inappropriate for use in therapy when backriding is needed. It's stride may be too short, quick and choppy (as is that of most ponies); the combined weight of the client and backrider may additionally shorten the stride and decrease the movement imparted to the client, negating any therapeutic benefit. The horse's width can vary, but if the client's hip and pelvic mobility is adequate, a wider base of support is preferable.

The horse's quality of movement and flexibility is extremely important, particularly in therapy. The horse should be balanced, symmetrical, and able to "track up" (at the walk, the hind foot steps forward and past the hoofprint of the same side forefoot) even with the weight of two riders. It should be able to bend with equal flexibility to either side. The horse should be able to vary his stride length in response to cues from the leader or when on long reins, without losing rhythm. This requires careful initial training, and a maintenance training regimen, by a skilled horse expert. Activities such as longing, cavalletti work, and training in the dressage style will help strengthen the horse's back and abdominal muscles.

The backriding horse should receive a gradual introduction to its task. Since backriding requires the horse to carry additional weight in an area of the back unused to it, the horse should be allowed to strengthen its back by practicing backriding with gradually increasing weight in the backrider's position. The length of the practice sessions should also gradually increase. It is very reasonable to assume that a horse unaccustomed to backriding will suffer at least muscle soreness and soft tissue trauma in the loin area. To help prevent this, a several week introduction to backriding could occur. During the first week, the horse could carry up to a 150 pound person in the normal riding position, with a small child of 50 pounds or less in the backriding position, for five minutes per session, at two or three sessions per week. Over the next few weeks the backrider's weight and the session duration could progressively increase, dependent on the needs of the therapeutic riding program, and the anticipated weight of the clients who may utilize that horse. A slow introduction to backriding in this manner may also clearly indicate what the horse's ability and weight tolerance will comfortably be, before an injury occurs.

There are other ways to minimize trauma to the horse's back. One is to limit backriding sessions with an individual horse to twice per week, and no more than one half-hour per session, coupled with a good maintenance training regimen. During a backriding session, the horse should be kept to an engaged medium or working walk when possible. It should be constantly monitored for signs of distress which may be related to backriding. These can include a change of mood or reluctance to work; flinching or uneasiness during grooming, saddling, or mounting; decreased hind leg stride length; pain and muscle spasm in the back, and also the poll; and unsoundness. When backriding, heavy pads which allow the horse's sweat to evaporate, or wick it away, should be used. A very high density closed cell foam pad which does not "bottom out" under the riders will distribute pressure; such foam does not have to be particularly thick to be effective. Often a combination of pads provides the best result.

It is inappropriate to backride with the client in a saddle, as the backrider is even further behind the client than without. Easing onto the horse during the mounting process enables the animal to accommodate to the weight more easily. Warming the horse up prior to the backriding session and cooling down after helps; in both instances, activities which encourage the horse to elongate and round the back, use the abdominal, and stretch its legs forward and under itself are appropriate. After a session, particularly in cold weather, a pad or blanket over the back for a short time will prevent rapid loss of body heat and resultant cramping. It is interesting to think that all these concepts--warm-up, cool-down, muscle strengthening, and so on--are very familiar subjects to not only therapists, but all those who appreciate personal physical fitness. If these same concepts are applied to horses used for backriding, the animals will retain their usefulness and health longer in all aspects of the program.

The riding program staff, volunteers and environment require careful consideration when backriding is utilized. The leader must be an experienced, knowledgeable horse handler who can recognize the signs of the horse's moods, and who can react appropriately to its behavior. The leader should be attentive to the instruction, needs and safety of the backrider and/or therapist. A minimum of one sideaide is required; two are strongly recommended, and more may be needed. While the backrider ensures the client's safety, the sideaides are responsible for assisting the backrider to maintain his or her balance. The sideaides may need to stabilize the backrider at his/her hips, thighs, knees or feet during the session; this may also be helpful during the client's dismount. The sideaides should only provide physical contact to the backrider for stability when and where needed, as indicated by the backrider. If the client is a larger adult, additional sideaides may be needed to help the backrider maintain the client's position. The sideaides should be of a height and strength appropriate to the needs of that particular session. They should be trained specifically for their responsibilities during backriding, as these differ from other types of sessions. The need for a sufficient number of well-trained sideaides during a backriding session should never be underestimated, as the result may be injury to both backrider and client.

The physical environment used for backriding should be considered prior to its use. It is preferable that the environment be quiet, clear of obstacles, reasonably distraction free, and enclosed by a fence with the gate shut. The footing should be even and soft, without rocks or significant debris. An indoor arena may best provide these components as well as further limiting the sometimes overwhelming array of sensory stimuli of the program site. Appropriate music can enhance an indoor session by providing a regular rhythm to which the horse can walk and by alleviating boredom for the staff and client. The site should also be safe because it is predictable--that is, reasonably free from unexpected, noisy events which might frighten the horse.

The equipment used in backriding is specific to both this technique and to the needs of the client. As noted, a saddle is not used due its negative impact on the position of the backrider. The horse should be well-padded to protect its back and for the comfort of the client and backrider. The type of pad chosen to be directly under the client will be determined by the client's stability, weight and balance. A pad which provides less friction, and allows the client to slide a little easier, might be chosen to facilitate improving the client's sense of midline and balance. A sheepskin often provides great comfort and may be less aversive to touch for the client with tactile hypersensitivity. The pads are held in place by a surcingle, which is also chosen for specific reasons. Considerations in the choice of a surcingle include the number and position of the handles, and its overall width. A vaulting surcingle may provide security and handles for upper extremity weightbearing. A vaulting surcingle which is narrow and with the handles placed well toward the withers of the horse is preferable because it takes up less space, is better accommodated by clients with decreased range of motion at the hips, and more easily reached. An anti-cast roller, with its centered handle, is easily accessible by client and backrider, should it be needed, and again usually accommodated by clients with decreased hip range of motion, but does take up space, and can make weightbearing through the hands on the horse's withers impossible. A surcingle without handles may be the least in the way but leaves the client or backrider without a handhold. While it is hoped that the session is safe enough that the backrider will not need a handhold, he or she may prefer one. Finally, the use of a helmet by both the backrider and client is usually considered an essential safety feature. The helmet should have an attached harness, no brim or a flexible brim. If the client's head control or posture is impaired by a regular riding helmet, a lightweight helmet may be chosen. For this client, the North American Riding for the Handicapped Association, Inc.,'s Guidelines for the use of a lightweight Helmet should be consulted.

The use of backriding as a therapy or teaching technique can be very effective. However, for the many reasons discussed herein, the choice of backriding should not be lightly made. It is a safe technique for therapeutic riding clients only when all safety concerns have been successfully addressed. The selection, training, and maintenance of the backriding horse will always truly show whether our use of the horse is humane and ethical, because the potential for harm to the animal through the use of this technique is both known and preventable. Clearly, the credo "Do No Harm" is one to be adhered to where backriding is concerned. Yet when correctly and safely done, backriding can provide a tremendously effective technique for improvement--and enjoyment--in therapeutic riding.

References
North American Riding for the Handicapped Association. (1990). *Backriding Guidelines*. Denver, CO.
Barnes, T. (1990). Houston, TX
Stanford, E. (1983). *Guidelines for Backriding*. unpublished educational seminar.
Glasow, B. (1983). *Putting Backriding into Proper Perspective*. NAHRA News, Denver, CO

24.07 NDT AND EQUINE-ASSISTED THERAPY: A LESSON REVIEW

Joann Benjamin, PT

Physical and occupational therapists have many treatment techniques they may use to treat a client effectively. They will generally choose techniques with which they are most familiar and which they judge will be the most beneficial to the client.

Neurodevelopmental treatment (NDT) is one technique which has been used extensively in the therapy clinic. The therapists who use this approach will have had training beyond that received in school, for working with children and adults. NDT is commonly utilized with clients who have neurological disorders. Let us review a single lesson in which the equine-assisted therapy will take a NDT approach.

Audrey is an 11 year old girl who suffered a closed head injury (CHI) two years ago when she was struck by a car. She was a typical nine year old prior to the accident. She is still very active, bright, personable and loves animals. Audrey's mother is interested in having her daughter ride in a therapy program. She has obtained a referral from Audrey's pediatrician and from her therapists.

The physical therapist (P.T.) in the program evaluated Audrey and reports the following: Audrey has functional use of her left side. The muscles on her right side are tight and resist stretching (hypertonus). Audrey carries her right arm close to her chest with elbow bent and hand fisted (flexor pattern). She stands 'crooked,' leaning to the right, and has difficulty rotating to the left (right trunk hypertonus). Audrey can walk for short distances (10-15 feet) with her mother's help or with a cane. Her steps are unequal and her balance is poor. She exaggerates stepping with her right leg and tends to turn her ankle under. This walking pattern gets worse the further she walks.

The therapist explains that this client demonstrates abnormal postural tone. Normal tone is "muscle tonus high enough to maintain posture against gravity, but low enough to move through it" (Sherrington, in Bobath, 1982). In other words, muscles need to have enough tension to support the body upright without being so tense that movement cannot occur. Audrey is unable to move easily against her tense muscles. This prevents her from effectively adapting to changes in position (balance) or from initiating voluntary smooth movements. When she has to increase her effort to move as when she walks, she repeats the abnormal movement patterns while increases the amount of muscle activity. Her nervous system is unable to control the excessive muscle activity and therefore her muscle tightness increases; this further restricts normal movement. This is now a vicious cycle.

Audrey also lacks symmetry in her posture and in her movements. The therapist explains that this is, in part, a result of Audrey's asymmetrical muscle tension; it is greater on the right than on the left. She has shown this posture for two years. Her sensory feedback system (proprioception) has adapted to this posture and accepts it as "normal." When Audrey is placed in proper alignment, she feels off balance. The same holds true for her movement patterns. She has moved in abnormal patterns for so long that the sensation of this movement has repeatedly entered her nervous system. Audrey no longer recognizes normal movement patterns as correct.

According to NDT theory, "normal movements need a background of normal tonus" in order to exist (Bobath 1982). Therefore, the "aim of NDT treatment should be to change the abnormal patterns of movement (Bobath 1982)" or to break the abnormal cycle of movement and sensory feedback. The control of abnormal activity results in the ability to develop normal postural responses, to initiate functional movement and to experience the sensation of normal movement. Through the experience of normal movement, one hopes that Audrey will develop more appropriate muscle activity: both automatic (unconscious) postural responses and voluntary movement.

Specific NDT handling techniques are applied by the certified therapist to decrease abnormal muscle tone and to encourage (facilitate) normal movement. The therapist works with a team of assistants (sidewalker, a horse handler) who are critical to the success of the session. Awareness of NDT principles and objectives makes every team member a contributor to the therapy experience.

In Audrey's case, as soon as she arrives at the arena the therapeutic riding team should begin to involve her in activities appropriate for her. Because Audrey will show signs of increased tone when walking a long distance, she is encouraged to use her wheelchair instead. With activities such as grooming, she will perform tasks which are a challenge, but not so difficult that they induce stress (increased tone). Throughout, Audrey should be positioned so that she can participate in activities while maintaining midline, not turning or leaning to her favored side.

When she is ready to mount her horse from the ramp, she will require assistance - enough help so that she is not struggling, yet, allowing her to do as much of the mount as she is able. The therapist positions Audrey on the horse in a symmetrical posture which will help to prevent abnormal patterns. Additionally, the therapist will avoid positions that cause Audrey discomfort, as pain will increase her abnormal tone.

When Audrey is comfortably astride the horse, her right leg is flexed more than her left. Even so, the therapist is certain to check that her weight is distributed evenly on her seat bones so that she can have a solid, midline base of support. Her trunk is supported by the therapist who facilitates symmetrical posture. Audrey has her hands on a weight bearing platform (Bryn Mawr Rehabilitation Hospital) at the horse's withers. This helps to encourage an upright trunk (shoulders over pelvis) while providing sensory input through the arms. Weight bearing will help to normalize tone in the limbs as well as in the trunk.

The therapist has the horse handler work the horse at a rhythmic walk along the rail as horse, rider, and therapist accommodate to each other. They begin to the right, with gentle turns at the corners, because Audrey is stronger in this direction. The movement of the horse, the weight bearing of the arms and trunk, along with reflex inhibiting techniques by the therapist all help to decrease Audrey's muscle tension. As Audrey's muscle tone decreases towards normal, her position on the horse improves; her pelvis, with the therapist's facilitation, begins to move into a neutral posture from a slumped position (posterior tilt). Her right leg positions more easily downward without squeezing the horse (adduction), her right arm shows less fisting of the hand and supports more weight. Audrey is more symmetrical from left to right; she now sits easily in midline. Her body is more supple and she now moves in rhythm with the horse. As she feels a decrease of muscle tension (hypertonus), the therapist chooses to facilitate greater postural response from Audrey. The therapist asks for changes of direction, then across the arena. Turns by the horse require Audrey to lengthen her trunk, primarily on the long side of the turn. The therapist can help facilitate this trunk elongation in conjunction with the horse's movement. Elongation and shortening of the trunk is essential for activities such as reaching and walking.

The therapist now has Audrey work on skills to enhance upper-trunk-on-lower-trunk movement such as twisting, bending forward toward the horse's neck, and lateral bending. The horse generates lower-trunk-on-upper-trunk movement as the therapist manually facilitates postural control and stability of the upper trunk in good alignment. The therapist concentrates on the child's trunk control because the trunk is the basis for all other movement. Audrey has been moved through a symmetrical, midline position. The movement of the trunk is over a stable base of support (pelvis) in good alignment (neutral pelvic tilt). Audrey begins to demonstrate improved trunk mobility as a result of her increased trunk stability. Both mobility and stability are directly dependent on normal muscle tone.

As Audrey develops better control in her trunk, the therapist is able to concentrate more on her arms and legs. Her right arm and leg may well have relaxed simply due to the decrease in hypertonus achieved in her trunk. Further decrease in muscle tension is achieved through handling methods (reflex inhibiting positions). As the decrease in tone occurs, the therapist will be facilitating muscle activity in the limbs. She asks Audrey to perform skills and assists as necessary. The therapist is looking for Audrey to achieve successful movement without inducing abnormal patterns. The child, with her therapist's help reaches out and touches parts of the horse, plays with a ball and handles large rings. At the end of the lesson, Audrey is integrating several of the skills the therapist helped facilitate. For instance, as Audrey places a ring in a mailbox she demonstrates:

1. A stable base (pelvis) in neutral alignment
2. Weight shifting toward the mailbox which requires elongation of the reaching (weight bearing) side, and shortening of the opposite side of the trunk
3. Movement of the upper trunk on the lower trunk
4. Voluntary, controlled movement of the arm
5. Resumption of midline posture upon completion of the task

At the end of the session, Audrey dismounts to the ramp. The therapist chooses to have Audrey dismount by bringing her right leg over the horse's neck and turning to sit on the horse sideways before standing on the ramp platform. The sidewalkers are careful to help support Audrey's trunk, and the leader is careful to monitor the horse from the front. It seems Audrey requires much less assistance than when mounting. She is able to initiate lifting her leg over the horse's neck, her trunk muscles show greater control in this off-balance posture. The therapist then has Audrey walk to her wheelchair. She continues to monitor the effort that Audrey must put forth to walk and facilitates when needed. This gives the therapist a chance to see what functional gains Audrey has made as a result of her riding session.

The riding session has been successful in achieving certain neurodevelopmental objectives appropriate for this child. Audrey's muscle tone is decreased to the point where more normal movement can take place. Audrey has an improved sense of midline orientation, she is comfortable when positioned in midline and her postural muscles help to maintain a symmetrical alignment. The increased stability of her trunk allows her to gain more active function of her trunk and extremities.

During the session, the horse provides the child with a tremendous amount of sensory input through movement. By inhibiting her abnormal tone to allow freer movement, the therapist helps Audrey to integrate the movement stimuli received from the horse. Her normal balance reactions are encouraged as the horse moves. The horse is the three dimensional movement stimulus, the therapist is the facilitator. Audrey benefits from the influence of both.

The therapist will take a similar approach on subsequent sessions, increasing the challenge as Audrey progresses. The therapist schedules Audrey twice per week, for 30 minute sessions. Re-evaluation is ongoing though she will formally re-evaluate Audrey at the end of eight weeks to determine continuation of the program. She will also contact the Audrey's primary therapists to monitor progress in other areas, and to integrate functional goals for Audrey with theirs.

As Audrey continues her equine-assisted therapy one can expect to see improvements throughout her trunk and limbs. She will demonstrate improved stability and midline orientation, as well as increased control of the trunk and extremities. Improved function, both on and off the horse is the ultimate goal. All along, the horse and the therapist will work closely to provide Audrey with normal sensory input, and a means through decreasing her abnormal movement, to integrate those sensations to reproduce the normal movement Audrey once knew.

References
Bobath, B. (1982) *Adult Hemiplegia: Evaluation and Treatment.* 2nd ed. London: Heinemann.
Bryn Mawr Rehabilitation Hospital. Physical Therapy Department, 414 Paoli Pike, Malvern, PA. 19355 USA. 215-251-5560.

24.08 RHYTHMIC FACILITATION - A METHOD OF TREATING NEUROMOTOR DISORDERS USING THE RHYTHM AND MOVEMENT OF THE WALKING HORSE

Jill Wham, Dip OT/NZ, OTR

DEFINING RHYTHMIC FACILITATION
Rhythmic facilitation is a neuromotor facilitation technique which is synchronized with the movement and rhythm of a walking horse. The horse provides the mobility and the rhythm, the occupational therapist organizes the client into an optimum posture and augments and mobilizes action with rhythmic facilitation (Wham, 1990). The rhythmical movement of the horse needs to be carefully analyzed in order to use this technique.

THE RHYTHM AND MOVEMENT OF THE WALKING HORSE
The horse has been described as a walking simulator machine (Riede, 1988). The movement is not like that of riding in a car or wheelchair, but is three-dimensional and rhythmical. The horse produces a pulse through its back which works against the client's forward, upward and lateral movements (Figure 1) (Riede, 1988). A posterior view of a client who is wearing reflective markers down the spine and across the buttocks (level with the hip joints) was video taped. This shows that as the horse walks an upward pulse is transmitted rhythmically and alternately through the clients left and right side of the pelvic girdle. The movement is absorbed through lateral flexion of the lumbar spine and elevation of the pelvis alternately on the left and then right. The markers above the waist remain in a neutral position (Figure 2).

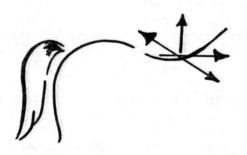

FIGURE 1.

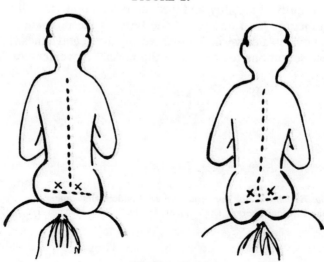

FIGURE 2.

566

When analyzed further, it was observed that the elevation of the pelvis coincides with the stance phase of the horse's hind leg on the same side, i.e., during the stance phase of the left hind leg, the horse's rump elevates on the left side, the client experiences pelvic elevation on the left and the lumbar spine side flexes accordingly to absorb the movement. The same movement can be observed from a posterior view when the person walks. During the stance phase of each leg the pelvis is elevated and the lumbar spine side flexes to absorb the movement. Videos comparing the posterior views of the client with those of the walker show that the same quality and dimensions of movement are experienced. A lateral view of the client shows that with each step there is a corresponding opening and closing (flexion/extension) of the hip joint (Figure 3). The client's hip is thrust forward and the lumbar vertebrae "ripple" to absorb the forward impulsion through the horse's back. This occurs alternately at each hip during the stance phase of the horse's hind leg. It is this action which brings in a rotational movement into the client's trunk, invaluable for inhibiting spasticity and reducing abnormally high muscle tone in cerebral palsy.

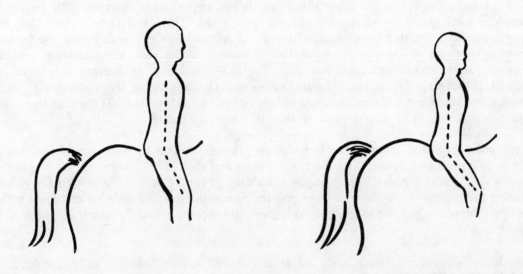

FIGURE 3.

Thus as the horse walks, the rider's lumbar spine, hips, thighs and associated musculature of the pelvic girdle and abdominal muscles act as "shock absorbers" while the upper body remains still. The implications are exciting in the field of rehabilitation related to neuromotor disorders such as cerebral palsy and head injuries. The ability to experience and learn the normal movement patterns and balance reactions necessary to sit, stand and walk is dependent on stability and freedom of movement in the pelvic girdle and trunk.

As in hippotherapy the client can be placed in a variety of other positions. These may include: supine lying along the length of the horse, sitting backwards, propping on extended arms or forearms, and lying prone across the horse. The emphasis can be upon developing stability in these positions or using a rhythmic technique to facilitate movement, for example: rolling along the horses back. Rhythmic facilitation techniques may also be used by the therapist while backriding. **In this case the therapist needs to be very well seated and able to feel the left, right, upward and forward pulses of the horse's walk.** A simple numnah (saddle pad) and surcingle are favored as providing the optimal benefit in terms of using the horse's shape, warmth, and movement.

SPECIFIC RHYTHMIC FACILITATION TECHNIQUES
The therapist must first be able to assess the client and analyze the aspects of the posture to be targeted for work. The most suitable position or positions to be used on the horse are selected, and after the mounting procedure the therapist helps the client settle into a relaxed and comfortable position. Warm-up procedures may be used initially, such as breathing, upper body exercises or creative visualization techniques, such as those used by Sally Swift (1985). The therapist directs the horse's pace and shape via the leader. For example, a slower pace may often be required

but the horse will be expected to make itself into a rounded outline and track up so that the movement through its back is fluid and rhythmical.

The horse leader is required to keep the horse's steps uniform and to encourage his (horse) concentration to be upon his work. It is important that the horse's rhythm and movement is not broken or that he not become distracted and turn his head or alter his shape. A leading technique similar to "long reining" can be used where the leader stands just behind the horse's ear, placing one hand over his neck to make contact with the reins onto the bit. The leader then "rides" the horse from the ground using the reins and voice commands instead of leg aids. The horse is trained to an advanced level of obedience and is capable of producing the rounded outline, fluidity of movement and concentration expected in good dressage.

The therapist walks beside the horse and firmly attaches one hand <u>over the client's thigh onto the surcingle or numnah</u>. Often a second sidewalker works on the other side of the horse, opposite the therapist. The purpose for holding onto the numnah or surcingle as opposed to the client's leg or waist is two-fold: 1) safety and 2) as an "anchoring point" for using rhythmic facilitation techniques. Although the horses are highly trained and the leaders are skilled and competent, the therapist and sidewalker must always be aware of the horse's instinctive potential to shy. Any environment has its surprises to which a horse may react. The disabled client often does not have necessary protective reactions and is likely to sustain a more severe injury than others if he falls. Being firmly attached to the horse means that if the horse shies, the client will remain anchored on by the two sidewalkers. If the situation continues to be dangerous, the sidewalkers will be in a position to take the client off safely.

As an anchoring point for a rhythmic facilitation technique, the attachment to the horse itself allows the therapist to be sensitive to and work in harmony with the horse's pace and rhythm. The support given to the client can be varied. The sidewalker's arm may rest lightly on the rider's leg or it may be used to anchor the client firmly onto the horse. Placing the arm closer to the hips gives greater proximal support and helps the client with poor pelvic and trunk stability. Supporting closer to the knee is a more distal contact and the client will need to work harder to stay balanced.

When using rhythmic facilitation techniques, the therapist times her own stride length and has to synchronize exactly with the horse's hind legs. When backriding, the therapist feels the horse's rhythmic pulse and will be able to identify exactly when each of the horse's hind legs are striking the ground. Using this rhythmical pattern (left... right... left... right... /one... two ... one... two...) the therapist can time the use of her hands to augment the horse's mobilizing action.

Three examples of this technique are outlined as followed:
   A. <u>To improve pelvic mobility</u>, the therapist uses the forward pulse of the horse and during the stance phase of the hind leg, she augments the forward movement of the client's hip. The heel of the hand and the flat of the fingers are applied just below the ischial spine (Figure 4), and pressure is used to alternately push the client's hips forward with the horse's movements. The client needs to be seated with good alignment of the body. This is observed as recommended in classical riding books. The client is encouraged to sit tall with the ear, shoulder and hip all being in the same vertical plane. This classical position may be modified to further augment the forward impulse through the client's hips by the rider leaning back slightly. This moves the ear-shoulder-hip line behind the vertical and the movement is exaggerated through the client's hip.

This rhythmic facilitation technique is effective with clients who have restricted mobility in the hips, e.g., spastic diplegia, spastic quadriplegia. It may also be used to challenge the client with low muscle tone and/ or poor pelvic stability. It should be noted that if the therapist's timing does not coincide with the horse's rhythm, the desired mobilizing action will be blocked.

B. <u>To improve symmetry, in particular emphasis is on even weight bearing through both seat bones</u>. Most clients with a neuromotor problem show asymmetry in their sitting position. There is often more weight distributed through one side than the other. When asked to transfer some of this weight to sit evenly, they are not able to maintain this symmetry for long. Their body schema (i.e., the perception of themselves in space) has altered so that sitting asymmetrically feels correct and sitting evenly may feel strange and insecure. The asymmetry is easily identified by walking behind the horse and observing the rider. Sometimes they may be placing so much weight on one side that they have slipped off the midline of the horse's back. The horse must be halted and the client brought back to the centre before the rhythmic facilitation technique can be used. Once the client is re-centered, the horse walks on and the therapist can now facilitate for symmetry. The client is "asked" to shift his weight distribution by rhythmic pressure bring applied upward and into the client's hip on the 'heaviest' side (Figure 5 - point **X**).

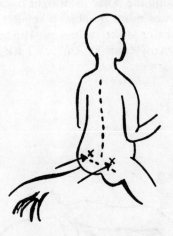

FIGURE 4. POINTS OF PRESSURE APPLIED BELOW THE ISCHIAL SPINE

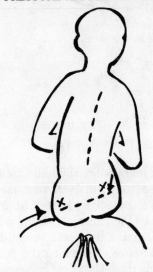

FIGURE 5. POINT Y AND X

Compression downward may also be used to "ask" the client to sit into the horse's movement on their 'lightest' side (figure 5--point **Y**). The stance phase of the hind leg on the 'lightest' side of the client is used in this case to encourage him to sit into the upward pulse of the horse's walk. As the client practices, the therapist can be lighter with her hands and can gradually replace the facilitation with verbal prompts or visualization techniques. A horse walks comfortably at 75 steps per minute, which translates into over 2000 steps per half hour. This gives over 1000 opportunities to practice the skill. In this case the skill is weight-bearing on the right side in sitting (Figure 5). In this way the client can accept and learn to tolerate the new sensation of symmetry.

C. <u>To decrease scoliosis</u> , the client is positioned supine along the length of the horse's back. The therapist places one hand over the client's thigh and onto the numnah at the withers. The other hand is placed under the client's axilla. As the horse walks, a rhythmic stretch is applied to match the elongating action of the horse's side, i.e., during the stance phase of the hind leg on the same side. For example, a client who needs elongation on his left side will be stretched rhythmically on the left during the horse's elongation or stance phase of the horse's left hind leg. The assistant sidewalker can help by bracing against the client's thoracic region to assist the elongation (Figure 6). This uses similar key points to the three point bracing systems used in modular seating systems for children with scoliosis. Walking the horse in straight lines or various side circles can vary the amount of elongation used. As the client becomes more "pliable" a smaller circle can be tolerated (the elongation is on the outer edge of the circle) and a greater stretch achieved. The results of this method of stretching for clients with scoliosis have been promising in many cases at Ambury Park Riding Center *.

FIGURE 6.

The above examples illustrate some of the many ways rhythmic facilitation can be used in hippo- therapy. As the therapist becomes more attuned to the horse itself and its rhythm, facilitation techniques can be worked in harmony with the horse. The therapist may work on foot walking herself in time with the horse's hind legs, or on top of the horse as in backing. The rhythm is the key to the client's learning with the repetition and expectation provided by the horse, and mental application of the client and therapist. A well-trained horse and leader ensure that each step is identical to the last, giving the client a chance to practice the postural skill over and over until it is mastered. A positive expectation is generated with the rhythm. The client knows what to expect and when. He is able to anticipate, prepare himself posturally and respond adaptively.The expectation is one of success and there is no time to be bored or complacent as the horse keeps moving. The rhythm does not wait for the client, but "*asks*" him to "*do it now*" .... *now* ...*now*".

When neuromuscular facilitation techniques are used in harmony with the horse's rhythmic movement, specific therapeutic goals can be targeted. Rhythmic facilitation can be used to develop improved muscle tone, head control, trunk righting reactions, pelvic stability, hip mobility, postural extension against gravity, symmetry and other functional goals. These, along with the cognitive and social aspects of development achieved by clients are the basis for major accomplishments such as independent sitting, standing and walking needed for occupational roles.

* In a research study by Dr. Jill Calveley, children with this problem showed improved sitting balance following a course of therapy using this method.

Conclusion:

RHYTHMIC FACILITATION - A THREE POINT MODEL

Rhythmic facilitation is a method of treating neuromotor disorders using the rhythmic action of a walking horse. The <u>horse</u> provides the mobility and rhythm, the <u>therapist</u> organizes the client into a desirable position to benefit and augments the mobilizing action with <u>rhythmic facilitation</u>.

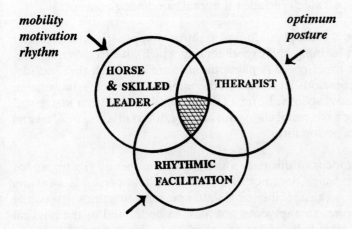

mobility
motivation
rhythm

HORSE & SKILLED LEADER

THERAPIST

optimum posture

RHYTHMIC FACILITATION

augmentive movement

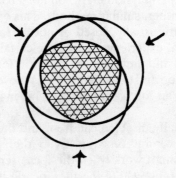

The three interlinking elements merge together so that all work simultaneously and harmoniously to become one operation. The client, the most important person, is the nucleus of the operation and the more these circles merge, the greater the benefit to him.

References:

Bertoli, D. (1988). "Effect of Therapeutic Horse Riding on Posture in Children with Cerebral Palsy." *Proceedings of the 6th International Therapeutic Riding Congress*. Toronto, Canada.

Calveley, J. (1988). The Effect of the Horse Riding upon Sitting Balance in People with Cerebral Palsy. *Proceedings from the 6th International Congress of Therapeutic Riding*. Toronto, Canada.   (from H, Brcko. 19 Alcaine Court, Thornhill, Ontario, Canada L3T 2G8.

Dacum Hippotherapy Curriculum Committee. (1988), October. *National Hippotherapy Project 3/91*. Warwick: New York

Glasow, B. *Division of Vaulting for Disabled*. Warwick: New York.

North American Riding for the Handicapped Medical Subcommittee. (1988). Therapeutic Riding Classifications.

Reide, D. (1988). *Physiotherapy on the Horse*. Madison: Omnipress.

Swift, S. (1985). *Centered Riding*. North Pomfret: David and Charles.

Tebay, J.M., Rowley, L.L., Copeland, J.C., Glasow, B.L. (1988). Training Physical and Occupational Therapists as Hippotherapy Specialists.

Wham, J. (1990). Abstract, paper presented at the New Zealand Association of Occupational Therapists Jubilee Conference. Christchurch, New Zealand.

24.09 HIPPOTHERAPY WITH THE CONSIDERATION OF REMEDIAL EDUCATION

Gundula Hauser, PT, Special Educator

During the past years, modern physics has demonstrated that the universe is a dynamic whole which cannot be divided and in which all parts interrelate and react to one another. This idea of systemic interrelatedness of all living organisms has become part of today's scientific thought. The same holistic approach can also be found in the field of social education whenever we look at a human being as a mind-body (or bio-psychological) entity.

At the beginning of the **Modern Age**, philosophy introduced the separation of body and spirit in medicine which led to a body of research solely tied to body chemistry and function. This can no longer be maintained. For a long time, remedial education has been connected too closely with purely scientific medicine. Under the new holistic approach it may be more aptly called "educational therapy" which includes the total mind/body concept.

Hippotherapy--physiotherapy on horseback--tends to use a neurophysiological treatment approach modeled after Bobath or other, similar methods. This opens avenues of learning and experimenting which, due to movement restrictions, are usually closed or not part of spontaneous experience. A physiotherapeutic approach that includes visual-spatial experiences may raise certain aspects to a conscious level when it is combined with active movement. Movements and their patterns occur in form of actions and reactions. Lorenz (1973) called this "pattern matching." The execution and the end result of a movement depends on the connection with and the differentiation of a "mental image" and an "outward reality." This involves the whole personality.

With physically disabled children, and they are the main focus of this paper, the physiotherapeutic treatment has the above task and function. Every therapeutic approach which does not deal with the whole person is a failure. It simply cannot work when the focus remains on the physical disability or isolated physical functions. Especially in hippotherapy, where the therapeutic helpmate is a horse, therapy does not have to be limited to the physical defects. Therefore a background in social education may provide helpful insights for use in this treatment method.

Many approaches, based on different training methods, provide insight into the mind-body relationship. As a physiotherapist, this author primarily relies on a medical and kinesiological approach. As a special educator, this same author plans which cognitive goal she wants to introduce and how she wants to direct the child toward it. Central to her work is the sensory approach. Each of the senses must be addressed and brought into consciousness. This begins with seeing, hearing, smelling and touching, and it includes the vestibular and proprioceptive senses. Much too often, these last two sensory systems are not taken into consideration.

When a child approaches the horse or is led to it, the author attaches great importance to the fact that the child looks at the horse, establishes contact, and talks to it. The child perceives the reaction of the animal to his attentions whether this is manifested by a look or a turning of his head or ears in his direction. Further more, the author likes to let the children put their ears against the horse's rump to listen to the sounds in his stomach and to try to perceive the heartbeat. This approach to the horse is carefully measured but intensive and even includes perceiving the horse's smell. In addition, the child touches the horse using gentle strokes from the shoulder to the neck and nostrils.

When the child finally gets on the horse's back, he literally loses the ground under his feet. For a child with vestibular dysfunction, this can be a rather unpleasant experience. But the fun of sitting on the horse's back helps him accept and overcome this initial difficulty. On horseback, the child may listen to the horse's steps, the rhythm of the walk or trot. At each step the child's joints and muscles must adapt to his moving support: the horse's back. The child may be asked to carry out some of the exercises with his eyes closed to eliminate one of the senses. This, in turn, stimulates the tactile and proprioceptive senses and produces an increased awareness of his own body and the ongoing movement. In the area of social interaction, hippotherapy entails a meeting of two living beings, as manifested by the child/horse relationship. As mentioned above, the child is encouraged from the beginning to make contact with the horse. His ability to relate to others is important for the development of his self-image. Unlike the people around him, the horse is not concerned with his physical defects. This may be very important to many disabled children as they often meet people with frightened or worried expressions or encounter other negative reactions.

The therapeutic exercise of lying prone or supine on the horse creates an intense contact which further enhances the child/horse relationship. Many children express this by saying: "You are so warm and soft" or "your mane tickles my nose" and other, similar words. As much as possible, the child decides when to walk or trot.. A well trained horse that reacts appropriately to the child's commands allows the child to experience cooperative behavior. The therapist is involved in the child's socio-emotional development by helping him improve his relationship with the horse. Thereby she becomes part of the confidence-based relationship, child-horse-therapist.

Client-centered conversation may be used as part of the preparation. This is an approved technique used in psychotherapy. If possible, the child should be prepared for the experience on his way to the horse. This may include a discussion of what the child will tell the horse or what exercises he wants to do this time. He should also have the opportunity to decide beforehand, if he wants to try a new exercise or if he wants to continue with the familiar ones.. In any case, the child must be given the opportunity to free himself from all emotional and mental preoccupation with his daily life to be free for new experiences on horseback. In therapy the feelings and experiences are made conscious through the dialogue. Soon the child will be enjoy expressing himself with word such as: "the horse pushes me, hop, hop, hop.." or "the horse rocks me, back and forth, back and forth, "verbally reproducing the rhythm of the horse's steps. He thereby connects his experiences with words which also improves his later recall. In the discussion following the therapy, we do not only reflect the content of the session, we go beyond that and try to make the child recall what he felt, smelled, and heard through the use of visualization and imagery.

In addition, we use relaxation exercises similar to the ones used in psychotherapy. The author, for instance, likes to have the child lie down on the horse facing backwards. That means, the child's head is on the croup, and his arms point to the horse's tail. The author then proceeds to let the child experience the first steps of a modified autogenic training: the experience of heaviness and warmth. This gives the child the ease to let his head, body, arms and legs sink heavily into the soft coat of the horses. Additionally, the experience of warmth is made more readily accessible by the warmth of the horse's body.

A child's positive behavioral responses can be reinforced by the therapist. Through dialogue and visual-motor experiences, the child is able to learn, especially in the area of social interactions. The therapist demonstrates different movements and stimulates the child with the help of mimicry and gestures to copy the movements in mirror symmetry. In addition, any arising anxiety on the part of the child at any time during the therapy must be accepted and dealt with by the therapist. It should mentioned that by training the proprioceptive and vestibular senses alone, the child will get an improved body scheme. This leads to greater self awareness and ultimately to an improved self image. A well developed self-image will result in greater self-confidence, and with that he will become less fearful. When these initial problems and fears have been overcome, the therapist can create new demands and new goals thereby leading the child, step by step, towards a fuller, more satisfying life.

Through hippotherapy, disabled children can discover the often unknown pleasure of being physically active. When steady problem solving, coupled with positive reinforcement through success experiences leads to an increase in motivation and in the pleasure of learning, the child is ready to learn new skills and to reach toward the next higher level of function. It is, of course, not possible or even necessary to use the whole range of therapeutic approaches in any one session, but a background knowledge or some training in special education and psycho-therapeutic techniques are desirable for physiotherapists, especially for those working with children.

In Austria and many other countries, more emphasis is placed on separating hippotherapy and the psycho-educational aspects of therapeutic riding than on finding ways of connecting these two methods. This report is designed to do away with all fragmentation and to give prominence to the connecting element-the child as a mind/body entity, in short: the total child.

Reference
Lorenz, K. (1973). Die Ruckseite des Spiegels, Munchen, Germany.

24.10 ASSESSMENT AND ADAPTATIONS IN RIDING THERAPY FOR THE CLIENT FOLLOWING A CEREBRAL VASCULAR ACCIDENT

Victoria Haehl, BS, PT

Diagrams by Victoria Vallee

A cerebral vascular accident (CVA) or stroke occurs when circulation of blood to a part of the brain is disrupted. This condition has a high incidence among both young and old but is more common in adults. Changes in a person's physical, emotional, mental, speaking and writing abilities may occur. Blood supply to the brain can be altered by:
1. An arteriosclerotic thrombosis--an artery becomes slowly clogged with a clot.
2. An embolism--a blood clot travels from another part of the body and becomes lodged in an artery in the brain.
3. Intercranial hemorrhage--due to hypertension (high blood pressure), an aneurysm, or atrioventricular malformation (Biery et al, 1989).

In humans one side of the brain controls function on the opposite side of the body. A person whose CVA occurred in the right side of the brain will demonstrate a weakness on the left side. This is called a left hemiparesis or hemiplegia. Though most persons who have a CVA will have either a right or left hemiparesis, each one will be different depending on the type and location of the insult, the size of the area involved, the length of time from onset, and the age and physical condition before the onset.

In addition to difficulties with weakness, a CVA can cause problems with regulating the muscle tone or tension that provides a normal muscle with a state of readiness. The tone may be abnormally high, low or fluctuating. An individual may demonstrate different tonal quality in different parts of the body, and it may vary depending on the person's body position. Spasticity refers to a muscle's response to quick stretch, and this may be observed or felt as resistance. The terms "tone" and "spasticity" are frequently used to describe motor control difficulties that arise following a CVA. Although each rider with a CVA is different, there are some alterations which occur that can be generalized. These are listed below.

Left brain injury:
1. Decreased control and sensation on the right side of the body
2. Speech and language impairment
3. Decreased memory related to language
4. A slow and cautious style of interaction with the environment

Right brain injury:
1. Decreased control and sensation of the left side of the body
2. Decreased ability to judge space and size
3. Left side neglect or inattention to the side
4. Decreased memory or decreased attention span
5. A quick and impulsive style of interaction with the environment

ASSESSMENT
Persons entering a therapeutic riding program should be carefully evaluated. It is important to look at how the head, arms, trunk and legs work as a whole, not as separate parts. The same need for the holistic view is especially true for the person who has suffered a cerebral vascular accident. Although it is tempting to focus attention solely to the side of the body with less control, therapists' and instructors' observations should be all-inclusive. Reference should also be made to the report of the physical and occupational therapists, as well as the speech pathologist, who have been working with the rider to glean any pertinent information. If a therapist is available at the therapeutic riding facility to perform evaluations, a full evaluation can be undertaken. Figure 1 shows an example of an initial therapeutic riding physical therapy evaluation.

PHYSICAL THERAPY (EQUINE-ASSISTED THERAPY) EVALUATION
(EVALUATION FOR PHYSICAL THERAPY TREATMENTS)

DATE OF EVALUATION_____

NAME _____ BIRTH DATE _____

DIAGNOSIS _____

   (MEDICAL HISTORY: SEIZURES, SURGERIES, ACCIDENTS) _____

   HIP X RAYS___MEDICATION_____ASSISTIVE DEVICES USED_____

W/C _____ BRACES _____ SPLINTS _____

A. MOTOR BEHAVIOR
   (PURPOSEFUL VS RANDOM RESPONSES TO HANDLING, REFLEX ACTIVITY [ATNR, STNR], GRASP-VOLUNTARY VS INVOLUNTARY,
   COORDINATION, RESPIRATORY, GROSS ORAL MOTOR FUNCTION).

_____

B. MOTOR FUNCTION ABILITY

HEAD CONTROL

SITTING _____ SUPPORTED _____ UNSUPPORTED _____

STANDING _____ SUPPORTED _____ UNSUPPORTED _____

BED MOBILITY_____

ROLLING_____

SUPINE TO SIT_____

SIT TO SUPINE_____

GAIT_____

TRANSFER STATUS_____

CAR_____

SIT TO STAND_____

STAND TO SIT_____

POSTURE_____

SITTING_____

STAND_____

C. BALANCE
   (EQUILIBRIUM REACTIONS, RIGHTING REACTIONS, SITTING, STANDING, STATIC, DYNAMIC, QUADRUPED)

_____

D. TONE   E. RANGE OF MOTION

NECK_____

TRUNK_____

    RIGHT U E_____

    LEFT   U E_____

    RIGHT L E_____

    LEFT   L E_____

F. COGNITIVE/PERCEPTUAL

EXPRESSIVE SPEECH/LANGUAGE_____

LANGUAGE COMPREHENSION

HEARING_____

FOLLOWING COMMANDS	1 STEP_____, 2 STEP_____, 3 STEP_____, COMPLEX_____
ATTENTION SPAN	POOR [0-1 MIN]_____, FAIR [1-5 MIN]_____, GOOD [5+ MIN]_____
FRUSTRATION TOLERANCE	POOR_____, FAIR_____, GOOD_____.
PROBLEM SOLVING	POOR_____, FAIR_____, GOOD_____.
COOPERATION	POOR_____, FAIR_____, GOOD_____.

FIGURE 1

(EVALUATION FOR PHYSICAL THERAPY TREATMENTS) CONTINUED

G. SPECIAL CONSIDERATIONS

_____

_____

H. CHANGES OBSERVED WITH INITIAL TREATMENT

_____

_____

RECOMMENDED PROGRAM

FREQUENCY AND DURATION _____

HIPPOTHERAPY   DEVELOPMENTAL VAULTING   REMEDIAL VAULTING   OTHER

HELMET   SIDEWALKER   1 OR 2, BACKRIDER

MOUNTING: RAMP   BLOCK   LEG UP   VAULT ON

ASSISTANCE NEEDED

LONGEING: THERAPEUTIC LONGEING   GROUND DRIVING   LONGEING/CIRCLE

DISMOUNTING: RAMP   BLOCK   SLIDE OFF   ASSISTANCE NEEDED

LONG TERM GOALS (6 MONTHS)

_____

_____

Communication should be ongoing between the therapeutic riding team members and any active rehabilitation team members to make the experience most beneficial to the rider. The physician who makes the referral and signs the authorization should certainly receive periodic updates on the client's progress. It is often useful to invite members of the rehabilitation team to a hippotherapy session to observe. Prior to the initial session, invite the rider to tour the facility and possibly observe hippotherapy in action. This may be a suitable time to screen the rider and describe the purpose of hippotherapy/therapeutic riding.

Some additional concerns that should be noted if present on the initial assessment include hypertension, heart problems, osteoarthritis and back problems such as degenerative disc disease and stenosis. The rider's physician should be consulted if any questions arise. Also, your facility should have a list of conditions that contraindicate participation

576

in riding therapy. Further be aware that individuals with CVA disabilities may become more stiff and sore following riding sessions, thus requiring additional warm-up/cool-down time and shorter riding sessions.

THE IMPORTANCE OF OBSERVATION

Learning to be a good observer is key to the assessment of riders on and off the horse. "How are they sitting in the car when they arrive?" "How do they get out of the car?" "Is assistance required?" "Are they ambulatory or in a wheelchair?" "Do they use a cane?" "Does walking on uneven ground look like a new experience for them?" and "Do they seem fearful in the unfamiliar surroundings?" Observing their first visit to the barn can provide very useful information in determining riding strategies and goals. It can indicate how best to assist the rider and what horse and equipment may be the most appropriate for him. After meeting the rider, his family and friends, and concluding parts of the initial evaluation, have the rider indicate what he hopes to accomplish during the hippotherapy/therapeutic riding sessions. Your goals should be made with this in mind. As in any therapeutic setting, goals can be altered as progress is made or interests change.

The individual who has had a cerebral vascular accident resulting in a hemiparesis may demonstrate limitations in the joints, pain, changes in sensation and an impaired ability to feel where a body part is (proprioception). The physical therapist's evaluation should be able to provide specific information regarding the rider's physical status, but an observation of the rider on the horse provides other critical information.

TRUNK AND HEAD

An important observation to make on or off the horse is, what is the trunk (top of the shoulders to bottom of pelvis) doing? An optimal view of the rider's trunk and upper extremities can be made by sitting the rider on a pad or sheepskin and surcingle. Weather and provision for modesty permitting, have the client disrobe as much as possible (provide T-shirts) so that you can see his posture before the horse moves. This is important because the horse's movement may have the most impact on the rider's trunk. As stated by Detlev Riede, MD in his book, *Physiotherapy on the Horse*, "according to Baumann (1978), Kunzle (1979), and Kluwer (1983), the three dimensional movement of the horse's back simulates the human gait." During normal gait the trunk moves in anterior/posterior, lateral, rotational, and superior/inferior directions (Figure 2).

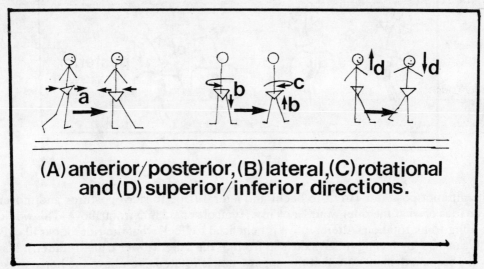

(A) anterior/posterior, (B) lateral, (C) rotational and (D) superior/inferior directions.

FIGURE 2.

The movement of the horse provides the rider's trunk with the components of normal human gait and positions him in a more normal upright posture which is difficult to duplicate in the therapeutic setting. Although the rider is sitting, the lower extremities are allowed to partially extend, unlike sitting in a chair. The lower extremities are brought closer to the plumb line of the pull of gravity on the horse than in sitting, making the posture resemble standing. In addition, the freedom of the lower extremities allows them to react to the movement of the horse and rider's trunk, resembling the demands of movement during gait (Figure 3).

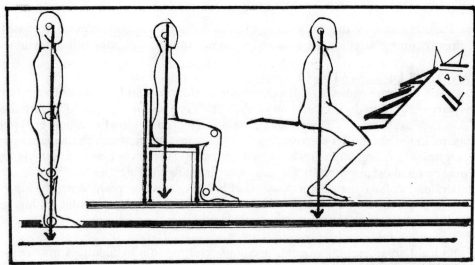

FIGURE 3.

A variety of trunk postures can be observed. If a video camera is available, it may be useful to film the rider from all angles to capture what your eye might miss. The rider may also find this interesting. But do not be surprised if he is somewhat shocked. Most people have no idea what they look like in action. Figure 4 illustrates some common poor postures observed. Standing directly behind the horse enables the therapist to see the asymmetries that frequently accompany a CVA. While these result from one side of the trunk functioning better than the other, remember that the whole trunk is reacting to the effects of the CVA, not only the hemiparetic side. Make sure both sides are carefully assessed.

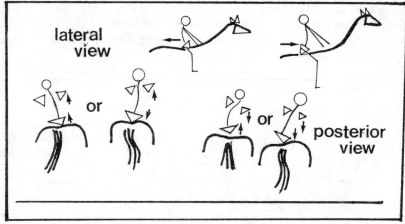

FIGURE 4.

In addition to the anterior/posterior (front to back) and lateral (side to side) postures and movements, it is also important to get an idea of what the rider would look like if you observed him from above. This would give important information regarding trunk rotation. Alternately it is beneficial to "feel" what the rider looks like. Place your hands on the pelvis. You can "see" by feeling if one side is in front of the other (lower trunk rotation). Hands on the back of the ribs below the scapula demonstrate that the upper trunk is rotated. Now have the horse walk on and observe the impact of the horse's three dimensional movement on the client's trunk.

Although this description of assessment provides clues for observing the rider for specific body parts, it is important to step back frequently to observe the whole. Many persons with hemiparesis will have problems with disassociation. Disassociation can be described as the ability to move one body part separately from another. Examples of disassociation are the ability to move the scapula on the thorax or move the lower extremity on the pelvis without moving the entire trunk. Problems with disassociation can best be seen by looking at the person as a whole. The therapist may see that the movement of the horse assists in disassociating body parts while the client passively sits on the horse.

The head position can also be influenced by motor control, sensory, perceptual or visual difficulties. Take note of whether the rider has full or partial range of motion in the neck. Due to any one or combination of these factors, the rider may not hold his head in midline (center). A head-forward posture may be a result of poor postural habits acquired from prolonged sitting following the CVA.

UPPER EXTREMITIES

The postures that the upper extremity assumes are numerous. An important observation to be made is at the shoulder. Due to abnormal positioning of the scapula and humerus, impaired motor control and soft tissue changes, the glenohumeral (shoulder) joint may become subluxed. This is a mal-alignment in which the head of the humerus can move interiorly, anteriorly or superiorly relative to the scapula. If the rider is unaware of this condition or is unable to inform the instructor or therapist, the limitation can be detected by feeling the top of the shoulder joint on both shoulders and observing the position of the scapula on the thorax. It is advisable to discuss this situation with the physical or occupational therapist treating the rider. Looking below the shoulder, be aware of the position of the arm in relation to the body; is it held behind, out to the side, or in front of the trunk, how does it change when the rider and horse begin to move? Pay particular attention to the hand, the wrist and fingers may be good indicators of how the client is reacting to the riding challenge. Clawing of the fingers and flexing of the wrist generally accompany the rider's sense of compromised balance or mal-alignment of the shoulder or trunk. (Similar changes can be seen in the toes and ankle).

Observe carefully the effect of the movement of the horse on the posture of the upper extremity. If it appears to be becoming more tight, it may be necessary to reassess the present activity, if improving posture is a goal of that session. It may also indicate that it is time for a break, a change in activity, or that the rider is fatigued. Continue to evaluate, observe and modify as the session progresses. Be aware that movement of the horse and movement of any part of the body can affect other parts of the body. This can especially be seen in the upper extremity. Pain should be closely monitored and avoided. If it persists or increases, riding may need to be discontinued until the therapist can further evaluate and treat the problem.

LOWER EXTREMITIES

Evaluating the lower extremity is sometimes difficult due to the various clothing: pants, boots, braces and equipment (i.e., stirrups, leathers). When making your initial observations and for periodic follow-up, it may be beneficial to use a sheepskin or pad secured by a surcingle. Remove braces and roll up pant legs. Knowing how the lower extremity reacts to the horses's movements, changes in direction and halts give a better understanding of how the legs will posture in the stirrup or brace. If the rider can wear shoes (no boots or brace), the ankle can be assessed more clearly. Make observations, as for the trunk and upper extremities, from all angles. Follow this by observing the whole body, horse and lower extremity relationship. A common posture for the involved foot is one of supination, in which the ankle turns in, the bottom of the foot points down and in. The toes may also claw. This posture may affect the type of stirrup chosen. A broader surface of support in addition to a variety of aids that can be placed on the ankle or foot may be beneficial to improve the posture. (Some suggestions are discussed in the treatment section.) The physical therapist working with the client may have some suggestions.

Balance should be assessed off the horse in a variety of positions: sitting, standing, and quadruped (hands and knees). On the horse, take note of the rider's trunk posture as well as any need for the support of his hands and/or from the sidewalker to maintain himself. Also record what the horse's walk is like, including its speed, amplitude and what direction of movement seems most prominent. How the rider tolerates this movement reflects his balancing capabilities.

During the observation/evaluation process the horse has already initiated the treatment session. The instructor or therapist need only facilitate this. In the beginning of each session, a warm-up period is advantageous. The horse should have received some conditioning or warm-up time prior to the rider mounting. Generally, it is best to start with riding long straight lines along the outside rail of the arena in both directions to make the rider feel more secure, balanced and prepared. This will also give the instructor time to quickly reassess posture and balance. The horse can proceed at a slow, medium or fast walk, depending on the rider's balance. Vary the horse's stride from short to extended. The rider may be more comfortable starting the session holding onto the surcingle handle with one or both hands. This makes the rider less tense and more able to feel the movement of the horse.

TREATMENT STRATEGIES TO FACILITATE RIDING

This description of various treatment ideas will address a rider who is on a horse with a surcingle, pad or sheepskin, long reins driven from behind (or being led) and two sidewalkers. Certainly, a saddle would not interfere with many of the activities proposed and may improve the rider's balance enabling him to perform more challenging activities. If stirrups are used for lower extremity weight bearing and the posture of the foot continues to change significantly, i.e., toes pointing down with heel up (plantar flexion of the ankle) or the bottom of the foot turning inward (supination), alternative positioning or equipment should be considered. A variety of ankle-foot-orthoses (AFO) are prescribed following a CVA. Some allow for motion at the ankle joint. The articulated AFO has hinges at the ankle to allow dorsiflexion (Figure 5). Other AFO's, depending on their rigidity, may also provide some support but allow for the movement necessary. Be careful to observe where the orthotic device ends under the foot. This may interfere with weight bearing on the stirrup in the proper portion of the foot. If the foot does not plantarflex excessively, but instead the sole turns inward (straining the lateral structures of the ankle and placing the ankle at risk for injury) an ankle airsplint may be of assistance (Figure 6). This support straps on with Velcro, does not limit dorsiflexion or plantar-flexion and limits medial/lateral movement at the ankle. There are also elastic wrap supports, which may be all that is required.

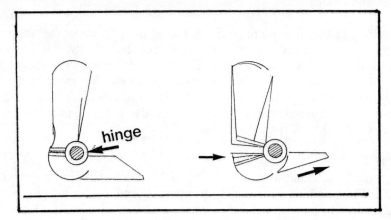

FIGURE 5.

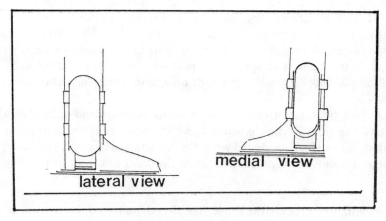

FIGURE 6.

Stirrups may be modified to fit the needs of the rider. The Devonshire Boot is a covering that encloses the front portion of the stirrup to prevent the foot from sliding through. Stirrup modifications such as rubber wedges should not be used without consulting a physical therapist. Remember that as the rider becomes more accomplished on the horse, these additional supports may need modification or may no longer be necessary.

When the lower extremity is not supported by a stirrup it is free to swing with the movement of the horse. This may assist in pelvic-lower extremity disassociation resulting in freer movement at the hip and ultimately better gait for the rider. The abducted slightly externally rotated position of the hip on the horse may improve the hips' range of motion. At a walk the pelvis is also being passively moved on the femur which passively mobilizes the hip joint. Relaxation of tight muscles of the hip, knee and ankle may be observed as the client continues during a session or series of sessions. By observing the rider from behind, an appreciation of leg length (reflecting tightness in muscles or pelvic obliquity) may be obtained. Changes in riding direction, doing circles, serpentine, figure eights, and lateral work may influence the lower extremity therapeutically.

The physical therapist may have some specific techniques that can be performed during the riding session for handling the hemiparetic lower extremity. For example, if the lower extremity tends to pull up, forward and inward; then if the therapist can give a gently, slowly sustaining slight down and out pull above the knee, and downward pull behind the heel momentarily at the halt, this may assist in relaxing the tightened muscles. The therapist should be consulted prior to actively manipulating the rider's extremities.

Following a CVA, as noted in the assessment section, the upper-extremity may assume a variety of postures that are related to the position of the trunk, the available range of motion in the joints, muscle tightness, motor control, sensation and, usually, the anxiety level of the rider. After the initial warm-up walking on the long sides of the arena, if the rider has been instructed in any self range of motion that can be performed sitting, this may be carried out by the rider with the horse halted or at the walk if feasible. It may also be helpful for the rider to perform some weight-bearing activities on the upper extremity as the horse walks on or at the halt. Positions can vary depending on the upper extremity. Some suggestions include placing the hands on the thighs, on the horse's neck, on the surcingle handle, or on the shoulders or arms of the sidewalkers. Dowels may also be positioned to allow weight bearing (Figure 7). If the rider is able to tolerate riding backward weight bearing with hands on the horse's haunches can be a great position. There is a lot of movement, proprioception and scapula/thoracic disassociation provided to the upper extremity and upper trunk in this posture. Frequently the upper extremity cannot fully extend at the elbow, wrist or fingers or does not have the control to maintain an extended position. It may be useful to use assistive positioning such as the upper extremity weight-bearing platform developed by Susan Christie, physical therapist and rehabilitation engineer at Bryn Mawr Rehabilitation Hospital in Malvern, Pennsylvania (Figure 8). It enables the rider to weight bear on a solid surface without fully extending the joints of the upper extremity. There are also a variety of plastic balls that can be placed between the rider's thigh and the body of the horse, at the surcingle handle or on the platform

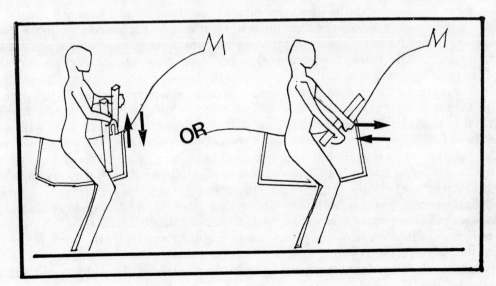

FIGURE 7.

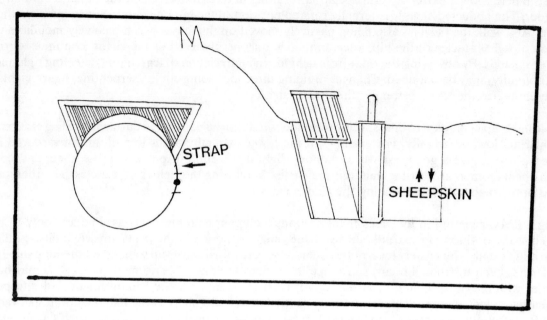

FIGURE 8.

that may assist the positioning of the wrist and fingers. If the rider is more involved in controlling the movement of the horse, adaptive reins (ladder, Humes) and adaptive gloves may be of assistance. These must be carefully monitored so there is not the danger of an inability to release if the rider needs to dismount in an emergency. Various non-weight-bearing activities that include the rider supporting his own upper extremity, and reaching in all available pain-free directions, may assist in function. Allowing the arm to swing freely at the side may also be beneficial. This is what arms normally do during gait. It may be the only opportunity that the rider has to experience this normal movement response, since usually a cane is in the hand of the stronger arm.

POSITIONING ADJUSTMENTS

A major impact of the horse's movement can be seen in the rider's trunk. Frequently following the initial few minutes of warm-up, the rider may be feeling a need to adjust his seat. Or it may be suggested to improve the symmetry, which will alter his experience of the horse's movement. Many times in therapy, improving symmetry of the trunk is a goal. The postural control of the trunk, head, and neck is key in the rehabilitation of the rest of the body. As the horse walks and the rider's pelvis is moved, the remainder of the trunk (spine, ribs, scapula and clavicle) reacts to these movements. These movements should be encouraged (not necessarily exaggerated) to insure the rider is not "fixing" or holding the pelvis. By observing the trunk, the instructor or therapist can decide what horse movement may be most beneficial to the rider. Transitions within the walk from slow to fast to slow, as well as to halt and back to walk, can assist in facilitating control anteriorly and posteriorly by activating the abdominals and the back extensors. The abdominals are often weaker on the affected side, which may cause the trunk to rotate back or ribs to flair as the rib cage loses it abdominal anchor (Ryerson, et al 1988). Abdominal control is very important to trunk control. Various figures can be used to move the pelvis laterally or rotating one side forward in relation to the other. By hopping on the horse yourself, you can feel which side of your pelvis or which scapula is tending to lower or raise, and which side of your trunk is working harder to stay symmetrical or balanced on the horse. Use your imagination. Try various moves to help with trunk control--side pass, shoulder in, and obstacles for the horse to step over. Using poles to create labyrinths for the horse to walk through combines transitions, changes in directions and amplitudes of movement. Changing the rider's position will also place new demands on his trunk, i.e., backward, sitting sideways, or forward, with both legs toward one side as if riding side saddle. The horse's movement will move the pelvis in relation to the upper trunk. Also encourage the upper trunk to move on the pelvis in a controlled way rotating in both directions, while the horse proceeds through a variety of changes and directions. Have the rider reach forward to either of the horse's shoulders or up the horse's neck on either side. By experiencing all of these movements yourself on the horse you will be familiar with the specific demands placed on the rider. The qualities of rhythm, timing and speed of movement may also be effected by a CVA. These may be improved by the work on the horse. Make sure that the rider is breathing normally and is relaxed at all times. This work to affect the trunk is key and cannot be duplicated in any other therapeutic setting.

The rider's head posture should also be addressed. There may be other factors beside the hemiparesis which contribute to the abnormal posturing of the head. With certain visual disturbances the rider may have limitations in the range of vision which may effect head positioning. The rider may also have a limited awareness or attention to the hemiparetic side, termed "neglect." Frequent changes in direction, circles and other figures, while instructing the rider to look in that direction with eyes and head forward may help this problem. Having dressage letters or other visual cues in the arena, or playing catch, may also be beneficial in promoting good head movement.

As the rider has been proceeding to move in response to the movement of the horse and in response to verbal cues from the instructor or therapist, staying on the horse has always been a goal. Fear of falling, especially for older individuals who have frequently experienced falls, may be strong. Side walkers, a well trained horse, driver and instructor or therapist can all help to ease this fear. This will allow the rider not to tense his muscles, to get better balance and react to the changing demands placed upon his vestibular, oculomotor and neuromuscular systems. As the rider sees himself better balanced on the horse, he may also see an improvement in his balance off the horse sitting, standing, and walking, off the horse. Bier and Kauffman (1989) sited studies conducted by Hall, Hulac, and Myers (1983) and Fox, Lawlar, and Luttges (1984) showing improvement in balance from riding. Bier and Kauffman went on to examine the effects of therapeutic riding on the balance of eight individuals with mental retardation. By measuring their balance in a variety of postures off the horse in standing and quadruped position prior to and after a six month therapeutic riding program the authors were able to document improvements. Each instructor is encouraged to monitor each rider's physical and functional status so that similar data can be gathered to support the use of the horse in the rehabilitation process.

MOUNTING AND DISMOUNTING
Since many disabled persons cannot mount and dismount in the usual ways, various aids and adaptations may be needed to make those activities possible. A ramp and mounting platform are desirable when dealing with adult riders. Children are more easily assisted by lifting them onto the horse from the ground. Additional factors such as pain, joint instability and limitations in the available range of motion may impair mounting from the ground. If a saddle is being used, slightly lowering the stirrup and assistance from the side walkers may be all that is necessary. When using a mounting platform, a variety of techniques may be used. The physical or occupational therapist working with the rider may be of more assistance in recommending a suitable transfer technique, especially if the rider is to be transferred from a wheelchair. If the rider is in a wheelchair, either that individual or a family member should be able to tell which direction of movement--left or right--is easiest. When assisting the rider in a wheelchair it may be safest and more practical to remove the footrest and the arm rest closest to the horse. Make sure that good body mechanics are used. The therapist's back should not be compromised.

If the rider has limited ambulatory skills, it may be best to have him first sit sideways on the horse prior to swinging one leg over the neck of the horse. Be prepared to support the trunk and assist the lower extremity swinging over the side. The rider will typically lose his balance backward and may not have sufficient hip range of motion to complete this mounting technique. If the rider is able to balance a short time on one leg with some support, an alternative method is to have the rider face the head of the horse, hold on to the handle of the surcingle or to the therapist and swing a leg over and sit. It may be easiest for a rider to stand on the stronger leg while swinging the involved lower extremity over the horse. Dismounting can be performed either way. It is helpful to have a chair on the platform so that the rider can sit after the ride.

CONCLUSION

This discussion has considered the physical assessment, observation, treatment and benefits for the client with CVA and his response to the horse in equine-assisted therapy. Look at the rider as a whole, consult rehabilitation team members and set obtainable goals with the rider. During and after treatment observe the rider's response to the horse, monitor for ill effects as well as the positive responses seen, and adapt the activities appropriately. But do not forget to help your riders have some fun and then watch their self-esteem rise.

References

Baumann, (1979). *Therapeutic Exercise on Horseback for Children with Neurogenic Disorders of Movement.* 3rd International Congress. England.

Bier, M.J., Kauffman, N. (1989). "The Effects of Therapeutic Horseback Riding on Balance." *Adapted Physical Activity Quarterly.* 221-229.

Bobath, B., (1978), *Adult Hemiplegia, Evaluation and Treatment.* Second Edition, London: William Heinemann Medical Books Limited.

Carr, S., Gordon, G. H. (1987). *Movement Science for Physical Therapy and Rehabilitation.* Maryland, Aspen Publishers.

Conti, D. (1984). *Post-Stroke Adapted Exercise Program.* (Informational Pamphlet): American Heart Association.

Davies, P. (1985). *Steps to Follow: A Guide to the Treatment of Adult Hemiplegia.* Germany: Sprirges-Verlag.

Fox, V. M., Lawlar and Luttges, M. W. (1984). "Pilot Study of Novel Test Instrumentation to Evaluate Therapeutic Horseback Riding" *Adapted Physical Activity Quarterly.* 1, 30-36.

Hall, S. J., Hulac, G. M., and Myers, J. E. (1983). *Improvement Among Participants in a Therapeutic Riding Program.* Unpublished manuscript, Washington State University, April.

Kluwer, C. (1982). On the Psychology of Riding/Vaulting. *Proceedings of the 4th International Congress.*

Kunzle, (1982). The Effect of the Horse's Movement on the Patient. *Proceedings of the 4th International Congress.*

Riede, D. (1988). *Physiotherapy on the Horse.* Wisconsin: Omnipress.

Ryerson, S., Levit, K.(1988). *Physical Therapy of the Shoulder.* New York: Churchill, Livingstone, Chapter: The Shoulder in Hemiplegia, 105-131.

Ryerson, S., Levit, K. (1988). *Physical Therapy of the Foot and Ankle.* New York: Churchill, Livingstone, Chapter: The Foot in Hemiplegia. 109-141.

Documents in these Proceedings. *Sixth International Riding Therapeutic Congress.* (1989). Toronto: Canada.

Haehl, Victoria, PT, BS. NDT certified (adult). consulting--All Seasons Riding Academy and other Bay Area therapeutic riding centers; member--NAHRA, Bay Area Equines for Sports & Therapy.

24.11 EQUINE-ASSISTED THERAPY WITH AN ADULT CLIENT WITH CEREBRAL PALSY

Barbara T. Engel, MEd, OTR

Joe is a 25 year old man born with athetoid quadriplegia, severe spasms and associated pathological reflex reactions. He has moderate scoliosis which remains flexible in the upper trunk and static in the hip area. Joe has received intensive neurodevelopmental (NDT) treatment since he was six months old. He has participated in *Conductive Education* technique (see section 23.04) for the last few years with his mother.

Joe began riding when he was about 12 years old with a social riding group. He needed a great deal of support from sidehelpers and a horse leader. He was learning how to direct the horse using one hand.

At 19 years, Joe began in-home occupational therapy to increase functional living skills. When he was first seen at home, Joe was able to feed himself, type with one finger and walk with maximum support using scissoring gait. He was unable to roll over in bed, come to sitting position or help with his dressing. He could not sit without back and side supports. Generally, his sensory registration of touch or position sense (the ability to sense where his limbs were) was poor.

After 6 months of in-home therapy, the occupational therapist visited a new riding program Joe had joined. She began visiting the center once a week to advise the riding instructor in positioning techniques and skills to enhance Joe's riding. Coordination of the home program and the riding program began. At the end of 18 months of in-home therapy, Joe was sitting independently on a bench, moving independently in bed, was able to come to sitting position and assist in dressing and bathing. He learned to use the phone, to sign his name, and to make a sandwich. In the riding program, Joe was using a Western saddle and could sit with minimal support from two sidehelpers or moderate support using a bareback pad and a surcingle. Therapy at home was discontinued at that time (Figure 1).

At age of 24, Joe began equine-assisted therapy one time a week. He sat fairly well on a saddle pad holding on to a vaulting girth surcingle handle but he needed support from the two sidehelpers for balance in turns and transitions at a walk. He controlled the horse using ladder reins only. He could not use his legs or seat aids. Hippotherapy was used to facilitate relaxation, back rotation, equilibrium reactions, develop a deep seat and back extension. Initially this involved 80% of the session but was reduced to 20% within four months (Figure 2).

Occupational therapy uses purposeful activities to regain function. Joe's posture has improved and his increased relaxed state now allows him to ride independently for a period of time with near normal posture and use of limbs without associated reactions of other limbs. He practices speech through repeating the dressage exercises and counting poles or turns and some times singing to help him relax.

Joe feels good when he can control his horse and perform challenging exercises. He is motivated to improve his riding skills and work toward completing a dressage test. The exercises are kept at a level that does not stress his physical system nor decrease his postural control. Schooling figures challenge him mentally and increase his sequential and spatial skills. He is learning to use his legs one at a time in movement patterns he has never learned before, to turn the horse and to stop the horse by using a deep seat, sitting back while keeping his hands quiet. Therapy techniques are constantly used to facilitate his functional movements. Riding continues as long as Joe's posture and functional movements remain coordinated or he requests to stop.

Joe's riding experience involves hippotherapy, equine-assisted therapy, followed by a short session of sports riding. Hippotherapy and equine-assisted therapy are directed by the therapist with the riding instructor supervising the horse. The sports riding is directed by the instructor with the therapist providing assistance regarding his physical mobility. For example, Joe was working on performing a correct circle. After making two circles, he began to collapse falling in at the waist. The therapist directed the instructor to change the direction of the circles and to circle at each end of the arena. This allowed Joe to rotate to each direction yet allowed him to regain the trunk straightness on the long side of the arena between circles.

FIGURE 1.
JOE IS WORKING WITH HIS INSTRUCTOR IN A RIDING LESSON

FIGURE 2
AFTER JOE HAD COMPLETED HIPPOTHERAPY AND WAS BEGINNING THE RIDING PART OF THE SESSION

Summary:
Joe's riding experiences have provided him with therapy which directly affected his functional living skills in an activity which he could use independently with pride. Joe is now riding without support from the sidehelpers or any assistance from the horse handler. He learned a dressage test which he can perform without a reader (a person reading the dressage test during a performance). He is beginning to sit to the trot for several strides at a time and maintaining good head control. Joe is also gaining more control over his posture and arm movements. His speech has improved so that others can understand some basic words. As a result of generally improved function he is able to hold a part time, paid, computer job at a local hospital.

24.12   THE REHAB RANCH: A RESIDENTIAL RIDING THERAPY CAMP

Kate Zimmerman, MBA, PT

THE DREAM

In the summer of 1980, the author was sitting on a deck overlooking San Francisco Bay with a fellow therapist and future partner, tossing around ideas on how to combine therapy they had been performing at Children's Hospital Medical Center (CHMC), in Oakland, California, with their favorite outdoor activities. They decided to investigate the possibility of running a summer camp for children with physical disabilities, which set in motion a series of events leading to the creation of a non-profit corporation called REHAB CAMPS, Incorporated.

The author learned to ride as a child in Montana. She spent summers on her uncle's ranch riding whenever she had a chance. She had been introduced to the concept of therapeutic riding through a course at All Seasons Riding Academy (ASRA)* where she spent three months cleaning stables, riding, and learning how to work with disabled children astride the horse. As a physical therapist, she found it very exciting to use the horse as a treatment modality as well as an adapted recreational activity, and gained the knowledge of the value of the horse in therapy. At the time the notion of the camp had developed, horses became the main focus that would be initiated during the camp experience.

THE BEGINNING

The next year, professional friends were signed up to be on the board of directors of REHAB CAMPS, INC. Funds were raised from a variety of sources, grants were written, and pleas were made for donations from local corporations. In the fall of 1981 the earnest planning of the camp had began. Staff was recruited from local therapy programs and a site and clients were all that was needed now. The camp began in June, 1982 and continued for four years. Some clients came back each year. It was an immensely gratifying learning experience at best, a tiring and frustrating one at its worst.

THE SITE

Initially, the group explored the possibility of renting established camps with riding facilities. These were all too expensive for REHAB CAMP's fledgling budget. Through the contacts of ASRA, the group found a riding enthusiast who held the lease on a riding concession at the Grant Ranch, in Hall's Valley east of San Jose. The use of the site was a donation for the first year's operation. There was open land for tents, primitive showers, stables, and a riding arena. After a survey of Grants's Ranch for wheelchair accessibility by a team of physical therapists, it was decided that this site was suitable. The team readily agreed to the free use of the land.

A ramp was constructed for wheelchair users. Barbecue pits were built. A portable shed and an above ground pool were purchased. To augment the one public restroom on the grounds, Porta-potties were rented. A member of the Board of Directors obtained the use of a recreational vehicle for the executive staff, and tents for campers were obtained from the U.S. Army. Refrigeration was another problem, but the team managed the first year with one refrigerator and a couple of big ice chests. The group simply made the operation work.

The second and third years that the camp was in operation were much easier as the host of the camp added facilities. A barn was built which was used for the director's living quarters and office. A netting and tarp covered area was built for eating and daytime activities that made campers and ranch staff more comfortable. The fourth year was the most comfortable of all. Because of an increase in funding, the group was able to rent a real camp with a pool, cabins, and indoor toilets. There were some steep hills at this locations but with paved paths. Wheelchair users needed to have someone to help push them up the hills. A real benefit of renting an established camp was that the proprietors provided meals and a program director to augment the group's staff.

---

* All Seasons Riding Academy, Fremont, California.

THE CAMPERS

The first year, from connections at CHMC, a group of 16 clients was selected for the first two-week session of the camp. In selecting the client/campers, finding a homogeneous group that could participate in activities together was of primary concern. The actual physical diagnosis was not as important since the director felt that establishing common ground for developing relationships in the weeks to come was more important.

The author had been a camp director at a large camp which accepted clients with a mixture of cognitive and physical disabilities. Through this experience she had learned the difficulties of program planning for groups too diverse to engage in similar activities or even to engage each other in relationships. As both the author's and her co-director's specialty was physical therapy, their focus became primarily clinical for boys and girls with physical disabilities. Another criteria for client selection was age. The clients needed to be old enough to spend two weeks away from home. The age ranged selected was from seven to sixteen years.

A review of the camp records indicates that the acceptance policy was liberal. During the four years there were clients who were blind and those who were severely disabled, needing one-on-one attention. Other clients had only mild disabilities and could assist in the care of the dependent campers. Clients' diagnoses included spinal muscle atrophy, cerebral palsy, spina bifida, equinus varus (club foot), closed head trauma, polio, and muscular dystrophy.

THE STAFF

Recruitment and selection of counselors evolved around identifying people with an interest in working with young physical challenged campers. The staff found the local colleges fertile ground, especially those with therapy, special education, and recreational therapy programs. Word was spread among professional co-workers and friends. A warm response and offers were received for volunteers. The staff included high school students with riding background, therapists with years of pediatric experience, and the mothers of the executive staff. A pediatrician joined the staff at the camp the first year and remained with the group as a consultant in the years to follow. Including the executive staff, the group always had at least one-on-one staff-to-camper ratios. Counselor-to-camper ratio was from one-on-one to one-on-three depending on campers' needs and abilities.

Due to the needs of the campers, the group recruited at least two nurses per session to help with potential problems that could and did arise. In the first year of REHAB CAMP, the staff found the camp needed the two nurses almost all the time in dealing with constipation, seizures, pressure sores and sunburn. The University of California San Francisco Hospital was the main source for nurses. The first year REHAB CAMP was fortunate to find an experienced rider who was also a nurse, and she later became a co-director of the program. It was surprising to find such a wealth of experienced and willing people, once the needs for staff was made known to the community.

CAMP PROGRAM AND TRAINING

REHAB CAMP program planning differed from that in the usual summer camp for disabled children in that it tried to focus on physical therapy in combination with recreation. Arts and crafts programs were taught by occupational therapists and occupational therapy students with an emphasis on cognitive learning. A purely recreational program was also offered with activities like dances, campfire sings, and story telling. The physical therapy staff provided pool and riding programs with an emphasis on physical therapy.

Training for the staff consisted of one to two day on-site sessions prior to the camp openings. The staff was trained in areas of:
- basic health care
- CPR (cardiopulmonary resuscitation)
- the nature of disabilities to be seen
- the general schedule of camp days
- the activities offered
- brainstorming on programming ideas
- campfire songs and stories
- campers profiles specific to the counselors assigned to them

The directors had produced manuals for reference for all the counselors. In addition, the directors sent out information about each camper to the staff prior to the first meeting. The directors made every attempt to cover all possible areas of concern to the staff, including job descriptions and schedules of a normal camp day. Each counselor reviewed the charts of the campers assigned her. The first year, young camp and executive staff did it all: camper care and attention, food buying and cooking, horse care and preparation, tent set up and maintenance, and a major part of program planning and implementation. The second and third years, we had additional assistance. This left more time for the executive staff to plan and implement the programs and made an enormous difference in the quality of the camp.

A DAY AT CAMP
A typical day's schedule at camp:

6:30 am	out of bed for staff and counselors.
6:30-7:30 am	readying campers for breakfast.
7:30 am	breakfast, announcements, and a brief staff meeting.
8:50-9:00 am	preparing for morning activities
9:00-10:30 am	activities began with choices of:

- riding
- arts and crafts
- individual therapy/group exercise
- swimming

10:50- Noon	rotating groups, same activities offered
Noon-1:30 pm	lunch and clean up
1:30-2:00 pm	rest and organization for afternoon activities.
2:00-3:00 pm	rotating groups in the same activity
3:00-4:00 pm	same as above, plus fishing
4:00-5:00 pm	rest and prepare for dinner
5:00-6:30 pm	dinner
6:30-7:00 pm	free time
7:00-8:30 pm	campfire activities/special dances

The stated schedule proved to be demanding for both campers and counselors and in later years it was amended to give more time between activities and for meals. The staff learned to make allowances for the most disabled persons in the group. This included cutting back on the number of activities offered to give everyone, especially staff, more time to breathe and relax.

This was the planned schedule. The staff had to make allowances for the weather. Because there was a lake in Hall's Valley, lake activities were incorporated into the daily schedule. Some campers caught fish which were cooked for dinner. The fourth year's site of REHAB CAMP had to adapt its activities to the schedule of an established camp which it was apart of. Nevertheless, most of the therapy activities were accommodated along with the many other activities the management had to offer.

THE RIDING PROGRAM
The first year the riding program consisted of simply getting everyone used to a horse and also to the use of a horse as a therapeutic modality. The approach was very basic--teaching care of the horse, grooming, bridling and saddling. The riding program focused on learning the basic commands of walk, halt, trot, turns, and simple patterns.

In the years to follow, a surcingle was used for a vaulting program and backriding was used to facilitate therapeutic reactions. Both recreational and therapeutic riding sessions were incorporated, with different goals for different campers. For therapy sessions, a longe line and a surcingle was used, with two side-walkers, an occasional backrider, and a therapist in the ring at all times. Altering the gaits of the horse was used to facilitate equilibrium reactions and for trunk strength; prone work across the horse, and sitting to kneeling exercises were performed for strength and balance. The use of a longe line gave more control over the horse and provided more security in trying the different gaits. The covered arena at the Grant Ranch provided a controlled environment for the horses and riders.

For the recreational program, one-forth of the campers could ride alone while the rest of the campers needed at least a leader. Many needed sidewalkers. In years two and three, there were more horses to choose from and the staff screened and trained the mounts to suit the individual needs of the campers. The author had received additional training in New York with Barbara Glasow (Winslow, NY Clinic 1982). This contributed greatly to the approaches used in years two and three.

The fourth year, REHAB CAMP used the horses provided by the YMCA camp. While this may sound ideal for a riding camp, it was not the optimal arrangement for a therapeutic program. It was necessary to screen each horse and train the ones that were suitable for disabled riders. The riding director and her YMCA staff accommodated to this new approach well and were trained to help.

SUMMARY

The four years that the Rehab Camps was in operation were exciting times. The directors created as they went along, evaluating, criticizing, changing, and improving from year to year. They accomplished what they set out to do, which was to prove that recreation and therapy can be combined in an outdoor setting where clients stay for an extended period of time. The staff did notice changes in the campers which included:

- increased self confidence
- increased physical abilities
- improved attitudes toward the therapists and therapy
- increased ability to take care of themselves
- increased ability to ask for help when it was needed

The results of the camp have not been put into numbers. But the directors do believe that in two concentrated weeks one can make a change. The directors also watched themselves grow, as they dealt with the challenges of creating something from nothing. They dealt well with problems and avoided serious problems or accidents. What was learned during these years were:

- the complexity of the daily lives of the clients, what their lives and challenges are all about, and how immense their needs were,
- the value of dedicated professional directors who have time to lend to such a worthwhile project,
- the value of the volunteers who contributed their time to make the project become reality,
- the value of dreams and of individual visions of potential reality,
- the value of the blind faith that sometimes, somehow things will work,
- to prepare for the worst, yet hope for the best,
- to know that everything that can go wrong will.

Camps like Rehab Camp need to happen. Pediatric therapy must be taken out of the white-walled clinics and made a part of the lives our client's live, or would like to live. Having the responsibility for clients for two weeks is an enormous undertaking which requires a lot of work and planning, but it is one of the most gratifying experiences this author has had in her therapy career.

25 THE APPLICATION OF RECREATIONAL THERAPY PRINCIPLES IN THERAPEUTIC RIDING

Gloria Hamblin, RTR

Recreational therapy uses participation in leisure activities to improve functional behavior and physical condition in clients while giving them the opportunity to acquire skills and knowledge. Therapeutic riding blends elements of therapy and education into a fun recreational activity which includes a living creature-the horse. Ultimately the goal is to use horses and riding as a vehicle by which clients challenge themselves to achieve their potential. The objective could be improved physical fitness, better socialization skills, or independent recreational riding. Ideally it could be all of these together producing an increase in self-esteem, control, and freedom.

Therapeutic horseback riding is but one aspect of recreational therapy, which includes a wide variety of pursuits from bowling to painting to drama. According to the National Therapeutic Recreation Society, "The purpose of therapeutic recreation is to facilitate the development, maintenance, and expression of an appropriate leisure lifestyle for individuals with physical, mental, emotional, or social limitations" (NTRS 1982). To do this the therapist designs programs with one or more goals:
1. Therapy--to improve functional behaviors
2. Leisure education--to expose the client to activities allowing them to gain new knowledge and skills
3. Recreation participation--to generate voluntary involvement in recreational activities

These goals, while generally pursued simultaneously, are emphasized to different degrees at different times, depending on the needs and abilities of the client. In therapeutic riding the goals of each session will be tailored to each client by talking with parents, caretakers, doctors, teachers or other therapists, and, most importantly, with the client himself. An appropriate treatment program can then be set up, implemented, and periodically assessed.

A recreational therapist in a therapeutic riding program, may work with clients who are at the lower levels of functional ability, such as persons with brain-injuries who live in a group home setting. In this situation the therapist may need to work on appropriate group interaction and socialization skills in order to conduct a productive group lesson. This would be in addition to teaching basic riding, grooming, and stable management skills. The client will learn to participate in a group lesson, and to visit with the volunteers in a socially acceptable manner. He may also work to increase physical stamina and balance by gradually increasing the time spent on horseback and the number and difficulty of the exercises he performs. As he continues to ride, an improvement in his control of the horse may also be observed.

As the client progresses and possibly is discharged from the group home to his family or to live independently, the goal of leisure education comes into focus. Now the client may have questions about equestrian events in his new neighborhood or need a referral to another riding program or regular riding stable. Where can he continue to learn about horses, horseshows, clinics, trail rides, or horse clubs that are available to him? He may well need continued guidance.

The last goal area mentioned is recreation participation, and would here refer to recreational riding or riding as sport. This includes participation in horse shows, trail rides, or lessons. These can occur in a therapeutic riding program or can be found at a regular training stable. The disabled client who is high functioning may come to a program just to learn to ride. He then progressively challenges himself to ride better and gain more knowledge.

It is clear that the three goals: therapy, leisure education, and recreational activity overlap a great deal and are often sought concurrently. A client who has had a stroke illustrates the model of the three areas of service well. A 55 year old man began riding eight months after a stroke left him with hemiplegia. He was naturally withdrawn and depressed about his condition. He had been forced to sell the business he had run all his life. He began to ride at weekly intervals with a leader and two sidewalkers, and to speak of his early twenties when he rode frequently and received a good bit of instruction. He progressed to riding independently and no longer needed a cane to walk. He learned about a horse science program at a local community college where he enrolled. The stables and horses became his avocation. He assisted the program where he rode by training new volunteers and often oriented new disabled riders. He purchased his own horse which he now cares for independently and has received an AA degree. It is easy to see that he has adjusted well to his disability and his leisure time is full and rewarding.

Ken Mobily (1985) in the *Therapeutic Recreation Journal* concludes that therapeutic recreation practitioners should "induce in their clients perceptions of control, responsibility and freedom". Showing clients the choices available and encouraging them to become self motivated, the recreational therapist who works in a riding program can offer the rider a myriad of benefits, from improved physical enhancement to social skills. Using therapy, leisure education and recreational activity, people with disabilities can be helped to achieve their fullest potential, increasing not only their own physical abilities and riding skills, but also their sense of self-esteem and independence that accompanies it.

References:
Mobily, K.E. 1985. A Philosophical Analysis of Therapeutic Recreation: What does it mean to say "We Can Be Therapeutic"? part 2, *Therapeutic Recreation Journal*, 18, no. 2, 2.
Approved by the Board of Directors of the National Branch of the National Recreation and Parks Association) May 1982. NTRS. (1982)

26 DEVELOPMENTAL RIDING THERAPY: HISTORY AND EVOLUTION

Jan Spink, MA

HISTORY AND EVOLUTION OF THE NEW HARMONY SYSTEM

Riding therapy (health care or treatment focus) in rehabilitation has an interesting and complex history. This chapter describes how therapeutic riding has evolved nationally and internationally over the past twenty five years. An understanding of the historical foundations, the strengths and the limitations of various approaches, is necessary to appreciate the need for and the components of Developmental Riding Therapy (D.R.T.^{Sm}).

THE FIRST 25 YEARS: THE UNITED STATES, BRITAIN, AND WEST GERMANY

The first twenty-five years of therapeutic riding in North America were characterized by enthusiasm, dedication, and devotion to the often quoted phrase, "The outside of a horse is good for the inside of a man." (Ogilviy, 1869). In response, numerous programs and philosophies of riding therapy were developed and offered to a wide range of clients. Like most evolutionary fields, however, it was also characterized by an overall dearth of definition, use of loosely applied terminology, and evidence of high variability in areas of quality control, professional training, and competence.

In response to these circumstances, a comprehensive review and comparative analysis of therapeutic riding in the United States, Great Britain, and West Germany was conducted (Spink, 1982). All three countries had been using the horse specifically to benefit the disabled for about twenty-five years. The review focused primarily on medical and psychological treatment techniques which used horseback riding as a therapeutic medium. Also investigated were the elements of educational and sport programs and whether client placement within these programs was appropriate for client needs. Five West German programs from the Kuratorium of Therapeutic Riding (1985) were studied thoroughly to identify characteristics and dimensions of interest in riding therapy. Also included were on-site reviews of Britain's two most recognized riding programs for the disabled. A similar review of five long-standing and representative American programs was also conducted. A total of twelve programs were included in the review.

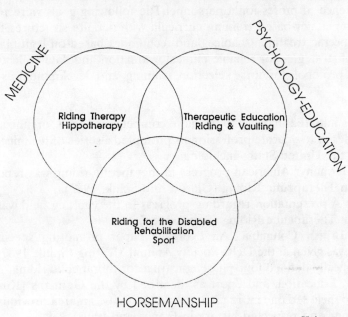

Original German Model

FIGURE. 1.1 THREE CIRCLE GERMAN

Heipertz, 1981.

593

The reviewer assumed the importance of defining competency-based models to guide professional development and structured approaches to client evaluation and treatment. It was apparent from this study that only the Germans had developed a set of structured educational standards to guide the activities of professionals in the field of riding therapy. In fact, as early as 1970, a basic model delineating three areas most relevant to their country's operation had been defined. These areas were Medicine, Education, and Sport.

Because sub-specialty areas linked to clearly defined treatment approaches were described early, the Germans attracted to the field many professionals (physicians, psychologists, special educators and physical therapists) who were interested in integrating equestrian activities with rehabilitation. Systematic study of the outcomes of riding therapy ensued, as many of these professionals used their associations with universities and teaching hospitals to conduct studies to further a scientific understanding of the method (Laban Centre). This enabled therapeutic riding to be recognized in Germany as a valid treatment option in medicine, psychology and education. As a result, the emerging field in that country was operating successfully under a standardized structure by 1982. It had also yielded a variety of replicable treatment methods for specific disorders such as multiple sclerosis and scoliosis, to name just two (Heipertz, 1981).

The United States and Great Britain appeared to have no structured visual schematic to help frame or guide the early development and organization of riding therapy. The initial appeal of equine use to benefit the disabled seemed to be greater for lay-horsemen and riding instructors than for professionals in medicine, education and psychology. Consequently, therapeutic riding in these two countries developed more as a recreational or adapted group sport activity than as a specific remedial or treatment activity.

Even in view of the lack of structure, a handful of professionals in both Great Britain and the United States entered the field initially out of a desire to blend their clinical training with their personal interests in equestrian activities. Unfortunately, these individuals did not have the benefit of specialty training in using the horse as a therapeutic agent. In most cases they were working in isolation and without support from a substantive, national knowledge base. However, in spite of the lack of available training programs, relevant clinical literature, and mentorships, innovative and creative approaches were developed. These simply were not substantiated by systematic study, training or research.

The 1982 review yielded several specific areas which potentially could improve the quality of programs in the United States and Great Britain. These directions for improvement were projected to foster structure for training programs and competence of professional personnel.The following goals were recommended:
   a) Creation of competency-based training curricula with definite structures for professional development
   b) Promotion of specific treatment choices and techniques based on legitimate rationales
   c) Development of strategies for reliable clinical evaluation and data collection
   d) Specification of protocols for horse selection, training, and development as related to specialty areas (Spink, 1982).

A concerted effort was initiated in order to promote competency-based, organizational approaches similar to the German model. This desire to educate professionals prompted a series of technical papers and presentations across Europe, Canada, and the United States including:
   ◘ Hamburg, Germany: American progress in therapeutic riding was reported at the Fourth International Congress On Therapeutic Riding (Glasow and Spink, 1982).
   ◘ Milan, Italy: A presentation regarding progress in the vaulting field was given at the Fifth International Congress On Therapeutic Riding (Spink, 1985).
   ◘ Vancouver, British Columbia: An overview paper promoting specialization and competency-based approaches was given at the Delta Society Annual Meeting (Spink, 1987). This paper supported adopting a new, specifically defined four-phase construct for therapeutic riding. This construct included the areas of Medicine, Education, and Sport as identified by the Germans (Kuratorium of Therapeutic Riding, 1985). It also included one more area, psychomotricity, an area previously unknown in the United States but with a long and respected history in France and Italy.

○ Toronto, Ontario: This paper supported the same theme and recommended that American and Canadian therapeutic riding organizations adopt the expanded, four phase construct in order to attract a wider array of clinical professionals. It was presented at the Sixth International Congress On Therapeutic Riding (Spink, 1988).

○ Houston, Texas: The final paper in this series presented more detail about the creation of theoretical structure and methodology which embody the systems approach called developmental riding therapy. It was presented as the McCulloch Memorial Lecture at the Annual Meeting of the Delta Society. (Spink, 1990). Although most American programs had become familiar with the basic three-phase German construct by 1988, the need to develop and incorporate other professional disciplines to expand the organizational construct was emphasized in the later presentations. A structured model for integrating other disciplines into a schema of riding therapy was the result.

A FOUR PHASE MODEL FOR US THERAPEUTIC RIDING:
a progressive model for physicians, therapists, educators, and riding instructors

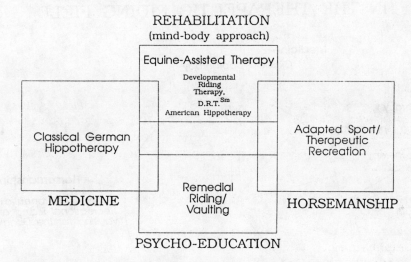

Copyright 1992 Spink.

FIGURE 1.2 FLOW CHART APPROACH FOR CLIENT PLACEMENT IN PROGRAM

The overall goal for these presentations was to inform practicing and incumbent professionals of the potential treatment scope and broad applicability the horse offers to clients with special needs. A more comprehensive model and treatment system was expected to facilitate significant understanding and recognition of specific equine-assisted therapies such as developmental riding therapy as a legitimate rehabilitation approach. By standardizing treatment techniques and quantifying the objectives and goals of client intervention, the field hoped to attract the interest of researchers and clinicians alike.

The need for credible, empirical research focusing on the therapeutic application of the horse is acute in North America. The organizational model proposed was expected to influence a positive trend toward more systematic study and more formalized, university-based, training. The increasing demand for training and certification programs in the medical, psychomotor, and educative use of the horse reflects an appreciation for the diverse applications. Attracting a wide array of skilled professionals from medicine, physical, occupational and speech therapy, rehabilitation/ psycho motricity, psychology, clinical social work, special education, and adapted physical education would strengthen the foundations of the entire field and help ensure its future viability.

The addition of psychomotricity as the fourth specialty area is intended to stimulate further professional expansion and client treatment opportunities. In D.R.T.^{Sm}, the basic tenets of psychomotricity have been synthesized to yield an innovative and eclectic systems approach. The approach incorporates treatment techniques previously unavailable in either classic hippotherapy or remedial riding and vaulting. It invites the participation of five health or education professions which previously had limited formal involvement or recognition within the field. These specific fields are occupational therapy, rehabilitation or psychomotricity, speech therapy, special education and psychology.

Attracting occupational therapists who are trained in sensory integration as well as in developmental and psychological domains is important to the process of D.R.T.^{Sm}. This system also provides a properly defined area of practice for psychomotorical or rehabilitation specialists who have graduate level training in psychology, movement, and mind/body integration techniques. Speech and Language pathologists are included here because of their advanced training in language development, speech production, and cognitive re-education. Special educators and psychologists, with their training in affective and cognitive development as well as therapeutic intervention strategies, are also integrated. The following schematic illustrates how all the various professions can be viewed within one broad field.

AN ESTIMATION OF SUB-SPECIALIZATIONS IN THE THERAPEUTIC RIDING FIELD

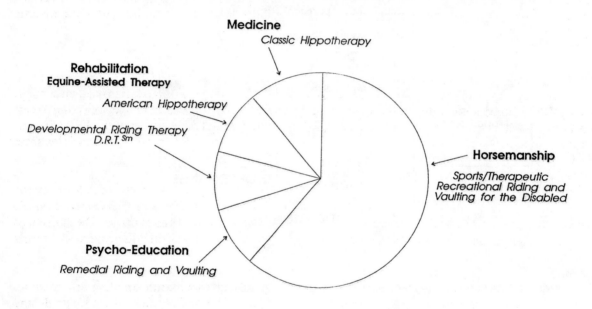

FIGURE 1.3 THE PIE GRAPH

The contribution of each specialty area has been estimated for this illustration. Currently, there is no information available to accurately assess current (or desirable) contributions from individual professions. An important direction for the future might be to identify the optimal mix of these professions to ensure quality programming. Until then, it is assumed that the needs of each client dictate the prescription for an individualized mix of contributing professional expertise. The next section of this chapter details the concepts of psychomotricity and rehabilitation. Traditional theory and methodology which influenced the development of this specialty use of the horse is chronologically described. Finally, the new American treatment approach termed Developmental Riding Therapy (D.R.T.^{Sm}) is outlined. This therapeutic approach is organized within a comprehensive framework that New Harmony Foundation refers to as the New Harmony System of D.R.T.^{Sm}.

PSYCHOMOTRICITY: HISTORY AND DEFINITION

Psychomotricity is a psycho-medical specialty area which was developed in the late 1940'S in response to the need to treat motor disorders that were not caused by neurological trauma or lesions (Barwick, 1986). Official recognition was granted in 1963 when the French Ministry of Education began to require training at the graduate level and certification for psychomotor therapists. Psychomotricity has evolved significantly since that time.

Sylvie Barwick, a French psychomotor therapist practicing in England, clearly describes the theoretical basis of psychomotricity when she writes:

"Unlike most other medical or psychological professions whose approach tends to consider either physical or psychological symptoms, psychomotricity concerns the progressive development of both the psyche and the soma and their interaction under the influence of organic maturation and social stimuli. It considers the individual in his psychosomatic entirety thus rejecting the traditional dichotomy between "mind" and "body" stemming from Cartesian philosophy. It reunites man within himself and observes him in action with his environment. It aims at building an individual whose healthy psychomotor development reflects his mental and physical ease and harmony." (Barwick, 1986)

There are many therapeutic applications and modalities used in the field. Related expressive therapies employed by psychomotor or rehabilitation specialists include art, dance and drama approaches. Psychomotricity also incorporates various popular approaches to movement such as those developed by Laban (Laban Center, England), Alexander (1985), Feldenkrais (1981), and Ayres (1974). Clearly, this comprehensive specialty which integrates emotion with language development and movement experience/education can be applied to the field of therapeutic riding.

HISTORY AND PHILOSOPHY

In the developmental phases of riding therapy, especially in the United States and Great Britain, it appeared that selected types of clients were not receiving optimal benefits from group recreational riding sessions, hippotherapy, or remedial group vaulting or riding. Most of these clients experienced specific deficits in the following areas: learning, language, behavior, sensory integration and visual perception and movement quality. What is now formalized as Developmental Riding Therapy (D.R.T.^{Sm}) began as an effort to blend movement principles from classic hippotherapy with developmental positions and sequences.

It also incorporated specific perceptual-motor, cognitive, and affective development skills in order to meet the needs of these particular clients. A surcingle was used as it allowed the client more freedom of movement on the horse. Initially, the approach was referred to as developmental vaulting, a form of riding therapy. The objectives of the approach were strictly therapeutic and therefore quite different from those established in programs of sports or gymnastic vaulting (Spink, 1985).

In the early 1980's, programs throughout the United States began to include developmental vaulting as a method. Instructors and therapists incorporated various isolated movements and exercises and began to use a surcingle and pad instead of a saddle to facilitate movement while astride. It appeared, however, that the concepts on which developmental vaulting was based were not being as thoroughly integrated as the specific techniques.

This left practitioners ill-prepared to coordinate and combine these specialized techniques to create individualized programs for clients. There also appeared to be incomplete rationale for equipment selection and modification of activities. The overall tendency was to develop an emphasis on the isolated motor tasks which most resembled traditional vaulting. In addition, there seemed to have been a breakdown in practitioners' abilities to interpret and integrate techniques which specifically addressed cognition, affect and perceptual-motor skills. Subsequently, the original holistic theory and complex methodology of developmental vaulting had been unintentionally fragmented and not applied as an integrated treatment system.

In order to correct any confusing resemblance to gymnastic vaulting and to clarify the goal of rehabilitation through riding therapy, the specialty approach was re-named the New Harmony System of Developmental Riding Therapy (D.R.T.^{Sm}) in 1987. New Harmony's primary project focus is to develop and test methodology and techniques in therapeutic riding and treat clients with specific central nervous system disorders. The Foundation's multi-purpose, non-profit educational programs also serve to provide national and international exchange in various fields of study such as psychomotricity and the human-animal bond.

This newly integrated approach is an evolutionary hybrid which preserves its psychomotoric integrity but extends its attention to other client systems as well. New Harmony utilizes the U.S. Patent and Trade Commission's protocol for service marks (Sm) which signify and protect methodological uniqueness of service areas.

A FOUR PHASE MODEL FOR US THERAPEUTIC RIDING:
a progressive model for physicians, therapists, educators, and riding instructors

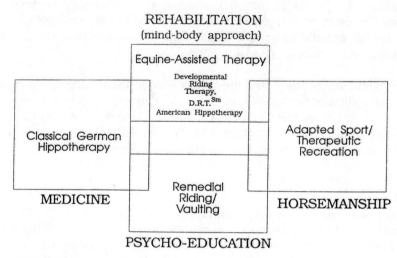

Copyright 1992 Spink.

FIGURE 1.4 THE NEW HARMONY FOUR PHASE CONSTRUCT

Figure 1.4 represents the New Harmony four phase construct for therapeutic riding. Here, D.R.T.Sm lies within a continuum, between the medical application of the horse (hippotherapy), psycho-education (remedial riding/vaulting), and horsemanship (sport/therapeutic recreational riding/vaulting for the disabled). The New Harmony system is distinct because of the population it serves and the inclusion of six mandatory elements which embody its definitive approach. The movement and horse handling components are derived in part from the movement principles of classic hippotherapy.

The fundamental, prerequisite elements are as follows:

1) Individual or partner sessions with active therapist input
2) The use of developmental positions on the horse which directly correlate with specifically controlled movement challenges from the horse
3) Development of the inter-relationships of the client, therapist and horse
4) Specific adaptations in selection of equipment
5) Selected components of riding and vaulting skills
6) The use of equine-adapted, purposeful activities

(Spink, 1990).

Hippotherapy is a method which focuses on benefiting clients who have mild to severe movement dysfunction from a purely medical or physical rehabilitation orientation. D.R.T.Sm is different in that it is distinctly designed to address clients with deficits in learning, language, behavior, cognition, and/or general movement competency. D.R.T.Sm can be a complement to hippotherapy or a much needed transition between these specific medical techniques and the group work which characterizes psycho-education and sport or therapeutic recreation. It also serves as an entry point for clients whose skills are not yet developed enough for remedial group riding or gymnastic vaulting.

598

To become a capable developmental riding therapist, one must demonstrate accurate clinical judgment, keen awareness, and a strong equestrian background. Subsequently, a text called *Developmental Riding Therapy: The Horse in Psycho-motoric and Psycho-education*[Sm] will be available by 1992 which will specifically detail the use of the specialty system. Candidates for training in the system must already possess entry-level professional credentials at the graduate level in one of the following five fields:

1. Psychomotricity/ rehabilitation therapy
2. Special education with training in movement approaches
3. Educational, clinical, counseling psychology or neuro-psychology, and/or licensed clinical social work, with training in movement approaches
4. Speech therapy
5. Occupational therapy (O.T.R. or O.T.R.\L)

Developmental riding therapy requires significant skill in the areas of dressage, specialized horse handling techniques, and basic vaulting. Mastery of a standardized set of horsemanship competencies is mandatory to qualify as a developmental riding therapist. It requires considerable professional dedication to devote the time necessary to understand the complex marriage of theory, ideology, and methodology embodied in this specialty approach. A significant amount of personal recreational time must be devoted to dressage, as necessary riding skills need to be maintained and/or developed to a minimum of <u>first level dressage</u>.

New Harmony aims to provide systematic, competency-based training programs for professional specialists who want to use the horse as a treatment agent. More thoroughly trained professionals yield better treatment opportunities as well as improved treatment results for clients. Selectively developed horses also greatly enhance quality control as the field evolves. Finally, it is projected that the combination of all these factors will attract increased interest in the study of outcomes achieved from combining carefully screened clients, systematically trained therapists and selectively developed horses within a structured system of treatment in which horses are the medium.

A DEVELOPMENTAL RIDING THERAPY SESSION

Profile #3
Name: Felicia
Age: 7

<u>General Diagnoses:</u> Central Nervous System Dysfunction
<u>Present Level of Performance</u>

I. Sensation, Perception, and Motricity:
   Felicia has a mild decrease in tone (hypotonia) mostly in her trunk and upper extremities. She has a very subtle hand tremor in some fine motor activities. She appears dyspraxic when running, skipping, and hopping. There is evidence of proximal instability throughout her shoulder girdle during movements involving upper extremities. Equilibrium reactions are slightly delayed. [Sm]

II. Cognition:
   Felicia has above average verbal skills but has delayed performance skills. Standardized testing reports indicate that she has visual perceptual problems in the realm of spatial relationships and form constancy. She appears to have some attention deficits. She also has some mild articulation problems in a structured, screened environment.

III. Affect:
Felicia displays some mild impulsivity and verbal inappropriateness during physical activity. This may be an adaptive avoidance technique she employs in order to control her environment and some underlying apprehension about physical challenges. She has considerable difficulty with staying in the moment. She is constantly talking about what is next or later versus what is being done right now, even if her safety depends on her awareness of what is happening currently.

Treatment Outline

I. Sensation, Perception, and Motricity:
A. Target Goals
   Bilateral Control
   Static and Dynamic Balance
   Motor Planning

B. Strategies
   1. Improve upper body strength and hand stability in fine motor tasks.
   2. Improve motor planning or praxis areas via organizing and controlling her body movements as she performs D.R.T.^{Sm} position sequences. Start with slow, graded movement challenges from horse.
   Then proceed with basic dynamic variance progressions within walk using straight lines, in curved figures progressing to slow trotting shifts. Trot work should be graded back down to straight lines during the transition phase. Use the T.T. initially, then move to C.C.L. for trot work once she is ready for a higher level of challenge to her equilibrium.

First establish correct postural alignment and good balance reactions sitting upright and forwards on horse. Incorporate the dynamic variance progression, gradually adding in more challenging figures and more abrupt rhythm changes. Grade up to some low level sitting trot work including walk/trot/walk transitions. Then, build in activities that focus on improving upper body strength with D.R.T.^{Sm} position sequences such as quadruped and full kneel forwards and backwards, horse sit-ups, prone prop backwards, ball work, all at walk again. For eye/hand control, use placement of colored clothes pins in the horse's mane, lace horse cut-out cards, or place felt cut-out animals on rump of horse with double sticky tape.

Grade up challenge in D.R.T.^{Sm} positions by manipulating movement of horse to increase her sense of adaptability and competence. This may include slow, steady sitting trot work on a large circle. Add rein use in component parts after evidence of good control and alignment in upper body areas and when emerging confidence is consistent with movement performance. Use a moderate to wide horse with a flat, low amplitude trot.

II. Cognition:
A. Target Goals
   Concentration and Select Attention
   Problem Solving

B. Strategies
   1. Improve ability to focus attention for one hour session with progressively fewer prompts while decreasing impulsivity.
   2. Utilize small components of guiding horse, halt/walk/halt and steering in and out of obstacles to reinforce praxis areas.

Felicia has the ability and the proclivity for responding to technical language and an instructing voice. Take advantage of her cognitive strengths (language processing, vocabulary, memory, causal relationships) to prepare her for physical challenges. Verbally define a task or movement pattern as it is demonstrated. Use highly descriptive language that defines very specific and finite steps of the task. Then repeat the verbal input as she practices the movement. After repeated practice, remove the excess words from the prompts until only key words or phrases remain. Eventually eliminate all verbal cues except for the initial request.

To help her practice clear articulation, first work on the enunciation of individual words directly related to her therapy routine. Once she concisely pronounces the words individually, have her describe her actions as she is doing them. A more motivating exercise is to have her explain to the horse what she is going to do on its back. This helps her stay in the moment by matching her verbal expression with her motor output. She can also use her mastered pronunciations to "instruct" the therapist or an assistant through a familiar task by allowing her to assume the role of teacher.

III. Affect:
  A. Target Goals
       Self Image
       Risk Taking
       Perseverance

  B. Strategies
       1. Decrease avoidance tendencies and empower her self esteem
       2. Improve fluency of emotional range from one of being totally stuck to moving on through resolve of frustrations, anxiety, etc.
       3. Increase her introspective abilities to monitor her feelings about self in regard to things she perceives as potentially difficult or threatening

Task analyzing and discussing an activity before it is performed should relieve a lot of Felicia's avoidance tendencies. Focus on her abilities to do each step of an exercise. Discuss rational consequences of typical difficulties in performing said task. Acknowledge what she is feeling and why she may feel that way. Emphasize the positive feelings of accomplishment, pride, happiness, and even mild relief when an activity perceived as risky is successfully completed. Provide her with the opportunity to be a role model for a peer and/or to demonstrate her abilities to a parent or friendly audience.

PRECAUTIONS: STANDBY GUARDING IN ALL TASKS

photograph by Sue Dent Sounder

FIGURE 1.5: A TREATMENT SESSION

REFERENCES

Barwick, S. (1986). Psychomotor therapy. In **Therapy through movement**, edited by Lorraine Burr. Nottingham, England: Nottingham Rehab Limited.

Glasow, B., Spink, J. (1982). Therapeutic riding in the United States. Report presented to the *Fourth International Congress on Therapeutic Riding*, Hamburg, West Germany.

Heipertz, W. (1977). **Therapeutic riding, medicine, education and sports**. (English translation), Greenbelt Riding Association, Ottawa: Canada.

Ogilviy, W. H. (1869). A Scottish poet. Referenced for New Harmony by Alexander McKay Smith and Peter Winnants of **The Chronicle of the Horse**.

Spink, J. (1982). A comparative review of medical and psycho-educational techniques in therapeutic riding. Unpublished master's thesis, Goddard Graduate Program, Vermont College.

Spink, J. (1985). A categorical approach to vaulting for the disabled. Report presented to the *Fifth International Congress on Therapeutic Riding*, Milan, Italy.

Spink, J. (1986). *The adjunctive use of the horse in therapy: A progression.* Unpublished seminar reference material.

Spink, J. (1987). *Rx: The horse.* Presentation to the Delta Society Annual Meeting, Vancouver, British Colombia.

Spink, J. (1988). A four phase construct for therapeutic riding. Report presented to the *Sixth International Congress on Therapeutic Riding,* Toronto, Canada.

Spink, J. (1990). A model application for the horse in riding therapy: the Michael McCulloch Memorial Award lecture, *Delta Society* Annual Meeting: Houston, Texas.

Kuratorium for Therapeutisches Reiten. (1985). German film converted to U.S. video format. **The horse in medicine, education and sport**. Available from the Delta Society, Renton, Washington. (See suggested contacts)

Brown, O., Tebay, J. (1991). "Standards and accreditation for therapeutic riding centers - A model". The proceedings of the *7th International Therapeutic Riding Congress,* Aarhus, Denmark. (See chapter 3.03 in this book.)

SUGGESTED CONTACTS OR READING:

Delta Society
P.O. Box 1080
Renton, Washington 98057
Tel. 206/226-7357

North American Riding for the
Handicapped Association, Inc.
P.O. Box 33150
Denver, Colorado 80233
Tel. 303/452-1212

American Hippotherapy Association
Contact Person: Nancy McGibbon, P.T.,
President
Box 647
Green Valley, Arizona 85622
*Written information only

United States Dressage Federation
(USDF)
(Training Level and First Level Test
Series)
1212 O Street, P.O. Box 80668
Lincoln, Nebraska 68501
Tel. 402/474-7632.

New Harmony Institute (N.E.A.T. Project)
Contact Person: Jan Spink, M.A.,
President
Morven Park International Equestrian
Institute
Route #4, Box 43 (Rt. #740)
Leesburg, Virginia, 22075 U.S.A.
*written information only

27 SPEECH-LANGUAGE PATHOLOGY ADDRESSED IN THE RIDING SETTING

Ruth Dismuke-Blakely, MS/CCC-SLP

The speech-language pathologist is constantly challenged to find treatment settings and activities that will allow maximum integration of the various components of speech and language in meaningful fashion. Language is simply a set of symbols used to represent reality. We tend to present language as being made up of grammatical or syntactic structures that have semantic meaning and that are used for a variety of communicative functions. Speech is one tool by which one conveys our language symbols to another. Written words as well as sign language would be other tools by which communication is conveyed to others.

Current treatment models used with in speech and language disorders are oriented toward the provision of services using real experiences and activities that allow the therapist to include various physiological and perceptual input. These models are described as being placed in pragmatically loaded, experientially based settings.

Riding therapy offers a ready-made "pragmatically loaded, experientially-based setting for addressing speech and language disability. The speech-language pathologist can develop a highly integrated and highly specialized treatment program through careful consultation with physical and occupational therapists. The activities of riding and the activities related to it offer a motivating and meaningful context in which to address the broad realm of communicative disability. The three dimensional movement of the horse offers controlled stimulation to the neural pathways involved in speech and language functioning. The strong neurological/perceptual components of riding can be manipulated by the speech pathologist in consultation with the occupational therapist to provide a more integrated treatment plan. The stimulation provided by the movement of the horse appears to provide vestibular and other perceptual input that in effect can be used to facilitate the client's receptiveness to therapy. Arousal states, and subsequently, attentional focus can be brought to a more normal level, making the time spent in treatment more productive. The postural elements of riding can be used for enhancement of basic speech processes (respiratory control, phonation, intensity, pitch, and articulation). The activity of riding and learning horsemanship skills offer natural communicative opportunities between client and therapist. In short, riding therapy provides a flexible yet dynamic setting for speech and language intervention.

Barring medical contraindication, a broad range of clients with all manner of cognitive, communicative, motoric, perceptual, and behavioral deficits are able to receive productive speech and language therapy in the riding therapy setting. Age groups served may range anywhere from infants requiring an intensive early stimulation/intervention up through school-age children and adults. Both developmentally disabled and trauma clients are seen. The format and content of therapy will depend entirely upon the treatment needs of each particular patient to be seen. All therapy services must be provided by a licensed, ASHA certified speech-language pathologist. It should be remembered that speech and language therapy "on horseback" uses treatment goals, criteria for reaching goals, and remediation procedures that are standard to the field of speech and language pathology.

Developing the Therapy Session

Prior to the initiation of speech and language therapy in the riding setting, the speech-language pathologist will have evaluated the patient with regard to deficit areas using standard assessment tools. The written treatment plan should parallel those written for more traditional treatment settings. An example goal for a child with language disability might read, "Ben will reduce discourse errors to fewer than 20% occurring in a 150 utterance conversational language sample." One for a client with a voice disorder might read, "Susan will demonstrate sustained phonation in two-word phrases at a level of 90% accuracy over 10 trials." The riding setting is simply the context in which these goals will be addressed. Therefore, it is not professionally appropriate to write treatment goals that reflect the acquisition of specific riding skills any more than it would be appropriate to write goals that reflect specific achievements on other therapy activities (say skills involved in the use of baking cookies as a language experience).

As the speech-language pathologist writes the treatment plan, it is appropriate to give some discussion to the manner in which therapy is to be provided. A paragraph detailing that "...Tom's therapy will be administered in the context of a structured riding therapy setting using a variety of intervention techniques...these techniques will include..." is fine. Often, the therapist will need to refer to how the three dimensional movement of the horse will be manipulated to address a specific goal. However the therapist need not go into extreme detail. It is not the case that a speech-language pathologist puts down on paper every therapy activity and/or stimulus that she might use in the course of a client's treatment.

Once treatment goals have been established, the speech-language pathologist is charged with the task of analyzing how those goals might be addressed in the riding therapy setting. There are many different modes of handling clients in this setting. The theme of horses and riding offers a dynamic and flexible content area for facilitation of more efficient communication skills whatever the cognitive, motoric, behavioral, perceptual and communicative levels a client might demonstrate. Due to the powerful physiological components of riding, it is important that the speech-language pathologist be in close communication with the occupational and physical therapists involved with her clients. Because of the tremendous sophistication of the riding setting itself, the speech-language pathologist also needs to maintain consultation with the horse professional on the staff as well.

As therapy is established, clients are typically seen either individually or in very small groups. Sessions will last from thirty minutes to ninety minutes, with a one hour session being the average. The ideal therapy situation involves the speech-language clinician and from one to three therapy aides depending on the physical problems of the client and the nature of the therapy setting. These therapy aides should have professional horse knowledge so as to provide safety constraints, especially if the therapist herself is not a horsewoman. The number of aides will depend upon the physical needs of the individual clients and the nature of the riding setting itself. The type of riding equipment used will be mandated by the cognitive, perceptual, motor, and behavioral needs of the patient. The choice of the horse will also be mandated by these needs.

Once the proper equipment and horse have been selected, the client can be managed in a number of ways, depending upon treatment goals. Possibilities include being lead from the ground with side walkers, having a back rider, having a side rider, or riding independently with monitoring. Many times it is appropriate to use alternative positions for the client on horseback (side sitting, back sitting, laying prone over the horse, or other positions) to facilitate certain physiological effects for more efficient speech and language production (back sitting to stimulate thoracic/abdominal muscle tone for a patient with low tone and poor respiratory function, for example). Teaching riding skills is not the primary emphasis, but rather the remediation of the communicative disability. Therefore the communication needs of the client will dictate the nature of the session. Each client's therapy management should be designed to address not only the speech-language goals, but the goals established by any other therapists on the team as well. The riding session is thus designed to reflect a true interdisciplinary treatment plan for the patient. Each therapist on the team becomes a good "technician" for the other therapists involved.

The speech-language pathologist should do a task analysis of the various opportunities present in the riding setting for targeting the treatment goals of her client. She then carefully integrates her remediation strategies and techniques into the setting. Tasks such as identifying and catching the horse, grooming, tacking and untacking, discussion the physical attributes of the horse, learning the basic elements of maneuvering the horse, carrying out designated patterns and movements on horseback, learning to care for the horse, and problem solving naturally arising issues are but a few of the activities available.

The riding setting can be designed to reflect as little or as much content structure as is deemed appropriate for any given client. Many well conducted speech-language therapy sessions on horseback have the appearance of nothing more than a very detailed riding lesson. The linguistically based processes required to "listen and repeat" the steps involved in tacking up the horse, for example, offer a naturally occurring, but easily manipulated stimulus activity for the clinician to use in addressing auditory processing deficits or language production breakdowns. The planning of a three step obstacle course can be used to target sequencing difficulties while training some verbal rehearsal strategies ("Ride over two logs, go around a yellow cone, and stop by a black square.")

The speech-language pathologist is able to address deficits in all of the structural aspects of speech and language (phonology, syntax, semantics), the pragmatics of language, language for problem- solving, conceptual development, processing breakdown, and general linguistic organization and efficiency. Secondary language concerns (reading, writing) can be successfully integrated into the riding setting, as can the use of augmentative or alternative communicative modalities.

One of the more valuable aspects of speech and language therapy in the riding setting lies in the continuity of the stimulus material. As the client is introduced to the riding setting, tasks will be at a very basic level. The speech-language pathologist expands upon the theme of horsemanship as the client is able to demonstrate some basic horse knowledge, always building upon the same reference point. As more sophisticated horse skills are acquired, the speech-language clinician can address more subtle and more abstract elements of cognitive-linguistic functioning. Because there are ever- expanding levels of horse knowledge, the clinician does not easily run out of stimulus material. In addition, the client does not have to reorient to a new therapy activity each session. This is a particular benefit of the riding setting.

Documentation of the client's progress in the riding therapy setting is done much as in a clinical setting. Session by session notes are often required, with formal assessments done periodically. Of particular value is the use of trained and untrained probe measures designed to tap into specific areas of ability or disability. They should be consistent in design for pre-and post-evaluation purposes. The use of video or audio taping of therapy sessions is invaluable for reviewing client functioning and treatment effectiveness. As treatment data is generated, progress summaries are written up in standard report fashion.

Specific Treatment Strategies
It is beyond the scope of this discussion to detail all of the speech and language therapy options available in the riding setting. What follows is a short description of some client management strategies to stimulate ideas for speech-language pathologists interested in the use of riding therapy for their clients.

Populations with Severe and Profound Problems
Effective stimulation for the low functioning client is very accessible in the riding setting. It is often difficult to find a salient stimulus activity for clients functioning in the severe and profound range of intellectual ability. Such clients are typically motivated by the movement of the horse, and are thus more readily focused. A basic requisite for communication lies in demonstration of "communicative intent" or the need to represent something through use of a symbol--be it vocal, gestural, pictorial. Using a gross gesture and/or vocalization to indicate "horse go" can generate a motivating and successful activity for the severe/profound client. As he discovers that he is able to "control" the horse using a communication symbol, the foundation for a more broad based communication system is laid. Simultaneously, the movement patterns of the horse provide powerful vestibular stimulation that typically arouses the client to a level of increased spontaneous vocalization. The speech-language pathologist then has more vocal output to work with and is able to generate a more accurate idea of the client's potential in expressive and receptive areas of communicative functioning.

Clients With Language Processing Deficits
Clients who demonstrate any of a broad range of linguistically-based processing deficits benefit dramatically from the strong neurological and psychological elements of the riding setting. The activity of riding provides an ideal situation in which to create a meaningful learning environment. As the client learns to move the horse through various maneuvers, he is involved in the coordination and organization of a number of cognitive, perceptual, motor, and linguistic elements. Consider, for example what is involved in retaining and executing the following directive: "Walk around in a circle and over the log before you stop your horse". Using a small group format, with clients alternately instructing each other, maximizes the opportunity for addressing both expressive and receptive deficits. Showing the client the natural consequences of being vague or nonspecific can be achieved by having a therapy aide carry out the client's instructions in literal fashion. For example, with the client stating "Put it on", the saddle blanket might be placed on the horse's neck. The patient did not specify where the blanket was to go. Another excellent technique is to use flow charts for mapping out various activities and maneuvers in the riding

setting, to facilitate better organization and retention skills. The riding setting offers a virtually unlimited variety of processing tasks that can be manipulated by the speech-language pathologist.

Integration of Speech-Language Therapy with Occupational Therapy * (See next page illustration)
Combining speech-language therapy with occupational therapy in the riding setting greatly facilitates the effectiveness of both. Speech and language is a higher level cortical function in human brain, and is greatly influenced by now the client's neurological system is functioning at other levels. Using a team approach within the same session, each therapist is able to make assessments and/or alterations to treatment in a "hands-on" fashion. Most of the clients seen in therapeutic riding have multiple handicaps, and the constant monitoring by both the speech-language pathologist and the occupational therapist enables the professionals to better serve the client. In the case of a person with sensory-integrative dysfunction, for example, the occupational therapist can supervise the optimal degree of vestibular input, the levels of arousal, perceptual defensiveness, and subtleties of functioning that might impact speech and language. The speech-language pathologist can provide strategies for facilitating more efficient communication functioning. In addition, working together, therapists are able to generate a differential diagnosis of the client's deficits.

Summary Statement
The provision of speech and language therapy services through the manipulation of the riding therapy setting offers a highly flexible and powerful approach to the habilitation/rehabilitation of persons with all manner of communication disabilities. The examples of therapy application previously discussed are but a few of the ways in which the riding setting can be used in this application. It is important to recognize that treatment of communication disabilities is a very complex and sophisticated science. The use of therapeutic riding is also a very complex and sophisticated science. When implemented together by licensed speech-language therapists and trained horse professionals, the scope of the services available in the riding setting is limited only by the creativity of the individual speech-language pathologist involved.

THE SENSORY INTEGRATION - COGNITIVE/LINGUISTIC CONNECTION

Sensory Input To The
Individual
⇓

Reception By System
Through Sensory
Receptors   I
⇓   N
                   P
                   U
Perception And The T
Decoding Of Sensory
Input
⇓

Interpretation And
Integration Of Sensory   COGNITIVE PROCESSING
Input At The CNS Level

⇓

Storage In CNS-   Integration Of The   Organization Of   Retrieval Of The
Short And Long   ⇒   Information Into   ⇒   Stored Information ⇒ Information From
Term Processes   Conceptual Knowledge   Together With   Storage Of Knowledge
                                                 Previous Knowledge   In The Mind

Linguistic Message
Is Conveyed
⇑

Production Of The
Verbal Thought
O   Through Voice,
U   Graphics, Gesture
T   ⇑
P
U   Formulation Into A
T   Verbal Thought To
     Be Communicated
     ⇑

Selective/Analysis
Of Information For
Verbalization

⇑

©

Sensory input is provided from auditory, visual, tactile, vestibular,proprioceptive, gustatory, and olfactory channels. Disorders in sensory processing and sensory integration can occur at any level or at several levels. These breakdowns result in the individual trying to deal with his environment based on faulty information. Incorrect incoming information leads to the formulation of faulty knowledge and conceptualization. Difficulties in sensory processing and/or integration can create severe disorganization in the individual. Deficits in the filtering and regulating of incoming sensory information can block the individual's ability to engage in effective and/or efficient communication on both receptive and expressive levels. The application of knowledge and communicating with that knowledge is made in effective by breakdowns in sensory integration.

Ruth Dusmuke-Blakely,MS/CCC-SLP
Kristy Kranz, MOTR/L

28 PSYCHOLOGICAL TREATMENT WITH THE HORSE

28.01 USING VAULTING LESSONS AS "REMEDIAL-EDUCATION"*

Antonius Kroger[1]

Preliminary Remarks

1.1. Definition

The concept of ""* addresses the educational, psychological, psychotherapeutic, rehabilitative and socially integrating aspects of the use of horses to help individuals of all ages with various disabilities and disturbances.

The focus is on using horses to benefit individuals developmentally, emotionally and behaviorally rather than to teach riding as a sport. The individual is addressed holistically in his or her interaction with the horse, whether riding or vaulting. Holistically means physically, mentally, emotionally and socially.

1.2. Group Size

An ideal group size is six children or adolescents. This:
- Allows for various subgroups of two or three for specific lessons
- Guarantees each participant the opportunity to recognize the limits of his or her abilities and thereby provides a basis for realistic self-assessment
- Makes abandoning favoritism possible
- Provides opportunities for cooperation
- Kindles the participants' courage to try new things by allowing them to observe and then imitate each other
- Allows group members to increasingly differentiate between horse and vaulter by counting the rhythmical movements of the horse's gaits. This requires the riders to hold still during the exercise
- Gives the individual participant enough time to recover his attention, concentration and overcome the fear after having exerted himself to his maximum ability.

A smaller group size may be preferable:
- When the experience of the vaulting instructor is so limited that if difficulties of a social nature were to arise, the riding instruction would be abandoned
- If the disabilities of the participants are so severe (i.e., their ability to participate as members of a group is so limited) that in the beginning, remedial-education riding and vaulting could only be done effectively either individually or in a correspondingly smaller group

1.3. Staff

The primary actors in an effective program of healing instruction in vaulting are:
- The group of participants
- A specially trained and reliable horse with a soft and easy canter
- A trained vaulting teacher whose constant concern is to teach in a professional manner

* (Healing Instruction) is a literal translation of the German term Heilpaedagogik. Since the concept is distinct from that commonly described in English by the word, it is here given its literal form (Translator). The term used in English is "remedial-education riding and vaulting" and will be used in this paper.

Translated from German by Eberhard W. Teichmann

Anyone else who wants to be present in order to "help" can do so only by not being actively involved in what is going on in the program. The "helper" must only observe and privately take note of what is happening in the group and with individual participants.

This person (helper) can reflect back to the vaulting instructor how the vaulter's actions and reactions move him or her toward his or her goal. This feedback can be used to better plan future lessons, (cf. section III ff.). A bystander or "helper" must never do things such as entertaining those children who are not vaulting, or lifting participants onto the horses or intervening in conflict situations. (cf. section II.2)

Parents are seldom able to perform the functions of a helper described above and for that reason, if they want to be present during the lesson, they should only be observers from a distance away from the group.

II. The Vaulting Lesson in Remedial-Education Riding and Vaulting

II. 1. Preparation (grooming and saddling) of the Vaulting Horse.
The participants help in caring for, grooming and saddling the horse. However, they alone must decide how near or far from the horse they want to be, which activities they want to be involved in, when and how much. The vaulting instructor should respect their choices. Otherwise, their natural interest in living things might be smothered and their motivation to make contact with the horse, extinguished.

II. 2. The Warm and Suppling of the Horse and the Vaulter
Especially in the beginning phase of therapy, the stability of the instructor is most important to children with social and emotional difficulties.

In order to maintain the horse as the primary medium for correcting the participant's personality development, the connection between horse and rider during the vaulting lesson should not be restricted in any way. The vaulting teacher is the person who maintains the participant's attention on the horse. Through appropriate initiatives, he controls the horse, and this is his means of education. That is the reason for excluding other reference persons (i.e., "helpers").

The first task for the participants in a lesson in remedial-education riding and vaulting is for them to establish, by themselves, their starting order for that lesson. Any child or adolescent is capable of learning this process of creating order in his or her group. It always needs to be done in relationship to the horse. While this is happening, the instructor is warming up the horse in the ring near where the group is so that the participants can become involved in suppling the horse immediately after they have established their riding order.

It is good to involve the whole group in suppling the horse. The movements of the horse form the basis for all the demands made on the participants--both inside and outside the ring. This activity around the horse can be conceived as multiform "games" played around the horse. Noteworthy is Bernhard Ringbeck's description of these in the book, *Heilpaedagogisches Reiten und Volti* (1990).

II.3. Exercises on the Horse

II.3.1. Exercises for individuals
The individual participant does his or her exercises on the horse in the order determined by the group; the person just finishing helps the person next in line onto the horse. Even more effective from the point of view of enhancing group process--if also more difficult--is to have the participant helped onto the horse by the person following him or her. If the group can also agree that the consequence of a person not helping is to miss his or her turn for that round, the participants' self discipline is quickly established.

If there are difficulties in helping someone onto the horse, others from the group may help. It does not matter whether help is asked for or given without asking. If help is not given or it is ineffective, the instructor can model giving help in an exemplary way.

610

Depending on the level of concentration in the group or the general spirit of the participants, the exercises for individuals are done in order and each exercise is repeated two or three times. The exercises are based on the six obligatory vaulting exercises. Those exercises that are accomplished in stride are soon attempted--often in the first hour--at a canter. In that way individuals can be kept at the edge of their capability at the moment, whether that capability be in concentration, in bodily attention, in physical strength or in overcoming fear. Since the ability to make this maximum effort in healing instructional vaulting is so limited in these participants, and their turns so brief, typically everyone in a group can have two turns on the horse in a period of about fifteen minutes.

II.3.2. Exercises with a partner
In the very first vaulting lesson, exercises for individuals should be followed by simple exercises with a partner. The purpose of this is for relaxation and for the participants to begin to establish social and emotional ties with each other. Exercises for three soon follow those for two. These exercises are carried out for a longer period of time. They help the participants in many ways, and especially: to focus on another being (both horse and rider); to concentrate; to accept the boundaries of other participants; to further the ability to accept close physical contact; and to comprehend the good nature of the horse.

During this group phase of the lesson when group harmony seems difficult to maintain, the vaulting instructor has a good opportunity to keep all the participants actively involved by having them make observations. The three bystanders might observe:
- How long the exercise lasts
- Which of the participants carries out the vaulting exercise correctly
- Who begins to speak first on the horse
- What sequence of exercises the vaulters invent
- Whether the following group does everything correctly
- During how many paces of the horse does the hind person stand
- Which hand does the front person put on their head
- With which hand does the front person praise the horse
- And much, much more. . . !

With time, remedial-education riding and vaulting becomes calmer and more creative. Also the motivation of the participants increases.

II.3.3. Requested Exercises
Toward the end of the vaulting lesson, each participant may request to do an exercise or exercise sequence of his or her choice. He or ahe may choose the gait of the horse, whether he or she is do the exercise alone, with one other or two others or even whether or not to do an exercise at all.

II.4. Care of the Horse
The care of the horse at the conclusion of the exercises is a way to acknowledge its contributions. This care includes:
- Praising the horse after the vaulting lesson by patting and stroking it
- Feeding it small treats such as apples, oats, and so forth
- Cooling it down in the arena by walking it in hand
- Removing the tack
- Taking the longe line, the whip and the saddle to the tack room
- Leveling the surface of the ring
- Leading the horse to its stall, removing the bridle and cleaning the bit
- Spreading shavings in the stall and blanketing the horse, if necessary
- Taking leave of the horse and the trainer

III. After the lesson, preparing for the next lesson

If an observer was present for the vaulting lesson, his or her help is invaluable in preparing for the next lesson. In this regard, the following might be taken into account:

- Was the management of the horse proper--when was something missing--
- Were the goals for each individual children achieved
- Were the agreed upon arrangements upheld
- For whom should a goal be changed
- How might a change be introduced and developed
- Were the corrections, i.e., the reinforcements appropriate to and for the conceptual level of the participants
- When and how did the instructor engage in a power struggle with a participant and thereby abandon the partnership
- What was obvious during the lesson regarding mutual attraction or rejection within the group members as it affected the partnership interaction
- Should a consequence for frequent misbehavior be arrived at democratically within the group

USING "REMEDIAL EdUCATION RIDING AND VAULTING TO CHANGE THE BEHAVIOR OF ELEMENTARY STUDENTS

Project History

This project involved children from an elementary school who where in the first three grades. The school doctor identified eight out of seventy first grade children whom he felt needed special attention, i.e., their motor functioning was unusual and conspicuous. Seven of these eight children were in one class. The author would like to note but not elaborate on the observation that motor deficiencies in children often have behavioral consequences. The author also noted that four out of these seven children were so severely disturbed socially that classroom instruction with them was very difficult. At the end of the first semester, the school principal offered to give the classroom teacher an hour a week free from her regular duties in order to work with these most socially disturbed students to develop their social skills. The teacher, in searching for something to strongly motivate these students, came across my work in teaching vaulting as the head of a school for special children and asked me to work with the four most affected boys. The parents of these boys were informed about the proposed instruction which was to take place in a series of four session, each for a month. And arrangements were made regarding which parents would transport the children to and from the riding arena at what times.

Course of the Project

The author held the first social training session on February 7, 1990. In it he explained vaulting to the children. The author recieved the expected result that all four children wanted to try it. They were also willing to accept my conditions for beginning each of the four possible series of sessions (each lasting a month) until summer vacation began. These conditions were as follows: "whoever 'hits' another person no more than eight times in each of the Wednesday sessions of a given month may participate in the next month." The point of this arrangement was to indicate unacceptable behavior in an objective way. The idea was that if these children could merely be made aware of their asocial behavior without being judged for it, it would be easier for them to work on changing it.

In the session on February 14, everything went according to plan. Three of the boys went on to canter during their first lesson. Only the most disturbed boy, whose aggressions were unpredictable, wanted only to walk the horse. He is the one labeled **S** in Table 1. The results of this vaulting lesson in terms of the boys' motivation and behavior in their regular classroom was nothing short of unbelievable. The student labeled as **P**, who regularly was involved in an average of eight major physical altercations each class day, abruptly stopped fighting and continued not to fight for the following five school days.

The tension engendered by this maximum effort in self control broke into chaos on February 21. However, before this happened, the author took **P** for a private vaulting lesson as a reward for his accomplishments. In his car on the way back to school after the lesson, **P** remarked, "I don't think I can do it again next week." Since the other three students wanted the same privilege of a private lesson, individual standards of social behavior for achieving it were set for each of them. If any of them met these standards for five days, they would have an additional private

On February 28, two of the children had earned a private session. On the next Wednesday, three had earned one. On March 14, a planned show was held in which, by the way, no fights occurred. On March 14, all the boys had met their requirements so that the classroom session in social behavior was canceled. In the following week, only two of the students earned an extra session. But one of them was S for whom this seemed to be the first time that any kind of therapy had worked. S had been continuously in either group or individual therapy since the age of four, none of which had shown any results until the present. After an Easter vacation of three weeks, all of the children forgot to pick up their cards from the teacher. They did not notice until there were no vaulting lesson on April 25.

Since these four children had managed to rapidly increase control over their behavior (as evidenced by the proportion of them earning extra lessons: 50% in the first interim period, 75% in the second, and 83% in the third), their parents definitely wanted the sessions to continue. Thus, these sessions became a regular arrangement in the next school year, this time with six participants (five boys and one girl). We expanded the group not because I could fit six children into my car, but because adding two more to the original four seemed to us important in a group dynamic sense. It seemed an important step in integrating the first four difficult students into a wider group.

Startfolge = Starting Order
Einfuehrung = Introduction
Osterferien = Easter Vacation
Projektwoche = Project Week

TRANSLATION FROM GERMAN TO ENGLISH

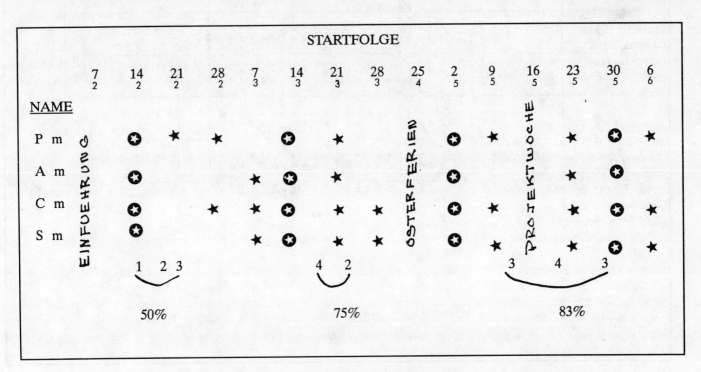

FIGURE 1.   MOTIVATIONAL REMEDIAL-EDUCATION RIDING AND VAULTING
FOR ELEMENTARY SCHOOL STUDENTS AS A BETTER WAY TO CONTROL BEHAVIOR?

Translation of German terms into English as they relate to Figure 2.	
Anzahl=number V. Lehrer Verhindert=prevented (from attending) by teacher Herbstferien=fall vacation Schulfrei=no school Ferien=vacation Osterferien=Easter vacation Feiertag=holiday	Anzahl der starts = number of special sessions a - Schulische Vorbedingung nicht erfuellt = academic conditions not met St - Verweis im stall = reprimand in the stall Sa - Sandwerfen = throwing sand Arabic numbers--arab. ziffer--Taetlichkeiten = acts of assault Roman number--roem. ziffer = verpasste starts = missed starts

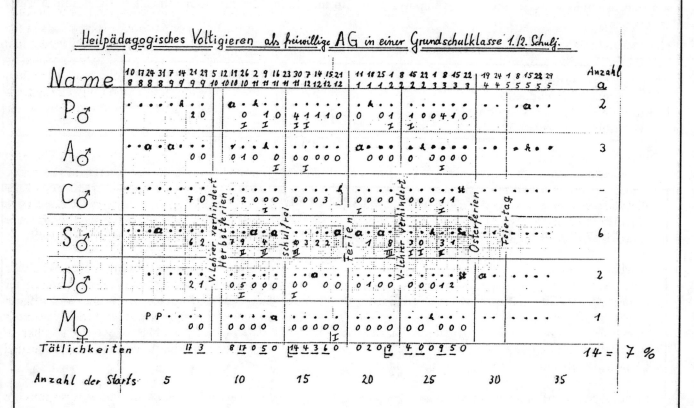

FIGURE 2. REMEDIAL-EDUCATION RIDING AND VAULTING AS A VOLUNTARY ASSOCIATION IN THE FIRST AND SECOND GRADES OF AN ELEMENTARY SCHOOL.

Figure 2 graphically displays the number of vaulting starts for the individual children in the period from the beginning of August, 1990 to the end of May, 1991. Thirty four events are tabulated in chronological order. The project continued as a voluntary working relationship outside of the required hours of instruction. Six children out of a class of twenty four were involved. Conditions for participation that were not related to vaulting were retained in the second year of the program since they had been so effective during the first year. In doing that, however, we instituted something that I had formerly rejected. I will come back to that later.

In Figure 2 the dots indicate that student participated at that time. **K** means that the participant missed the session because of illness. A means that the student did not participate because he or she did not meet the conditions set by the school in order to be able to do so. For **P** that was so twice, for **A** three times, and for **C** not at all. St means non-participation because of a warning in the previous hour by stable staff. **S** did not meet the conditions six times, **D** two times, and **M** once. The last column gives the sum of the **A**'s.

The Arabic numerals give information about serious physical altercations during the vaulting. That was hardly observed among the four children during the first school year. During the second year, some of it might be explained by the increase in size of the group, although the two new children did not trust themselves to become socially active during that time. In addition, **D** showed strong motor disturbances. I see further explanations in the fact that the sessions were no longer new and unusual and also in that in the larger group, the participants had to establish their starting order at the beginning of each session. The problems that arose could only be solved by force in the beginning. Telling the children that the horse could not stand being around this kind of violent problem solving because it would become afraid of the vaulting only helped for awhile. They then fought away from the horse so that it could not react to them. That at least was a step toward becoming more considerate, which was something the children were not able to be at all in the rest of their lives.

In order to make some progress in tackling this issue, I recruited a student teacher to secretly make a checklist of serious conflict and how often who was involved during the next hour. In doing that, the severity of the blows, the length of the fight and the instigator were all to be ignored. All she was to register was the frequency of the conflicts because this was what the children could most easily relate to. On september 9th, seventeen incidents were secretly recorded on the list. At the end of the hour, each participant was asked how often he or she thought they had participated in a conflict. The result of questioning them had little to do with what had been recorded.

Before the beginning of the next session, I asked each participant to guess how many times he or she would be involved in a conflict. That guess was also recorded by the student teacher and at the end of the hour that number was compared with the number on the checklist, which was now being recorded openly. Over time and without exception, all the children developed a certain pride in their ability to predict what they would do. From November on, the guesses were no longer registered because the children could relatively reliably count the number of conflicts they had been in. They did this regularly in the car on the trip back to school. The vaulting proceeded with less incidents and became progressively more performance oriented.

The Roman numerals indicate missed opportunities for starting a vaulting round. Each participant was responsible for noting his or her starting order for that day. Whoever did not approach the horse in the ring at the end of the previous rider's turn without being reminded, was passed over without either having an extra turn or being admonished for missing one. It was made clear to the childrn that they were free to pass on their turn if they were afraid or if they did not feel like going at the moment.

For lack of space, an analysis of the last row will be foregone: the frequency of physical assault. I do want to mention that the group was able to democratically arrive at certain arrangements on occasion. A warning from the stable staff and throwing sand while the horse was in the area resulted in the loss of one session and the loss of five "points." Leaving the arena building without permission during the vaulting lesson meant being without supervision. The consequence for that was loss of the session.

During the last three months a further rule was established that whoever lost his or her point card also lost the privileges contained in those points.

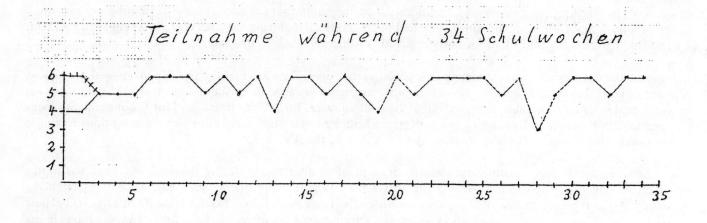

0 participants	0	= 0%		4 participants	2	= 6%
1 "	0	= 0%		5 "	11	= 32%
2 "	0	= 0%		6 "	20	= 59%
3 "	1	= 3%				

FIGURE 3. PARTICIPATION DURING 34 WEEKS OF SCHOOL

This graph displays the number of participants in the individual vaulting lessons. For fairness sake, those participants who missed because of illness (which happened eight times) are marked as being in attendance. For a total of 34 occasions:

20 times	all 6 children took part	= 59% of the time
11 times	5 children took part	= 32% of the time
2 times	4 children took part	= 6% of the time
1 time	3 children took part	= 3% of the time

The results speak for themselves! A further point is clear. Out of 2OO possible starts only 14 (7%) could not be used because the conditions for doing them had not been met. The author finds this last result rather puzzling since he had totally abandoned using conditions for participating in vaulting some time ago as the result of negative experiences. In thinking further about the question of why the setting of conditions in this project was so helpful. The author made the following conclusions:

- My earlier conditions were probably not concrete enough
- The author did not give enough consideration to the principle of small steps in necessary changes
- The timing of the conditions in relation to the desired changes was insufficient
- Often the conditions were substantially and too rapidly changed to respond immediately to variations in misbehavior
- Last but not least: the conditions were not directed enough at the reasons for the misbehavior; only when one knows the reasons for a misbehavior is a real behavior change possible.

The author finds the foregoing remarks confirmed by the following example. During vaulting a participant, totally deficient in group skills, began for the first time in his life to take requests that were directed at the whole group as being relevant to him as well. In addition, the more his interest in achieving was awakened, the more he changed his behavior. His conditions for participating were not to hit others in the classroom and not to take others' things away and then destroy them.

616

After summer vacation, these rules soon were applied to his behavior in the whole school building. Six weeks later they applied to his instruction in all his subjects. By the end of December, any fighting on the school property was grounds for denying him "points." The chart shows that even after his interest in achievement suddenly declined in October after fall vacation, his hitting and breaking of others' things was relatively contained. From that time on, he resisted participating in any instruction other than vaulting and was involved only in things that had nothing to do with school. He became increasingly animal-like, inflexible, and inadvertently got into physical altercations with his classmates more and more often, thus the five absences during this period until the end of January. All the efforts of his teachers, his parents and the principal to get him to participate again seemed to make him all the more determined to swim against the current. He was about to be transferred to a special school for Developmental Assistance which his parents had agreed to but had not yet undertaken because his mother had been in the hospital and had not yet returned home.

At this point I need to talk about the timing which I mentioned earlier. In January, when I confronted him about not working, he said: "Why should I? I didn't fight and I didn't take things away from people and break them, so I'm allowed to do the vaulting." As a result, on the first of February I decided to risk totally changing the conditions for his participating in the vaulting. I did this in the classroom in front of a number of his classmates. I made it clear to him that his next vaulting lesson was his last unless he decided to work in all his school classes in four out of five days. How he behaved was irrelevant. Therefore, today was his final vaulting lesson. All his classmates, all his teachers and even I believed (about 90% certain) that today <u>was</u> his last lesson.

Summary

In a video showing the "last" vaulting lesson with S on the horse, it shows how he almost immediately follows my requests twenty three times in a row. On the ride back to school in the car with the others, he quietly added the following remark to the chatter of the other children: "You'll see."

Suddenly on the next day of school, he began to work continuously from class to class. He was allowed to participate in the vaulting five weeks in a row. Then he had to take a break because of throwing sand but after that he started regularly eighteen times until the end of school. He behaved unobtrusively, radiated inner contentment, traded tender behaviors with his father (which he had not been able to do before), and was promoted to the third grade without comment.

Finally, here are a few words about the other five children, all of whom overcame similarly tense situations.
- **P** and **D** demonstrated first in vaulting and later in the classroom that they are with certainty not learning disabled.
- **A** was also spared being sent to the special school for Developmental Assistance.
- **M** stopped sucking his thumb, is more self confident in his schoolwork and expresses his own ideas and wants.

<u>Final Observation</u>
Remedial-education riding and vaulting (Healing Instructional Vaulting) is an exceptionally productive educational tool not only for special schools but also for regular school children. It is indispensable for any elementary school from a preventive point of view.

Reference
Ringbeck, B. (1990). *Heilpaedagogisches Reiten und Volti*. edited by Marianne Gaeng, Munich and Basel: E. Reinhard.

28.02   SPIRITUAL PSYCHOLOGY: AN APPROACH TO THERAPEUTIC RIDING

Barbara Rector-Morken, MA

Sierra Tucson Adolescent Care is a private psychiatric hospital for severely emotionally disturbed adolescents who have substance, chemical or behavioral abuse problems. The treatment philosophy is of a traditional Western (cultural) medical model interfaced with emerging experiential therapeutic modalities, including wilderness experience, riding therapy, 18 feet wall climbing, ropes course, dance and the arts, all of which are oriented within the Twelve Steps of Recovery Framework.

Sierra Tucson's Integrated Riding Resource Program's (STIRRUP) purpose is to elevate the troubled adolescent's self-esteem through the therapeutic use of the horse and the horse experience. Carefully structured sessions provide safe nurturing opportunities to elicit an expanded awareness, develop multi-sensory integration and contribute to an increased capacity for individuation. Healthy, conscious choice-making is practiced and mastered. Relationship skills are developed; communication, interpersonal and intimacy skills are crafted, practiced and worked.

The horse experience includes mounted skill lessons, T.T.E.A.M work, basic stable management skills, farrier and minor veterinarian techniques in a comprehensive curriculum of cognitive learning and hands on practicums. Riding activities develop self-awareness, build confidence, cultivate concentrations, and self-discipline. Posture, balance, coordination, strength and flexibility are improved. Riding is especially valuable for people who have impaired mobility and/or limited awareness of being "in their body." Exercising the spirit is as important as exercising the body. The horse provide a unique vehicle for both of these essentials. The horse opens previously closed doors for people with physical, mental and emotional disabilities.

EQUINE FACILITATED PSYCHOTHERAPY, A TWELVE STEP APPROACH

1. We admitted we were powerless over alcohol--that out lives had become unmanageable.
2. We came to believe that a Power greater than ourselves could restore us to sanity.
3. We made a decision to turn our will and our lives over to the care of God as we understood Him.
4. We made a search and fearless moral inventory of ourselves.
5. We admitted to God, to ourselves, and to another human being, the exact nature of our wrong doings.
6. We were entirely ready to have God remove all these defects of our character.
7. We humbly asked him to remove our shortcomings.
8. We made a list of all persons we had harmed, and became willing to make amends to them all.
9. We made direct amends to such people whenever possible, except when to do so would injure them or others.
10. We continued to take personal inventory and when we were wrong, promptly admitted it.
11. We sought through prayer and meditation to improve our conscious contact with God as we understood Him, praying only for knowledge of His will for us and the power to carry that out.
12. Having had a spiritual awakening as the result of these steps, we try to carry the message to persons who are alcoholics, and to practice these principles in all our affairs.

Equine Facilitated Psychotherapy is an experiential treatment method utilizing horses to assist with access to the psyche's inner processes. The experience of the horse and the relational dynamics of human to horse brings forth to conscious awareness certain habitual patterns of thought within the client that serve to shape his experience of reality. A specific conceptual framework, a template (map) of a person's way of being in the world of matter, substance, and form, emerges in the close observation of the developing relationship between client and horse.

It is the nature of the horse's association with man to always be in the process of "being trained". Every interaction, each facet and nuance of communication between horse and human is a continuous learning and teaching situation.

These human-animal (horse) interactions serve as conscious practice for developing personal choices about feelings and behavior that enhance the quality of life, in the stable as well as in the external world's ordinary experiences. The recovery process evokes conscious awareness of the rules by which one lives one's life. Working a Twelve Step Program makes possible an objective assessment of how helpful such behavior and thought patterns are to the creation of quality-life experience in the here and now.

Therapeutic riding instructors use the process of learning to ride as a tool for developing intimate relationship skills. They teach the art of joining with the horse in a partnership of communication to develop mutual rhythm, harmony, balance, and alignment: all helpful attitudes and postures for process living in "real" life. Therapeutic riding instructors teach these skills on all levels: mental, physical, emotional, and spiritual.

In the STIRRUP program, the most valuable aids are the focused mind filled with purposeful intent aligned with the big-hearted energy of desire and a "want to" attitude. Students are taught the skills of being fully present "in their own bodies" while attuning their energies to those of their horse.[1] Beginning mounted work is done on the longe line with the horse wearing side-reins. The student becomes accustomed to accommodating his body to the horse's movements. Once independent, they each practice simple school figures on the circle, turn through the circle, transitions through walk, trot, and canter in a 60 foot longe pen. The experience of the horse's movement produces relaxation of tense rigid muscles. New sensory input is absorbed throughout the entire physiological system. The significant relationship of personal body language and the focused mind to the horse's response produced with the application of subtle classical "aids" is reinforced continuously through successful practice on a well-schooled therapy horse.

Mounted work is done on the longe with the instructor demonstrating the lesson skills to be "mastered." A "seasoned" client begins to practice these skills and when he feels confident and ready, he becomes the "teacher-coach" for the next client. The last client "teaches" the primary counselor or counselor aide. Generally there is time in the lesson for several "rounds" of teacher-student coaching; an ideal ratio is 3 clients and a counselor, with instructor and therapy horse. The process of experiencing the role of both student and teacher is a powerful anchoring technique for newly acquired information and skills.

Basic aids for the mounted work are framed within the Twelve Step Program language and tied to the concepts of the recovery process. Graduation to independent mounted work first in the longe pen and then the riding arena is generally dependent on the client's ability to align his minds and his body for the short duration of the practice work. Twenty minutes is about maximum time that these clients can work in this intensive energy processing environment. The STIRRUP program works weekly with the primary group therapy members (6 clients), their primary counselor, and their counselor aide. Initially these people are divided into two groups to learn basic barn safety, elementary grooming, tacking skills, and attend a basic equine psychology lecture.

The STIRRUP program barn contains within its equine personalities the labeled dysfunctional family components of "identified client", co-dependent, acting-out scapegoat, hero/achiever, lost child and various combination there-of. Clients are invited to walk through the barn and pick out the horse they notice most. The one horse that seems to call to them with its particular energy, appearance and behavioral characteristics. Invariably the client chooses a horse that represents to them their own role in the dysfunctional family. Over the course of treatment as the client reaches some insight and acceptance of self their preference in horses shifts to reflect a particular treatment issue that has emerged in the course of their process work.

---

[1] Phase used to describe survival skill of disassociation, a defense mechanism first described by Freud to explain the process whereby a portion of the mind "travels" elsewhere while the body continues to function on "auto pilot". An example is while driving your car over a much traveled and familiar route, you suddenly snap to awareness that you're further along than you realized. Where were "you" or a portion of your mind while your body continued driving the car. Ego 'you' had disassociated, i.e., a portion of conscious mind split off in daydream or fantasy trip from full conscious ware presence in the body.

Story of Elliott

One of the STIRRUP program horses, T.S. Elliott, has volunteered to serve as the challenging, acting-out, and behaviorally difficult adolescent of the barn herd. All barns include, within their equine group, exact duplicates of the human family constellation prevalent in local collective consciousness. So, our barn contains the labeled dysfunctional family components of "identified client," co-dependent, acting-out scapegoat, hero/achiever, lost child, and various combinations there-of. Elliott makes it difficult for you to like him. He pins his ears and bares his teeth when you enter his stall. He is mouthy and "lippy" as you halter him. If tied too loose for grooming, he will continually dive his nose to the butt of the person cleaning his hooves. Why is Elliott even in our program barn, you may ask. Why? He represents that scapegoat, acting-out, "bad" child within us all. He craves love. His life experience has taught him a distorted way of asking for and giving love, recognition, and attention. Our task in the barn for both clients and staff is to model for Elliott more healthy, helpful forms of asking for and receiving attention, recognition, and love.

The adolescent clients have designed a remedial treatment/training plan for Elliott. The plan mandates lots of "positive" response for appropriate behavior no matter how small seeming or insignificant. Elliott is worked in the round pen with the John Lyon's body language longe techniques. No equipment other than the handler (client) in the center holding a longe whip is used. The clients learn the significance of body language, personal boundaries (personal body space), and the power of the focused, attentive mind. Elliott is given lots of verbal praise.

In mounted work, Elliott is challenged by his riders to fit in and conform to the discipline of arena exercises. All are careful to ask Elliott to produce an effort he is capable of, while gently stretching his capacity for disciplined work. The other day, a significant gain was achieved when, without benefit of a lead rider, Elliott and a client produced a straight walk of regular cadence and harmony over the ground pole. Elliott was praised for his efforts. The client warded him by dismounting, running up the stirrups, and loosening his girth.

Clients have more than once been heard saying in the barn, "Elliott makes it hard to like him. He is like us. He needs treatment." Yes, and he is capable of change. He is capable of being remediated. And if for some reason he were experienced as an active danger to himself or others, he would, like the clients, be isolated and given a time-out until he stabilized. Then, he would be reassessed and evaluated for either re-admission to the STIRRUP Program or for a transfer to a more appropriate living situation to best meet his needs for optimum functioning in the life experience.

Story of Shasta: A spiritual Archetype

The STIRRUP program barn also contains, within its herd members, representatives for the various archetypical aspects of psyche. Carl Gustau Jung characterized psyche as an organizing locus for the myth-creating level of mind he called the collective unconscious. The collective unconscious is an unlimited reservoir of latent primordial image linking all humanity.

These innate behavior patterns are what Jung termed archetypes, an original model, a prototype of a behavioral matrix. Jung said, "Just as instincts compel man to conduct a life that is specifically human, so the archetypes compel intuition and apprehension to form specifically human patterns." The archetype image represents to consciousness innate predisposition for responding to typical human situations or being in human relationships. Some major archetype images described by Jung are Persona, Shadow, Anima, Animus, Wise Old Man, Great Mother, Miraculous Child, Hero/Savior, and Self (these are represented among our herd).

The other day, in a budget discussion, a corporate executive invited me to justify "that little hay-burning pony." He was referring to Shasta, our aged (28 years) palomino Shetland pony who only occasionally pulls a jogging cart.

Currently, Shasta resembles the classic chubby "Thewell" pony wearing her blonde fluffy winter coat body clipped with a large heart emblazoned on her rump and the shaggy, shaggy leggings of a mini-Clydesdale.

She came to the STIRRUP program suffering from not being used or feeling useful in her work. Our clients created an individual treatment plan for her remediation which includes much love and appreciation. Love is demonstrated through frequent grooming, long slow walks on a leadline and cross country long reining practice. Most important of all (Shasta, clients and staff) she is given complete freedom in the barn and stable yard.

Complete freedom? Yes! She is allowed to mosey about, or run, or buck, or zip in and out of wherever she pleases. She has, however, one "off limits" activity. Apparently, there is always an "off limits" in every life. Shasta's is the <u>field of dreams</u>: the lush, green, irrigated playing field used by the recreational therapy department for its multi-purpose outdoor games. It is located just adjacent to our STIRRUP program barn area. On rare occasions, usually when that same executive is about, Shasta forgets herself. She will wander over to the tempting lushness of the green, green field. The field has a very expensive underground irrigation system that is not designed to tolerate pony prints. A fairly sharp shout in her direction from the barn staff or an alert client sends her zipping back to the stable yard at a rapid clip. Shasta is most frequently seen on a leadline between an adolescent client and primary counselor who are "walking her out" as part of her remedial conditioning program. Some valuable one-on-one psychotherapy is also occurring as client and counselor join efforts in helping Shasta with her rehabilitation regimen. There is also the added element of mutual support as the trio is astonished by the therapeutic instructor to take no "guff" from the maintenance and grounds personnel who are fond of providing jesting remarks centered around the theme of "walking that funny dog."

Archetypically, Shasta represents that precious perfect core element of us all. She is. She is love energy. You feel, see, sense, and know love with Shasta. She represents that core aspect of our inner self that needs no justification for being. Being is enough. She is precious. She is perfect.

Spiritually, Shasta anchors for us our inner knowing of ourselves as essential elements, integral to humanity's function. Our being is enough. No justification is needed. No activity or achievement is required. Our essential energy is vital and important to the functioning totality of our collective experience. We are enough. And Shasta's very presence reminds us of this truth. She represents the healing in our shame. She is perfect just the way she is. Core energy. Love.

A recent post session processing group revealed some significant connections and insights gained by the clients during a typical primary group experience. A young fourteen year old girl severely depresses with active suicide ideation accessed some deeply buried rage in her frustrated attempts to use one rein in each hand. (She was only comfortable with neck reining.) Her deeply felt shame at not being able to achieve success while trying something new was blocking her ability to even function. Staff urged her to use this frustration energy to make clear to the horse her wishes (to have the horse stay on the rail of the 60 feet round pen and not cut into the middle of the circle). She became more and more awkward and disjointed as her frustration level elevated. Finally, in tears she stopped and heaved out--

> "I can't do this. I'm no good. I can't do anything right. I'm worthless. I give up."
> "And isn't that exactly your attitude facing life?" suggests staff gently.
> "What? Well, yes I guess it is." Her tears are flowing openly.
> "And that's why you're here in out hospital; to acquire tools for changing your attitude."

As the tears stopped she was willing to take several deep breaths and to listen intently to the instructor/therapist who coached her in precisely how to take her horse back out to the rail, one rein in each hand with a focused, intentional mind. She told her inner critic out loud to "take a break" while she suspended all judgement about her feelings of awkwardness and allowed her body-mind to follow the coaching directions. Shortly, the client and her horse achieved unity and a semblance of harmony with walk-trot transitions. Eventually, a lovely sitting trot was produced by the team (the client, horse, and therapeutic instructor also functioning as therapist).

Post session processing tied together the awkward frustration feelings of those new to recovery and the use of the Twelve Steps as healing tools for improving the quality of one's daily experience of life. It begins by letting go of "control" and admitting to needing help.

The group closes by standing to form a circle, arms linked about waists and repeating out loud the Serenity Prayer--

"God, grant me serenity
to accept the things I cannot change,
the courage to change the things I can,
and the wisdom to know the difference."

Reference
O'Connor, P. (1985). *Understanding Jung, Understanding Yourself.* New York: Paulist Press.
Frager, R., Fadiman, J. (1984). *Personality and Personal Growth.* New York: Harper and Row.
Alcoholics Anonymous. (1976). Alcoholics Anonymous Word Services, Inc. New York, N.Y.
Zlukau, G. (1990). *The Seat of the Soul.* Simon and Schuster, Inc.

GENERAL GLOSSARY OF TERMS USED IN THERAPEUTIC RIDING PROGRAMS AND EQUINE-ASSISTED THERAPY.

AAT: Animal-assist therapy.

ABDOMEN: The part of the body between the chest and the hips.

ABDUCTION: To move away from the center of the body.

ABDUCTOR: A muscle that moves a limb away from the center of the body.

ABNORMAL: That which is not normal.

ABNORMAL FATIGUE: Limited endurance.

ABNORMAL REFLEXES: Reflexes that are pathological.

ABNORMAL TONE: Muscle tone which is to high and too low.

ACTIVITIES OF DAILY LIVING: components of every day living which may include self-care, work, play/leisure activities.

A.D.L: Abbreviation for activities of daily living. Normal tasks we do each day to survive.

ACUTE: That which has a rapid onset and a short duration.

ADAPT: To use old knowledge to suit a new situation.

ADAPTIVE REACTION: (adaptive behavior). An appropriate change in behavior to an environmental demand.

ADAPTIVE RIDING: Adjusting the riding equipment and environment to accommodate riders with disabilities.

ADDUCTION: To move toward the center of the body.

ADDUCTOR: A muscle that moves a limb toward the center of the body.

AEROBIC: Using oxygen.

AGRAPHIA: Loss of ability to write.

AGGRESSIVE: Being pushy, forceful, or assertive.

AHSA: American Horse Show Association - regulates and governs horse shows in the US.

AIDS: Communication with the horse - natural: legs, hands, weight, voice.

AIDS: Artificial: Spurs, whip, martingale.

AIDS, LIGHT: A term used to describe the subtle use of the seat, leg, hand aids.

ALEXIA: Inability to recognize or comprehend printed/written words.

AMBULATORY: Those who move about independently by walking.

AMPUTATION: To cut off.

ANATOMICAL POSITION: Face forward with palms of hands facing forward.

ANATOMY: The structure of an organism.

ANKLE BOOTS: Worn by the horse to protect his lower leg joints.

ANTICONVULSANT: That which prevents seizures or convulsions.

ANXIETY: Feelings of being frightened, stressed, tense or in danger.

APATHY: The lack of drive or ambition. Emptiness.

APRAXIA: The inability to perform a purposeful movement though the ability to move the limb is there.

ARTHRITIS: Pain or inflammation of a joint or surrounding area.

ARTICULATION: (In speech). The coordination of the muscles and systems that produce speech and the production of speech sounds.

ARTIFICIAL RIDING AIDS: Spurs or whip used by the rider to communicate with the horse.

ASHA: American Speech, Language and Hearing Association. (CCC): Certificate of Clinical Competence.

ASSIMILATES: To incorporate, comprehend, to absorb.

ASSISTIVE/ADAPTIVE EQUIPMENT: Special devices which assist an individual to perform tasks involved in daily living tasks (including riding).

ASYMMETRICAL: Not the same on both sides - lack of sameness.

ASYMMETRICAL TONIC NECK REFLEX: When the head turns to one side, the arms and leg on the chin side become straight while the arm and leg on the skull side will bend - an automatically reaction without intent.

ATAXIA: Muscular incoordination, tremor like movements, especially when voluntary movements are attempted.

ATHETOSIS: A condition causing irregular snake like movements.

ATROPHY: Wasting away or very weak muscle.

ATTENTION DEFICIT DISORDER: The inability to attend or to focus onto a task for any length of time.

ATTIRE: The clothing worn by a rider, including riding boots, hat, breeches, jodhpurs, chaps, jacket, shirt and gloves.

AUTOMATIC: Something that occurs instinctively or with out effort.

AUTOMATIC REFLEXES:

BABBLING: Repetitive speech sounds.

BACK: A two-beat diagonal gait in reverse; also called "Rein back".

BACK-RIDING: When a therapist or instructor rides behind a client/program rider.

BALANCE IN MOVEMENT: A state of equilibrium of the horse.

BALANCE-DYNAMIC: The ability to maintain equilibrium during movement.

BALANCE-STATIC: The ability to maintain equilibrium while still.

BEAT: When one or more feet strike the ground; or the rhythmical beat of gait including the beat of suspension.

BEDDING: (horse term) Wood-shavings or straw used as soft padding in the horse's stall.

BEHAVIORAL: Action and conducts of human or horse.

BEHAVIORAL ASSESSMENT: A systematic and quantitative method for observing and assessing behavior.

BELLBOOTS: (over reach boots). Rubber bell shaped boots worn over the coronet and hoof to protect the horse's front feet from "over-stepping" (hitting) with the hind feet.

BENDING: (flexion). To stretch, to the response of the rider's aid, his body around the rider's leg, to shape himself to the curve of the circle or turn.

BHSAI: British Horse Society Assistant Instructor.

BHSI: British Horse Society Instructor.

BILATERAL: Involving two sides.

BILATERAL INTEGRATION: Ability to perform purposeful movement that requires interaction between both sides of the body in a smooth and refined manner.

BIT: A piece of metal, rubber or plastic which goes into the horse's mouth and attaches to the reins and the headstall.

BIT LEAD: A single lead attached to a ring from which double straps with snaps extend and attach to the bit rings of the bridle.

BIT RINGS: The rings on each side of the bit where the bit lead or reins attach.

BITE REFLEX: A swift, uncontrolled biting action produced by stimulation of the oral cavity--may be difficult to release. Abnormal reaction.

BOBATH TECHNIQUE: A treatment technique developed by Karl and Bertha Bobath.

BODY CONCEPT: The human conscious awareness of one's body and its parts.

BODY IMAGE: Subjective picture people have of their physical appearance.

BODY LANGUAGE: Using one's body to express oneself.

BODY-MIND CONNECTION: The integration of mental and physical function.

BODY POSITIONS:

    ANTERIOR-Toward the front.

    MEDIAL-Toward the middle.

    POSTERIOR-DORSAL-Toward the back or back part.

    LATERAL-Toward the outside.

    SUPERIOR-Upper or above.

    INFERIOR-Underside.

    PRONE-Lying on the stomach.

    SUPINE-Lying on the back.

    ERECT-Being upright.

    FLEXION-To bend.

    PROXIMAL-Closest to the midline of the body.

    DISTAL-Farthest from the middle of the body.

    INTERNAL-The inside.

    EXTERNAL-The outside.

    ROTATION-The process of turning.

    EXTERNAL ROTATION-Turning outward.

BODY SCHEME: The unconscious awareness of one's body and the position of it's parts.

BOLTING: The horse makes a sudden move, runs away.

BONDING: Developing a close meaningful attachment with another person or animal.

BONE AGE: Age as judged resorption of bone from bone development; It is compared.

BOWED TENDON: Damage caused by overstretching of the lower leg tendon.

BREAST PLATE: (horse term). A strap which fits across the chest of the horse and is attached to the saddle to prevent the saddle from slipping down the back of the horse.

BREECHES: Riding pants worn with knee-high boots.

BRUSHING BOOTS: Protective coverings worn over the long bone of the horse's leg to prevent injury.

BUTAZOLIDIN: (BUTE). A common medicine given to animals for pain and as an anti-inflammatory drug.

BUTTOCKS: The fleshy part of the body posterior to the hip.

CADENCE: Rhythm and impulsion which provides the gait extra quality and is expressed by an energetic lifting of the feet from the ground.

CANTER: Three beats footfall (with a beat of suspension). The second to fastest gait of a horse.

CANTLE: The back part of a saddle.

CARDIAC: Related to the heart.

CARDIOVASCULAR: The complex systems which includes the heart, arteries, capillaries and veins by which the blood is propelled through the body.

CARDIOVASCULAR ACCIDENT (CVA):

CAREGIVER: Any person who takes responsibility for the care of another - can be a parent or non-related person.

CAST: "to be cast". The horse lies down and rolls in such a way that he cannot get up without help.

CAVALRY: Soldiers on horseback.

CAVALLETTI: Poles suspended on two crossbars or blocks. A very small jump.

CAVESSON: A leather noseband on a headstall (bridle).

CENTER OF GRAVITY: A point at which the downward force by mass and gravity is equivalent or balanced on either side of a fulcrum.

CENTRAL NERVOUS SYSTEM-CNS: Related to the brain and spinal cord.

CERVICAL: Related to the neck.

CHAIN SHANK: A chain attached to a lead line.

CHANGE OF REIN: "Change of hand" change of direction.

CHAPS: Leather seatless "overalls" worn on the legs of the rider. Used with the Western attire. Worn for protection of the rider's legs in both English and Western riding especially in training or schooling.

CHEWING ON THE BIT: A good sign of relaxation and acceptance of the bit when other signs also indicate relaxation.

CHRONIC: A condition which has been there a long time and may be permanent.

CHRONOLOGICAL AGE: The actual time elapsed since the birth of living individuals.

CINCH: An American term used for girth. A strap that secures a western saddle.

CIRCUMDUCTION: Circular movement of a joint.

CLAVICLE: (human). A bone of the shoulder girdle.

CNS: Central nervous system.

COGNITION: Conscious process of knowledge, perception, understanding, and reasoning.

COGNITIVE SKILLS: Quality and quantity of comprehension, concentration, problem solving, judgment, communication, sequential abilities, conceptualization, and integration of learning.

COLIC: Mild to severe pain in the digestive system of the horse.

COLLECTION: To gather the horse in an organized manner of balance and motion, engaging the hindquarters, compressing the horse between the buttocks and shoulder, to place the horse on the bit with a relaxed and flexed jaw.

COLT: A male horse under four years.

CONFORMATION: Dependent on the bone structure and how the parts interrelate.

CONTACT: (on the bit). Dependent on the horse's correct use of his body, balance, submission, power of his hind legs, softening of the neck muscles.

CONTRACTURE: Fixed resistance to passive stretch of a muscle resulting in limitation of range of motion of a joint.

CORTICAL BLINDNESS: Loss of visual sensation, including light and dark, blink reaction due to disturbance of the cerebral visual center.

COMPENSATION: The ability to make up for deficiencies.

CONFORMATION: The physical structure of a horse.

CONGENITAL: Inherited traits, present at birth.

CONTACT: The amount of "feel" in the reins linking the hands to the bit

CONTRA-INDICATION: That which is not advisable or should not be attempted.

CONTRACTURE: A joint which is in a fixed and immobile position.

COORDINATION: Parts working together in groups, harmoniously.

CORTICAL BLINDNESS: Damage to that part of the brain that interprets sight. There is no damage to the eye itself.

CRIBBING: The horse anchors his teeth into a horizontal, fixed surface and arches neck and inhales air. A bad habit due to boredom.

CROUP: The rear end (rump) of a horse.

CRUTCH: A special staff used to assist in walking.

CUES: Western term for aids.

DEEP SEAT: The ability to relax and sit close to the horse's spine (in the saddle).

DEFECT: Any abnormality of structure.

DEFICIT: An impairment or lack in some area.

DEFORMITY: Any deviation from the normal shape and form.

DEVELOPMENT: The normal process of maturation of a living being.

DEVELOPMENTAL DELAY: Slow development in child growth or occurring later than normal.

DEVELOPMENTAL DISABILITY: Significantly impaired function in one or more areas with the onset before twenty-one years of age.

DEXTERITY: The skill and spontaneity in performing physical activities.

DIAGONAL: The diagonal pair of legs the rider rises to in the "posting" or "rising" trot. Generally rising to the outside diagonal (outside foreleg, and inside hind leg). Also a schooling figure used to "change the rein" by moving diagonally from one corner of the arena to another.

DIAGNOSIS: Identifying a problem or disease.

DISABILITY: Any failure of function or shill.

DISLOCATION: Displacement of a bone from its joint.

DISOBEDIENCE: The horse refuses to obey aids or commands which are well presented to him.

DISORIENTATION: Inability of a person to judge time, place or person.

DISTAL: Farthest from trunk.

DISTRACTIBILITY: The inability to pay attention to one task.

DECUBITUS: A pressure sore or skin breakdown.

DOWNWARD TRANSITION: Changing to a slower gait when riding.

DRESSAGE: The basic training is a systematic, progressive training to achieve balance, suppleness, submission and facilitating the horse's performance of normal tasks.

DRESSAGE TEST: A test to determine the level of training.

DRIVING AIDS: The combination of seat and legs used to drive the horse forward.

DRIVING WITH LONG LINES: Guiding the horse from the ground by walking at the rear or side of the horse, using long reins attached to the bit.

DROPPINGS: The horse's waste or manure.

DYSFUNCTION: Impaired or poor function in some area.

DYNAMIC: Moving, change.

DYNAMIC EQUILIBRIUM: Maintaining balance during a moving exercise.

DYSLEXIA: Dysfunction in reading and in comprehension of written material.

DYSTROPHY: Wasting away.

ECHOLALIA: Constantly repeating words or phrases which have just been heard.

EDEMA: A build up of fluid in the body tissue.

ELEVATION: To raise up.

ELEVATION: (HORSE TERM) - A good spring to the stride.

ELICIT: To bring about or make something happen.

EMOTIONAL LIABILITY: Not having control of one's emotions.

EMPATHY: While maintaining one's sense of self, the ability to recognize and share the emotions and state of mind of another person.

ENCODING: (cognitive). Those processes or strategies used to initially store information in memory.

ENGAGEMENT: Putting the hindquarters in a position under the horse to create energy and impulsion to forward movement.

ENVIRONMENT: Everything outside of oneself.

ENVIRONMENT ADAPTATIONS: Changes in structural or positional changes designed to facilitate independence/safety of daily living such as ramps, bars.

EQUILIBRIUM: A state of balance. Equal.

EQUILIBRIUM REACTIONS: A group of reflexes which act together to produce a state of balance.

EQUINE: Pertaining to the horse.

EQUINE-ASSISTED THERAPY: A therapy procedure used by health care professionals when the horse is used as a modality.

EQUITATION: The art of riding a horse.

EVALUATION: The process of collecting and interpreting data, through observation, interview, tests, and record review.

EVERSION: Duck feet - turning the feet out.

EXPRESSIVE LANGUAGE: Expressing thought through words, writing and body expression.

EXTENSION: Proceeds from proper collection; the horse covers as much ground as possible, with a long stride, but maintaining the original rhythm.

EXTREMITY: The limbs of the body such as legs and arms.

EYE-HAND COORDINATION: When the eyes and hands integrate their actions.

FACILITATION TECHNIQUES: Selection, grading, and modification sensory input which attempts to stimulate function/movement in an impaired body part.

FACILITATOR: A person or thing who helps to make something happen.

FACILITATORY: A process used to helps to make something happen.

FALLING IN/OUT: Falling into the circle-not remaining straight-allowing a shoulder or hindquarters to fall in. Falling out of the circle with shoulder or hindquarters out.

FARRIER: The shoesmith who cares for the horse's hooves.

FAR SIDE: The right side of the horse.

FEI: Federation Equestre Internationale - organization governing international competition.

FELDENKRAIS PRACTITIONER: A person who has completed the four year program of study under the direction of the Feldenkraise Institute.

FLEXION: Flexing the jaw or yielding the jaw.

FEMUR: Seat bone (ischia).

FIGURE EIGHT: Riding two connecting circles. A schooling figure.

FIGURE GROUND: The visual separation of an object from its background.

FILLY: A female horse under four years.

FINE MOTOR: Relates to the fine motor movements, especially the hands and eyes.

FLACCID MUSCLE: One that is limp or spongy, unable to contract.

FLAG: A gymnastic exercise.

FLEXION: (HORSE TERM) Act of lateral bending. Bending of the horse's neck and body with relaxation of the jaw in response to direct aids.

FLEXOR: A muscle or group of muscles which cause a joint to bend.

FOAL: A horse under one year.

FOCUS: Ability to center, to concentrate on a focal point or issue.

FOOTFALL: The placement of the horse's hoof on the ground.

FORGING: When a horse hits the sole of his front foot with the toe of his back foot on the same side.

FOREHAND: Front section of the horse - forelegs, shoulder, neck, and head.

FORWARD SEAT: Rider sits with his weight through the thighs and knees, over the stirrups. A English style of riding used to stay in balance during jumping and cross-country riding.

FREE WALK: A walk on a "loose rein" (long rein) to allow the horse to stretch his neck.

GAIT: (in humans). A style of movement with the legs.

GAIT: (in horses). The way of going, also known as paces - the natural way the horse moves - walk, trot, canter, gallop.

GALLOP: A gait with four beats to each stride. The horse's fastest gait.

GELDING: A castrated male horse. One no longer a stallion.

GENETIC: Having to do with origin, to genes.

GIMMICK: A term used in horse training referring to short cuts used to gain specific action rather than using a solid training method.

GIRTH: The measurement of the circumference of a horse's body behind the withers.

GIRTHING: To tighten the girth of the saddle.

GOAL: The end that one strives to attain.

GROSS MOTOR: Relates to the large movements of the body.

GROSS MOTOR COORDINATION: Motor behavior concerned with posture, locomotion ranging from early developing behavior to developing fine tuned balance.

GROUND TIE: Horse stands still when the lead rope is dropped to the ground.

GYMKHANA: Mounted contest of events. A competition where the rider's skill is tested.

GYMNASTIC MOVEMENTS: Physical exercises.

HABITUAL PATTERN: An action which has become automatic compared to an action which requires observation-focus and/or thought.

HACKAMORE: A bitless bridle.

HACKING: Riding out. Trail ride, trekking. A ride in the country or on a bridle path.

HALF PASS: A Dressage movement in which the horse moves forward and sideways at the same time.

HAND: Unit of measurement (4 inches, 10.2 cm) used to determine the height of a horse - measured from ground to withers.

HANDICAP: (human). Any condition which impedes an individual's development, opportunities, expectations and activities.

HAUNCHES: The hindquarters of a horse.

HEAD COLLAR: (Halter in USA) Used to lead a horse without a bit.

HEMISPHERE: Related to the right and left parts of the brain.

HORSE LENGTH: Eight feet; distance between horses.

HORSEMANSHIP: The art of riding, understanding the needs and care of the horse.

HUMAN-ANIMAL BONDING:
HYPERACTIVE: Excessive movement and energy.
HYPEREXTEND: To move a limb beyond the normal straightened range.
HYPERSENSITIVITY: Being over responsive to some stimulation.
HYPERTONIC: Too much tone in a muscle.
HYPOTONIC: Too little tone in a muscle.

ILIAC CREST: The top or superior portion of the pelvis.
IMPULSION: The energy generated by the hindquarters of the horse. The desire of the horse to move forward.
IMPULSIVE BEHAVIOR: One who has an impelling need to do some thing.
INCONTINENT: The inability to control the muscles of the bladder causing urine to escape.
INDEPENDENT SEAT: (independent aids). When a rider can use his arms, legs, hands, and seat independent of each other. One does not influence the other while riding.
INHIBIT: To restrain a process or function.
INHIBITORY: A process used to stop an action (stop a muscle from becoming stiff) by modifying sensory input.
INSIDE LEG: The leg on the inside of the arena or ring or the bend of the horse which can be on the outside of the ring.
INTEGRATION: The useful and harmonious incorporation and organization of old and new information.
INTELLIGENCE: The measured capacity of learned ability.
INTERNAL ROTATION: To turn inward toward the body.
INVERSION: Turning the foot in - pigeon toed.
INVOLUNTARY: Actions which cannot be controlled.
IRONS: The metal part of the English stirrup.
ISCHIAL TUBEROSITY: A protuberance of the ischium upon which the body rests in sitting.

JOG: A slow trot in Western riding.
JOINT: A place of union or junction of two or more bones.

KINESTHESIA: The ability to sense position and movement of a limb or body part.
KINETIC ACTIVITIES: Those activities which require motion.
KNOWLEDGE: Acquaintance with fact, awareness, understanding, that which is grasped by the mind.

LAME: The horse moves unevenly or limps.
LATERALITY: The stronger or dominant side of the body.
LATIGO: The cinching strap on a Western saddle which secures the girth to the saddle.
L.E.: The abbreviation for lower extremity.
LEAD: Specific footfall pattern at the canter or lope- the inside legs on a circle, reaches farther forward than the outside legs.
LEAD LINE, LEAD STRAP: A rope with which to lead a horse.
LEATHERS: Heavy straps which attach the stirrup irons to the saddle.
LEG YIELDING: Moving the horse sideways and forward with one's legs.
LENGTHENING OF STRIDE: Increasing the length of the stride within a set frame.
LIGAMENT: Connective tissue that attach bone to bone.
LIMB: A leg or arm.
LONG-REINING: Controlling the horse from the ground by means of long-reins attached to the bit.
LONGEING: (lungeing). Using a longe-rein (long rein) attached to a cavesson or bit of the bridle and the horse performs circles around the trainer who stands in the center holding the rein.
LONGE CAVESSON: A head collar with a well-padded, snugly fitted noseband with swivel rings attached to the noseband to which the lunge line is attached.
LONGE WHIP: A five to six foot whip used in lungeing a horse to provide the aids or impulsion.
LOPE: A three-beat gait used in Western riding.
LORDOSIS: An exaggerated front to back curve of the spine.
LUMBAR: The lower part of the spine.

MACROCEPHALIA: A head that is larger than normal.
MARE: A female horse over four years.
MICROCEPHALIA: A head that is smaller than normal.
MIDLINE: The center point of the body from head to toe.
MINIMAL BRAIN DAMAGE: (SOFT SIGNS). Damage to the nervous system that is not visible to the eye, does not affect intelligence but may affect how one functions.
MOBILITY: To move.
MOTOR PLANNING: The ability to carry out purposeful motor movements.
MOTOR SYSTEM: All parts of the body that have to do with movement.
MOUNTED: Sitting on a horse.
MULTI-HANDICAPPED: A person with more than one disability.
MUSCLES: Body fibers that contract and cause movement.
MUSCLE MOVEMENT-OVERFLOW: Immitative movements, fisting, or flaring of the second hand <u>not</u> involved in a one handed task which is being performed by the first hand (normal till about age 8.)
MUSCLE TONE: Tension of a muscle.

MUSCULAR: Having to do with muscles.
MYELINATION: The process of accumulating myelin during development.

NATURAL AIDS: Riding aids. The rider's legs, seat, weight, hands, and voice are used to communicate with and control the horse.
NEAR SIDE: The left side of the horse.
NECK-REINING: A method of guiding a horse used in Western riding.
NEURO: Relating to the nervous system.
NEURODEVELOPMENTAL: Having to do with the neurological development of a person related to the development of the nervous system.
NEUROMUSCULAR: Having to do with the muscles and the nerves.
NEUROMUSCULAR STIMULATION: Techniques used by health care professionals to stimulate specific neurological reactions.
NUMNAH: A saddle shaped pad used under a saddle.
NYSTAGMUS: A normal involuntary rapid movement of the eyeball which occurs as a result of quick stops, body rotations or changes in any directions.

OFF SIDE: The right side of the horse.
ON THE AIDS: When the horse is responding and attentive to the rider's aids.
ON THE BIT: The position of the horse's head (the face is close to the vertical) at which the rider can most easily exercise control and the horse freely accepting the contact with the rider through the reins. The hind legs are engaged and well under the body.
ONTOGENETIC: (Ontogeny). The origin and development of an organism - not related environment or evolution.
OUTSIDE LEG: The rider's leg on the outside of the ring, circle or bend.
OVER-REACH: When horse hits his front heels with the hind toes.

PACE: Same as gait.
PACE: Also used to describe a-two-beats-to-each-stride with both legs on one side moving together.
PADDOCK: A small enclosure near the stable.
PARALYSIS: Temporary or permanent loss of function.
PARALYSIS: CATEGORIES OF INVOLVEMENT-
    MONOPLEGIA involves one limb.
    HEMIPLEGIA involves one side of the body.
    PARAPLEGIA involves both of the legs.
    DIPLEGIA involves all limbs but more severe in the legs.
    QUADRIPLEGIA involves all four limbs.
    TRIPLEGIA involves three limbs.
PARESIS: Partial or incomplete paralysis.
PATHOLOGICAL: Abnormal. Diseased.
PELHAM: A single bit used with four reins. A modified full bridle (one with two bits).
PELVIC: (pelvis). The basin-shaped bone formed by the pelvic girdle and adjoining bones of the spine.
PERCEPTUAL DISORDER: A disorder involving mental processing.
PERCEPTUAL-MOTOR: Recognition of a stimuli with a motor response.
PERFORMANCE SKILLS: Motor skills, sensory integration, psychological/intrapersonal skills, cognitive skills, social/interpersonal skills.
PHYLOGENIC: Origin and development of a species.
PHYSICALLY CHALLENGED: A person with a disability who pursues activities regardless of his or her handicap.
PINCER GRASP: To grasp with the thumb against the fingers; a pinch.
PLANTAR FLEXION: Bending the ankle down - toes down.
POLL: Junction of the skull with the first vertebrae; the prominent top of the horse's head.
PONY: Any horse that stands under fourteen point two hands (14.2) or fifty-eight inches (147.3 cm).
POOR WAY OF GOING: Gait that is not symmetrical.
POSITIONING: Placing body parts in correct skeletal alignment.
POSTING: "Rising trot". The rising and descending of the rider with the rhythm of the trot.
POSTURAL ADJUSTMENT: The change of ones posture in response to changes in the environment.
POSTURAL REACTIONS: Changes in postural position in reaction to gravity.
PREDISPOSE: Make susceptible to a condition.
PRIMITIVE REFLEXES OR RESPONSES: Reflexes present at birth which aid in normal development and than disappear during growth.
PROGNOSIS: The anticipated results of an illness or treatment.
PROPRIOCEPTION: The normal ongoing awareness of the position, balance and movement of posture of ones body in space without visual input or looking.
PROTECTIVE REACTIONS: Automatic reflexes which help to protect the body.
PULMONARY: Related to the lungs.
PULSE: Rhythmic throbbing of an artery related to the beat of the heart.
PURPOSEFUL ACTIVITY: A task or skill that has a functional goal (picking up rings and putting them on a pole) in contrast to an exercise of moving the arm up and down in repetition.

RANGE OF MOTION: (ROM). Degree of free movement of a joint.
REACTIONS: Response to a stimuli.
REFLEX: Automatic predicable responses of the body to changes in position.
REGRESSION: To decrease function, go backward, get worse.
REHABILITATION: The restoration process for a disabled person designed to increase his function to maximum level of ability.
REIN BACK: (same as BACK). To back a horse. A two-beat diagonal gait.
RESPIRATION: Pertaining to breathing.

RIGIDITY: Inflexible or stiffness.

RIGHTING: A reaction that assists (human or horse) to the upright position.

RISING TROT: Same as posting.

RHYTHM: Regularity of footfall or the sequenced placement of a horse's feet during gait.

SACRUM: The tail bone (5 fused bones of the lower spine).

SCAPULA: The large bone which forms the back of the shoulder girdle.

SCHOOLING: Training a horse for what he is intended to do.

SCHOOLING FIGURES: Movements performed to train the horse and rider.

SCOLIOSIS: Abnormal side to side curvature of the spine.

SEAT: The position a rider takes on a horse.

SELF-CARRIAGE: Resulting from the yielding of the jaw and correct impulsion, the horse remains light, imbalance, relaxed, and self-impelled.

SENSATION: The reception of stimuli such as touch, pain, taste, smell, vision, hearing, temperature, vestibular, proprioception/kinesthesia, stereognosis.

SENSE ORGANS: Eyes, ears, nose, touch, joints through which sensation is received.

SENSORY INTEGRATION: The amount and quality of development and integration of somatosensory functions, reflected in reflex, sensory degree, posture, motor activity and praxis, form and space perception, body schema and self concept.

SENSORIMOTOR: The motor response to sensory input.

SEQUENTIAL: One following the other in an orderly form.

SEQUENTIAL BEHAVIOR: The natural stages of development of the infant to adulthood.

SERPENTINE: Series of half circles and straight lines crossing from one side of an arena to the other; a schooling exercise.

SHAPING: A technique used to changer behavior through sequential modeling of behavior patterns to gain specific results.

SHORTENING OF STRIDE: Decreasing the length of the stride within a set frame.

SHOULDER GIRDLE: The system of bones that support the upper limbs (human) the scapula, clavicle.

SHOULDER-IN: The horse is slightly bent around the in-side leg of the rider; the horse's leg inside leg passes and crosses the outside leg.

SHUNT: A medically inserted tubular device to drain fluid from one place to another.

SHYING: The horse startles, is spooked by a moving object.

S.I.: Abbreviation for sensory integration.

SITTING TROT: The rider sits deep in the saddle and maintains contact with the saddle while trotting.

SNAFFLE BIT: A type of bit with a jointed or unjointed mouthpiece with rings attached at each end.

SOUND: (horse term). Free from any abnormal deviation in structure or function which interferes with the usefulness of the horse.

SPASM: Sudden involuntary contraction of a muscle.

SPASTICITY: Increased muscle tone which is the result of resistance to stretching the muscles.

SPATIAL ORIENTATION: The ability to align one's self in space.

SPATIAL RELATIONS: The ability to perceive the position of two or more objects in relation to each other.

SPECIAL NEEDS INFANT/CHILDREN: Those who have disabilities or disease which require special care.

SPLINTER SKILLS: Skills taught out of the normal order of developmental sequence.

SPOOK: When a horse is frightened by something, becomes nervous, shies, jumps or runs in response.

SPOOK PROOF: A horse with a good temperament who has be trained not to react to environmental influences which interfere with riding tasks.

STALL: A small enclosure in which to keep a horse.

STANCE: The weight bearing phase of a stride.

STATIC: Remaining the same, no movement.

STERNUM: The flat narrow bone in the center of the chest.

STRAIGHTNESS: Occurs when both sides of the horse's physiques are fully and evenly developed enabling the horse to maintain an even bend of the body and neck on curves and straightness on the long side.

STRIDE: One complete circuit of the stepping of all four feet.

STRUCTURING ENVIRONMENT: The organization of a person's environment, time, activities, and level of skill required in order to enhance function.

SUPPLENESS: The horse stretches length wise and sideways, allowing the back to raise and legs to move freely.

SUPPORT: To sustain, to hold, to prop, to bolster.

SUPPORT REACTIONS: A reflex reaction which occurs when a person leans off balance - leg straightens to support weight, hand goes out to the side when leaning to side.

SURCINGLE: A strap that goes around the girth of a horse.

SWING THROUGH: During movement, it is the non-weight bearing phase of a stride.

SYMMETRICAL: The same on each side (mirror image).

SYNERGIES-ABNORMAL: Abnormal primitive patterns of motion which is often seen with CNS damaged individuals (a stereotype movement may be seen in flexing the arm which cannot be altered at will.

TACKING UP: To put tack on a horse.

TACTILE: Related to touch.

TACTILE DEFENSIVENESS: Cannot tolerate or is sensitive to being touched.

TEMPO: Speed of the rhythm.

TONUS: (tone). The state of a muscle-tight, loose or normal.

TRACKING-UP: The placement of the hind feet behind, into, or in front of the print of the forefeet as the horse walks or trots.

TRAINING EXERCISES: Circles, serpentines, leg yielding, shoulder-in, turns, half-halts, lengthening and collecting pace.

TRANSFER: To move from one place to another.

TRANSITION: (horse term). To change from one gait to another and changing the stride with in a gait.

TRAVERS: A dressage movement in which the horse is slightly bent around the inside leg of the rider and positioned at a 30 degree angle to the line of the track it follows.

TREE: (horse term)(saddle tree). The wooden, nylon or metal frame of a saddle.

TROT: A swinging two-beat foot-fall in which diagonal legs move together--a period of suspension after each footfall.

TURNING OUT: To put the horse into a field, large corral or paddock.

U.E.: Abbreviation for upper extremity.

UPWARD TRANSITION: (horse term). Changing to a faster gait.

VAULTING: Gymnastics on a moving horse.

VAULTING BARREL: A barrel constructed to aid vaulter in the perfection of vaulting exercises.

VAULTING SURCINGLE: A leather girth with two secure handles, which fits around the horse.

VERTEBRA: Bones which enclose the spinal cord.

VESTIBULAR: The brain mechanism which influences balance, muscle tone, visual muscles and the body's posture against gravity.

VETERINARIAN: (DMV). A doctor of veterinary medicine who treats animals.

VITAL ORGANS: Parts of the body which are critical to life such as the heart, lungs, stomach.

WALK: A four-beat gait.

WEIGHT-BEARING: When weight is balance on a limb or body; stance phase during movement.

WHIP: A flexible stick used to aid the horse by enforcing the rider's leg aid.

WRAPPING: (horse term). Used to protect the horse's legs.

XENOPHON: (c.430-350 BC). The writer of the first organized material on the art of riding.

Blakiston's Gould Medical Dictionary, Fourth Edition: (1979). New York, McGraw-Hill Book Co.

Christiansen, C; Baum, C. (1991). *Occupational Therapy: Overcoming Human Performance Deficits,*

Summerhays, R. S. *Summerhays' Encyclopaedia for Horsemen.* (1988). London: Threshold Books.

Umphred, D.A. (1985). *Neurological Rehabilitation.* St Louis: The C.V. Mosby Co.

REFERENCES FROM TEXT AND OTHER SOURCES FOR THERAPEUTIC RIDING

RIDING TRAINING

British Horse Society. *You and Your Pony; Beginning, Intermediate and Advanced Level of Horsemanship.* Order from Miller's Tack. East Rutherford, NJ.
British Horse Society. *The Instructor's Handbook.* London: Threshold Books, LTD.
Brownson, L. (1990). *Polocrosse Practice for Individuals and Teams.*

Canadian Equestrian Federation. *Manual of Basic Driving.* Canadian Horse Council.

Froissard, J. (1967). *Equitation.* Cranbury, N.J.: A.S. Barnes and Co.

German National Equestrian Federation. (1985). *The Principles of Riding.* New York: Arco Publishing Inc.

Hadfield, M. (1989). *The Manual of Horsemanship.* British Horse Society and Pony Club. London: Threshold Books.
Harris, C. (1985). *Fundamentals of Riding.* London: J.A. Allen.
Hedlund, G. (1988). *This is Riding: Dressage, Jumping, Eventing in Word and Pictures.* Middletown: Half Halt Press.
Henriques, P. (1987). *Balanced Riding.* Gaithersburg: Half Halt Press.
Hill, C. (1988). *From the Center of the Ring.* Pownal VT: Garden Way Publishing Book
Hill, C. (1991). *Becoming An Effective Rider.* Pownal: Storey Communication.

Inderwick, S. (1986). *Lungeing the Horse and Rider.* North Pomfret: David & Charles Inc.

Lewis, A. (1975). *A Guide to Basic Riding Instruction.* London: J.A. Allen and Co., Ltd.
Littauer, V.S. (1974). *Commonsense Horsemanship.* New York: Arco Publishing Co.

Mager, R. F. (1962). *Preparing Instructional Objectives.* Palo Alto: Fearon Publishers.
Macdonald, J.W. (1987). *Riding to Music.* London:J.A. Allen.
Morris, G. H. (1981). *George Morris Teaches Beginners to Ride.* Garden City: Doubleday & Co.
Mortimer, M. (1983). *The Riding Instructor's Handbook.* North Pomfret: David & Charles Inc.
Museler, W. (1984). *Riding Logic.* Arco Publishing, Inc.

Pastene, H.A. (1987). *Riding Contact: As a Function of Equipment and the Mental Side of Riding.* Hilton Head Island: Cooper Clark Co.
Palardy, J. M. (1971). *Elementary School Curriculum.* New York: MacMillan Co. 44, 60-66,104-109,146, 165.
Podhajsky, A. (1967). *The Complete Training of Horse and Rider.* Garden City: Doubleday & Co. 82.
Podhajsky, A. (1968). *My Horses, My Teachers.* Garden City: Doubleday and Co. 14, 79.
Podhajsky, A. (1973). *The Riding Teacher.* Garden City: Doubleday & Co.
Richter, J. (1986). *The Longeing Book.* New York: Prentice Hall Press. 17.
Roberts, P. (1987). *Teaching the Child Rider.* London: J.A. Allen & Co.

Schusdziarra, H, Schusdziarra V. (1985). *An Anatomy of Riding.* Briarcliff: Breakthrough Publications.
Sivewright, M. (1984). *Thinking Riding.* London: J.A. Allen.
Soloman, D. S. (1982). *Teaching Riding.* Univ. of Oklahoma Press, Norman, OK.
Storl, W. (1987). *Riding to Music.* Millwood: Breakthrough Publications.
Swift, S. (1985). *Centered Riding.* North Pomfret: David & Charles Inc.

Tellington, W., Tellington-Jones, L.(1979). *Endurance and Competitive Trail Riding.* New York: Doubleday.
Townley, A. (1990). *Natural Riding.* Millwood: Breakthrough Publications.

Wallace, G., & Kaufman, J.M. (1978). *Teaching Children with Learning Problems.* (2nd ed). Columbus: Charles E. Merrill Publishing Co. 105.
Wanless. M. (1987). *The Natural Rider.* New York: Summit.
Wanless. M. (1992). *Riding With Your Mind.* North Pomfret: Trafalgar Square Publishing.
Wolfe, F. (1990). *Polocrosse Strategy.* Warwick, NY.
Wright, G; Kelly, M. (1975). *The Riding Instructor's Manual.* Garden City: Doubleday & Co.

HORSE CARE

Adams, O.R. (1972). *Lameness in Horses.* 2nd ed. Fort Collins: Lea & Febiger. 340.
Ainslie, T., & Ledbetter, B. (1980). *The Body Language of Horses.* New York: William Marrow & Co.,Inc. 34.
Alcock, J. (1976). *Animal Behavior, An Evolutionary Approach.* Sunderland: Sinauer Associates, Inc. 199.

Bennett, D. (1988). *Principles of Conformation Analysis, Vol I.* Gaithersburg: Fleet Street Publishing Corporation.
Bennett, D. (1989). *Principles of Conformation Analysis, Vol II.* Gaithersburg: Fleet Street Publishing Corporation.
Bennett, D. (1991). *Principles of Conformation Analysis, Vol III.* Gaithersburg: Fleet Street Publishing Corporation.

Borton, A. (1990). *Selection of the Horse*. In J.W. Evans, A. Borton, H.F. Hintz, & L.D. Van Vleck. *The Horse*. New

Blazer, D. (1982). *Horses Seldom Burp! How to Keep Them Happy and Well*. La Jolla: A.S. Barnes & Co. Inc.

Bromily, M. (1987). *Equine Injury and Therapy*. New York: Howell Book House Inc.

Condax, K.D.(1979). *Horse Sense*. Causes and Correction of Horse and Rider Problems. New York: Prentice Hall Press.

Current Therapy in Equine Medicine: Philadelphia: W.B. Saunders.

Dorrance, T. (1987). *True Unity*. Tuscarora: Give-It-A-Go Enterprises Publisher, NV 1987.

Equus Staff. (1980). "Cleaning the Sheath". 32. Gaithersburg: Fleat Street Corporation, MD.

Evans, J.W. (1989). *Horses: A Guide to Selection, Care, and Enjoyment*. New York: W.H. Freeman and Company.

Evans, J.W., A. Borton, H.F. Hintz, and L.D. Van Vleck. (1990). *The Horse*. New York: W.H. Freeman and Company.

German National Equestrian Federation. (1987). *Horse Management*. Gaithersburg: Half Halt Press.

Gonzales, A. (1986). *Proper Balance Movement*. Manassas: REF Publishing.

Green, Ben K. (1969). *Horse Conformation*. Northland Press, A Justin Co.

Hamilton, S. (1978). Man's Impact on Behavior, *Equus* 9, Gaithersburg: Fleat Street Corporation, MD.

Harris, S.E. (1977). *Grooming to Win*. New York: Charles Scribner's Sons.

Henriques, P. (1991) *Conformation*. Buckingham, GB: Threshold Books.

Houpt, K. (1980). Two is a Herd. *Equus*. 35 Gaithersburg: Fleat Street Corporation, MD.

Hunt, R. (1978). *Thinking Harmony with Horses*. Fresno: Pioneer Publishing Co.

Kellon, E.M. (1986). *The Older Horse*. Millwood: Breakthrough Publications.

Kellon, E.M. (1990). *First Aid For Horses*. Millwood: Breakthrough Publications.

Kidd. J. (1984). *The Better Horse*. New York: Arco Publishing Inc.

Kilby, E. (1981). How Smart is Your Horse. *Equus* 46, 22. Gaithersburg: Fleet Street Corporation, MD.

Kilby, E. (1987). Where Weathers is always Front Page News. *Equus*. 110. 40-41, 62.

Kiley-Worthington, M. (1987). *The Behavior of Horses: In Relation to Management and Training*. London: J.A. Allen Co.

King, P.A. (1990). "Your Horse's Vital Signs". *Horseplay*.

Kinnish, M.K. (1988). *Healthy Hooves Their Care and Balance*. Gaithersburg: Fleet Street Publishing Corp.

Klimke, R. (1969). *Cavalletti*. London: J.A. Allen & Co. LTD. 131.

Klimke, R. (1985). *Basic Training of the Young Horse*. London: J.A. Allen & Co. LTD. 131.

Lichtner-Hoyer, P. (1991). *Complete Cavalletti*. Ossining: Breakthrough Publications.

Liebermann, B. (1980). The Sense of It All. *Equus*. Farmingdale: Fleet Street Publishing Corp. 34-39, 57.

Lyon, W. (1984). *First Aid Hints for the Horse Owner*. Glasgow: William Collins Sons & Co Ltd.

Lyons, John; Browning, S. (1991). *Lyons on Horses*. New York: Doubleday.

Lyles, L.L. (1980). *Horseman's Handbook*. Santa Rosa: California State Horsemen's Assoc. 28.

Merck Veterinary Manual. Rahway, N.Y.: Merck and Co.

McNab, J.R., Poplawski, V. (1988). Sharing the Experience of the World if the Horse. *Proceedings of the 6th International Therapeutic Congress*. Toronto, Canada.

Maynard, L.A., J.K. Loosli, H.F. Hintz, and R.G. Warner. (1979). *Animal Nutrition*. Seventh edition. McGraw-Hill Book Co.

McBane, S. (1980). *Keeping a Horse Outdoors*. North Pomfret: David & Charles Inc. 13-17.

McCall, J. (1988). *Influencing Horse Behavior: A Natural Approach to Training*. Loveland: Alpine Publications.

Naviaux, J. L. (1985). *Horses in Health and Disease*. Second edition. Philadelphia: Lea and Febiger.

NRC. (1989). *Nutrient Requirements of Horses*. Fifth revised edition. National Academy of Sciences, Washington, DC.

Oliver, R.,Langrish, B. (1991). *A Photographic Guide To Conformation*. London: J.A. Allen & Co. Ltd.

Pascoe, E. (1986). *The Horse Owner's Preventive Maintenance Handbook*, New York: Charles Scribner's & Sons.

Perrault, G. *The New Horse Owner Illustrated Manual*. Ottawa: Editions Grand Prix Reg'd.

Peyre-Ferry, M. (1990). Waking Up the Sluggish Horse. *Horse Illustrated*. 5.

Rees, L. (1985). *The Horse's Mind*. New York: Prentice Hall Press. 27, 125.

Richardson, J. (1981). *Horse Tack*. New York: William Morrow & Co, Inc. 22-25.

Richter, J. (1986). *The Longeing Book*. New York: Prentice Hall Press. 17

Robinson, D.W., L.M. Slade. (1974). *The Current Status of Knowledge on the Nutrition of Equines*. J. Animal Science.

Roomey, J. (1974). *The Lame Horse*. Cranbury, NJ: A.S. Barnes.

Savitt, S. (1981). *Draw Horses*. New York: Bonanza.

Schramm, U. (1986). *The Undisciplined Horse*. London: J.A. Allen.

Smallwood, P. (1988). *The Manual of Stable Management: Care of the Horse*. Middletown: Half Halt Press.

Smallwood, P. (1988). *The Manual of Stable Management: The Horse*. British Horse Society. Gaithersburg: Half Halt Press.

Smythe, R.H. (1965). *The Mind of the Horse*. Lexington: Stephen Greene Press.

Smythe, R.H. (1975). *The Horse Structure and Movement*. 2nd Ed. Revised by P.C. Goody. London: J.A. Allen & Co Ltd.

Sumner, D.W. (1976). *Breaking Your Horse's Bad Habits*. Millwood: Breakthrough Publishing.

Summerhays, R.S. (1988). *Summerhays' Encyclopedia for Horsemen*. Rev. ed. London: Threshold Books. Schramm, U. (1986). *The Undisciplined Horse*. London: J.A. Allen.

Tellington-Jones, L., Bruns, U. (1985). *The Tellington-Jones Equine Awareness Method*. Millwood: Breakthrough Publications.

Tellington-Jones, L., Taylor, S. (1992). *The Tellington TTouch*. New York: Viking Penguin.

Vavra, R. (1979). *Such is the Real Nature of Horses*. New York: William Morrow & Company, Inc.

Wallace, M. (1991). Emergency Care. *Equus*. 166, 52-55 95-97.

Watkins, V. (1986). *Trimming and Clipping*. London: Threshold Books.

Way, R.F. (1983). *The Anatomy of the Horse*. Millwood:Breakthrough Publications.

Williams, M. (1976). *Practical Horse Psychology*. No. Hollywood: Wilshire Book Co.

Williamson, M.B. (1977). *Applied Horse Psychology*. Houston: Cordova Publisher Inc. 2-42.

Wood, C.H., S.G. Jackson, (1988). *Basic Horse Nutrition*. Lexington: University of Kentucky Cooperative Extension Service.

THERAPEUTIC RIDING

American Vaulting Association: *American Vaulting Association Rule Book*. Saratoga, CA.

Armstrong-Esther, C.A.. Myco. F., Sandelands, M.L. (1985). An Examination of the Therapeutic Benefits of the Horseback Riding Technique Used by the Lethbridge Handicapped Riding Association. *Proceedings of the 5th International Congress on Therapeutic Riding*.

Bauer, Joseph J. (1972). *Riding for Rehabilitation*. Toronto: Canadian Stage and Arts Publications Ltd.

Baumann, (1979). *Therapeutic Exercise on Horseback for Children with Neurogenic Disorders of Movement*. 3rd International Congress. England. Shakesville Publishing Co.

Bier, M.J., Kauffman, N. (1989). "The Effects of Therapeutic Horseback Riding on Balance." *Adapted Physical Activity Quarterly*. 221-229.

Bly, L. (1983). *The Components of Normal Movement During the First Year of Life and Abnormal Motor Development*. Chicago: NDT Assoc. Inc.

Brock, B. (1987). *Effect of Therapeutic Horseback Riding on Physically Disabled Adults*. Doctoral Dissertation: Indiana University.

Cotton, E. (no date given). *The Hand as a Guide to Learning*. London: The Spastics Society.

Davies, J.A. (1968, 1988 revised). *Reins of Life*. London: J A Allen. An Instructional and Informative Manual on Riding for the Disabled.

Davies, J.A. *Riding in Rituore*. London: J.A. Allen & Co. Ltd.

DePauw, K.P. (1986). Horseback riding for individuals with disabilities: programs, philosophy, and research. *Adapted Physical Activity Quarterly*, 3, 3, 217-226.

Donahue, K. (1986). Centered riding for the physically disabled rider. Abstract of paper presented at *Delta Society International Conference*. Boston, MA.

Engel, B.T. (1988). *Bibliography for Therapeutic Riding, Sport, Education, Medicine*. Barbara Engel Therapy Services: 10 Town Plaza, Suite 238, Durango, CO 81301.

Engel, B.T., et al. (1989). *The Horse, The Handicapped and the Riding Team*. Barbara Engel Therapy Services: 10 Town Plaza, Suite 238, Durango, CO. 81301.

Feldenkrais, M. (1977). *Awareness Through Movement*. New York: Harper & Row.

Feldenkrais, M. (1981). *The Elusive Obvious*. Cupertino: Meta Publications.

Finnie, N.R. (1975). *Handling the Young Cerebral Palsied Child at Home*. New York: E.P.Dutton & Co., Inc.

Fox, V. M. (1986 Winter). Measurement device for therapeutic horseback riding. *People-Animals-Environment*. 33.

Fox, V. M., Lawlar and Luttges, M. W. (1984). "Pilot Study of Novel Test Instrumentation to Evaluate Therapeutic Horseback Riding". *Adapted Physical Activity Quarterly*. 1, 30-36.

Good. C. L. (1986). Psychosocial aspects of riding for adult disabled equestrians. Abstract of paper presented at *Delta Society International Conf*. Boston, Guyton, A. (1964). *Function of the Human Body*. Philadelphia: W.B. Sanders Co. MA.

Hall, S. J., Hulac, G. M., Myers, J. E. (1983). *Improvement Among Participants in a Therapeutic Riding Program*. Unpublished manuscript, Washington State University, April.

Hanna, T. (1980). *The Body of Life*. New York: Random House.

Hanna, T. (1988). *Somatics: Reawakening the Mind Control of Movement, Flexibility, and Health*. Addison-Wesley Publishing Co.

Heipertz, W. (1981). *Therapeutic Riding, Medicine, Education and Sports*. English translation, Greenbelt Riding Association, Ottawa: Canada.

Hulsey-Chickering, Robin. (1979). *Horseback Riding for the Hearing Impaired: A Practical Guide and Suggested Signs*. From Riding High Inc, 2392 D. Half Moon Dr., St Louis, MO 63114.

Johnson, L.M., Elitsky, L., Bailey, D. (1990). A holistic approach to therapeutic riding. Abstract of paper presented at *Delta Society Ninth Annual Conference*, October 11-13, 1990.

Jollinier, M. (1989). Horse riding activity and psycho-social re-education in problem children. Abstract of paper presented at *5th International Conference on the Relationship between Humans and Animals*. Monaco.

Joswick, F., Kittredge, M., McCowan, L. et al. (1986). *Aspects and Answers*. Michigan: Cheff Center.

Knickerbocker, B. M. (1980). *A Holistic Approach to the Treatment of Leaning Disorders*. Thorofare: Charles B. Slack, Inc.

Lawrence, E.A. (1982). *Rodeo: An Anthropologist Looks at The Wild and the Tame*. Chicago: Univ of Chicago Press.
Lawrence, E.A. (1985). *Hoofbeats and Society: Studies of Human-Horse Interactions*. Bloomington:Indiana Univ. Press.
Lawrence, E.A. (1988). Horses in Society. *Anthrozoos*. Vol 1, no 4, Spring.
Leff, M., el al. (1988). *Guide to Therapeutic Groundwork*. Washington, DC: National Center for Therapeutic Riding.
Longden, M.L. (1984). Teaching Disabled Riders. Blackburn: Acacia Press PTY. LTD.
Longden, M., Lane, B. (1988) Riding Instructors: the Vital Link. *Proceedings of the 6th International Therapeutic Congress*. Toronto, Canada.

Mayberry, R. (1978). The mystique of the horse is strong medicine: Riding as therapeutic recreation. *Rehabilitation Literature*.
McCowan, L. (1972). *It is Ability That Counts*. Augusta MI: Cheff Center.
Mobily, K.E. 1985. A Philosophical Analysis of Therapeutic Recreation: What does it mean to say "We Can Be Therapeutic"? part 2, *Therapeutic Recreation Journal*, 18, no. 2, 2.
Morrow, D. *Handicap System to Equalize Degrees and Types of Disabilities in Riding Competitions*. VARHA, Inc., P.O. Box 226, Franklin, PA 16323.

NARHA Handbook. North American Riding for the Handicapped. Denver: NARHA. 1988.

O'Daniel, K. (1986). Horseback Riding for Handicappers. *4-H Youth Programs*, Cooperative Extension Service. Michigan State University.

Piaget. J. (1963). *The Origins of Intelligence in Children*. New York: W.W. Norton & Co. 1963.

Tebay, J. & Schlesinger, R. (1986 Spring). Riding therapy as a contraindication for Down syndrome individuals with atlantoaxial instability. *People-Animals-Environment*. 31-32.

Seaman, J.A., DePauw, K.P. (1979). *The New Adapted Physical Education*. Palo Alto: Mayfield Publishing Co.
Special Olympics International, Inc. (1988). *Official Special Olympics Summer Sports Rules*. (1988). 1250 New York Avenue, N,W. #5OO, Washington. DC
Special Olympics International, Inc. (1989). *Special Olympics Equestrian Sports Skills Program*. 1350 New York Ave., Suite 500. Washington D.C.

United States Pony Club (1984). *Bandaging*. West Chester: United States Pony Club, Inc.
United States Pony Club (1984). *Longeing*. West Chester: United States Pony Club, Inc.
United States Pony Club (1984). *Vaulting Manual*. West Chester: United States Pony Club, Inc.

EQUINE-ASSISTED THERAPY AND RELATED INFORMATION

Affolter, F.D. (1991). *Perception, Interaction, and Language*. Berlin: Springer-Verlag.
Alexander, G. (1985). *Eutony*. Great Neck: Felix Morrow.
Ayres, A. J. (1974). *Sensory Integration and Learning Disorders*. Los Angeles: Western Psychological Services.

Barnes, M., Crutchfield, C., Heriza, C., Hardman, S. (1990). *Reflex and Vestibular Aspects of Motor Control, Motor Development and Motor Learning*. Atlanta:
Basmajian, J.V. (1964). *Primary Anatomy*. Baltimore: The Williams and Wilkins Co.
Bertoli, D. (1988). "Effect of Therapeutic Horse Riding on Posture in Children with Cerebral Palsy." *Proceedings of the 6th International Therapeutic Riding Congress*. Toronto, Canada.
Bobath, B. (1978). *Adult Hemiplegia, Evaluation and Treatment*. Second Edition, London: William Heinemann Medical Books Limited.
Bobath, B. (1985). *Abnormal Postural Reflex Activity Caused by Brain Lesions*. Rockville: Aspen Systems Corp.
Boehme, R. (1988). *Improving Upper Body Control*. Tucson: Therapy Skill Builders.

Calveley, J. (1988). The Effect of Horse Riding Upon Sitting Balance in People with Cerebral Palsy. *Proceedings of the 6th International Therapeutic Congress*. Toronto, Canada.
Carr, S., Gordon, G. H. (1987). *Movement Science for Physical Therapy and Rehabilitation*. Maryland, Aspen Publishers.
Cambell, M., Harris-Ossman. (1990). *Adult Positions, Transitions, and Transfers*. Tucson: Therapy Skill Builders.
Chakerian, D. (1991).*The Effect of Upper Extremity Weight Bearing on Hand Function in Children with Cerebral Palsy*. NDTA Newsletter 9/7.
Copeland, J.C. (1986). A study of four physically disabled riders with twenty-five years of combined riding experience. Abstract of paper presented at the *Delta Society International Conference*. Boston, MA.
Copeland, J.C. (1989). Therapeutic riding as a treatment adjunct after selective posterior lumbar rhizotomy surgery. Abstract of paper presented at 5th *International Conference on the Relationship between Humans and Animals*. Monaco.
Copeland, J.C., McGibbon, N., & Freeman, G. (1990). Theoretical perspectives in therapeutic riding. Abstract of paper presented at *Delta Society Ninth Annual Conference,* October 11-13.

Dismuke, R.P. (1981). Therapeutic horsemanship. *The Quarter Horse Journal*. 34-37.
Dismuke, R.P. (1984). Rehabilitative horseback riding for children with language disorders. In R.K. Anderson, B.L. Hart, & L.A. Hart (Eds), *Pet Connection*. 131-140. Minneapolis: University of Minneapolis, Center to Study.
Dismuke-Blakely, R.P. (1990). Combined speech/language and occupational therapy through rehabilitative riding. Abstract of paper presented at *Delta Society Ninth Annual Conference*.

Donahue, K. (1988). The Use of Hippotherapy as an Adjunct Treatment for Traumatic Brain Injured Clients. *Proceedings of the 6th International Therapeutic Congress*. Toronto, Canada.

Glasow, B. (1986). Hippotherapy The Horse as a Therapeutic Modality. *People-Animals-Environment*. 30-31.

Glasow, B. *Division of Vaulting for Disabled*. Warwick: New York. *North American Riding for the Handicapped Medical Subcommittee*. (1988). Therapeutic Riding Classifications.

Hauser, G. (1988). Hippotherapy Under the Aspect of Therapeutic Pedagogics. *Proceedings of the 6th International Therapeutic Congress*. Toronto, Canada.

Heipertz, W. (1981). *Therapeutic Riding: Medicine, Education, Sport*. Canadian Equestrian Federation, 333 River Road, Ottawa, Ontario D1L 8B9.

Illingworth, R. S. *The Development of the Infant and Young Child*. Edinburgh: Churchill Livingstone. 1980. 1-12, 146-168.

Kluwer, C. (1982). On the Psychology of Riding/Vaulting. *Proceedings of the 4th International Congress*.

Knickerbocker, B.M. (1980). *A Holistic Approach to the Treatment of Learning Disorders*. Thorofare, Charles B. Slack, Inc.

Kunzle. (1982). The Effect of the Horse's Movement on the Patient. *Proceedings of the 4th International Congress*.

Kuratorium for Therapeutisches Reiten. 1985. German film converted to U.S. video format. *The Horse in Medicine, Education and Sport*. Available from the Delta Society, Renton, Washington. (See suggested contacts).

Nelson, A. J. (1974). Functional Ambulation Profile. *Physical Therapy*. 54: 1059.

Riede, D. (1988). *Physiotherapy on the Horse*. Delta Society, 321 Burnett Ave. So., Renton WA.

Shores, M. (1974). Footprint Analysis in Gait Documentation. *Physical Therapy*. 60: 1163-1167.

Spink 1982. *A Comparative Review of Medical and Psycho-educational Techniques in Therapeutic Riding*. Unpublished master's thesis, Goddard Graduate Program, Vermont College.

Spink 1985. A categorical approach to vaulting for the disabled. Report presented to the *Fifth International Congress on Therapeutic Riding*. Milan, Italy.

Spink 1986. *The Adjunctive use of the Horse in Therapy: A Progression*. Unpublished seminar reference material.

Spink 1987. Rx: The horse. Presentation to the *Delta Society Annual Meeting*, Vancouver, British Colombia.

Spink 1988. A four phase construct for therapeutic riding. Report presented to the *Sixth International Congress on Therapeutic Riding*, Toronto, Canada.

Spink 1990. A model application for the horse in riding therapy: the Michael McCulloch Memorial Award lecture, *Delta Society Annual Meeting*: Houston, Texas.

Walsh, L. (1989). The therapeutic value of horseback riding and the developmental milestones accomplished through horseback riding. Abstract of paper presented at *5th International Conference on the Relationship between Humans and Animals*, Monaco.

Wham, J. (1990). *Hippotherapy Specialists*. presented at the New Zealand Association of Occupational Therapists Jubilee Conference. Christchurch, NZ.

VIDEO REFERENCES

Centered Riding with Sally Swift. Two videos-part I and part II, describes in detail the Sally Swift's techniques on Centered Riding. Order from Miller's Tack. East Rutherford, NJ.

Challenged Equestrians. Therapeutic Riding, a description of all phases of therapeutic riding. Order from Winslow Therapeutic Riding Unlimited, Warwick, NY. 10990.

The Horse in Sport-*Driving*. Equestrian Video Library. The Gladstone Equestrian Assoc. Library. GEA, P.O. Box 119, Gladstone, NJ. 07934

Advanced Classic Driving with Larry Poulin. Video. The Morgan Horse Club. PO Box 960, Shelburne, VT 05482-0960.

Contact the Carriage Association of America, Inc., R.D. 1. Box 115, Salem, NJ 08079 for information on the following.

Kellogg, C. *Driving the Horse in Carriage*.

Walrond, S. *A Guide to Driving Horses*.

Ganton, D. *Drive On*.

Norris, A. *Harnessing Up*

Norris, A. *Driving*.

The Therapeutic Application of the Horse's Movements. C.A.R.D., Canada. 19 Alcaine Court, Thornhill, Ontario, Canada L3T 2G8.

T.E.A.M Method of Horse Care and Training. 5 Videos by L. Tellington-Jones. Order from T.E.A.M; or major tack shops.

Awareness Through Movement; Riding With Awareness; T.E.A.M. Learning Part I & Part II; TTouch for Body, Tail, Legs; TTouch for Neck and Head. Published by Lawlor Productions, 3262 Holiday Court, Suite 202, La Jolla, CA.

Horse Health Care Series. A Six Series video which cover all aspects of horse care. Order from Miller's Tack. East Rutherford, NJ.

From the Ground Up. Care and handling, grooming and exercising the horse presented to educate the non-horse person to the intermediate horse handler. Order from Miller's Tack. East Rutherford, NJ.

Suggested Contacts

American Hippotherapy Association
Santa Rita Ranch, Box 647
Green Valley, AZ 85622
602-625-8678

Delta Society
P.O. Box 1080 Renton, Washington 98057
206-226-7357

North American Riding for the Handicapped
Association, Inc.
P.O. Box 33150, Denver, CO 80233
303-452-1212

The Federation of Riding for the Disabled
International
Wootton Hall
New Milton, Hampshire, UK BH 25 5SJ UK
0044-425-611-065

Canadian Therapeutic Riding Association
Box 1055, Guelph, Ontario N1H 6J6 Canada
519-767-0700

Riding for the Disabled (RDA)
Avenue R, National Agriculture Centre
Kenilworth, Warwickshire, UK CV8 2LY

Association of Special People Inspired to
Riding Excellence.
RD 4 Box 115, Malvern, PA 19355

Special Olympics International, Inc.
Special Olympics Equestrian Sports Program.
1350 New York Ave., Suite 500
Washington, D.C. 20005.
202-628-8298

United States Cerebral Palsy Association
34518 Warren Road, #264
Westland, MI 48185

T.T.E.A.M.
Santa Fe, New Mexico 87501-0793
505-455-2945
FAX 505-455-7233

American Vaulting Association
PO Box 3663
Saratoga, CA 95070-1663

United States Pony Club
329 South High Street,
West Chester, PA 19382
215-436-0300

American Horse Show Association (AHSA)
201 S. Capital Ave., Suite 430
Indianapolis, IN 46225
317-237-5252

National 4-H Council
7100 Connecticut Avenue
Chevy Chase, MD 20815

American Horse Council
1700 "K" St. NW, Suite 300
Washington, DC 20006

United States Dressage Federation (U.S.D.F.)
(Training Level and First Level Test Series)
1212 "O" Street, P.O. Box 80668
Lincoln, Nebraska 68501
402-474-7632.

The British Horse Society
National Equestrian Centre
Kenilworth, Warwickshire, UK CV8 2LR

Canadian Equestrian Federation
1600 James Ainsmith Drive
Gloucester, Ontario K1B 5N4
613-748-5632

American Polocrosse Association
601 Rustic Road, Durango, CO 81301.

National Association of Driving for the
Disabled (NADD)
87 Main Street, Fort Plain, NY 13339.

Kuratorium Fur Therapeutisches Reiten
Freiherr-Von-Langen Strasse 13
4410 Warendorf, Germany

A.N.I.R.E.
Associazione Nazionale Italiana
Di Riabilitazione Equestre
Riconosciuta Con D.P.R. 8 Luglio
1986 N 610 Del Capo Dello Stato, Italy

RDA Association of Australia, Inc.
1st Floor, 1 Cookson Street
Camberwell 3124, Victoria, Australia

New Zealand RDA Inc.
PO Box 5095, New Plymouth, NZ

American Occupational Therapy Assoc.
1383 Piccard Drive
PO Box 1725
Rockville, MD 20850
301-948-9626

American Physical Therapy Assoc.
1111 N. Fairfax Street.
Alexandria, VA. 22314
703-684-2782

Sensory Integration International
1402 Cravens Avenue
Torrance, CA 90501
310-533-8338

Neuro-Developmental Treatment Assoc.
PO Box 70
Oak Park, IL 60303
312-386-2445

Clearinghouse on the Handicapped
US Dept of Education
Switzer Building, Rm. 3132
Washington, D.C. 20036-2319
202-732-1241

National Handicapped Sports & Recreation
Association.
1145 19th St., NW, Suite 717
Washington, DC 20036
301-652-7505

Federation Equestre Internationale (FEI)
Avenue Mon-Repos 24, PO Box 157, CH-100
Lausanne, Switzerland

Miller's Harness Co., Inc.
235 Murray Hill Parkway
East Rutherford, NJ 07073
1-800-553-7655
Tack, apparel, books, videos

Dover Saddlrey
Box 5837
Hollister, MA 01746
1-800-989-1500
Tack, apparel, books, videos

The Blok-Mico Fence Co.
615 Howard Street
Findlay, OH 45840
419-422-5220
Cavalletti Bloks

State Line Tack, Inc.
PO Box 428, Plaistow,
NH 03865
1-800-228-9208
Tack, horse care and apparel

Phelan's
10 Liberty Ship Building
184 Schoolmaker Point
Sausalito, CA 94965
415-332-6001
Riding apparel and tack

FlagHouse
150 N. MacQuesten Pkwy
Mt Vernon, NY 10550
800-221-5185
Athletic and game equipment, mats

Damart
1811 Woodbury Ave.
Portsmouth, NH 03805
Extra warm clothing

Tandy Leather Co.
Dept HI 792, PO Box 2934
Ft. Worth Tx 76113
Leather, tools and findings

Breakthrough Publications
Millwood, NY 10546

Patagonia
P.O. Box 8900
1609 W. Babcock St.
Bozeman, MT 59715
1-800-336-9090
Special warm riding clothing